Lecture Notes in Computer Science

Commenced Publication in 1973
Founding and Former Series Editors:
Gerhard Goos, Juris Hartmanis, and Jan van Leeuwen

Lecture Notes in Computer Science

Hiroshi Yoshiura   Kouichi Sakurai
Kai Rannenberg   Yuko Murayama
Shinichi Kawamura (Eds.)

Advances
in Information
and Computer Security

First International Workshop on Security, IWSEC 2006
Kyoto, Japan, October 23-24, 2006
Proceedings

 Springer

Volume Editors

Hiroshi Yoshiura
The University of Electro-Communications, Faculty of Electro-Communications
Tokyo, Japan
E-mail: yoshiura@hc.uec.ac.jp

Kouichi Sakurai
Kyushu University, Faculty of Information Science and Electrical Engineering
Fukuoka, Japan
E-mail: sakurai@csce.kyushu-u.ac.jp

Kai Rannenberg
Goethe University Frankfurt, Institute of Business Informatics
Frankfurt, Germany
E-mail: Kai.Rannenberg@m-lehrstuhl.de

Yuko Murayama
Iwate Prefectural University, Faculty of Software and Information Science
Iwate, Japan
E-mail: murayama@iwate-pu.ac.jp

Shinichi Kawamura
Toshiba Corporation, Corporate Research and Development Center
E-mail: shinichi2.kawamura@toshiba.co.jp

Library of Congress Control Number: 2006934578

CR Subject Classification (1998): E.3, G.2.1, D.4.6, K.6.5, K.4.1, F.2.1, C.2, J.1

LNCS Sublibrary: SL 4 – Security and Cryptology

ISSN   0302-9743
ISBN-10   3-540-47699-7 Springer Berlin Heidelberg New York
ISBN-13   978-3-540-47699-3 Springer Berlin Heidelberg New York

Springer is a part of Springer Science+Business Media

springer.com

© Springer-Verlag Berlin Heidelberg 2006

Typesetting: Camera-ready by author, data conversion by Scientific Publishing Services, Chennai, India
Printed on acid-free paper   SPIN: 11908739   06/3142   5 4 3 2 1 0

Preface

It was our pleasure to hold the International Workshop on Security 2006 (IWSEC 2006) this year in Kyoto and to publish the proceedings as a volume of the Lecture Notes in Computer Science series.

The workshop was our first trial in that two major academic society groups on security in Japan, viz. ISEC and CSEC, jointly organized it; ISEC is a technical group on information security of the Institute of Electronics, Information and Communication Engineers (IEICE), and CSEC is a special interest group on computer security of the Information Processing Society of Japan (IPSJ). It was Ryoichi Sasaki, the former head of CSEC, who proposed holding such an international workshop in Japan for the first time, two years ago. The two groups supported his idea and started organizing the workshop. CSEC has its annual domestic symposium, the Computer Security Symposium (CSS), in October for three days, and we decided to organize the workshop prior to CSS this year.

The initial aim of the workshop was primarily to provide young researchers with the opportunity to present their work in English. However, due to more submissions than we had anticipated, the quality of the accepted papers became far better than we had expected.

The conference received 147 submissions, out of which the program committee selected 30 for presentation. These proceedings contain the final versions of the accepted papers, which the authors finalized on the basis of comments from the reviewers. Since these revisions were not subject to editorial review, the authors bear full responsibility for the contents of their papers.

The reviewing process was a challenging task. Each submitted paper was reviewed by at least three members of the program committee. The individual reviewing phase was followed by a Web-based discussion. Papers over which the reviewers significantly disagreed were further reviewed by external experts. On the basis of the comments and scores given by the reviewers, the final decisions on acceptance were made at a one-day meeting of the program committee at the University of Electro-Communications.

We appreciate the hard work of the organizing committee members. In particular, the workshop would not have been possible without the members of the Advisory Committee. The members of the program committee also made important contributions through their sincere reviews and discussions. We thank them for their intellectual contributions as well as their hard work. The expertise of the external reviewers improved the quality of the selection process. The reviewing and discussion processes were greatly facilitated by the Web-based system, which was developed by Wim Moreau and Joris Claessens, under the guidance of Bart Preneel. We are sincerely grateful to them.

Finally, we would like to thank the authors who submitted papers. We hope that you find the book interesting and informative.

October 2006   Yuko Murayama and Shinichi Kawamura
                    Hiroshi Yoshiura, Kouichi Sakurai, and Kai Rannenberg

Organization

IWSEC (International Workshop on Security) 2006 was organized by ISEC and CSEC. ISEC is a technical group of IEICE (The Institute of Electronics, Information and Communication Engineers) on information security, and CSEC is a SIG (Special Interest Group) of IPSJ (Information Processing Society of Japan) on computer security.

General Co-chairs

Yuko Murayama (Iwate Prefectural University, Japan)
Shinichi Kawamura (Toshiba Corporation, Japan)

Advisory Committee

Norihisa Doi (Chuo University, Japan)
Akira Hayashi (Kanazawa Institute of Technology, Japan)
Hideki Imai (Chuo University, Japan)
Günter Müller (University of Freiburg, Germany)
Eiji Okamoto (University of Tsukuba, Japan)
Ryoichi Sasaki (Tokyo Denki University, Japan)
Shigeo Tsujii (Institute of Information Security, Japan)

Program Committee Co-chairs

Hiroshi Yoshiura (University of Electro-Communications, Japan)
Kouichi Sakurai (Kyushu University, Japan)
Kai Rannenberg (Goethe University Frankfurt, Germany)

Program Committee

Thomas Berson (Anagram Labs, USA)
Bob Blakley (Texas A&M University, USA)
Soon Ae Chun (City University of New York, USA)
Kyo-il Chung (ETRI, Korea)
George Davida (University of Wisconsin-Milwaukee, USA)
Hiroshi Doi (Institute of Information Security, Japan)
Paul Dowland (University of Plymouth, UK)
Isao Echizen (Hitachi, Ltd., Japan)
Mahmoud T. El-Hadidi (Cairo University, Egypt)
Jan Eloff (University of Pretoria, South Africa)

Kiyoshi Tanaka (Shinshu University, Japan)
Toshiaki Tanaka (KDDI Co., Japan)
Masato Terada (Hitachi, Ltd., Japan)
Masayuki Terada (NTT DoCoMo, Inc., Japan)
Doug Tygar (UC Berkeley, USA)
Ryuya Uda (Tokyo University of Technology, Japan)
Tetsutaro Uehara (Kyoto University, Japan)
Vijay Varadharajan (Macquarie University, Australia)
Teemupekka Virtanen (Helsinki University of Technology, Finland)
Jozef Vyskoc (VaF, Slovak Republic)
Hajime Watanabe (AIST, Japan)
Duncan Wong (City University of Hong Kong, Hong Kong)
Chuan-Kun Wu (Chinese Academy of Sciences, China)
Bin Xiao (Hong Kong Polytechnic University, Hong Kong)
Sung-Ming Yen (National Central University, Taiwan)
Maki Yoshida (Osaka University, Japan)
Moti Yung (RSA Laboratories, USA)
Jianying Zhou (Institute for Infocomm Research, Singapore)
Albin Zuccato (Karlstad University, Sweden)

External Reviewers

Chien-Ning Chen, Chun-I Fan, Hsi-Chung Lin, Hung-Min Sun,
Chih-Hung Wang, Bin Zhang, Philip Feng, Xiaojian Tian, Guomin Yang,
Robert Zhu, Osamu Takahashi, Fumitaka Yura, Kevin R.B. Butler,
Patrick Traynor, Will Enck, Joonsang Baek, Shane Balfe, Tanmoy Kanti Das,
Maria Papadaki, Sotiris Ioannidis, Matthew Burnside, Angelos Stavrou,
Michael Locasto, Stelios Sidiroglou, Yunho Lee, Jeeyeon Kim, Hyunjue Kim,
Heasuk Jo, Keunwoo Rhee, Seokhyang Cho, Isaac Agudo, Jose A. Montenegro,
Pablo Najera, Jose A. Onieva, Xinyi Huang, Shidi Xu, Koichiro Akiyama,
Kouichi Fujisaki, Yuichi Komano, Tatsuyuki Matsushita, Hideyuki Miyake,
Hirofumi Muratani, Hanae Nozaki, Satoshi Ozaki, Hideo Shimizu, Wook Shin,
Hyung Chan Kim, Koji Chida, Shin'ichiro Matsuo, Kazuomi Oishi,
Koutarou Suzuki, Keisuke Tanaka, Siu-Leung Chung, Meng Ge, Jinyang Shi,
Hongwei Sun, Xibin Zhao, Meng Ge, Hongwei Sun, Daniel R.L. Brown,
Benoit Chevallier-Mames, Bok-Min Goi, Javier Herranz, Anthony T.S. Ho,
Benoit Libert, Qibin Sun, Tamir Tassa, Bogdan Warinschi, Kazuo Ohta,
Tetsuya Izu, Miyako Ohkubo, Mitsugu Iwamoto, Santoso Bagus,
Kazuki Yoneyama, Hyun A. Park, Kyu Young Choi, Nam Su Chang,
Taek Young Youn, Ik Rae Jeong, Jeong Jae Yu, Bum Han Kim, Chang Ho Hong,
Ryohei Fujimaki, Tsutomu Murase, Masayuki Nakae, Kazuo Yanoo, Jeen Kim,
Dang Nguyen Duc, Vo Duc Liem, Divyan M. Konidala, Uday K. Tupakula,
Ching Lin, Keisuke Takemori, Hiroshi Aono, Makoto Iguchi, Takeshi Okamoto,
Tetsu Iwata, Koji Okada, Kouya Tochikubo, Toshihiko Matsuo,
Naonobu Okazaki, Kazuhiro Ono, Yoshiaki Terashima, Hirosato Tsuji,

Haruko Kawahigashi, Ryuichi Kitaichi, Naishin Seki, Seiji Munetoh,
Sachiko Yoshihama, Takeo Yoshizawa, Megumi Nakamura, Yuji Watanabe,
Takuya Mishina, Seigo Arita, Keisuke Hakuta, Goichiro Hanaoka, Martin Hell,
Kentaro Imafuku, Tsuyoshi Nishioka, Katsuyuki Okeya, Hisayoshi Sato,
Hirotaka Yoshida, Sang Rae Cho, Jong-Gook Ko, Dosung Ahn.

Local Organizing Committee

Steering Chairs:	Yuko Murayama (Iwate Prefectural University, Japan)
	Shinichi Kawamura (Toshiba Corporation, Japan)
Program Chairs:	Hiroshi Yoshiura (University of Electro-Communications, Japan)
	Kouichi Sakurai (Kyushu University, Japan)
Finance Chair:	Masato Terada (Hitachi, Ltd., Japan)
Publicity Chairs:	Masakatsu Nishigaki (Shizuoka University, Japan)
	Ryuya Uda (Tokyo University of Technology, Japan)
	Mitsuru Matsui (Mitsubishi Electric Co., Japan)
	Tsuyoshi Takagi (Future University Hakodate, Japan)
Local Arrangement Chairs:	Tetsutaro Uehara (Kyoto University, Japan)
	Masakatsu Morii (Kobe Univesity, Japan)
Publication Chairs:	Hiroaki Kikuchi (Tokai University, Japan)
	Masahiro Mambo (University of Tsukuba, Japan)
	Kanta Matsuura (The University of Tokyo, Japan)
Registration Chairs:	Masato Terada (Hitachi, Ltd., Japan)
	Masayuki Terada (NTT DoCoMo, Inc., Japan)
Award Chairs:	Hiroshi Doi (Institute of Information Security, Japan)
	Atsuko Miyaji (Japan Advanced Institute of Science and Technology, Japan)
Liaison Chair:	Toshiaki Tanaka (KDDI Co., Japan)

Table of Contents

Authentication

Security for Multimedia

Network Security

Encryption and Key Exchange

Cryptanalysis and Implementation

Access Control

ID-Based Ring Signature Scheme Secure in the Standard Model

Man Ho Au[1], Joseph K. Liu[2], Tsz Hon Yuen[3], and Duncan S. Wong[4]

[1] Centre for Information Security Research
School of Information Technology and Computer Science
University of Wollongong
Wollongong 2522, Australia
mhaa456@uow.edu.au
[2] Department of Computer Science
University of Bristol
Bristol, BS8 1UB, UK
liu@cs.bris.ac.uk
[3] Department of Information Engineering
The Chinese University of Hong Kong
Shatin, N.T., Hong Kong
thyuen4@ie.cuhk.edu.hk
[4] Department of Computer Science
City University of Hong Kong
Kowloon, Hong Kong
duncan@cityu.edu.hk

Abstract. The only known construction of ID-based ring signature schemes which maybe secure in the standard model is to attach certificates to non-ID-based ring signatures. This method leads to schemes that are somewhat inefficient and it is an open problem to find more efficient and direct constructions. In this paper, we propose two such constructions. Our first scheme, with signature size linear in the cardinality of the ring, is secure in the standard model under the computational Diffie-Hellman assumption. The second scheme, achieving constant signature size, is secure in a weaker attack model (the selective ID and selective chosen message model), under the Diffie-Hellman Inversion assumption.

1 Introduction

Identity-based (ID-based) cryptosystem, introduced by Shamir [16], eliminated the need for checking the validity of the certificates. In an ID-based cryptosystem, public key of each user is easily computable from a string corresponding to this user's identity (e.g. an email address, a telephone number, etc.). A private key generator (PKG) then computes the private keys from a master secret for the users. This property avoids the necessity of certificates and associates an implicit public key (user identity) to each user within the system.

Ring signature is a group-oriented signature with privacy concerns. A user can sign anonymously on behalf of a group on his own choice, while group members can be totally unaware of being conscripted in the group. Any verifier can be

H. Yoshiura et al. (Eds.): IWSEC 2006, LNCS 4266, pp. 1–16, 2006.

convinced that a message has been signed by one of the members in this group, but the actual identity of the signer is hidden.

ID-based ring signature combines the property of ring signature and ID-based signature. The first construction is in [20]. Since then, several construction have been proposed [11,3,21,12,9]. The above scheme are all based on pairings with signature size linear in the cardinality of the ring. Non-pairing-based approach can be found in [2]. The first constant-size construction appears in [10]. Independent work was given in [14]. Both of them use accumulator. Later [19] point out a flaw in [14] and outline a patch. All existing constructions are only secure in the random oracle model.

There are only a few number of ring signature scheme secure in the standard model. One is a generic scheme based on standard signature, public-key encryption and ZAP proof system; and a second, more efficient ring signature scheme but supporting only 2 users[4]. Another one is an independent work by Chow *et. al.* without utilizing encryption and ZAP but rely on a new assumption [8]. Recently, independent of our work, Wei and Yuen have proposed a Hierarchical Identity-Based Threshold Ring Signature scheme in the standard model [18].

Our Contribution. We give two direction construction for ID-Based ring signature scheme. Signature size of the first scheme is linear with the cardinality of the ring. We prove that it is secure under the computational Diffie-Hellman assumption. Signature size of the second scheme is constant. We prove that the second scheme is secure under the Diffie-Hellman Inversion assumption in the selective-ID, selective chosen message attack model. In terms of signature size and computational cost, our schemes outperform schemes constructed indirectly following the generic approach described above.

2   Preliminaries

2.1   Security Models

An ID-Based $(1, n)$ Ring Signature scheme is a tuple of probabilistic polynomial-time (PPT) algorithms below:

- **Setup.** On input an unary string 1^λ where λ is a security parameter, the algorithm outputs a master secret key s and a list of system parameters param that includes λ and the descriptions of a user secret key space $\mathcal{D}$, a message space $\mathcal{M}$ as well as a signature space Ψ.
- **Extract.** On input a list param of system parameters, an identity $ID_i \in \{0,1\}^*$ for a user and the master secret key s, the algorithm outputs the user's secret key $d_i \in \mathcal{D}$. When we say identity ID_i corresponds to user secret key d_i or vice versa, we mean the pair (ID_i, d_i) is an input-output pair of **Extract** with respect to param and s.
- **Sign.** On input a list param of system parameters, a group size n of length polynomial in λ, a set $\{ID_i \in \{0,1\}^* | i \in [1, n]\}$ of n user identities, a message $m \in \mathcal{M}$, and a secret key $\{d_j \in \mathcal{D} | j \in [1, n]\}$, the algorithm outputs an ID-based $(1, n)$ ring signature $\sigma \in \Psi$.

- **Verify.** On input a list param of system parameters, a group size n of length polynomial in λ, a set $\{ID_i \in \{0,1\}^* | i \in [1,n]\}$ of n user identities, a message $m \in \mathcal{M}$, a signature $\sigma \in \Psi$, it outputs either valid or invalid.

Correctness. An ID-Based $(1,n)$ Ring Signature scheme should satisfy the *verification correctness* – signatures signed by honest signers are verified to be invalid with negligible probability.

2.2   Security Requirement

A secure ID-Based $(1,n)$ Ring Signature scheme should be *unforgeable* and *anonymous* which will be defined in a similar way to that of a traditional ring signature scheme.

Unforgeability. It should not be possible for an adversary to forge any signature just from the identities of the group members. We specify a security model which mainly captures the following two attacks:

1. Adaptive chosen message attack
2. Adaptive chosen identity attack

Adaptive chosen message attack allows an adversary to obtain message-signature pairs on demand during the forging attack. Adaptive chosen identity attack allows the adversary to forge a signature with respect to a group chosen by the adversary. To support adaptive chosen message attack, we provide the adversary the following oracle queries.

- **Extraction oracle** ($\mathcal{EO}$): On input ID_i, $d_i \leftarrow$ **Extract**(param, ID_i) is returned . The oracle is stateful, meaning that if $ID_i = ID_j$, then $d_i = d_j$.
- **Signing oracle** ($\mathcal{SO}$): $\mathcal{A}$ chooses a group of n identities $\{ID_i\}_{i \in [1,n]}$ and a message m, the oracle outputs a valid ID-based $(1,n)$ ring signature denoted by $\sigma \leftarrow$ **Sign**(param, n, $\{ID_i | i \in [1,n]\}, m$). The signing oracle may query the extraction oracle during its operation.

Let $\mathcal{U} = \{ID_1, \cdots, ID_N\}$ be a set of identities. An adversary $\mathcal{A}$ with oracles $\mathcal{EO}$ and $\mathcal{SO}$ *succeeds* if it outputs $(L, m, \sigma) \leftarrow \mathcal{A}^{\mathcal{SO},\mathcal{EO}}(\mathcal{U})$, such that it satisfies **Verify**(param, L, m, σ) = valid, where $L \subseteq \mathcal{U}$ and $|L| = n$ with restriction that (L, m) should not be in the set of oracle queries and replies between $\mathcal{A}$ and $\mathcal{SO}$, and $\mathcal{A}$ is not allowed to make an Extraction query on any identity $ID \in L$.

The advantage of an adversary $\mathcal{A}$ is defined to be

$$\mathbf{Adv}_{\mathcal{A}} = \Pr[\mathcal{A} \text{ succeeds}]$$

Definition 1 (Unforgeability). *An adversary $\mathcal{A}$ is said to be an (ϵ, t, q_e, q_s)-forger of an ID-based $(1,n)$ ring signature scheme if $\mathcal{A}$ has advantage at least ϵ, runs in time at most t, and makes at most q_e and q_s extraction and signing oracles queries respectively. A scheme is said to be (ϵ, t, q_e, q_s)-unforgeable if no (ϵ, t, q_e, q_s)-forger exists.*

Note that it cannot achieve the unforgeability in the stronger sense that the adversary produces a different signature on the same message and the same list of identities, as described in [1,13] since our proposed scheme does not enjoy this level of stronger security.

Anonymity. It should not be possible for an adversary to tell the identity of the signer with a probability larger than $1/n$, where n is the cardinality of the ring, even assuming that the adversary has unlimited computing resources.

Definition 2 (Anonymity). *An ID-based $(1, n)$ ring signature scheme is unconditional anonymous if for any group of n users with identity $\{ID_1, \cdots, ID_n\}$, any message m and signature $\sigma \leftarrow \mathbf{Sign}(param, n, \{ID_i | i \in [1, n]\}, m)$, any adversary $\mathcal{A}$, even with unbounded computational power, cannot identify the actual signer with probability better than random guessing. That is, $\mathcal{A}$ can only output the identity of the actual signer with probability no better than $1/n$.*

2.3 Bilinear Pairing

We briefly review bilinear pairing. We use the following notation [?]. Let $\mathbb{G}_1$ and $\mathbb{G}_2$ be two (multiplicative) cyclic groups of prime order p. Let g be a generator of $\mathbb{G}_1$, and $\hat{e}$ be a bilinear map such that $\hat{e} : \mathbb{G}_1 \times \mathbb{G}_1 \to \mathbb{G}_2$ with the following properties:

1. *Bilinearity:* For all $u, v \in \mathbb{G}_1$, and $a, b \in \mathbb{Z}$, $\hat{e}(u^a, v^b) = \hat{e}(u, v)^{ab}$.
2. *Non-degeneracy:* $\hat{e}(g, g) \neq 1$.
3. *Computability:* It is efficient to compute $\hat{e}(u, v)$ for all $u, v \in \mathbb{G}_1$.

2.4 Intractability Assumptions

We review some intractability assumptions in bilinear groups.

Definition 3 (Computational Diffie-Hellman (CDH) Problem). *Given a group G of prime order p with generator g and elements $g^a, g^b \in G$ where a, b are selected uniformly at random from $\mathbb{Z}_p^*$, the CDH problem in G is to compute g^{ab}.*

We say that the (ϵ, t)-CDH assumption holds in a group G if no algorithm running in time at most t can solve the CDH problem in G with probability at least ϵ.

Definition 4. *(n-DHI problem) The n-Diffie-Hellman Inversion problem is that, given $g, g^\alpha, g^{\alpha^2}, \ldots, g^{\alpha^n} \in G$, for unknown $\alpha \in \mathbb{Z}_p^*$, to compute $g^{1/\alpha}$.*

Definition 5. *(n-DHI* problem) The n-Diffie-Hellman Inversion* problem is that, given $g, g^\alpha, g^{\alpha^2}, \ldots, g^{\alpha^n} \in G$, for unknown $\alpha \in \mathbb{Z}_p^*$, to compute $g^{\alpha^{n+1}}$.*

The n-DHI problem and n-DHI* problem are proven equivalent in [22]. We say that the (ϵ, t, n)-DHI* assumption holds if no algorithm running in polynomial time t can solve a random instance of the n-DHI* problem with non-negligible probability ϵ.

3   The Proposed Scheme

Our proposed ID-based ring signature scheme is motivated from the signature scheme in [15,6] and the encryption scheme in [17].

3.1   Construction

Let $H_u : \{0,1\}^* \rightarrow \{0,1\}^{n_u}$ and $H_m : \{0,1\}^* \rightarrow \{0,1\}^{n_m}$ be two collision-resistant hash functions for some $n_u, n_m \in \mathbb{Z}$. They are used to create identities and messages of the desired length respectively. The proposed scheme is defined by the following algorithms.

Setup. Select a pairing $e : \mathbb{G}_1 \times \mathbb{G}_1 \rightarrow \mathbb{G}_2$ where the order of $\mathbb{G}_1$ is p. Let g be a generator of $\mathbb{G}_1$. Randomly select $\alpha \in_R \mathbb{Z}_p$, $g_2 \in_R \mathbb{G}_1$ and compute $g_1 = g^\alpha$. Also select randomly the following elements:

- $u', m' \in_R \mathbb{G}_1$
- $\hat{u}_i \in_R \mathbb{G}_1$ for $i = 1, \ldots, n_u$. Let $\hat{U} = \{\hat{u}_i\}$.
- $\hat{m}_i \in_R \mathbb{G}_1$ for $i = 1, \ldots, n_m$. Let $\hat{M} = \{\hat{m}_i\}$.

The public parameters param are $(e, \mathbb{G}_1, \mathbb{G}_2, g, g_1, g_2, u', \hat{U}, m', \hat{M})$ and the master secret key is g_2^α.

Extract. Let $u_j = H_u(ID_j)$ for user j with identity ID_j, where $j \in \mathbb{Z}$. Let $u_j[i]$ be the i-th bit of u_j. Define $\mathcal{U}_j \subset \{1, \ldots, n_u\}$ to be the set of indicies such that $u_j[i] = 1$.

To construct the private key, d_j, of identity ID_j, randomly selects $r_{u_j} \in_R \mathbb{Z}_p$ and compute $d_j = \left(g_2^\alpha (U_j)^{r_{u_j}}, g^{r_{u_j}} \right) = (D_j^{(1)}, D_j^{(2)})$ where $U_j = u' \prod_{i \in \mathcal{U}_j} \hat{u}_i$.

Sign. Let $L = \{ID_1, \ldots, ID_n\}$ be the list of n identities to be included in the ring signature, including the one of the actual signer. To sign a message $m \in \{0,1\}^*$, compute $\mathfrak{m} = H_m(m, L)$. Let $\mathfrak{m}[i]$ be the i-th bit of $\mathfrak{m}$ and $\mathcal{M} \subset \{1, \ldots, n_m\}$ be the set of indicies i such that $\mathfrak{m}[i] = 1$.

Let the signer be indexed π, where $\pi \in [1, n]$, with private key $d_\pi = (D_\pi^{(1)}, D_\pi^{(2)})$. Randomly select $r_1, \ldots, r_n, r_\mathfrak{m} \in_R \mathbb{Z}_p$, compute $U_j = u' \prod_{i \in \mathcal{U}_j} \hat{u}_i$ for $j = 1, \ldots, n$ and

$$\sigma = \left(D_\pi^{(1)} \left(\prod_{j=1}^n (U_j)^{r_j} \right) \left(m' \prod_{i \in \mathcal{M}} \hat{m}_i \right)^{r_\mathfrak{m}}, g^{r_1}, \ldots, g^{r_{\pi-1}}, D_\pi^{(2)} g^{r_\pi}, g^{r_{\pi+1}}, \right.$$

$$\left. \ldots, g^{r_n}, g^{r_\mathfrak{m}} \right)$$

$$= (V, R_1, \ldots, R_n, R_\mathfrak{m})$$

Verify. Given a signature $\sigma = (V, R_1, \ldots, R_n, R_\mathfrak{m})$ for a list of identities L on a message m, a verifier first computes $\mathfrak{m} = H_m(m, L)$, $U_j = u' \prod_{i \in \mathcal{U}_j} \hat{u}_i$ for $j = 1, \ldots, n$

and checks whether $e(V, g) \stackrel{?}{=} e(g_2, g_1) \left(\prod_{j=1}^{n} e(U_j, R_j) \right) e(m' \prod_{i \in \mathcal{M}} \hat{m}_i, R_m)$
Output valid if the equality holds. Otherwise output invalid.

Correctness. It is easy to see that the signature scheme is correct, as shown in following:

$$e(V, g) = e\left(g_2^{\alpha} (U_{\pi})^{r_{u_{\pi}}} (U_1)^{r_1} \dots (U_n)^{r_n} (m' \prod_{i \in \mathcal{M}} \hat{m}_i)^{r_m}, g \right)$$

$$e(V, g) = e\left(g_2^{\alpha} (U_1)^{r_1} \dots (U_{\pi})^{r_{u_{\pi}} + r_{\pi}} \dots (U_n)^{r_n} (m' \prod_{i \in \mathcal{M}} \hat{m}_i)^{r_m}, g \right)$$

$$= e(g_2, g)^{\alpha} e(U_1, g)^{r_1} \dots e(U_{\pi}, g)^{r_{u_{\pi}} + r_{\pi}} \dots e(U_n, g)^{r_n} e(m' \prod_{i \in \mathcal{M}} \hat{m}_i, g)^{r_m}$$

$$= e(g_2, g_1) e(U_1, R_1) \dots e(U_n, R_n) e(m' \prod_{i \in \mathcal{M}} \hat{m}_i, R_m)$$

3.2   Security Analysis

We will prove that our proposed scheme is unconditional anonymous and existentially unforgeable under a chosen message and identity attack, in the standard model.

Theorem 1 (Anonymity). *The scheme proposed in Section 3 is unconditional anonymous.*

Proof. In the signature $\sigma = (V, R_1, \dots, R_n, R_m)$, $\{R_i\}, i \in [1, n] \setminus \pi$ and R_m are randomly generated which provide no information on the actual signer. $R_{\pi} = g^{r_{u_{\pi}}} g^{r_{\pi}}$. r_{π} is randomly generated by the actual signer. $r_{u_{\pi}}$ is randomly generated by the master which is independent to any user. Thus R_{π} is also randomly distributed. V is in the form of $g_2^{\alpha} (U_1)^{r_1} \dots (U_{\pi})^{r_{u_{\pi}} + r_{\pi}} \dots (U_n)^{r_n} (m' \prod_{i \in \mathcal{M}} \hat{m}_i)^{r_m}$. Using the same argument, $r_1, \dots, r_{u_{\pi}} + r_{\pi}, \dots, r_n, r_m$ are random numbers while α is the master's secret key. All of them provide no information on the actual signer. It is no better for the adversary to do a wild guess. Our proposed scheme is unconditional anonymous. □

For unforgeability, our scheme relies on the hardness of CDH problem, which is stated as below:

Definition 6 (Computational Diffie-Hellman (CDH) Problem). *Given a group G of prime order p with generator g and elements $g^a, g^b \in G$ where a, b are selected uniformly at random from $\mathbb{Z}_p^*$, the CDH problem in G is to compute g^{ab}.*

We say that the (ϵ, t)-CDH assumption holds in a group G if no algorithm running in time at most t can solve the CDH problem in G with probability at least ϵ.

Theorem 2 (Existential Unforgeability). *The 1-out-of-n ID-based ring signature scheme proposed in Section 3 is (ϵ, t, q_e, q_s)-unforgeable, assuming that*

the (ϵ', t')-*CDH assumption holds in* $\mathbb{G}_1$, *where* $\epsilon' \geq \frac{\epsilon}{2^{n+3}(q_e + q_s)^n (n_u + 1)^n q_s (n_m + 1)}$,
$t' = t + O\Big((q_e n_u + q_s(nn_u + n_m))\rho + (q_e + nq_s)\tau\Big)$ *and* ρ *and* τ *are the time for a multiplication and an exponentiation in* $\mathbb{G}_1$ *respectively.*

Proof. Assume there is a (ϵ, t, q_e, q_s)-adversary $\mathcal{A}$ exists. We are going to construct another PPT $\mathcal{B}$ that makes use of $\mathcal{A}$ to solve the CDH problem with probability at least ϵ' and in time at most t'.

$\mathcal{B}$ is given a problem instance as follow: Given a group $\mathbb{G}_1$, a generator $g \in \mathbb{G}_1$, two elements $g^a, g^b \in \mathbb{G}_1$. It is asked to output another element $g^{ab} \in \mathbb{G}_1$. In order to use $\mathcal{A}$ to solve for the problem, $\mathcal{B}$ needs to simulates a challenger and the oracles (the extraction oracle and the signing oracle) for $\mathcal{A}$. $\mathcal{B}$ does it in the following way.

Setup. Let $l_u = 2(q_e + q_s)$ and $l_m = 2q_s$. $\mathcal{B}$ randomly selects two integers k_u and k_m such that $0 \leq k_u \leq n_u$ and $0 \leq k_m \leq n_m$. Also assume that $l_u(n_u + 1) < p$ and $l_m(n_m + 1) < p$ for the given values of q_e, q_s, n_u and n_m. It randomly selects the following integers:

- $x' \in_R \mathbb{Z}_{l_u}$; $z' \in_R \mathbb{Z}_{l_m}$; $y', w' \in_R \mathbb{Z}_p$
- $\hat{x}_i \in_R \mathbb{Z}_{l_u}$, for $i = 1, \ldots, n_u$. Let $\hat{X} = \{\hat{x}_i\}$.
- $\hat{z}_i \in_R \mathbb{Z}_{l_m}$, for $i = 1, \ldots, n_m$. Let $\hat{Z} = \{\hat{z}_i\}$.
- $\hat{y}_i \in_R \mathbb{Z}_p$, for $i = 1, \ldots, n_u$. Let $\hat{Y} = \{\hat{y}_i\}$.
- $\hat{w}_i \in_R \mathbb{Z}_p$, for $i = 1, \ldots, n_m$. Let $\hat{W} = \{\hat{w}_i\}$.

We further define the following functions for binary strings $\mathfrak{u}_j$ and $\mathfrak{m}$ where $\mathfrak{u}_j = H_u(ID_j)$ for an identity $ID_j, j \in Z$ and $\mathfrak{m} = H_m(m, L)$ for a message m and a list of identities L, as follow:

$$F(\mathfrak{u}_j) = x' + \sum_{i \in \mathcal{U}_j} \hat{x}_i - l_u k_u \quad \text{and} \quad J(\mathfrak{u}_j) = y' + \sum_{i \in \mathcal{U}_j} \hat{y}_i$$

$$K(\mathfrak{m}) = z' + \sum_{i \in \mathcal{M}} \hat{z}_i - l_m k_m \quad \text{and} \quad L(\mathfrak{m}) = w' + \sum_{i \in \mathcal{M}} \hat{w}_i$$

$\mathcal{B}$ constructs a set of public parameters as follow:

$$g_1 = g^a, \quad g_2 = g^b$$
$$u' = g_2^{-l_u k_u + x'} g^{y'}, \quad \hat{u}_i = g_2^{\hat{x}_i} g^{\hat{y}_i} \ \text{ for } \ 1 \leq i \leq n_u$$
$$m' = g_2^{-l_m k_m + z'} g^{w'}, \quad \hat{m}_i = g_2^{\hat{z}_i} g^{\hat{w}_i} \ \text{ for } \ 1 \leq i \leq n_m$$

Note that the master secret will be $g_2^\alpha = g_2^a = g^{ab}$ and we have the following equations: $U_j = u' \prod_{i \in \mathcal{U}_j} \hat{u}_i = g_2^{F(\mathfrak{u}_j)} g^{J(\mathfrak{u}_j)}$ and $m' \prod_{i \in \mathcal{M}} \hat{m}_i = g_2^{K(\mathfrak{m})} g^{L(\mathfrak{m})}$. All public parameters are passed to $\mathcal{A}$.

Oracles Simulation. $\mathcal{B}$ simulates the extraction and signing oracles as follow:

(*Extraction oracle.*) Upon receiving a query for a private key of an identity ID_j, B compute $\mathfrak{u} = H_u(ID_j)$. Although $\mathcal{B}$ does not know the master secret, it can still construct the private key by assuming $F(\mathfrak{u}_j) \neq 0 \bmod p$. It randomly chooses $r_{u_j} \in_R \mathbb{Z}_p$ and computes the private key as $d_{u_j} = (D_j^{(1)}, D_j^{(2)}) = \left(g_1^{-\frac{J(\mathfrak{u}_j)}{F(\mathfrak{u}_j)}} (U_j)^{r_{u_j}}, g_1^{-\frac{1}{F(\mathfrak{u}_j)}} g^{r_{u_j}} \right)$

By letting $\tilde{r}_{u_j} = r_{u_j} - \frac{a}{F(\mathfrak{u}_j)}$, it can be verifier that d_{u_j} is a valid private key, shown as follow:

$$
\begin{aligned}
D_j^{(1)} &= g_1^{-\frac{J(\mathfrak{u}_j)}{F(\mathfrak{u}_j)}} (U_j)^{r_{u_j}} \\
&= g_1^{-\frac{J(\mathfrak{u}_j)}{F(\mathfrak{u}_j)}} (g_2^{F(\mathfrak{u}_j)} g^{J(\mathfrak{u}_j)})^{r_{u_j}} \\
&= g^{-\frac{a J(\mathfrak{u}_j)}{F(\mathfrak{u}_j)}} (g_2^{F(\mathfrak{u}_j)} g^{J(\mathfrak{u}_j)})^{r_{u_j}} \\
&= g^{-\frac{a J(\mathfrak{u}_j)}{F(\mathfrak{u}_j)}} (g_2^{F(\mathfrak{u}_j)} g^{J(\mathfrak{u}_j)})^{\frac{a}{F(\mathfrak{u}_j)}} (g_2^{F(\mathfrak{u}_j)} g^{J(\mathfrak{u}_j)})^{-\frac{a}{F(\mathfrak{u}_j)}} (g_2^{F(\mathfrak{u}_j)} g^{J(\mathfrak{u}_j)})^{r_{u_j}} \\
&= g^{-\frac{a J(\mathfrak{u}_j)}{F(\mathfrak{u}_j)}} g^{ab} g^{\frac{a J(\mathfrak{u}_j)}{F(\mathfrak{u}_j)}} (g_2^{F(\mathfrak{u}_j)} g^{J(\mathfrak{u}_j)})^{\tilde{r}_{u_j}} \\
&= g^{ab} (g_2^{F(\mathfrak{u}_j)} g^{J(\mathfrak{u}_j)})^{\tilde{r}_{u_j}} = g_2^a (g_2^{F(\mathfrak{u}_j)} g^{J(\mathfrak{u}_j)})^{\tilde{r}_{u_j}} = g_2^a (U_j)^{\tilde{r}_{u_j}}
\end{aligned}
$$

and $D_j^{(2)} = g_1^{-\frac{1}{F(\mathfrak{u}_j)}} g^{r_{u_j}} = g^{r_{u_j} - \frac{a}{F(\mathfrak{u}_j)}} = g^{\tilde{r}_{u_j}}$ To the adversary, all private keys given by $\mathcal{B}$ are indistinguishable from the keys generated by the true challenger.

If $F(\mathfrak{u}_j) = 0 \bmod p$, since the above computation cannot be performed (division by 0), the simulator aborts. To make it simple, the simulator will abort if $F(\mathfrak{u}_j) = 0 \bmod l_u$. The equivalency can be observed as follow. From the assumption $l_u(n_u + 1) < p$, it implies $0 \leq l_u k_u < p$ and $0 \leq x' + \sum_{i \in \mathcal{U}_j} \hat{x}_i < p$ ($\because x' < l_u, \hat{x}_i < l_u, |\mathcal{U}_j| \leq n_u$). We have $-p < F(\mathfrak{u}_j) < p$ which implies if $F(\mathfrak{u}_j) = 0 \bmod p$ then $F(\mathfrak{u}_j) \bmod l_u$. Hence, $F(\mathfrak{u}_j) \neq 0 \bmod l_u$ implies $F(\mathfrak{u}_j) \neq 0 \bmod p$. Thus the former condition will be sufficient to ensure that a private key can be computed without aborting.

(*Signing oracle.*) For a given query of a signature on the list of identities $L = \{ID_1, \ldots, ID_n\}$ and a message m [1], $\mathcal{B}$ first computes $\mathfrak{u}_j = H_u(ID_j)$ and $\mathfrak{m} = H_m(m, L)$.

If $F(\mathfrak{u}_j) \neq 0 \bmod l_u$ for some $j \in [1, n]$, $\mathcal{B}$ randomly selects $\pi \in_R \mathcal{J}$ where $\mathcal{J}$ is the set of integers j such that $F(\mathfrak{u}_j) \neq 0 \bmod l_u$. $\mathcal{B}$ just constructs a private key for π as in the extraction oracle query, then use the **Sign** algorithm described in the proposed scheme to create a signature on L and m.

If $F(\mathfrak{u}_j) = 0 \bmod l_u$ for *all* $j \in [1, n]$, $\mathcal{B}$ tries to construct the signature in a similar way to the construction of private key in an extraction oracle query. Assume $K(\mathfrak{m}) \neq 0 \bmod l_m$. Using the aforementioned argument, it implies $K(\mathfrak{m}) \neq 0 \bmod p$ provided that $l_m(n_m + 1) < p$. The signature can be constructed by first randomly selecting $r_1, \ldots, r_n, r_\mathfrak{m} \in_R \mathbb{Z}_p$ and computing

---

[1] Note that $\mathcal{A}$ is not allowed to make any extraction oracle query on any ID_j, where $ID_j \in L$.

$$\sigma = \left(\left(\prod_{j=1}^{n} (U_j)^{r_j} \right) g_1^{-\frac{L(m)}{K(m)}} \left(m' \prod_{i \in \mathcal{M}} \hat{m}_i \right)^{r_m} , g^{r_1}, \ldots, g^{r_n}, g_1^{-\frac{1}{K(m)}} g^{r_m} \right)$$

$$= \left(g_2^a \left(\prod_{j=1}^{n} (U_j)^{r_j} \right) \left(m' \prod_{i \in \mathcal{M}} \hat{m}_i \right)^{\tilde{r}_m} , g^{r_1}, \ldots, g^{r_n}, g^{\tilde{r}_m} \right)$$

where $\tilde{r}_m = r_m - \frac{a}{K(m)}$. If $K(m) = 0 \mod l_m$, the simulator aborts.

Output Calculation. If $\mathcal{B}$ does not abort, $\mathcal{A}$ will return a list of identities $L^* = \{ID_1^*, \ldots, ID_n^*\}$ and a message m^* with a forged signature $\sigma^* = (V, R_1, \ldots, R_n, R_m)$ on L^* and m^* with probability at least ϵ. $\mathcal{B}$ checks whether the following conditions are fulfilled:

1. $F(u_j^*) = 0 \mod p$ for *all* $j \in [1, n]$, where $u_j^* = H_u(ID_j^*)$.
2. $K(m^*) = 0 \mod p$, where $m^* = H_m(m^*, L^*)$.

If not all the above conditions are fulfilled, $\mathcal{B}$ aborts. Otherwise $\mathcal{B}$ computes and outputs

$$\frac{V}{R_1^{J(u_1^*)} \ldots R_n^{J(u_n^*)} R_m^{L(m^*)}} = \frac{g_2^a (U_1)^{r_1} \ldots (U_n)^{r_n} \left(m' \prod_{i \in \mathcal{M}} \hat{m}_i \right)^{r_m}}{g^{J(u_1^*)r_1} \ldots g^{J(u_n^*)r_n} g^{L(m^*)r_m}}$$

$$= \frac{g_2^a \left(g_2^{F(u_1^*)} g^{J(u_1^*)} \right)^{r_1} \ldots \left(g_2^{F(u_n^*)} g^{J(u_n^*)} \right)^{r_n} \left(g_2^{K(m^*)} g^{L(m^*)} \right)^{r_m}}{g^{J(u_1^*)r_1} \ldots g^{J(u_n^*)r_n} g^{L(m^*)r_m}}$$

$$= g_2^a = g^{ab}$$

which is the solution to the CDH problem instance.

Probability Analysis. For the simulation to complete without aborting, we require the following conditions fulfilled:

1. Extraction queries on an identity ID have $F(u) \neq 0 \mod l_u$, where $u = H_u(ID)$.
2. Sign queries (L, m) will either have $F(u_j) \neq 0 \mod l_u$, for some $j \in [1, n]$ where $ID_j \in L$, or $K(m) \neq 0 \mod l_m$ where $m = H_m(m, L)$.
3. $F(u_j^*) = 0 \mod l_u$ for all $j \in [1, n]$ where $ID_j^* \in L^*$ and $K(m^*) = 0 \mod l_m$.

For ease of analysis, we will bound the probability of a subcase of this event.

Let $u_1, \ldots, u_{q_I}$ be the output of the hash function H_u appearing in either extract queries or in sign queries not involving any of the challenge identity included in L^*, and let $m_1, \ldots, m_{q_M}$ be the output of the hash function H_m in the sign queries involving the challenge list of identities L^*. We have $q_I \leq q_e + q_s$ and $q_M \leq q_s$. We also define the events A_i, A^*, B_ℓ, B^* as follow:

$$A_i : F(u_i) \neq 0 \mod l_u \qquad \text{where } i = 1, \ldots, q_I$$
$$A^* : F(u_j^*) = 0 \mod p \qquad \text{for all } j \in [1, n] \text{ where } ID_j^* \in L^*$$
$$B_\ell : K(m_\ell) \neq 0 \mod l_m \qquad \text{where } \ell = 1, \ldots, q_M$$
$$B^* : K(m^*) = 0 \mod p$$

The probability of $\mathcal{B}$ not aborting is

$$\Pr[\text{not abort}] \geq \Pr\left[\left(\bigwedge_{i=1}^{q_I} A_i \wedge A^*\right) \wedge \left(\bigwedge_{\ell=1}^{q_M} B_\ell \wedge B^*\right)\right]$$

Note that the events $\left(\bigwedge_{i=1}^{q_I} A_i \wedge A^*\right)$ and $\left(\bigwedge_{\ell=1}^{q_M} B_\ell \wedge B^*\right)$ are independent.

The assumption $l_u(n_u + 1) < p$ implies if $F(\mathfrak{u}) = 0 \bmod p$ then $F(\mathfrak{u}) = 0 \bmod l_u$. Since k_u, x' and $\hat{X}$ are randomly chosen,

$$\Pr[A^*] = \prod_{j=1}^{n} \Pr[F(\mathfrak{u}_j^*) = 0 \bmod p \wedge F(\mathfrak{u}_j^*) = 0 \bmod l_u]$$

$$= \prod_{j=1}^{n} \Pr[F(\mathfrak{u}_j^*) = 0 \bmod l_u] \Pr[F(\mathfrak{u}_j^*) = 0 \bmod p \mid F(\mathfrak{u}_j^*) = 0 \bmod l_u]$$

$$= \left(\frac{1}{l_u} \frac{1}{n_u + 1}\right)^n$$

On the other hand, we have $\Pr\left[\bigwedge_{i=1}^{q_I} A_i | A^*\right] = 1 - \Pr\left[\bigvee_{i=1}^{q_I} \overline{A_i} \mid A^*\right] \geq 1 - \sum_{i=1}^{q_I} \Pr[\overline{A_i} \mid A^*]$ where $\overline{A_i}$ denote the event $F(\mathfrak{u}_i) = 0 \bmod l_u$.

Also note that the events $F(\mathfrak{u}_{i_1}) = 0 \bmod l_u$ and $F(\mathfrak{u}_{i_2}) = 0 \bmod l_u$ are independent, where $i_1 \neq i_2$, since the outputs of $F(\mathfrak{u}_{i_1})$ and $F(\mathfrak{u}_{i_2})$ will differ in at least one randomly chosen value. Also since the events A_i and A^* are independent for any i, we have $\Pr[\overline{A_i}|A^*] = 1/l_u$ and

$$\Pr\left[\bigwedge_{i=1}^{q_I} A_i \wedge A^*\right] = \Pr[A^*] \Pr\left[\bigwedge_{i=1}^{q_I} A_i | A^*\right]$$

$$= \left(\frac{1}{l_u(n_u + 1)}\right)^n \left(1 - \frac{q_I}{l_u}\right)$$

$$\geq \left(\frac{1}{l_u(n_u + 1)}\right)^n \left(1 - \frac{q_e + q_s}{l_u}\right)$$

$$= \left(\frac{1}{2(q_e + q_s)(n_u + 1)}\right)^n \left(1 - \frac{1}{2}\right)$$

$$(\text{ by setting } l_u = 2(q_e + q_s)) = \frac{1}{2^{n+1}(q_e + q_s)^n(n_u + 1)}$$

Using similar analysis technique for signing queries we can have

$$\Pr\left[\bigwedge_{\ell=1}^{q_M} B_\ell \wedge B^*\right] \geq \frac{1}{4q_s(n_m + 1)}$$

By combining the above result, we have

$$\Pr[\text{not abort}] \geq \Pr\left[\left(\bigwedge_{i=1}^{q_I} A_i \wedge A^*\right) \wedge \left(\bigwedge_{\ell=1}^{q_M} B_\ell \wedge B^*\right)\right]$$

$$\geq \frac{1}{2^{n+3}(q_e + q_s)^n (n_u + 1)^n q_s (n_m + 1)}$$

If the simulation does not abort, $\mathcal{A}$ will produce a forged signature with probability at least ϵ. Thus $\mathcal{B}$ can solve for the CDH problem instance with probability

$$\epsilon' \geq \frac{\epsilon}{2^{n+3}(q_e+q_s)^n(n_u+1)^n q_s(n_m+1)}$$

Remark: We note that since n is included as the exponent of the denominator, we suggest that n may not be too large in order to claim its security.

Time Complexity Analysis. The time complexity of $\mathcal{B}$ is dominated by the exponentiation and multiplication operations for large values of n_u and n_m performed in the extraction and signing queries.

There are $O(n_u)$ and $O(nn_u + n_m)$ multiplications and $O(1)$ and $O(n)$ exponentiations in the extraction and singing stage respectively. The time complexity of $\mathcal{B}$ is $t + O\Big(\big(q_e n_u + q_s(nn_u + n_m)\big)\rho + (q_e + nq_s)\tau \Big)$ □

4   Constant-Size Identity Based Ring Signature

We propose a constant-size identity based ring signature without random oracles. The size of the signature is independent of the size of the ring. However, this scheme has a restriction on the maximum number of signers of the ring when the private key is extracted from the identity. Furthermore, the scheme is provably secure in a weak model for unforgeability, namely selective-identity, selective chosen message attack. The security model of selective-identity can be found in [7]. This model is used in some identity based schemes. The difference from the standard model is that the adversary gives the challenge identity at the beginning of the security game, and the query of the challenge identity (or its prefix) to the extraction oracle is forbidden.

In this section, we use a security model in unforgeability which extends the selective-identity model. We introduce the selective-identity, selective chosen message attack model. The difference from the adaptive identity and adaptive chosen message attack model is that the adversary gives the challenge identity and challenge message at the beginning of the unforgeability game, the query of the challenge identity to the extraction oracle is forbidden, and the query of the challenge identity and the challenge message together to the signing oracle is forbidden.

4.1   Construction

Our scheme is motivated from the encryption scheme in [5]. Let $H_u : \{0,1\}^* \to \mathbb{Z}_p^*$ and $H_m : \{0,1\}^* \to \mathbb{Z}_p^*$ be two collision-resistant hash functions. They are used to create identities and messages of the desired length respectively. The proposed scheme is defined by the following algorithms.

Setup. Select a pairing $e : \mathbb{G}_1 \times \mathbb{G}_1 \to \mathbb{G}_2$ where the order of $\mathbb{G}_1$ is p. Let g be a generator of $\mathbb{G}_1$. Randomly select $\alpha \in_R \mathbb{Z}_p$, $g_2 \in_R \mathbb{G}_1$ and compute $g_1 = g^\alpha$. Also select randomly the following elements:

- $u', m' \in_R \mathbb{G}_1$
- $\hat{u}_i \in_R \mathbb{G}_1$ for $i = 1, \ldots, n + 1$. Let $\hat{U} = \{\hat{u}_i\}$.

The public parameters param are $(e, \mathbb{G}_1, \mathbb{G}_2, g, g_1, g_2, u', \hat{U})$ and the master secret key is g_2^{α}.

Extract. To generate a private key for ID, let id$= H_u(ID)$. For $1 \leq i \leq n + 1$, the algorithm picks a random $r_i \in \mathbb{Z}_p^*$ and computes:

$$SK_{ID,i} = \left(g_2^{\alpha}(u' \hat{u}_i^{\mathrm{id}})^{r_i}, \quad g^{r_i}, \quad \hat{u}_1^{r_i}, \quad \ldots, \quad \hat{u}_{i-1}^{r_i}, \quad \hat{u}_{i+1}^{r_i}, \quad \ldots, \quad \hat{u}_{n+1}^{r_i}\right)$$
$$= (a_i, \ b_i, \ c_{i,1}, \ \ldots, \ c_{i,i-1}, \ c_{i,i+1}, \ \ldots, \ c_{i,n+1})$$

Sign. Let $L = \{ID_1, \ldots, ID_{n'}\}$ be the list of $n' < n$ identities to be included in the ring signature, including the one of the actual signer at index π. Let id$_i = H_u(ID_i)$ for $i = 1, \ldots, n'$. To sign a message $M \in \{0,1\}^*$, let m$= H_m(M, L)$. The signer picks random $t \in \mathbb{Z}_p$, and uses $SK_{ID,\pi}$ to compute:
$V = a_{\pi} \cdot (\prod_{j=1, j \neq \pi}^{n'} c_{\pi,j}^{\mathrm{id}_j}) \cdot c_{\pi,n'+1}^{\mathrm{m}} \cdot (\hat{u}_1^{\mathrm{id}_1} \cdots \hat{u}_{n'}^{\mathrm{id}_{n'}} \cdot \hat{u}_{n'+1}^{\mathrm{m}} \cdot u')^t$, $R = b_{\pi} \cdot g^t$ The signature σ is (V, R).

Verify. Given a signature $\sigma = (V, R)$ for a list of identities $L = \{ID_1, \ldots, ID_{n'}\}$ on a message M, a verifier first computes m$= H_m(M, L)$ and id$_i = H_u(ID_i)$ for $i = 1, \ldots, n'$ and then checks whether $\hat{e}(g, V) \stackrel{?}{=} \hat{e}(g_1, g_2) \cdot \hat{e}(R, \hat{u}_1^{\mathrm{id}_1} \cdots \hat{u}_{n'}^{\mathrm{id}_{n'}} \cdot \hat{u}_{n'+1}^{\mathrm{m}} \cdot u')$ Output valid if the equality holds. Otherwise output invalid.

Correctness. The scheme is correct as shown in the following:

$$\hat{e}(g, V) = \hat{e}(g, a_{\pi} \cdot (\prod_{j=1, j \neq \pi}^{n'} c_{\pi,j}^{\mathrm{id}_j}) \cdot c_{\pi,n'+1}^{\mathrm{m}} \cdot (\hat{u}_1^{\mathrm{id}_1} \cdots \hat{u}_{n'}^{\mathrm{id}_{n'}} \cdot \hat{u}_{n'+1}^{\mathrm{m}} \cdot u')^t)$$
$$= \hat{e}(g, g_2^{\alpha} \cdot (\hat{u}_1^{\mathrm{id}_1} \cdots \hat{u}_{n'}^{\mathrm{id}_{n'}} \cdot \hat{u}_{n'+1}^{\mathrm{m}} \cdot u')^{r_{\pi}+t})$$
$$= \hat{e}(g_1, g_2) \cdot \hat{e}(R, \hat{u}_1^{\mathrm{id}_1} \cdots \hat{u}_{n'}^{\mathrm{id}_{n'}} \cdot \hat{u}_{n'+1}^{\mathrm{m}} \cdot u')$$

4.2   Security Analysis

Theorem 3 (Anonymity). *The scheme proposed in Section 4 is unconditional anonymous.*

Proof. In the signature $\sigma = (V, R)$, $R = g^{r_{\pi}} g^t$. t is randomly generated by the actual signer. r_{π} is randomly generated by the master which is independent to any user. Thus R is a random number. V is in the form of $g_2^{\alpha} (\hat{u}_1^{\mathrm{id}_1} \cdots \hat{u}_{n'}^{\mathrm{id}_{n'}})^{r_{\pi}+t}$. Using the same argument, $r_{\pi} + t$ is a random number while α is the master's secret key. All of them provide no information on the actual signer. It is no better for the adversary to do a wild guess. Our proposed scheme is unconditional anonymous. $\square$

Theorem 4. *The 1-out-of-$(n - 1)$ ID-based ring signature scheme proposed in section 4 is (ϵ, t, q_e, q_s)-unforgeable under the selective-ID attack model, assuming that the (ϵ', t', n)-DHI* assumption holds in $\mathbb{G}_1$ and H_u, H_m are collision* *resistant hash functions, where* $\epsilon' \geq \epsilon \left(1 - \frac{1}{p}\right)^{q_e} \left(1 - \frac{1}{p^2}\right)^{q_s}$, $t' = t + O\left((q_e + q_s)n\rho\right) + O\left((q_e + q_s)n\tau\right)$ *and* ρ *and* τ *are the time for a multiplication and an exponentiation in* $\mathbb{G}_1$ *respectively.*

Proof. Assume there is a (ϵ, t, q_e, q_s)-adversary $\mathcal{A}$ exists. We are going to construct another PPT $\mathcal{B}$ that makes use of $\mathcal{A}$ to solve the n-DHI* problem with probability at least ϵ' and in time at most t'.

Setup. $\mathcal{B}$ is given the n-DHI* tuple $(g, g^x, \ldots, g^{x^n})$. The game begins with $\mathcal{A}$ sends the challenge identity $L^* = \{ID_1^*, \ldots, ID_{n-1}^*\}$ and the challenge message M^* to $\mathcal{B}$. Denote $\mathsf{id}_j^* = H_u(ID_j^*)$ for $1 \leq j \leq n-1$ and $\mathsf{id}_n^* = H_m(M^*, L^*)$. $\mathcal{B}$ picks a random $\gamma \in \mathbb{Z}_p$ and assigns $g_1 = g^x, g_2 = g^{x^n} \cdot g^\gamma$. $\mathcal{B}$ picks random $\gamma_1, \ldots \gamma_{n+1} \in \mathbb{Z}_p$ and sets $\hat{u}_j = g^{\gamma_j} g^{-x^{n-j+1}}$, for $1 \leq j \leq n$. It also picks a random $\delta \in \mathbb{Z}_p$ and computes $u' = g^{\delta + \sum_{j=1}^n x^{n-j+1} \mathsf{id}_j^*}$. $\mathcal{B}$ gives $\mathcal{A}$ the public parameters $\mathsf{param} = (g, g_1, g_2, u', \hat{u}_1, \ldots, \hat{u}_n)$. The corresponding (unknown) master secret key is $g_2^x = g^{x(x^n + \gamma)}$.

Oracle Simulation. $\mathcal{B}$ simulates the extraction and signing oracles as follow:

(*Extraction oracle.*) Upon receiving a query for a private key of an identity ID, if $H_u(ID) = H_u(ID_1^*)$, $\mathcal{B}$ declares failure and exits. Otherwise the simulator chooses a random $\tilde{r}_1 \in \mathbb{Z}_p$. Denote $\mathsf{id} = H_u(ID)$ and $r_1 = \frac{x}{(\mathsf{id} - \mathsf{id}_1^*)} + \tilde{r}_1$ and compute:

$$a_1 = g^{x\gamma} \cdot Z \cdot g^{x^n \tilde{r}_1 (\mathsf{id}_1^* - \mathsf{id})} \quad \text{where} \quad Z = \left(g^{\delta + \mathsf{id}\gamma_1} \cdot \prod_{i=2}^n g^{x^{n-i+1} \mathsf{id}_i^*}\right)^{r_1}$$

$$b_1 = g^{r_1} = g^{x/(\mathsf{id} - \mathsf{id}_1^*)} g^{\tilde{r}_1}$$

$$c_{1,2} = \hat{u}_2^{r_1} = g^{(\gamma_2 - x^{n-1})\left(\frac{x}{(\mathsf{id} - \mathsf{id}_1^*)} + \tilde{r}_1\right)}$$

$$\vdots$$

$$c_{1,n} = \hat{u}_2^{r_1} = g^{(\gamma_n - x)\left(\frac{x}{(\mathsf{id} - \mathsf{id}_1^*)} + \tilde{r}_1\right)}$$

Refer to [5] for the well-formedness of the secret key. The computation for $(a_i, b_i, c_{i,j})$ where $1 \leq i \leq n-1$ are similar and hence are omitted.

(*Signing oracle.*) For input identities $L = (ID_1, \ldots, ID_{n'})$ and message M, denote $\mathsf{id}_j = H_u(ID_j)$ for $1 \leq j \leq n'$ and $\mathsf{id}_{n'+1} = H_m(M, L)$. If $\{\mathsf{id}_1, \ldots, \mathsf{id}_{n'+1}\}$ is the same as $\{\mathsf{id}_1^*, \ldots, \mathsf{id}_n^*\}$ or is a prefix of it, $\mathcal{B}$ declares failure and exits. Otherwise there exists a $k \leq n$ such that $\mathsf{id}_k \neq \mathsf{id}_k^*$. We set k be the smallest such index. To answer the query, $\mathcal{B}$ derives for the secret key of identity id_k as in the extraction oracle, and then computes the signature using the secret key.

Output Calculation. Finally, $\mathcal{A}$ returns a signature σ^* for message M^* and signers L^*. Notice that L^* and M^* is given at the beginning of the selective-ID game and the total length of id_i^* is n. We denote $\sigma^* = (V^*, R^*)$. Therefore we can set $R^* = g^{\bar{r}}$ for some $\bar{r} \in \mathbb{Z}_p$. Then:

$$V^* = g_2^\alpha (u' \prod_{i=1}^n \hat{u}_i^{\mathrm{id}_i^*})^{\bar{r}}$$

$$= g_2^\alpha (g^\delta \prod_{j=1}^n g^{x^{n-j+1}\mathrm{id}_j^*} \prod_{i=1}^n (\frac{g^{\gamma_i}}{g^{x^{n-i+1}}})^{\mathrm{id}_i^*})^{\bar{r}}$$

$$= g_2^\alpha (g^\delta \prod_{i=1}^n g^{\gamma_i \mathrm{id}_i^*})^{\bar{r}} = g_2^\alpha (g^{\delta + \sum_{i=1}^n (\gamma_i \mathrm{id}_i^*)})^{\bar{r}}$$

Therefore $\mathcal{B}$ returns $g^{x^{\ell+1}} = g_2^\alpha / g^{x\gamma} = V^*/(R^{*\delta + \sum_{i=1}^\ell (\gamma_i I_i^*)} g^{x\gamma})$ as the solution.
Probability Analysis. For the simulation to complete without aborting, we require the following conditions fulfilled:

1. Extraction queries on an identity ID have $H_u(ID) = H_u(ID_1^*)$.
2. Sign queries for $\{\mathrm{id}_1, \ldots, \mathrm{id}_{n'+1}\}$ is not the same as $\{\mathrm{id}_1^*, \ldots, \mathrm{id}_n^*\}$ or is a prefix of it.

We define the events A_i, B_ℓ as follow:

$$A_i : H_u(ID_i) \neq H_u(ID_1^*) \qquad \text{where } i = 1, \ldots, q_e$$
$$B_\ell : \{\mathrm{id}_{\ell,1}, \ldots, \mathrm{id}_{\ell,n'_\ell+1}\} \neq \{\mathrm{id}_1^*, \ldots, \mathrm{id}_{\bar{n}}^*\} \qquad \text{where } \ell = 1, \ldots, q_s, \ 2 \leq \bar{n} \leq n$$

The probability of $\mathcal{B}$ not aborting is $\Pr[\text{not abort}] \geq \Pr\left[\left(\bigwedge_{i=1}^{q_e} A_i\right) \wedge \left(\bigwedge_{\ell=1}^{q_s} B_\ell\right)\right]$
Note that the events $\left(\bigwedge_{i=1}^{q_e} A_i\right)$ and $\left(\bigwedge_{\ell=1}^{q_s} B_\ell\right)$ are independent.

The assumption that H_u and H_m are collision resistant hash functions implies:
$\Pr[A_i] = 1 - \frac{1}{p}$ and $\Pr[B_i] = 1 - (\frac{1}{p})^{n'_i + 1}$
By combining the above result, we have

$$\Pr[\text{not abort}] \geq \Pr\left[\left(\bigwedge_{i=1}^{q_e} A_i\right) \wedge \left(\bigwedge_{\ell=1}^{q_s} B_\ell\right)\right]$$
$$= \left(1 - \frac{1}{p}\right)^{q_e} \prod_{i=1}^{q_s} \left(1 - (\frac{1}{p})^{n'_i + 1}\right) \geq \left(1 - \frac{1}{p}\right)^{q_e} \left(1 - \frac{1}{p^2}\right)^{q_s}$$

If the simulation does not abort, $\mathcal{A}$ will produce a forged signature with probability at least ϵ. Thus $\mathcal{B}$ can solve for the DHI* problem instance with probability
$\epsilon' \geq \epsilon\left(1 - \frac{1}{p}\right)^{q_e} \left(1 - \frac{1}{p^2}\right)^{q_s}$
Time Complexity Analysis. The time complexity of $\mathcal{B}$ is dominated by the exponentiation and multiplication operations for large values of n_u and n_m performed in the extraction and signing queries.

There are $O(n)$ multiplications and $O(n)$ exponentiations in the both extraction and singing stage. The time complexity of $\mathcal{B}$ is $t + O\left((q_e + q_s)n\rho\right) + O\left((q_e + q_s)n\tau\right)$ $\qquad \square$

Full Unforgeability. As shown in many identity-based schemes in the literature with selective-ID security model, we can always turns a proof in selective-ID security model into a proof of adaptive-ID model by hashing the identity prior to using it. However the reduction introduces a 2^d multiplicative security loss factor in the standard model, where d is the length of the output of the hash function. The same result can be applied to our scheme. For the selective chosen message attack, the case is similar to the selective-ID model. We can turn the proof into a proof of adaptive chosen message attack model by hashing the message. However the reduction introduces a $2^{d'}$ multiplicative security loss factor in the standard model, where d' is the length of the output of the hash function for message.

5 Conclusion

In this paper, we have proposed two new ID-based ring signature schemes which are secure in the standard model. Our first scheme, with signature size linear in the cardinality of the ring, is secure in the standard model under the computational Diffie-Hellman assumption. The second scheme, achieving constant signature size, is secure in a weaker attack model (the selective ID and selective chosen message model), under the Diffie-Hellman Inversion assumption. It also applies certain limitation on the size of the ring in the signature.

It remains an open problem to construct a scheme that is secure in the strongest model with constant size signature while removing all limitations on the size of ring.

References

1. M. Abe, M. Ohkubo, and K. Suzuki. 1-out-of-n signatures from a variety of keys. In *Proc. ASIACRYPT 2002*, pages 415–432. Springer-Verlag, 2002. Lecture Notes in Computer Science No. 2501.
2. M. Au, J. K. Liu, P. P. Tsang, and D. S. Wong. A suite of id-based threshold ring signature schemes with different levels of anonymity. Cryptology ePrint Archive, Report 2005/326, 2005. http://eprint.iacr.org/.
3. A. K. Awasthi and S. Lal. ID-based Ring Signature and Proxy Ring Signature Schemes from Bilinear Pairings. Cryptology ePrint Archive, Report 2004/184, 2004. http://eprint.iacr.org/.
4. A. Bender, J. Katz, and R. Morselli. Ring signatures: Stronger definitions, and constructions without random oracles. In *TCC 2006*, volume 3816 of *Lecture Notes in Computer Science*, pages 60–79. Springer, 2006.
5. D. Boneh, X. Boyen, and E.-J. Goh. Hierarchical identity based encryption with constant size ciphertext. In *Proc. EUROCRYPT 2005*, volume 3494 of *LNCS*, pages 440–456. Springer, 2005.
6. X. Boyen and B. Waters. Compact group signatures without random oracles. In *Advances in Cryptology—EUROCRYPT 2006*, volume 4004 of *Lecture Notes in Computer Science*, pages 427–444. Springer-Verlag, 2006.
7. R. Canetti, S. Halevi, and J. Katz. A forward-secure public-key encryption scheme. In *Proc. EUROCRYPT 2003*, volume 2656 of *Leture Notes in Computer Science*, pages 255–271. Springer-Verlag, 2003.

8. S. S. M. Chow, J. K. Liu, V. K. Wei, and T. H. Yuen. Ring signatures without random oracles. In *ASIACCS 06*, pages 297–302. ACM, 2006.
9. S. S. M. Chow, S.-M. Yiu, and L. C. K. Hui. Efficient identity based ring signature. In *ACNS 2005*, volume 3531 of *Lecture Notes in Computer Science*, pages 499–512. Springer, 2005.
10. Y. Dodis, A. Kiayias, A. Nicolosi, and V. Shoup. Anonymous identification in ad hoc groups. In *EUROCRYPT 2004*, volume 3027 of *LNCS*, pages 609–626. Springer-Verlag, 2004.
11. J. Herranz and G. Sáez. A provably secure ID-based ring signature scheme. Cryptology ePrint Archive, Report 2003/261, 2003. `http://eprint.iacr.org/`.
12. C.-Y. Lin and T.-C. Wu. An identity-based ring signature scheme from bilinear pairings. Cryptology ePrint Archive, Report 2003/117, 2003. `http://eprint.iacr.org/`.
13. J. K. Liu and D. S. Wong. Linkable ring signatures: Security models and new schemes (extended abstract). In *ICCSA 2005*, volume 3481 of *LNCS*, pages 614–623. Springer-Verlag, 2005.
14. L. Nguyen. Accumulators from Bilinear Pairings and Applications. In *CT-RSA 2005*, volume 3376 of *LNCS*, pages 275–292, 2005.
15. K. Paterson and J. Schuldt. Efficient identity-based signatures secure in the standard model. Cryptology ePrint Archive, Report 2006/080, 2006. `http://eprint.iacr.org/2006/080/`.
16. A. Shamir. Identity-Based Cryptosystems and Signature Schemes. In *CRYPTO 1984*, volume 196 of *LNCS*, pages 47–53, 1984.
17. B. Waters. Efficient identity-based encryption without random oracles. In *Proc. EUROCRYPT 2005*, volume 3494 of *LNCS*, pages 114–127. Springer-Verlag, 2005.
18. V. Wei and Y. H. Yuen. (hierarchical identity-based) threshold ring signatures. http://eprint.iacr.org/2006/193/, 2006.
19. F. Zhang and X. Chen. Cryptanalysis and improvement of an id-based ad-hoc anonymous identification scheme at ct-rsa 05. Cryptology ePrint Archive, Report 2005/103, 2005. `http://eprint.iacr.org/`.
20. F. Zhang and K. Kim. ID-Based Blind Signature and Ring Signature from Pairings. In *ASIACRYPT 2002*, volume 2501 of *LNCS*, pages 533–547. Springer-Verlag, 2002.
21. F. Zhang and K. Kim. Efficient ID-Based Blind Signature and Proxy Signature from Bilinear Pairings. In R. Safavi-Naini and J. Seberry, editors, *Information Security and Privacy, 8th Australasian Conference, ACISP 2003, Wollongong, Australia, July 9-11, 2003, Proceedings*, volume 2727 of *Lecture Notes in Computer Science*, pages 312–323. Springer, 2003.
22. F. Zhang, R. Safavi-Naini, and W. Susilo. An efficient signature scheme from bilinear pairings and its applications. In *PKC 2004*, volume 2947 of *Lecture Notes in Computer Science*, pages 277–290. Springer, 2004.

A Short Verifier-Local Revocation Group Signature Scheme with Backward Unlinkability

Toru Nakanishi and Nobuo Funabiki

Dept. of Communication Network Engineering, Okayama University, Japan
{nakanisi, funabiki}@cne.okayama-u.ac.jp

Abstract. Previously Verifier-Local Revocation (VLR) group signature schemes from bilinear maps were proposed. In VLR schemes, only verifiers are involved in the revocation of a member, while signers are not involved in the revocation. Thus, the schemes are suitable for mobile environments. Furthermore, the previously proposed schemes satisfy an important property, the backward unlinkability. It means that even after a member is revoked, signatures produced by the member before the revocation remain anonymous. This property is needed in case a member leaves voluntarily or in case of a stolen key. In this paper an improved scheme is proposed, where the group signatures are shorter. This is achieved using a different assumption, DLDH assumption, and improving zero-knowledge proofs in the group signatures. The length of the proposed group signatures is about 53% of that of the previous ones.

Keywords: group signature, revocation, backward unlinkability, bilinear maps, DLDH assumption.

1 Introduction

A *group signature scheme* [8,1,14,2,7,16,5,6,13,12] allows a group member to anonymously sign a message on behalf of a group, where a group manager controls the membership of members. Then, often a third party can cancel the anonymity of signatures to trace the signers (This topic is out of scope in this paper). Another important topic in the group signature scheme is membership revocation [14,2,7,16,5,6,12]. Namely, the membership of a member can be disabled without influencing the other members.

The simplest revocation method is that the manager changes the group public key and secret keys of all members except the revoked member to re-distribute the keys [2]. However, the other members' loads are large. A better solution is to broadcast a small public membership message to all signers and verifiers, as in [7,16,5]. Although the costs of signers are better, the signer still has to obtain some data depending on the size of the group (or the number of revoked members) whenever signing. On the other hand, there is another approach [14,2,6,12], where some revocation messages are only sent to verifiers, although the verifiers need the computational cost depending the number of revoked members. Since the signers' costs are lower, this type is suitable for mobile environments where

H. Yoshiura et al. (Eds.): IWSEC 2006, LNCS 4266, pp. 17–32, 2006.

mobile hosts anonymously communicate with the servers. We refer to this type as *Verifier-Local Revocation* (VLR) group signature scheme, as in [6,12].

In [14,2], VLR group signature schemes based on the strong RSA assumption are proposed. However, the schemes have some drawbacks on efficiency. The first scheme of [14] and the scheme of [2] suffer from the inefficiency of signing, due to the used inefficient zero-knowledge proofs. The second scheme of [14] forces a signer to compute $O(T)$ exponentiations at every time interval, where T is the total number of time intervals.

In [6], a VLR group signature scheme from bilinear maps is proposed, where the traceability (i.e., unforgeability) is based on the q-SDH (Strong DH) assumption and the anonymity is based on the Decision Linear DH (DLDH) assumption. The advantage of this scheme is that signatures are short, since the elliptic curves can be adopted. However, unfortunately, this scheme [6] does not satisfy *backward unlinkability*. This property means that even after a member is revoked, signatures produced by the member before the revocation remain anonymous. Namely, in the scheme [6], the anonymity of signatures produced before the revocation is compromised. In case a member leaves voluntarily or in case of a stolen key, the anonymity of signatures before leaving should be ensured.

In [12], improved schemes with the backward unlinkability are proposed. The schemes introduce time intervals like [14]. Then, by obtaining a revocation token of a revoked member at a time interval from the manager, verifiers can check whether a group signature at the corresponding interval was made by the revoked member. Thus, by releasing only tokens after the revocation, the signature after the revocation can be detected, while the previous signatures can still be anonymous. The anonymity with the backward unlinkability is proved under the Decision BDH (DBDH) assumption.

In this paper, we propose a short VLR group signature scheme with the backward unlinkability. Let $e : G_1 \times G_2 \to G_T$ be a bilinear map on groups G_1, G_2, G_T with the same prime order. Then, the previous group signature [12] includes a G_T element. Using MNT curves [11], G_T elements are represented as 1020 bit strings, while G_1 elements are represented as 171 bit strings. On the other hand, the proposed group signature excludes G_T elements, and thus the signature is shorter. This is achieved by utilizing the DLDH assumption, on which the scheme [6] is also based. In addition to excluding G_T elements, we improve the efficiency of the signature, using the efficient zero-knowledge proof technique, which is derived from the technique in [9]. In the above setting, our group signature needs only 1533 bits, while the previous one needs 2893 bits. Therefore, the length of our signature is about 53% of that of the previous one.

Remark 1. Recently, a short VLR group signature scheme is independently proposed [15], which is based on another assumption, Decisional Tripartite DH (DTDH) assumption [10]. However, since the signature includes a G_2 element, it becomes longer than the case where the signature includes only G_1 elements, which is our signature. In addition, the zero-knowledge proof in our signature is improved, compared with the signature in [15] whose zero-knowledge proof is

Table 1. Comparisons among VLR schemes from bilinear maps

Scheme	Sig. len. (bits)	Comp. cost of revocation check (# of bilinear map comp.)	Assumptions	Backward unlinkability
[6]	1192	2	q-SDH, DLDH	No
[12]	2893	1	q-SDH, DBDH	Yes
[15]	2557	2	q-SDH, DTDH	Yes
Proposed	1533	2	q-SDH, DLDH	Yes

similar to [12]. Using MNT curves, the signature in [15] is 2557 bits, though our signature is only 1533 bits.

Among VLR schemes from bilinear maps including [15], we show the comparisons w.r.t. important factors (i.e, signature length, computational cost of revocation check, assumptions, and backward unlinkability) in Table 1. Since the dominant computational cost in VLR schemes is caused in the revocation check in the signature verification, we compare the cost of revocation check per revoked member, based on the number of the bilinear map computations.

2   Model and Security Definitions

We show a model of VLR group signature scheme with backward unlinkability in [12], which is extended from [6].

Definition 1. *A VLR group signature scheme with backward unlinkability consists of the following algorithms:*

KeyGen(n, T)**:** *It is a probabilistic algorithm on inputs n, which is the number of members, and T, which is the number of time intervals. It outputs a group public key gpk, an n-element vector of members' secret keys $\boldsymbol{gsk} = (\boldsymbol{gsk}[1], \ldots, \boldsymbol{gsk}[n])$, and an $n \times T$-element vector of revocation tokens $\boldsymbol{grt} = (\boldsymbol{grt}[1][1], \ldots, \boldsymbol{grt}[n][T])$, where $\boldsymbol{grt}[i][j]$ indicates the token of member i at time interval j.*

Sign$(gpk, j, \boldsymbol{gsk}[i], M)$**:** *This takes as inputs the group public key gpk, the current time interval j, a secret key $\boldsymbol{gsk}[i]$, and a message $M \in \{0,1\}^*$, and outputs the signature σ.*

Verify$(gpk, j, RL_j, \sigma, M)$**:** *This takes as inputs gpk, j, a set of the revocation tokens RL_j at the time interval j, a signature σ, and the message M. Then, it outputs either valid or invalid. The validity means that σ is a correct signature on M at interval j w.r.t. gpk, and that the signer is not revoked at the interval j.*

Remark 2. In this model, when member i is revoked at interval j, the manager has to publish the revocation tokens $\boldsymbol{grt}[i][j], \ldots, \boldsymbol{grt}[i][T]$.

Then, the security requirements, *Correctness*, *Traceability*, and *BU-anonymity*, are defined as follows [12].

Definition 2 (Correctness). *Correctness requires that for all* $(gpk, \boldsymbol{gsk}, \boldsymbol{grt}) =$ **KeyGen**(n, T), *all* $j \in [1, T]$, *all* RL_j, *all* $i \in [1, n]$, *and all* $M \in \{0, 1\}^*$,

$$\mathbf{Verify}(gpk, j, RL_j, \mathbf{Sign}(gpk, j, \boldsymbol{gsk}[i], M), M) = valid \iff \boldsymbol{grt}[i][j] \notin RL_j.$$

As well as [6,12], we introduce implicit tracing algorithm: For any interval j, using the revocation token $\boldsymbol{grt}[i][j]$ of all members, the implicit tracing algorithm can trace the signer from a valid signature-message pair (σ, M).

The following traceability requirement captures the unforgeability of group signatures, introduced first by [3]. Consider the following traceability game between an adversary $\mathcal{A}$ and a challenger, where $\mathcal{A}$ tries to forge a signature that cannot be traced to one of members corrupted by $\mathcal{A}$.

Setup: The challenger runs **KeyGen**(n, T), and obtains $gpk, \boldsymbol{gsk}$, and $\boldsymbol{grt}$. He provides $\mathcal{A}$ with gpk and $\boldsymbol{grt}$, and sets U with empty.

Queries: $\mathcal{A}$ can query the challenger about the following.

  Signing: $\mathcal{A}$ requests a signature on an arbitrary message M for an arbitrary member i at an arbitrary interval j. The challenger responds the corresponding signature.

  Corruption: $\mathcal{A}$ requests the secret key of an arbitrary member i. The challenger adds i to U, and responds the key.

Output: Finally, $\mathcal{A}$ outputs a message M^*, an interval j^*, a set $RL_{j^*}^*$ of revocation tokens, and a signature σ^*.

Then, $\mathcal{A}$ wins if (1) **Verify**$(gpk, j^*, RL_{j^*}^*, \sigma^*, M^*) = valid$, and (2) σ^* traces to a member outside of the coalition, i.e, $U \setminus RL_{j^*}^*$ or the trace is failure, and (3) $\mathcal{A}$ did not obtain σ^* by making a signing query at M^*.

Definition 3 (Traceability). *Traceability requires that for all PPT $\mathcal{A}$, the probability that $\mathcal{A}$ wins the traceability game is negligible.*

The following BU-anonymity requirement captures the anonymity with the backward unlinkability. Consider the following BU-anonymity game.

Setup: The challenger runs **KeyGen**(n, T), and obtains $gpk, \boldsymbol{gsk}$, and $\boldsymbol{grt}$. He provides $\mathcal{A}$ with gpk.

Queries: At the beginning of every interval $j \in [1, T]$, the challenger announces the beginning of j to $\mathcal{A}$, where j is incremented. At the current interval j, $\mathcal{A}$ can query the challenger about the following.

  Signing: $\mathcal{A}$ requests a signature on an arbitrary message M for an arbitrary member i at the current interval j. The challenger responds the corresponding signature.

  Corruption: $\mathcal{A}$ requests the secret key of an arbitrary member i.

  Revocation: $\mathcal{A}$ requests the revocation of an arbitrary member i at the current interval j. The challenger responds $\boldsymbol{grt}[i][j]$.

Challenge: $\mathcal{A}$ outputs a message M and two members i_0 and i_1. The corruption of i_0 and i_1 must not be requested. Furthermore, the revocations of i_0 and i_1 must not be requested before the current interval j_0 (including j_0). The challenger chooses $\phi \in_R \{0, 1\}$, and responds the signature on M of member i_ϕ at the current interval j_0.

Restricted Queries: Similarly, $\mathcal{A}$ can make the signing queries, corruption queries, and revocation queries, while the time interval is incremented. However, $\mathcal{A}$ cannot query the corruptions of i_0 and i_1, and the revocations of i_0 and i_1 at the interval j_0 (Note that the revocations of i_0 and i_1 after j_0 is permitted).

Output: Finally, $\mathcal{A}$ outputs a bit ϕ' indicating its guess of ϕ.

If $\phi' = \phi$, $\mathcal{A}$ wins. We define the advantage of $\mathcal{A}$ as $|\Pr[\phi' = \phi] - 1/2|$.

Definition 4 (BU-Anonymity). *BU-anonymity requires that for all PPT $\mathcal{A}$, the advantage of $\mathcal{A}$ on the BU-anonymity game is negligible.*

3 Preliminaries

3.1 Bilinear Groups

Our scheme utilizes bilinear groups and bilinear maps as follows:

1. G_1, G_2 and G_T are multiplicative cyclic groups of prime order p,
2. g_1 is a generator of G_1, and g_2 is a generator of G_2,
3. ψ is an efficiently computed isomorphism from G_2 to G_1, with $\psi(g_2) = g_1$,
4. e is an efficiently computed bilinear map: $G_1 \times G_2 \to G_T$, i.e., (1) for all $u, u' \in G_1$, all $v, v' \in G_2$, $e(uu', v) = e(u, v)e(u', v)$ and $e(u, vv') = e(u, v)e(u, v')$, and (2) $e(g_1, g_2) \neq 1$.

Such an e can be constructed by Weil or Tate parings on the elliptic curves. As mentioned in [5,6], the Tate paring on MNT curves [11] gives us the efficient implementation, where $G_1 \neq G_2$ and ψ can be implemented by the trace map.

3.2 Assumptions

Our scheme is based on the q-SDH assumption [5,6,12] and the DLDH assumption [5,6].

Definition 5 (q-SDH Assumption). *For all PPT algorithm $\mathcal{A}$, the probability*

$$\Pr[\mathcal{A}(g_1, g_2, g_2^{\gamma}, \ldots, g_2^{(\gamma^q)}) = (g_1^{(1/\gamma+x)}, x) \wedge x \in Z_p^*]$$

is negligible, where $g_2 \in_R G_2$ $(g_1 = \psi(g_2))$ and $\gamma \in_R Z_p^*$.

Definition 6 (Decision Linear DH (DLDH) Assumption on G_2). *For all PPT algorithm $\mathcal{A}$, the probability*

$$|\Pr[\mathcal{A}(u, v, h, u^a, v^b, h^{a+b}) = 0] - \Pr[\mathcal{A}(u, v, h, u^a, v^b, h^c) = 0]|$$

is negligible, where $u, v, h \in_R G_2$ and $a, b, c \in_R Z_p^*$.

Based on the q-SDH assumption, the DL (Discrete Logarithm) assumption on G_2 also holds.

Definition 7 (DL Assumption on G_2). *For all PPT algorithm $\mathcal{A}$, the probability*

$$\Pr[\mathcal{A}(g_2, g_2^\gamma) = \gamma]$$

is negligible, where $g_2 \in_R G_2$ and $\gamma \in_R Z_p^*$.

3.3   Proving Relations on Representations

As well as [6,12], we adopt signatures converted by Fiat-Shamir heuristic (using a hash function) from zero-knowledge proofs of knowledge (PK), where a signer can convince a verifier of knowledge with relations on representations. We call the signatures SPKs. The SPKs we adopt are the generalization of the Schnorr signature. We introduce the following notation.

$$SPK\{(x_1, \ldots, x_t) : R(x_1, \ldots, x_t)\}(M),$$

which means a signature of message M by a signer who knows secret values $x_1, \ldots, x_t$ satisfying a relation $R(x_1, \ldots, x_t)$. In this paper, the following SPKs on G_1, G_T are utilized.

SPK **of Representation:** An SPK proving the knowledge of a representation of $C \in G_1$ to the bases $f_1, f_2, \ldots, f_t \in G_1$ on message M is denoted as

$$SPK\{(x_1, \ldots, x_t) : C = f_1^{x_1} \cdots f_t^{x_t}\}(M).$$

This can be also constructed on group G_T.

SPK **of Representations with Equal Parts:** An SPK proving the knowledge of representations of $C, C' \in G_1$ to the bases $f_1, \ldots, f_t \in G_1$ on message M, where the representations include equal values as parts, is denoted as

$$SPK\{(x_1, \ldots, x_u) : C = f_{i_1}^{x_{j_1}} \cdots f_{i_v}^{x_{j_v}} \wedge C' = f_{i'_1}^{x_{j'_1}} \cdots f_{i'_{v'}}^{x_{j'_{v'}}}\}(M),$$

where indices $i_1, \ldots i_v, i'_1, \ldots i'_{v'} \in \{1, \ldots, t\}$ refer to the bases $f_1, \ldots, f_t$, and indices $j_1, \ldots j_v, j'_1, \ldots, j'_{v'} \in \{1, \ldots, u\}$ refer to the secrets $x_1, \ldots, x_u$. This SPK can be extended for different groups G_1 and G_T with the same order p, as follows.

$$SPK\{(x_1, \ldots, x_u) : C = f_{i_1}^{x_{j_1}} \cdots f_{i_v}^{x_{j_v}} \wedge C' = f'^{x_{j_1}}_{i'_1} \cdots f'^{x_{j'_{v'}}}_{i'_{v'}}\}(M),$$

where $C, f_1, \ldots, f_t \in G_1$, and $C', f'_1, \ldots, f'_t \in G_T$.

In the random oracle model, the SPK can be simulated without the knowledge using a simulator in the zero-knowledge-ness of the underlying PK. Moreover, the SPK has an extractor of the proved secret knowledge given two accepting protocol views whose commitments are the same and whose challenges are different.

4   Proposed Scheme

4.1   Idea

The previous scheme [12] is informally as follows. In [12], the case of $G_1 = G_2$ is described, which can be easily extended to the case of $G_1 \neq G_2$. Here, we describe the case of $G_1 \neq G_2$. The group public key is $gpk = (g_1, g_2, g_2^\gamma, h_j)$, where $h_j \in G_2$ for all $1 \leq j \leq T$, and secret key $\boldsymbol{gsk}[i]$ of member i is an SDH pair (A_i, x_i) s.t. $A_i = g_1^{1/(\gamma+x_i)}$. Then, the group signature consists of $T_3 = e(g_1^{x_i}, h_j)^\beta$, $T_4 = g_1^\beta$ for $\beta \in_R Z_p^*$ and the SPK proving the correctness and the ownership of A_i corresponding to x_i. The revocation token at interval j is $B_{ij} = h_j^{x_i}$. Then, by checking $T_3 = e(T_4, B)$ for all revocation tokens B at interval j, it can be checked whether T_3 includes a token of a revoked member. On the other hand, the revocation tokens at different interval j' do not satisfy the above checking. However, the signature includes a G_T element, $T_3 = e(g_1^{x_i}, h_j)^\beta$. When MNT curves are used, T_3 is 6 times longer than the values from G_1, and thus the signature is long.

Here, we construct a VLR group signature scheme, where a signature includes only G_1 elements and Z_p^* elements. In the previous scheme, since the BU-anonymity is based on the DBDH assumption including the bilinear map e, the signature includes $e(g_1^{x_i}, h_j)^\beta$. On the other hand, the proposed scheme is based on a different assumption, the DLDH assumption that does not include e. The proposed scheme is informally as follows. The group public key gpk and secret key $\boldsymbol{gsk}[i]$ are the same as the previous scheme. Then, the group signature of i consists of $T_2 = \psi(f)^{\beta+x_i}$ and $T_3 = \psi(h_j)^\beta$ together with the SPK, where f is a hashed value on G_2. The revocation token at interval j is $B_{ij} = \psi(h_j)^{x_i}$. By $e(T_2, h_j) \neq e(BT_3, f)$ for all $B \in RL_j$, it can be checked whether the signature is not revoked. In the construction, it is desired to exclude longer G_2 elements from the signature. This is why $f \in G_2$ is computed by both signer and verifier via a hush function from the public information and a short random nonce. Only the nonce is included in the signature.

In the proof of the BU-anonymity, regard u, v, h, u^a, v^b and h^{a+b} in the DLDH assumption as $u = g_2, v = h_j, h = f, u^x = g_2^{x_i}, v^b = h_j^\beta$ and $h^{a+b} = f^{\beta+x_i}$. Then, informally the DLDH assumption means that $h^{a+b} = f^{\beta+x_i}$ and a random h^c are indistinguishable, namely $T_3 = \psi(f)^{\beta+x_i}$ does not reveal any information on x_i. The formal proof is described later.

In addition, we improve the efficiency on the SPK proving the ownership of A_i. The construction is derived from [9]. Let T_1 be the commitment of A_i. T_1 is computed by $T_1 = A_i\tilde{g}^\alpha$, where $\tilde{g}$ is a public element from G_1 and α is a random factor chosen by the signer. In the previous scheme [12], for the commitment of A_i, the signer proves the knowledge of A_i s.t. $A_i = g_1^{1/(\gamma+x_i)}$ directly, using another commitment. Thus, forging a group signature implies forging an SDH pair, which breaks the q-SDH assumption. The SPK is for the secrets x_i, α, and for more 3 secrets. On the other hand, in the proposed group signature, the knowledge of T_1 s.t. $T_1 = (g_1\tilde{g}^{\alpha\gamma+\zeta})^{1/(\gamma+x_i)}$ is proved in the SPK (If $\zeta = \alpha x_i$, it implies $T_1 = A_i\tilde{g}^\alpha$). This proof can be achieved by only T_1 and the SPK for secrets x_i, α and another secret ζ. Thus, the signature size and computational cost are improved. For a forged group signature proving the knowledge of T_1, the corresponding A_i can be computed using a discrete logarithm of $\tilde{g}$ to g_1 without the knowledge of γ, which leads to the security proof of the traceability. This proof is described later.

Remark 3. Although this improvement of SPK is derived from [9], our SPK is simpler, since the forms of A_i and T_1 are simpler. This is why the security proof is different from that in [9].

4.2   Proposed Algorithms

In addition to bilinear groups (G_1, G_2) with isomorphism ψ and bilinear map e, we employ hash function H_0 and H with respective ranges G_2 and Z_p, which are treated as random oracles.

KeyGen(n, T): This key generation algorithm is given the number of members and the number of time intervals, and computes keys as follows.

1. Select a generator $g_2 \in G_2$ and set $g_1 = \psi(g_2)$. Additionally, select $\tilde{g} \in_R G_1$ and $h_j \in_R G_2$, and set $\hat{h}_j = \psi(h_j)$ for all $j \in [1, T]$.
2. Select $\gamma \in_R Z_p^*$ and compute $w = g_2^\gamma$.
3. Select $x_i \in_R Z_p^*$ and compute $A_i = g_1^{1/(\gamma + x_i)}$ for all $i \in [1, n]$.
4. Compute $B_{ij} = \hat{h}_j^{x_i}$ for all i and j.

The group public key gpk is $(g_1, g_2, \tilde{g}, h_1, \ldots h_T, w)$. Each member's secret key $\boldsymbol{gsk}[i]$ is (A_i, x_i). The revocation token at interval j of member with secret (A_i, x_i) is $\boldsymbol{grt}[i][j] = B_{ij}$. Output $(gpk, \boldsymbol{gsk}, \boldsymbol{grt})$.

Sign$(gpk, j, \boldsymbol{gsk}[i], M)$: The inputs of this signing algorithm are $gpk = (g_1, g_2, \tilde{g}, h_1, \ldots h_T, w)$, the current time interval j, the signer's secret $\boldsymbol{gsk}[i] = (A_i, x_i)$ and a signed message $M \in \{0, 1\}^*$. We assume that M includes the time interval j in order to bind the signature to the interval. The algorithm is as follows:

1. Pick a random nonce $r \in_R Z_p$. Compute $f = H_0(gpk, M, r) \in G_2$. Then, compute $\hat{f} = \psi(f)$, and $\hat{h}_j = \psi(h_j)$.
2. Select randoms $\alpha, \beta \in_R Z_p^*$.
3. Compute $T_1 = A_i \tilde{g}^\alpha$, $T_2 = \hat{f}^{\beta + x_i}$, $T_3 = \hat{h}_j^\beta$.
4. Set $\zeta = \alpha x_i$. Then, compute

$$V = SPK\{(\alpha, \beta, x_i, \zeta) :$$
$$\wedge\, e(T_1, w)/e(g_1, g_2) = e(\tilde{g}, g_2)^\zeta e(\tilde{g}, w)^\alpha / e(T_1, g_2)^{x_i}$$
$$\wedge\, T_2 = \hat{f}^{\beta + x_i} \wedge T_3 = \hat{h}_j^\beta\}(M).$$

This SPK proves the knowledge $\alpha, \beta, x_i, \zeta$ s.t. $T_1 = (g\tilde{g}^{\alpha\gamma + \zeta})^{1/(\gamma + x_i)}$, $T_2 = \hat{f}^{\beta + x_i}$, and $T_3 = \hat{h}_j^\beta$. The proof is described in Lemma 2. Concretely, compute SPK V as follows.

(a) Pick blinding factors $r_\alpha, r_\beta, r_{x_i}, r_\zeta \in_R Z_p$.
(b) Compute

$$R_1 = e(\tilde{g}, g_2)^{r_\zeta} e(\tilde{g}, w)^{r_\alpha} / e(T_1, g_2)^{r_{x_i}}$$
$$R_2 = \hat{f}^{r_\beta + r_{x_i}}$$
$$R_3 = \hat{h}_j^{r_\beta}$$

(c) Compute a challenge $c \in Z_p$ as

$$c = H(gpk, j, M, T_1, T_2, T_3, R_1, R_2, R_3).$$

(d) Compute responses $s_\alpha = r_\alpha + c\alpha$, $s_\beta = r_\beta + c\beta$, $s_{x_i} = r_{x_i} + cx_i$, and $s_\zeta = r_\zeta + c\zeta$ in Z_p.

Output the group signature $\sigma = (r, T_1, T_2, T_3, c, s_\alpha, s_\beta, s_{x_i}, s_\zeta)$.

Verify$(gpk, j, RL_j, \sigma, M)$: The inputs are $gpk = (g_1, g_2, \tilde{g}, h_1, \ldots h_T, w)$, the current time interval j, the revocation list RL_j that consists of $\boldsymbol{grt}[i][j]$ for all revoked i at the interval j, a target signature $\sigma = (r, T_1, T_2, T_3, c, s_\alpha, s_\beta, s_{x_i}, s_\zeta)$ and the message $M \in \{0,1\}^*$.

1. **Signature Check.** Check that σ is valid, by checking the SPK V, as follows.
   (a) Compute $\hat{h}_j = \psi(h_j)$, $f = H_0(gpk, M, r)$, and $\hat{f} = \psi(f)$.
   (b) Retrieve

   $$\tilde{R}_1 = (e(\tilde{g}, g_2)^{s_\zeta} e(\tilde{g}, w)^{s_\alpha} / e(T_1, g_2)^{s_{x_i}})(e(g_1, g_2)/e(T_1, w))^c$$
   $$\tilde{R}_2 = \hat{f}^{s_\beta + s_{x_i}} (1/T_2)^c$$
   $$\tilde{R}_3 = \hat{h}_j^{s_\beta} (1/T_3)^c$$

   (c) Check the challenge c as

   $$c = H(gpk, j, M, T_1, T_2, T_3, \tilde{R}_1, \tilde{R}_2, \tilde{R}_3).$$

2. **Revocation Check.** Check that the signer is not revoked at the interval j, by checking $e(T_2, h_j) \neq e(B_{ij}T_3, f)$ for all $B_{ij} \in RL_j$.
   Consider the case of $T_2 = \hat{f}^{\beta + x_i}$, $T_3 = \hat{h}_j^\beta$ and $B_{ij} = \hat{h}_j^{x_i}$. Then, $e(T_2, h_j) = e(\hat{f}^{\beta + x_i}, h_j) = e(\hat{f}, h_j)^{\beta + x_i}$. On the other hand, $e(B_{ij}T_3, f) = e(\hat{h}_j^{x_i} \hat{h}_j^\beta, f) = e(\hat{h}_j, f)^{\beta + x_i}$. Let $f = h_j^\zeta$ for some $\zeta \in Z_p^*$. Then, $e(\hat{f}, h_j) = e(\psi(h_j), h_j)^\zeta = e(\hat{h}_j, f)$. Thus, in this case, $e(T_2, h_j) = e(B_{ij}T_3, f)$. Namely, the revoked signature can be detected.

5 Security

Since the correctness is straightforward, only BU-anonymity and traceability are shown.

5.1 BU-Anonymity

Theorem 1. *The proposed scheme satisfies the BU-anonymity in the random oracle model under the DLDH assumption.*

The following lemma implies the above theorem.

Lemma 1. *Suppose adversary $\mathcal{A}$ breaks the BU-anonymity of the proposed scheme with the advantage ε and q_H hash queries and q_S signature queries. Then, we can construct $\mathcal{B}$ that breaks the DLDH assumption on G_2 with the advantage $(1/nT - q_S q_H/p)\varepsilon$.*

Proof. The input of $\mathcal{B}$ is $(u, v, h, u^a, v^b, Z) \in G_2{}^6$, where $a, b \in_R Z_p^*$ and either $Z = h^{a+b}$ or $Z = h^c$ for $c \in_R Z_p^*$. $\mathcal{B}$ decides which Z it is given by communicating with $\mathcal{A}$, as follows.

Setup. $\mathcal{B}$ simulates **KeyGen**(n, T) as follows.

1. $\mathcal{B}$ picks $i^* \in_R [1, n]$ and $j^* \in_R [1, T]$.
   $\mathcal{B}$ sets $g_2 = u$, and $g_1 = \psi(g_2)$. Furthermore, $\mathcal{B}$ selects $\tilde{g} \in_R G_1$. Additionally, $\mathcal{B}$ selects $r_j \in_R Z_p^*$ and computes $h_j = g_2^{r_j}$ for all $j \in [1, T]$ except j^*. For j^*, $\mathcal{B}$ sets $h_{j^*} = v$. For all j, $\mathcal{B}$ sets $\hat{h}_j = \psi(h_j)$.
2. As usual, $\mathcal{B}$ selects $\gamma \in_R Z_p^*$ and computes $w = g_2^\gamma$.
3. As usual, $\mathcal{B}$ selects $x_i \in_R Z_p^*$ and computes $A_i = g_1^{1/(\gamma + x_i)}$ for all $i \in [1, n]$ except i^*. For i^*, define $x_{i^*} = a$ and $A_{i^*} = g_1^{1/(\gamma + a)}$, which are unknown for $\mathcal{B}$.
4. As usual, $\mathcal{B}$ computes $B_{ij} = \hat{h}_j^{x_i}$ for all i except i^* and all j. For i^*, $\mathcal{B}$ sets $B_{i^* j} = \psi((u^a)^{r_j}) = \psi(g_2^{a r_j}) = \hat{h}_j^a$ except for j^*. For i^* and j^*, define $B_{i^* j^*} = \psi(v^a) = \hat{h}_{j^*}^{x_{i^*}}$, which is also unknown.

Note that simulated h_j and B_{ij} have the same distributions as the real, due to $a, x_i, r_j \in_R Z_p^*$.

Hash Queries. At any time, $\mathcal{A}$ can query the hash functions H_0 and H. $\mathcal{B}$ responds with random values with consistency.

Phase 1. $\mathcal{A}$ can request signing queries, corruption queries, and revocation queries at any time interval j. If $i \neq i^*$, then $\mathcal{B}$ uses the secret key of i to respond to the query as usual. If $i = i^*$, $\mathcal{B}$ responds as follows.

Signing Queries: $\mathcal{B}$ computes a simulated group signature of i^*, depending on j as follows.

Case of $j \neq j^*$:

1. $\mathcal{B}$ selects $r \in_R Z_p$ and $\beta, \delta \in_R Z_p^*$. In addition, $\mathcal{B}$ sets $f = h_j^\delta$, $\hat{f} = \psi(f)$, and $\hat{h}_j = \psi(h_j)$.
2. $\mathcal{B}$ selects $T_1 \in_R G_1$. Furthermore, $\mathcal{B}$ computes $T_2 = \hat{f}^\beta B_{i^* j}^\delta = \hat{f}^\beta \hat{h}_j^{x_i^* \delta} = \hat{f}^{\beta + x_i^*}$, and $T_3 = \hat{h}_j^\beta$.

3. $\mathcal{B}$ computes the simulated SPK V by using the simulator of the perfect zero-knowledge-ness, which includes the backpatch of the hash function. If the backpatch is failure, $\mathcal{B}$ outputs a random guess $\omega' \in_R \{0,1\}$ and aborts. Furthermore, $\mathcal{B}$ defines $f = H_0(gpk, M, r)$. If this backpatch is failure, $\mathcal{B}$ also outputs a random guess and aborts.

Case of $j = j^*$:

1. $\mathcal{B}$ selects $r \in_R Z_p$ and selects $\beta, \delta \in_R Z_p^*$. In addition, $\mathcal{B}$ sets $f = u^\delta$, $\hat{f} = \psi(f)$, and $\hat{h}_j = \psi(h_j)$.
2. $\mathcal{B}$ selects $T_1 \in_R G_1$. Furthermore, $\mathcal{B}$ computes $T_2 = \psi(u^\beta(u^a))^\delta = \psi(f^{\beta+x_i^*}) = \hat{f}^{\beta+x_i^*}$, and $T_3 = \hat{h}_j^\beta$.
3. This is the same as in Case of $j \neq j^*$.

Then, $\mathcal{B}$ responds signature $\sigma = (r, T_1, T_2, T_3, V)$ to $\mathcal{A}$. Note that each value in σ has the same distribution as the real, due to $\alpha \in_R Z_p^*$ in the real and $T_1 \in_R G_1$ in the simulation, and due to the perfect zero-knowledge-ness of SPK.

Revocation Queries: If $j \neq j^*$, $\mathcal{B}$ responds B_{i^*j}. Otherwise (i.e., $j = j^*$), $\mathcal{B}$ outputs a random guess $\omega' \in_R \{0,1\}$ and aborts.

Corruption Queries: $\mathcal{B}$ outputs a random guess $\omega' \in_R \{0,1\}$ and aborts.

Challenge. $\mathcal{A}$ outputs a message M, the current time interval j and two members i_0, i_1 to be challenged. If $j \neq j^*$, $\mathcal{B}$ outputs a random guess $\omega' \in_R \{0,1\}$ and aborts. Otherwise, $\mathcal{B}$ picks $\phi \in_R \{0,1\}$. Then, if $i_\phi \neq i^*$, $\mathcal{B}$ outputs a random guess $\omega' \in_R \{0,1\}$ and aborts. Otherwise, $\mathcal{B}$ responds the following simulated group signature of i^* and j^*.

1. $\mathcal{B}$ selects $r \in_R Z_p$, regards b as β which is unknown, and sets $f = h$, $\hat{f} = \psi(f)$, and $\hat{h}_{j^*} = \psi(h_{j^*})$.
2. $\mathcal{B}$ selects $T_1 \in_R G_1$. Furthermore, $\mathcal{B}$ sets $T_2 = \psi(Z)$ and $T_3 = \psi(v^b) = \hat{h}_{j^*}^\beta$. Note that if $Z = h^{a+b}$, $T_2 = \psi(h^{a+b}) = \hat{f}^{\beta+x_{i^*}}$.
3. $\mathcal{B}$ computes the simulated SPK V by using the simulator of the perfect zero-knowledge-ness. Furthermore, $\mathcal{B}$ defines $f = H_0(gpk, M, r)$.

Phase 2. This is the same as Phase 1.

Output. $\mathcal{A}$ outputs its guess $\phi' \in \{0,1\}$. If $\phi = \phi'$, $\mathcal{B}$ outputs $\omega' = 1$ (implying $Z = h^{a+b}$), and otherwise outputs $\omega' = 0$ (implying $Z = h^c$).

Now, we evaluate the advantage of the guess of $\mathcal{B}$. Let $\omega \in \{0,1\}$ denote whether the input Z is h^c ($\omega = 0$) or h^{a+b} ($\omega = 1$). Let **abort** be the event that $\mathcal{B}$ aborts. Then, we have $\Pr[\omega = \omega'|\textbf{abort}] = 1/2$. On the other hand, assume that $\mathcal{B}$ does not abort. If $\omega = 0$, i.e., $Z = h^c$, then the challenged signature has no information on x_{i^*}. Thus, $\Pr[\omega' = 0|\overline{\textbf{abort}} \wedge \omega = 0] = 1/2$. If $\omega = 1$, i.e., $Z = h^{a+b}$, then $\mathcal{B}$ perfectly simulates the real and thus $\mathcal{A}$ guesses correctly with the advantage ε. Therefore, we obtain $\Pr[\omega' = 1|\overline{\textbf{abort}} \wedge \omega = 1] = 1/2 + \varepsilon$.

Putting everything together, we obtain the advantage of $\mathcal{B}$'s guess, as follows.

$$|\Pr[\mathcal{B}(u, v, h, u^a, v^b, h^{a+b}) = 0] - \Pr[\mathcal{B}(u, v, h, u^a, v^b, h^c) = 0|$$
$$= |\Pr[\omega' = 0|\omega = 1] - \Pr[\omega' = 0|\omega = 0]|$$
$$= |(1 - \Pr[\omega' = 1|\omega = 1]) - \Pr[\omega' = 0|\omega = 0]|$$
$$= |1 - \Pr[\mathbf{abort}]\Pr[\omega' = 1|\overline{\mathbf{abort}} \wedge \omega = 1]$$
$$- \Pr[\overline{\mathbf{abort}}]\Pr[\omega' = 1|\overline{\mathbf{abort}} \wedge \omega = 1]$$
$$- \Pr[\mathbf{abort}]\Pr[\omega' = 0|\overline{\mathbf{abort}} \wedge \omega = 0]$$
$$- \Pr[\overline{\mathbf{abort}}]\Pr[\omega' = 0|\overline{\mathbf{abort}} \wedge \omega = 0]|$$
$$= |1 - \Pr[\mathbf{abort}](\frac{1}{2} + \frac{1}{2}) - \Pr[\overline{\mathbf{abort}}]((\frac{1}{2} + \varepsilon) + \frac{1}{2})|$$
$$= \Pr[\overline{\mathbf{abort}}]\varepsilon.$$

In the rest, we evaluate $\Pr[\overline{\mathbf{abort}}]$. If the guesses of i^* and j^* are correct, $\mathcal{B}$ aborts only when the backpatch is failure in the signing query. The probability that a specific signature causes the failure is at most q_H/p, as well as [6]. Thus, for all signature queries, the probability that $\mathcal{B}$ aborts due to the failure of the backpatch is at most $q_S q_H/p$. On the other hand, since $\mathcal{A}$ has no information on i^* and j^* and $\phi \in_R \{0, 1\}$, the probability that $\mathcal{B}$ correctly guesses i^* and j^* is at least $1/nT$. Thus, $\Pr[\overline{\mathbf{abort}}] \geq 1/nT - q_S q_H/p$.

Therefore, the advantage that $\mathcal{B}$' guesses ω is at least $(1/nT - q_S q_H/p)\varepsilon$. $\quad\square$

5.2   Traceability

Before proving the traceability, we show that the SPK V proves $T_1 = (g_1 \tilde{g}^{\alpha\gamma+\zeta})^{1/(\gamma+x_i)}$, $T_2 = \hat{f}^{\beta+x_i}$, and $T_3 = \hat{h}_j^{\beta}$.

Lemma 2. SPK V proves the knowledge $\alpha, \beta, x_i, \zeta$ s.t. $T_1 = (g_1 \tilde{g}^{\alpha\gamma+\zeta})^{1/(\gamma+x_i)}$, $T_2 = \hat{f}^{\beta+x_i}$, and $T_3 = \hat{h}_j^{\beta}$.

Proof. By the knowledge extractor for V, we can obtain $\alpha, \beta, x_i, \zeta$ s.t.

$$e(T_1, w)/e(g_1, g_2) = e(\tilde{g}, g_2)^{\zeta} e(\tilde{g}, w)^{\alpha}/e(T_1, g_2)^{x_i}, \qquad (1)$$
$$T_2 = \hat{f}^{\beta+x_i}, \qquad (2)$$
$$T_3 = \hat{h}_j^{\beta}. \qquad (3)$$

From (1), the equation $e(T_1, w)e(T_1, g_2)^{x_i} = e(\tilde{g}, g_2)^{\zeta} e(\tilde{g}, w)^{\alpha} e(g_1, g_2)$ holds. The left hand is equal to $e(T_1, wg_2^{x_i})$. The right hand is equal to $e(\tilde{g}, g_2^{\zeta} w^{\alpha})e(g_1, g_2)$. Thus, the equation $e(T_1, wg_2^{x_i}) = e(\tilde{g}, g_2^{\zeta} w^{\alpha})e(g_1, g_2)$ holds. Define $\tilde{g} = g_1^{\eta}$ and $T_1 = g_1^{\theta}$. Then, since $w = g_2^{\gamma}$, we obtain the following equations.

$$e(g_1^{\theta}, g_2^{\gamma} g_2^{x_i}) = e(g_1^{\eta}, g_2^{\zeta} g_2^{\alpha\gamma})e(g_1, g_2)$$
$$e(g_1, g_2)^{\theta(\gamma+x_i)} = e(g_1, g_2)^{\eta(\zeta+\alpha\gamma)+1}$$

Thus, $\theta(\gamma + x_i) = \eta(\zeta + \alpha\gamma) + 1 \pmod{p}$, which means $T_1 = g_1^{(\eta(\zeta + \alpha\gamma) + 1)/(\gamma + x_i)} = (g_1 \tilde{g}^{\alpha\gamma + \zeta})^{1/(\gamma + x_i)}$. Furthermore, from (2) and (3), the extracted x_i satisfies $T_2 = \hat{f}^{\beta + x_i}$ and $T_3 = \hat{h}_j^\beta$ for the extracted β. $\square$

Now, we show the traceability.

Theorem 2. *The proposed scheme satisfies the traceability in the random oracle model under the q-SDH assumption.*

The following lemma implies the above theorem.

Lemma 3. *Suppose adversary $\mathcal{A}$ breaks the traceability of the proposed scheme with the advantage ε and q_H hash queries and q_S signature queries. Then, we can construct $\mathcal{B}$ that breaks the $(n+1)$-SDH assumption with the advantage $(\varepsilon/n - 1/p)/(4q_H)$ or $\mathcal{B}'$ that breaks the DL assumption on G_2 with the advantage $(\varepsilon/n - 1/p)/(4q_H)$.*

Proof Sketch. Consider the following framework with $\mathcal{A}$, which is derived from the proof in [6,12].

Setup. It is given $g_1, g_2, w = g_2^\gamma$, and n pairs (A_i, x_i). For each $i \in [1, n]$, either $s_i = 1$ indicating that an SDH pair (A_i, x_i) is known, or $s_i = 0$ indicating that x_i is known but A_i is unknown. Pick $\eta \in_R Z_p^*$, and compute $\tilde{g} = g_1^\eta$. Furthermore, as usual, choose $h_j \in_R G_2$ for all $j \in [1, T]$ and compute $B_{ij} = \psi(h_j^{x_i})$ for all i, j. Then, run $\mathcal{A}$ on $gpk = (g_1, g_2, \tilde{g}, h_1, \ldots, h_T, w)$ and $grt = (B_{11}, \ldots, B_{nT})$.

Hash Queries. At any time, $\mathcal{A}$ can query the hash functions H_0 and H. Respond with random values with consistency.

Signing Queries. $\mathcal{A}$ queries a signature on message M at member i and interval j. If $s_i = 1$, respond a signature using the secret key (A_i, x_i). If $s_i = 0$, pick $r \in_R Z_p$, $T_1 \in_R G_1$, and $\beta \in_R Z_p^*$. Then, compute $f = H_0(gpk, M, r)$, $T_2 = \psi(f)^{\beta + x_i}$ and $T_3 = \psi(h_j)^\beta$. Furthermore, obtain a simulated SPK V using the simulator of the SPK, which includes the backpatch of the hash function. Respond (r, T_1, T_2, T_3, V).

Corruption Queries. $\mathcal{A}$ requests the secret key at member i. If $s_i = 0$, then abort. Otherwise, respond requested key (A_i, x_i).

Output. Finally, $\mathcal{A}$ outputs a forged signature $\sigma^* = (r^*, T_1^*, T_2^*, T_3^*, V^*)$ including a secret key A^*. Using all B_{ij}, we can identify the member. If the identification fails (i.e., the member is outside of all i), output σ^*. Otherwise, some i is identified. If $s_i = 0$, then output σ^*. Otherwise (i.e., $s_i = 1$), abort.

Then, there are two types of forger on the above framework. Type 1 forger forges a signature of the member who is different from all i. Type 2 forger forges a signature of the member i whose corruption is not requested.

For q-SDH instance $(g_1, g_2, g_2^\gamma, \ldots, g_2^{\gamma^q})$, we can obtain $g_1, g_2, w = g_2^\gamma$ and $q - 1$ SDH pairs (A_i, x_i), using the technique of [4]. On the other hand, any SDH pair besides these $q - 1$ pairs can be transformed a solution of the q-SDH instance, which means that the q-SDH assumption is broken, using the same technique. As well as [6,12], we treat two types of forger differently.

Type 1. Given $(n+1)$-SDH instance, obtain n SDH pairs (A_i, x_i) with (g_1, g_2, w). Then, perform the framework with Type 1 forger $\mathcal{A}$ (i.e., all $s_i = 1$). $\mathcal{A}$ finally outputs a signature with secret key A^* s.t. $A^* \neq A_i$ for all i. In this case, the simulation is perfect, and thus $\mathcal{A}$ succeeds with advantage ε.

Type 2. Given n-SDH instance, obtain $n-1$ SDH pairs (A_i, x_i), which distributes n pairs, and set $s_i = 1$. For the unfilled entry at random index i^*, select $x_{i^*} \in_R Z_p^*$ (A_{i^*} is unknown), and set $s_{i^*} = 0$. Then, perform the framework with type 2 forger $\mathcal{A}$. In this case, it succeeds only if $\mathcal{A}$ never requests the corruption of i^*, but forges the signature including A_{i^*}. As discussed in [6], the value of i^* is independent $\mathcal{A}$'s view. Thus, the probability that $\mathcal{A}$ outputs the signature of i^* is at least ε/n.

Now we show how to obtain another SDH pair beyond the given $q-1$ SDH pairs, using the framework with Type 1 or Type 2. We can rewind the framework to obtain two forged signatures on the same message M and the same interval j, where the commitments in the SPK V are the same but the challenges and responses are different. As shown in [6], by the forking lemma, the successful probability is at least $(\varepsilon' - 1/p)^2/(16q_H)$, where ε' is the probability that the framework on each forger succeeds. Thus, using the extractor of the SPK V in Lemma 2, we can obtain a tuple $(\alpha^*, x^*, \zeta^*, T_1^*)$ s.t. $T_1^* = (g_1 \tilde{g}^{\alpha^* \gamma + \zeta^*})^{1/(\gamma + x^*)}$, $e(T_2^*, h_j) = e(\psi(h_j)^{x^*} T_3^*, f)$ and $x^* \neq x_i$ for all i with the probability $(\varepsilon' - 1/p)^2/(16q_H)$.

After the extraction, check $-\eta\alpha^* x^* + 1 + \eta\zeta^* = 0 \pmod{p}$. If it is true, abort. Otherwise (i.e., $-\eta\alpha^* x^* + 1 + \eta\zeta^* \neq 0 \pmod{p}$), consider the following equations, using $\tilde{g} = g_1^\eta$.

$$
\begin{aligned}
T_1^* &= (g_1 \tilde{g}^{\alpha^* \gamma + \zeta^*})^{1/(\gamma + x^*)} \\
&= (g_1^{1 + \eta(\alpha^* \gamma + \zeta^*)})^{1/(\gamma + x^*)} \\
&= (g_1^{\eta\alpha^* (\gamma + x^*) - \eta\alpha^* x^* + 1 + \eta\zeta^*})^{1/(\gamma + x^*)} \\
&= g_1^{\eta\alpha^*} g_1^{(-\eta\alpha^* x^* + 1 + \eta\zeta^*)/(\gamma + x^*)}
\end{aligned}
$$

Thus, the equation $T_1^* g_1^{-\eta\alpha^*} = g_1^{(-\eta\alpha^* x^* + 1 + \eta\zeta^*)/(\gamma + x^*)}$ holds. Since $-\eta\alpha^* x^* + 1 + \eta\zeta^* \neq 0 \pmod{p}$, this implies $T_1^* g_1^{-\eta\alpha^*/(-\eta\alpha^* x^* + 1 + \eta\zeta^*)} = g_1^{1/(\gamma + x^*)}$. Thus, we obtain another SDH pair (A^*, x^*), where $A^* = T_1^* g_1^{-\eta\alpha^*/(-\eta\alpha^* x^* + 1 + \eta\zeta^*)}$.

Let ε'' be the probability that $\mathcal{A}$ outputs the group signature for $(\alpha^*, x^*, \zeta^*, T_1^*)$ s.t. $-\eta\alpha^* x^* + 1 + \eta\zeta^* \neq 0 \pmod{p}$. Putting everything together, we have shown the following. Using Type 1 forger, we can solve the $(n+1)$-SDH instance with $(\varepsilon'' - 1/p)^2(16/q_H)$. Using Type 2 forger, we can solve the n-SDH instance with $(\varepsilon''/n - 1/p)^2(16/q_H)$. We can guess the type of forger with the probability $1/2$. Therefore, the pessimistic Type 2 forger implies the latter.

Finally, we consider the different game for the case of $-\eta\alpha^* x^* + 1 + \eta\zeta^* = 0 \pmod{p}$. Then, given $g_2, \tilde{g} = g_2^\eta$ for an unknown η, we can break the DL assumption on G_2, using $\mathcal{A}$, as follows. Set $\tilde{g} = \psi(\bar{g}) = g_1^\eta$. For $(g_1, g_2, \bar{g})$, conduct the above framework with $\mathcal{A}$. In the framework, choose γ and compute all SDH pairs, as usual. Then, $\mathcal{A}$ outputs the group signature for $(\alpha^*, x^*, \zeta^*, T_1^*)$ s.t. $-\eta\alpha^* x^* + 1 + \eta\zeta^* = 0 \pmod{p}$ (Otherwise, abort). Thus, $\eta(\alpha^* x^* - \zeta^*) = 1 \pmod{p}$. Since $\eta \neq 0$, we obtain $\eta^{-1} = \alpha^* x^* - \zeta^* \pmod{p}$. This is the discrete logarithm of g_2 to the base $\bar{g}$. By the similar discussion to the above case, the advantage of this game is $((\varepsilon - \varepsilon'')/n - 1/p)^2(16/q_H)$. Note that $\mathcal{A}$ can guess which game is given with just probability $1/2$.

If $\varepsilon'' \geq \varepsilon/2$, we can break the $(n+1)$-SDH assumption with the advantage of at least $(\varepsilon/n - 1/p)^2(4/q_H)$. Otherwise (i.e., $\varepsilon'' < \varepsilon/2$), since $\varepsilon - \varepsilon'' > \varepsilon/2$, we can break the DL assumption with the advantage of at least $(\varepsilon/n - 1/p)^2(4/q_H)$.   □

6   Efficiency

We compare the efficiency of the proposed scheme to the previous scheme [12].

Signature Length. For the bilinear groups G_1, G_2 with bilinear map e and isomorphism ψ, we can adopt the elliptic curves proposed in [11] called MNT curves. The use of MNT curves can make the representations of elements in G_1 short. Then, one can take the order p to be 170-bit prime, and the representations of G_1, G_T can be expressed in 171 and 1020 bits, respectively [6].

The proposed group signature includes 3 elements from G_1 and 6 elements from Z_p. In the above setting, this group signature is 1533 bits or 192 bytes. Although the previous group signature is described in case of $G_1 = G_2$, it can be extended in case of $G_1 \neq G_2$. In the extended case, the previous group signature includes 3 elements from G_1, 1 element from G_T and 8 elements from Z_p. In the above setting, this group signature is 2893 bits or 362 bytes. Therefore, the length of our signature is about 53% of that of the previous one.

Performance. The signature generation requires 6 multi-exponentiations, 1 isomorphism computation and 1 bilinear map computation (plus 1 isomorphism computation and 2 bilinear map computations that can be pre-computed). The verification requires 3 multi-exponentiations, 1 isomorphism computation and $2 + 2|RL_j|$ bilinear map computations (plus 3 bilinear map computations that can be pre-computed). In the previous scheme, the signature generation requires 10 multi-exponentiations and 1 bilinear map computation (plus 3 bilinear map computations that can be pre-computed). The verification requires 6 multi-exponentiations and $2 + |RL_j|$ bilinear map computations (plus 4 bilinear map computations that can be pre-computed).

Therefore, in the signature generation cost, our signature is better. However, in the verification, although the multi-exponentiation costs in our scheme is better, the dominant bilinear map computation cost depending on the size of the revocation list is worse (almost double), which is overhead of our scheme.

7   Conclusion

We have been proposed a short VLR group signature scheme with the backward unlinkability. Although the verification cost is worse (almost double), the length of the proposed group signature is about 53% of that of the previous one [12]. In addition, the signature generation cost is also reduced.

Our future works are to implement the proposed scheme, and to apply it to the anonymous authentication in mobile environments.

References

1. G. Ateniese, J. Camenisch, M. Joye, and G. Tsudik, "A practical and provably secure coalition-resistant group signature scheme," Proc. CRYPTO 2000, LNCS 1880, pp.255–270, 2000.
2. G. Ateniese, D. Song, and G. Tsudik, "Quasi-efficient revocation of group signatures," Proc. FC 2002, LNCS 2357, pp.183–197, 2003.
3. M. Bellare, D. Micciancio, and B. Warinschi, "Foundations of group signatures: Formal definitions, simplified requirements, and a construction based on general assumptions," Proc. EUROCRYPT 2003, LNCS 2656, pp.614–629, 2003.
4. D. Boneh and X. Boyen, "Short signatures without random oracles," Proc. EUROCRYPT 2004, LNCS 3027, pp.56–73, 2004.
5. D. Boneh, X. Boyen, and H. Shacham, "Short group signatures," Proc. CRYPTO 2004, LNCS 3152, pp.41–55, 2004.
6. D. Boneh and H. Shacham, "Group signatures with verifier-local revocation," Proc. ACM-CCS '04, pp.168–177, 2004.
7. J. Camenisch and A. Lysyanskaya, "Dynamic accumulators and application to efficient revocation of anonymous credentials," Proc. CRYPTO 2002, LNCS 2442, pp.61–76, 2002.
8. D. Chaum and E. van Heijst, "Group signatures," Proc. EUROCRYPT '91, LNCS 547, pp.241–246, 1991.
9. J. Furukawa and H. Imai, "An efficient group signature scheme from bilinear maps," Proc. ACISP 2005, LNCS 3574, pp.455–467, 2005.
10. F. Laguillaumie, P. Paillier, and D. Vergnaud, "Universally convertible directed signatures," Proc. ASIACRYPT 2005, LNCS 3788, pp.682–701, 2005.
11. A. Miyaji, M. Nakabayashi, and S. Takano, "New explicit conditions of elliptic curve traces for FR-reduction," IEICE Trans. Fundamentals, vol.E84-A, no.5, pp.1234–1243, 2001.
12. T. Nakanishi and N. Funabiki, "Verifier-local revocation group signature schemes with backward unlinkability from bilinear maps," Proc. ASIACRYPT 2005, LNCS 3788, pp.533–548, 2005.
13. L. Nguyen and R. Safavi-Naini, "Efficient and provably secure trapdoor-free group signature schemes from bilinear pairings," Proc. ASIACRYPT 2004, LNCS 3329, pp.372–386, 2004.
14. D.X. Song, "Practical forward secure group signature schemes," Proc. ACM-CCS '01, pp.225–234, 2001.
15. Z. Sujing and L. Dongdai, "A shorter group signature with verifier-location revocation and backward unlinkability." Cryptology ePrint Archive: Report 2006/100, 2006.
16. G. Tsudik and S. Xu, "Accumulating composites and improved group signing," Proc. ASIACRYPT 2003, LNCS 2894, pp.269–286, 2003.

Sound Computational Interpretation of Symbolic Hashes in the Standard Model

Flavio D. Garcia and Peter van Rossum

Institute for Computing and Information Sciences,
Radboud University Nijmegen, The Netherlands
{flaviog, petervr}@cs.ru.nl

Abstract. This paper provides one more step towards bridging the gap between the formal and computational approaches to the verification of cryptographic protocols. We extend the well-known Abadi-Rogaway logic with probabilistic hashes and we give a precise semantic interpretation to it using Canetti's oracle hashes. These are probabilistic polynomial-time hashes that hide all partial information. Finally, we show that this interpretation is computationally sound.

1 Introduction

The analysis of security protocols is being carried out mainly by means of two different techniques. On the one hand, from a logical perspective, messages are seen as algebraic objects, generated by some grammar from elementary objects such as keys, nonces, and constants. Cryptographic operations are seen as algebraic operations which are unbreakable. Attackers are typically modelled as so-called Dolev-Yao attackers [DY83], having total control over the network, having no computational limitations, and being only (but absolutely) incapable of breaking cryptographic operations. These logical methods are appealing, because they are relatively easy to use and capture most mistakes commonly made in security protocols.

On the other hand, from a complexity-theory perspective, messages are seen as bit strings and cryptographic operations as functions on bit strings satisfying certain security properties [Gol01]. An attacker here is a resource bounded probabilistic algorithm, limited by running time and/or memory, but capable of breaking cryptographic operations, if that is computationally feasible. The complexity based methods are more general and more realistic, but also more complex.

In the last few years much research has been done to relate these two perspectives [AR02, AJ01, MW04, Her05]. Such a relation takes the form of a function mapping algebraic messages m to (distributions over) bit strings $[\![m]\!]$. This map should relate messages that are observationally equivalent in the algebraic world (meaning that a Dolev-Yao attacker can see no difference between them) to indistinguishable distributions over bit strings (meaning that a computationally

H. Yoshiura et al. (Eds.): IWSEC 2006, LNCS 4266, pp. 33–47, 2006.

bounded adversary can only with negligible probability distinguish the distributions). Such a map allows one to use algebraic methods, possibly even automated, to reason about security properties of protocols and have those reasonings be valid also in the computational world.

The work carried out in the literature on relating these two perspectives mainly deals with symmetric encryption [AR02, MW04] and public key encryption [Her05]. Micciancio and Warinschi [MW04] briefly but explicitly question if this logical approach can be extended to, among other things, collision resistant hashes. Backes, Pfitzmann, and Waidner [BPW06] show that in their simulatability framework [PW00] a sound interpretation of hashes cannot exist, but that it is possible to give a sound interpretation of formal hashes in the simulatability framework using random oracles.

The problem with hashes is that in the algebraic world $h(m)$ and $h(m')$ are indistinguishable for a Dolev-Yao attacker if the attacker does not know m and m'. In the computational world, however, the normal security definition — it must be computationally infeasible to compute any pre-image of a hash value or a hash collision [RS04] — does not guarantee that the hash function hides all partial information about the message; hence there is no guarantee that $[\![h(m)]\!]$ and $[\![h(m')]\!]$ are computationally indistinguishable. A possible solution to this can be found in the work of Canetti and others [Can97a, CMR98] on perfectly one-way functions (a.k.a. oracle hashing). These are computable probabilistic hash functions that hide all partial information of their input (see Section 3.3 for a definition and an example).

Our Contribution. We propose an extension to the commonly used Abadi-Rogaway logic of algebraic messages introducing a *probabilistic hash operator* $h^r(m)$ in the logic, next to the probabilistic symmetric encryption operator $\{\!|m|\!\}_k^r$. Just as the original logic introduces a $\square$-operator to put in place of undecryptable ciphertext (for us $\square^r$, since we also deal with repetitions of ciphertexts), we introduce a $\boxtimes^r$-operator to put in place of the hash of an unknown message. In the computational world, we interpret h as a perfectly one-way function and prove that the resulting interpretation is sound.

It is relatively easy to see that the interpretation of messages like $\langle m, h^r(n, 0)\rangle$ and $\langle m, h^r(n, 1)\rangle$ are computationally indistinguishable whenever the adversary can not learn n from m. If, however, the adversary can learn n from m, then the messages are not observationally equivalent. The main technical difficulty that has to be overcome is that the adversary can learn part of the argument of the hash from the context, as for example in the message $\langle k, h^r(n, k)\rangle$.

Overview. Section 2 introduces the message algebra, including the probabilistic encryption and probabilistic hash operators. It also defines the observational equivalence relation on messages. Section 3 then introduces the computational world, giving the security definitions for encryption and hashes. In Section 4 the semantic interpretation $[\![-]\!]$ is defined and Section 5 proves the soundness of this interpretation. Finally, Section 6 discusses further research directions.

2   The Algebraic Setting

This section describes the message space and the observational equivalence extending the well-known Abadi-Rogaway logic [AR02] of algebraic messages with hashes. These messages are used to describe cryptographic protocols and the observational equivalence tells whether or not two protocol runs are indistinguishable for a global eavesdropper. Here a protocol run is simply the concatenation of all the messages exchanged in the run.

Definition 2.1. Key is an infinite set of *key symbols*, Nonce an infinite set of *nonce symbols*, Const a finite set of *constant symbols*, and Random an infinite set of *randomness labels*. Keys are denoted by $k, k', \ldots$, nonces by $n, n', \ldots$, constants by $c, c', \ldots$, and randomness labels by $r, r', \ldots$. There is one special key called $k_\square$ and for every randomness label r there is a special nonce called $n_\boxtimes^r$. Using these building blocks, *messages* are constructed using algebraic encryption, hashing, and pairing operations:

$$\text{Msg} \ni m := c \mid k \mid n \mid \{\!|m|\!\}_k^r \mid \text{h}^r(m) \mid \langle m, m \rangle \mid \square^r \mid \boxtimes^r .$$

Here k and n do not range over all keys/nonces, but only over the non-special ones. Special symbols ($\square^r$ and $\boxtimes^r$) are used to indicate undecryptable ciphertexts or hash values of unknown messages. When interpreting messages as (ensembles of distributions over) bit strings, we will treat $\square^r$ as if it were $\{\!|0|\!\}_{k_\square}^r$ and $\boxtimes^r$ as if it were $\text{h}^r(n_\boxtimes^r)$.

A message of the form $\{\!|m|\!\}_k^r$ is called an *encryption* and the set of all such messages is denoted by Enc. Similarly, messages of the form $\text{h}^r(m)$ are called *hash values* and the set of all these messages is denoted by Hash. Finally Box denotes the set of all messages of the form $\square^r$ or $\boxtimes^r$. The set of all messages that involve a "random choice" at their "top level", i.e., Key $\cup$ Nonce $\cup$ Enc $\cup$ Hash $\cup$ Box, is denoted by RanMsg.

The *closure* of a set U of messages is the set of all messages that can be constructed from U using tupling, detupling, and decryption. It represents the information an adversary could deduce knowing U.

Definition 2.2 (Closure). Let U be a set of messages. The *closure* of U, denoted by $\overline{U}$, is the smallest set of messages satisfying:

1. Const $\subseteq \overline{U}$;
2. $U \subseteq \overline{U}$;
3. $m, m' \in \overline{U} \implies \langle m, m' \rangle \in \overline{U}$;
4. $\{\!|m|\!\}_k^r, k \in \overline{U} \implies m \in \overline{U}$;
5. $\langle m, m' \rangle \in \overline{U} \implies m, m' \in \overline{U}$.

For the singleton set $\{m\}$, we write $\overline{m}$ instead of $\overline{\{m\}}$.

We define the function *encpat*: Msg $\to$ Msg as in Abadi-Rogaway [AR02] which takes a message m and reduces it to a pattern. Intuitively, this is the pattern that an attacker sees in a message given that he knows the messages in U. This function does not replace hashes. Formally, it is defined as follows:

$$encpat(m) = encpat(m, \overline{m})$$

where

$$encpat(\langle m_1, m_2 \rangle, U) = \langle encpat(m_1, U), encpat(m_2, U) \rangle$$

$$encpat(\{\!|m|\!\}_k^r, U) = \begin{cases} \{\!|encpat(m, U)|\!\}_k^r, & \text{if } k \in U; \\ \square^{\mathcal{R}(\{\!|m|\!\}_k^r)}, & \text{otherwise.} \end{cases}$$

$$encpat(\mathrm{h}^r(m), U) = \mathrm{h}^r(encpat(m, U))$$

$$encpat(m, U) = m \quad \text{in any other case.}$$

Here $\mathcal{R} \colon \mathrm{Enc} \cup \mathrm{Hash} \hookrightarrow \mathrm{Random}$ is an injective function that takes an encryption or a hash value and outputs a tag that identifies its randomness. We need this tagging function to make sure that the function $encpat$ is injective. That is, we need to make sure that distinct undecryptable messages get replaced by distinct boxes and similarly for $hashpat$ below.

Now we define the function $hashpat \colon \mathrm{Msg} \to \mathrm{Msg}$ which takes a message m and reduces all hashes of unknown (not in U) sub-messages, to $\boxtimes$. This function does not replace encryptions. Formally:

$$hashpat(m) = hashpat(m, \overline{m})$$

where

$$hashpat(\langle m_1, m_2 \rangle, U) = \langle hashpat(m_1, U), hashpat(m_2, U) \rangle$$

$$hashpat(\{\!|m|\!\}_k^r, U) = \{\!|hashpat(m, U)|\!\}_k^r$$

$$hashpat(\mathrm{h}^r(m), U) = \begin{cases} \mathrm{h}^r(hashpat(m, U)), & \text{if } m \in U; \\ \boxtimes^{\mathcal{R}(\mathrm{h}^r(m))}, & \text{otherwise.} \end{cases}$$

$$hashpat(m, U) = m \quad \text{in any other case.}$$

Naturally, we now define $pattern$ as $pattern = encpat \circ hashpat$.

Example 2.3. Consider the message

$$m = \langle \{\!|\{\!|1|\!\}_{k'}^{r'}, \mathrm{h}^{\tilde{r}}(n)|\!\}_k^r, \mathrm{h}^{\hat{r}}(k), k \rangle.$$

Then $\quad hashpat(m) = \langle \{\!|\{\!|1|\!\}_{k'}^{r'}, \boxtimes^t |\!\}_k^r, \mathrm{h}^{\hat{r}}(k), k \rangle, \quad$ because n is not in $\overline{m}$,

and $\quad pattern(m) = \langle \{\!| \square^s , \boxtimes^t |\!\}_k^r, \mathrm{h}^{\hat{r}}(k), k \rangle, \quad$ because k' is not in $\overline{m}$,

where $t = \mathcal{R}(\mathrm{h}^{\tilde{r}}(n))$ and $s = \mathcal{R}(\{\!|1|\!\}_{k'}^{r'})$.

Definition 2.4 (Observational Equivalence). Two messages m and m' are said to be *observationally equivalent*, notation $m \cong m'$, if there is a type preserving permutation σ of $\mathrm{Key} \cup \mathrm{Nonce} \cup \mathrm{Box}$ such that $pattern(m) = pattern(m')\sigma$. Here $pattern(m')\sigma$ denotes simultaneous substitution of x by $\sigma(x)$ in $pattern(m')$, for all $x \in \mathrm{Key} \cup \mathrm{Nonce} \cup \mathrm{Box}$.

From the original setting in [AR02] we inherit the requirement that messages must be acyclic for the soundness result to hold.

Definition 2.5 (Acyclicity). Let m be a message and k, k' two keys. The key k is said to *encrypt* k' *in* m if m has a sub-message of the form $\{m'\}_k^r$ with k' being a sub-message of m'. A message is said to be *acyclic* if there is no sequence $k_1, k_2, \ldots, k_n, k_{n+1} = k_1$ of keys such that k_i encrypts k_{i+1} in m for all $i \in \{1, \ldots, n\}$.

3 The Computational Setting

This section gives a brief overview of the concepts used in the complexity theoretic approach to security protocols. Much of this is standard; the reader is referred to [GB01, BDJR97] for a thorough treatment of the basic concepts, to [AR02] for the notion of *type-0 security* for cryptographic schemes (see Section 3.2 below), and to [Can97a] for the notion of *oracle hashing* (see Section 3.3 below).

In the computational world, messages are elements of Str := $\{0, 1\}^*$. Cryptographic algorithms and adversaries are probabilistic polynomial-time algorithms. When analyzing cryptographic primitives, it is customary to consider probabilistic algorithms that take an element in Param := $\{1\}^*$ as input, whose length scales with the security parameter. By making the security parameter large enough, the system should become arbitrarily hard to break.

This idea is formalized in the security notions of the cryptographic operations. The basic one, which is what is used to define the notion of semantically equivalent messages, is that of *computational indistinguishability* of probability ensembles over Str. Here a *probability ensemble over* Str is a sequence $\{A_\eta\}_{\eta \in \mathbb{N}}$ of probability distributions over Str indexed by the security parameter.

Definition 3.1 (Computational Indistinguishability). Two probability ensembles $\{A_\eta\}_\eta$ and $\{B_\eta\}_\eta$ are *computationally indistinguishable* if for every probabilistic polynomial-time algorithm A, for all polynomials p, and for large enough η,

$$\mathbb{P}[x \xleftarrow{\$} A_\eta; A(1^\eta, x) = 1] - \mathbb{P}[x \xleftarrow{\$} B_\eta; A(1^\eta, x) = 1] < \frac{1}{p(\eta)}.$$

After a brief interlude on probabilistic polynomial-time algorithms in Section 3.1, we give the formal definition of an encryption scheme and its security notion in Section 3.2 and of oracle hashing in Section 3.3.

3.1 Probabilistic Algorithms

In Definition 3.1, the notion of probabilistic polynomial-time algorithm was already used. Because we explicitly use two different views of these algorithms and in order to fix notation, we give a more precise definition.

Definition 3.2. Coins is the set $\{0, 1\}^\omega$, the set of all infinite sequences of 0's and 1's. We equip Coins with the probability distribution obtained by flipping a fair coin for each element in the sequence.

Definition 3.3. The result of running a probabilistic algorithm A on an input $x \in \text{Str}$ is a probability distribution $A(x)$ over Str. When we need to explicitly write the randomness used while running A, we write $A(x, \rho)$ with $\rho \in \text{Coins}$. Using this notation, $A(x)$ and $[\rho \xleftarrow{\$} \text{Coins}; A(x, \rho)]$ are the same probability distribution. When confusion is unlikely, we will also denote the support of this probability distribution, $\{y \in \text{Str} | \mathbb{P}[\rho \xleftarrow{\$} \text{Coins}; A(x, \rho = y)] > 0\}$, by $A(x)$.

Now suppose that A runs in polynomial time p. Then running A on x cannot use more than $p(|x|)$ coin flips. Letting $\text{Coins}_{p(|x|)}$ denote the uniform probability distribution on $\{0, 1\}^{p(|x|)}$, we get that the probability distribution $A(x)$ can also be written as $[\rho \xleftarrow{\$} \text{Coins}_{p(|x|)}; A(x, \rho)]$.

3.2 Encryption Scheme

For each security parameter $\eta \in \mathbb{N}$ we let $\text{Plaintext}_\eta \subseteq \text{Str}$ be a non-empty set of *plaintexts*, satisfying that for each $\eta \in \mathbb{N}$: $\text{Plaintext}_\eta \subseteq \text{Plaintext}_{\eta+1}$ as in Goldwasser and Bellare [GB01]. Let us define $\text{Plaintext} = \bigcup_\eta \text{Plaintext}_\eta$. There is a set $\text{Keys} \subseteq \text{Str}$ of *keys* and also a set $\text{Ciphertext} \subseteq \text{Str}$ of *ciphertexts*. Furthermore, there is a special bit string $\bot$ not appearing in Plaintext or Ciphertext. An *encryption scheme Π* consists of three algorithms:

1. a (probabilistic) key generation algorithm $\mathcal{K} \colon \text{Param} \to \text{Keys}$ that outputs, given a unary sequence of length η, a randomly chosen element of Keys;
2. a (probabilistic) encryption algorithm $\mathcal{E} \colon \text{Keys} \times \text{Str} \to \text{Ciphertext} \cup \{\bot\}$ that outputs, given a key and a bit string, a possibly randomly chosen element from Ciphertext or $\bot$;
3. a (deterministic) decryption algorithm $\mathcal{D} \colon \text{Keys} \times \text{Str} \to \text{Plaintext} \cup \{\bot\}$ that outputs, given a key and a ciphertext, an element from Plaintext or $\bot$.

These algorithms must satisfy that the decryption (with the correct key) of a ciphertext returns the original plaintext. The element $\bot$ is used to indicate failure of en- or decryption, although there is no requirement that decrypting with the wrong keys yields $\bot$.

Now we define type-0 security of an encryption scheme as in [AR02], which is a variant of the standard semantic security definition, enhanced with some extra properties. In particular a type-0 secure encryption scheme is which-key concealing, repetition concealing and length hiding. We refer to the original paper for motivation and explanations on how to achieve such an encryption scheme. The notion of type-0 security makes slightly unrealistic assumptions on the encryption scheme. However our result on hashes does not significantly depend on the specific security notion for the encryption scheme. As in [MP05, Her05], it is possible to replace type-0 security by the standard notion of ind-cpa or ind-cca by adapting the definition of *encpat*. For simplicity of the exposition, throughout this paper we adopt the former security notion.

Definition 3.4. An *adversary (for type-0 security)* is a probabilistic polynomial-time algorithm $A^{\mathcal{F}(-),\mathcal{G}(-)} \colon \text{Param} \to \{0, 1\}$ having access to two probabilistic oracles $\mathcal{F}, \mathcal{G} \colon \text{Str} \to \text{Str}$. The *advantage* of such an adversary is the function $\text{Adv}_A \colon \mathbb{N} \to \mathbb{R}$ defined by

$$\mathrm{Adv}_A(\eta) = \mathbb{P}[\kappa, \kappa' \xleftarrow{\$} \mathcal{K}(1^\eta); A^{\mathcal{E}(\kappa,-),\mathcal{E}(\kappa',-)}(1^\eta) = 1] -$$
$$\mathbb{P}[\kappa \xleftarrow{\$} \mathcal{K}(1^\eta); A^{\mathcal{E}(\kappa,0),\mathcal{E}(\kappa,0)}(1^\eta) = 1].$$

Here the probabilities are taken over the choice of κ and κ' by the key generation algorithm, over the choices of the oracles, and over the internal choices of A. An encryption scheme $\langle \mathcal{K}, \mathcal{E}, \mathcal{D} \rangle$ is called *type-0 secure* if for all polynomial-time adversaries A as above, the advantage Adv_A is a negligible function of η. This means that for all positive polynomials p and for large enough η, $\mathrm{Adv}_A(\eta) \leq \frac{1}{p(\eta)}$.

In the sequel we need an extra assumption on the encryption scheme, namely that the ciphertexts are well-spread as a function of the coins tosses of $\mathcal{E}$. It means that for *all* plaintexts μ and *all* keys κ, no ciphertext is exceptionally likely to occur as the encryption of μ under κ. Note that this does not follow from, nor implies type-0 security. Also note that every encryption scheme running in cipher block chaining mode automatically has this property: the initial vector provides the required randomness.

Definition 3.5 (Well-spread). An encryption scheme $\langle \mathcal{K}, \mathcal{E}, \mathcal{D} \rangle$ is said to be *well-spread* if for every polynomial p,

$$\forall \eta \gg 1. \forall x \in \mathrm{Ciphertext}. \forall \kappa \in \mathcal{K}(1^\eta). \forall \mu \in \mathrm{Plaintext}_\eta: \ \mathbb{P}[\mathcal{E}(\kappa, \mu) = x] < \frac{1}{p(\eta)}.$$

3.3 Oracle Hashing

The underlying secrecy assumptions behind formal or Dolev-Yao hashes [DY83] are very strong. It is assumed that given a hash value $f(x)$, it is not possible for an adversary to learn any information about the pre-image x. In the literature this idealization is often modelled with the random oracle [BR93]. Such a primitive is not computable and therefore it is also an idealization. Practical hash functions like SHA or MD5 are very useful cryptographic primitives even though this functions might leak partial information about their input. Moreover, under the traditional security notions (one-wayness), a function that reveals half of its input is considered secure. In addition, any deterministic hash function f leaks partial information about x, namely $f(x)$. Through this paper we consider a new primitive introduced by Canetti [Can97a] called *oracle hashing*, that mimics what semantic security is for encryption schemes. This hash function is probabilistic and therefore it needs a verification function, just as in a signature scheme. A *hash scheme* consists of two algorithms $\mathcal{H}$ and $\mathcal{V}$. The probabilistic algorithm $\mathcal{H}$: Param $\times$ Str $\to$ Str takes a unary sequence and a message and outputs a hash value; the verification algorithm $\mathcal{V}$: Str $\times$ Str $\to \{0,1\}$ that given two messages x and c correctly decides whether c is a hash of x or not. As an example we reproduce here a hash scheme proposed in the original paper. Let p be a large (i.e., scaling with η) safe prime. Take $\mathcal{H}(x) = \langle r^2, r^{2 \cdot h(x)} \mod p \rangle$, where r is a randomly chosen element in $\mathbb{Z}_p^*$ and h is any collision resistant hash function. The verification algorithm $\mathcal{V}(x, \langle a, b \rangle)$ just checks whether $b = a^{h(x)} \mod p$.

Canetti gives essentially two security notions for such a hash scheme. The first one, *oracle indistinguishability*, guarantees that an adversary can gain no information at all about a bit string, given its hash value (or rather, with sufficiently small probability). The second one is an appropriate form of collision resistance. It guarantees that an adversary cannot (or rather, again, with sufficiently small probability) compute two distinct messages that successfully pass the verification test with the same hash value.

Definition 3.6. A hash scheme $\langle \mathcal{H}, \mathcal{V} \rangle$ is said to be *oracle indistinguishable* if for every family of probabilistic polynomial-time predicates $\{D_\eta : \text{Str} \to \{0,1\}\}_{\eta \in \mathbb{N}}$ and every positive polynomial p there is a polynomial size family $\{L_\eta\}_{\eta \in \mathbb{N}}$ of subsets of Str such that for all large enough η and all $x, y \in \text{Str} \setminus L_\eta$:

$$\mathbb{P}[D_\eta(\mathcal{H}(1^\eta, x)) = 1] - \mathbb{P}[D_\eta(\mathcal{H}(1^\eta, y)) = 1] < \frac{1}{p(\eta)}.$$

Here the probabilities are taken over the choices made by $\mathcal{H}$ and the choices made by D_η. This definition is the non-uniform [Gol01] version of oracle indistinguishability proposed by Canetti [Can97a] as it is finally used throughout the proof (See the full version [Can97b], Appendix B).

Definition 3.7 (Collision Resistance). A hash scheme $\langle \mathcal{H}, \mathcal{V} \rangle$ is said to be *collision resistant* if for every probabilistic polynomial time adversary A, the probability

$$\mathbb{P}[\langle c, x, y \rangle \xleftarrow{\$} A(1^\eta); x \neq y \wedge \mathcal{V}(x, c) = \mathcal{V}(y, c) = 1]$$

is a negligible function of η.

4   Interpretation

Section 2 describes a setting where messages are algebraic terms generated by some grammar. In Section 3 messages are bit strings and operations are given by probabilistic algorithms operating on bit strings. This section shows how to map algebraic messages to (distributions over) bit strings. This interpretation is very much standard. We refer to [AR02, AJ01, MW04] for a thorough explanation. In particular this section introduces notation that allows us to assign, beforehand, some of the random coin flips used for the computation of the interpretation of a message. This notation becomes useful throughout the soundness proof.

Definition 4.1. For every message m and set of messages V we define the set $\text{R}(m, V) \subseteq \text{RanMsg}$ of *random messages in m relative to V* as follows: if $m \in V$, then $\text{R}(m, V) = \emptyset$, otherwise

$$\text{R}(c, V) = \emptyset \qquad\qquad \text{R}(\{\!|m|\!\}_k^r, V) = \text{R}(m, V) \cup \{k, \{\!|m|\!\}_k^r\}$$
$$\text{R}(n, V) = \{n\} \qquad\qquad \text{R}(\text{h}^r(m), V) = \text{R}(m, V) \cup \{\text{h}^r(m)\}$$
$$\text{R}(k, V) = \{k\} \qquad\qquad \text{R}(\langle m_1, m_2 \rangle, V) = \text{R}(m_1, V) \cup \text{R}(m_2, V)$$
$$\text{R}(\square^r, V) = \{k_\square, \square^r\} \qquad\qquad \text{R}(\boxtimes^r, V) = \{n_\boxtimes^r, \boxtimes^r\}.$$

The set of *random messages in* m is defined as $\mathrm{R}(m) := \mathrm{R}(m, \emptyset)$ and the set of *random messages in* m *relative to* m' as $\mathrm{R}(m, m') := \mathrm{R}(m, \{m'\})$.

Note that $\mathrm{R}(m)$ is nearly equal to the set of all sub-messages of m that are in RanMsg; the only difference is that $\mathrm{R}(m)$ also may contain the special key $k_\square$ or special nonces $n_\boxtimes^r$. When interpreting a message m as (ensembles of distributions over) bit strings (Definition 4.4 below), we will first choose a sequence of coin flips for all elements of $\mathrm{R}(m)$ and use these sequences as source of randomness for the appropriate interpretation algorithms.

Also note that $\mathrm{R}(m, m')$ is the set of all random messages in m except those that *only* occur as a sub-message of m' (see Definition 4.5 below).

Example 4.2. Let m be the message $\langle k, \{0\}_k^r, \mathrm{h}^{r'}(\{0\}_k^r, n), n'\rangle$ and let $\tilde{m}$ be the message inside the hash: $\langle\{0\}_k^r, n\rangle$. Then the randomness in m is $\mathrm{R}(m) = \{k, \{0\}_k^r, \mathrm{h}^{r'}(\{0\}_k^r, n), n', n\}$, the randomness inside the hash is $\mathrm{R}(\tilde{m}) = \{\{0\}_k^r, k, n\}$, and the randomness that occurs only outside the hash is $\mathrm{R}(m, \mathrm{h}^{r'}(\tilde{m})) = \mathrm{R}(m) \setminus \{\mathrm{h}^{r'}(\tilde{m}), n\}$. The randomness that is shared between the inside of the hash and the outside of the hash is $\mathrm{R}(m, \mathrm{h}^{r'}(\tilde{m})) \cap \mathrm{R}(\tilde{m}) = \{\{0\}_k^r\}$.

Definition 4.3. For every finite set X we define $\mathrm{Coins}(X)$ as $\{\tau\colon X \to \mathrm{Coins}\}$. We equip $\mathrm{Coins}(X)$ with the induced product probability distribution. Furthermore, for every message m we write $\mathrm{Coins}(m)$ instead of $\mathrm{Coins}(\mathrm{R}(m))$.

An element of τ of $\mathrm{Coins}(m)$ gives, for every sub-message m' of m that requires random choices when interpreting this sub-message as a bit string, an infinite sequence $\tau(m')$ of coin flips that will be used to resolve the randomness.

Now we are ready to give semantic to our message algebra. We use $\mathcal{E}$ to interpret encryptions, $\mathcal{K}$ to interpret key symbols, and $\mathcal{H}$ to interpret for hashes. We let $\mathcal{C}\colon \mathrm{Const} \to \mathrm{Str}$ be a function that (deterministically) assigns a constant bit string to each constant identifier. We let $\mathcal{N}\colon \mathrm{Param} \to \mathrm{Str}$ be the nonce generation function that, given a unary sequence of length η, chooses uniformly and randomly a bit string from $\{0, 1\}^\eta$.

Definition 4.4. For a message m, a value of the security parameter $\eta \in \mathbb{N}$, a finite set U of messages containing $\mathrm{R}(m)$, and for a choice $\tau \in \mathrm{Coins}(U)$ of (at least) all the randomness in m, we can (deterministically) create a bit string $[\![m]\!]_\eta^\tau \in \mathrm{Str}$ as follows:

$$[\![c]\!]_\eta^\tau = \mathcal{C}(c) \qquad\qquad [\![\{m\}_k^r]\!]_\eta^\tau = \mathcal{E}([\![k]\!]_\eta^\tau, [\![m]\!]_\eta^\tau, \tau(\{m\}_k^r))$$

$$[\![k]\!]_\eta^\tau = \mathcal{K}(1^\eta, \tau(k)) \qquad\qquad [\![\mathrm{h}^r(m)]\!]_\eta^\tau = \mathcal{H}(1^\eta, [\![m]\!]_\eta^\tau, \tau(\mathrm{h}^r(m)))$$

$$[\![n]\!]_\eta^\tau = \mathcal{N}(1^\eta, \tau(n)) \qquad\qquad [\![\square^r]\!]_\eta^\tau = \mathcal{E}([\![k_\square]\!]_\eta^\tau, \mathcal{C}(0), \tau(\square^r))$$

$$[\![\langle m_1, m_2\rangle]\!]_\eta^\tau = [\![m_1]\!]_\eta^\tau[\![m_2]\!]_\eta^\tau \qquad\qquad [\![\boxtimes^r]\!]_\eta^\tau = \mathcal{H}(1^\eta, [\![n_\boxtimes^r]\!]_\eta^\tau, \tau(\boxtimes^r)).$$

Note that $[\![m]\!]_\eta^\tau = [\![m]\!]_\eta^{\tau|_{\mathrm{R}(m)}}$. For a fixed message m and $\eta \in \mathbb{N}$, choosing τ from the probability distribution $\mathrm{Coins}(\mathrm{R}(m))$ creates a probability distribution $[\![m]\!]_\eta$ over Str:

$$[\![m]\!]_\eta := [\tau \xleftarrow{\$} \mathrm{Coins}(m); [\![m]\!]_\eta^\tau].$$

Note that although the codomain of $\tau \in \mathrm{Coins}(m)$ is Coins, the set of *infinite* bit strings, when interpreting a fixed message m at a fixed value of the security parameter η, only a predetermined *finite* initial segment of each sequence of coin flips will be used by $\mathcal{K}, \mathcal{N}, \mathcal{E}$, and $\mathcal{H}$ (cf. Definition 3.3). Denoting by $\mathrm{Coins}_\eta(m)$ the probability distribution (on $\{\tau\colon \mathrm{R}(m) \to \mathrm{Str}\}$) that is actually being used when computing $[\![m]\!]_\eta$, we could also write

$$[\![m]\!]_\eta = [\tau \xleftarrow{\$} \mathrm{Coins}_\eta(m); [\![m]\!]_\eta^\tau].$$

Furthermore, letting η range over $\mathbb{N}$ creates an ensemble of probability distributions $[\![m]\!]$ over Str, namely $[\![m]\!] := \{[\![m]\!]_\eta\}_{\eta \in \mathbb{N}}$.

Definition 4.5. We will also need a way of interpreting a message as a bit string when the interpretation of certain sub-messages has already been chosen in some other way. For this, let e be a function from some set $\mathrm{Dom}(e) \subseteq \mathrm{Pat}$ to Str and let $\tau \in \mathrm{Coins}(U, \mathrm{Dom}(e))$ with U a finite set of messages containing $\mathrm{R}(m)$. We interpret a message m using e whenever possible and τ otherwise: if $m \in \mathrm{Dom}(e)$, then $[\![m]\!]_\eta^{e,\tau} = e(m)$, otherwise

$$[\![c]\!]_\eta^{e,\tau} = \mathcal{C}(c) \qquad\qquad [\![\{\!|m|\!\}_k^r]\!]_\eta^{e,\tau} = \mathcal{E}([\![k]\!]_\eta^\tau, [\![m]\!]_\eta^{e,\tau}, \tau(\{\!|m|\!\}_k^r))$$

$$[\![k]\!]_\eta^{e,\tau} = \mathcal{K}(1^\eta, \tau(k)) \qquad\qquad [\![\mathrm{h}^r(m)]\!]_\eta^{e,\tau} = \mathcal{H}(1^\eta, [\![m]\!]_\eta^{e,\tau}, \tau(\mathrm{h}^r(m)))$$

$$[\![n]\!]_\eta^{e,\tau} = \mathcal{N}(1^\eta, \tau(n)) \qquad\qquad [\![\square^r]\!]_\eta^{e,\tau} = \mathcal{E}([\![k_\square]\!]_\eta^{e,\tau}, \mathcal{C}(0), \tau(\square^r))$$

$$[\![\langle m_1, m_2 \rangle]\!]_\eta^{e,\tau} = [\![m_1]\!]_\eta^{e,\tau} [\![m_2]\!]_\eta^{e,\tau} \qquad\qquad [\![\boxtimes^r]\!]_\eta^{e,\tau} = \mathcal{H}(1^\eta, [\![n_\boxtimes^r]\!]_\eta^{e,\tau}, \tau(\boxtimes^r)).$$

Definition 4.6. We also need a way of pre-specifying some of the random choices to be made when interpreting a message. For this, let $\tau \in \mathrm{Coins}(U)$ for some finite set of messages U. Then for every $\eta \in \mathbb{N}$ and every message m, the distribution $[\![m]\!]_\eta^\tau$ is obtained by randomly choosing coins for the remaining randomness labels in m. Formally,

$$[\![m]\!]_\eta^\tau := [\tau' \xleftarrow{\$} \mathrm{Coins}(\mathrm{R}(m) \setminus U); [\![m]\!]_\eta^{\tau \cup \tau'}],$$

where $\tau \cup \tau' \in \mathrm{Coins}(m)$ denotes the function which agrees with τ on $U \cap \mathrm{R}(m)$ and with τ' on $\mathrm{R}(m) \setminus U$.

This can also be combined with the previous way of preselecting a part of the interpretation. For a function e from a set $\mathrm{Dom}(e) \subseteq \mathrm{Pat}$ to Str and $\tau \in \mathrm{Coins}(U)$ as above, we define $[\![m]\!]_\eta^{e,\tau} := [\tau' \xleftarrow{\$} \mathrm{Coins}(\mathrm{R}(m) \setminus U); [\![m]\!]_\eta^{e,\tau \cup \tau'}]$.

5 Soundness

This section shows that the interpretation proposed in the previous section is computationally sound. Throughout this section we assume that the encryption scheme $\langle \mathcal{K}, \mathcal{E}, \mathcal{D} \rangle$ is type-0 secure (or ind-cca with *encpat* modified as in [Her05, MP05]) and well-spread, and that the probabilistic hash scheme $\langle \mathcal{H}, \mathcal{V} \rangle$ is oracle indistinguishable and collision resistant.

The following lemma uses all these assumptions. It claims that if you pre-specify some, but not all, of the sequences of coins to be chosen when interpreting a message m, then no single bit string x is exceptionally likely to occur as the interpretation of m.

Lemma 5.1 *Let m be a message, $U \subsetneq \mathrm{R}(m)$. Let p be a positive polynomial. Then*

$$\forall \eta \gg 1. \forall \tau \in \mathrm{Coins}(U). \forall x \in \mathrm{Str} : \mathbb{P}[\alpha \xleftarrow{\$} \llbracket m \rrbracket_\eta^\tau; \alpha = x] < \frac{1}{p(\eta)}.$$

Proof. The proof follows by induction on the structure of m. See the full version of this paper [GR06]. ∎

Theorem 5.2 *Let m be a message with a sub-message of the form $\mathrm{h}^r(\tilde{m})$. Assume that $\tilde{m} \notin \overline{m}$. Take $m' := m[\mathrm{h}^r(\tilde{m}) := \boxtimes^s]$, where $s = \mathcal{R}(\mathrm{h}^r(\tilde{m}))$. Then $\llbracket m \rrbracket \equiv \llbracket m' \rrbracket$.*

Proof. Assume that $\llbracket m \rrbracket \not\equiv \llbracket m' \rrbracket$, say $A \colon \mathrm{Param} \times \mathrm{Str} \to \{0,1\}$ is a probabilistic polynomial-time adversary and p a positive polynomial such that

$$\frac{1}{p(\eta)} \leq \mathbb{P}[\mu \xleftarrow{\$} \llbracket m \rrbracket_\eta; A(1^\eta, \mu) = 1] - \mathbb{P}[\mu \xleftarrow{\$} \llbracket m' \rrbracket_\eta; A(1^\eta, \mu) = 1] \qquad (1)$$

for infinitely many $\eta \in \mathbb{N}$. We will use this to build a distinguisher as in Definition 3.6 that breaks oracle indistinguishability of $\langle \mathcal{H}, \mathcal{V} \rangle$.

Let $\eta \in \mathbb{N}$, abbreviate $\mathrm{R}(m, \tilde{m}) \cap \mathrm{R}(\tilde{m})$ to U and let $\tau \in \mathrm{Coins}(U)$. Note that τ chooses coin flips for the randomness that occurs both inside and outside the hash. Then define a probabilistic polynomial-time algorithm $D_\eta^\tau \colon \{0,1\}^* \to \{0,1\}$ as follows.

> **algorithm** $D_\eta^\tau(\alpha)$:
> $\mu \xleftarrow{\$} \llbracket m \rrbracket_\eta^{\{\mathrm{h}^r(\tilde{m}) \mapsto \alpha\}, \tau}$
> $\beta \xleftarrow{\$} A(\eta, \mu)$
> **return** β

This algorithm tries to guess if a given bit string α was drawn from $\llbracket \mathrm{h}^r(\tilde{m}) \rrbracket_\eta^\tau$ or from $\llbracket \boxtimes^s \rrbracket_\eta^\tau = \llbracket \mathrm{h}^s(n_{\boxtimes}^s) \rrbracket_\eta^\tau$. It does so by computing an interpretation for m as follows. The sub-message $\mathrm{h}^r(\tilde{m})$ is interpreted as α; the randomness that is shared between the inside of the hash ($\tilde{m}$) and the rest of the message is resolved using hard-coded sequences of coin flips τ. It then uses the adversary A to guess if the resulting interpretation was drawn from $\llbracket m \rrbracket_\eta$ (in which case it guesses that α was drawn from $\llbracket \mathrm{h}^r(\tilde{m}) \rrbracket_\eta$) or from $\llbracket m' \rrbracket_\eta$ (in which case it guesses that α was drawn from $\llbracket \boxtimes^s \rrbracket_\eta$).

Even though τ has values in Coins, i.e., infinite strings, this is still a well-defined probabilistic polynomial-time algorithm, as it uses only a finite, predetermined amount of bits from τ (cf. Definitions 3.3 and 4.4). However, $(1^\eta, \alpha) \mapsto D_\eta^\tau(\alpha)$ would not be a well-defined probabilistic polynomial-time algorithm.

Now consider one of the infinitely many values of η for which (1) holds. Using D_η^τ we can rephrase (1) as follows:

$$\frac{1}{p(\eta)} \leq \mathbb{P}[\tau \xleftarrow{\$} \mathrm{Coins}_\eta(U), \alpha \xleftarrow{\$} [\![h^r(\tilde{m})]\!]_\eta^\tau; D_\eta^\tau(\alpha) = 1] -$$

$$\mathbb{P}[\tau \xleftarrow{\$} \mathrm{Coins}_\eta(U), \alpha \xleftarrow{\$} [\![\boxtimes^s]\!]_\eta^\tau; D_\eta^\tau(\alpha) = 1]$$

$$= \sum_{\tau \in \mathrm{Coins}_\eta(U)} \Big(\mathbb{P}[\alpha \xleftarrow{\$} [\![h^r(\tilde{m})]\!]_\eta^\tau; D_\eta^\tau(\alpha) = 1] -$$

$$\mathbb{P}[\alpha \xleftarrow{\$} [\![\boxtimes^s]\!]_\eta^\tau; D_\eta^\tau(\alpha) = 1] \Big) \cdot \mathbb{P}[T \xleftarrow{\$} \mathrm{Coins}_\eta(U); T = \tau]$$

$$= \sum_{\tau \in \mathrm{Coins}_\eta(U)} \Big(\mathbb{P}[\alpha \xleftarrow{\$} [\![\tilde{m}]\!]_\eta^\tau; D_\eta^\tau(\mathcal{H}(1^\eta, \alpha)) = 1] -$$

$$\mathbb{P}[\alpha \xleftarrow{\$} [\![n_\boxtimes^s]\!]_\eta^\tau; D_\eta^\tau(\mathcal{H}(1^\eta, \alpha)) = 1] \Big) \cdot \mathbb{P}[T \xleftarrow{\$} \mathrm{Coins}_\eta(U); T = \tau].$$

Note that τ selects the randomness that is shared between the inside of the hash and the outside of the hash; when α is drawn from $[\![\tilde{m}]\!]_\eta^\tau$ the randomness that appears only inside the hash is chosen (and the assumption on $\tilde{m}$ means that there is really something to choose); $\mathcal{H}$ chooses the randomness for taking the hash; and D_η^τ itself resolves the randomness that appears only outside the hash. This means that there must be a particular value of τ, say $\bar{\tau}_\eta$, such that

$$\frac{1}{p(\eta)} \leq \mathbb{P}[\alpha \xleftarrow{\$} [\![\tilde{m}]\!]_\eta^{\bar{\tau}_\eta}; D_\eta^{\bar{\tau}_\eta}(\mathcal{H}(1^\eta, \alpha)) = 1] - \mathbb{P}[\alpha \xleftarrow{\$} [\![n_\boxtimes^s]\!]_\eta^{\bar{\tau}_\eta}; D_\eta^{\bar{\tau}_\eta}(\mathcal{H}(1^\eta, \alpha)) = 1]. \quad (2)$$

Gathering all $D_\eta^{\bar{\tau}_\eta}$ together for the various values of η, let D be the non-uniform adversary $\{D_\eta^{\bar{\tau}_\eta}\}_{\eta \in \mathbb{N}}$. Note that we have not actually defined $D_\eta^{\bar{\tau}_\eta}$ for all η, but only for those (infinitely many) for which (1) actually holds. What D does for the other values of η is irrelevant.

We will now show that D breaks the oracle indistinguishability of $\langle \mathcal{H}, V \rangle$. For this, let $L = \{L_\eta\}_{\eta \in \mathbb{N}}$ be a polynomial size family of subsets of Str. We have to show that for infinitely many values of η, there are $x, y \in \mathrm{Str} \setminus L_\eta$ such that D meaningfully distinguishes between $\mathcal{H}(1^\eta, x)$ and $\mathcal{H}(1^\eta, y)$.

Once again, take one of the infinitely many values of η for which (1) holds. Continuing from (2), a short computation (see the full version of this paper [GR06]) gives

$$\frac{1}{p(\eta)} \leq \frac{1}{2p(\eta)} + \sum_{\substack{\alpha \in [\![\tilde{m}]\!]_\eta^{\bar{\tau}_\eta} \setminus L_\eta \\ \beta \in [\![n_\boxtimes^s]\!]_\eta^{\bar{\tau}_\eta} \setminus L_\eta}} \Big[\Big(\mathbb{P}[D_\eta^{\bar{\tau}_\eta}(\mathcal{H}(1^\eta, \alpha)) = 1] - \mathbb{P}[D_\eta^{\bar{\tau}_\eta}(\mathcal{H}(1^\eta, \beta)) = 1] \Big)$$

$$\cdot \mathbb{P}[[\![\tilde{m}]\!]_\eta^{\bar{\tau}_\eta} = \alpha] \cdot \mathbb{P}[[\![n_\boxtimes^s]\!]_\eta^{\bar{\tau}_\eta} = \beta] \Big]. \quad (3)$$

Now suppose that for all $\alpha \in [\![\tilde{m}]\!]_\eta^{\bar{\tau}_\eta} \setminus L_\eta$ and all $\beta \in [\![n_\boxtimes^s]\!]_\eta^{\bar{\tau}_\eta} \setminus L_\eta$ we have

$$\mathbb{P}[D_\eta^{\bar{\tau}_\eta}(\mathcal{H}(1^\eta, \alpha)) = 1] - \mathbb{P}[D_\eta^{\bar{\tau}_\eta}(\mathcal{H}(1^\eta, \beta)) = 1] < \frac{1}{2p(\eta)}.$$

Then, continuing from (3), we get a contradiction:

$$\frac{1}{p(\eta)} < \frac{1}{2p(\eta)} + \sum_{\substack{\alpha \in [\![\tilde{m}]\!]_\eta^{\bar{\tau}_\eta} \setminus L_\eta \\ \beta \in [\![n_\boxtimes^s]\!]_\eta^{\bar{\tau}_\eta} \setminus L_\eta}} \frac{1}{2p(\eta)} \cdot \mathbb{P}[[\![\tilde{m}]\!]_\eta^{\bar{\tau}_\eta} = \alpha] \cdot \mathbb{P}[[\![n_\boxtimes^s]\!]_\eta^{\bar{\tau}_\eta} = \beta]$$

$$= \frac{1}{2p(\eta)} + \frac{1}{2p(\eta)} \sum_{\substack{\alpha \in [\![\tilde{m}]\!]_\eta^{\bar{\tau}_\eta} \setminus L_\eta \\ \beta \in [\![n_\boxtimes^s]\!]_\eta^{\bar{\tau}_\eta} \setminus L_\eta}} \mathbb{P}[[\![\tilde{m}]\!]_\eta^{\bar{\tau}_\eta} = \alpha] \cdot \mathbb{P}[[\![n_\boxtimes^s]\!]_\eta^{\bar{\tau}_\eta} = \beta]$$

$$\le \frac{1}{2p(\eta)} + \frac{1}{2p(\eta)}.$$

Therefore, there must be an $x \in [\![\tilde{m}]\!]_\eta^{\bar{\tau}_\eta} \setminus L_\eta$ and a $y \in [\![n_\boxtimes^s]\!]_\eta^{\bar{\tau}_\eta} \setminus L_\eta$ such that

$$\frac{1}{2p(\eta)} \le \mathbb{P}[D_\eta^{\bar{\tau}_\eta}(\mathcal{H}(1^\eta, x)) = 1] - \mathbb{P}[D_\eta^{\bar{\tau}_\eta}(\mathcal{H}(1^\eta, y)) = 1].$$

Hence D breaks oracle indistinguishability, contradicting the assumption on $\langle \mathcal{H}, \mathcal{V} \rangle$. $\square$

Theorem 5.3 (Abadi-Rogaway) *Let m be an acyclic message. Suppose that for every sub-message $h^r(\tilde{m})$ of m, $\tilde{m} \in \overline{m}$. Then $[\![m]\!] \equiv [\![encpat(m)]\!]$.*

Proof. The proof follows just like in Abadi-Rogaway [AR02]. Interpreting hashes here is straightforward because their argument is always known, by assumption. We refer the reader to the original paper for a full proof. $\square$

Theorem 5.4 (Soundness) *Let m and m' be acyclic messages. Then $m \cong m' \implies [\![m]\!] \equiv [\![m']\!]$.*

Proof. The assumption that $m \cong m'$ means that there is a permutation σ of Key $\cup$ Nonce $\cup$ Box such that $pattern(m) = pattern(m')\sigma$. Therefore we get $[\![pattern(m)]\!] \equiv [\![pattern(m')]\!]$. By definition of $pattern$, $[\![encpat \circ hashpat(m)]\!] \equiv [\![encpat \circ hashpat(m')]\!]$. Now, by applying Theorem 5.3 two times, we obtain $[\![hashpat(m)]\!] \equiv [\![hashpat(m')]\!]$. Finally, by repeatedly applying Theorem 5.2 on both sides we get $[\![m]\!] \equiv [\![m']\!]$. $\square$

6   Conclusions and Future Work

We have proposed an interpretation for formal hashes that is computationally sound. For the proof we considered non-uniform adversaries and the assumption that the encryption scheme is type-0 secure and well-spread and that the hash scheme is oracle indistinguishable and collision resistant. This paper considers passive adversaries. It would be interesting to study whether this result can be extended to active adversaries. Another interesting research direction would be proving completeness for this extended logic.

Acknowledgements. We are thankful to David Galindo for providing the reference to [Can97a] and insightful comments.

References

[AJ01]   Martín Abadi and Jan Jürjens. Formal eavesdropping and its computational interpretation. In Naoki Kobayashi and Benjamin C. Pierce, editors, *Proceedings of the Fourth International Symposium on Theoretical Aspects of Computer Software (TACS'01)*, volume 2215 of *Lecture Notes in Computer Science*, pages 82–94. Springer, 2001.

[AR02]   Martín Abadi and Phillip Rogaway. Reconciling two views of cryptography (the computational soundness of formal encryption). *Journal of Cryptology*, 15(2):103–127, 2002.

[BDJR97]   Mihir Bellare, Anand Desai, Eron Jokipii, and Philip Rogaway. A concrete security treatment of symmetric encryption. In *38th Annual Symposium on Foundations of Computer Science (FOCS'97)*, pages 394–405. IEEE, 1997.

[BPW06]   Michael Backes, Birgit Pfitzmann, and Michael Waidner. Limits of the reactive simulatability/UC of Dolev-Yao models with hashes. Cryptology ePrint Archive, Report 2006/014 (http://eprint.iacr.org/2006/068), 2006.

[BR93]   Mihir Bellare and Phillip Rogaway. Random oracles are practical: A paradigm for designing efficient protocols. In *Proceedings of the 1st ACM CCS*, pages 62–73. ACM, 1993.

[Can97a]   Ran Canetti. Towards realizing random oracles: Hash functions that hide all partial information. In Burt Kaliski, editor, *Advances in Cryptology, 17th Annual International Cryptology Conference (CRYPTO'97)*, volume 1294 of *Lecture Notes in Computer Science*, pages 455–469. Springer, 1997.

[Can97b]   Ran Canetti. Towards realizing random oracles: Hash functions that hide all partial information. Cryptology ePrint Archive, Report 1997/007 (http://eprint.iacr.org/1997/007), 1997.

[CMR98]   Ran Canetti, Danielle Micciancio, and Omer Reingold. Perfectly one-way probabilistic hash functions (preliminary version). In *Proceedings of the Thirtieth Annual ACM Symposium on Theory of Computing (STOC'98)*, pages 131–140. ACM, 1998.

[DY83]   Danny Dolev and Andrew C. Yao. On the security of public key protocols. *IEEE Transactions on Information Theory*, 29(2):198–208, 1983.

[GB01]   Shafi Goldwasser and Mihir Bellare. *Lecture Notes on Cryptography*. 2001. http://www-cse.ucsd.edu/~mihir/papers/gb.html.

[Gol01]   Oded Goldreich. *Foundations of Cryptography*, volume 1. Cambridge University Press, 2001.

[GR06]   Flavio D. Garcia and Peter van Rossum. Sound computational interpretation of formal hashes. Cryptology ePrint Archive, Report 2006/014 (http://eprint.iacr.org/2006/014), 2006.

[Her05]   Jonathan Herzog. A computational interpretation of Dolev-Yao adversaries. *Theoretical Computer Science*, 340(1):57–81, 2005.

[MP05]   Daniele Micciancio and Saurabh Panjwani. Adaptive security of symbolic encryption. In Joe Kilian, editor, *Theory of Cryptography: Second Theory of Cryptography Conference (TCC'05)*, volume 3378 of *Lecture Notes in Computer Science*, pages 169–187. Springer, February 2005.

[MW04]   Daniele Micciancio and Bogdan Warinschi. Completeness theorems of the Abadi-Rogaway logic of encrypted expressions. *Journal of Computer Security*, 12(1):99–129, 2004.

[PW00]   Birgit Pfitzmann and Michael Waidner. Composition and integrity preservation of secure reactive systems. In *Proceedings of the 7th ACM CCS*, pages 245–254, 2000.

[RS04]   Phillip Rogaway and Thomas Shrimpton. Cryptographic hash-function basics: Definitions, implications, and separations for preimage resistance, second-preimage resistance, and collision resistance. In Bimal Roy and Willi Meier, editors, *Fast Software Encryption: 11th International Workshop (FSE'04)*, volume 3017 of *Lecture Notes in Computer Science*, pages 371–388. Springer, 2004.

A Requirement Centric Framework for Information Security Evaluation

Reijo Savola

VTT Technical Research Centre of Finland, Kaitoväylä 1, 90570 Oulu, Finland
Reijo.Savola@vtt.fi

Abstract. Information security evaluation of software-intensive systems typically relies heavily on the experience of the security professionals. Obviously, automated approaches are needed in this field. Unfortunately, there is no practical approach to carrying out security evaluation in a systematic way. We introduce a general-level holistic framework for security evaluation based on security behaviour modelling and security evidence collection, and discuss its applicability to the design of security evaluation experimentation set-ups in real-world systems.

Keywords: Information security evaluation, security metrics, security modeling, security testing.

1 Introduction

Products and services, and the technical infrastructures that enable them are showing a strong trend towards convergence and networking. At the same time, industrial companies and other organizations are creating very complex value nets to design and manufacture products and to maintain them. These trends, together with pressure from information security and privacy legislation, are increasing the need for adequately tested and managed information security solutions in software intensive systems and networks. The lack of appropriate information security solutions might have serious consequences for business and the stakeholders.

Security evaluation, testing and assessment techniques are needed to be able find adequate solutions. Seeking *evidence* of the actual information security level or performance of systems still remains an ambiguous and undeveloped field. To make progress in the field there is a need to focus on the development of better experimental techniques, better security metrics and models with practical predictive power [4].

Security evidence can be used both for quantitative and qualitative analysis methods. Evidence is more useful when they are meaningful for most of the systems lifecycle:

- **During research and development,** security evidence helps researchers to develop more secure solutions and to find design vulnerabilities. Research-oriented security evidence can be constructed using analytical models that take account of factors contributing to security and the cross-relationships of components. Research-oriented metrics can concentrate on the critical parts, especially the technical challenges.

H. Yoshiura et al. (Eds.): IWSEC 2006, LNCS 4266, pp. 48–59, 2006.

- **During system implementation,** security evidence can be used to find design and implementation vulnerabilities as a part of security engineering. These are also based on analytical models. If security metrics are part of a security engineering process, they are more valuable.
- **During the system maintenance phase,** security evidence can be used for preservation of the achieved security level during possible updates, integration or modifications, and to find implementation vulnerabilities. From the point of view of the security engineering process, a technical system can be constantly in the system maintenance phase. In addition to preservation of the security level, this level can be improved using feedback obtained from the application of security evidence information.

The main contribution of this study is to introduce a holistic approach to security evaluation based on evidence collection and to discuss the evidence collection process in practice. The rest of this paper is organized as follows. Section 2 discusses security metrics and their relationships in general, Section 3 presents our theoretical security modelling and evaluation framework, Section 4 analyses how evidence collection can be done in practice with the help of the framework, and, finally, Section 5 discusses future work and Section 6 gives conclusions.

2 Background

The wide majority of the available security metrics approaches offering evidence information have been developed for evaluating security policies and the maturity of security engineering processes. The most widely used of these maturity models is the Systems Security Engineering Capability Maturity Model SSE-CMM (ISO/IEC 21827) [8]. Other well-known models are Trusted Computer Security Evaluation Criteria (TCSEC, The Orange Book) (TCSEC 1985) [17] and Common Criteria (CC) [7]. In connection with policy and process metrics, it is extremely important to evaluate the security functionality of products at the technical level, without forgetting their life cycle management. The goal of the whole process of seeking of security evidence should be targeted at understanding information security threats and vulnerabilities of the product and its usage environment holistically.

Jonsson [9] sorts the methods of security measurement into the following techniques: risk analysis, certification and measures of the intrusion process:

- *Risk analysis* is an estimation of the probability of specific intrusions and their consequences and costs, and it can be thought of as a trade-off to the corresponding costs for protection,
- *Certification* is the classification of the system in classes based on design characteristics and security mechanisms. "The 'better' the design is, the more secure the system."
- *Measures of the intrusion process* means statistical measurement of a system based on the effort it takes to make an intrusion. "The harder it is to make an intrusion, the more secure the system."

In addition to these methods, it is justifiable to consider *auditing* and *security evaluation* as measurement techniques for information security. Most technical security analysis is currently performed using penetrate-and-patch or "tiger team" tactics. The security level is evaluated by attempting to break into a system under evaluation, exploiting previously known vulnerabilities. If a break-in attempt is successful, the vulnerability is patched. Penetrate-and-patch tactics have been used by special security testing professionals whose methods and tools have not been made public knowledge. There are several problems with penetrate-and-patch: it requires experienced professionals, the actual testing is carried out too late, and the patches are often ignored and even sometimes introduce new vulnerabilities. Most of the technical testing metrics are meant for the unit or source code level. Various methods for system security evaluation and assessment have been proposed in the literature, see e.g. [2, 12, 13, 19]. These frameworks are conceptual and help in understanding the problem area. However, these frameworks do not offer aggregated means for practical security evaluation or the testing process.

3   Framework for Seeking Evidence of Security

In the following we introduce our holistic framework for model-based information security evaluation or testing of software-intensive systems. This collection of constructs and abstractions forms the basis of our approach to seeking evidence of security in a system. Please note that the framework could be expressed in a formal way using various types of representations, such as Labelled Transition Systems (LTSs). However, in this paper we discuss the implications of the framework for practical security testing and evaluation rather than intending to formalize the framework.

3.1   Role of Threat Analysis

The most important task in the whole process of security evaluation is to identify security risks and threats, taking enough assumptions of the attackers' capabilities into account. A subtask in threat analysis is to identify valuable *assets* that may be subject to security risks. An asset is something in the context of the system that is to be protected. A threat description can be represented, e.g., by *threat / asset* combinations. A holistic and cross-disciplinary threat picture of the system controls the development of security solutions. Threats that are possible during the whole life cycle of the system under evaluation must be considered.

It must be noted that the collection of security threats to a system is not static. Security algorithms and other solutions are cracked and new vulnerabilities are found every now and then. Even complete platforms or communication protocol structures can be compromised. As a consequence, a system's threat landscape is constantly changing, possibly reflecting different kinds of trends. A *weak* signal is a factor for change hardly perceptible at present but which will constitute a strong trend in the future. Some weak signals can represent on-going or anticipated changes in the threat landscape. The actual change in time can happen in small steps or in one leap. In the former case, the trend could be exposed, if weak signals presenting the steps could be detected [11].

Example 1. We denote the original set of identified threats in a system by T, consisting of the threat factors T_0, T_1, T_2,…T_n. Later, the effect of discipline D_x is introduced into the system. This effect manifests itself as a weak signal type of threat τ_x, which can or cannot be identified. In the former case, T is updated to $T := T \cup \tau_x$. In the latter case, the effect of D_x remains a hidden threat represented by the undetected weak signal τ_x. $\square$

3.2 Role of Security Requirements

The goal of defining security requirements for a system is to map the results of risk and threat analysis to practical security requirement statements that manage (cancel, mitigate or maintain) the security risks of the system under investigation. Security requirements are constraints on functional requirements intended to reduce vulnerabilities. Security mechanisms are then developed to fulfil the requirements. Haley *et al.* [6] represent an interesting method for deriving security requirements from threat descriptions. They derive the security requirements using an iterative process where each iteration recomposes the threat descriptions with the functional requirements. Iterations are required because identifying and eliminating vulnerabilities will often create new vulnerabilities.

The security requirements play a crucial role in the security evaluation. The requirements guide the whole process of security evidence collection. For example, security metrics can be developed based on requirements: If we want to measure security behaviour of an entity in the system, we can compare it with the explicit security requirements, which act as a "measuring rod".

All applicable *dimensions* (or *quality attributes*) of security should be addressed in the security requirements definition. See e.g. [1] for a presentation of quality attribute taxonomy. Well-known general dimensions include confidentiality, integrity, availability, non-repudiation and authenticity. Quality attributes like usability, robustness, interoperability, etc., are important requirements too. In fact, an unusable security construct can even turn out to be a security threat.

The safety community has developed a standard approach to solving the problem of requirements relevance, and the similarity between safety and security implies that it would be well worth considering if something similar could be done for security [3]. For example, Security Importance Levels (SILs) could be used for categorizing non-security requirements in terms of their security relevance and Security Evidence Assurance Levels (SEALs) could be used to enforce the additional measures needed to develop the more security-critical parts of systems.

It must be noted that one cannot easily define a general-level security requirement list that could be used for different kinds of systems. The actual requirements and role of the security dimensions heavily depends on the system itself, and its context and use scenarios.

3.3 Modelling Entities and Their Cross Relationships

It is obvious that in order to be able to evaluate security systematically, a model of the security behaviour of a system is needed. To make a decision about whether a system is secure, we need evidence that (i) each software or hardware component and subcomponent and (ii) the composition formed from them, taking account of cross-relationships, are secure. Essentially, the process of security evaluation takes use scenarios and the context of the system into account. In addition to this structural classification of entities, it is important to find the behavioural entities in the system.. In order to help investigate the security behaviour of a system, we define *security action, atomic security action and security behaviour*:

Definition 1. (*security action*) A security action, a_r, is a behavioural entity of a system that has some effect, either incremental or decremental, on the security defined by a certain security requirement, r, of a system.   □

Definition 2. (*atomic security action*) An atomic security action, a, is a security action that cannot be split into other security actions. It is the lowest level of observable security behaviour.   □

Definition 3. (*security behaviour of a system*) The security behaviour, A, of a system consists of a composition of atomic security actions of all the security requirements of the system that take their cross-relationships into account.   □

The security behaviour of the system, expressed using suitable modelling language, is the basis model of the system under security evaluation. For example, a pattern language could be used to describe the security actions and security behaviour.

Security actions can represent one or several dimensions or quality attributes of security. We define the dimensions of a security action in the following:

Definition 4. (*dimensions of security action*) A security action, a_r, having effect on security requirement r, has an impact, $i(a_r,u)$, and a probability, $p(a_r,v)$.   □

Definition 5. (*impact of security action*) The impact $i(a_r,u)$ of security action a_r is the estimate of its impact in scale [-1,1] to security requirement r. If the impact increases security, it is positive; u is the uncertainty of the impact estimate, between [0,1], where 1 presents complete certainty.   □

Definition 6. (*probability of security action*) The probability $p(a_r,v)$ of security action a_r is the estimated probability of the security action to be realized with uncertainty, v.   □

It is important to notice that impact analysis of security actions is within the focus of our approach. After all, we are interested what the impact of a system's security behaviour is on the whole – i.e. the overall impact.

Definition of the actual security actions in the system under investigation is a challenging task. In practice, this task may turn out to be impossible due to the amount of functionality and use scenarios in practical systems. Real-world implementations are far too complex for this kind of analysis. There is a need for automated and easily applicable and standardized technical methods for software implementation to ensure and measure security, e.g. standard secure memory management support and component-level life cycle management support.

Modelling the security behaviour is an iterative process. Voas [18] states that we do not know *a priori* whether the security of a system composed of two components, A and B, can be determined merely from knowledge of the security of A and B. Rather, the security of the composite is based on more than just the security of the individual components – it hinges on the cross-relationships. Both the atomic behaviour and cross-relationships have to be known and analysed in an iterative way.

Security behaviour of a system could be modelled using tree representations, such as Attack Trees [15], evaluation criteria, such as Common Criteria [7], several formal approaches and semi-formal approaches, such as UML and its security extension UMLSec [10]. Perhaps the most interesting method is to develop security patterns [16]. A security pattern describes a particular recurring security problem that arises in specific contexts and presents a well-proven generic scheme for its solution. In practice, a chosen set of security patterns could guide the process of defining security requirements. Security behaviour with adequate set of security actions could be associated to these patterns. The key elements of security patterns include the following:

- **Name:** a label representing the structure,
- **Context:** general conditions,
- **Problem:** a statement that defines the problem that will be solved by the security pattern, and
- **Solution:** solution of the problem.

3.4   Evidence Information

Security evidence is gathered from various sources as input to the decision process of security evaluation. The evidence collection should be arranged in a way that supports evaluation of security behaviour and security actions. We classify the types of security evidence information into three categories:

- **Measured Evidence.** The process of gathering measured or assessed information uses security metrics as its basis. Table 1 lists some examples of measured security evidence. Measured evidence can be collected during security testing or in a security audit based on pre-defined metrics.
- **Reputation Evidence.** Reputation of software or hardware constructs, or their origin, is an important class of evidence. A software company in charge of implementing a product might have some confidential knowledge of the security of different software components. Table 2 lists some examples of reputation evidence. Reputation evidence can be collected from experience of R&D departments and be based on general-level knowledge.
- **Tacit Evidence.** In addition to the measured and reputation evidence, there might be some "silent" or "weak" signals of security behaviour. The subjectivity level of tacit evidence might be higher than in the case of measured and reputation evidence. Collection of tacit evidence is typically an ad hoc process. Senior security experts and "tiger teams" play an important role in this kind of evidence.

The objectivity level of the evidence varies a lot. In many cases, even the measurements are arranged in a highly subjective manner. Typically, no single measured value is able to capture the security value of a system. Thus, several pieces of security evidence have to be combined.

Table 1. Examples of measured evidence

Dimension	Metric types
Confidentiality	Use of compartmentalization in memory use
Confidentiality	Encryption strength
Integrity	Result of one-way hash function
Integrity	Robustness of data synchronization algorithm
Availability	Validation result of access control rules
Usability	Amount of user interaction needed

Table 2. Examples of reputation evidence

Metric types
Reputation of practices of subcontractor
Reputation of implementation results of subcontractor
Reputation of a software version
Reputation of a software component provider
Reputation of a standard used in the implementation
Reputation of an integrator

3.5 Trust Assumptions

A *trust assumption* is a decision to trust the given properties of some domain and to go no further in the analysis [5]. Trust assumptions set the boundaries for the need for evidence. Trust assumptions can be made e.g. based on reputation evidence: if we trust a software version fully, there is no need to investigate it at more detailed level.

Trust assumptions can make the security evaluation process feasible by taking a certain risk to assume that the object left out of more detailed investigation is trusted.

3.6 Decision Process

The most final phase of security evaluation is the decision process. The overall goal of the decision process is to make an assessment and form conclusions on the information security level or performance of the system under investigation. The decision process can be split into sub-decisions based on the security action model.

The decision process can be carried out in the following way:

1. For each security requirement and security action composition, seek evidence and estimate the probability and impact of that action, taking cross-relationships and trust assumptions into account.
2. Estimate the overall impact of the gathered evidence on each security requirement
3. Make a decision whether the security of the system with regard to the requirements is at a sufficient level.

In a high abstraction level, the overall impact of all security actions on a security requirement can be defined as follows:

Definition 7. (*overall impact*) The overall impact of all security actions on a security requirement is

$$I = \sum_{t=0}^{T} w_t \cdot p_t \cdot i_t \tag{1}$$

where I is the overall impact, T the number of all security actions of a security requirement, and w_t is a weighting factor, p_t a probability and i_t the impact of security action t on the requirement under investigation. The weighting factor depends on time and context.

4 Modelling Example

We discuss the constructs presented in the previous section with help of a highly simplified authorization example based on [14] representing the most usual authorization rule, on which most other (more complex) access control models are based, see. Fig. 1.

In authorization we are interested who is authorized to access specific resources in a system. Granted permissions (authorizations) for security subjects accessing protected objects need to be indicated explicitly. Otherwise, any subject could access any resource. In the class diagram of Fig. 1., the class Subject describes an active entity, which attempts to access a resource in some way. The class Object represents the resource to be protected. The association between the subject and the object is authorization ("isAuthorizedFor"). The association class Right describes the access type (e.g. read or write) the subject is allowed to perform on the corresponding object.

In the following, we give examples of how our framework can be related to this example. However, we do not aim at a complete analysis. Let us assume that only the *confidentiality* requirements of the system specification are concerned. In reality, other security dimensions are affected by authorization too.

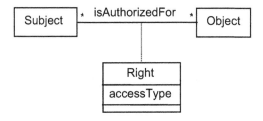

Fig. 1. A simplified authorization pattern

4.1 Subject

A security action associated with the class Subject can be, e.g., a *request* from a process asking to read from a protected file. Let us assume that the system allows this kind of request from both authenticated and unauthenticated sources. In the latter case the assumption is that the request can come from a local process. The following types of *request* security actions might be possible, depending in the design, e.g.:

- (*req1*) request from an authenticated process authorized to access the file,
- (*req2*) request from an authenticated process not authorized to access the file,
- (*req3*) request from an impersonating process that has been able to go through the authentication,
- (*req4*) request from an unauthenticated process authorized to access the file, and
- (*req5*) request from an unauthenticated process not authorized to access the file.

Obviously, *req1* is an atomic security action within *req3*. Note that *req3* contains other atomic security actions too. In this case *req1* is dependent on them. If there are no mechanisms to detect the impersonating process at this stage (e.g. additional authentication), an attacker might be able to access a protected file.

The impact of *req3* can be estimated based on evidence of the criticality of the information contained in the protected file. The probability evidence of *req3* can be based on, e.g., interface descriptions and authentication mechanism evaluation. Usually, the impact of *req3* is negative on the security.

4.2 Object

The object of our example, a protected file, might have, e.g., directly critical information or indirectly critical key or certificate information, enabling the impersonator to continue his or her attack and cause more harm. Related security actions include:

- (*f_access1*) access to a file with no directly or indirectly confidential information,
- (*f_access2*) access to a file with indirectly confidential but no directly confidential,
- (*f_access3*) access to a file with directly confidential but no indirectly confidential information, and
- (*f_access4*) access to a file with directly and indirectly confidential information.

"Confidential information" here means information that is confidential to the subject. Recognizably, all the listed security actions, except *f_access1*, have varying degrees of negative impact on the security.

If the system has some additional protection mechanisms for file access, the security actions associated with this protection, e.g., *encrypt_file* and *ask_decrypt_key*, have a positive impact on the confidentiality requirements.

4.3 Authorizer

The association "isAuthorizedFor" can be validated by an authorizer. As an input, the authorizer receives access requests from a process and decides whether a process has the right to access the protected file. The following security actions, e.g., are needed:

- (*check_read_right*) check the read right of the process requesting a read access,
- (*authorize_req*) authorize the process to read from the file,
- (*not_authorize_req*) forbid the process to read from the file,
- (*upd_rd_r*) update read rights, and
- (*authenticate_right_change*) authenticate the party asking for right change.

The functionality of authentication and errors enabled by poor design might lead to, e.g. *upd_rd_r_wrong_unintent*, *upd_rd_r_wrong_intent*, and *update_rd_r_correctly* – all of which are atomic security actions of *upd_rd_r*.

4.4 Design and Implementation

The actual design and implementation generates more security actions; e.g., failure to compartmentalize critical parts of the system, such as the authorizer, or programming errors generate more negative security actions. In practice, the security actions discussed above include several atomic security actions.

5 Practical Considerations

In the previous section we presented an approach to security modelling and evaluation. Unfortunately, in practice, a thorough modelling of security behaviour is only possible in a few ideal cases. Typically, today's software-intensive products are very complex, their functionality is not well documented and often has unknown dependencies. Development of an ambiguous security behaviour model at an atomic security action level is a very challenging and time-consuming task.

The practical needs for security evaluation are often limited too. This results to a situation in which we should be able to try to find the security actions that are most critical and most typical. To reach the desired security level it is not important to try and measure every part and component that affects security. Instead, we need enough evidence to make trade-off decisions.

We propose the following process to carry out practical-level security evaluation:

- **Risk and threat analysis.** Carry out risk and threat analysis of the system and its use environment if not carried out before. In real-world engineering, risk and threat analysis are not carried out adequately. Consequently, the set of security requirements might not be sufficient.
- **Define security requirements** in a way that they can be compared with the security actions of the system. Based on the threat analysis, define the security requirements for the system, if not yet defined. These are lacking in many practical systems.
- **Prioritize security and other requirements.** The most critical and most often needed security requirements should be paid the most attention.
- **Model the security behaviour.** Based on the prioritized security requirements, identify the functionality of the system that forms the security actions and their dependencies in a priority order.
- **Gather evidence** from measured, reputation and tacit security information.
- **Estimate the probabilities and impacts of security actions** based on the evidence.
- **Aggregate the results from the probability and impact estimation** to form a clear picture of whether or not the system fulfils the security requirements. and context.

6 Discussion and Future Work

A practical security evaluation framework based on the ideas discussed in this paper requires a lot of future development. In the following we list some goals for the future work.

A suitable language needs to be developed to formalize and express security actions and their cross-dependencies, as well as security requirements. Both the system security behaviour and requirements need to be expressed in a way that it is possible to compare them. A language able to express behavioural patterns is a good candidate for this purpose. Security patterns are currently under development in the pattern community. Security patterns augmented with semantics representing security properties could offer a feasible means to model security requirements and security behaviour of systems. Possibly, the use of fuzzy logic might be connected to that kind of language. A mechanism to describe the interactions and cross-dependencies of security actions is needed.

A knowledge base of typical security constructs should be established to offer pattern information on their security behaviour. The security actions of a system can be expressed using patterns. Typical constructs include encryption elements, firewalls, proxies, compartmentalization, inter-process communication, access control mechanisms and authentication mechanisms. The information needs to be collected experimentally to enable development of the knowledge base.

Security evaluation or testing can be done in practice if this kind of knowledge base support could be used for security behaviour modelling and suitable security requirement documentation of the system is available. Furthermore, the process of evidence collection from different sources, and aggregation of it, should be developed using experimental information from real-world systems.

7 Conclusions

We have discussed the problem of information security evaluation in the context of software-intensive systems. There are no systematic means of carrying out security evaluation. In this paper we have presented a conceptual holistic framework for security modelling and evaluation with some practical considerations. The framework is based on evidence collection and security requirement centred impact analysis.

This is not a rigorous solution and future work needs to be done on developing a suitable language for expressing security requirements and security behaviour in an unambiguous way. A collection of security patterns would be very helpful in modelling the security behaviour when carrying out security testing or experimentation.

In practical security evaluation, requirements should be prioritized and the system modelled only to the extent needed to conform to the trust assumptions. Full modelling of practical systems is not feasible without automated approaches that are might be very challenging to develop.

References

1. Avizienis A., Laprie J.-C., Randell B. and Landwehr C.: Basic Concepts and Taxonomy of Dependable and Secure Computing. In: IEEE Transactions on Dependable and Secure Computing, Vol. 1, No. 1, January/March, (2004) 11-33
2. Brocklehurst S., Littlewood B., Olovsson T. and Jonsson E.: On Measurement on Operational Security. In: IEEE AES Systems Magazine, Oct. (1994) 7-15
3. Firesmith D. G. (2005) Analyzing the Security Significance of System Requirements. In: Symposium on Requirements Engineering for Information Security (SREIS), August 25, 2005, Paris. (2005)
4. Greenwald M., Gunter C., Knutsson B., Seedrov A., Smith J. and Zdancewic S.: Computer Security is not a Science (but it should be). In: Large-Scale Network Security Workshop, Landsdowne, VA, March 13-14 (2003)
5. Haley C. B., Laney R. C., Moffett J. D. and Nuseibeh B.: Using Trust Assumptions in Security Requirements Engineering. In: 2nd International iTrust Workshop on Trust Management in Dynamic Open Systems, 15-17 September, Imperial College, London, UK (2003)
6. Haley C. B., Laney R. C. and Nuseibeh B.: Deriving Security Requirements from Crosscutting Threat Descriptions. In: AOSD 04, March, Lancaster, UK (2004)
7. ISO/IEC 15408: Common Criteria for Information Technology Security Evaluation, Version 2.2 (2004)
8. ISO/IEC 21827: Information Technology – Systems Security Engineering – Capability Maturity Model (SSE-CMM) (2002)
9. Jonsson, E.: Dependability and Security Modelling and Metrics, Lecture Slides, Chalmers University of Technology, Sweden (2003)
10. Jürjens J.: UMLSec: Extending UML for Secure Systems Development. In: UML 2002 – The Unified Modeling Language, Vol. 2460 of LNCS, Springer (2002) 412-425
11. Kajava J. and Savola R.: Weak Signals in Information Security Management. In: Proceedings of the International Conference on Computational Intelligence and Security (CIS) 2005, Part II, Xi'an, China, December 15-19, Springer (2005) 508-517
12. McDermid J.A. and Shi, Q.: A Formal Approach for Security Evaluation. In: Proceedings of the 7th Annual Conference on Computer Assurance, Systems Integrity, Software Safety, Process Security (1992) 47-55
13. Nicol D., Sanders W. H., Trivedi K. S.: Model-Based Evaluation: From Dependability to Security. In: IEEE Transactions on Dependable and Secure Computing, Vol. 1, No. 1, January/March (2004) 48-65
14. Priebe T., Fernandez E. B., Mehlau J. I. and Pernul.: A Pattern System for Access Control. In: 18th Annual IFIP WG 11.3 Conf. on Data and Applications Security, Sitges, Spain, 235-249 (2004)
15. Schneier B.: Attack Trees. In: Doctor Dobb's Journal, December (1999) 21-29
16. Schumacher M. and Roedig U.: Security Engineering with Patterns. In: Pattern Languages of Programs, September 11-15, Monticello, Illinois (2001)
17. Trusted Computer System Evaluation Criteria, "Orange Book", U.S. Department of Defense Standard, DoD 5200.28-std (1985)
18. Voas, J.: Why is it so Hard to Predict Software System Trustworthiness from Sofware Component Trustworthiness? In: Proceedings of the 20th IEEE Symposium on Reliable Distributed Systems (2001)
19. Voas J., Ghosh A., McGraw G., Charron F. and Miller K.: Defining an Adaptive Software Security Metric from a Dynamic Software Failure Tolerance Measure. In: Proceedings of the 11th Annual Conference on Computer Assurance, Systems Integrity, Software Safety, Process Security (1996)

A Model-Based Method for Security Configuration Verification

Hiroshi Sakaki, Kazuo Yanoo, and Ryuichi Ogawa

Internet Systems Research Laboratories, NEC Corporation,
1753, Shimonumabe, Nakahara-Ku, Kawasaki, Kanagawa, Japan
h-sakaki@cq.jp.nec.com, k-yanoo@ab.jp.nec.com,
r-ogawa@bq.jp.nec.com

Abstract. Various kinds of access control mechanisms have been employed in today's computer systems to protect confidential information. Since high expertise is required for the system configuration maintenance, detecting vulnerabilities due to configuration errors is a difficult task. In this paper, we propose a model-based configuration verification method that can find complex errors of two major access control mechanisms, network packet filtering and file access control. This method constructs an information flow model using the configurations of the two mechanisms and verifies whether the system is configured to suffice access policies defined by system administrators. Through the development of a prototype system and its experimental use, we confirmed that the proposed method could discover configuration errors of Web servers that might cause information leakage.

1 Introduction

Various kinds of access control mechanisms are employed in today's computer systems to protect confidential information. Administrators should maintain configurations of these mechanisms properly. But the configurations are often described in different formats and maintained by different administrators. Also the access control mechanisms often work collaboratively, so that one small configuration change can affect many other ones. Still, the whole configurations must be subject to the same security policies to keep information secret. The administrators must take proper action in all such situations. Therefore verifying whether the configurations satisfy given security policies is a quite difficult task, requiring high expertise both on security and network management.

For example, suppose we have to verify the configurations of a simple server client system as shown in Fig. 1. The system employs only two major access control mechanisms, packet filtering and file access control, but they are implemented in several different ways such as:

- Packet filtering rules in the Firewall
- A File access control list of operating system on the Web Server
- IP-based access control rules of Apache on the Web Server
- A File access control list of Apache on the Web Server
- Packet filtering rules of a Personal Firewall on the Client

H. Yoshiura et al. (Eds.): IWSEC 2006, LNCS 4266, pp. 60–75, 2006.

We need to read the configuration files, usually written in different formats, to see if any erroneous configurations exist. We also need to compare them according to the network topology, because a configuration mismatch of two different access control mechanisms can be a security hole and should be regarded as a configuration error.

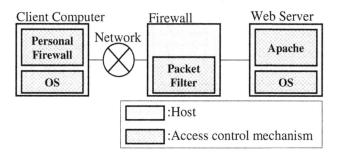

Fig. 1. Example of simple server client system

We also should consider the layered structure of applications. The software implementation usually has a layered structure and access control mechanisms are usually implemented with the middleware or the platform software. For example the access control mechanism of Apache depends on the OS as shown in Fig. 2. In this case we say that the Apache is an *upper* access control mechanism, and the OS is a *lower* one. In Web Server (A) in the figure, the user id "sakaki" on the Apache is identified as "nobody" by the OS, and a file "/data/" is identified as "/var/www/htdocs/data/" by the OS. When administrators verify whether "sakaki" can read "/var/www/htdocs/", they have to take account of these dependencies and check not only whether the user "sakaki" has a read access right but also whether "nobody" has a read access right.

In addition, administrators have to consider that the layered structure varies according to system configurations. For example, they should take into account whether a super server such as Xinetd is installed (Web Server (B)). If Xinetd is installed and it is configured to execute Apache, administrators have to consider the IP-based access control on Xinetd as shown in the Web Server (B).

Thus, the verification requirements are summarized as follows:

(1). Configurations of a packet filtering mechanisms and a file access control mechanism should be verified.
(2). The combination based on network topology should be verified.
(3). The combination based on layered structure of access control mechanisms should be verified.

For these requirements, we propose a model-based verification method for detecting erroneous configurations, called the Information Leakage Path AnalysiS (LPAS) Method. It verifies whether a system is configured to suffice access policies defined by system administrators.

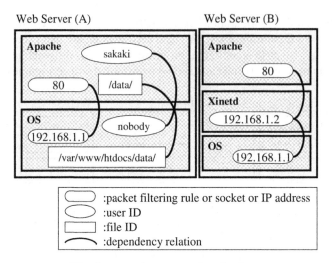

Fig. 2. Layered structure of applications

In this paper, we describe details of the LPAS Method, and show an experimental implementation of a prototype to verify a DMZ network. Through the development of a prototype system and its experimental use, we confirmed that the proposed method could discover configuration errors of Web servers that might cause information leakage.

This paper is structured as follows. In Section 2 we define the LPAS Method. In Section 3 we define access policies used in the verification. In Section 4 we explain the verification algorithm. In Section 5 we describe an implementation prototype of the LPAS Method. In Section 6 we describe a verification experiment. In Section 7 we describe related work.

2   LPAS Method

2.1   Overview

The LPAS Method is a model-based verification method using an information flow model. The method collects configurations such as file access control mechanisms of OS and packet filtering rules of firewalls. It makes a model that describes an information flow, and detects unauthorized access paths throughout an entire system. It therefore enables us to detect vulnerabilities due to configuration errors or misplacement of documents, and fix these configuration errors.

The LPAS Method is composed of three modules: Model Generator, Translator, and Verifier (Fig.3). The Model Generator collects packet filtering rules and access control lists to generate the LPAS Model. The Translator generates policy matching rules from Access Policies and Category Specifications. The Verifier verifies the LPAS Model with the rules.

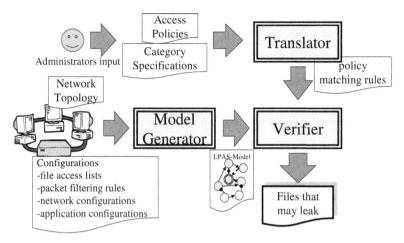

Fig. 3. Overview of LPAS Method

2.2 Definition

The LPAS Model, which is constructed from the configuration parameters of a target system, describes all possible access paths from users to files. In order to meet the requirements given in Section 1, the model is fundamentally built over the four elements shown in Definition 1.

Definition 1. LPAS Model is a tuple (C_P, C_F, LS, T), where:

(A) A packet filtering C_P is a set of authorized network accesses such that $C_P \subseteq S \times S$, where S is a set of sockets in the target system.

(B) A file access control C_F is a set of authorized file accesses such that $C_F \subseteq U \times F$, where U is a set of user or group identities, and F is a set of file identities.

(C) A Network topology T is a graph G over physical network nodes such that $G = (N, E)$, where E ($\subseteq N \times N$) is a set of pairs of physically adjacent network nodes, where N a set of network nodes identified by specific IP addresses..

(D) A Layered Structure LS is a relation among elements ($\subseteq U \cup F \cup S \cup C_P \cup N$) on different access control mechanisms.

This definition is designed to ensure that we can generate the four elements *independently*. By analyzing configurations of each access control mechanism, we can generate C_P and C_F without regard to configurations of other access control mechanisms. T can be taken from a network management system such as OpenView[5]. LS can be generated from the system configuration and specifications of each access control mechanism.

Since we can generate an entire system model by combining independently generated models, our method is more scalable and feasible than previously proposed method such as [10].

In order to impose actual security configurations on the remaining components, we make the components more detailed as follows.

A detailed model of C_P :

An actual rule of packet filtering is specified with the following elements:

- A source end point identified with a pair of an IP address and a port number.
- A destination end point identified with a pair of an IP address and a port number.

In order to impose these elements on C_P, we define $s \in S$ as a pair of an IP address and a port number such that $s = (ip, port)$, where ip is an IP address of s, and *port* is a port number that s may use in communication time.

A detailed model of C_F :

In real systems, file access control is performed to access control lists (ACLs) on individual network nodes. Generally, an ACL can be viewed as a set of *file permissions*, each of which specifies a triple of a user identity, a file identity, and an authorized action such as "read" and "write." Such file permissions are modeled as "canRead" and "canWrite" relations which are defined as follows.

Definition 2. "canRead" relation F_R is a set of pairs of a user identity $u \in U$ and a file identity $f \in F$ such that $(f, u) \in F_R$ if and only if there is a file permission that allows a user identified with u to read a file identified with f . Similarly, "canWrite" relation F_W is a set of pairs such that $(u, f) \in F_W$ if and only if there is a file permission that allows a user identified with u to write a file identified with f .

Definition 3. A user network node relation UN is a set of pairs of a user u and a socket s such that $(u, s) \in UN$. N_R and N_W are subsets of UN , which mean "canRead" and "canWrite" relations from u to s , respectively.

A detailed model of LS :

A layered structure is described in Section 1. For example, a user with the identity "sakaki" on the access control mechanism such as an Apache may be identified as a user with the identity "nobody" on the *lower* access control mechanisms such as an OS. In another case, he may be identified as "root" when using *setuid* applications. Regarding file identities, we can find similar cases in *file aliases*. For example, if the Apache is configured with "alias /test/ = /var/www/test/", the file identity "/var/www/test/" on the OS is treated as the file identity "/test/" on the Apache. To identify such ambiguity, we introduce the following identity relationships.

Definition 4. R_U is a user identity relation such that $\forall u_1, u_2; (u_1, u_2) \in R_U$ if and only if both u_1 and u_2 identify an identical user. Also, R_F is a file identity relation such that $\forall f_1, f_2; (f_1, f_2) \in R_F$ *if and only if* that both f_1 and f_2 identify an identical file.

In addition to the layered structure between files and users, we also consider the layered structure among network elements.

For example, if the access control mechanism of the Xinetd is configured as Web Server (B) in Fig. 2, packets coming from the network node n on the OS are firstly sent to the packet filtering c_P on the Xinetd, and then sent to the socket s on the Apache. On the other hand, if the access control mechanism of Apache is configured as Web Server (A), packets coming from the node n on the OS are directly sent to the socket s on the Apache.

To identify such ambiguity, we introduce relations among sockets, network nodes, and packet filtering rules. The relations stand when elements ($\in N \cup S \cup C_P$) on the lower access control mechanism communicate with other elements ($\in S \cup C_P$) on the upper access control mechanism.

Definition 5. $R_{NI} (\subseteq N \times C_P)$ is a binary relation such that $(n, c_P) \in R_{NI}$ if and only if an incoming packet through the network node n is evaluated by the packet filter c_P. $R_{NO} (\subseteq C_P \times N)$ is reverse of R_{NI}, where $(c_P, n) \in R_{NO}$ if and only if an outgoing packet from packet filter c_P is sent to the network node n. To be concise, we denote $R_{NI} \cup R_{NO}$ by R_N.

Similarly $R_S (\subseteq S \times C_P \cup C_P \times S)$ and $R_{NS} (\subseteq N \times S \cup S \times N)$ are defined for relation between sockets and a packet filtering rules, and sockets and network nodes, respectively.

The following subsection shows an example of the LPAS Model generation from actual system configurations.

2.3 Example LPAS Model

Fig. 4 shows a graphical example of an LPAS Model. It represents a server client system such as that in Fig. 1, and the Web Server is configured as Web Server (B) in Fig.2. To save space, we describe only details of the Web Server.
Apache is configured as follows:

(1) Basic authentication is enabled, and a user named *sakaki* is defined.
(2) Only authenticated users can read /secret/sec.html.
(3) Files in the /w directory are served as Web contents.
(4) The server accepts connection on port 80.
(5) Apache process runs as the user *nobody*.
Linux OS is configured as follows:
(6) IP address of the Web Server is 192.168.2.3.
(7) The user *nobody* can read files in /w directory.
Xinetd is configured as follows:
(8) Only the hosts with IP address 192.168.1.2 can connect Apache via port 80.

The Model Generator reads and analyzes the above configurations, and generates the nodes and the arcs in Fig.4. For example, it generates R_F arcs for (3), R_U arcs for (5), F_R arcs on Linux for (7), and F_R arcs on Apache for (2).

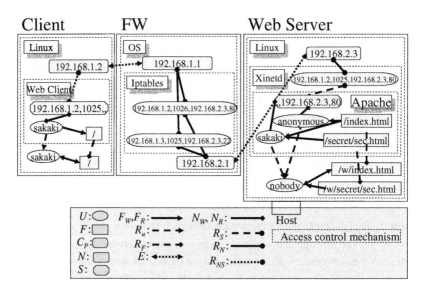

Fig. 4. Graphical example of an LPAS Model

3   Access Policy

In general, an access policy is modeled as an *access matrix* such as (S, O, A), where S is a set of subjects (e.g., users), O is a set of objects (e.g., files), and A is a set of actions (e.g., read and write). We take an access matrix model enhanced with service-based conditions C so that it becomes (S, O, C, A). This enhanced model allows us to specify unauthorized access paths including an untrusted service such as a Web application with no SSL functionality or authentication process.

Furthermore, as a practical policy specification, we introduce *category specifications* for users, files and services (e.g., user roles, confidential level for documents and service functionalities, respectively) as well as *domain specifications* that correspond to network domains.

An Access Policy used in an LPAS based verification method is formalized as follows.

Definition 6. An Access Policy is a set of tuples $(c_S, d_s, c_O, d_o, s_C, a)$. Each component is defined as follows:

- $c_S (\in C_S)$ is a subject category, where C_S is a predefined set of subject categories. A user-category relation $R_{UCS} (\subseteq U \times C_S)$ is defined such that $(u, c_S) \in R_{UCS}$, if u is a member of c_S.

- $d_S (\in D_S)$ is a subject domain, where D_S is a predefined set of subject domains. A user-domain relation $R_{UDS} (\subseteq U \times D_S)$ is defined such that $(u, d_S) \in R_{UDS}$, if u is located on d_S.

- $c_O (\in C_O)$ is an object category. A file-category relation $R_{FCO} (\subseteq F \times C_O)$ is defined such that $(f, c_O) \in R_{FCO}$.
- $d_O (\in D_O)$ is a object domain. A file-domain relation $R_{FDO} (\subseteq F \times D_O)$ is defined such that $(f, d_O) \in R_{FDO}$, if f is located on d_O.
- $s_C (\in S_C)$ is a service category that specifies a condition with respect to access paths from S to O. S_C is a predefined set of service categories. A network-category relation $R_{SSC} (\subseteq S \times S_C)$ is defined such that $(s, s_C) \in R_{SSC}$, if s is specified by s_C.
- a is an action such as read and write.

Note that most of the category specifications (i.e., R_{UCS}, R_{UDS}, R_{FCO}, R_{FDO} and R_{SSC}) can be constructed automatically, so that the administrator can specify access policies easily. R_{UCS} and R_{UDS} can usually be retrieved from directory services, and R_{FDO} is constructed by scanning files on the computer. R_{SSC} is small enough for the administrator to define it, and R_{FCO} may be constructed by analyzing the contents of the files [1].

Usually an Access Policy has two types, one to permit policies, and the other to deny policies. In this paper, we use only the latter to detect information leakage. Therefore, we describe Access Polices as follows:

(1). deny("any user", "Inlab", "any file", "DMZ", "unencrypted password", read)
This means that no users on Inlab may read any file on servers in DMZ segment via services that use unencrypted passwords.
(2). deny("temporary personnel", "any domain", "personal", "internal server", "any service", write)
This means that temporary personnel must not write personal files on internal servers in any service.

4 Verification Algorithm

The Verification Algorithm validates an LPAS Model in three steps as follows:

(1). Generate policy matching rules from access policies.
(2). Enumerate *possible information flows,* which describe permissive information flows on file access mechanisms, without regard to packet filtering mechanisms.
(3). Check that no possible information flows violate the matching rules, with regard to packet filtering mechanisms.
(4). Report access paths that may cause information leakage.

These steps are described below.

In the first step, the Translator translates access policies into policy matching rules. Policy matching rules $PM (\subseteq U \times F \times S \times \{read, write\})$ is a set of unauthorized access paths such that $\forall u, f, s; (u, f, s, read) \in PM$ if and only if the Access Policy prohibits the user u from *read*ing the file f via the service s.

An Access Policy $deny(c_S, d_U, c_O, d_F, s_C, a)$ is translated to PM, such that $\forall u, f, s; (u, f, s, a) \in PM$ if and only if $(u, c_S) \in R_{UCS} \wedge (u, d_S) \in R_{UDS} \wedge (f, c_O) \in R_{FCO} \wedge (f, d_O) \in R_{FDO} \wedge (s, s_C) \in R_{SSC}$ holds.

In the second step, the Verifier constructs a directed graph $M' = (N', E')$, where $N' = U \cup F \cup N \cup C_P \cup S$, $E' = N' \times N'$, and every $e \in E'$ satisfies all of the following conditions:

(1). $e \in R_P \cup R_N \cup R_S \cup R_{SN} \cup N_R \cup N_W \cup F_R \cup F_W \cup E$ (refer again to Section 3).

(2). if $e \in F_R$, for every $e = (f, u)$, the following conditions must be satisfied:

    (a) $\forall f', u'; ((f, f') \in R_F) \wedge ((u, u') \in R_U) \Rightarrow (f', u') \in F_R$, and

    (b)   for any such (f', u'), (f', u') also satisfies condition (2).

(3). if $e \in F_W$, for every $e = (u, f)$, the following conditions must be satisfied:

    (a) $\forall f', u'; ((f, f') \in R_F) \wedge ((u, u') \in R_U) \Rightarrow (u', f') \in F_W$, and

    (b)   for any such (u', f'), (u', f') also satisfies condition (3).

Conditions (2) and (3) imply that the upper file access is permitted only if the lower access control mechanism allows users access between corresponding files and users.

Each path in M' represents a *possible information flow*, which describes a permitted information flow on file access mechanisms, without regard to packet filtering mechanisms.

In the third step, the Verifier detects paths (called unauthorized paths) in the directed graph M' that violate given policy matching rules. For a policy matching rule $m = (f, u, s, a)$, the procedure identifies the unauthorized paths with respect to m as follows:

(1)   Iterate the following steps for each directed path $ES = (e_1, e_2, ..., e_n)$, where ES is a directed path from f to u in M' (if $a = read$), or from u to f in M' (if $a = write$).

(2)   If ES does not include s, then there is no unauthorized path with respect to m.

(3)   Let e_j be the first occurrence of an element of N_W in ES, and let e_k be the first occurrence of an element of N_R in ES. If neither e_j nor e_k exist, output ES as an unauthorized path with respect to m. Note that if ES includes at least two socket nodes, then both of e_j and e_k exist. Since for any socket node s, s is adjacent to a user node according to Definitions 2 and 6.

(4)   Let $ES_{jk} = (e_j, ..., e_k)$ be a substring of ES. Note that $j < k$ always holds and every edge in ES_{jk} is a member of $N_R \cup N_W \cup R_P \cup R_N \cup R_S \cup R_{NS} \cup E$ (by definition of the LPAS Model).

(5)   Let (i_1, p_1) be the source pair of an IP address and a port number, which corresponds to the socket node s_k connected with e_k. Similarly, let (i_2, p_2) be the destination pair, which corresponds to the socket node s_j connected with e_j. If there exists a packet filter ($\in C_P$) that blocks a packet from (i_1, p_1) to (i_2, p_2), then ES is not an unauthorized path.

(6) If there are other elements of N_W in the rest of $ES(=(e_{k+1}, ..., e_n))$, repeat (3) to (6). Otherwise, output ES as an unauthorized path with respect to m.

Step (2) ensures that any possible information flow that does not include s is not an unauthorized path. Steps (3)-(5) ensure that any possible information flow that includes packet filtering that prohibits communication between e_j and e_k is not an unauthorized path.

5 Implementation

In this section, we describe the implementation of a prototype of the LPAS Method (Fig. 5) which is composed of the Agents, the Manager, and the Policy Editor.

Each agent corresponds to an access control mechanism, and is deployed on the target system. The Manager and the Policy Editor are deployed on the LPAS Server.

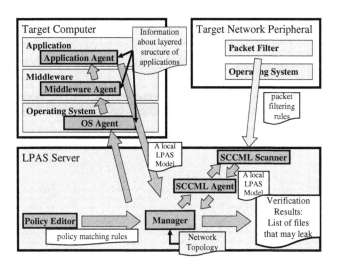

Fig. 5. Implementation of LPAS Method

The Agents implement the Model Generator method, which collects configurations of a target system and generates LPAS Models. Policy Editor implements the Translator method, which translates the Access Policies given by the administrator into policy matching rules. The Manager implements the Verifier method, which integrates models generated by the Agents and verifies whether the LPAS Model satisfies the policy matching rules.

5.1 Agents

In Fig. 5, when the Manager sends a request for creating a local LPAS Model of the Target Computer, the OS Agent is invoked to collect configurations of the OS such as file paths, user IDs and file permissions. After creating a model for the OS, the OS Agent invokes another agent for the upper access control mechanisms according to the layered structure. In this way, each invoked agent generates a model for each application and merges it into the local LPAS model that reflects the layered structure.

As for network peripherals such as routers and firewalls, we employ a common agent, SCCML Agent, instead of implementing different agents for each peripheral. The agent adopts a common file format, SCCML, for describing packet filtering rules written in different formats [2]. We also employ SCCML Scanners which collect the configurations of major routers and firewalls and translate them into rules in SCCML format. With the translated rules SCCML Agent can generate a local LPAS Model of various kinds of network peripherals.

5.2 Policy Editor and Manager

Policy Editor implements Policy Input UI and the Translator. The Policy Input UI displays domains and categories of users, files and service in menu format. The administrator can define policies merely by selecting category and domain from the menu with the Policy Input UI (Fig. 6).

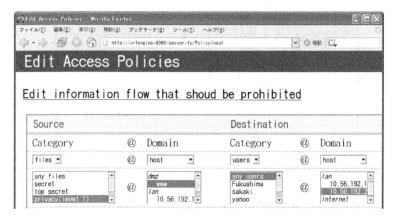

Fig. 6. View of editing Access Policy

After input is completed, the Translator translates the Access Policy into the policy matching rules based on category specifications.

The Manager collects local LPAS Models generated by the Agent and generates an integrated LPAS Model from these models with network topology information. The Manager then verifies whether the integrated model satisfies the given access policies.

6 Verification Experiment

6.1 Verification Target

To evaluate the LPAS Method, we select a verification target whose configurations are shown in Fig. 7. The target system has a WWW Server, a CISCO Router, a number of clients in an external network (CEN) and other clients in an internal network (CIN). The router is a gateway between the CIN and the CEN. The WWW Server provides documents for R&D division members with the domain "www-i.example.co.jp", and also provides documents for other divisions with "www-e.example.co.jp". These two domains are implemented by the virtual host mechanism of Apache. The WWW Server also has the secret document "secret.html", and it provides this document with "http://www-i.example.co.jp/p/secret/secret.html". Users in CEN cannot access with this URL because the IP-based access control mechanism of the Apache is enabled.

There are three configuration files related to the Apache, one for the global configuration for the Apache, one for the internal virtual host, and one for the external virtual host. The WWW Server has about 5300 files, and the SCCML Scanner has 10 compiled rules of the router in SCCML format.

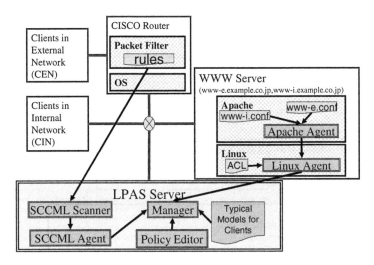

Fig. 7. Block diagram of experimental system

Two agents are installed on the WWW Server, one for the OS, and the other for the Apache. The former collects file permissions of the OS, and the latter reads and analyzes configuration files of the Apache. The SCCML Agent and the SCCML Scanner are located on the LPAS Server. The SCCML Scanner reads the configuration of the router via tftp, and translates it into the SCCML format. And then the SCCML Agent generates a local LPAS Model of the router by analyzing the packet filtering rules written in the SCCML format.

Instead of describing the whole information flow of all clients, we employ typical client models of common client behavior and configurations such as Internet Explorer. The Manager combines these typical models and models generated by Agents into an integrated LPAS Model, and verifies whether the integrated model satisfies the following policy.

deny("any user", "CEN", "secret", "WWW", "any service", "read")

This policy means that CEN users must not read secret files on the WWW Server.

6.2 Experimental Results

Fig. 8 shows experimental results we obtained. The top of the figure shows a list of files that may leak, and the bottom shows a list of configuration files that may cause information leakage. It takes 18 minutes for the Manager to verify whether the LPAS Model satisfies the Access Policies.

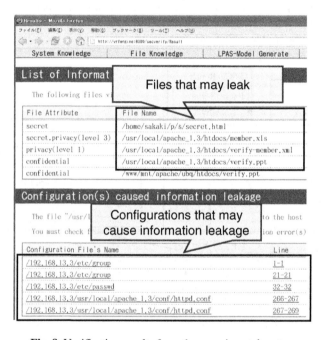

Fig. 8. Verification results from the experimental system

An information leakage path is detected as shown in Fig. 9. The path means that the user "user" in the CEN can access the file "/home/usr/public_html/s/secret.html" via port 80. The configuration vulnerability that causes this information leakage path is the lack of configurations of IP-based access control rules of the Apache. This is because the directory "/public_html/" is selected as the UserDir of the Apache, so that it can be read via both virtual hosts.

Therefore, the administrator must have configured IP-based access control on both virtual hosts to prevent information leakage. However, he or she overlooked the fact that the Apache configuration is divided into three files, and did not configure IP-based access control on the virtual host with "www.e-example.co.jp".

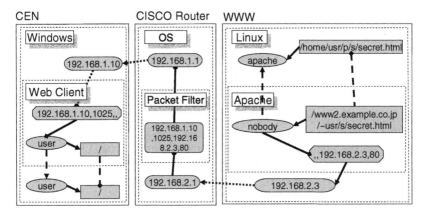

Fig. 9. Detected information leakage path

7 Related Work

Several vulnerability assessment tools have been proposed and used for detecting system configuration errors. They can be classified into two categories: signature-based and model-based.

Most practical vulnerability assessment tools [3, 4] are signature-based. They scan for weak passwords to assess the security of password files, check whether any files can be modified, and find potentially vulnerable services such as anonymous ftp. Signature-based tools detect vulnerabilities based on signatures defined in advance. Therefore, even though they can detect obvious configuration errors such as world-readable password files, they cannot detect configuration errors caused by inconsistent configurations.

Attack Graph[6,7,8] is a model-based method that employs model checking for vulnerability analysis. An attack graph represents relations of vulnerabilities and exploits. The method verifies whether an attack graph may reach an undesired condition when several vulnerabilities exist. Although Attack Graph can detect potential configuration vulnerabilities, developing an attack graph requires a high level of expertise. The method also requires high computational power for reasoning, and thus we consider Attack Graph to be too complex for detecting misconfigurations of access control mechanisms.

MulVAL[10] employs Datalog for expressing vulnerabilities and system configurations. When a policy such as *allow(Everyone, read, webPages)* is given, the Datalog engine decides whether it holds or not. Although MulVAL focuses on vulnerability assessment, it can be used for configuration verification. Being based on Datalog, it has more expressive power than the LPAS method. On the other hand, MulVAL does not provide mechanisms for collecting network configurations. Administrators thus have to provide *host access control lists* that express all accesses between hosts allowed by the network. Thus MulVAL is rather difficult to use and too error-prone for ordinary users.

ISM [9] is another model-based configuration verification method that employs Datalog. Its target objective is very similar to that of the LPAS method: detecting policy violations caused by inconsistent configurations of access control mechanisms. However, the paper does not address how to construct models from network configurations.

8 Conclusion and Future Work

This paper described a model-based analysis method, which we call the Information Leakage Path Analysis (LPAS) Method, for detecting configuration vulnerabilities. The method collects the parameters of two major access control mechanisms: access control and packet filtering. Its Model Generator constructs an LPAS Model that represents information flows. Its Translator translates access policies defined by the administrator into policy matching rules. Its Verifier then verifies whether the LPAS Model satisfies access policies.

To evaluate the method's feasibility, we implemented a prototype system. Experiments with it show that the LPAS System can find configuration vulnerabilities of a live Web server.

While the LPAS Method promises to reduce system configuration maintenance costs and time, a few problems remain to be resolved when we apply it to large practical systems. One known problem is that long computation time is required for model generation. This is because the file element generation method is straightforward; creating a new file element for every file used in applications, so that searching identity relations among the elements is time-consuming. To resolve this issue, we are going to reduce the number of file elements by mapping files which have the same ACLs onto one file element. In general, most files in the same directory have the same ACLs, therefore this method will reduce the size of the model substantially.

Another known problem is that the LPAS Model is not expressive enough to describe network systems that deploy NAT and VPN. To resolve this issue we are going to extend the LPAS Model by introducing NAT relation between a global IP address and a set of local IP addresses and improve the verification algorithm so that it can handle NAT relations.

As for the implementation, development cost of the agents might be a serious problem. Because we need to develop agents for each application that has access control mechanisms with a programming language such as Java, it requires a large amount of effort and expertise to develop them. One possible way to resolve this issue is to design a declarative scripting language for describing information flows in an application. Because non-experts can develop agents easily by using this language, it can reduce the development cost of the agents.

References

1. Hosomi, H. Sakaki and R. Ogawa, "An Information Leakage Risk Evaluation Method Based on Sensitive Document Detection and Security Configuration Validation (2) Sensitive Document Detection with Text and Structure Analysis", the 67th National Convention of IPSJ, 2005 (in Japanese)
2. S. Okajo, K. Matsuda, R. Ogawa, A Policy Description Language for Policy-based Security Management, 2004-CSEC-027, Vol.2004 No.129, December 2004 (in Japanese)

3. Nessus Vulnerability Scanner, http://www.nessus.org/

4. Symantec Enterprise Security Manager, http://www.symantec.com/Products/enterprise?c=prodinfo&refId=855

5. HP OpenView, http://h50146.www5.hp.com/products/software/management/openview/

6. C. Phillips, L.P. Swiler, A graph-based system for network-vulnerability analysis, Proceedings of the 1998 workshop on New security paradigms, pages 71 – 79 , 1998

7. C.R. Ramakrishnan, R. Sekar, Model-based Analysis of Configuration Vulnerabilities, Journal of Computer Security Volume 10, Numbers 1-2 / 2002 pages189-209, 2003

8. S. Cheung, U. Lindqvist, M. W. Fong, Modeling Multistep Cyber Attacks for Scenario Recognition, Proceedings of the Third DARPA Information Survivability Conference and Exposition (DISCEX III), Washington, D.C., Volume I, pages 284–292, April 22–24, 2003

9. S. Bhatt, W. Horne, J. Pato, S. R. Rajagopalan, P. Rao, Model-based validation of enterprise access policies, HPL-20050152(R.1), 2006

10. X. Ou, S. Govindavajhala, A.W.Appel, MulVAL:A Logic-based Network Security Analyzer, 14th Usenix Security Symposium, 2005

Personal Computer Privacy: Analysis for Korean PC Users

Young Chul Kwon, Sang Won Lee, and Songchun Moon

Graduate School of Management,
Korea Advanced Institute of Science and Technology(KAIST),
207-43 Cheongryang, Dongdaemun, Seoul 130-722, Korea
{yck, sangwonlee, scmoon}@kgsm.kaist.ac.kr

Abstract. In this paper, we introduce our own two-year experiments to acquire sensitive personal information from discarded hard disks which we had obtained with no ease in Korean second-hand PC markets. With careful scanning, we found that most of hard disks were not adequately cleaned, and had a plenty of confidential and sensitive personal data, which could be utilized in crimes like identity theft. Collected private data, analyzed based on the concept of identifiable individual, amounted to 4,526 persons worth of data, including 3,584 resident registration numbers. The result also indicated that discovered data items of each person were revealed to display a wide spectrum of sensitivity level.

Keywords: privacy, data forensics.

1 Introduction

Data in hard disks from discarded personal computers could be a substantial privacy threat. Although hard disks must be disposed after permanent erasure, many companies retire corporate PCs without concern for their data[8]. Nowadays, safe disposal of old computers becomes quite difficult in terms of overwriting time overhead. It is time-consuming to completely erase disks of enormous capacity, e.g. hundreds or thousands gigabytes, as the time required for overwriting a whole drive increases roughly in proportion to its size. Moreover, to comply the environmental regulations for disposing electronic equipments, enterprises choose to leave retired drives reusable rather than to destroy or degauss them. Since most of used hard drives are usually placed on sale to public or donated to charity, potential criminals could find no difficulty in acquiring them in a legitimate manner.

Actually, recent researches revealed that a considerable amount of personal information has been found in hard drives purchased from second-hand markets. For instance, in the analysis of used disks from U.K.'s PC markets[6], more than half of disks contained customers' and stakeholders' private information. They had identifiable names, contact details, and credit card numbers, which are enough to be cloned in crimes such as identity theft. From a recent survey[5], the majority of reported cases of identity theft seem to originate offline rather than

H. Yoshiura et al. (Eds.): IWSEC 2006, LNCS 4266, pp. 76–87, 2006.

online. As well as traditional methods such as stolen wallet or theft of paper mail, used hard disk could be a good offline source for identity thieves.

However, preventing leakage of used PC's data has paid less attention to individuals at privacy risk. Conventional study focused on the protection of confidential information merely in perspective of corporations. Note that previous researches mainly discussed what would be the number of overwrites[4][10] for safe sanitization. We will at this time instead attempt to answer more profound questions like "What part of data is potentially privacy-critical?" and "What kind of data is particularly vulnerable to identity-related crimes?" Our discussion on these questions will help corporations and governments to establish PC retirement policy based on customers' privacy sensitivity.

Chapter 2 presents an overview of previous study on second-hand PC markets. In chapter 3 we propose a standard procedure to evaluate experiments on PC privacy from the viewpoint of individuals. We also introduce assumptions on personal identifier and sensitivity criterion of private information. Chapter 4 is dedicated to the two-year experiments based on hard drives that we had obtained with no ease from Korean second-hand PC markets. The analysis results are shown and then classified into our taxonomy for privacy sensitivity. In chapter 5 we conclude with new research ideas.

2   Related Works

A number of recent researches on second-hand PC market reported the possibility of data leakage. They generally addressed canonical sanitization methods like three-time overwriting strategy adopted in U.S. Department of Defense[10], which could also be a guidance for corporates. They, however, have been limited to revelation of simple-minded list of recovered data elements or document files. Inattention has been paid to inspections like whether recovered data items would violate personal privacy.

One of the attempts, Garfinkel et al.[3] of MIT, purchased 158 hard drives mostly from eBay online auction service in 2002. Careful scanning has revealed more than 5,000 credit card numbers, medical reports, detailed financial information, several gigabytes of personal e-mails and pornography. Jones[6] in U.K. discovered that from the 92 hard disks from internet auctions, computer fairs, and a computer recycler, 49 of them(53 percent) had identifiable names and 47(51 percent) had details of personal information. We see from Table 1 that the ratio of properly sanitized disks ranged from 9 to 17 percent of each sample. Most of drives were not completely wiped and therefore contained recoverable files.

We were able to note that there is no standard procedure to conduct analysis of used hard disks that takes privacy impact on individuals seriously. Data items of each person from drives were revealed to display a wide spectrum of privacy threat levels, as for the instance the social security number of a person is considered to possess a heavier privacy weight than the name of the person. Once a SSN has been counterfeited, criminals could access not only person name but other crucial personal information in major public or private databases that use SSN as search key. Studies like [2] have revealed how SSN is vulnerable to various privacy intrusions. In this sense, the name and the SSN might be treated separately for privacy sensitivity designation. Although summary results of previous studies, as in Table 1, could contribute to address security awareness levels of a certain community like countries, the major metrics used in them, for example number of hard drives or recovered files, merely do not convey anything meaningful for the real privacy threat on individuals.

Table 1. Analysis by Number of Drives Examined

No. of drives / Degree of erase	Garfinkel et al. [3]	Jones [6]
(All functional)	129	92
Completely overwritten (No file structures contained)	12 (9 percent)	16[1](17 percent)
Data removal attempted[2]	79 (61 percent)	44 (48 percent)
Recoverable data remained	81 (63 percent)	74 (80 percent)
Personal information remained	N/A[3]	49 (53 percent)

[1] 12 of the 16 were procured from a computer recycling company.
[2] Simple-minded efforts like simple deletion of files as well as disk formatting other than complete overwriting had been applied.
[3] List of personal data items like credit card numbers had been merely been reported.

3   Experiment Design

3.1   Analysis Process

Fig. 1 shows the experiment process of analyzing hard disks. We follow the process that computer-literate people recover data by use of a general-purpose PC and software. Our analysis focuses on functional hard disks, which can be accessed with the tools and techniques available to computer literate users. Winnowing functional hard disks is to check whether they are connected to PC or not. General recovery software and office tools extract files from target disks and check sensitive personal information from the files. Extracted personal information is used in statistics and summarization with the privacy sensitivity criteria that is introduced in Section 3.3.

3.2   Assumptions on Personal Identifier

Because our data analysis counts each identifiable person, we need to choose appropriate attributes for personal identifier. We mainly use resident registration numbers and full names as the key attributes representing each individual. Resident registration number is a representative number that identifies each Korean citizen. It is made up of 13 digits and has the meaning of birth date (year, month,

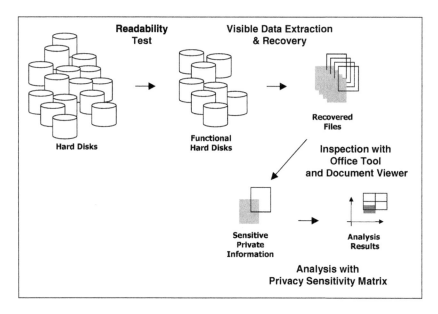

Fig. 1. Analysis Process for Used Hard Disks

and day) and birth place code in itself. In that RRN is an individual identifier which is endowed by government, it is similar to social security number (SSN) in U.S. However, SSN is subject to restriction for use, and if one declines to offer his or her SSN, it does not make against his or her advantage for services. On the other hand, RRN is widely used for recognizing a person's identity in the private sectors as well as the public ones. RRN should be essentially offered for most services in Korea. Therefore, RRN has more impact on individuals' privacy in Korea than SSN do in U.S. We treat each RRN found in hard disks on the Assumption 1 and 2.

Assumption 1. (Uniqueness of Resident Registration Numbers): A discovered RRN is used as a unique key attribute.

Assumption 2. (Validity of Resident Registration Numbers): All the RRN discovered are valid. That is, because they indicate actual persons, criminals could misuse them for identity theft.

A full name is utilized instead if discovered personal data does not have RRN. Our usage of full names is based on the Assumption 3.

Assumption 3. (Using Full Names as Personal Identifier): A full name with family or given name is enough to be used as an individual identifier. In one disk, a different person with the same name is handled as a same individual.

3.3 Privacy Sensitivity Matrix for Used Personal Computers

To describe data found on recovered disk drives based on the privacy impact on each PC user, we created privacy sensitivity matrix(see Fig. 2).

Privacy sensitivity level on the y-axis is the level of users' perception of sensitive data. Users' perception of high sensitivity level means that users are hardly willing to provide their private information in return for personalized service. Ackerman's privacy classification survey[1] reported that only 1 percent of their sample felt comfortable with revealing their social security numbers, and 3 percent with their credit card numbers respectively. Less than 20 percent of the respondents were comfortable about disclosure of phone numbers, income, and medical information. To the contrary, more than half of the sample would give away their full names, age, email addresses, and preferences for TV show. In brief, there is enormous difference of privacy sensitivity among personal attributes.

Type of data on the x-axis is divided into *profile-related information* and *identity-related information*. This classification is originated from Spiekermann et al.[9] regarding users' privacy preferences in electronic commerce environment. Identity-related information means data items with which one can surely infer a specific person. Profile-related information is usually appended to identity-related data and describes users' profile(See Fig. 2 for examples). The risk of private information owned by third-party incorporates privacy risk and impersonation leading to fraud(= identity theft)[7]. Our sensitivity matrix embraces these two types of risk – profile-related information is related to privacy risk and identity-related information to identity theft.

4 Our Experiment

4.1 Acquisition of Used Hard Disks

How to obtain a sufficiently large number of used hard disk drives was the major concern for this study. We have spent almost a half year to collect them only through customer-to-customer online auction markets. We had tried other ways to see if by any chance there is any possibility to get some of recycled PCs that are regularly, most of cases in three years basis, disposed to second-hand PC markets or to charity organization.

In the early four months of the experiment, we made a round of the recycling centers administrated by the Seoul Metropolitan Government and examined whether we were able to obtain used PCs for analysis. However, we apprehended that used PCs of the recycling centers were not suited to our experiment for the following reasons. Firstly, most of used PCs have no hard disk needed for analysis. A hard disk is longer lived than other computer components and is compatible with other computers with various function and performance. So as soon as a PC was put into a recycling center, the hard disk in it is extracted by used computer dealers and is resold at a used computer market like an online auction. Secondly, although we obtain a used PC with a hard disk, there are

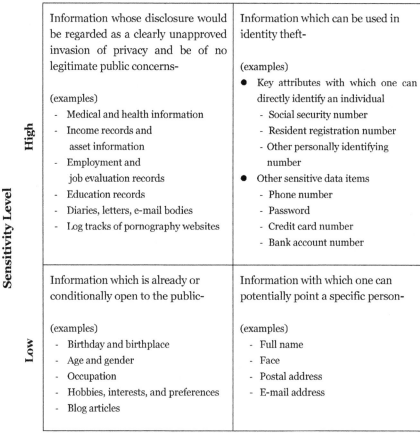

Fig. 2. Privacy Sensitivity Matrix

many cases when we could not analyze further because careless recycling process makes a hard disk damaged or disabled. That is to say, almost all PCs of the recycling centers were nothing but ferrous scraps destined for abolition or decomposition. Finally, we were obliged to give up collecting disks through the recycling centers.

As another trial, we promoted to obtain disks through used computer whole sellers. We tried to analyze data after purchasing 30 used hard disks at a time at a store in Yongsan Electronic Market, the largest computer market in Korea. However, we could not use these disks for analysis because of the uniformity of samples. From the information on disk labels, we checked out that all the 30 hard disks were used at a bankrupt internet cafe. We were not able to find out meaningful data because the outward appearances, capacities, manufacturers, and options of all the hard disks were one and the same, and then all the hard disks were initialized as a condition of factory shipment through professional complete deletion of disk sellers. We decided that to obtain a large amount of disks through used computer whole sellers were not inconsistent with our experimental goal, which intended to explore the possibility to find out personal information from discarded PCs in Korea.

To increase the possibility of detecting personal information, we brought to a conclusion that we should purchase only through customer-to-customer purchasing, which of course requires tedious works. For one purchasing, we bought one to three disks and avoided more than four disks from sellers who sold in large quantities. The purchasing was carried out two times, 30 disks in August to December 2003 and the rest 25 in January to April 2005, mostly through internet auction service (http://www.auction.co.kr). The total purchasing cost for 55 used hard disks amounts to 400,000 Korean Won($\simeq$ 400 U.S. Dollar). Before carrying out data analysis, we numbered each hard disk and wrote its outward appearance and physical specification for each. We also put down sellers' information with referring to sales for each hard disk. In case of buying hard disks by use of internet auctions, minimal personal information (name, telephone number, address) should be mutually exchanged between sellers and buyers. So, under favor of personal information of second-hand sellers within hard disks through internet auctions, malicious buyers are prone to make easy valuable information of sellers.

4.2   Initial Examination

As the first phase of analyzing disks, we first connected each drive to a computer running Windows XP operating system and conducted recognition operations. And then we wrote whether each disk is recognized or not and whether each is formatted or not. After recognition process on 55 disks, we discovered that 17 disks were out of physical order and so we extracted files from the rest 38 disks. Of the functional 38 disks, only two (5 percent) were found to be gone through a complete erasure. 16 (42 percent) had one or more identifiable names. Table 2 shows the initial analysis results by the number of drives.

Table 2. Initial Analysis by Number of Drives Examined

No. of drives / Degree of erase	Our experiment
(All functional)	38
Completely overwritten (No file structures contained)	2 (5 percent)
Data removal attempted[1]	17 (45 percent)
Recoverable data remained	30 (80 percent)
Personal information remained	16 (42 percent)

[1] Simple-minded efforts like simple deletion of files as well as disk formatting other than complete overwriting had been applied.

4.3   Data Extraction and Recovery

Data extraction process for each hard disk is composed of three following stages:

1. *Extracting regular files*: Seeking all files that are visible and have names, attributes, and contents in file systems (temporary files in folders like 'recycle bin' and internet cache files are included.)
2. *Recovering deleted files and remained data blocks*: Separating some recoverable files by use of data recovery programs.
3. *Storing files*: Securing files from above two stages for further analysis.

Through the above stages, we extracted 3.2 gigabytes worth of data from 30 hard disks. For separating files that have the high possibility of including personal information among data, we explore each file system of disks in search of file extension. The target file extensions are as follows; HWP as a Korean word processor file of Hangul and Computer Co. Ltd., DOC, XLS, PPT, MDB as MS Office tool files of Microsoft Corp., PDF as a universally used document file, and DBF as a database file. Beyond these files, we found out some files with the following extension like PST as a MS Outlook file and MBX as a MS Outlook Express email file. We so added them to the target data for detailed examination.

We examined some files among target files with the exception of damaged files and default example files provided by application programs. And we separated personal information of special concern and made a database with their contents, the number of target persons, and field names. As a result, we discovered variously sensitive personal information from personal profiles to secret documents. Collected personal information amounted to 4,526 identifiable individuals. Among them, the number of private information data including resident registration number is 3,584.

4.4   Results of Data Analysis

Data recovery produced the result that the majority of detected personal information is concentrated on several disks that would be used in enterprises. We were able to infer the name of some organizations in which 12 hard disks of totally 38 functional ones were used. All the distinguished organizations are enterprises that cover a construction company, a national heath insurance company, an insurance company, and an IT solution company. We grasped that the rest 26 disks would be used by individuals or unidentified organizations.

To make a more detailed study, we classified all personal information with regard to the privacy sensitivity matrix(in Fig. 2 of Section 3.3). After we understood identifiable name in each personal data, we grouped and counted individual-related information of both profile-related and identity-related information from low to high level of sensitivity. We found personal information of more than low level in 16 hard disks, and show the detection record of personal information for each disk. From seven disks originated from enterprises, there was 4,478 people worth of personal information, which includes 3,566 RRNs and other sensitive identity-related and profile-related data. 9 disks from individuals

Table 3. Detailed Analysis Result for disks (from enterprises)

Disk#	Num. of Exposed People[1]	Private Information with *High* Sensitivity Level		Remarks
		Profile-related	Identity-related	
30	315	Income records: insurance default like economic poverty and physical disorder	315 RRNs[2] & 51 insurance numbers	From an excel file including insurance defaulters' list in National Health Insurance
31	237	Employment records: Official orders of personnel like results of promotion exams	Phone numbers	In a national health insurance company
39	512	Education and income records & unemployment insurance for industrial disasters: accident details, disease names, prospected medical fee, disorder grade	471 RRNs of employees and outsourcing laborers	In a construction company
45	373	Education records of insurance sales persons: contract accomplishment and its ranking	115 RRNs of employees (mainly insurance sales persons)	In a life insurance company
46	2,935	Contract records of customers in 250 WAV files recorded in 2001 and 2002	2,665 RRNs, insurance numbers and a number of bank accounts	In a life insurance company
47	85	Academic background, contract accomplishment, job career, and discipline result of insurance sales persons		From secret documents for educating employees' customer responses or conversation skills in a life insurance company
51	21	Cookies from pornographic websites		Containing 10 design drawings in an IT solution company

[1] Num. of Exposed People: Numbers of people whose private data is exposed with the basis on ones' identifiable names

[2] RRN: Resident Registration Number

had 48 people worth of personal information with 18 RRNs. (See Table 3 and 4 for detailed list of number of exposed people and private data with only high sensitivity level found in each disk.)

Table 4. Detailed Analysis Result for disks (from individuals)

Disk#	Num. of Exposed People	Private Information with *High* Sensitivity Level		Remarks
		Profile-related	Identity-related	
2	1	Adult sites		
3	4	Education records	4 RRNs	From a resume with family members' information
20	3	Education & income records	3 RRNs	
21	21	Education records	Phone numbers	Containing address books
23	5	60 megabytes worth of e-mails	1 RRN	
24	1	Diaries		
28	1	Cookies & about 3,200 of pornographic photos		
40	1	A letter to friend		
53	11	Cookies from pornographic websites	10 RRNs of members of an amateur anglers' club	From emails made when joining a club

Most of sensitive personal information is discovered in the hard disks used in enterprises. A number of Excel files including laborers' records of industrial disaster victims or medical checkups were discovered in only one hard disk used in a construction company. These files also have medical information including personal history of disasters and disorder grades. In three disks used at a branch of national health insurance, extremely sensitive information for more than 300 insurance defaulters was found with economic poverty, facility accommodation, and physical disorder. In another three disks used at certain insurance company in Korea, we detected customers' names and resident registration numbers of approximately 2,650 persons in one Excel file and then did approximately 250 WAV files recorded for training employees for canvassing insurance products. By thorough examination of these files recording conversation between employees and customers, we had additional finds with resident registration numbers from insurance contract histories of 11 persons.

Even though an examination of personally-used disks did not find more personal information than we expected, it found many private emails or diaries, resumes with resident registration numbers, and guidance records for student's life. One of disks contained membership applicant information for an amateur anglers' club, which included resident registration number, address, and so forth for each member. For catching personal propensity for information retrieval on the internet, we researchers specially explored web site addresses and caches in cookies. And as a result, we were able to get traces exploring pornography sites in 6 disks.

5   Conclusion

We demonstrated the possibility to acquire much personal information easily from hard disks in Korean second-hand PC markets. We also made clear that a part of hard disks was used in enterprises although all of disks were bought from individuals. As the analysis results, hard disks from enterprises have much more abundant and sensitive personal information than those from individuals. This could be a proof that disks including sensitive personal information was hidden away by internal employees and distributed in the markets without any complete-erasure procedure for inside files.

Penalties may be imposed when violation of data-privacy and computer-disposal regulations is occurred. For instance, Health Insurance Portability and Accountability Act[11] in U. S. addresses the security and privacy of health information. According to this Act, if violation is committed with the intent to sell, transfer, or use identifiable health information for commercial advantage, personal gain, or malicious harm individually, the fine or imprisonment will be levied. Hence, the enterprises of today should manage and supervise the life cycle from obtainment to abolition of personal information in making direct use of personal information systematically. The taxonomy of data analysis we proposed will make a contribution to assess the protection degree of personal information especially in enterprises.

This paper has a limitation that the sensitivity taxonomy of personal information is not detailed sufficiently and is dependent on subjective judgment. To set up more correct policy for securing personal information, classification standards according to the sensitivity of personal information should be clearer. Our proposed taxonomy, in addition, has another limitation that does not consider the cultural relativity although it complies with a common idea of society. A further study on positive analysis of the importance of private information according to demographic differences is needed.

References

1. Ackerman, M.S., Cranor, L.F. and Reagle, J.: Privacy in E-Commerce: Examining User Scenarios and Privacy Preferences. In Procs. of 1st ACM Conference on Electronic Commerce., Denver, Colorado, U.S.A. (1999)
2. Berghel, H.: Digital Village: Identity Theft, Social Security Numbers, and the Web. Communications of the ACM **43**(2) (2000) 17–21
3. Garfinkel, S.L. and Shelat, A.: Remembrance of Data Passed: A Study of Disk Sanitization Practices. IEEE Security and Privacy **1**(1) (2003) 17–27
4. Gutmann, P.: Secure Deletion of Data from Magnetic and Solid-State Memory. In Procs. of 6th USENIX Security Symposium, San Jose, California, U.S.A. (1996)
5. Javelin Strategy and Research: 2005 Identity Fraud Survey Report.

6. Jones, A.: How Much Information Do Organizations Throw Away? Computer Fraud and Security **2005**(3) (2005) 4–9
7. Schneier, B.: Risks of Third-party Data. Communications of the ACM **48**(5) (2005) 136
8. Shein, E.: Die Hard (Drive). CFO Magazine (2004)
9. Spiekermann, S., Grossklags, J. and Berendt, B.: E-privacy in 2nd Generation E-commerce: Privacy Preferences Versus Actual Behavior. In Procs. of 3rd ACM Conference on Electronic Commerce., Tampa, Florida, U.S.A. (2001)
10. U.S. Department of Defense: DoD 5220.22-M National Industrial Security Program Operating Manual (1995)
11. U.S. Public Law 104-191: Health Insurance Portability and Accountability Act of 1996.

Short Traceable Signatures Based on Bilinear Pairings

Seung Geol Choi[1], Kunsoo Park[2], and Moti Yung[1]

[1] Dept. of Computer Science, Columbia University, USA
{sc2506, moti}@cs.columbia.edu
[2] Dept. of Computer Science and Engineering, Seoul National University, Korea
kpark@theory.snu.ac.kr

Abstract. We propose a short traceable signature scheme based on bilinear pairings. Traceable signatures, introduced by Kiayias, Tsiounis and Yung (KTY), support an extended set of fairness mechanisms (mechanisms for anonymity management and revocation) when compared with the traditional group signatures. Designing short signatures based on the power of pairing has been a current activity of cryptographic research, and is especially needed for long constructions like that of traceable signatures. The size of a signature in our scheme is less than one third of the size in the KTY scheme and about 40% of the size of the pairing based traceable signature (which has been the shortest till today). The security of our scheme is based on the Strong Diffie-Hellman assumption and the Decision Linear Diffie-Hellman assumption. We prove the security of our system in random oracle model using the security model given by KTY.

Keywords: traceable signatures, group signatures, anonymity, cryptographic protocols, bilinear pairings.

1 Introduction

Group signatures, introduced by Chaum and van Heyst [11], provide anonymity for signers. Any member of the group can sign messages, but the resulting signature keeps the identity of the signer secret. Because unconditional anonymity may be a very dangerous tool against public safety, in case of dispute about the signed message group signatures allow the group manager to open the signature and identify its originator. In this respect, group signatures can be said to incorporate a *fairness* mechanism.

Traceable signatures, introduced by Kiayias, Tsiounis and Yung [13], support an extended set of fairness mechanisms (mechanisms for anonymity management and revocation) when compared with the traditional group signature schemes. Consider the following scenario: a certain member of the group is suspected of illegal activity. Its identity was revealed by opening a signature value. It is then necessary to detect the signatures issued by this member so that his/her transactions are traced. The only solution with existing group signature schemes is to have the group manager open all signatures. However, this solution have two

H. Yoshiura et al. (Eds.): IWSEC 2006, LNCS 4266, pp. 88–103, 2006.

problems. First, since all signatures are opened the solution violates the privacy of all group members. Second, since only the group manager can open signatures it impairs scalability. We need some parallel mechanism for scalability. Traceable signatures support three different types of traceability :

1. signature opening : as in group signature, reveal the signer of a given signature
2. user tracing : check whether a signature was issued by a given user; it can be applied to all signatures by designated tracing agents running in parallel
3. signature claiming : the signer of a signature provably claims a given signature that he/she has signed.

Therefore, the above scenario can be solved with user tracing if we use traceable signatures.

Kiayias, Tsiounis and Yung (hereafter KTY) gave a formal security model through three security requirements: misidentification, anonymity, framing. If the adversary is able to generate a signature whose originator is not traced by the group manager, the scheme is not secure against misidentification. Given a signature and two members of which one is its originator, if the adversary can identify its originator no better than randomly, the scheme has anonymity. The adversary succeeds in framing an honest user, if he generates a signature that is wrongly traced to an innocent user. The KTY scheme [13] is secure under the Strong RSA and Decisional Diffie-Hellman assumptions. We note that in concurrent independent work, Bellare et al. [7,8] gave a formal security model for group signatures with a security model which is nearly the same as that of KTY [13].

Traceable signature with the above scalable anonymity is suitable for various applications and extends the reach of e-commerce while allowing users extended anonymity. In a typical web based commerce, it may be desired that the service provider does not know the user, yet that there is a mechanism that a tracing authority (either as a law enforcement mechanisms for illegal activity or as a routine mechanisms like billing by a bank) will be able at a different layer to expose users selectively. The notion of "anonymous non-repudiation" that indeed combines both anonymity at the service provider level, but identification at another layer has high potential in many application domains.

Recent pairing based signatures: Boneh et al. [6] noticed that bilinear maps can shorten signature schemes; this started a line of research of employing pairings in order to shorten signatures. Boneh et al. [5] devised a short group signature scheme using bilinear pairings. The size of a signature is under 200 bytes that offer approximately the same level of security as a regular RSA signature of the same length. The scheme used the Strong Diffie-Hellman (SDH) and Decision Linear Diffie-Hellman (DLDH) assumptions. Nguyen and Safavi-Naini. [16] also introduced a group signature scheme using bilinear pairings. The size of its signature is slightly bigger than that of [5], but the scheme has stronger anonymity. They also introduced a traceable signature scheme using El Gamal public key encryption under the assumptions above. Boyen and Waters [9] gave the group signature scheme without random oracles but the scheme is not practical in that the size of a signature grows logarithmically in the number of group members. Ateniese et al. [2] devised practical group signature scheme without random oracles. Their scheme is based on the Strong LRSW, q-EDH, and Strong SXDH assumptions.

Our Result: We extend the result of [5] to construct a traceable signature scheme with the length of signatures 362 byte long (just about the size of three RSA signatures), which is shorter than those of [13] and [16], which are 1200 byte and 900 byte long, respectively. In contrast to the previous schemes that need two separate parts for tracing and claiming [13,16], we use one part for the two procedures, which is possible with the help of bilinear pairing, and therefore we get shorter signature size. In spite of its shorter length, the security level of our scheme is the same as of the schemes using bilinear pairings. We used the SDH and DLDH assumptions given by [5].

2   Preliminaries

2.1   Bilinear Pairings

We first review a few concepts related to bilinear pairings. Let $\mathbb{G}_1, \mathbb{G}_2$ be cyclic additive groups generated by P_1 and P_2, respectively, both with prime order p, and $\mathbb{G}_T$ be a cyclic multiplicative group of order p. Suppose there is an isomorphism $\psi : \mathbb{G}_2 \to \mathbb{G}_1$ such that $\psi(P_2) = P_1$. A bilinear pairing is a function $e : \mathbb{G}_1 \times \mathbb{G}_2 \to \mathbb{G}_T$ with the following properties.

- Non-degeneracy : $e(P_1, P_2) \neq 1$
- Bilinearity : For all $Q_1 \in \mathbb{G}_1, Q_2 \in \mathbb{G}_2$ and $a, b \in \mathbb{Z}_p$, $e(aQ_1, bQ_2) = e(Q_1, Q_2)^{ab}$.
- Computability : For all $Q_1 \in \mathbb{G}_1, Q_2 \in \mathbb{G}_2$, there is an efficient algorithm to compute $e(Q_1, Q_2)$.

We assume that p is about 2^{170}. $\mathbb{G}_1$ and $\mathbb{G}_2$ are assumed to be subgroups with order p of an elliptic curve group where possibly $\mathbb{G}_1 = \mathbb{G}_2$. $\mathbb{G}_T$ is a subgroup with order p of a finite field of size about 2^{1024}. We note that the bilinear groups of Rubin and Siverberg [18] or Miyagi et al. [15] can be used. We denote the generation algorithm of bilinear pairings by $\mathcal{G}_{BP}$ throughout this paper.

2.2   SDH Representation

Let $\mathbb{G}_1, \mathbb{G}_2$ be cyclic additive groups of prime order p where possibly $\mathbb{G}_1 = \mathbb{G}_2$. Let P_1 be a generator of $\mathbb{G}_1$ and P_2 a generator of $\mathbb{G}_2$. The q-Strong Diffie Hellman (q-SDH) problem in $(\mathbb{G}_1, \mathbb{G}_2)$ is defined as follows [5]: Given $(q + 2)$-tuple $(P_1, P_2, \gamma P_2, \ldots, \gamma^q P_2)$ as input, output a pair $(\frac{1}{\gamma+x} P_1, x)$ where $x \in \mathbb{Z}_p^*$. The advantage of an algorithm $\mathcal{A}$ for the q-SDH problem is defined as follows:

$$\mathbf{Adv}_{\mathcal{A}}^{q\text{-SDH}}(k) = \Pr \left[\begin{array}{l} \mathcal{A}(\mathcal{G}, \gamma P_2, \ldots, \gamma^q P_2) = \left(\frac{1}{\gamma+x} P_1, x\right) \wedge x \in \mathbb{Z}_p^* \quad \text{where} \\ \mathcal{G} = (p, \mathbb{G}_1, \mathbb{G}_2, \mathbb{G}_T, P_1, P_2, e) \leftarrow \mathcal{G}_{BP}(1^k) \\ \gamma \xleftarrow{R} \mathbb{Z}_p^* \end{array} \right]$$

We define the q-Strong Diffie-Hellman assumption. This assumption was used by Boneh and Boyen [4] to construct short signatures.

Definition 1. q-Strong Diffie-Hellman (q-SDH) Assumption. *For every PPT algorithm $\mathcal{A}$, $\mathbf{Adv}_{\mathcal{A}}^{q-\mathsf{SDH}}(k)$ is negligible in k.*

We next define an SDH representation. The representation is similar to a discrete-log representation of an arbitrary power in the KTY scheme [13].

Definition 2. SDH representation. *For $\mathcal{G} = (p, \mathbb{G}_1, \mathbb{G}_2, \mathbb{G}_T, P_1, P_2, e)$ and (Q, R) where $Q \in \mathbb{G}_1, R = \gamma P_2 \in \mathbb{G}_2$ with unknown γ, an SDH representation is a tuple (A, x, t) with $A \in \mathbb{G}_1$ and $x, t \in \mathbb{Z}_p^*$ such that $A = \frac{1}{\gamma + t}(xP_1 + Q)$. Note that the tuple satisfies $e(A, tP_2 + R) = e(xP_1 + Q, P_2)$.*

In this work we will be interested in the following computational problem.

Definition 3. One more SDH representation problem. *Given K SDH representations for $\mathcal{G} = (p, \mathbb{G}_1, \mathbb{G}_2, \mathbb{G}_T, P_1, P_2, e)$ and (Q, R), one more SDH representation problem is to find another SDH representation.*

Lemma 1. *Under the q-SDH assumption, it is infeasible for a PPT algorithm to solve one more SDH representation problem with $K = q$.*

2.3   Linear Encryption

Let $\mathbb{G}_1$ be a cyclic additive group of prime order p, and let X, Y, Z be generators of $\mathbb{G}_1$. The Decision Linear Diffie-Hellman problem in $\mathbb{G}_1$ is defined as follows [5]: Given $X, Y, Z, aX, bY, cZ \in \mathbb{G}_1$ as input, output **yes** if $a + b = c$ and no otherwise. The advantage of an algorithm $\mathcal{A}$ for the Decision Linear Diffie-Hellman problem is defined as follows:

$$\mathbf{Adv}_{\mathcal{A}}^{\mathsf{DLDH}}(k) = \left| p_k^{(0)} - p_k^{(1)} \right|$$

where

$$p_k^{(i)} = \Pr \begin{bmatrix} \mathcal{A}(\mathcal{H}, aX, bY, cZ) = \mathsf{yes} \text{ where} \\ \mathcal{H} = (p, \mathbb{G}_1, X, Y, Z) \leftarrow \mathcal{G}_{DL}(1^k) \\ a, b \xleftarrow{R} \mathbb{Z}_p^* \\ c \leftarrow a + b \text{ if } i = 0 \\ c \xleftarrow{R} \mathbb{Z}_p^* \text{ otherwise} \end{bmatrix}.$$

We define the Decision Linear Diffie-Hellman assumption. This assumption was used by Boneh et al. [5] to construct short group signatures.

Definition 4. Decision Linear Diffie-Hellman (DLDH) assumption. *For every PPT algorithm $\mathcal{A}$, $\mathbf{Adv}_{\mathcal{A}}^{\mathsf{DLDH}}(k)$ is negligible in k.*

The DLDH assumption gives rise to the Linear encryption (LE) scheme [5]. This scheme is semantically secure against chosen-plaintext attacks, assuming the DLDH assumption holds.

Definition 5. Linear encryption. *With* $M \in \mathbb{G}_1$, *along with arbitrary generators* X, Y *and* Z *of* $\mathbb{G}_1$, *linear encryption* LE *with public key* X, Y *and* Z *is as follows:*

$$LE(M) = (r_1 X, r_2 Y, M + (r_1 + r_2)Z)$$

where $r_1, r_2 \in \mathbb{Z}_p$ *is randomly chosen.*

Lemma 2. *[5] Under the DLDH assumption, linear encryption is secure against chosen-plaintext attacks.*

3   Zero-Knowledge Protocol for an SDH Representation

We assume that $\mathcal{G} = (p, \mathbb{G}_1, \mathbb{G}_2, \mathbb{G}_T, P_1, P_2, e), Q \in \mathbb{G}_1, R = \gamma P_2 \in \mathbb{G}_2$ with unknown γ are given as specified in Section 2. Let X, Y, Z be generators of $\mathbb{G}_1$, and W a generator of $\mathbb{G}_2$. A zero-knowledge protocol for an SDH representation (A, x, t) is as follows.

Protocol 1. The prover chooses exponents $r_1, r_2, r_3 \xleftarrow{R} \mathbb{Z}_p$, $d_1 \leftarrow tr_1, d_2 \leftarrow tr_2$, and then computes the following values:

$$T_1 \leftarrow r_1 X, \quad T_2 \leftarrow r_2 Y, \quad T_3 \leftarrow A + (r_1 + r_2)Z,$$
$$T_4 \leftarrow r_3 W, \quad T_5 \leftarrow e(P_1, T_4)^x \quad .$$

Note that T_1, T_2 and T_3 constitute a Linear encryption of the value A. Note also that if we precalculate the value $e(P_1, W)$, we can compute $T_5 = e(P_1, W)^{r_3 x}$ with just one exponentiation on $\mathbb{G}_T$ avoiding the expensive pairing calculation of $e(P_1, T_4)^x$. Now, the prover and the verifier execute a proof of knowledge of values $(r_1, r_2, d_1, d_2, t, x)$ which satisfy the following equations:

$$r_1 X = T_1, \quad r_2 Y = T_2,$$
$$t T_1 - d_1 X = O, \quad t T_2 - d_2 Y = O,$$
$$e(P_1, T_4)^x = T_5,$$
$$e(T_3, P_2)^t \cdot e(Z, P_2)^{-d_1 - d_2} \cdot e(Z, R)^{-r_1 - r_2} \cdot e(P_1, P_2)^{-x} = e(Q, P_2)/e(T_3, R) \quad .$$

This proof is a typical 3-move honest verifier zero-knowledge proof for discrete logarithm relation set. For the first move, the prover randomly chooses $b_{r_1}, b_{r_2}, b_{d_1}, b_{d_2}, b_t, b_x$ from $\mathbb{Z}_p$, and then computes the following values:

$$B_1 \leftarrow b_{r_1} X, \quad B_2 \leftarrow b_{r_2} Y,$$
$$B_3 \leftarrow b_t T_1 - b_{d_1} X, \quad B_4 \leftarrow b_t T_2 - b_{d_2} Y,$$
$$B_5 \leftarrow e(P_1, T_4)^{b_x},$$
$$B_6 \leftarrow e(T_3, P_2)^{b_t} \cdot e(Z, P_2)^{-b_{d_1} - b_{d_2}} \cdot e(Z, R)^{-b_{r_1} - b_{r_2}} \cdot e(P_1, P_2)^{-b_x},$$

He sends $(T_1, \ldots, T_5, B_1, \ldots, B_6)$ to the verifier, who sends a random challenge value $c \xleftarrow{R} \mathbb{Z}_p$ to the prover as a second move. The prover computes and sends back the values in response to the verifier as the last move:

$$s_{r_1} \leftarrow b_{r_1} + cr_1, \quad s_{r_2} \leftarrow b_{r_2} + cr_2, \quad s_{d_1} \leftarrow b_{d_1} + cd_1,$$
$$s_{d_2} \leftarrow b_{d_2} + cd_2, \quad s_x \leftarrow b_x + cx, \quad s_t \leftarrow b_t + ct \quad .$$

The verifier checks if the following equations hold; if they hold the verifier accepts, otherwise he rejects.

$$s_{r_1} X \stackrel{?}{=} cT_1 + B_1 \tag{1}$$

$$s_{r_2} Y \stackrel{?}{=} cT_2 + B_2 \tag{2}$$

$$s_t T_1 - s_{d_1} X \stackrel{?}{=} B_3 \tag{3}$$

$$s_t T_2 - s_{d_2} Y \stackrel{?}{=} B_4 \tag{4}$$

$$e(P_1, T_4)^{s_x} \stackrel{?}{=} T_5^c \cdot B_5 \tag{5}$$

$$e(T_3, P_2)^{s_t} \cdot e(Z, P_2)^{-s_{d_1} - s_{d_2}} \cdot e(Z, R)^{-s_{r_1} - s_{r_2}} \cdot e(P_1, P_2)^{-s_x}$$
$$\stackrel{?}{=} (e(Q, P_2)/e(T_3, R))^c \cdot B_6 \quad . \tag{6}$$

Lemma 3. *Protocol 1 is complete.*

Lemma 4. *There exists a simulator for the transcripts of Protocol 1 for an honest verifier under the DLDH assumption.*

Lemma 5. *There exists an extractor for Protocol 1.*

Proof. We allow an extractor to rewind a prover in the protocol to the point just before the prover is given a challenge c. Then, the extractor can obtain two protocol transcripts :

$$(T_1, \ldots, T_5, B_1, \ldots, B_6, c, s_{r_1}, s_{r_2}, s_{d_1}, s_{d_2}, s_x, s_t)$$
$$(T_1, \ldots, T_5, B_1, \ldots, B_6, c^*, s_{r_1}^*, s_{r_2}^*, s_{d_1}^*, s_{d_2}^*, s_x^*, s_t^*) \quad .$$

First observe that, from (1), $B_1 = s_{r_1} X - cT_1 = s_{r_1}^* X - c^* T_1$ from which we obtain $(c - c^*)T_1 = (s_{r_1} - s_{r_1}^*)X$ and it follows that $\tilde{r}_1 = (s_{r_1} - s_{r_1}^*)(c - c^*)^{-1} \pmod{p}$ satisfies $\tilde{r}_1 X = T_1$. In a similar fashion we obtain from (2) $\tilde{r}_2 = (s_{r_2} - s_{r_2}^*)(c - c^*)^{-1} \pmod{p}$ which satisfies $\tilde{r}_2 Y = T_2$.

Next we have, from (5), $B_5 = e(P_1, T4)^{s_x}/T_5^c = e(P_1, T4)^{s_x^*}/T_5^{c^*}$ from which we obtain $e(P_1, T4)^{s_x - s_x^*} = T_5^{c - c^*}$ and it follows that $\tilde{x} = (s_x - s_x^*)(c - c^*)^{-1} \pmod{p}$ satisfies $e(P_1, T4)^{\tilde{x}} = T_5$.

Next we have, from (3), $B_3 = s_t T_1 - s_{d_1} X = s_t^* T_1 - s_{d_1}^* X$ from which we obtain $(s_t - s_t^*)T_1 = (s_{d_1} - s_{d_1}^*)X$. Since $\tilde{r}_1 X = T_1$, we have $(s_{d_1} - s_{d_1}^*) = \tilde{r}_1(s_t - s_t^*) \pmod{p}$. Similarly, we have from (4) $(s_{d_2} - s_{d_2}^*) = \tilde{r}_2(s_t - s_t^*) \pmod{p}$.

Finally, dividing two instances of (6), we obtain

$$(e(Q, P_2)/e(T_3, R))^{(c - c^*)}$$
$$= e(T_3, P_2)^{(s_t - s_t^*)} \cdot e(Z, P_2)^{-(s_{d_1} - s_{d_1}^*) - (s_{d_2} - s_{d_2}^*)} \cdot$$
$$e(Z, R)^{-(s_{r_1} - s_{r_1}^*) - (s_{r_2} - s_{r_2}^*)} \cdot e(P_1, P_2)^{-(s_x - s_x^*)}$$
$$= e(T_3, P_2)^{(s_t - s_t^*)} \cdot e(Z, P_2)^{-\tilde{r}_1(s_t - s_t^*) - \tilde{r}_2(s_t - s_t^*)} \cdot$$
$$e(Z, R)^{-(s_{r_1} - s_{r_1}^*) - (s_{r_2} - s_{r_2}^*)} \cdot e(P_1, P_2)^{-(s_x - s_x^*)} \quad .$$

Taking $(c - c^*)$-th roots, we have

$$
\begin{aligned}
&e(Q, P_2)/e(T_3, R) \\
&= e(T_3, P_2)^{\tilde{t}} \cdot e(Z, P_2)^{\tilde{t}(-\tilde{r_1} - \tilde{r_2})} \cdot e(Z, R)^{-\tilde{r_1} - \tilde{r_2}} \cdot e(P_1, P_2)^{-\tilde{x}} \\
&= e(T_3, \tilde{t}P_2) \cdot e(-(\tilde{r_1} + \tilde{r_2})Z, \tilde{t}P_2) \cdot e(-(\tilde{r_1} + \tilde{r_2})Z, R) \cdot e(\tilde{x}P_1, P_2)^{-1},
\end{aligned}
$$

where $\tilde{t} = (s_t - s_t^*)(c - c^*)^{-1} (\mathrm{mod}\ p)$. This can be rearranged as

$$
e(\tilde{x}P_1 + Q, P_2) = e(T_3 - (\tilde{r_1} + \tilde{r_2})Z, \tilde{t}P_2 + R) \quad .
$$

Thus the extractor obtains an SDH representation $(T_3 - (\tilde{r_1} + \tilde{r_2})Z, \tilde{x}, \tilde{t})$. □

By the three lemmas above, the following holds.

Theorem 1. *Protocol 1 is an honest-verifier zero-knowledge proof of knowledge for an SDH representation under the DLDH assumption.*

4   The Traceable Signature Scheme

This section describes our traceable signature scheme. With Theorem 1, we obtain from Protocol 1 a signature scheme secure in the random oracle model by applying the Fiat-Shamir heuristic [1,12]. In our construction, in order to reduce the length of a signature we use a variant of the Fiat-Shamir heuristic used by Ateniese et al. [3], where the challenge c is included in the signature instead of $B_1, \ldots, B_6$. We verify the validity of the signature by checking whether the output of the random oracle is equal to the challenge c.

A traceable signature scheme consists of nine operations Setup, Join/Iss, Sign, Verify, Open, Reveal, Trace, Claim, Claim_Verify. The operations are executed by the active participants of the system, which are identified by the group manager, tracing agents, and a set of users.

Setup(1^k). For a given security parameter 1^k, the system is setup as follows:

$$
\begin{aligned}
&\mathcal{G} = (p, \mathbb{G}_1, \mathbb{G}_2, \mathbb{G}_T, P_1, P_2, e) \leftarrow \mathcal{G}_{BP}(1^k), \\
&\gamma \xleftarrow{R} \mathbb{Z}_p^*, \quad Q \xleftarrow{R} \mathbb{G}_1, \quad R \leftarrow \gamma P_2, \quad W \xleftarrow{R} \mathbb{G}_2 \setminus \{1_{\mathbb{G}_2}\}, \\
&Z \xleftarrow{R} \mathbb{G}_1 \setminus \{1_{\mathbb{G}_1}\}, \quad \xi_1, \xi_2 \xleftarrow{R} \mathbb{Z}_p^*, \quad X \leftarrow \xi_1^{-1} Z, \quad Y \leftarrow \xi_2^{-1} Z \quad .
\end{aligned}
$$

The system public key $\mathcal{Y}$ is $(\mathcal{G}, Q, R, W, X, Y, Z)$. The group manager's private key $\mathcal{S}$ is (γ, ξ_1, ξ_2). The scheme also selects an hash function $H : \{0, 1\}^* \to \mathbb{Z}_p$, which is to be considered as a random oracle here.

Join($\mathcal{Y}$)/Iss($\mathcal{Y}, \mathcal{S}$). By executing Join operation, a user joins this system. On the other part, when received a join request, the group manager gives a certificate to the requester by executing Iss operation. The Join/Iss operation is performed in a secure channel. The details are as follows.

1. A user i generates non-adaptive random x_i (see 4.2 in [16]) and sends $x_i P_1$ to the group manager. We will denote the i-th user's membership secret by $\mathsf{sec}_i = x_i$.

2. The group manager selects $t_i \xleftarrow{R} \mathbb{Z}_p^*$, computes $A_i = \frac{1}{t_i + \gamma}(x_i P_1 + Q)$, and then sends (i, A_i, t_i) to the user i. We will denote the i-th user's membership certificate by $\mathsf{cert}_i = (A_i, t_i)$.

3. The user i checks if (A_i, t_i) satisfies $e(A_i, t_i P_2 + R) = e(x_i P_1 + Q, P_2)$, and then stores $(i, \mathsf{cert}_i, \mathsf{sec}_i)$.

4. We will denote the join transcript between the the group manager and i-th user by $\mathsf{transcript}_i = (C_i = x_i P_1, A_i, t_i)$. The group manager stores $\mathsf{transcript}_i$ in the join transcript table $\mathsf{transcripts}$.

$\mathsf{Sign}(m, \mathcal{Y}, \mathsf{cert}_i, \mathsf{sec}_i)$. A member i of the group can sign a message m using this operation with his certificate $\mathsf{cert}_i = (A_i, t_i)$ and his secret $\mathsf{sec}_i = x_i$.

1. Compute the values $T_1, \ldots, T_5, B_1, \ldots, B_6$ using (A_i, x_i, t_i) according to Protocol 1.

2. Compute c using the hash function :

$$c \leftarrow H(m, T_1, \ldots, T_5, B_1, \ldots, B_6) \quad .$$

3. Compute the values $s_{r_1}, s_{r_2}, s_{d_1}, s_{d_2}, s_x, s_t$ using c according to Protocol 1.

4. The signature is $\sigma = (T_1, \ldots, T_5, c, s_{r_1}, s_{r_2}, s_{d_1}, s_{d_2}, s_x, s_t)$. If each of $T_1, \ldots, T_4$ is 170 bits, T_5 is 1024 bits, and $c, s_{r_1}, \ldots, s_t$ are 170 bits each, the signature size is about $(170 \times 11 + 1024)/8 = 362$ bytes.

$\mathsf{Verify}(m, \sigma, \mathcal{Y})$. The signature σ of message m can be verified with this operation.

1. Parse σ as $(T_1, \ldots, T_5, c, s_{r_1}, s_{r_2}, s_{d_1}, s_{d_2}, s_x, s_t)$.

2. Reconstruct $\tilde{B}_1, \ldots, \tilde{B}_6$ using equations (1)-(6).

3. Check if the following equation holds:

$$c \stackrel{?}{=} H(m, T_1, \ldots, T_5, \tilde{B}_1, \ldots, \tilde{B}_6) \quad .$$

Return 1 if it holds and return 0 otherwise.

$\mathsf{Open}(\sigma, \mathcal{Y}, \mathcal{S})$. The group manager can find who signed the signature σ of m with this operation.

1. Parse σ as $(T_1, \ldots, T_5, c, s_{r_1}, s_{r_2}, s_{d_1}, s_{d_2}, s_{x_i}, s_{t_i})$.

2. Compute $\tilde{A} = T_3 - (\xi_1 T_1 + \xi_2 T_2)$ using (ξ_1, ξ_2) from $\mathcal{S}$.

3. Look up i in the join transcript table $\mathsf{transcripts}$ such that $A_i = \tilde{A}$ and return i.

$\mathsf{Reveal}(i, \mathsf{transcripts})$. The group manager can obtain the tracing information of user i with this operation. User i is a suspicious user (e.g., detected by an Open operation).

1. Return C_i of $\mathsf{transcript}_i = (C_i = x_i P_1, A_i, t_i)$ in the join transcript table $\mathsf{transcripts}$. Note that only the group manager can access the join transcript table $\mathsf{transcripts}$.

Trace$(\sigma, C, \mathcal{Y})$. Tracing agents trace the signature generated by a suspicious user. The input C is a tracing information of the suspicious user given by the group manager. By executing this operation, tracing agents check whether σ is generated by the suspicious user. Note that all the signatures can be checked efficiently when many tracing agents execute this operation in parallel.

1. Parse σ as $(T_1, \ldots, T_5, c, s_{r_1}, s_{r_2}, s_{d_1}, s_{d_2}, s_x, s_t)$.
2. Check if the following equation holds: $e(C, T_4) \stackrel{?}{=} T_5$.
   Return 1 if it holds and return 0 otherwise.

Since $C = x_j P_1$ where j is the suspicious user $e(C, T_4)$ can be rewritten as $e(P_1, T_4)^{x_j}$. If the originator of σ is i, we have $T_5 = e(P_1, T_4)^{x_i}$. Therefore, if $i = j$ this procedure will return 1.

Claim$(\sigma, \mathcal{Y}, \mathrm{sec}_i)$. The originator i of the signature σ can claim that he is its originator with this protocol.

1. Parse σ as $(T_1, \ldots, T_5, c, s_{r_1}, s_{r_2}, s_{d_1}, s_{d_2}, s_x, s_t)$.
2. Generate a proof of knowledge of the value x which satisfies $e(P_1, T_4)^x = T_5$, and return the proof τ. This is possible because if the prover is the real originator of σ, sec_i will be x_i such that $e(P_1, T_4)^{x_i} = T_5$.

Claim_Verify$(\sigma, \tau, \mathcal{Y})$. The output of Claim τ is verified with this operation.

1. Parse σ as $(T_1, \ldots, T_5, c, s_{r_1}, s_{r_2}, s_{d_1}, s_{d_2}, s_{x_i}, s_{t_i})$.
2. Verify the proof τ.

5   Correctness of the Traceable Signature Scheme

In this section we will prove the correctness of our scheme in the model of KTY [13].

Definition 6. Correctness of a Traceable Scheme. *A traceable signature scheme with security parameter k is* **correct** *if the following four conditions are satisfied (with overwhelming probability in k). Let* Sign$_\mathcal{U}$ *be the signing mechanism of user $\mathcal{U}$ and* Claim$_\mathcal{U}$ *its corresponding claim mechanism and $\mathcal{S}$ the group manager's private key.*

1. **Sign-Correctness:** *For all m,* Verify$(m, \mathrm{Sign}_\mathcal{U}(m)) = 1$.
2. **Open-Correctness:** *For any m,* Open$(\mathrm{Sign}_\mathcal{U}(m), \mathcal{S}) = \mathcal{U}$.
3. **Trace-Correctness:** *For any m,* Trace$(\mathrm{Sign}_\mathcal{U}(m), \mathrm{Reveal}(\mathcal{U})) = 1$; *on the other hand* Trace$(\sigma, \mathrm{Reveal}(\mathcal{U})) = 0$ *for any $\sigma \leftarrow \mathrm{Sign}_{\mathcal{U}'}(m)$ with $\mathcal{U}' \neq \mathcal{U}$.*
4. **Claim-Correctness:** Claim_Verify$(m, \sigma, \mathrm{Claim}_\mathcal{U}(\sigma)) = 1$ *for all $m, \sigma \leftarrow$* Sign$_\mathcal{U}(m)$.

Theorem 2. *The traceable signature scheme of Section 4 is correct.*

6   Security Model of the Traceable Signature Scheme

We introduce in this section the security model of KTY [13].

6.1   Oracles

The security definitions will be formulated via experiments in which an adversary's attack capabilities are modelled by providing it with access to certain oracles. Oracles shares the following variables with each other.

- state: It contains the join transcript, certificates and secrets of users which are obtainable in the system's perspective.
- n : It is a counter that stores the number of users joining the system.
- Sigs : It contains signatures generated by Q_{sig} oracle.
- Revs : It contains the members revealed by Q_{reveal} oracle.
- U^p : It is a set of private users which are not corrupted.
- U^a : It is a set of users in corruption type A. We say that the user i falls in corruption type A if the adversary controls the user i. In this case $(i, \text{cert}_i, \text{sec}_i)$ is leaked to the adversary.
- U^b : It is a set of users in corruption type B. We say that the user i falls in corruption type B if the transcript during the join procedure is exposed to the adversary. In this case (i, cert_i) is leaked to the adversary.

The various oracle specifications are listed below.

- $Q_{\mathcal{Y}}()$. This oracle returns $(n, \mathcal{Y})$. It allows the adversary to learn the public-information of the system.
- $Q_{\mathcal{S}}()$. This oracle returns $\mathcal{S}$. It allows the adversary to corrupt the group manager.
- $Q_{p-join}()$. This oracle simulates Join/Iss protocol in private, increases the user count n by 1, and sets state $\leftarrow$ state$\|(n, \text{transcript}_n, \text{cert}_n, \text{sec}_n)$. It also adds n into U^p and transcripts $\leftarrow$ transcripts $\|$ $(n, \text{transcript}_n)$.
- $Q_{a-join}()$. This oracle allows the adversary to introduce an adversarially controlled user to the system. The introduced user falls in corruption type A. Firstly, the oracle initiates Join/Iss protocol with the adversary. In the protocol, the oracles takes the role of the group manager and the adversary the prospective user. When the protocol terminates successfully, the oracle increases n by 1 and sets state $\leftarrow$ state$\|(n, \text{transcript}_n, \text{cert}_n, \perp)$. It also adds n into U^a and transcripts $\leftarrow$ transcripts $\|$ $(n, \text{transcript}_n)$.
- $Q_{t-join}()$. This oracle is identical to the $Q_{p-join}()$ oracle except that at the end it transmits $(\text{cert}_n, \text{sec}_n)$ to the adversary and adds n to U^a (not U^p). As explained in [13], the statistical difference between Q_{a-join} and Q_{t-join} is negligible. Therefore, we can always replace Q_{a-join} with Q_{t-join} when it is hard to simulate the behavior of Q_{a-join}.
- $Q_{b-join}()$. This oracle allows the adversary as the group manager to introduce users. Users introduced with this oracle falls in corruption type B. Firstly, the oracle initiates Join/Iss protocol with the adversary. In the protocol, the oracles takes the role of the prospective user and the adversary the group manager. When the protocol terminates successfully, the oracle increases n by 1 and sets state $\leftarrow$ state$\|(n, \perp, \text{cert}_n, \text{sec}_n)$. It also adds n into U^b. It does not modify the join transcript table transcripts since this oracle behaves as a user.

- $Q_{sig}(i, m)$. This oracle returns a signature of message m by the i-th user. It parses state and if it discovers an entry of the form $(i, \cdot, cert_i, sec_i)$ it produces a traceable signature σ using $cert_i$ and sec_i. If no such entry is found or $i \in U^a$, it returns $\bot$. When it successfully produces σ, it sets Sigs $\leftarrow$ Sigs$\|(i, \sigma)$.
- $Q_{reveal}(i)$. This oracle returns the output of Reveal$(i, transcripts)$. Note that it returns $\bot$ when user i does not exist or $i \in U^b$. It also adds i into Revs.

6.2   Security Definitions of Traceable Signatures

Definition 7. *A traceable signature scheme is said to be* **secure** *if it satisfies security against misidentification, anonymity, and framing attacks.*

Misidentification Attacks. In a misidentification attack the adversary is allowed to control a number of users of the system (Q_{a-join}, Q_{p-join}). The adversary is also allowed to observe the operation of the system while users are added and they produce signatures ($Q_{p-join}, Q_{sig}, Q_{reveal}$). Finally, the adversary is required to produce a signature that does not open to any of the users controlled by the adversary or that does not trace to any of the users controlled by the adversary.

Experiment $\mathbf{Exp}_{\mathcal{A}}^{mis}(k)$
  $(\mathcal{Y}, \mathcal{S}) \leftarrow$ Setup(1^k);
  $(m, \sigma) \leftarrow A(Q_{\mathcal{Y}}, Q_{p-join}, Q_{a-join}, Q_{sig}, Q_{reveal})$;
  If Verify$(m, \sigma, \mathcal{Y}) = 0$ then return 0;
  If Open$(\sigma, \mathcal{Y}, \mathcal{S}) \notin U^a$ or $\bigwedge_{i \in U^a}$ Trace$(\sigma, $Reveal$(i)) = 0$ then return 1;
  return 0;

Definition 8. *A traceable signature scheme is secure against misidentification attacks if for any PPT algorithm* $\mathcal{A}$ $\mathbf{Pr}[\mathbf{Exp}_{\mathcal{A}}^{mis}(k) = 1]$ *is negligible in* k.

Framing Attacks. In a framing attack, the adversary is allowed to act as a group manager. The adversary is also allowed to observe the operation of the system while users are added and they produce signatures. There are two types of successful framing attacks. First, the adversary may construct a signature that opens or traces to an innocent user. Second, it may claim a signature that was generated by another user as its own. Note that in this attack the adversary observes the operations as a group manager which are simulated through $Q_{\mathcal{S}}$, Q_{b-join}, and Q_{sig} oracles.

Experiment $\mathbf{Exp}_{\mathcal{A}}^{fra}(k)$
  $(\mathcal{Y}, \mathcal{S}) \leftarrow$ Setup(1^k);
  $(m, \sigma, \tau) \leftarrow A(Q_{\mathcal{Y}}, Q_{\mathcal{S}}, Q_{b-join}, Q_{sig})$;
  If Verify$(m, \sigma, \mathcal{Y}) = 0$ then return 0;
  If Open$(\sigma, \mathcal{Y}, \mathcal{S}) \in U^b$ or $\bigvee_{i \in U^b}$ Trace$(\sigma, $Reveal$(i)) = 1$ then return 1;
  If $\left(\bigvee_{i \in U^b} (i, \sigma) \in $ Sigs$\right) \wedge ($Claim_Verify$(\sigma, \tau) = 1)$ then return 1;
  return 0;

Definition 9. *A traceable signature scheme is secure against framing attacks if for any PPT algorithm $\mathcal{A}$ $\mathbf{Pr}[\mathbf{Exp}_{\mathcal{A}}^{\mathrm{fra}}(k) = 1]$ is negligible in k.*

Anonymity Attacks. In an anonymity attack, the adversary operates in two stages called play and guess. In the play stage, the adversary is allowed to join the system through $\mathsf{Q}_{\mathsf{a-join}}$ oracles. The adversary is also allowed to observe the operation of the system while users are added and they produce signatures through $\mathsf{Q}_{\mathsf{p-join}}, \mathsf{Q}_{\mathsf{sig}}$, and $\mathsf{Q}_{\mathsf{reveal}}$ oracles. At end of the play stage, the adversary returns a message and two target users he does not control, and then receives a signature of the message he returned. In the guess stage, the adversary tries to guess which of the two produced the signature.

Experiment $\mathbf{Exp}_{\mathcal{A}}^{\mathrm{anon}}(k)$
$\quad (\mathcal{Y}, \mathcal{S}) \leftarrow \mathsf{Setup}(1^k);$
$\quad (aux, m, i_0, i_1) \leftarrow A(\mathsf{play} : \mathsf{Q}_{\mathcal{Y}}, \mathsf{Q}_{\mathsf{p-join}}, \mathsf{Q}_{\mathsf{a-join}}, \mathsf{Q}_{\mathsf{sig}}, \mathsf{Q}_{\mathsf{reveal}});$
$\quad \text{If } (i_0 \notin U^p) \vee (i_1 \notin U^p) \vee (i_0 \in \mathsf{Revs}) \vee (i_1 \in \mathsf{Revs}) \text{ then return } 0;$
$\quad b \xleftarrow{R} \{0,1\}, \quad \sigma \leftarrow \mathsf{Sign}(m, \mathcal{Y}, \mathsf{cert}_{i_b}, \mathsf{sec}_{i_b});$
$\quad b^* \leftarrow A(\mathsf{guess}, \sigma, aux : \mathsf{Q}_{\mathcal{Y}}, \mathsf{Q}_{\mathsf{p-join}}, \mathsf{Q}_{\mathsf{a-join}}, \mathsf{Q}_{\mathsf{sig}}, \mathsf{Q}_{\mathsf{reveal}});$
$\quad \text{If } (i_0 \in \mathsf{Revs}) \vee (i_1 \in \mathsf{Revs}) \text{ then return } 0;$
$\quad \text{If } b = b^* \text{ then return } 1;$
$\quad \text{return } 0;$

Definition 10. *A traceable signature scheme is secure against anonymity attacks if for any PPT algorithm $\mathcal{A}$ $\left| \mathbf{Pr}[\mathbf{Exp}_{\mathcal{A}}^{\mathrm{anon}}(k)] - \frac{1}{2} \right|$ is negligible in k.*

6.3 Security of Our Scheme

These lemmas show the security properties.

Lemma 6. *Under the q-SDH assumption, our scheme is secure against misidentification attacks provided that the number of joined users is less than or equal to q (an adaptable "assumption parameter" that does not influence the complexity).*

Proof. Let $\mathcal{A}$ be an adversary that violates security against misidentification, We construct an algorithm $\mathcal{B}$ which solves one more representation problem using the attacker $\mathcal{A}$. SDH representations for $\mathcal{G} = (p, \mathbb{G}_1, \mathbb{G}_2, \mathbb{G}_T, P_1, P_2, e)$ and (Q, R) are given as $\mathsf{Refs} = \{(A_l, t_l, x_l)\}_{l=1}^q$. $\mathcal{B}$ chooses $W \xleftarrow{R} \mathbb{G}_2, Z \xleftarrow{R} \mathbb{G}_1$ and $\xi_1, \xi_2 \xleftarrow{R} \mathbb{Z}_p^*$. It then sets $X \leftarrow \xi_1^{-1} Z, Y \leftarrow \xi_2^{-1} Z$. $\mathcal{B}$ simulates oracles allowed to $\mathcal{A}$ as follows.

- $\mathsf{Q}_{\mathcal{Y}}()$. It returns n and $(\mathcal{G}, Q, R, W, X, Y, Z)$.
- $\mathsf{Q}_{\mathsf{p-join}}()$. $\mathcal{B}$ increments n by one, and chooses $A \xleftarrow{R} \mathbb{G}_1$ and $t, x \xleftarrow{R} \mathbb{Z}_p^*$. It sets $\mathsf{cert}_{\mathsf{n}} \leftarrow (A, t), \mathsf{sec}_{\mathsf{n}} \leftarrow x$. It then sets $\mathsf{state} \leftarrow \mathsf{state} \, || (\mathsf{n}, \perp, \mathsf{cert}_{\mathsf{n}}, \mathsf{sec}_{\mathsf{n}})$ and $\mathsf{transcripts} \leftarrow \mathsf{transcripts} || (\mathsf{n}, \perp)$. Also, $\mathcal{B}$ adds n into U^p.

- Q_{t-join}. $\mathcal{B}$ increments j which is a counter representing how many SDH representations have been consumed and then gets $\mathsf{Refs}_j = (A_j, x_j, t_j)$ from Refs. It gives $(\mathsf{cert}_n = (A_j, t_j), \mathsf{sec}_n = x_j)$ to $\mathcal{A}$. It then sets $\mathsf{state} \leftarrow \mathsf{state}$ $||(n, \perp, \mathsf{cert}_n, \mathsf{sec}_n)$ and $\mathsf{transcripts} \leftarrow \mathsf{transcripts}||(n, \perp)$. Also, $\mathcal{B}$ adds n into U^a.

- $Q_{sig}(i, m)$. If $i \notin U^p$, $\mathcal{B}$ returns "fail" to $\mathcal{A}$. If $i \in U^p$, it simulates Protocol 1 with cert_i from state and get a signature σ, which is is possible because Protocol 1 has a simulator. Also, $\mathcal{B}$ sets $\mathsf{Sig} \leftarrow \mathsf{Sig}||(i, \sigma)$. Note that the value c which is selected by the simulator during simulation must be stored in the hash oracle such that the hash oracle should keep the random oracle property.

- $Q_{reveal}(i)$. $\mathcal{B}$ searches from state an entry of the form $(i, \cdot, \cdot, \mathsf{sec}_i = x_i)$, and returns $C_i = x_i P_1$. It also adds i into Revs.

Let (m, σ_1^*) be a successful output of algorithm $\mathcal{A}$. Using the general forking lemma [14], $\mathcal{B}$ can get another pair (m, σ_2^*) which is also valid. Because Protocol 1 has a knowledge extractor, an SDH representation $(\tilde{A}, \tilde{x}, \tilde{t})$ used in signing m can be extracted.

Now we have two alternative cases: (i) $\mathsf{Open}(\sigma, \mathcal{Y}, \mathcal{S}) \notin U^a$. It means that $\tilde{A}$ is not equal to any A_i for those $i \in U^a$. As a result, we solved one more SDH representation problem. In the second case we have: (ii) $\bigwedge_{i \in U^a} \mathsf{Trace}(\sigma, \mathsf{Reveal}(i)) = 0$. It means that $\tilde{x}$ is not equal to any x_i for those $i \in U^a$. Again we solved one more SDH representation problem. $\qquad \square$

Lemma 7. *Under the assumption of infeasibility of discrete logarithm in $\mathbb{G}_1$, our scheme is secure against framing attacks.*

Proof. Let $\mathcal{A}$ be an adversary that violates security against framing attacks. We construct an algorithm $\mathcal{B}$ which solves a problem of discrete logarithm in $\mathbb{G}_1$ using the attacker $\mathcal{A}$. $\mathcal{B}$ is given P_1 and $S = \rho P_1 \in \mathbb{G}_1$ as input, and $\mathcal{B}$ wants to find ρ. We assume $\mathbb{G}_1$ is a group such that $\mathcal{G} = (p, \mathbb{G}_1, \mathbb{G}_2, \mathbb{G}_T, P_1, P_2, e)$ is easily obtained. $\mathcal{B}$ selects $Q \xleftarrow{R} \mathbb{G}_1$, $R \leftarrow \gamma P_2$ with $\gamma \xleftarrow{R} \mathbb{Z}_p^*$, and $W \xleftarrow{R} \mathbb{G}_2$. It also chooses $\xi_1, \xi_2, y \xleftarrow{R} \mathbb{Z}_p$ and $Y \leftarrow y P_1$ and then set $Z \leftarrow \xi_2 Y$, $X \leftarrow \xi_1^{-1} Z$. Then, $\mathcal{Y}$ becomes $(\mathcal{G}, Q, R, W, X, Y, Z)$ and $\mathcal{S}$ becomes (γ, ξ_1, ξ_2). $\mathcal{B}$ simulates oracles allowed to $\mathcal{A}$ as follows.

- $Q_{\mathcal{Y}}()$. $\mathcal{B}$ returns n and $\mathcal{Y}$.
- $Q_{\mathcal{S}}()$. $\mathcal{B}$ returns $\mathcal{S}$.
- $Q_{b-join}()$. $\mathcal{B}$ increments n by one. In the 1st step of Join/Iss procedure, $\mathcal{B}$ chooses $x_n' \xleftarrow{R} \mathbb{Z}_p^*$, and supplies $x_n' P_1 + S$ as the $x_n P_1$ value. It receives the tuple (A_n, t_n) from $\mathcal{A}$, in the 2nd step. When the procedure is finished successfully, it sets $\mathsf{cert}_n \leftarrow (A_n, t_n)$, $\mathsf{sec}_n \leftarrow x_n' + \rho = x_n$ where ρ is unknown. It then appends $(n, \perp, \mathsf{cert}_n, \mathsf{sec}_n)$ to state. Finally, it adds i into U^b.
- $Q_{sig}(i, m)$. If $i \in U^b$, $\mathcal{B}$ extracts $\mathsf{cert}_i = (A_i, t_i)$ and $\mathsf{sec}_i = x_i' + \rho$ from state. Then it chooses $r_1, r_2, r_3 \xleftarrow{R} \mathbb{Z}_p^*$, and sets $T_1, \ldots, T_5$ as follows :

$$T_1 \leftarrow r_1 X, \quad T_2 \leftarrow r_2 Y, \quad T_3 \leftarrow A_i + (r_1 + r_2) Z,$$
$$T_4 \leftarrow r_3 W, \quad T_5 \leftarrow e(x_i' P_1 + S, T_4) = e((x_i' + \rho) P_1, T_4) = e(P_1, T_4)^{x_i} \quad .$$

And then it simulates Protocol 1 and get a signature σ. This is possible because Protocol 1 has a simulator. Also, it sets Sigs $\leftarrow$ Sigs$||(i,\sigma)$. Note that the value c which is selected by the simulator during simulation must be stored in the hash oracle such that the hash oracle should keep the random oracle property.

Let $(m, \sigma_1^*, \tau_1^*)$ be a successful output of algorithm $\mathcal{A}$. Now we have three cases: (i) Open$(\sigma_1^*, \mathcal{Y}, \mathcal{S}) \in U^b$. Using the general forking lemma [14], $\mathcal{B}$ can get another pair (m, σ_2^*) which is also valid. Moreover with the knowledge extractor in Protocol 1, an SDH representation $(\tilde{A}, \tilde{x}, \tilde{t})$ used in signing m can be extracted. Let $i \in U^b$ be the result of Open. Then, $\tilde{x}$ is equal to sec$_i$, which means $\tilde{x} = x_i' + \rho$. Therefore $\mathcal{B}$ can find ρ. In the second case we have: (ii) $\bigvee_{i \in U^b}$ Trace$(\sigma_1^*, \text{Reveal}(i)) = 1$. It can also extract an SDH representation $(\tilde{A}, \tilde{x}, \tilde{t})$ using a similar method to the case (i). We get also here $\tilde{x} = \text{sec}_i = x_i' + \rho$. Therefore $\mathcal{B}$ can find ρ. In the final case we have: (iii) $(\bigvee_{i \in U^b}(i, \sigma_1^*) \in \text{Sigs}) \wedge (\text{Claim\_Verify}(\sigma_1^*, \tau_1^*) = 1)$ Using the general forking lemma [14], $\mathcal{B}$ can get another proof τ_2^* for σ_1^*. Then with a knowledge extractor (actually it is a subpart of the extractor in Protocol 1), a secret $\tilde{x}$ used for claim can be extracted. Let i be such that $(i, \sigma_1^*) \in \text{Sigs}$. Then, we have $\tilde{x} = \text{sec}_i = x_i' + \rho$. Therefore $\mathcal{B}$ can find ρ.   □

Lemma 8. *Under the assumption of semantic security of Linear encryption, our scheme is secure against anonymity attacks.*

Proof. Let $\mathcal{A}$ be an adversary that violates security against anonymity. We construct an algorithm $\mathcal{B}$ which breaks the semantic security of Linear encryption using the attacker $\mathcal{A}$. $\mathcal{B}$ is given $X, Y, Z \in \mathbb{G}_1$ as input which are a public key for Linear encryption, and tries to break the semantic security of this encryption scheme.

We assume $\mathbb{G}_1$ is a group such that $\mathcal{G} = (p, \mathbb{G}_1, \mathbb{G}_2, \mathbb{G}_T, P_1, P_2, e)$ is easily obtained. $\mathcal{B}$ selects $Q \xleftarrow{R} \mathbb{G}_1$ and $R \leftarrow \gamma P_2$ where $\gamma \xleftarrow{R} \mathbb{Z}_p^*$. It also selects $W \xleftarrow{R} \mathbb{G}_2$, and set $\mathcal{Y}$ to $(\mathcal{G}, Q, R, W, X, Y, Z)$. $\mathcal{B}$ simulates oracles allowed to $\mathcal{A}$ as follows.

- $Q_{\mathcal{Y}}()$. $\mathcal{B}$ returns n and $\mathcal{Y}$.
- $Q_{\text{p-join}}()$. $\mathcal{B}$ increments n by one, and chooses $A \xleftarrow{R} \mathbb{G}_1$ and $t, x \xleftarrow{R} \mathbb{Z}_p^*$. It sets cert$_n \leftarrow (A, t)$, sec$_n \leftarrow x$. It then sets state $\leftarrow$ state $||(n, \perp, \text{cert}_n, \text{sec}_n)$ and transcripts $\leftarrow$ transcripts$||(n, \perp)$. Also, $\mathcal{B}$ adds n into U^p.
- $Q_{\text{t-join}}()$. $\mathcal{B}$ generates an SDH representation (A_j, x_j, t_j) for $(\mathcal{G}, Q, R)$ which is possible because it knows γ, and then gives (cert$_n = (A_j, t_j)$, sec$_n = x_j$) to $\mathcal{A}$. It sets state $\leftarrow$ state $||(n, \perp, \text{cert}_n, \text{sec}_n)$ and transcripts $\leftarrow$ transcripts$||(n, \perp)$. Also, $\mathcal{B}$ adds n into U^a.
- $Q_{\text{sig}}(i, m)$. If $i \notin U^p$, $\mathcal{B}$ returns "fail" to $\mathcal{A}$. If $i \in U^p$, $\mathcal{B}$ finds cert$_i = (A_i, t_i)$ and sec$_i = x_i$ from state, and encrypts A_i using the given public key (X, Y, Z). The resulting cipher-text will be T_1, T_2, T_3, and then it sets $T_4 \leftarrow r_3 W, T_5 \leftarrow e(P_1, T_4)^{x_i}$ where $r_3 \xleftarrow{R} \mathbb{Z}_p^*$. It simulates Protocol 1 to generate a signature. This is possible because Protocol 1 has a simulator.

Table 1. Comparison of number of operations and signature length (in bytes)

		KTY	Nguyen et al.	Ours
	exponentiations	19	11	6
sign	scalar multiplications	0	19	10
	pairing computations	0	1	1
	exponentiations	17	6	7
verify	scalar multiplications	0	14	8
	pairing computations	0	3	3
	signature length	1206	917	362

Also, it sets Sigs ← Sigs$||(i, \sigma)$. Note that the value c which is selected by the simulator during simulation must be stored in the hash oracle such that the hash oracle should keep the random oracle property.
- $Q_{reveal}(i)$. $\mathcal{B}$ searches $sec_i = x_i$ from state, and returns $x_i P_1$. It also adds i into Revs.

When $\mathcal{A}$ returns i_0 and i_1 to $\mathcal{B}$ as a challenge after play stage, $\mathcal{B}$ returns A_{i_0} and A_{i_1} as a challenge. $\mathcal{B}$ will be given the cipher-text (T_1', T_2', T_3') of A_{i_b}, where b is unknown. It generates a signature σ' containing (T_1', T_2', T_3') using a simulator for Protocol 1, and the value c must also be stored in a hash oracle. It returns σ' to $\mathcal{A}$. Let b^* be the output of $\mathcal{A}$ after the guess stage. $\mathcal{B}$ returns b^*. If $\mathcal{A}$ breaks anonymity, then it is obvious that $\mathcal{B}$ also breaks semantic security. □

As a result of the lemmas we conclude the following:

Theorem 3. *Under the q-SDH assumption, infeasibility of discrete logarithm in $\mathbb{G}_1$, and the semantic security of Linear encryption, our traceable signature scheme is secure provided that the number of joined users is less than or equal to q .*

7   Efficiency

In this section we compare our scheme with previous schemes in terms of the signature length and the number of important operations such as exponentiations, scalar multiplications and pairing computations. We summarize the result in Table 1. we did not include pre-computable operations such as $e(P_1, P_2)$ in the number of pairing computations. While the numbers of operations are comparable in the three schemes, the signature length of our scheme is much shorter than those of the previous schemes.

8   Conclusion

We presented a traceable signature scheme based on Strong Diffie-Hellman and Decision Linear Diffie-Hellman assumptions. The scheme uses bilinear pairings, and we get a signature under 400 bytes when any of the curves in [6] are used. We have proved the correctness and security of our scheme.

References

1. M. Abdalla, J. An, M. Bellare, and C. Namprepre. From identification to signatures via the Fiat-Shamir transform: Minimizing assumptions for security and forward-security. *EUROCRYPT 2002, LNCS, Springer.*
2. G. Ateniese, J. Camenisch, S. Hohenberger, and B. Medeiros. Practical Group Signatures without Random Oracles. *Cryptology ePrint Archive, Report 2005/385, http://eprint.iacr.org/.*
3. G. Ateniese, J. Camenisch, M. Joye, and G. Tsudik. A practical and provably secure coalition-resistant group signature scheme. *Crypto 2000, LNCS, Springer.*
4. D. Boneh, X. Boyen. Short Signatures Without Random Oracles. *EUROCRYPT 2004, LNCS, Springer.*
5. D. Boneh, X. Boyen, and H. Shacham. Short Group Signatures. *Crypto 2004, LNCS, Springer.*
6. D. Boneh, B. Lynn, and H.Shacham. Short signatures from Weil pairing. *Asiacrypt 2001, LNCS, Springer.*
7. M. Bellare, D. Micciancio, and B.Warinshci. Foundations of group signatures: Formal definitions, siimplified requirements, and a construction based on general assumptions. *EUROCRYPT 2003, LNCS, Springer.*
8. M. Bellare, H. Shi, C. Zhang. Foundations of group signatures: The case of dynamic groups. *Cryptology ePrint Archive, Report 2004/077, http://eprint.iacr.org/.*
9. X. Boyen and B. Waters. Compact Group Signatures Without Random Oracles. *Cryptology ePrint Archive, Report 2005/381, http://eprint.iacr.org/.*
10. J. Camenisch. Efficient and generalized group signatures. *EUROCRYPT 1997, LNCS, Springer.*
11. D. Chaum and E. van Heyst. Group signatures. *EUROCRYPT 1991, LNCS, Springer.*
12. A. Fiat and A. Shamir. How to prove yourself: Practical solutions to identification and signature problems. *Crypto 1986, LNCS, Springer.*
13. A. Kiayias, Y. Tsiounis, and M. Yung. Traceable Signatures. *EUROCRYPT 2004, LNCS, Springer.*
14. A. Kiayias and M. Yung. Group signatures: Efficient constructions and annymity from trapdoor-holders. *Cryptology ePrint Archive, Report 2004/076. http://eprint.iacr.org/.*
15. A. Miyaji, M. Nakabayashi, and S. Takano. New explicit conditions of elliptic curve traces for FR-reduction. *IEICE Trans. Fundamentals, E84-A(5):1234-43, May 2001.*
16. L. Nguyen and R. Safavi-Naini. Efficient and Provably Secure Trapdoor-free Group Signatures Schemes from Bilinear Pairings. *Asiacrypt 2004, LNCS, Springer.*
17. D. Pointcheval and J. Stern. Security arguments for digital signatures and blind signatures. *Journal of Cryptology, 13(3):361-396, 2000.*
18. K. Rubin and A. Silverberg. Supersingular Abelian varieties in cryptology. *Crypto 2002, LNCS, Springer.*
19. C. Schnorr. Efficient signature generation by smart cards. *Journal of Cryptology, 4(3):161-174, 1991.*

Ring Signature with Designated Linkability

Joseph K. Liu[1], Willy Susilo[2], and Duncan S. Wong[3,*]

[1] Department of Computer Science
University of Bristol
Bristol, BS8 1UB, UK
liu@cs.bris.ac.uk
[2] Centre for Information Security Research
School of Information Technology and Computer Science
University of Wollongong
Wollongong 2522, Australia
wsusilo@uow.edu.au
[3] Department of Computer Science
City University of Hong Kong
Hong Kong, China
duncan@cityu.edu.hk

Abstract. Ring signatures enable a user to sign a message so that a ring of possible signers is identified, without revealing exactly which member of that ring actually generated the signature. This concept has been used to construct new cryptographic applications, such as designated signatures, concurrent signatures, etc. To avoid being abused, the concept of *linkable* ring signatures was introduced. In this concept, when two ring signatures are produced by the same signer, then anyone can *link* the signatures. In this paper, we introduce a new concept called *linkable ring signature with designated linkability* that lies between the two. In this new concept, the ring signatures remain anonymous from the public's point of view. However, they can *only* be *linked* by a designated party, whenever necessary. This notion allows the privacy of the signer, but additionally, it also limits the receiver from being abused. We present a generic construction for such schemes, and proceed with an instantiation of our generic construction that is built from the existing linkable ring signature scheme due to Liu *et al.*

Keywords: ring signature, linkable ring signature, spontaneous group signature.

1 Introduction

The ability to communicate anonymously is requisite for any privacy preserving interactions, in particular in the applications on the Internet era. The are many cryptographic primitives proposed in the literature for supporting anonymity. Among these protocols, ring signature [19] is one of the fundamental primitives

---

* The author was supported by a grant from CityU (Project No. 9360087).

H. Yoshiura et al. (Eds.): IWSEC 2006, LNCS 4266, pp. 104–119, 2006.

that is promising to solve this problem. Ring signature schemes allow a signer to generate a signature on behalf of the group of users in such a way that everyone can be sure that the signature is generated by one of the group members, but no one can identify who the signer is. Unlike group signature [8], there is no group manager. Thus the group formation of ring signature is spontaneous, or setup-free. Moreover, no one is able to revoke anonymity. The privacy is even stronger than group signature.

However, sometimes too strong anonymity is not suitable for some applications. For example, ring signatures can be abused as explained in [16]. Liu *et al.* addressed this issue by proposing a new notion of linkable ring signature. In this notion, the identity of the signer in a ring signature remains anonymous, but two ring signatures can be linked if they are signed by the same signer. Linkable ring signatures are suitable in many different practical applications, such as e-voting and e-cash [20]. Original ring signatures cannot be used for e-voting because any double votes cannot be detected as they are unlinkable. No one is able to find out whether any two signatures (with two votes) are generated by the same voter or not. Linkable ring signatures solve this problem by allowing the public to detect for any signer producing two or more signatures (votes).

Note that linkability is compulsorily embedded into the signature instead of voluntarily added in linkable ring signatures. If the signer refuses to add the correct linking information, the whole signature is invalid. In other words, linkability is enforced by the verifier. The signer cannot decline to do so. This is different from voluntarily added linkability. In this case, whether allowing the signature to be linked or not can be decided by the signer. This issue is also explained in [16].

Since the introduction of linkable ring signature, it remains unknown if the signers can actually control on *who* can determine linkability. Conventional linkable ring signature allows the public to do so and the signers have no control on it. In some situations, we require the linkability feature to be controllable. By "controllable", we mean that the linkability can only be performed by a designated party, and *not* by everyone. Consider the following example for this situation.

We re-consider the scenario of leaking a secret as suggested in [19]. A member of CIA agents solicits information to the press. To ensure that the information is valid, the information must satisfy the following conditions: 1) it is signed by a CIA member (without any necessity to know who the signer is), 2) it is verified that the signature has been constructed correctly by one of the group member, and 3) to avoid being abused, the signature can be linked by a designated party only. In this example, the signature produced by the CIA member must be verifiable by anyone, but the signature can be linked *only* by the press media, to convince the media that the secret is leaked by the same person since the movement maybe continue from time to time. In this situation, we cannot employ a group signature, since they require a group manager to do the setup stage and key distribution. A standard ring signature is also not suitable, since the media is not able to determine whether a serial of secret information is leaked by the same person or not. Unfortunately, we cannot directly employ the notion of linkable ring signature either, since the linking ability should *not* be conducted by anyone, *except* a designated party (the press media). Otherwise, it gives CIA more information in finding out the member who leaks the secret many times. (They may use some non-cryptographic method to do so, if they know that different secret information is in fact leaked by the same person.)

1.1   Our Contribution

In this paper, we answer the above question affirmatively by proposing the notion of *ring signature with designated linkability*. In the new notion, the linkability feature can only be conducted by a designated party, and we generalize this by having *t-out-of-n* users who are designated to *link* signatures. We present a generic construction for such schemes, and we proceed with a specific instantiation of the generic construction based on Liu *et al.*'s linkable ring signature scheme.

1.2   Related Work

Ring signature was formalized by Rivest *et al.* [19] in 2001 although the concept was first suggested by Cramer *et al.* [13] in 1994. A number of variants were proposed later, including threshold [5,22,17,10], identity-based [23,10,11], constant size [14], blind ring signature [7] and improved security [4,12].

The notion of linkable ring signature was first proposed by Liu *et al.* [16] in 2004. Their construction is based on the ring signature scheme by Abe *et al.* [1]. A separable and threshold linkable ring signature scheme was proposed later on by Tsang *et al.* [21]. Separability allows different users to choose their own type of keys. It also provides a threshold option. Tsang and Wei [20] proposed another scheme on linkable ring signature which achieves a constant size signature length independent of the number of users involved in the ring. Liu and Wong [18] proposed an enhanced security model on linkable ring signature scheme. They also provided two instantiations. Recently, an identity-based linkable ring signature scheme [2] is proposed, which is based on the strong RSA assumption.

1.3   Paper Organization

The rest of the paper is organized as follows. We specify the security models of a linkable ring signature scheme with designated linkability in Sec. 2. A generic construction is then given in Sec. 3. It is followed by a specific instantiation of the generic scheme in Sec. 4. Finally we conclude the paper in Sec. 5.

2   Security Models

In this section, we give a formal definition of a ring signature scheme with designated linkability and then specify the security requirements of such a scheme.

2.1   Syntax

A $(1, n)$-*linkable ring signature scheme with* (t', n')-*designated linkability* is a quadruple $(Gen, Sig, Ver, Link)$ of polynomial-time algorithms. The first two algorithms are randomized.

Key Generation $(x, y) \leftarrow Gen(1^k)$ takes a security parameter $k \in \mathbb{N}$ and outputs a private key x and a public key y.

Signature Generation $\sigma \leftarrow Sig(1^k, n, t', n', x, L, L', m)$ takes security parameter k, integers $n, t', n' \in \mathbb{N}$ such that $t' \le n'$, private key x, an n-element set L of public keys including the one corresponding to x, an n'-element set L' of public keys, and a message m, and outputs a signature σ. Each of n and n' are considered to be some polynomial in k.

Signature Verification $1/0 \leftarrow Ver(1^k, n, t', n', L, L', m, \sigma)$ is a Boolean algorithm which takes k, n, t', n', L, L', m, (as in Sig) and signature σ, returns 1 or 0 for accept or reject, respectively.

Signature Linking $1/0 \leftarrow Link(1^k, n, t', n', L, L', \mathcal{D}_{t'}, m_1, m_2, \sigma_1, \sigma_2)$ takes security parameter k, integers n, t', n', n-element set L of public keys, n'-element set L' of public keys, t'-element set $\mathcal{D}_{t'}$ of private keys, messages m_1, m_2, and signatures σ_1, σ_2, such that $Ver(1^k, n, t', n', L, L', m_1, \sigma_1) = 1$ and $Ver(1^k, n, t', n', L, L', m_2, \sigma_2) = 1$, returns 1 or 0 for linked or unlinked, respectively.

Signature Correctness. We require that for any message $m \in \{0, 1\}^*$, any n-element public key set L that includes the public key corresponding to x, and any n'-element public key set L', provided that all keys in L and L' are generated by Gen,

$$Ver(1^k, n, t', n', L, L', m, Sig(1^k, n, t', n', x, L, L', m)) = 1$$

where $1 \le t' \le n'$.

Linking Correctness. We require that for any messages $m_1, m_2 \in \{0, 1\}^*$, any n-element public key set L, and any n'-element public key set L', provided that all keys are generated by Gen, and any $\sigma_1 \leftarrow Sig(1^k, n, t', n', x_1, L, L', m_1)$, $\sigma_2 \leftarrow Sig(1^k, n, t', n', x_2, L, L', m_2)$ such that the corresponding public keys of x_1 and x_2 are in L respectively, any t'-element private key set $\mathcal{D}_{t'}$ such that the corresponding public keys are in L',

$$Link(1^k, n, t', n', L, L', \mathcal{D}_{t'}, m_1, m_2, \sigma_1, \sigma_2) = \begin{cases} 1 & \text{if } x_1 = x_2 \\ 0 & \text{otherwise.} \end{cases}$$

Discussions. In the specification above, n represents the 'ring' size of the ring signature. It corresponds to the set L which contains the signers who can generate a signature on behalf of the signers in L. n' is the number of users in L' who can determine the linkability of any two signatures generated by some signer in L. Intuitively, we require that at least t' users in L' have to work jointly in order to determine the linkability. We emphasize on the requirement of having a threshold number of users collaborate before being able to determine the linkability because this feature affects significantly on the privacy of the signer. This is one of the major differences between the original linkable ring signature and our notion (with designated linkability). In the original linkable ring signature, anyone (the public) can determine linkability.

Also note that L and L' can be chosen independently. The 'ring' L can be entirely different from the group L' of users who are responsible for determining linkability. It can also be the case that L and L' are coupled together. The relationship between L and L' should be determined by the target applications. In our definition above and construction in the later part of this paper, we consider the general setting of them. This is another major difference between the original linkable ring signature and ours.

2.2   Security Requirements

The security of a $(1, n)$-linkable ring signature with (t', n')-designated linkability has three aspects: unforgeability, signer anonymity and linkability.

Unforgeability.   Consider a *universal* set of public keys denoted by $\mathcal{U} = \{y_1, \cdots, y_N\}$. Assume that each public key in $\mathcal{U}$ is generated by Gen and N is some polynomial in security parameter k. To capture adaptive chosen message attack, we provide the adversary a signing oracle $\mathcal{SO}$. $\mathcal{SO}(\hat{L}, \hat{L}', t', \hat{m})$ takes an n-element subset $\hat{L}$ and an n'-element subset $\hat{L}'$ of $\mathcal{U}$, an integer t' such that $1 \leq t' \leq n'$, and message $\hat{m}$, produces a signature $\hat{\sigma}$ such that $Ver(1^k, \hat{n}, \hat{t}', \hat{n}', \hat{L}, \hat{L}', m', \sigma') = 1$.

Definition 1 (Existential Unforgeability against Chosen Message and Public Key Attacks).   *A $(1, n)$-linkable ring signature scheme with (t', n')-designated linkability is unforgeable if, for any probabilistic polynomial-time algorithm $\mathcal{A}$ with signing oracle $\mathcal{SO}$, it is negligible in k that $(L, L', t', m, \sigma) \leftarrow \mathcal{A}^{\mathcal{SO}}(1^k, \mathcal{U})$ such that $Ver(1^k, n, t', n', L, L', m, \sigma) = 1$, where $L, L' \subseteq \mathcal{U}$, $|L| = n$, $|L'| = n'$, $1 \leq t' \leq n'$, and $m \in \{0, 1\}^*$. Restriction is that (L, m) should not be in the set of oracle queries between $\mathcal{A}$ and $\mathcal{SO}$.*

Signer Anonymity.   Our definition is based on an enhanced model for the original linkable ring signature due to Liu and Wong [18]. When compared with the original model in [16], their enhanced model allows the adversary to corrupt ring members (i.e. obtaining their private keys), adaptively obtain signatures from $\mathcal{SO}$ and choose a ring of possible signers to challenge. Below are the details.

Consider an experiment with two stages: choose and guess. In the choose stage, an adversary $\mathcal{A}$ with signing oracle $\mathcal{SO}$ chooses two subsets L and L' of $\mathcal{U}$ and a message $m \in \{0, 1\}^*$, where L is to define the ring members and L' is to define the designated parties for determining linkability. This is denoted by

$$(L, L', n, n', t', m, State) \leftarrow \mathcal{A}^{\mathcal{SO}}(1^k, \mathcal{U}, \mathsf{choose})$$

where *State* is some state information which can be passed to the guess stage, $L, L' \subseteq \mathcal{U}$, $|L| = n$, $|L'| = n'$, and $1 \leq t' \leq n'$. Let $L = \{y_{i_1}, \cdots, y_{i_n}\}$. In the guess stage, $\mathcal{A}$ is given access to not only the signing oracle $\mathcal{SO}$, but also a corruption oracle $\mathcal{CO}$. $\mathcal{CO}(\pi')$ takes as input any $\pi' \in \{i_1, \cdots, i_n\}$ and returns the private key $x_{\pi'}$ corresponding to the public key $y_{\pi'} \in L$. The objective of $\mathcal{A}$ in the guess stage is to determine the public key in L whose private key is used to generate a given signature σ which is properly generated with respect to m, L and L'. This is denoted by

$$\xi \leftarrow \mathcal{A}^{\mathcal{SO},\mathcal{CO}}(1^k, n, t', n', L, L', m, \sigma, State, \mathcal{U}, Priv_{N-n}, \text{guess})$$

where $\xi \in \{i_1, \cdots, i_n\}$ and $Priv_{N-n}$ is the set of private keys corresponding to the public keys in $\mathcal{U} \setminus L$. Below is the complete description of the experiment.

Experiment $\mathbf{Exp}_{\mathcal{A}}^{\text{anon}}(k, N)$
  For $i = 1, \cdots, N$, $(x_i, y_i) \leftarrow Gen(1^k)$ with fresh coin flips
  Set $\mathcal{U} = \{y_1, \cdots, y_N\}$
  $(L, L', n, n', t', m, State) \leftarrow \mathcal{A}^{\mathcal{SO}}(1^k, \mathcal{U}, \text{choose})$
  $\pi \overset{R}{\leftarrow} \{i_1, \cdots, i_n\}$, $\sigma \leftarrow Sig(1^k, n, t', n', x_\pi, L, L', m)$.
  $\xi \leftarrow \mathcal{A}^{\mathcal{SO},\mathcal{CO}}(1^k, n, t', n', L, L', m, \sigma, State, \mathcal{U}, Priv_{N-n}, \text{guess})$
  If $\mathcal{A}$ failed, the experiment halts with failure
  If $\mathcal{A}$ did not query $\mathcal{CO}$ with π then
        return 1 if $\xi = \pi$, otherwise return 0
  Else the experiment halts with failure
An experiment succeeds if it halts with no failure. We denote by

$$\mathbf{Adv}_{\mathcal{A}}^{\text{anon}}(k, N) = \Pr[\mathbf{Exp}_{\mathcal{A}}^{\text{anon}}(k, N) = 1 \mid \text{Experiment succeeds}] - \frac{1}{n - t}$$

the advantage of the adversary $\mathcal{A}$ in breaking the anonymity of a linkable ring signature scheme with designated linkability where t is the number of private keys that A has corrupted using $\mathcal{CO}$.

Definition 2 (Signer Anonymity). *A linkable ring signature scheme with designated linkability is signer anonymous if for any integer N, for any probabilistic polynomial-time adversary $\mathcal{A}$, the function $\mathbf{Adv}_{\mathcal{A}}^{\text{anon}}(\cdot, N)$ is negligible.*

Note that $\mathcal{A}$ can obtain signatures for any messages and subgroups of $\mathcal{U}$ by querying $\mathcal{SO}$. This also captures an attacking scenario where an adversary may try to find out the authorship of a signature instance through collecting signatures generated for different subgroups of $\mathcal{U}$ [18].

Designated Linkability. Usually similar approach as above, we specify three experiments for capturing the following attacks concerning designated linkability:

1. A group member generates two signatures such that $Link$ returns 0.
2. (Framing) After learning some signature and the identity of the group member who generates that signature, a different group member generates another signature such that $Link$ returns 1 on these two signatures.
3. A group of parties wants to determine the linkability of two signatures even when the group does not have enough private keys (i.e. smaller than t') with respect to L'.

The last item above is the only additional requirement when compared with the security requirements of a conventional linkable ring signature scheme.

Experiment $\mathbf{Exp}_{\mathcal{A}}^{\mathrm{link1}}(k, N)$

1. For $i = 1, \cdots, N$, $(x_i, y_i) \leftarrow Gen(1^k)$ with fresh coin flips;
2. set $\mathcal{U} = \{y_1, \cdots, y_N\}$;
3. $\pi \leftarrow \mathcal{A}^{\mathcal{SO}}(1^k, \mathcal{U}, \mathsf{choose})$ where $\pi \in \{1, \cdots, N\}$;
4. $(L, L', n, t', n', m_1, m_2, \sigma_1, \sigma_2) \leftarrow \mathcal{A}^{\mathcal{SO}}(1^k, x_\pi, \mathcal{U}, \mathsf{sign})$
    where $L, L' \subseteq \mathcal{U}$, $|L| = n$, $|L'| = n'$, $1 \le t' \le n'$, $y_\pi \in L$, and
    $Ver(1^k, n, t', n', L, L', m_i, \sigma_i) = 1$, for $i = 1, 2$;
5. if $(L, L', t', m_i, \sigma_i)$, $i = 1, 2$, are not in the set of oracle queries and replies
    between $\mathcal{A}$ and $\mathcal{SO}$ then
    return $1 - Link(1^k, n, t', n', L, L', \mathcal{D}_{t'}, m_1, m_2, \sigma_1, \sigma_2)$
        where $\mathcal{D}_{t'}$ is the set of t' private keys such that the corresponding
        public keys are in L';
6. else the experiment halts with failure.

The experiment above captures Attack 1. The adversary is only given one private key while it tries to produce two signatures which are determined to be unlinked by the algorithm **Signature Linking**.

Experiment $\mathbf{Exp}_{\mathcal{A}}^{\mathrm{link2}}(k, N)$

1. For $i = 1, \cdots, N$, $(x_i, y_i) \leftarrow Gen(1^k)$ with fresh coin flips;
2. set $\mathcal{U} = \{y_1, \cdots, y_N\}$;
3. $(L, L', n, t', n', \pi_1, m_1) \leftarrow \mathcal{A}^{\mathcal{SO}}(1^k, \mathcal{U}, \mathsf{choose_1})$
    where $L, L' \subseteq \mathcal{U}$, $|L| = n$, $|L'| = n'$, $y_{\pi_1} \in L$, $1 \le t' \le n'$;
4. $\sigma_1 \leftarrow Sig(1^k, n, t', n', x_{\pi_1}, L, L', m_1)$;
5. $\pi_2 \leftarrow \mathcal{A}^{\mathcal{SO}}(1^k, \mathcal{U}, L, L', t', \pi_1, m_1, \sigma_1, \mathsf{choose_2})$
    where $\pi_2 \in L \setminus \{\pi_1\}$;
6. $(m_2, \sigma_2) \leftarrow \mathcal{A}^{\mathcal{SO}}(1^k, \mathcal{U}, x_{\pi_2}, L, L', \pi_1, m_1, \sigma_1, \mathsf{sign})$
    such that $Ver(1^k, n, t', n', L, L', m_2, \sigma_2) = 1$;
7. if $(L, L', t', m_i, \sigma_i)$, $i = 1, 2$, are not in the set of oracle queries and replies
    between $\mathcal{A}$ and $\mathcal{SO}$ then
    return $Link(1^k, n, t', n', L, L', \mathcal{D}_{t'}, m_1, m_2, \sigma_1, \sigma_2)$
        where $\mathcal{D}_{t'}$ is the set of t' private keys such that the corresponding
        public keys are in L';
8. else the experiment halts with failure.

This experiment captures Attack 2. The adversary tries to generate a signature with a different signer from another one, while the two different signatures are linked.

Experiment $\mathbf{Exp}_{\mathcal{A}}^{\mathrm{link3}}(k, N)$

1. For $i = 1, \cdots, N$, $(x_i, y_i) \leftarrow Gen(1^k)$ with fresh coin flips;
2. set $\mathcal{U} = \{y_1, \cdots, y_N\}$;
3. $(L, L', n, t', n', \pi_0, \pi_1, m_0, m_1) \leftarrow \mathcal{A}^{\mathcal{SO}}(1^k, \mathcal{U}, \mathsf{choose_1})$
    where $L, L' \subseteq \mathcal{U}$, $|L| = n$, $|L'| = n'$, $y_{\pi_0}, y_{\pi_1} \in L$, $1 \le t' \le n'$;
4. $\sigma_0 \leftarrow Sig(1^k, n, t', n', x_{\pi_0}, L, L', m_0)$;

5. $b \xleftarrow{R} \{0,1\}$;
6. $\sigma_1 \leftarrow Sig(1^k, n, t', n', x_{\pi_b}, L, L', m_1)$;
7. $T \leftarrow \mathcal{A}^{\mathcal{SO}}(1^k, \mathcal{U}, n, t', n', L, L', \pi_0, \pi_1, m_0, m_1, \sigma_0, \sigma_1, \mathsf{choose}_2)$
   where $T \subseteq L'$ and $|T| < t'$;
8. $b' \leftarrow \mathcal{A}^{\mathcal{SO}}(1^k, \mathcal{U}, n, t', n', L, L', \pi_0, \pi_1, m_0, m_1, \sigma_0, \sigma_1, T, \mathcal{D}_T)$
   where $b' \in \{0,1\}$ and $\mathcal{D}_T = \{x_i\}_{i \in T}$;
9. if any of $(L, L', t', m_i, \sigma_i)$, $i = 0, 1$, is in the set of oracle queries and replies
   between $\mathcal{A}$ and $\mathcal{SO}$, the experiment halts with failure;
10. if $b' = b$, return 1; otherwise return 0.

The experiment above captures Attack 3. The adversary is only given strictly less than t' private keys of the designated parties. Two signatures are given to the adversary, with only 1/2 probability that they are linked. The adversary is to tell whether these two signatures are linked or not.

We denote by

$$\mathbf{Adv}_{\mathcal{A}}^{\mathrm{link}}(k, N) = \Pr[\mathbf{Exp}_{\mathcal{A}}^{\mathrm{link1}}(k, N) = 1 \mid \text{Experiment succeeds}] +$$
$$\Pr[\mathbf{Exp}_{\mathcal{A}}^{\mathrm{link2}}(k, N) = 1 \mid \text{Experiment succeeds}] +$$
$$(\Pr[\mathbf{Exp}_{\mathcal{A}}^{\mathrm{link3}}(k, N) = 1 \mid \text{Experiment succeeds}] - 1/2)$$

the advantage of the adversary $\mathcal{A}$ in breaking the linkability of a linkable ring signature scheme with designated linkability.

Definition 3 (Designated Linkability). *A linkable ring signature scheme has designated linkability if for any integer N, for any probabilistic polynomial-time adversary $\mathcal{A}$, the function $\mathbf{Adv}_{\mathcal{A}}^{\mathrm{link}}(\cdot, N)$ is negligible.*

Remark: In the security models of unforgeability and designated linkability above, the adversaries are not given any access to the corruption oracle. This essentially follows the original model of unforgeability given by Abe *et al.* [1] and the comparable model for linkability of linkable ring signature given by [16,18]. We adopt this *weaker* model because in our schemes described in the subsequent sections, we assume the existence of linkable ring signature schemes that are secure in the sense of those previously proposed models. We leave the security analysis of our schemes under the stronger model, that is, corruption oracle is also provided to adversaries in both unforgeability model and the designated linkability model, as our future work.

3   The Generic Construction

We now propose the generic construction of a $(1, n)$-ring signature scheme with (t', n')-designated linkability.

3.1   Basic Idea

A conventional linkable ring signature scheme [16,21,20,18] uses an *event-based linking tag* in such a way that a signer cannot generate two different tags for two different signatures in any particular event. The linking tag is attached to a signature so that the public can link a signer's signature with another signature generated by the same signer by simply examining the value of the associated tags.

The idea of our generic construction is to adopt the concept of event-based linking tag but change the method of tag examination so that at least t' out of n' designated users have to work together for doing so.

One obvious approach is to encrypt the linking tag using a threshold encryption algorithm. However, if we solely use threshold encryption, the signer can cheat by generating a fake linking tag since no one, except those designated users can decrypt and verify the validity of the linking tag. The public, however, cannot do the checking. Note that we still require the validity of the signature (including the validity of the linkability) to be publicly verifiable. For solving this problem, we need to do the threshold encryption while at the same time allowing the public to verify the following:

- the encrypted linking tag can only be decrypted by any t'-subset of a designated group of n' users; and
- the actual signer cannot generate fake linking tag.

These requirements can be satisfied by a combined use of some well-studied techniques in some special way.

3.2   Details

Let $\theta : \mathcal{E} \times G_1 \rightarrow G_2$ be a one-way homomorphic mapping family indexed by event $e \in \mathcal{E}$, where $\mathcal{E}$ is the event space and G_1, G_2 are some groups of the same order. For any $e \in \mathcal{E}$, define $\theta_e(s)$ by $\theta(e, s)$. Also define $\theta_e^{-1}(S)$ to be s such that $\theta(e, s) = S$. Assume that it is hard to determine $\theta_e^{-1}(S) \stackrel{?}{=} \theta_{e'}^{-1}(S')$, if e and e' are uniformly chosen at random from $\mathcal{E}$, and for some $S, S' \in G_2$.

For any integers $t', n' \in \mathbb{N}$ such that $1 \leq t' \leq n'$, let $\Lambda_{t',n'}^{\theta_e}$ be the share generation function of a verifiable secret sharing (VSS) scheme [9,15] that takes a secret $s \in G_1$ and produces n' shares $s_1, \cdots, s_{n'}$ (each of them is in G_1), $S = \theta_e(s)$, $C_i = \theta_e(s_i)$, $1 \leq i \leq n'$, and some auxiliary information aux^1. The VSS scheme ensures that any t' of the shares are enough to recover s, but it is computationally infeasible to recover s if only $t'-1$ shares or less are known. Let $\Phi_{t',n'}^{\theta_e}$ be the share verification function of the VSS scheme that takes $S, C_1, \cdots, C_n$ and aux, and outputs 1 or 0. If the output is 1, it implies that $\theta_e^{-1}(S) = s$, and $\theta_e^{-1}(C_i) = s_i$ for $i = 1, \cdots, n$. In other words, this is the verification of the n shares. Let $Construct_e$ be the secret *commitment* reconstruction function which takes inputs of any t' values of C_i's and aux to reconstruct S. Readers can consider the underlying VSS scheme to be the one described in [15].

We now start describing the scheme.

---

[1] If the scheme of [15] is used, the auxiliary information aux will be some $t'-1$ elements in G_2.

Key Generation. On input a security parameter $k \in \mathbb{N}$, the algorithm randomly picks $x \in_R G_1$, and then sets private key to x and public key $y := \theta_g(x)$ where $g \in \mathcal{E}$ is a public parameter chosen randomly but fixed throughout the generation of all the public key pairs used in the system.

Signature Generation. We use $\mathsf{Enc}_i(m)$ to denote the public key encryption function of a designated user (indexed by) i in L' on a plaintext m, and use $\mathsf{LRing}_{x_\pi, L, e'}(m)$ to denote a linkable ring signature signing function which takes a private key x_π and a set L of public keys with an event identity $e' \in \mathcal{E}$ on message m, and generates a linkable ring signature with a linking tag $\theta_{e'}(x_\pi)$ (to be precise, it takes the first component of x_π only). Let $\mathsf{LRingVer}_{L, e'}(m, \sigma')$ be the corresponding linkable ring signature verification function which outputs 1 if the signature σ' is a valid with respect to m and L.

Let $H : \{0, 1\}^* \to \mathcal{E}$ be a hash function. For security analysis, we consider H to behave as a random oracle [3]. The signature generation algorithm on message m is described as follows:

1. Set $e \leftarrow H(L)$ and call it the *real* event identity.
2. Randomly choose a *virtual* event identity $e' \in_R \mathcal{E}$ such that $e' \neq e$, and compute a *virtual* linking tag $\tilde{y}' \leftarrow \theta_{e'}(x_\pi)$.
3. Compute shares and associated information using the VSS scheme

$$(x_{\pi(1)}, \cdots, x_{\pi(n')}, S, C_1, \cdots, C_{n'}, aux) \leftarrow \Lambda_{t', n'}^{\theta_{e'}}(x_\pi),$$

   where $S = \theta_{e'}(x_\pi)$ and $C_i = \theta_{e'}(x_{\pi(i)})$, $1 \leq i \leq n'$. Since $S = \tilde{y}'$, we replace the occurrence of S with $\tilde{y}'$ in the rest of the scheme.
4. Compute ciphertext $E_i = \mathsf{Enc}_i(\theta_e(x_{\pi(i)}))$, for $1 \leq i \leq n'$. Note that we use the *real* event identity e here.
5. Construct a non-interactive Proof-of-Knowledge (PoK) to show that all E_i and C_i are formed correctly, for $1 \leq i \leq n'$, that is,

$$PK\{\alpha_i : \ E_i = \mathsf{Enc}_i(\theta_e(\alpha_i)) \ \wedge \ C_i = \theta_{e'}(\alpha_i)\}(m)$$

   (For the notation of the proof-of-knowledge protocol, we refer readers to [6]).
6. Compute a linkable ring signature $\sigma' \leftarrow \mathsf{LRing}_{x_\pi, L, e'}(m\|Trans)$ where $Trans$ is the non-interactive PoK in Step (5). Note that we use the virtual event identity e' here and therefore the linking tag of σ' is $\tilde{y}'$.

The signature is $\sigma(m) = (e', \sigma', \tilde{y}', E_1, C_1, \cdots, E_{n'}, C_{n'}, aux, Trans)$.

Signature Verification. Given a list of public keys L and a signature $\sigma(m)$ for message m in the format above, one can verify the signature as follows:

1. Verify if $\mathsf{LRingVer}_{L, e'}(m\|Trans, \sigma') = 1$.
2. Verify if $Trans$ is valid with respect to the non-interactive PoK as constructed in Step 5 of the signature generation above.
3. Verify if $\Phi_{t', n'}^{\theta_{e'}}(\tilde{y}', C_1, \cdots, C_{n'}, aux) = 1$.
4. Output accept if all verifications above are passed. Otherwise, output reject.

Signature Linking. To link two signatures, for each of the signatures, any t' of the n' verifiers corresponding to the public keys in L' first decrypt their corresponding ciphertexts E_i to obtain $\theta_e(x_{\pi(i)})$ and work together to reconstruct the linking tag $\theta_e(x_\pi)$ by applying $Construct_e$ on $\theta_e(x_{\pi(i)})$'s. If the linkable tags of the two signatures are the same, these verifiers will conclude that these signatures are generated by the same signer.

3.3   Security Analysis

Theorem 1. *The scheme proposed above satisfies the security requirements specified in Sec. 2.2 under the random oracle model [3] if the underlying linkable ring signature scheme LRing is unforgeable under the model of [1] and signer anonymous under the corresponding model of [18].*

Proof. (Sketch) We show its security in three aspects, namely **Unforgeability**, **Signer Anonymity** and **Designated Linkability**.

Unforgeability. It follows directly from the unforgeability of the underlying linkable ring signature scheme LRing under the model of [1]. The reason is that in Def. 1, the adversary is at most as powerful as the adversary in the unforgeability model defined by Abe et al. in [1]. The designated linkable ring signature scheme proposed above is therefore also unforgeable as it contains the linkable ring signature σ' generated by LRing as part of the signature.

Signer Anonymity. We argue signer anonymity part by part. The signature is $\sigma(m) = (e', \sigma', \tilde{y}', E_1, C_1, \cdots, E_{n'}, C_{n'}, aux, Trans)$. e' is uniformly distributed over $\mathcal{E}$. σ' is the signature generated by LRing which is signer anonymous under the model of [18], and the adversary in experiment $\mathbf{Exp}_{\mathcal{A}}^{anon}$ is at most as powerful as that in the corresponding model of [18]. We remain to analyze the remaining parts.

According to the configuration of experiment $\mathbf{Exp}_{\mathcal{A}}^{anon}$, without loss of generality, the adversary can obtain all the t' (or even n') private keys corresponding to the designated parties for determining linkability, as long as the actual signer's private key x_π is not corrupted. In other words, the adversary is able to obtain $\theta_e(x')$ from $\{E_i\}_{1 \le i \le n'}$, and $\theta_{e'}(x'')$ from $\{C_i\}_{1 \le i \le n'}$, where $e = H(L)$ while e' is uniformly chosen at random from $\mathcal{E}$ by the actual signer. Under the assumptions that H behaves as a random function [3] and it is hard to determine if $x' \overset{?}{=} x''$ from $\theta_e(x')$ and $\theta_{e'}(x'')$ (Sec. 3.2). Thus the signature is signer anonymous.

Note that $\mathcal{A}$ is able to tell whether user i is the actual signer, by testing whether $\tilde{y}' \overset{?}{=} \theta_{e'}(x_i)$ if it has the private key x_i. That is why we need to exclude those t possibility in our definition of signer anonymity.

Designated Linkability. According to the definition in Sec. 2.2, we investigate the security of our scheme in three experiments: $\mathbf{Exp}_{\mathcal{A}}^{link1}$, $\mathbf{Exp}_{\mathcal{A}}^{link2}$ and $\mathbf{Exp}_{\mathcal{A}}^{link3}$.

In $\mathbf{Exp}_{\mathcal{A}}^{link1}$, the adversary $\mathcal{A}$ is given only one private key x_π. It tries to produce two valid signatures such that they are unlinked.

Let $\sigma_{(i)}(m_{(i)}) = (e'_{(i)}, \sigma'_{(i)}, \tilde{y}'_{(i)}, E_{(i)}, C_{(i)}, \cdot)$ for $i = 1, 2$ be two valid signatures generated by $\mathcal{A}$ such that they are unlinked. Let $t_{(i)}$ be the reconstructed linking tag after decrypting the ciphertext components $E_{(i)}$'s from $\sigma_{(i)}$, for $i = 1, 2$. Since both signatures are unlinked, it implies that

$$t_{(1)} \neq t_{(2)} \tag{1}$$

According to the non-interactive PoK in Step (5) of the signature generation algorithm and the correctness of the underlying VSS, we have

$$t_{(i)} = \theta_e(x_{\pi_i}), \quad i = 1, 2. \tag{2}$$

and

$$\tilde{y}'_{(i)} = \theta_{e'_{(i)}}(x_{\pi_i}), \quad i = 1, 2. \tag{3}$$

for some private keys x_{π_1} and x_{π_2} whose public keys are included in L. Since θ is a deterministic function, from equation (1) and (2), we have

$$x_{\pi_1} \neq x_{\pi_2} \tag{4}$$

From equation (3) and (4), we have

$$\theta_{e'_{(1)}}^{-1}(\tilde{y}'_{(1)}) \neq \theta_{e'_{(2)}}^{-1}(\tilde{y}'_{(2)}). \tag{5}$$

$\tilde{y}'_{(1)}$ and $\tilde{y}'_{(2)}$ are the linking tag of the underlying linkable ring signature $\sigma'_{(1)}$ and $\sigma'_{(2)}$ respectively. From equation (5), it implies that the linkability security of the underlying linkable ring signature scheme is broken, since the adversary is only given one private key. Note that it is obvious that $\tilde{y}'_{(1)} \neq \tilde{y}'_{(2)}$ since $e'_{(1)} \neq e'_{(2)}$. However, a secure linkable ring signature scheme requires that the inverse of linking tag $\tilde{y}'_{(i)}$, that is, $\theta_{e'_{(i)}}^{-1}(\tilde{y}'_{(i)})$ should be the same as that for signature $\sigma'_{(i)}$, $i \in \mathbb{Z}$, generated by a single private key.

In $\mathbf{Exp}_{\mathcal{A}}^{\text{link2}}$, the adversary $\mathcal{A}$ is given a signature $\sigma_{(1)}$ generated by a private key x_{π_1} and then a private key x_{π_2} such that $x_{\pi_1} \neq x_{\pi_2}$. It tries to produce a valid signature $\sigma_{(2)}$ such that the two signatures are linked.

Assume it succeeds with non-negligible probability. We try to derive a contradiction to the fact that the adversary knows only one private key x_{π_2} which is equal to x_{π_1}. Let $t_{(i)}$ be the reconstructed linking tag by decrypting the ciphertext from $\sigma_{(i)}$, for $i = 1, 2$. Since $\sigma_{(1)}$ is generated according to the algorithm, we have

$$t_{(1)} = \theta_e(x_{\pi_1}) \tag{6}$$

Since both signatures are linked,

$$t_{(1)} = t_{(2)} \tag{7}$$

As $\sigma_{(2)}$ is a valid signature, using the above argument,

$$\theta_e^{-1}(t_{(2)}) = x \tag{8}$$

for some private key x whose public key is included in L. On the other side, we have

$$\theta_e(x_1) \neq \ldots \theta_e(x_{\pi_1-1}) \neq \theta_e(x_{\pi_1+1}) \neq \ldots \neq \theta_e(x_n) \neq t_{(1)} \tag{9}$$

From equation (8) and (9), we have

$$x = x_{\pi_1} \tag{10}$$

That is, $x_{\pi_1} = x_{\pi_2}$.

In $\mathbf{Exp}_{\mathcal{A}}^{\text{link3}}$, $\mathcal{A}$ is given two signatures and strictly less than t' private keys of the designated parties. It tries to tell whether two signatures are generated by the same signer or not, given that exactly half of the chance that the two signatures are linked.

Assume the underlying encryption scheme is secure. $\mathcal{A}$ cannot decrypt t' or more ciphertext and reconstruct $\theta_e(x_\pi)$ in both signatures. Obviously, $\tilde{y}'_{(1)} \neq \tilde{y}'_{(2)}$ since $e'_{(1)} \neq e'_{(2)}$. In addition, $\mathcal{A}$ cannot tell whether $\theta_{e'_{(1)}}^{-1}(\tilde{y}'_{(1)}) \overset{?}{=} \theta_{e'_{(2)}}^{-1}(\tilde{y}'_{(2)})$. $\tilde{y}'_{(1)}$ and $\tilde{y}'_{(2)}$ are indistinguishable to $\mathcal{A}$. The underlying linkable ring signatures $\sigma'_{(1)}$ and $\sigma'_{(2)}$ do not help either, since they are generated using different virtual events $e'_{(1)}$ and $e'_{(2)}$. Thus $\mathcal{A}$ needs to do a wild guess. The successful probability is negligibly greater than $1/2$. $\qquad\square$

4   A Specific Instantiation of Our Proposed Scheme

In this section, we give a concrete instantiation of the generic construction proposed above. The underlying linkable ring signature scheme is due to Liu et al. [16].

Let $G = \langle g \rangle$ be a group of prime order q such that the underlying discrete logarithm problem is intractable. Let $H_1 : \{0,1\}^* \to \mathbb{Z}_q$ and $H_2 : \{0,1\}^* \to G$ be some statistically independent cryptographic hash functions. We require that for any $\alpha \in \{0,1\}^*$, the discrete logarithm of $H_2(\alpha)$ to the base g in G is intractable. For $i = 1, \cdots, n$, each user i has a distinct public key y_i and a private key x_i such that $y_i = g^{x_i}$. Let $L = \{y_1, \cdots, y_n\}$ be the set of the n public keys of the ring included in the signature. For $j = 1, \cdots, n'$, each user j has a distinct public key y'_j and a private key x'_j such that $y'_j = g^{x'_j}$. All the private keys in the system are assumed to be chosen uniformly at random over $\mathbb{Z}_q$. Let $L' = \{y'_1, \cdots, y'_{n'}\}$ be the set of the n' public keys of the designated linkers (that is, any t' of them can determine the linkability of signatures with respect to L'.)

Signature Generation. For some message $m \in \{0,1\}^*$, a user (signer) indexed by π, where $1 \leq \pi \leq n$, uses his private key x_π and generates a $(1, n)$-ring signature with (t', n')-designated linkability, with respect to L as follows.

1. Compute the *real* event identity $e = H_2(L)$ and $\tilde{y} = e^{x_\pi}$.
2. Pick uniformly at random a *virtual* event identity $e' \in_R G$ and compute a virtual linking tag $\tilde{y}' = (e')^{x_\pi}$.

3. Randomly generate a polynomial $f(x) = \sum_{\ell=0}^{t'-1} a_\ell x^\ell$ of degree $(t'-1)$ over $\mathbb{Z}_q$ such that $f(0) = x_\pi$ (that is, $a_0 = x_\pi$). Compute $x_{\pi(j)} = f(j)$, for $j = 1, \ldots, n'$.

4. For $j = 1, \ldots, n'$, generate an ElGamal Encryption on plaintext $e^{x_{\pi(j)}}$. That is, compute the ciphertext $(A_j, B_j) = (g^{r_j}, y_i^{r_j} e^{x_{\pi(j)}})$ for some random $r_j \in_R \mathbb{Z}_q$.

5. For $j = 1, \ldots, n'$, compute $C_j = (e')^{x_{\pi(j)}}$. For $\ell = 1, \cdots, t'-1$, compute $\alpha_\ell = (e')^{a_\ell}$ where a_ℓ is the coefficient of the polynomial f. Let $aux = \alpha_1 \| \cdots \| \alpha_{t'-1}$.

6. For $j = 1, \ldots, n'$, construct a non-interactive proof-of-knowledge (PoK) on message m as follows:

$$PK\{(\lambda_j, \beta_j)_{1 \leq j \leq n'} : A_j = g^{\lambda_j} \wedge B_j = (y_j)^{\lambda_j} e^{\beta_j} \wedge C_j = (e')^{\beta_j}\}(m)$$

Let $\mathcal{T}$ be the concatenation of this non-interactive PoK and $(L', A_1, B_1, C_1, \ldots, A_{n'}, B_{n'}, C_{n'}, aux)$.

7. (Generate the signature) Pick uniformly at random $u \in_R \mathbb{Z}_q$, and compute

$$c_{\pi+1} = H_1(L, \mathcal{T}, \tilde{y}', m, g^u, (e')^u).$$

8. For $i = \pi+1, \cdots, n, 1, \cdots, \pi-1$, pick $s_i \in_R \mathbb{Z}_q$ and compute

$$c_{i+1} = H_1(L, \mathcal{T}, \tilde{y}', m, g^{s_i} y_i^{c_i}, (e')^{s_i} (\tilde{y}')^{c_i}).$$

9. Compute $s_\pi = u - x_\pi c_\pi \mod q$.

The signature is $\sigma_L(m) = (e', c_1, s_1, s_2, \cdots, s_n, \tilde{y}', \mathcal{T})$.

Signature Verification. On input a set of public keys L, a message m and a signature $\sigma_L(m) = (e', c_1, s_1, s_2, \cdots, s_n, \tilde{y}', \mathcal{T})$, the algorithm proceeds as follows.

1. For $i = 1, \cdots, n$, compute $z_i' = g^{s_i} y_i^{c_i}$, $z_i'' = (e')^{s_i} (\tilde{y}')^{c_i}$ and then $c_{i+1} = H_1(L, \mathcal{T}, \tilde{y}', m, z_i', z_i'')$ if $i \neq n$.

2. Check whether $c_1 \stackrel{?}{=} H_1(L, \mathcal{T}, \tilde{y}', m, z_n', z_n'')$. If not, reject.

3. (Verify the encryption) Compute $e = H_2(L)$ and verify the non-interactive PoK on $\mathcal{T}$. If it is not valid, reject.

4. (Verify the secret-sharing) For $j = 1, \ldots, n'$, check whether

$$C_j \stackrel{?}{=} \tilde{y}' \prod_{\ell=1}^{t'-1} (\alpha_\ell)^{j^\ell}$$

If all pass, output accept. Otherwise, output reject.

Signatures Linking. In order to link two signatures (corresponding to the same L), any t' out of n' users decrypt their corresponding ciphertext (A_j, B_j), for $j = 1, \ldots, t'$, to obtain $h^{x_{\pi(j)}}$ and work together to reconstruct h^{x_π}, which is the linking tag. If the linkable tag of any two signatures are the same, they are considered to be linked.

5   Conclusion

In this paper, we proposed a new concept called ring signature with designated linkability. The term "designated linkability" refers to a designated party who can *link* the ring signatures whenever required. In this paper, we generalize this concept by allowing the designated party to be a *t-out-of-n* recipients of the ring signatures. We presented a generic construction of such schemes, and proceed with an instantiation of our generic construction based on Liu *et al.* linkable ring signature scheme.

References

1. M. Abe, M. Ohkubo, and K. Suzuki. 1-out-of-n signatures from a variety of keys. In *Proc. ASIACRYPT 2002*, pages 415–432. Springer-Verlag, 2002. Lecture Notes in Computer Science No. 2501.
2. M. Au, J. K. Liu, P. P. Tsang, and D. S. Wong. A suite of id-based threshold ring signature schemes with different levels of anonymity. Cryptology ePrint Archive, Report 2005/326, 2005. `http://eprint.iacr.org/`.
3. M. Bellare and P. Rogaway. Random oracles are practical: A paradigm for designing efficient protocols. In *Proc. 1st ACM Conference on Computer and Communications Security*, pages 62–73. ACM Press, 1993.
4. A. Bender, J. Katz, and R. Morselli. Ring signatures: Stronger definitions, and constructions without random oracles. In *TCC 2006*, volume 3816 of *Lecture Notes in Computer Science*, pages 60–79. Springer, 2006.
5. E. Bresson, J. Stern, and M. Szydlo. Threshold ring signatures and applications to ad-hoc groups. In *Proc. CRYPTO 2002*, pages 465–480. Springer-Verlag, 2002. Lecture Notes in Computer Science No. 2442.
6. J. Camenisch and M. Stadler. Efficient group signature schemes for large groups. In *Proc. CRYPTO 97*, pages 410–424. Springer-Verlag, 1997. LNCS Vol. 1294.
7. T. Chan, K. Fung, J. Liu, and V. Wei. Blind spontaneous anonymous group signatures for ad hoc groups. In *ESAS 2004*, volume 3313 of *LNCS*, pages 82–94. Springer-Verlag, 2004.
8. D. Chaum and E. van Heyst. Group signatures. In *EUROCRYPT '91*, volume 547 of *Lecture Notes in Computer Science*, pages 257–265. Springer, 1991.
9. B. Chor, S. Goldwasser, S. Micali, and B. Awerbuch. Verifiable secret sharing and achieving simultaneity in the presence of faults. In *Proc. 26th IEEE Symp. on Foundations of Comp. Science*, pages 383–395, Portland, 1985. IEEE.
10. S. Chow, L. Hui, and S. Yiu. Identity based threshold ring signature. In *ICICS 2004*, volume 3506 of *LNCS*, pages 218–232. Springer-Verlag, 2005.
11. S. Chow, S. Yiu, and L. Hui. Efficient identity based ring signature. In *ACNS 2005*, volume 3531 of *LNCS*, pages 499–512. Springer-Verlag, 2005.
12. S. S. M. Chow, J. K. Liu, V. K. Wei, and T. H. Yuen. Ring signatures without random oracles. In *ASIACCS 06*, pages 297–302. ACM, 2006.
13. R. Cramer, I. Damgård, and B. Schoenmakers. Proofs of partial knowledge and simplified design of witness hiding protocols. In *Proc. CRYPTO 94*, pages 174–187. Springer-Verlag, 1994. LNCS Vol. 839.
14. Y. Dodis, A. Kiayias, A. Nicolosi, and V. Shoup. Anonymous identification in ad hoc groups. In *EUROCRYPT 2004*, volume 3027 of *LNCS*, pages 609–626. Springer-Verlag, 2004.

15. P. Feldman. A practical scheme for non-interactive verifiable secret sharing. In *Proc. 28th IEEE Symp. on Foundations of Comp. Science*, pages 427–438, Los Angeles, 1987. IEEE.

16. J. Liu, V. Wei, and D. Wong. Linkable spontaneous anonymous group signature for ad hoc groups. In *ACISP04*, pages 325–335. Springer-Verlag, 2004. Lecture Notes in Computer Science No. 3108.

17. J. Liu, V. Wei, and D. Wong. A separable threshold ring signature scheme. In *ICISC 2003*, pages 12–26. Springer-Verlag, 2004. Lecture Notes in Computer Science No. 2971.

18. J. K. Liu and D. S. Wong. Linkable ring signatures: Security models and new schemes (extended abstract). In *ICCSA 2005*, volume 3481 of *LNCS*, pages 614–623. Springer-Verlag, 2005.

19. R. Rivest, A. Shamir, and Y. Tauman. How to leak a secret. In *Proc. ASIACRYPT 2001*, pages 552–565. Springer-Verlag, 2001. Lecture Notes in Computer Science No. 2248.

20. P. P. Tsang and V. K. Wei. Short linkable ring signatures for e-voting, e-cash and attestation. In *ISPEC 2005*, volume 3439 of *LNCS*, pages 48–60. Springer-Verlag, 2005.

21. P. P. Tsang, V. K. Wei, T. K. Chan, M. H. Au, J. K. Liu, and D. S. Wong. Separable linkable threshold ring signatures. In *INDOCRYPT 2004*, volume 3348 of *LNCS*, pages 384–398. Springer-Verlag, 2004.

22. D. Wong, K. Fung, J. Liu, and V. Wei. On the RS-code construction of ring signature schemes and a threshold setting of RST. In *5th Intl. Conference on Information and Communication Security (ICICS 2003)*, pages 34–46. Springer-Verlag, 2003. Lecture Notes in Computer Science No. 2836.

23. F. Zhang and K. Kim. ID-Based blind signature and ring signature from pairings. In *Proc. ASIACRYPT 2002*, pages 533–547. Springer-Verlag, 2002. Lecture Notes in Computer Science No. 2501.

Ad Hoc Group Signatures*

Qianhong Wu[1], Willy Susilo[1], Yi Mu[1], and Fangguo Zhang[2]

[1] Center for Information Security Research, SITACS
University of Wollongong, Wollongong NSW 2522, Australia
{qhw, wsusilo, ymu}@uow.edu.au
[2] School of Information Science and Technology
Sun Yat-sen University, Guangzhou 510275, P.R. China
isszhfg@mail.sysu.edu.cn

Abstract. The main advantage of ring signatures is to ensure anonymity in ad hoc groups. However, since a group manager is not present in ad hoc groups, there is no existing way to identify the signer who is responsible for or benefit from a disputed ring signature. In this paper, we address this issue by formalizing the notion of *ad hoc group signature*. This new notion bridges the gap between the ring signature and group signature schemes. It enjoys the same advantage of ring signatures to provide anonymity whilst not requiring any group manager. Furthermore, it allows a member in an ad hoc group to provably claim that it has (not) issued the anonymous signature on behalf of the group. We propose the *first* construction of ad hoc group signatures that is provably secure in the random oracle model under the Strong RSA assumption. Our proposal is very simple and additionally, it produces a *constant size* signature length and requires constant modular exponentiations. This is to ensure that our scheme is very practical for ad hoc applications where a centralized group manager is not present.

1 Introduction

Anonymity has been a main concern in cryptography for years. Group signatures and ring signatures are the most popular notions for providing anonymity.

1.1 Group Signatures

In a group signature, any group member is allowed to anonymously generate signatures on behalf of the group. In case of dispute, a trusted group manager can *open* the group signature to trace the true signer. Group signatures were first introduced and implemented by Chaum and van Heyst [8]. The state-of-the-art group signature is the notion of *traceable signature* [16] which enjoys better traceability: (1) Tracing a given user can be applied to all signatures by agents running in parallel; (2) The signer can provably claim a given group signature that it has signed. Currently, the most efficient group signatures are due to [5] in the random oracle model and [1, 6] in the standard model.

---

* This work is supported by ARC Discovery Grant DP0557493 and the National Natural Science Foundation of China (No. 60403007).

H. Yoshiura et al. (Eds.): IWSEC 2006, LNCS 4266, pp. 120–135, 2006.
© Springer-Verlag Berlin Heidelberg 2006

Ateniese and Medeiros proposed an efficient group signature scheme [2] that is *without trapdoor* in the sense that, the system trapdoor is only used during the initialization to generate system parameters. The advantage of this property is that the same trapdoor information can be used to initiate different groups. In [20], Tsudik and Xu proposed a group signature initiated with an RSA integer N whose factorization is unknown for none of parties. In [11], Dodis *et al.* also exploited such an RSA integer to setup their system. In this paper, we use the similar idea to make the system available for more applications.

1.2   Ring Signatures

A ring signature is an alternative mean to achieve anonymity for ad hoc groups *without* any trusted manager. It is used to convince any third party that *at least* one member in an ad hoc group has indeed issued the signature on behalf of the group. Since its introduction in [19], the notion of ring signatures has attracted a lot of attention [11, 17, 21, 22]. There are some natural extensions such as threshold ring signatures and linkable/unlinkable ring signatures. In (t, n)-threshold ring signatures, the generation of a ring signature requires the involvement of at least t of n members, and yet the signature reveals nothing about the identities of the signers [22]. Linkable ring signatures [17] allow anyone to determine whether two signatures are signed by the same member. If a user signs only once on behalf of a group, the user still enjoys anonymity similar to that in conventional ring signatures.

The notion of ring signatures is attractive due to the following properties: (1) *Set-up free.* Ring signatures require no managers to initialize the system. All signers publish their public keys to form a public-key list and, any player wishing to generate a ring signature later appends its own public key to the list and can generate a valid ring signature. (2) *Cooperation-free.* It refers to the capability of having a ring member to produce a ring signature for any message independently. Hence, a ring signature requires no interactions or cooperations among ring members provided that all the members' public keys are known.

While having a simple group formation set up as an advantage, the size of ring signatures linearly depends on the group size, as the verifier needs to know at least the group description. However, as remarked in [11], in many scenarios, the group does not change for a long time. Hence, an appropriate measurement of ring signature complexity *does not* need to include the cost to describe the group. All the early constructions of ring signatures suffer from linearly increasing complexity related to the number of group members. Subsequent results incorporating techniques from *cryptographic accumulators* have successfully reduced the size of a ring signature. The state-of-the-art ring signatures enjoying a constant cost independent of group size have been proposed in [11, 21].

1.3   Motivations

While achieving privacy without any group manager is an advantage, in case of dispute, the originator of ring signatures *cannot be identified* due to the absence of a group manager for revoking anonymity. Furthermore, for most existing schemes, the anonymity is unconditional in the sense that, given the secret keys of all the possible signers, one can not determine the true signer of a ring signature. Such perfect privacy comes at a price. Consider the following scenarios.

(1) *Untraceable criminal.* A policeman detects a ring signature involving a serious crime and submits the signature to a judge as a witness. However, even if the judge forces all the ring members to show their secret key, it cannot determine who the criminal is. Then, what decision should the judge make and who will be responsible for the crime? Indeed, perfect privacy implies perfect crime.

(2) *Dilemma of lottery players.* Lottery players tend to require anonymity protection for fear of blackmail in case of winning the giant prize, while trust no third party for fear that the party may leak their identities. Hence, it seems that ring signatures enjoying unconditional anonymity is very applicable to such applications by signing the lottery numbers. However, when the winning lottery number is selected, the unlucky winner who luckily chose the winning number cannot prove that it is the true winner even if it exposes its private signing key!

The two scenarios show that unconditional privacy seems to be an attractive notion from the user's view point, nevertheless it can potentially be a very troublesome tool against public safety and can even be abused against the user itself. In the first case, we need the security property that *any innocent group member* can prove that it *did not* generate a given anonymous signature without the help of a group manager or leaking its private key. If a ring signature scheme is deniable in the sense that a non-signer group member can disavow a given ring signature, then it can prevent criminals maliciously from abusing anonymity of ring signatures. Due to the ad hoc property of ring signatures, such a denying functionality is indeed essential to make ring signature practical for some applications. In the second case, we need the security that *the true signer* can prove that it *did* generate a given anonymous signature without the help of a group manger or leaking its private key.

Theoretically, the second property is implied by the first property since all the group members except the true signer can deny the signature and the true signer is identified. However, from the viewpoint of applications, such a traceability derived from denying functionality is useless as it requires all the other group members to cooperate to trace the true signer. On the one hand, the ad hoc group may be too large to enable all the group members to deny one by one. On the other hand, the group members may refuse to deny the signature if they are not the true signer, for example the losers in the lotteries system. Hence, it is useful to integrate such *self-traceability* into ring signatures in practice and bridge the gap between ring signatures and group signatures, so that it can enjoy the advantages of both ad hoc property of ring signatures and traceability of group signatures.

1.4   Contributions

The main contributions in this paper include a more general mathematical model, a new functional notion of ad hoc group signatures, practical implementations, and their applications.

Collision quasi-resistant accumulator. In previous models (e.g., [11, 20]), only primes and RSA integers are allowed to be accumulated. The extension allows to accumulate any integers. We also notice that in several previous accumulator-based group/ring signatures, random values were obliviously accumulated but not covered in their models. The extension captures and fixes this discordance between the general model and its concrete implementations.

Ad hoc group signatures. The new notion has the same advantages of ring signatures, i.e, setup free and cooperation free, except the unconditional anonymity (else it contradicts to the traceability of group signatures). Furthermore, it enables a group member to *provably claim* that a given signature was generated by it or not. It addresses the *ownership dispute* in case of emergency and provides a general fair mechanism of privacy for self-organized groups. By dicing the anonymity-revoking functionality of group signatures to the distributed members, rather than a centralized manager, the new notion provides a generic technique to remove the trusted third party such as a group manager from the privacy systems. It enjoys more flexibility and practicality.

Practical instantiations of ad hoc group signatures. Efficient implementations are proposed with provable security in the random oracle model under the standard Strong RSA assumption and the Decisional Factorization Diffie-Hellman assumption. After the group key is pre-computed, only several (less than 10) modular exponentiations are required to generate or verify the signature and the tracing arguments. The signature and the tracing argument are both about 4 standard RSA signatures in length. It outperforms the state-of-the-art ring signatures due to Dodis *et al.* [11]. We show efficient applications of the proposed schemes to electronic lotteries, where a player can prove that it is the winner without a third party. The schemes are simple and practical.

Organization of the Paper. The remaining of the paper is organized as follows. The new notion of ad hoc signatures and its security are formalized in Section 2. In Section 3, we provide some preliminaries, including the complexity assumption and the underlying mathematical model. Section 4 proposes practical ad hoc signature schemes and details their security and performance. We show some potential applications of self-traceable signatures to electronic lotteries in Section 5, followed by the conclusion in the last section.

2 Definition of Ad Hoc Group Signatures

An ad hoc group signature scheme is a tuple of nine procedures $AHGS$=(PG, MG, GG, Sig, SV, Own, OV, Dny, DV).

- $\mathcal{Y} \leftarrow$ PG(1^λ) is a probabilistic polynomial-time (PPT) algorithm which, on input a security parameter λ, outputs a public description of the system including system-wide parameters such as collision-resistant hash functions.
- $(sk_i, pk_i) \leftarrow$ MG(1^λ) is a PPT algorithm which, on input a security parameter λ, outputs a secret/public key pair (sk_i, pk_i). We denote by SK and PK the list of possible secret keys and public keys, respectively.

- $y \leftarrow \mathtt{GG}(\mathcal{Y}, PK)$ is a PPT algorithm which, on input the output $\mathcal{Y} \leftarrow \mathtt{PG}(1^\lambda)$ and all the possible public keys PK of ad hoc group members, outputs y as the public key of the ad hoc group.
- $\sigma \leftarrow \mathtt{Sig}_{sk_i}^{AHGS}(m)$ is a PPT algorithm which, on input a secret key sk_i and message m, produces a signature σ on m.
- $1/0 \leftarrow \mathtt{SV}^{AHGS}(\sigma, m, y)$ is a deterministic polynomial-time algorithm which, on input the ad hoc group public key y and a message-signature pair (m, σ), returns 1 or 0 for *Valid* or *Invalid*, respectively.
- $\dot{\sigma} \leftarrow \mathtt{Own}_{sk_i}^{AHGS}(\sigma, m)$ is a PPT algorithm which, on input a secret key sk_i and a message-signature pair (m, σ), produces an ownership witness $\dot{\sigma}$.
- $1/0 \leftarrow \mathtt{OV}^{AHGS}(\sigma, m, \dot{\sigma}, y)$ is a polynomial-time algorithm which, on input y, a message-signature pair (m, σ) and an ownership witness $\dot{\sigma}$, returns 1 or 0 for *Yes* or *Failure*, respectively representing that member i is the author of (m, σ) and there is a failure.
- $\ddot{\sigma} \leftarrow \mathtt{Dny}_{sk_i}^{AHGS}(\sigma, m)$ is a PPT algorithm which, on input a secret key sk_i and a message-signature pair (m, σ), outputs a denying witness $\ddot{\sigma}$.
- $1/0 \leftarrow \mathtt{DV}^{AHGS}(\sigma, m, \ddot{\sigma}, y)$ is a polynomial-time algorithm which, on input the ad hoc group public key y, a message-signature pair (m, σ) and a denying witness $\ddot{\sigma}$, returns 1 or 0 for *Not* or *Failure*, respectively representing that member i is not the author of (m, σ) and there is a failure.

Remark 1. Generally speaking, the ability of an ad hoc group member to provably claim the ownership of an ad hoc group signature does not imply it can provably claim an ad hoc group signature was not generated by a particular group member even if it really did not produce the signature. On the contrary, the ability to provide the disavowal witness may imply the ability to provide ownership witness. However, such a signer tracing procedure is impractical since the non-signers may refuse to deny the ownership of signatures or the group is too large to enable the non-signers to deny one by one. So we capture these different functionalities by respective definitions.

2.1   Model of Adversaries

We model the behaviors of adversary Ad with a series of queries to a challenger CH, who controls all the communication channels of Ad and will validly answer all the necessary queries from Ad.

- $\mathcal{Q}_{ran}$. Ad queries with its chosen string and CH returns a random string. It is the standard random oracle query.
- $\mathcal{Q}_{pub}$. Ad queries for the public parameters of the system and CH returns the string $< \lambda, \mathcal{Y}, PK, y >$. This allows Ad to learn the public information of the system, i.e., the number of users and the public-key information.
- $\mathcal{Q}_{join}$. Ad runs $(sk_j, pk_j) \leftarrow \mathtt{MG}(1^\lambda)$ and queries with (sk_j, pk_j). CH checks whether (sk_j, pk_j) is a valid key pair. If not, it returns *null*. Else, it adds pk_j to the public key list. Then, it returns the updated $< \lambda, \mathcal{Y}, PK, y >$ to Ad and update the corresponding local records of the system. This query action allows Ad to introduce a new user to the system.

- $\mathcal{Q}_{skey}$. Ad queries with $pk_i \in PK$. CH checks whether $pk_i \in PK$. If not, it returns *null*. Else, it returns sk_i corresponding to $pk_i \in PK$. This query action allows Ad to corrupt the group members.
- $\mathcal{Q}_{sign}$. Ad queries with its chosen message m. CH returns an ad hoc group signature σ on m such that $\mathsf{SV}^{AHGS}(\sigma, m, y) = 1$, where $\sigma \leftarrow \mathsf{Sig}_{sk_i}^{AHGS}(m)$ with sk_i corresponding to a random $pk_i \in PK$. This query action allows Ad to get valid ad hoc group signatures.
- $\mathcal{Q}_{link}$. Ad queries with two message-signature pairs (m, σ) and (m', σ'), where $\mathsf{SV}^{AHGS}(\sigma, m, y) = 1$ and $\mathsf{SV}^{AHGS}(\sigma', m', y) = 1$. CH returns $1/0$ representing the fact that σ and σ' were generated with the same secret key or not. This query action allows Ad to learn the relation between signatures.
- $\mathcal{Q}_{trace}$. Ad queries with a message-signature pair (m, σ) and an integer j satisfying $pk_j \in PK$. CH returns $\dot{\sigma} \leftarrow \mathsf{Own}_{sk_j}^{AHGS}(\sigma, m)$ if $\sigma \leftarrow \mathsf{Sig}_{sk_i}^{AHGS}(m)$ and $i = j$, or $\ddot{\sigma} \leftarrow \mathsf{Dny}_{sk_j}^{AHGS}(\sigma, m)$ if $i \neq j$. This query action allows Ad to learn the relation between signatures and signers.

2.2 Security Properties of Ad Hoc Group Signatures

We proceed to characterize the various security properties that an ad hoc group signature scheme should satisfy. These properties except the correctness are defined via a series of two-stage experiments Exp.

Definition 1. (Correctness.) *An AHGS is correct if, for any $\lambda, I = poly(\lambda) \in \mathbb{N}, i \neq j \in \{1, \cdots, I\}$, $\mathcal{Y} \leftarrow \mathsf{PG}(1^\lambda)$, $(sk_i, pk_i) \leftarrow \mathsf{MG}(1^\lambda)$, $PK = \{pk_1, \cdots, pk_I\}$, $y \leftarrow \mathsf{GG}(\mathcal{Y}, PK)$, $m \leftarrow \{0,1\}^*$, $\sigma \leftarrow \mathsf{Sig}_{sk_i}^{AHGS}(m)$, $\dot{\sigma} \leftarrow \mathsf{Own}_{sk_i}^{RS}(\sigma, m)$, $\ddot{\sigma} \leftarrow \mathsf{Dny}_{sk_j}^{AHGS}(\sigma, m)$, it holds that $\mathsf{SV}^{AHGS}(\sigma, m, y) = 1$, $\mathsf{OV}^{AHGS}(\sigma, m, \dot{\sigma}, y) = 1$, and $\mathsf{DV}^{AHGS}(\sigma, m, \ddot{\sigma}, y) = 1$ except a negligible probability in λ.*

Definition 2. (Unforgeability.) *In the first stage, CH initializes the game by running $\mathcal{Y} \leftarrow \mathsf{PG}(1^\lambda)$, $(sk_i, pk_i) \leftarrow \mathsf{MG}(1^\lambda)$ and $y \leftarrow \mathsf{GG}(\mathcal{Y}, PK)$. Then, Ad is allowed to ask all the above queries (in an adaptive fashion). At the end of the first stage, Ad is required to choose a public list PK and a message m, where $\mathcal{Q}_{skey}(pk)$ for any $pk \in PK$ has never been queried. In the second stage, Ad is also allowed to ask all the above queries (in an adaptive fashion) except $\mathcal{Q}_{skey}$. At the end of the second stage, Ad is required to forge a string $\tilde{\sigma}$ satisfying: (1) $\mathcal{Q}_{sign}(m)$ has never been queried; (2) $\mathsf{SV}^{AHGS}(\tilde{\sigma}, m, y) = 1$. If Ad completes the experiment, $\mathtt{Exp} = 1$. Else, $\mathtt{Exp} = 0$. An AHGS scheme is unforgeable if for any PPT Ad, $\Pr[\mathtt{Exp}_{Unf}^{Ad}(\lambda) = 1] < \varepsilon(\lambda)$, where $\varepsilon(\lambda)$ is a negligible function in λ.*

Definition 3. (Anonymity.) *The first stage is the same as that of the Unforgeability game. At the end of the first stage, CH sends Ad two public keys $pk_{i_0}, pk_{i_1} \in PK$ and Ad is required to choose a message m, where $\mathcal{Q}_{skey}(pk)$ for any $pk \in PK$ has never been queried. Then CH tosses a fair coin $b \leftarrow \{0,1\}$ and sends $\sigma_{i_b} \leftarrow \mathsf{Sig}_{sk_{i_b}}^{AHGS}(m)$ to Ad. In the second stage, Ad is also allowed to ask all the above queries (in an adaptive fashion) except $\mathcal{Q}_{trace}(\sigma_{i_b})$, $\mathcal{Q}_{skey}(pk_{i_0})$, $\mathcal{Q}_{skey}(pk_{i_1})$ and $\mathcal{Q}_{link}(\sigma_{i_b}, \sigma')$ for any valid signature σ'. At the end of the second* stage, Ad *is required to output a bit* $\hat{b}$. *If* $\hat{b} = b$, **Exp** $= 1$. *Else,* **Exp** $= 0$. *An AHGS scheme is anonymous if for any PPT* Ad, $|\Pr[\textbf{Exp}_{Anon}^{Ad}(\lambda) = 1] - 1/2| < \varepsilon(\lambda)$.

Definition 4. (Self-traceability.) *It is defined by the following three two-stage experiments* **Exp**.

Experiment 1. The first stage is the same as that of the Unforgeability game. At the end of the first stage, Ad *is required to choose a message* m *and a public key list* $PK = PK_i \cup PK_j$, *where* $\mathcal{Q}_{skey}(pk)$ *for any* $pk \in PK_i$ *has never been queried while* $\mathcal{Q}_{skey}(pk)$ *for any* $pk \in PK_j$ *has been queried. Then,* CH *sends* $\sigma \leftarrow \text{Sig}_{sk_i}^{AHGS}(m)$ *to* Ad, *where* sk_i *corresponds to* $pk_i \in PK_i$. *In the second stage,* Ad *is also allowed to ask all the above queries except* $\mathcal{Q}_{skey}(pk)$ *for any* $pk \in PK_i$, $\mathcal{Q}_{trace}(\sigma, m)$ *and* $\mathcal{Q}_{link}(\sigma, m; \sigma', m')$, *where* $\text{SV}^{AHGS}(\sigma', m', y) = 1$. *At the end of the second stage,* Ad *is required to output a string* $\mathring{\sigma}$ *such that* $\text{OV}^{AHGS}(\sigma, m, \mathring{\sigma}, y) = 1$. *If* Ad *completes the experiment,* **Exp** $= 1$. *Else,* **Exp** $= 0$.

Experiment 2. The first stage is the same as that of the Unforgeability game. At the end of the first stage, Ad *is required to choose a message* m, *a public key list* $PK = PK_i \cup PK_j$, *where* $\mathcal{Q}_{skey}(pk)$ *for any* $pk \in PK_i$ *has never been queried while* $\mathcal{Q}_{skey}(pk)$ *for any* $pk \in PK_j$ *has been queried, and a string* $\tilde{\sigma}$ *satisfying: (1)* $\mathcal{Q}_{sign}(m)$ *has never been queried; (2)* $\text{SV}^{AHGS}(\tilde{\sigma}, m, y) = 1$. *In the second stage,* Ad *is also allowed to ask all the above queries except* $\mathcal{Q}_{skey}(pk)$ *for any* $pk \in PK_i$, $\mathcal{Q}_{trace}(\tilde{\sigma}, m)$ *and* $\mathcal{Q}_{link}(\tilde{\sigma}, m; \sigma', m')$, *where* $\text{SV}^{AHGS}(\sigma', m', y) = 1$. *At the end of the second stage,* Ad *is required to output a string* $\mathring{\tilde{\sigma}}$ *such that* $\text{DV}^{AHGS}(\sigma, m, \mathring{\tilde{\sigma}}, y) = 1$. *If* Ad *completes the experiment,* **Exp** $= 1$. *Else,* **Exp** $= 0$.

Experiment 3. The first stage is the same as that of the Unforgeability game. At the end of the first stage, Ad *is required to choose a message* m, *a public key list* $PK = PK_i \cup PK_j$, *where* $\mathcal{Q}_{skey}(pk)$ *for any* $pk \in PK_i$ *has never been queried while* $\mathcal{Q}_{skey}(pk)$ *for any* $pk \in PK_j$ *has been queried, and a string* $\tilde{\sigma}$ *satisfying: (1)* $\mathcal{Q}_{sign}(m)$ *has never been queried; (2)* $\text{SV}^{AHGS}(\tilde{\sigma}, m, y) = 1$. *In the second stage,* Ad *is also allowed to ask all the above queries (in an adaptive fashion). At the end of the second stage,* Ad *is required to output a secret key* sk_i *corresponding to a public key* $pk_i \in PK_i$, *and a string* $\mathring{\tilde{\sigma}} \leftarrow \text{Dny}_{sk_i}^{AHGS}(\tilde{\sigma}, m)$ *it holds that* $\text{DV}^{AHGS}(\tilde{\sigma}, m, \mathring{\tilde{\sigma}}, y) = 0$. *If* Ad *completes the experiment,* **Exp** $= 1$. *Else,* **Exp** $= 0$.

An AHGS is self-traceable if for any PPT Ad, $\Pr[\textbf{Exp}_{Trace}^{Ad}(\lambda) = 1] < \varepsilon(\lambda)$.

Definition 5. (Unlinkability.) *The first stage is the same as that of the Unforgeability game. At the end of the first stage,* Ad *is required to choose two messages* m, m' *and two public keys* $pk_{i_0}, pk_{i_1} \in PK$, *where* $\mathcal{Q}_{skey}(pk_{i_0})$ *and* $\mathcal{Q}_{skey}(pk_{i_1})$ *have never been queried. Then* CH *tosses two fair coins* $b, \tilde{b} \leftarrow \{0, 1\}$. CH *sends* $\sigma_{i_b} \leftarrow \text{Sig}_{sk_{i_b}}^{AHGS}(m)$ *and* $\sigma_{i_{\tilde{b}}} \leftarrow \text{Sig}_{sk_{i_{\tilde{b}}}}^{AHGS}(m)$ *to* Ad. *In the second stage,* Ad *is also allowed to ask all the above queries except* $\mathcal{Q}_{link}(\sigma_{i_b}, m; \sigma_{i_{\tilde{b}}}, m')$, $\mathcal{Q}_{trace}(\sigma_{i_b}, m)$, $\mathcal{Q}_{trace}(\sigma_{i_{\tilde{b}}}, m')$, $\mathcal{Q}_{skey}(pk_{i_0})$, $\mathcal{Q}_{skey}(pk_{i_1})$. *At the end of the second stage,* Ad *is required to output a bit* $\hat{b}$. *If* $\hat{b} = b \oplus \tilde{b}$, **Exp** $= 1$. *Else,* **Exp** $= 0$. *An AHGS is unlinkable if for any PPT* Ad, $|\Pr[\textbf{Exp}_{Unl}^{Ad}(\lambda) = 1] - 1/2| < \varepsilon(\lambda)$.

3   Mathematical Aspects

3.1   Complexity Assumptions

In this section we review the strong RSA assumption [3, 12] and suggest some useful related extensions. A number N is an RSA integer if $N=PQ$ where P and Q are safe primes: $P=2P'+1$, $Q=2Q'+1$, where both P' and Q' are prime. Let RSA_λ be the set of RSA integers of size λ, QR_N the set of quadratic residues.

Strong RSA Assumption [3, 12]. Given λ, a proper group $\mathbb{G}$ with unknown order, for any PPT attacker $\mathcal{A}$:

$$\Pr[z \leftarrow \mathbb{G}; (u, x) \leftarrow \mathcal{A}(1^\lambda, \mathbb{G}, z) : x \neq \pm 1 \land u^x = z] \leq \varepsilon(\lambda).$$

Strong RSA-DLP Assumption. Given λ, an order-unknown group $\mathbb{G}$ where Strong RSA holds, for any PPT attacker $\mathcal{A}$:

$$\Pr[g \leftarrow \mathbb{G}; (u, x, y) \leftarrow \mathcal{A}(1^\lambda, \mathbb{G}, g) : u^x = g^y \land x \neq 0 \land x \nmid y] \leq \varepsilon(\lambda).$$

Lemma 1. *The Strong RSA and the Strong RSA-DLP are equivalent.*

Proof. Clearly, any algorithm to solve the Strong RSA assumption can be transformed to solve the Strong RSA-DLP Assumption. We prove that an algorithm Ad can also be transformed to solve the Strong RSA assumption.

Given any Strong RSA challenge $(z, \mathbb{G})$, one runs Ad and obtains (u, x, y) such that $x \neq 0, 1, -1, u^x = z^y$. Note that $x \nmid y$. Let $\delta = \gcd(x, y)$. Then $1 < \delta < x$ and $x/\delta > 1$. From the extended Euclid algorithm, one finds α, β such that $\delta = x\alpha + y\beta$. It follows that $z = z^{x\alpha/\delta + y\beta/\delta} = (z^\alpha)^{x/\delta} u^{x\beta/\delta} = (z^\alpha u^\beta)^{x/\delta}$. Notice $x/\delta > 1$. One finds a solution $(z^\alpha u^\beta, x/\delta)$ to the Strong RSA challenge $(z, \mathbb{G})$. The transformation is clearly polynomial in λ.

In our security proofs, we will use the following candidate (weak) Decisional Factorization Diffie-Hellman (DFDH) assumption. Coarsely speaking, given g, h in a *proper* group $\mathbb{G}$ with unknown order and two RSA integers n_0, n_1, it is difficult to decide $\log_g h$ is a non-trivial factor of n_0 or n_1. Intuitively, as the factorization problem of RSA integers and the discrete logarithm problem in proper groups are widely believed difficult, it will be difficult to determine whether the two problems have the same solution. This assumption is not completely new. It was implicitly used before without specification [8]. However, to the best of our knowledge, there is no known efficient algorithm to reduce the DFDH problem to other widely-believed difficult problems to date. So we will specify it as a new candidate assumption and use it in our proofs.

DFDH Assumption. Given secure parameters λ, a *proper* group $\mathbb{G}$ with unknown order, for any PPT attacker $\mathcal{A}$:

$$\Pr\left[\begin{array}{l} n_0 = p_0 q_0 \leftarrow RSA_\lambda, p_1 \leftarrow \mathbb{Z}_{2^{|p_0|}} \\ g \leftarrow \mathbb{G}, b \leftarrow \{0, 1\}, h = g^{p_b} \end{array} \middle| \begin{array}{c} b' \leftarrow \mathcal{A}(1^\lambda, \mathbb{G}, n_0, g, h) \\ \land b' = b \end{array}\right] \leq \varepsilon(\lambda).$$

Note that p_1 is a *random* integer in the same size $|p_0|$ of prime p_0. To make the DFDH assumption hold, $\mathbb{G}$ must be chosen *properly* with unknown order to the attacker, for instance, the additive group of the points of elliptic curves over ring $\mathbb{Z}_N$, where $N \leftarrow RSA_\lambda$ [14]. However, we stress that one *cannot* directly use $\mathbb{Z}_N^*$ as $\mathbb{G}$ with unknown order since in this case, the Jacobi symbols of $gg^{p_0} = g^{p_0+1}$ $gg^{p_1} = g^{p_1+1}$ are distinguishable for prime p_0 and random integer p_1. To cover such groups $\mathbb{G}$, we slightly weaken the DFDH as follows.

Weak DFDH Assumption. Given secure parameters λ, a proper group $\mathbb{G}$ with unknown order, for any PPT attacker $\mathcal{A}$:

$$\Pr\left[\begin{array}{c} n_0 = p_0 q_0, n_1 = p_1 q_1 \leftarrow RSA_\lambda \\ g \leftarrow \mathbb{G}, b \leftarrow \{0,1\}, h = g^{p_b} \end{array} \middle| \begin{array}{c} b' \leftarrow \mathcal{A}(1^\lambda, \mathbb{G}, n_0, n_1, g, h) \\ \wedge b' = b \end{array} \right] \leq \varepsilon(\lambda).$$

3.2   Accumulators

An accumulator scheme, introduced in [4] and further developed in [3,11], allows aggregation of a large set of inputs into one constant-size value while keeping some useful property of the inputs. It has been shown as a powerful tool for efficiently constructing group signatures and ring signatures. We extend the notations to accumulate random strings.

An accumulator family is a pair $(\{\mathcal{F}_{\lambda \in \mathbb{N}}\}, \{\mathbb{X}_{\lambda \in \mathbb{N}}\})$ where $\mathcal{F}_\lambda$ is a sequences of families of functions such that each $f \in \mathcal{F}_\lambda$ is defined as $f : \mathbb{U}_f \times \mathbb{X}_f^{ext} \to \mathbb{U}_f$ for some $\mathbb{X}_f^{ext} \supseteq \mathbb{X}_\lambda$, and additionally the following properties are satisfied:

- *(Efficient generation)* There exists an efficient algorithm $\mathcal{G}(\cdot)$ that on input a security parameter 1^λ, outputs a random element f of $\mathcal{F}_\lambda$, possibly together with some auxiliary information Aux_f.
- *(Efficient evaluation)* Any $f \in \mathcal{F}_\lambda$ is computable in time polynomial in λ.
- *(Quasi-commutativity)* For all $\lambda \in \mathbb{N}, f \in \mathcal{F}_\lambda, u \in \mathbb{U}_f, x_1, x_2 \in \mathbb{X}_\lambda, f(f(u, x_1), x_2) = f(f(u, x_2), x_1)$.

Definition 6. *An accumulator is said to be collision quasi-resistant if for any $\lambda \in \mathbb{N}$ and any PPT attacker $\mathcal{A}$:*

$$\Pr\left[\begin{array}{c} (f, Aux_f) \leftarrow \mathcal{G}(1^\lambda) \\ u \leftarrow \mathbb{U}_f \end{array} \middle| \begin{array}{c} (x', w, X) \leftarrow \mathcal{A}(f, u, \mathbb{U}_f) \wedge w \in \mathbb{U}_f \\ \wedge X \subseteq \mathbb{X}_\lambda \wedge x' \notin X_{well} \wedge f(w, x') = f(u, X) \end{array} \right] \leq \varepsilon(\lambda).$$

where X_{well} is a well-determined set by X.

Definition 7. *Let π be a map (maybe not efficient) $\pi : \mathbb{X}_\lambda \times \{0,1\}^k \to \mathbb{X}'_{well}$, where k is a security parameter. Let $X \subseteq \mathbb{X}_\lambda$. The set $X_{well} = \pi(X \times \{0,1\}^k)$ is well-determined by X if there exists an efficient distinguisher, for any element $\beta \in \mathbb{X}'_{well}$, to determine whether $\beta \in X_{well}$. Else, the set X_{well} is not well-determined by X.*

Examples of a well-determined set. Let $X = \{x_1, \cdots, x_k\}$ where $x_i \leftarrow \mathbb{Z}_p^*$ for $i = 1, \cdots, n$, and p is a sufficient large strong prime and n a security parameter. Then $X_{well} = \{\beta : \beta | \prod_{i \in I}^{I \subseteq \{1,\cdots,k\}} x_i\}$ is well-determined by X due to the efficient Euclid algorithm. However, if n is sufficiently large, $\tilde{X}_{well} = \{\beta : \beta = \prod_{i \in I}^{I \subseteq \{1,\cdots,k\}} x_i \bmod p\}$ is not a well-determined set due to the difficulty of the well-known subset product problem and discrete logarithm problem.

Examples of a collision quasi-resistant accumulator. For a security parameter λ, the family $\mathcal{F}_\lambda$ consists of the following functions: $f : \mathbb{G} \times \mathbb{Z}_p^* \mapsto \mathbb{G}$, $f(u, x) = u^x$, where $\mathbb{G}$ is the corresponding group defined in the Strong RSA and DFDH assumptions. The well-determined set X_{well} by X is $\{\beta : \beta | \prod_{i \in \{1,\cdots,k\}} x_i\}$. Directly from lemma 1, we have the following corollary.

Corollary 1. *Under the Strong RSA assumption, the function family $f(u, x) = u^x$ defined above is a collision quasi-resistant accumulator.*

Remark 2. In [3], Baric and Pfitzman proposed an RSA-based accumulator to accumulate random strings m. They use an underlying RSA-based accumulator for primes and a conversion algorithm. Assume security parameters κ, ℓ and a collision resistant hash function $H(\cdot) : \{0,1\}^* \to \{0, 1, \cdots, 2^\ell - 1\}$. Given m, search for the smallest prime $p = 2^\kappa H(m) + \gamma$ by improving $\gamma \in \mathbb{N}$. Finally, accumulate the prime using an underlying RSA-based accumulator for primes. Our extension is much more efficient than Baric-Pfitzman approach, which requires a lot of primality tests. The cost is the DFDH assumption.

4 Proposed Ad Hoc Group Signature Schemes

In the ring signature schemes in the literature, there are a number of users and an associated PKI. Ad hoc subsets of the user population can be formed without the help of a group manager–but it is assumed that *each user has a registered public key correctly generated following the specifications of the system*. In our schemes, we also follow this pre-condition in the context of ad hoc group signatures.

4.1 Ad Hoc Group Signature with Linkability

In some applications, linkable anonymous signatures can be used to determine whether some players voted multiple times. In this section, we detail a simple yet efficient linkable ad hoc group signature scheme.

- **(System parameter generation.)** Let $\mathbb{G}$ be an order-unknown group in which the Strong RSA and the DFDH hold. $1 < \epsilon, \kappa, \ell, \ell_1, \lambda_1 < poly(\lambda)$ are security parameters, where $\ell_1 = (\ell - 2)/\epsilon - \kappa$. $1 < I < poly(\lambda)$ is the number of group members. $H(\cdot) : \{0, 1\}^* \to \mathbb{G}$ is a cryptographic hash function.
- **(Member key generation.)** $n_i \leftarrow RSA_\lambda$, where $n_i = p_i q_i, p_i \in \mathbb{S}(0, 2^{\ell_1}) = \{2^{\ell_1} + 1, \cdots, 2^{\ell_1} - 1\}, 2^\ell < q_i$. n_i is player i's ($i \in \{1, \cdots, I\}$) public key and p_i, q_i its private keys. $PK = \{n_i\}_{i=1}^I$ is the public key list. Note that the member's public key is RSA integers but the two factors are assumed in different length, for instance, p_i is in size of 510 bits while q_i in 737 bits.

- (**Group key generation.**) Choose a generator g of $\mathbb{G}$ *depending on* PK, for instance, the hash value of PK. Then, any one can compute $y = g^{n_1 n_2 \cdots n_I}$. The ad hoc group public key is $\{\lambda, \epsilon, \ell, \ell_1, \kappa, \mathbb{G}, g, y, H(\cdot), PK\}$.
- (**Signature generation.**) Compute $u = g^{n_1 n_2 \cdots n_I / p_i}$ in advance. For a message m, compute the following knowledge signature [9, 12, 7]:

$$\varrho = KS\{p_i : y = u^{p_i} \wedge p_i \in \mathbb{S}(0, 2^\ell)\}(m).$$

Output the signature $\sigma = (u, \varrho)$ on m.
- (**Signature verification.**) Check that $u \neq \pm y^{\pm 1}$ and the validity of the knowledge signature ϱ. Output 1 if all the checks hold. Otherwise, output 0.
- (**Tracing arguments generation.**) In case of dispute, member j can prove to the judge that it has (not) produced a given linkable ad hoc group signature σ by computing $\dot{y}_j = u^{p_j}, h = H(PK\|m\|g\|y\|u\|\sigma\|\dot{y}_j), w = h^{n_j}, \dot{h} = h^{q_j}$, and knowledge signature [9, 12, 7]:

$$\dot{\varrho} = KS\{p_j : \dot{y}_j = u^{p_j} \wedge w = \dot{h}^{p_j} \wedge p_j \in \mathbb{S}(0, 2^\ell)\}(m, \sigma).$$

Output self-tracing arguments $\ddot{\sigma} = \dot{\sigma} = (j, \dot{y}_j, \dot{h}, \dot{\varrho})$.
- (**Tracing witness verification.**) Compute h, w as the member j and check that $y_j \neq \pm u^{\pm 1}$, $w \neq \pm \dot{h}^{\pm 1}$ and the validity of the knowledge signature $\dot{\varrho}$. If any check does not hold, output *Failure*. Else, further check $\dot{y} \stackrel{?}{=} \dot{y}_j$. If the equality holds, member j produced the given ad hoc group signature. Else, member j did not produce it.

A straightforward verification shows that any legal ad hoc group member can generate ad hoc group signatures on any message accepted by the verification algorithm. For an ad hoc group signature, a group member can always provide a valid knowledge signature so that a judge can determine whether or not the given signature is generated by the member. Under the strong RSA assumption, the knowledge signature ϱ implies that signer knows $\hat{p}$ such that $g^{n_1 \cdots n_I} = u^{\hat{p}}$. From lemma 1, $\hat{p}|n_1 \cdots n_I$. Note that $\hat{p} \neq \pm 1 \in \mathbb{S}(0, 2^\ell)$. So $\hat{p}$ must be the unique smallest non-trivial factor of some $n_i \in PK$ and u is uniquely determined by $\hat{p}$. The knowledge signature $\dot{\varrho}$ convinces one that the prover's secret factor is equal to the factor involved in ϱ or not. So it can be used to determine whether member j generated the plain ring signature ϱ. Hence, the scheme is unforgeable, traceable and linkable. An algorithm to break the anonymity can be used to break the (weak) DFDH assumption.

Theorem 1. *The above ad hoc group signature scheme is correct. In the random oracle model, if the Strong RSA assumption holds, the above ad hoc group signature scheme is unforgeable, self-traceable and linkable. If the (weak) DFDH assumption holds, the above ad hoc group signature scheme is anonymous.*

Proof. Omitted due to page limitation. We refer the readers to the full version of this paper.

4.2   Ad Hoc Group Signature with Unlinkability

There are approaches to improve the basic linkable ad hoc group signature to an unlinkable one. The first approach is to let the generator g not be a component of the ad hoc group public keys. The generator g is now generated independently before producing different ring signatures, for instance, generated with a hash function as we suggested in the self-tracing procedure in the previous section. The other procedures of the above scheme keep unchanged. In this case, g is a part of the resulting anonymous signature. Following this approach, one indeed obtains the same scheme in [8]. Clearly, now the new anonymous signature is unlinkable and it is efficient in term of bandwidth consumption. However, the online computation is heavy and linear to the number of possible group members.

In the following, we suggest an alternative to achieve unlinkability. Every time, during the signing procedure, the group member will accumulate a random integer that is co-prime to all the public keys to blind the witness of accumulating the smaller prime factor of some RSA integer. The extended notion of accumulators allows accumulating random integers. This feature critically contributes efficiency improvements for our unlinkable ad hoc group signature. In the following, we will only specify the signing, verifying and tracing procedures, as the other parts remain unchanged as discussed earlier.

- **(Signing procedure.)** Randomly select $a \neq 0 \leftarrow \mathbb{S}(0, 2^{\ell_1})$ co-prime with p_i, and compute $z = y^a$, $v = u^a$, α, β satisfying $a\alpha + p_i\beta = 1$, $y_1 = y^\beta$ and the knowledge signature [9,12,7]:

$$\varrho = KS\{a, p_i, \alpha : z = y^a \wedge z = v^{p_i} \wedge y = z^\alpha y_1^{p_i} \wedge a \in \mathbb{S}(0, 2^\ell) \wedge p_i \in \mathbb{S}(0, 2^\ell)\}(m).$$

The resulting ad hoc group signature is $\sigma = (z, v, \beta, \varrho)$.
- **(Verification procedure.)** Compute $y_1 = y^\beta$ and verify $z \neq \pm y^{\pm 1}$, $v \neq \pm z^{\pm 1}$ and the validity of the knowledge signature ϱ. Output 1 if and only if all the checks hold.
- **(Tracing arguments generation.)** In case of dispute, a group member j can prove to the judge that a given ad hoc group signature σ was (not) generated by it without leaking its private key. As the above ad hoc group signature is not linkable, tracing the given signature will leak no information about the relation between of member j and other signatures.

$$\dot{z}_j = v^{p_j}, h = H(PK\|m\|g\|y\|\sigma\|\dot{z}_j)^2, w = h^{n_j}, \dot{h} = h^{q_j}$$
$$\dot{\varrho} = KS\{p_j : \dot{z}_j = v^{p_j} \wedge w = \dot{h}^{p_j} \wedge p_j \in \mathbb{S}(0, 2^\ell)\}(m, \sigma).$$

Output self-tracing arguments $\ddot{\sigma} = \dot{\sigma} = (j, y_j, \dot{h}, \dot{\varrho})$.
- **(Tracing arguments verification.)** The judge computes h, w as the prover and checks that $\dot{z}_j \neq \pm v^{\pm 1}$, $w \neq \pm \dot{h}^{\pm 1}$ and the validity of the knowledge signature $\dot{\varrho}$. If any check does not hold, the judge outputs *Failure*. Else, it further checks $z \overset{?}{=} \dot{z}_j$. If the equality holds, the judge declares that member j produced the given ad hoc group signature. Else, the judge declares that member j did not produce it.

Similar to the basic linkable ad hoc group signature, under the strong RSA assumption, the knowledge signature ϱ implies that signer knows co-prime integers $\hat{a}, \hat{p}$ such that $g^{an_1 \cdots n_I} = u^{\hat{p}}$. From lemma 1, $\hat{p}|an_1 \cdots n_I$. since $\hat{a}, \hat{p}$ are proven co-prime, it follows that $\hat{p}|n_1 \cdots n_I$. Note that $\hat{p} \neq \pm 1 \in \mathbb{S}(0, 2^\ell)$. So $\hat{p}$ must be the unique smallest non-trivial factor of some $n_i \in PK$. The unique u determined by $\hat{p}$ is masked by one-time random integer $\hat{a}$ in the form $v = u^{\hat{a}}$ for each signature. The knowledge signature $\dot{\varrho}$ convinces one that the prover's secret factor is equal to the factor involved in ϱ or not. So it can be used to determine whether member j generated the ad hoc group signature ϱ. Hence, the scheme is unforgeable, traceable. An algorithm to break the anonymity or unlinkability can be used to break the (weak) DFDH assumption.

Theorem 2. *The above ad hoc group signature scheme is correct. In the random oracle model, if the Strong RSA assumption holds, the above ad hoc group signature scheme is unforgeable and self-traceable. If the (weak) DFDH assumption holds, the ad hoc group signature scheme is anonymous and unlinkable.*

Proof. Omitted due to page limitation. We refer the readers to the full version of this paper.

Remark 3. Note that given a valid ad hoc group signature $\sigma = (z, v, \beta, \varrho)$ from member i, if the order of $\mathbb{G}$ is exposed to group member i, then group member i can deny that the ownership of σ. In this case, member i choose a random integers $p' \neq p_i, q'$ in the corresponding space such that $n_i = p'q' \mod \varphi(N)$ and compute $\dot{z}'_i = v^{p'_i}, h = H(PK||m||g||y||\sigma||\dot{z}'_i)^2, w = h^{n_i}, \dot{h} = h^{q'}, \dot{\varrho} = KS\{p'_i : \dot{z}'_i = v^{p'_i} \wedge w = \dot{h}^{p'_i} \wedge p'_i \in \mathbb{S}(0, 2^\ell)\}(m, \sigma)$. Since the knowledge signature is valid and $z \neq z'_i$, this forged denying arguments is valid. However, a group member $j \neq i$ cannot provably claim the ownership of σ even if member j knows the order of $\mathbb{G}$, due to the fact that p_i is uniquely determined by z and v and it is impossible for member j to compute $\dot{h}$ such that $\dot{h}^{p_i} = h^{n_j}$ if the discrete logarithm is difficult in $\mathbb{G}$ as assumed. The above discussion also shows the difference between ability to deny a signature and that to claim a signature.

4.3   Efficiency

In this section we summarize the performance of our schemes and compare them with the state-of-the-art ring signatures. The most efficient secure existing ring signatures are proposed by Dodis *et al.* in [11] which provides no self-traceability. We denote it by DKNS scheme and our ad hoc group signature scheme with linkability/unlinkability by LAHGS/ULAHGS scheme, respectively. Exp denotes the single-base exponentiation modulo a λ-bit RSA integer. For fairness, we compare it with our ad hoc group signatures enjoying the same functionalities without considering the tracing arguments. As suggested in [11], we will measure the complexity of signatures by the *actual complexity* without the description of the group and the calculation of group public keys.

In the above tables, we consider $\mathbb{G} = QR_N$ where N is an RSA integer with unknown factorization. Accordingly, the security relies on the weak DFDH assumption. But note that the schemes can be realized with more general case of

Table 1. Comparison of ring signatures with our ad hoc group signatures

	Length (bits)	Typical size	Generation	Verification
DKNS [11]	$5\lambda + \kappa + \epsilon(7.5\ell_1 + 5\kappa) - 5$	10363	22 Exp	18 Exp
Our LAHGS	$\lambda + \kappa + \ell - 1$	1920	1 Exp	2 Exp
Our ULAHGS	$2\lambda + 2\ell + \ell_1 + \kappa - 2$	4196	7 Exp	6 Exp

Table 2. Complexity of the tracing arguments

	Length (bits)	Typical size	Generation	Verification
Our LAHGS	$2\lambda + \kappa + \ell - 1 + \log I$	$2944 + \log I$	5 Exp	5 Exp
Our ULAHGS	$2\lambda + \kappa + \ell - 1 + \log I$	$2944 + \log I$	5 Exp	5 Exp

$\mathbb{G}$. We suggest typical security parameters as previous papers [16]: $\lambda = 1024, \kappa = 160, \epsilon = 1.1, \ell_1 = 510$. The computation complexity is in terms of modular exponentiations without any optimization, that is, a two-base exponentiation is calculated as two single-base exponentiations. Clearly, without considering the tracing arguments, our ad hoc group signatures dramatically improve the efficiency of the DKNS scheme. The tracing procedures are also efficient and independent of the group size. Moreover, a group member can judge whether it is the owner of a given signature with its private key only. It does not require the member's previous inner random coins.

We also noted that there are some independent works to bridge the gap between ring signatures and group signatures. In [15], Komano *et al.* presented the notion of deniable ring signatures which allowing a group member to deny a ring signature. Their notion is weaker and indeed covered in our ad hoc group signatures (see *Remarks 1,3*). In [18], Manulis proposed the notion of democratic group signatures which provides outsider anonymity while any group member can trace the signer. The democratic group signature requires *interactive group key* agreement, and additional *leave* and *join* sub-protocols. Moreover, the implementations in both [15] and [18] suffers from linear complexity regarding to the group scale while ours are independent of the group size.

5   Applications

There are many potential applications of ad hoc group signatures. In the following, we show direct applications to electronic lotteries. In a typical lottery one or more winners are chosen during a trusted process so that each purchased ticket has an equal chance to be chosen. This process is usually monitored by an outsider auditor which ensures the fairness of the protocol. As the process is random it cannot be repeated and the ticket purchasers must trust the process.

We use the same framework as [19]. Assume there is a bulletin and some necessary public information has been published on the bulletin including the order-hiding group $\mathbb{G}$. As previous schemes our lottery uses random numbers chosen by the players in order to output a number whose randomness is granted provided that at least one player chooses its number at random.

There are a few papers discussed how to implement the process to compute the result of winning number [19, 13]. In the following, we focus on the privacy of the lottery players. As we remarked in the introduction of the report, lottery players tend to require anonymity protection for fear of blackmail when winning the giant prize, while trust no third party for fear that the party may leak their identities. The unlinkable ad hoc group signatures can provide the players with the expected privacy. First, all lottery players register to the bulletin with their RSA public keys. Then the group public key can be computed. Second, the lottery players decide their lottery number and sign them using the unlinkable ad hoc group signature scheme in Section 4.2. They cast their lottery number (maybe, in the ciphertext form) and the signature to the bulletin. Finally, after the winning numbers are calculated out, the winners can prove that they are really the winners using the tracing arguments. In our scheme, a lottery has size about 0.53K bytes. The lottery scheme is very simple and efficient. It enjoys perfect privacy in the sense that no third party except that the lotteries issuer can determine the true identity of the winner and additionally, no other player's identity will be exposed. Moreover, the system initialization can be speeded up by letting the lotteries issuer generate $\mathbb{G}$ without affecting security of the lotteries applications (see Remark 3).

6   Conclusion

We outlined the usefulness of adding the self-traceability to ring signatures in practice, by proposing the notion of ad hoc group signatures. It provides a general fair mechanism of privacy protection for self-organized groups. It also provides a generic technique to remove the trusted third party such as a group manager from the privacy protection systems. Meanwhile, it dices the anonymity-revoking functionality of a conventional group signature to the distributed members, rather than a centralized manager. It is flexible and practical.

We implemented the notion using a slightly extended model of cryptographic accumulators with provable security in the random oracle model. The implementations are very efficient and elegant. After the group members are determined and the group key is computed, the space, time, and communication complexities of the relevant parameters and operations are constant. It outperforms the state-of-the-art ring signatures. Furthermore, a group member can judge whether or not it generated a given ad hoc group signature with its private key only. Hence, the notion of ad hoc group signatures is useful, and the proposed implementations are very efficient and practical.

Acknowledgments

The authors are indebted to Duncan S. Wong for his useful comments on the DFDH assumption and the anonymity of the linkable ad hoc group signature. The authors would like to thank Bo Qin for many discussions during the preparation of the versions of this paper.

References

1. G. Ateniese, J. Camenisch, S. Hohenberger and B. de Medeiros. Practical group signatures without random oracles. Cryptology ePrint Archive, Report 2005/385.
2. G. Ateniese, and B. de Medeiros. Efficient group signatures without trapdoors. Asiacrypt'03, LNCS 2894, pp. 246-268. Springer-Verlag, 2003.
3. N. Baric, B. Pfitzman. Collision-free accumulators and fail-stop signature schemes without trees. Eurocrypt'97, LNCS 1233, pp. 480-494, Springer-Verlag, 1997.
4. J. Benaloh and M. de Mare. One-way accumulators: a decentralized alternative to digital signatures. Eurocrypt'93, LNCS 765, pp. 274-285, Springer-Verlag, 1993.
5. D. Boneh and H. Shacham. Group signatures with verifier-local revocation. ACM-CCS 2004, pp.168-177, ACM Press, 2004.
6. X. Boyen and B. Waters. Compact Group Signatures Without Random Oracles. Eurocrypt 2006, to appear. Available at Cryptology ePrint Archive: 2005/381.
7. A. Chan, Y. Frankel, and Y. Tsiounis. Each Come - Easy Go Divisible Cash. Eurocrypt'98, LNCS 1403, pp. 561-575, Springer-Verlag, 1998.
8. D. Chaum, E. van Heyst. Group signatures. Eurocrypt'91, LNCS 547, pp. 257-265, Springer-Verlag, 1991.
9. J. Camenisch and M. Michels. A group signature scheme based on an RSA variant. Asiacrypt'98, LNCS 1514, pp. 160-174, Springer-Verlag, 1998.
10. J. Camenisch, M. Stadler. Efficient group signatures for large groups. Crypto'97, LNCS 1294, pp. 465-479, Springer-Verlag, 1997.
11. Y. Dodis, A. Kiayias, A. Nicolosi, and V. Shoup. Anonymous identification in ad hoc groups. Eurocrypt'04, LNCS 3027, pp. 609-626, Springer-Verlag, 2004.
12. E. Fujisaki and T. Okamoto. Statistical zero knowledge protocols to prove modular polynomial relations. Crypto'97, LNCS 1294, pp. 16-30, Springer-Verlag, 1997.
13. D. M. Goldschlag and S.G. Stubblebine. Publicly verifiable lotterie: applications of delaying functions. FC'98, LNCS 1465, pp. 214-226. Springer-Verlag, 1998.
14. K. Koyama, U. M. Maurer, T. Okamoto, and S. A. Vanstone. New public-key schemes based on elliptic curves over the ring Z_n. Crypto'91, LNCS 576, pp. 252-266. Springer-Verlag, 1991.
15. Y. Komano, K. Ohta, A. Shimbo1, and S. Kawamura. Toward the Fair Anonymous Signatures: Deniable Ring Signatures. CT-RSA'06, LNCS 3860, pp. 174-191. Springer-Verlag, 2006.
16. J. Kiayias, Y. Tsiounis, and M. Yung. Traceable signatures scheme. Eurocrypt 2004, LNCS 3027, pp. 571-589, Springer-Verlag, 2003.
17. J. K. Liu, V. K. Wei, and D. S. Wong. Linkable spontaneous anonymous group signature for ad hoc groups (extended abstract). ACISP'04, LNCS 3108, pp. 325-335. Springer-Verlag, 2004.
18. M. Manulis. Democratic Group Signatures on Example of Joint Ventures. To appear at ASIACCS'2006. Available at: http://eprint.iacr.org/2005/446.pdf.
19. R. L. Rivest, A. Shamir, and Y. Tauman. How to leak a secret. In Proc. Asiacrypt'01, LNCS 2248, pp. 552-565, Springer-Verlag, 2001.
20. G. Tsudik, S. Xu. Accumulating composites and improved group signing. Asiacrypt'03, LNCS 2894, pp. 269-286. Springer-Verlag, 2003.
21. Q. Wu, X. Chen, C. Wang, Y. Wang. Shared-key Signature and Its Application to Anonymous Authentication in Ad Hoc Group. ISC'04, LNCS 3225, pp.330-341, Springer-verlag, 2004.
22. D. S. Wong, K. Fung, J. K. Liu, and V. K. Wei. On the RS-code construction of ring signature schemes and a threshold setting of RST. ICISC'03, LNCS 2971, pp. 34-46, Springer-Verlag, 2003.

Rateless Codes for the Multicast Stream Authentication Problem

Christophe Tartary and Huaxiong Wang

Division of ICS, Department of Computing
Macquarie University, NSW 2109 Australia
{ctartary, hwang}@ics.mq.edu.au

Abstract. We study the multicast authentication problem when an opponent can drop, reorder and introduce data packets into the communication channel. We first study the packet authentication probability of a scheme proposed by Lysyanskaya, Tamassia and Triandopoulos in 2003 since our opponent model is based on theirs. Using a family of rateless codes called Luby Transform codes (LT codes) we design a protocol which allows any packet to be authenticated at the receiver with probability arbitrary close to 1. We also compare LT codes to other families of rateless codes which could be used in that context in order to minimize the packet overhead as well as the time complexity of encoding and decoding data.

Keywords: stream authentication, polynomial reconstruction, rateless codes.

1 Introduction

Multicast protocols enable data to be transmitted from one sender to many receivers via a communication network such as the Internet. The applications are as various as pay-TV, online games and military defense systems for instance. Nevertheless large-scale broadcasts prevent lost content from being retransmitted since the loss of any piece of data could generate an overwhelming number of redistribution requests at the sender. In addition the network can be under the influence of malicious users performing harmful actions on the data stream. Thus the security of broadcast transmission schemes depends on both network properties and opponents' computational power. Unconditionally secure schemes have been designed in [1, 4, 25] but either they can only be used for a single authentication or they require too large storage capacities. In this paper we will consider that opponents have bounded computational abilities.

In recent years several protocols were designed to deal with the multicast authentication problem [3]. Applications like stock quotes and pay-TV involve that the stream size can be large and eventually infinite. On the other hand the receivers must be able to authenticate data within a short period of delay upon reception. Since many protocols will transfer private or sensitive information, non-repudiation of the sender is required for most of them. Signing each packet[1] via digital signatures is impractical since they are generally time expensive to generate and verify. Using one-time or k-time signatures [6, 24] overcomes this drawback but their size is, in general, too large to be used

---

[1] Since the stream size is large, it is divided into small fixed-size entities called *packets*.

H. Yoshiura et al. (Eds.): IWSEC 2006, LNCS 4266, pp. 136–151, 2006.

for broadcasting due to bandwidth limitations. Thus to provide non-repudiation, most techniques rely on signature amortization. One signature is created and its overhead and time generation/verification are amortized over several packets using hash functions.

In order to deal with packet loss Perrig et al. designed EMSS [21] and MESS [21] where the hash of each packet is appended to several followers according to a specific pattern. One signature is generated from time to time and is always assumed to be received providing non-repudiation and allowing new users to join the communication group at any time. Using k-state Markov chains [20, 30] to model packet loss they computed bounds on packet authentication probability. Using augmented chains to distribute hashes, Golle and Modadugu [7] and Miner and Staddon [17] obtained other bounds. Unfortunately all these schemes rely on the reception of signed packets.

Wong and Lam [29] used Merkle-hash trees [16] to distribute hashes and solve the problem of reliable signature transmission. Their scheme can tolerate any packet loss and data injections but the size of the tag[2] is logarithmic in the number of packets per block[3]. As said earlier, bandwidth limitations prevent us from using such an approach.

To deal with packet loss without relying on reception of the signature packets one can split the signature into k parts where only l of them ($l < k$) are enough for recovery. Using error-correcting codes, Lysyanskaya et al. [14] developed a protocol which also tolerates data injections. Their approach was recently extended by Tartary and Wang [28]. Nevertheless none of these schemes provided bounds on packet authentication probability. In addition the rate of their linear code depends on some network parameters. If one of them changes then the whole structure of the code must be updated.

Our approach is motivated by the following observation. A necessary condition for all these schemes to authenticate a packet P (at the receiver) is to get an element $\tilde{P}$ containing P along with some hashes [7, 17, 21, 29] or code symbols [14, 19, 28]. If $\tilde{P}$ is dropped then P is definitely lost since such a $\tilde{P}$ is unique for each scheme. As these previous techniques we will process data stream packet per block of n elements: $P_1, \ldots, P_n$. Our technique can be seen as an extension of Lysyanskaya et al.'s approach which enables any receiver to recover all data packets $P_1, \ldots, P_n$ despite loss incurred during transmission. This constitutes a major improvement from existing techniques in the way that receivers not only authenticate what they received but also reconstruct what was lost. This is particularly beneficial when $P_1, \ldots, P_n$ represent audio or video information where our technique prevents frozen images and audio gaps to happen.

We propose to use Luby Transform (LT) codes to encode blocks of n data packets $P_1, \ldots, P_n$ into $\mathcal{N}$ symbols $E_1, \ldots, E_\mathcal{N}$ (the value of $\mathcal{N}$ is specified in Sect.3). LT codes were introduced by Luby [12] as the first practical realization of rateless codes to illustrate the Digital Fountain concept [2]. These codes are constructed in such a way that there exists a threshold value m (depending on n) such that any subset of $\{E_1, \ldots, E_\mathcal{N}\}$ having at least m distinct elements can be used to recover all n original packets $P_1, \ldots, P_n$ with good probability. By representing $E_1, \ldots, E_\mathcal{N}$ as coefficients of a particular polynomial and carefully choosing $\mathcal{N}$, the receiver will be able to run a reconstruction algorithm due to Guruswami and Sudan [8] and will recover that polynomial despite potential data injections performed by malicious users.

---

[2] We call *authentication tag* the extra information appended to a packet to prove its authenticity.

[3] In order to be processed, packets are gathered into fixed-size sets called *blocks*.

In [14], Reed-Solomon codes were used to design a multicast authentication scheme dealing with both packet loss and data injection. We will prove that its packet authentication probability (which has not been studied in [14]) does not exhibit an easy lower bound. In addition when a packet was dropped during transmission its content was definitely lost for the receivers. Combining a LT code with the polynomial reconstruction technique we design a broadcast protocol having two main advantages. First it allows the receivers to reconstruct erased data which is, to our knowledge, a new feature in the multicast authentication problem. Second it exhibits a minimal lower bound on the packet authentication probability which can be chosen arbitrary close to 1.

Since we will use the same opponent model as Lysyanskaya et al., we will prove that our scheme is as secure as theirs. Since its security depends on the consistency of the LT decoding (while Lysyanskaya et al.'s relies on Reed-Solomon codes' one), we will compare LT codes to other families of rateless codes including Online and Raptor codes [15, 26]. We will show that it is possible to achieve reasonable and constant packet overhead by using a modified version of LT codes. We will also enlighten that Raptor codes can provide good practical implementations for our scheme if they are used instead of LT codes. A digital signature will be used to ensure non-repudiation and to enable new members to join the communication group at any block boundary.

The paper is organized as follows. We will describe the scheme developed in [14] and analyze its packet authentication probability in the next section. In Sect. 3 we will develop our authentication protocol using LT codes. In Sect. 4 we will compare different families of rateless codes that could be used instead of LT codes. The last section will summarize our contribution to the multicast authentication problem.

2   Analysis of Lysyanskaya et al.'s Protocol

In this section we will shortly describe the scheme designed in [14]. We will first introduce the network model used in that paper. Then we will recall the tasks performed at the sender and the receiver to authenticate data and analyze the packet authentication probability of that approach since it has not been studied in the original paper [14]. Finally we will illustrate our result when the network exhibit a bursty loss pattern [20].

Network Model. The network is assumed to be under partial control of an opponent $\mathcal{O}$ who can drop and rearrange packets of his choice. He can also inject data into the channel. Since our main concern is the multicast authentication problem, we assume that a reasonable number of packets reaches the different receivers and not too many packets are injected by $\mathcal{O}$. Indeed if too many packets are dropped then data transmission becomes the main problem to solve since the small number of received elements would be useless even authenticated. On the other hand if $\mathcal{O}$ can introduce a large quantity of packets then $\mathcal{O}$ can potentially overflow the network and the major problem becomes strengthening the channel against denial-of-service attacks.

The stream is split into blocks of n packets and we introduce two parameters: $\alpha (0 < \alpha \leq 1)$ (the *survival* rate) and $\beta (\beta \geq 1)$ (the *flood* rate). It is assumed that at least αn original packets and a total of no more than βn packets reach each receiver.

Description of the Scheme. We need a collision-resistant hash function h [22] and a secure signature scheme $(\text{Sign}_{SK}, \text{Verify}_{PK})$ [27] the couple of keys of which (SK,PK) is created by a generator KeyGen. Denote $\{P_1, \ldots, P_n\}$ the block of n packets to be sent. The number BID denotes the block position within the whole stream. Each P_i is hashed into h_i by h. A signature σ is generated as: $\sigma := \text{sign}_{SK}(\text{BID}\|h_1\|\cdots\|h_n)$. The concatenation $\mathcal{C} := h_1\|\cdots\|h_n\|\sigma$ is encoded into $[c_1, \ldots, c_n]$ using the $[n, \rho n]_q$ binary systematic Reed-Solomon (SRS) code over $\mathbb{F}_q$ where q is a power of 2. Both ρ and q depend on α and β. The sender builds the set of n authenticated packets $\{AP_1, \ldots, AP_n\}$ to be emitted to the receivers via the network as: $\forall i \in \{1, \ldots, n\}$ $AP_i = \text{BID}\|i\|P_i\|c_i$.

When a receiver gets m elements $\{AP'_1, \ldots, AP'_m\}$ he first decomposes each of them as: $\text{BID}_i\|j_i\|P'_{j_i}\|c'_{j_i}$. He verifies that $\text{BID}_i = \text{BID}$ and builds the family $\{(j_1, c'_{j_1}), \ldots, (j_m, c'_{j_m})\}$. He checks that m is consistent with the values of the rates α and β. In order to deal with packet loss and data injections he uses an algorithm developed by Guruswami and Sudan [8] (GS-Decoder) to list-decode the SRS code. He gets a list of candidates for the signature verification. If one of them verifies the signature then this element must be $\mathcal{C}$ since the signature scheme is secure. Thus the receiver recovers the hashes of the original packets. What remains to achieve is to authenticate the original packets amongst the received ones. The receiver computes the hashes of the m packets $P'_{j_1}, \ldots, P'_{j_m}$ and look for matchings with the h_i's. Since h is collision resistant if $h'_{j_k} = h_i$ then $P'_{j_k} = P_i$. In this case P_i is said to have been *authenticated* by the receiver. Using this process he can find the original packets amongst data he received.

This authentication scheme deals with both packets loss and data injections and the communication group is joinable by new users at any block boundary. In addition no reliable transmission of the block signature is assumed. Nevertheless no study of its packet authentication probability was performed in [14]. We will now address this point.

Analysis of the Packet Authentication Probability. We call the action $\mathcal{O}$ performs on the stream a *modification pattern*. We first introduce the following definition:

Definition 1. *We say that a couple (α, β) of survival and flood rates is accurate for a network flow of n symbols if when data is sent per block of n elements, the receiver gets at least αn of them and receives no more than βn pieces of data (including opponent's injections). In addition (α, β) is unique (and called the accuracy of the network) if:*
(1) $\mathcal{O}$ can use a modification pattern $\mathcal{M}'$ allowing to receive (at least) one set of αn original packets with positive probability as well as a modification pattern $\mathcal{M}''$ allowing to receive (at least) one set of βn packets with positive probability and:
(2) $\mathcal{O}$ cannot use either a modification pattern allowing to receive less than αn original packets with a non-zero probability or a modification pattern allowing to receive more than βn packets with a non-zero probability

The previous definition means that the accuracy (α, β) is optimal in the sense that no receiver can get less than αn original elements but $\mathcal{O}$ can drop packets in such a way that at least one of the receivers can gets exactly αn of them (pattern $\mathcal{M}'$). It also means that no receiver can get more than βn elements but $\mathcal{O}$ can inject packets in such a way that at least one of the receivers can gets exactly βn elements (pattern $\mathcal{M}''$).

From now on, we consider that (α, β) is the accuracy of the network. The set of n elements of Definition 1 will be $\{AP_1, \ldots, AP_n\}$. Denote $\mathcal{F}$ the set of families having at least αn elements of $\{AP_1, \ldots, AP_n\}$. For any $\lambda \in \{\alpha n, \ldots, n\}$ we also define $\mathcal{F}_\lambda$ the subset of $\mathcal{F}$ consisting of families having exactly λ elements. Denote $\mathcal{M}$ the modification pattern used by $\mathcal{O}$. It induces a probabilistic distribution over $\mathcal{F}$ and therefore over $\{P_1, \ldots, P_n\}$. Our aim is to compute $P_\mathcal{M}(P_i$ is authenticated) for any $i \in \{1, \ldots, n\}$. Assume that we received a family of packets F for the block number BID. We denote $\hat{F}$ the subfamily of F consisting of the original packets. Since (α, β) is the accuracy of the network we have: $\alpha n \leq |\hat{F}| \leq |F| \leq \beta n$. We have the following theorem:

Theorem 1 ([28]). *If (α, β) is the accuracy of the network (for a flow n) then any received family F verifies the signature.*

Therefore we get for any i in $\{1, \ldots, n\}$:
$$P_\mathcal{M}(P_i \text{ is authenticated}) = P_\mathcal{M}(P_i \text{ is authenticated} \mid F \text{ verifies the signature})$$

According to [14] once F verifies the signature, P_i is authenticated if and only if there exists a received element $\text{BID}\|k\|P_k'\|c_k'$ such that $h(P_k') = h_i$. Given that h is collision resistant this happens if and only if $P_k' = P_i$. We have three cases. First, we have $AP_i = \text{BID}\|k\|P_k'\|c_k'$. Second, we have $AP_i \neq \text{BID}\|k\|P_k'\|c_k'$ but there is another original element $AP_j (j \neq i)$ such that $AP_j = \text{BID}\|k\|P_k'\|c_k'$ (this corresponds to the fact that a piece of data P_i has to be sent several times). Third, $\text{BID}\|k\|P_k'\|c_k'$ does come from the sender and therefore has been introduced by $\mathcal{O}$. Since $\mathcal{O}$ can eavesdrop the network, he knows all the AP_j's. Since he has no interest in helping the receivers to get original data, he will only introduce incorrect content. Thus we can claim the last two cases have a very small probability to happen and approximate the right hand side of the inequality by $P_\mathcal{M}(AP_i$ is received):

$$P_\mathcal{M}(P_i \text{ is authenticated}) \simeq P_\mathcal{M}(AP_i \text{ is received}) \tag{1}$$

Since AP_i is an original packet, we have: $P_\mathcal{M}(AP_i \text{ is received}) = P_\mathcal{M}(AP_i \in \hat{F})$. Furthermore the cardinality of $\hat{F}$ belongs to $\{\alpha n, \ldots, n\}$. So we can write:

$$P_\mathcal{M}(AP_i \in \hat{F}) = P_\mathcal{M} \left(\bigcup_{\lambda=\alpha n}^{n} \left\{ \hat{F} \in \mathcal{F}_\lambda \text{ and } AP_i \in \hat{F} \right\} \right)$$
$$= \sum_{\lambda=\alpha n}^{n} P_\mathcal{M}(\hat{F} \in \mathcal{F}_\lambda \text{ and } AP_i \in \hat{F})$$

The last equality comes from the fact that $\{\mathcal{F}_{\alpha n}, \ldots, \mathcal{F}_n\}$ is a partition of $\mathcal{F}$. The distribution induced by $\mathcal{M}$ may involve $P_\mathcal{M}(\hat{F} \in \mathcal{F}_\lambda) = 0$ for some values of λ. In this case $P_\mathcal{M}(AP_i \in \hat{F} | \hat{F} \in \mathcal{F}_\lambda)$ may not be uniquely defined [23] but the product $P_\mathcal{M}(AP_i \in \hat{F} | \hat{F} \in \mathcal{F}_\lambda) P_\mathcal{M}(\hat{F} \in \mathcal{F}_\lambda)$ is still equal to 0. Thus we get a unique value for $P_\mathcal{M}(AP_i \in \hat{F})$ as:

$$P_\mathcal{M}(AP_i \in \hat{F}) = \sum_{\lambda=\alpha n}^{n} P_\mathcal{M}(AP_i \in \hat{F} | \hat{F} \in \mathcal{F}_\lambda) P_\mathcal{M}(\hat{F} \in \mathcal{F}_\lambda) \tag{2}$$

By combining (1) and (2), we get an approximation of the packet authentication probability of Lysyanskaya et al.'s scheme as:

$$P_\mathcal{M}(P_i \text{ is authenticated}) \simeq \sum_{\lambda=\alpha n}^{n} P_\mathcal{M}(AP_i \in \hat{F} | \hat{F} \in \mathcal{F}_\lambda) P_\mathcal{M}(\hat{F} \in \mathcal{F}_\lambda) \tag{3}$$

Definition 1 tells us that there exists a pattern $\mathcal{M}'$ such that $P_{\mathcal{M}'}(\hat{F} \in \mathcal{F}_{\alpha n}) \neq 0$ so that the starting index value αn cannot be increased in the general setting.

Resistance against Bursty Loss. In [20], Paxson outlined that the Internet experienced bursty packet loss. Golle and Modadugu [7] and Miner and Staddon [17] designed schemes based on graph theory to resist multiple bursts of fixed lengths. We will illustrate an application of (3) when $\mathcal{M}$ is a multiple-burst pattern in order to approximate $P_{\mathcal{M}}(P_i$ is authenticated). In this case there are no packet injections so $\beta = 1$. Due to space limitations we only give milestones to follow and we refer the reader seeking more details to the extended version of this paper.

Definition 2. *A burst is a sequence a consecutive deletions. Two bursts are separated by at least one non-erased element.*

We must determine how many bursts can occur over $\{AP_1, \ldots, AP_n\}$ providing that at least αn of these elements are received.

Definition 3. *Let $(t_1, \ldots, t_n)$ be a n-tuple. We say that a burst of length $b (\leq n)$ starts (respectively ends) at t_i if the elements erased by the burst are $t_i, \ldots, t_{i+b-1}$ (respectively $t_{i-b+1}, \ldots, t_i$).*

Definition 4. *A tuple of positive integers $(\mathcal{B}_1, p_1, \ldots, \mathcal{B}_\delta, p_\delta)$ is called a δ-burst if for all $i \in \{1, \ldots, \delta\}$, $\mathcal{B}_i$ is the length of the ith burst occurring over a tuple $(t_1, \ldots, t_n)$ and starts at position p_i. $(\mathcal{B}_1, \ldots, \mathcal{B}_\delta)$ is called the δ-length of the δ-burst.*

It can be shown that in order to have a δ-burst over a set of n elements we must have: $n \geq \mathcal{B}_1 + \cdots + \mathcal{B}_\delta + (\delta - 1)$. Since at least αn original elements have to be received δ must not exceed $\min(\lfloor \frac{n+1}{2} \rfloor, (1 - \alpha)n)$ either. Once δ and the δ-length $(\mathcal{B}_1, \ldots, \mathcal{B}_\delta)$ are chosen, it can be proved that there are:

$$N = \sum_{i_\delta = 1}^{\xi+1} \sum_{i_{\delta-1}=1}^{i_\delta} \cdots \sum_{i_2=1}^{i_3} \sum_{i_1=1}^{i_2} 1$$

possibilities to choose the starting positions $(p_1, \ldots, p_\delta)$ where ξ is the unique natural integer such that: $n = \mathcal{B}_1 + \cdots + \mathcal{B}_\delta + (\delta - 1) + \xi$. This value N represents the number of ways one can build a δ-burst $(\mathcal{B}_1, p_1, \ldots, \mathcal{B}_\delta, p_\delta)$ over $\{AP_1, \ldots, AP_n\}$. Since we want AP_i to be received, we must determine the number N_i of such δ-bursts which do not erase AP_i. We can assume that $\mathcal{O}$ chooses any δ-burst with equal likelihood. Thus:

$$P_{\mathcal{M}}(AP_i \text{ is received}) = \frac{N_i}{N}$$

If we denote k_i (respectively k_i') the maximal number of bursts which can occur over $\{AP_1, \ldots, AP_{i-1}\}$ (respectively $\{AP_{i+1}, \ldots, AP_n\}$) then we have to compute how many Δ-bursts $(\mathcal{B}_1, p_1, \ldots, \mathcal{B}_\Delta, p_\Delta)$ can occur over $\{AP_1, \ldots, AP_{i-1}\}$ and how many $(\delta - \Delta)$-bursts $(\mathcal{B}_{\Delta+1}, p_{\Delta+1}, \ldots, \mathcal{B}_\delta, p_\delta)$ can occur over $\{AP_{i+1}, \ldots, AP_n\}$. The value Δ describes the set $I(i) := \{0, \ldots, k_i\} \cap \{\delta - k_i', \ldots, \delta\}$. As before, we can prove:

$$N_i^\Delta = \left(\sum_{i_\Delta=1}^{b_1} \sum_{i_{\Delta-1}=1}^{i_\Delta} \cdots \sum_{i_2=1}^{i_3} \sum_{i_1=1}^{i_2} 1 \right) + \left(\sum_{i_{\delta-\Delta}=1}^{b_2} \sum_{i_{\delta-\Delta}=1}^{i_{\delta-\Delta}} \cdots \sum_{i_2=1}^{i_3} \sum_{i_1=1}^{i_2} 1 \right)$$

where $b_1 = i - (\mathcal{B}_1 + \cdots + \mathcal{B}_\Delta + (\Delta - 1))$ and $b_2 = \mathcal{B}_1 + \cdots + \mathcal{B}_\Delta + \Delta + \xi - i + 1$. So we can approximate $P_\mathcal{M}(P_i$ is authenticated) to:

$$
\sum_{\Delta \in I(i)} \left(\sum_{i_\Delta=1}^{b_1} \sum_{i_{\Delta-1}=1}^{i_\Delta} \cdots \sum_{i_2=1}^{i_3} \sum_{i_1=1}^{i_2} 1 + \sum_{i_{\delta-\Delta}=1}^{b_2} \sum_{i_{\delta-\Delta}=1}^{i_{\delta-\Delta}} \cdots \sum_{i_2=1}^{i_3} \sum_{i_1=1}^{i_2} 1 \right)
$$
$$
\sum_{i_\delta=1}^{\xi+1} \sum_{i_{\delta-1}=1}^{i_\delta} \cdots \sum_{i_2=1}^{i_3} \sum_{i_1=1}^{i_2} 1
$$
(4)

We previously mentioned that Miner and Staddon [17] used p-random graphs to resist multiple bursts. Namely they considered that the bursts occurring in the network can only have a finite number ℓ of pairwise different length $\mathcal{B}_1, \ldots, \mathcal{B}_\ell$. They assumed that each burst of length $\mathcal{B}_i$ can occur up to λ_i times. Their scheme was able to deal with any distribution of these $\delta := \lambda_1 + \cdots + \lambda_\ell$ bursts. Here we consider that each burst of length $\mathcal{B}_i$ exactly occurs λ_i times. We denote L_δ the set of δ-length we can generate with this duplicating process. The cardinality of L_δ is the multinomial coefficient:

$$
\binom{\delta}{\mathcal{B}_1 \cdots \mathcal{B}_\ell}
$$

Once again we assume that any δ-length has the same probability to be chosen by the opponent $\mathcal{O}$. We denote $\mathbb{P}(L_\delta)$ the set of permutations of L_δ. $\mathcal{B} := (\mathcal{B}_1, \ldots, \mathcal{B}_1, \ldots, \mathcal{B}_\ell, \ldots, \mathcal{B}_\ell)$ is an element of L_δ (each $\mathcal{B}_i$ is iterated λ_i times). We deduce the packet authentication probability provided by Lysyanskaya et al.'s scheme.

$$
P_\mathcal{M}(P_i \text{ is authenticated}) = \binom{\delta}{\mathcal{B}_1 \cdots \mathcal{B}_\ell}^{-1} \sum_{\tau \in \mathbb{P}(L_\delta)} P_{\tau(\mathcal{B})}(P_i \text{ is authenticated}) \quad (5)
$$

where $P_\mathcal{M}(P_i$ is authenticated) is approximated by (4) when $\mathcal{M}$ is the loss pattern corresponding to the δ-length $\tau(\mathcal{B})$.

The efficiency of an authentication scheme can be defined as the smallest value of the packet authentication probability it provides. In other words, we are interested in $\min_{i \in \{1,\ldots,n\}} P_\mathcal{M}(P_i$ is authenticated). Formulae (4) and (5) do not provide a clear lower bound on this minimal probability and therefore practical efficiency of the scheme is hard to guess. This motivates a search for a new authentication scheme exhibiting a clear authentication probability. This can be achieved by using LT codes as we will describe in the next session of this paper.

3   LT Codes for Multicast Stream Authentication

In this section, we will give a multicast authentication protocol using LT codes which is robust against packet loss and data injection. As in Sect. 2 we allow $\mathcal{O}$ to use any pattern $\mathcal{M}$ (not only the multiple-burst one) respecting the accuracy of (α, β). Our technique also allows any new user to join the communication group at any block boundary and exhibits a lower bound for the packet authentication probability. We will first review the construction of LT codes. Then we will develop our authentication scheme, prove its security and exhibit a minimal bound for the packet authentication probability.

Construction of LT Codes. We briefly describe how to generate outputs for LT codes and how to decode data. A complete description of both processes can be found in [12].

Encoding. We have a fixed number of input symbols denoted by $I_1, \ldots, I_n$. In order to generate a new encoding symbol E, we use a probabilistic distribution called the Robust Soliton distribution to choose the degree[4] d of the symbol E. We randomly pick d elements amongst the input symbols: $I_{i_1}, \ldots, I_{i_d}$[5]. We generate E as the XOR of $I_{i_1}, \ldots, I_{i_d}$. Using this process we can generate as many encoding symbols as we want since we only need to run the Robust Soliton distribution to get a new one.

Decoding. When the receiver gets m encoding symbols $E_1, \ldots, E_m$ he first builds the bipartite graph used to compute $E_1, \ldots, E_m$[6]. We would like to point out that it can happen that not every I_i is on the left hand side. This is true in particular if m is small and the encoding symbols have small degrees. At the beginning of the decoding process no I_j's have been covered[7]. They are initialized with 0's. We first release[8] all E_k's with a single adjacent vertex to cover their unique neighbor. The set of covered input symbols not yet processed is called the *ripple* and denoted R. All previous covered symbols belong to R. At each step one element I_j is processed as follows:
1. Each neighbor N_j^k of I_j has its value XOR-ed with I_j's.
2. I_j is removed as a neighbor of these elements N_j^k. That is, the corresponding edges are removed from the graph.
3. For each N_j^k having one remaining neighbor in the new graph, N_j^k is released from the graph and covers its remaining neighbors which are added to R (for those which were not already in).
4. I_j is released from R (because it has no neighbors any longer).
Step 3 and 4 make the size of R vary. The decoding process ends when R is empty. It is successful when $I_1, \ldots, I_n$ have been released from R. We will use the following theorem to deal with packet loss occurring during data transfer.

Theorem 2 ([12]). *For $\delta \in (0, 1)$, the decoding process fails with probability at most δ from any set of $m := n + (R + \frac{R}{2} + \cdots + \frac{1}{n-R}) \ln \left(\frac{R}{\delta}\right)$ encoding symbols where $R := c \ln \left(\frac{n}{\delta}\right) \sqrt{n}$ for a positive constant c determined within the Robust Soliton distribution.*

---

[4] Any LT code can be represented as a bipartite graph with $I_1, \ldots, I_n$ as the left hand side vertices and all encoding symbols as right hand side vertices. An edge is drawn between I_j and the encoding symbol E if I_j has been used to compute E. I_j is said to be a *neighbor* of E (and conversely). We use the term *degree* to denote the number of neighbors a symbol has.

[5] This is how we build the bipartite graph representing the LT code.

[6] The positions of the input symbols XOR-ed to build an encoding symbol E_i are sent along with E_i [9].

[7] An input symbol I_j is said to be *covered* when it is the only adjacent vertex of an encoding symbol E_k. The covering operation is a XOR of the current value of I_j with E_k.

[8] A symbol is said to be *released* when we remove its representing vertex from the graph.

Our Authentication Protocol. We will consider the same opponent model as in Sect. 2 and the same definitions for (α, β), h and the signature scheme (KeyGen,Sign,Verify). As said before data is processed per block of n packets: $P_1, \ldots, P_n$. We assume that the sender published a list of irreducible polynomials over $\mathbb{F}_2$ (remember that for any positive integer r, we can always build a irreducible polynomial of degree r over $\mathbb{F}_2$ [11]). On this public list he also puts δ, n, α, β, PK as well as h and the verification algorithm Verify. We denote τ_{par} the tag representing the communication parameters, namely: $\tau_{\mathrm{par}} = n\|\alpha\|\beta\|\delta$. We assume that this tag is represented with a fixed number of bits b_{par}. We denote $\mathcal{H}$ the size of a hash produced by h and $\mathcal{S}$ the size of a signature. We first introduce the algorithm used by the sender.

Authenticator

Input: The private key SK, the network rates α, β, a block $\{P_1, \ldots, P_n\}$, its BID and the parameter δ.

1. Compute $\mathcal{N} = \begin{cases} \max(\lceil \frac{m}{\alpha} \rceil, \lceil \frac{\beta}{\alpha^2} \rceil) & \text{if } \frac{\beta}{\alpha^2} \notin \mathbb{N} \\ \max(\lceil \frac{m}{\alpha} \rceil, \frac{\beta}{\alpha^2} + 1) & \text{otherwise} \end{cases}$ where m is defined in Theorem 2.

Consider the n packets as input symbols for the LT code and build $\mathcal{N}$ encoding symbols: $E_1, \ldots, E_{\mathcal{N}}$. Each symbol E_i is along with the positions of its d_i neighbors $N_i^1, \ldots, N_i^{d_i}$. Compute the hashes: $\forall i \in \{1, \ldots \mathcal{N}\}\ h_i = h(E_i\|N_i^1\|\cdots\|N_i^{d_i})$.

2. Compute the block signature: $\sigma = \mathrm{Sign}_{\mathrm{SK}}(h(\mathrm{BID}\|\tau_{\mathrm{par}}\|h_1\|\cdots\|h_{\mathcal{N}}))$ and form the authentication tag $\tau = \tau_{\mathrm{par}}\|h_1\|\cdots\|h_{\mathcal{N}}\|\sigma$. Compute $k = \begin{cases} \lfloor \frac{\alpha^2 \mathcal{N}}{\beta} \rfloor & \text{if } \frac{\alpha^2 \mathcal{N}}{\beta} \notin \mathbb{N} \\ \frac{\alpha^2 \mathcal{N}}{\beta} - 1 & \text{otherwise} \end{cases}$.

Denote $\ell = k - [\mathcal{N}\mathcal{H} + \mathcal{S} + b_{\mathrm{par}}] + 1$ and pad τ with ℓ zeros: $\tau' = \tau\|0^\ell$.

3. Write τ' as the concatenation of $(k+1)$ elements of $\mathbb{F}_{2^r}$: $p_0\|\cdots\|p_k$. Compute $r = \max\left(\lceil \log_2(\mathcal{N}) \rceil, \left\lceil \frac{\mathcal{H}\mathcal{N} + \mathcal{S} + b_{\mathrm{par}}}{k+1} \right\rceil \right)$. Form the polynomial $P(X) = \sum_{i=0}^{k} p_i X^i$ and evaluate it in the first $\mathcal{N}$ points[9] of $\mathbb{F}_{2^r}$: $\forall i \in \{1, \ldots, \mathcal{N}\}\ y_i = P(i)$.

4. Form the authenticated packets: $\forall i \in \{1, \ldots, \mathcal{N}\}\mathrm{AP}_i = \mathrm{BID}\|i\|E_i\|N_i^1\|\cdots\|N_i^{d_i}\|y_i$

Output: $\{\mathrm{AP}_1, \ldots, \mathrm{AP}_{\mathcal{N}}\}$: set of authenticated packets

We first notice that even when the channel rates α, β change the structure of the LT code does not need to be modified since we keep working with the same inputs $P_1, \ldots, P_n$ and the same value c for the Robust Soliton distribution. Only the number $\mathcal{N}$ of encoding symbols to be generated increases. This is an advantage over Lysyanskaya et al.'s technique since the size of their field as well as the rate of their code have to be updated in case of modification of network rates. In addition it can be shown that the ratio $\frac{\mathcal{N}}{n}$ (as a function of n) is asymptotically bounded by a constant.

We now justify our choices for $\mathcal{N}, k, r$ and $P(X)$. In order to recover $P_1, \ldots, P_n$ with probability at least $1 - \delta$ despite loss, the integer $\mathcal{N}$ must verify $\alpha \mathcal{N} \geq m$. In addition we want to represent the hashes of these $\mathcal{N}$ encoding symbols as coefficients of a polynomial $P(X)$ of degree k over an extension of degree r of $\mathbb{F}_2$. We want k to be

---

[9] Since any element of $\mathbb{F}_{2^r}$ can be represented as $\lambda_0 Y^0 + \lambda_1 Y^1 + \ldots + \lambda_{r-1} Y^{r-1}$ where each λ_i belongs to $\mathbb{F}_2$. We define the first $\mathcal{N}$ elements as $(0, \ldots, 0), (1, 0, \ldots, 0), (0, 1, 0, \ldots, 0), (1, 1, 0, \ldots, 0)$ and so on until the binary decomposition of $(\mathcal{N} - 1)$.

as large as possible to minimize the extension degree r. The polynomial $P(X)$ will be evaluated in $\mathcal{N}$ different positions. The receiver must solve the polynomial reconstruction problem to recover $P(X)$. In order to run GS-Decoder, the sufficient condition exhibited by Guruswami and Sudan [8] is to have $T > \sqrt{kN}$ where N is the number of points used for the reconstruction, T the number of these points (x, y) such that $y = P(x)$. Due to the definition of (α, β) we have $T \geq \alpha \mathcal{N}$ and $\alpha \mathcal{N} \leq N \leq \beta \mathcal{N}$. Thus $(T > \sqrt{kN})$ is verified as soon as $0 \leq k < \frac{\alpha^2 \mathcal{N}}{\beta}$. Since we want to split τ' into several elements we have $k \geq 1$. Thus $\frac{\alpha^2 \mathcal{N}}{\beta} > 1$ which justifies the value of $\mathcal{N}$ at step 1. The optimality of k at step 2 follows.

Since $P(X)$ will be evaluated into $\mathcal{N}$ points we must have: $2^r \geq \mathcal{N}$. We want to represent τ as the concatenation $p_0 \| \cdots \| p_k$ the size of which is $(k + 1)r$ since each p_i is an element of $\mathbb{F}_{2^r}$. On the other hand the size of τ is $\mathcal{N} \mathcal{H} + \mathcal{S} + b_{\text{par}}$. Thus r must verify $(k + 1)r \geq \mathcal{N} \mathcal{H} + \mathcal{S} + b_{\text{par}}$. Therefore $r \geq \frac{\mathcal{H} \mathcal{N} + \mathcal{S} + b_{\text{par}}}{k + 1}$. This justifies both choices of ℓ and r at steps 2 and 3.

Now we describe a variant of the GS-Decoder called *Modified GS-Decoder* (MGS-Decoder) which will be used as a subroutine of our decoding algorithm.

MGS-Decoder

<u>Input</u>: The number of packets per block n, the network rates α, β, the degree of the polynomial k and N elements $\{(x_i, y_i), 1 \leq i \leq N\}$.

1. If $N > \beta n$ or we have less than αn distinct values (x_i, y_i) then the algorithm stops.
2. Run GS-Decoder on the N points to get the list L of all polynomials of degree at most k over $\mathbb{F}_{2^r}$ passing through at least αn of the N points.
3. Write the list L as: $L = \{L_1(X), \ldots, L_\mu(X)\}$. Write each element of L as: $L_i(X) =$
$$\sum_{j=0}^{k} \mathcal{L}_{ij} X^j$$ where $\forall i \in \{0, \ldots, k\} \mathcal{L}_{ij} \in \mathbb{F}_q$. Form the elements: $\mathcal{L}_i = \mathcal{L}_{i0} \| \cdots \| \mathcal{L}_{ik}$.

<u>Output</u>: $\{\mathcal{L}_1, \ldots, \mathcal{L}_\mu\}$: list of candidates

When the receiver gets data he first runs MGS-Decoder to build a list of elements (which are polynomial coefficients) and tests each of them until the signature is verified or the list exhausted. When the signature is recovered the receiver knows the hashes of the original encoding symbols of the LT code. Then he browses amongst the received packets to find as many original encoding symbols as he can. Due to the definition of α, there are at least $\alpha \mathcal{N}$ of them. Using the first $\alpha \mathcal{N}$ ones he attempts to decode the LT code to recover all the original packets $P_1, \ldots, P_n$. According to Theorem 2, this succeeds with probability at least $1 - \delta$. Here is the formal description of the algorithm.

Decoder

<u>Input</u>: The public key PK, the number of packets per block n, the network rates α, β, the block number BID, the parameter δ, the sender's list of irreducible polynomials and the set of received packets RP.

1. Compute $\mathcal{N}$. Write the packets as $\text{BID}_i \| j_i \| E_{j_i} \| N_{j_i}^1 \| \cdots \| N_{j_i}^{d_{j_i}} \| y_{j_i}$ and discard those having $\text{BID}_i \neq \text{BID}$ or $j_i \notin \{1, \ldots, \mathcal{N}\}$. Denote N the number of remaining packets. If $(N < \alpha n$ or $N > \beta n)$ then the algorithm stops.
2. Rename the set of received packets $\{\text{AP}'_1, \ldots, \text{AP}'_N\}$ and write each element as:

$AP'_i = BID\|j_i\|E_{j_i}\|N^1_{j_i}\| \cdots \|N^{d_{j_i}}_{j_i}\|y_{j_i}$ where $j_i \in \{1,\dots,\mathcal{N}\}$. Compute k and r. Get the irreducible polynomial of degree r from the sender's public list and run MGS-Decoder on the set $\{(j_i,y_{j_i}), 1 \le i \le N\}$ to get a list $\{c_1,\dots,c_\mu\}$ of candidates for signature verification. If MGS-Decoder rejects that set then the algorithm stops.

3. Compute ℓ. Initialize $h_i = \emptyset$ for $i \in \{1,\dots,\mathcal{N}\}$. Initialize $i = 1$. While the list has not been exhausted (and the signature not verified yet), we pick c_i. We first check if the ℓ last bits are zeros (we verify the length of the pad). If so, we write c_i as: $\tau^i_{\text{par}}\|h^i_1\| \cdots \|h^i_\mathcal{N}\|\sigma^i$. If $\tau^i_{\text{par}} = \tau_{\text{par}}$ then check whether $\text{Verify}_{\text{PK}}(h(BID\|\tau^i_{\text{par}}\|h^i_1\| \cdots \|h^i_\mathcal{N}),\sigma^i) = \text{true}$. In this case we set $h_j = h^i_j$ for $j \in \{1,\dots,\mathcal{N}\}$ and break out the loop. In any other cases we increment i by 1 and start again the while loop.

4. If $(h_1,\dots,h_\mathcal{N}) = (\emptyset,\dots,\emptyset)$ then the algorithm stops. Otherwise set $E'_\lambda = \emptyset$ for $\lambda \in \{1,\dots,\mathcal{N}\}$. For each AP'_i written as at step 2, if $h(E_{j_i}\|N^1_{j_i}\| \cdots \|N^{d_{j_i}}_{j_i}) = h_\lambda$ then $E_\lambda = E_{j_i}$, $d_\lambda = d_{j_i}$ and $\forall\xi \in \{1,\dots,d_{j_i}\}N^\xi_\lambda = N^\xi_{j_i}$.

5. Pick the first $\alpha\mathcal{N}$ non-empty elements E_μ and decode the LT code using the E_μ's as encoding symbols with degree d_μ and adjacent vertices positions $E^1_\mu,\dots,E^{d_\mu}_\mu$. Get n input symbols $\{P'_1,\dots,P'_n\}$ (where some of them can be empty).

Output: $\{P'_1,\dots,P'_n\}$: set of identified packets

Security of the Scheme. We will now analyze the security of our authentication scheme. We want the receivers to authenticate data despite malicious actions performed by $\mathcal{O}$. Similar to [14], we give the following definition:

Definition 5. (KeyGen,Authenticator,Decoder) *is a secure and (α,β)-correct probabilistic multicast authentication scheme if no probabilistic polynomial-time opponent $\mathcal{O}$ can win with a non-negligible probability to the following game:*

  i) *A key pair* (SK, PK) *is generated by* KeyGen

  ii) *$\mathcal{O}$ is given: (a) The public key* PK *and (b) Oracle access to* Authenticator *(but $\mathcal{O}$ can only issue at most one query with the same block identification tag* BID)

  iii) *$\mathcal{O}$ outputs* (BID, n,α,β,δ, RP)

$\mathcal{O}$ wins if one of the following happens:

  a) *(violation of the correctness property) $\mathcal{O}$ succeeds to output* RP *such that even if it contains $\alpha\mathcal{N}$ packets of some authenticated packet set* AP_i *for block identification tag* BID, *decoding failure probability δ and parameters n,α,β, the decoder authenticates some incorrect packets.*

  b) *(violation of the security property) $\mathcal{O}$ succeeds to output* RP *such that the decoder outputs $\{P'_1,\dots,P'_n\}$ which is non-empty and was never authenticated by* Authenticator *for the value* BID, *the probability δ and parameters n,α,β.*

The difference from the definition given in [14] is that the packets are authenticated by the receiver with certain probability. In short, even if the receiver gets a set RP having at least $\alpha\mathcal{N}$ original elements, the whole original set $\{P_1,\dots,P_n\}$ is recovered with some probability. Nevertheless Definition 5 involves that no incorrect packets can be authenticated. That is: $\forall i \in \{1,\dots,n\} P'_i \in \{\emptyset, P_i\}$ where P'_i denotes the ith

packet output by Decoder. Lysyanskaya et al. showed that their scheme is secure and (α, β)-correct. Following their arguments, we obtain the following result for ours.

Theorem 3. *Our scheme* (KeyGen,Authenticator,Decoder) *is secure and* (α, β)-correct.

Proof (Sketch). If the scheme is neither secure nor (α, β)-correct then $\mathcal{O}$ is able to create data packets which will be authenticated by the receiver after LT decoding at step 5. Nevertheless the LT decoding process is consistent. That is, if only correct encoding symbols are given to the decoder then it only outputs the corresponding input symbols (along with some empty symbols when the decoding process is not successful). Therefore $\mathcal{O}$ is able to create (at least) one fake symbol $\tilde{E}_i \| \tilde{N}_i^1 \| \ldots \| \tilde{N}_i^{\tilde{d}_i}$ such that its hash $\tilde{h}_i$ is a part of the element $\tilde{c}$ which successfully verified the signature at step 3. Since h is collision resistant, we have: $\forall j \in \{1, \ldots, \mathcal{N}\}\, \tilde{h}_i \neq h_j$. Thus $\tilde{c}$ was never signed by the sender and $\mathcal{O}$ is able to break the signature scheme. Due to space limitations we did not include the complete proof here. It can still be found in the extended version of this paper. It exhibits the necessity of using τ_{par} as a part of the authentication tag. $\square$

Thus our authentication scheme is as secure and correct as the technique developed in [14]. We will now study the packet authentication probability of our protocol.

Analysis of the Packet Authentication Probability. We now justify our use of LT codes to enable the receivers to recover all the n data packets $P_1, \ldots, P_n$ despite loss with probability close to 1 as claimed in Sect. 1. We assume that the receiver gets a set RP of packets. Since (α, β) is the network accuracy we have $|\text{RP}| \leq \beta \mathcal{N}$ and at least $\alpha \mathcal{N}$ original authenticated packets are amongst RP. As before we denote $\mathcal{M}$ the modification pattern used by $\mathcal{O}$. We fix i in $\{1, \ldots, n\}$. To be more concise we denote V_{RP} the probabilistic event $\{\text{RP verifies the signature}\}$. Using Bayes' theorem we get:

$$p_{\mathcal{M}}(P_i \text{ is authenticated}|V_{\text{RP}})\, p_{\mathcal{M}}(V_{\text{RP}})$$
$$=$$
$$p_{\mathcal{M}}(V_{\text{RP}}|P_i \text{ is authenticated})\, p_{\mathcal{M}}(P_i \text{ is authenticated})$$

Again, even if one of the events $\{P_i \text{ is authenticated}\}$ or V_{RP} is $p_{\mathcal{M}}$-negligible the previous equality is still true since both products would be 0. Due to the design of Decoder, a necessary condition to output packets is to verify the signature. So: $p_{\mathcal{M}}(V_{\text{RP}}|P_i \text{ is authenticated}) = 1$. On the other hand, since (α, β) is accurate RP always verifies the signature since MGS-Decoder outputs the list of all polynomials passing through at least $\alpha \mathcal{N}$ of the elements of RP. Thus the polynomial used by the sender belongs to that list and therefore the signature is verified. So: $p_{\mathcal{M}}(V_{\text{RP}}) = 1$. Thus we get: $p_{\mathcal{M}}(P_i \text{ is authenticated}) = p_{\mathcal{M}}(P_i \text{ is authenticated}|V_{\text{RP}})$ which can be written as:

$$p_{\mathcal{M}}(P_i \text{ is authenticated}) = p_{\mathcal{M}}(\text{All packets are authenticated}|V_{\text{RP}})$$
$$+$$
$$p_{\mathcal{M}}(\{P_i \text{ is authenticated}\} \cap \{\text{At least one } P_j \text{ is not authenticated}\}|V_{\text{RP}})$$

Since $p_{\mathcal{M}}(V_{\text{RP}}) = 1$, we deduce:

$$p_{\mathcal{M}}(\text{All packets are authenticated}|V_{\text{RP}}) = p_{\mathcal{M}}(\text{The LT code is successfully decoded})$$

In addition we have:

$$p_{\mathcal{M}}(\{P_i \text{ is authenticated}\} \cap \{\text{At least one } P_j \text{ is not authenticated}\}|V_{\text{RP}})$$
$$=$$
$$p_{\mathcal{M}}(\{P_i \text{ is authenticated}\} \cap \{\text{The LT code is not successfully decoded}\})$$

The last event is not $p_{\mathcal{M}}$-negligible in general since any symbol released from the ripple during the LT decoding process is consistent with the original input symbols [12]. Thus:

$$p_{\mathcal{M}}(P_i \text{ is authenticated}) \geq p_{\mathcal{M}}(\text{The LT code is successfully decoded}) \geq 1 - \delta$$

Since this is true for any value i, we deduce that:

$$\min_{i \in \{1,\dots,n\}} p_{\mathcal{M}}(P_i \text{ is authenticated}) \geq 1 - \delta$$

We also notice that this lower bound does not depends on the modification pattern $\mathcal{M}$.

4   Other Families of Rateless Codes

In this section we will compare the complexity in encoding/decoding of LT, Online and Raptor codes. Indeed the security, correctness and computation of the lower bound on the packet authentication probability only depend on the fact that the LT decoding algorithm is consistent which is also the case for Online and Raptor codes. In addition we will also compare these families to the modified LT codes introduced by Harrelson et al. [9]. In their work, they changed the construction of LT codes given by Luby [12] to fit them to their practical implementations without altering their optimality (i.e. if we generate enough symbols then we can have $\delta \simeq 0$). Their technique consists of modifying the way the neighbors of each encoding symbol E are chosen. As in [12], the degree d is chosen using the Robust Soliton distribution. Instead of uniformly choosing the d neighbors, Harrelson et al. proposed to uniformly choose two integers a and b and to generate the positions of the d neighbors as $a\,i + b$ for $i \in \{1, \dots, d\}$. Thus it is useless to append the neighbors to the encoding symbol for transmission since only $E\|a\|b\|d$ needs to be sent. This means that the overhead per encoding symbol has a fixed and much smaller size than in [12]. This is of particular interest in our case (step 4 of Authenticator) since our overhead per packet is particularly limited and such a fixed size helps to avoid data congestion due to irregular flow of information within the network.

   Contrary to block codes which use finite field operations to encode and decode data, these families of rateless codes rely on XOR operations over packets. Based on the work done in [9, 12, 15, 26] we built Table 1. Both Raptor and Online codes require preprocessing of data before encoding. In [15], Maymounkov proposed two different ways to do so for Online codes. The complexities shown in Table 1 correspond to the second method since the first technique involves a dependence between the packet authentication probability and the number of packets per block. The notation ϵ_δ means that the element depends on the decoding failure probability δ but is independent from n.

Table 1. Complexity comparison for different classes of rateless codes

	Average number XOR operations for decoding	Number of encoding symbols generated	Decoding failure probability	Encoding symbol overhead
LT codes	$O(n\log(n/\delta))$	$n + O(\sqrt{n}\log^2(n/\delta))$	δ	variable
LT codes (modified)	$O(n\log(n/\delta))$	$n + O(n^{5/6}\,\mathrm{polylog}(n, 1/\delta))$	δ	constant
Online codes	$O(n\log(1/\epsilon_\delta))$	$(1 + \epsilon_\delta)n$ (fixed $\epsilon_\delta > 0$)	$O(\delta^\eta)$ (fixed $\eta > 0$)	variable
Raptor codes	$O(n\log(1/\epsilon_\delta))$	$(1 + \epsilon_\delta)n$ (fixed $\epsilon_\delta > 0$)	δ	variable

According to Table 1, Online and Raptor codes seem to have better encoding and decoding complexities than LT codes. Nevertheless Raptor codes were designed for the Binary Erasure channel (BEC) since the efficiency of its preprocessing part relies on the existence on good pre-codes to achieve linear time for both encoding and decoding process. That is the property which is achieved by Tornado codes on BEC [13, 26]. Given our opponent model it is unlikely that BEC can be the modification pattern used by $\mathcal{O}$. Nevertheless a recent work by Palanki and Yedidia [18] suggests that Raptor codes can still be practically more efficient than LT codes for our authentication scheme. Indeed they implemented both classes of codes on Additive White Gaussian Noise Channel and Binary Symmetric Channel and noticed that, even on these channels, Raptor codes outperformed LT codes for decoding. Etesami et al. [5] performed analoguous implementations and their results exhibited the same behavior. They also showed that Raptor codes could perform quite well on any arbitrary symmetric channel.

As suggested by Harrelson at al. [9], it is possible to reduce the size of information to be transmitted and achieve a constant packet overhead at the cost of extra symbols for decoding (see Table 1). Since achieving a regular throughput within the communication channel avoids data congestion, substituting original LT codes by their modifications in our authentication protocol is recommended (the value of m in Theorem 2 has to be updated consequently). Since Raptor codes are the concatenation of an erasure code (as Tornado codes for instance) and a LT code, these modifications can also be applied to these codes. Therefore we believe that practical implementations of the authentication scheme described in Sect. 3 will be even more efficient when substituting LT codes by Raptor codes (exhibiting the same modifications for their internal LT coding).

Nevertheless these threshold values enabling recovery of the n data packets can still be too important for some applications. Karp et al. [10] gave a formula expressing the probability of non-decoding u packets amongst n after receiving a fixed value of encoding symbols which can be chosen by the sender. This can be useful if the application which will run the received packets has a tolerance rate for loss of content. The sender computes the number of packets he has to transmit in order to achieve at most this rate of non-recovered packets. In this case the lower bound computed on Sect. 3 is not valid any longer but the security and correctness of the scheme are still preserved.

5   Conclusion

In 2003, Lysyanskaya et al. [14] designed a multicast authentication scheme dealing with both packet loss and data injection. Unfortunately its packet authentication probability does not exhibit an easy lower bound and when a packet is dropped during transmission its content is definitely lost for the receivers. Our technique, which can be considered as an extension of theirs, has two main advantages. First it allows the receivers to reconstruct erased data which, to our knowledge, had never been achieved yet by any existing multicast stream authentication protocol using signature dispersion. Second it exhibits a minimal lower bound on the packet authentication probability which can be chosen arbitrary close to 1. Our reconstruction property relies on the fact that (α, β) is the network accuracy which can be hard to determine when the communication group size is large. Hopefully any couple $(\tilde{\alpha}, \tilde{\beta})$ such that $\tilde{\alpha} \leq \alpha$ and $\beta \leq \tilde{\beta}$ will also be fine for our scheme. This is at the cost of creating more encoding symbols to run GS-Decoder. Thus this couple of parameters has to be chosen carefully in order to respect the heterogeneity of the receivers without generating unnecessary data. Our scheme also allows new users to join the communication group at any time since each block of n packets contains its own signature. We also proposed to use a modified version of LT codes to achieve reasonable and fixed overhead per packet preventing the network from having too irregular variations of data flow. Given [5, 18], we also stress that Raptor codes could provide good implementations of our scheme if used instead of LT codes.

Acknowledgment

The authors would like to thank Professor Josef Pieprzyk for valuable conversations as well as the anonymous reviewers for their comments to improve the quality of this paper. This work was supported by the Australian Research Council under ARC Discovery Project DP0344444. The first author's work was also funded by an iMURS scholarship supported by Macquarie University.

References

[1] C. Blundo, A. De Santis, A. Herzberg, S. Kutten, U. Vaccaro, and M. Yung. Perfectly-secure key distribution for dynamic conferences. In *Advances in Cryptology - Crypto'92*, volume 740 of *LNCS*. Springer - Verlag, August 1992.

[2] J. W. Byers, M. Luby, and M. Mitzenmacher. A digital fountain approach to asynchronous reliable multicast. In *IEEE Journal on Selected Areas in Communications*, volume 20, October 2002.

[3] Y. Challal, H. Bettahar, and A. Bouabdallah. A taxonomy of multicast data origin authentication: Issues and solutions. In *IEEE Communications Surveys and Tutorials*, volume 6, October 2004.

[4] Y. Desmedt, Y. Frankel, and M. Yung. Multi-receiver/multi-sender network security: Efficient authenticated multicast/feedback. In *INFOCOM '92*, May 1992.

[5] O. Etesami, M. Molkaraie, and A. Shokrollahi. Raptor codes on symmetric channels. Available online at: http://www.cs.berkeley.edu/~etesami/raptor.pdf, preprint 2003.

[6]   R. Gennaro and P. Rohatgi. How to sign digital streams. In *Proceedings of the 17th Annual International Cryptology*. Springer-Verlag, August 1997.

[7]   P. Golle and N. Modadugu. Authenticating streamed data in the presence of random packet loss. In *Proceedings of the Symposium on Network and Distributed Systems Security (NDSS 2001)*. Internet Society, February 2001.

[8]   V. Guruswami and M. Sudan.   Improved decoding of Reed-Solomon and algebraic-geometric codes. In *IEEE Transactions on Information Theory*, May 1999.

[9]   C. Harrelson, L. Ip, and W. Wang. Limited randomness LT codes. In *41st Annual Allerton Conference on Communication, Control and Computing*, October 2003.

[10] R. Karp, M. Luby, and A. Shokrollahi. Finite length analysis of LT codes. In *International Symposium on Information Theory, 2004*, June 2004.

[11] R. Lidl and H. Niederreiter. *Introduction to Finite Fields and their Applications - Revised Edition*. Cambridge University Press, 2000.

[12] M. Luby. LT codes. In *43rd Annual IEEE Symposium on Foundations of Computer Science*. IEEE ComputeR Society, November 2002.

[13] M. Luby, M. Mitzenmacher, M. Shokrollahi, and D. Spielman. Efficient erasure correcting codes. In *IEEE Transactions on Information Theory*, volume 47, February 2001.

[14] A. Lysyanskaya, R. Tamassia, and N. Triandopoulos.   Multicast authentication in fully adversarial networks. In *IEEE Symposium on Security and Privacy*, November 2003.

[15] P. Maymounkov. Online codes. Technical report, New York University, November 2002.

[16] R. Merkle. A certified digital signature. In *Advances in Cryptology - Crypto'89*. Springer - Verlag, 1989.

[17] S. Miner and J. Staddon. Graph-based authentication of digital streams. In *IEEE Symposium on Security and Privacy*, May 2001.

[18] R. Palanki and J. S. Yedidia. Rateless codes on noisy channels. In *38th Annual Conference on Information Sciences and Systems*, March 2004.

[19] A. Pannetrat and R. Molva. Authenticating real time packet streams and multicasts. In *7th International Symposium on Computers and Communications*, July 2002.

[20] V. Paxson. End-to-end Internet packet dynamics. In *IEEE/ACM Transactions on Networking*, June 1999.

[21] A. Perrig and J. D. Tygar. *Secure Broadcast Communication in Wired and Wireless Networks*. Kluwer Academic Publishers, 2003.

[22] J. Pieprzyk, T. Hardjono, and J. Seberry. *Fundamentals of Computer Security*. Springer, 2003.

[23] M. M. Rao. *Conditional Measures and Applications (Second Edition)*. CRC Press, 2005.

[24] P. Rohatgi. A compact and fast hybrid signature scheme for multicast packet authentication. In *6th ACM Conference on Computer and Communications Security*, 1999.

[25] R. Safavi-Naini and H. Wang. New results on multi-receiver authentication code. In *Advances in Cryptology - Eurocrypt'98*, volume 1403 of *LNCS*. Springer - Verlag, June 1998.

[26] A. Shokrollahi. Raptor codes. Technical report, Digital Fountain, June 2003.

[27] D. R. Stinson. *Cryptography: Theory and Practice*. CRC Press, 1995.

[28] C. Tartary and H. Wang. Efficient multicast stream authentication for the fully adversarial network. In *WISA 2005*, volume 3786 of *LNCS*. Springer - Verlag, August 2005.

[29] C. K. Wong and S. S. Lam. Digital signatures for flows and multicasts. In *IEEE/ACM Transactions on Networking*, volume 7, August 1999.

[30] M. Yajnik, S. Moon, J. Kurose, and D. Towsley. Measurement and modeling of the temporal dependence in packet loss. In *IEEE Conference on Computer Communications*, 1999.

Crossing Borders: Security and Privacy Issues of the European e-Passport*

Jaap-Henk Hoepman, Engelbert Hubbers, Bart Jacobs,
Martijn Oostdijk, and Ronny Wichers Schreur

Institute for Computing and Information Sciences
Radboud University Nijmegen
P.O. Box 9010, 6500 GL Nijmegen, the Netherlands
{jhh, hubbers, bart, martijno, ronny}@cs.ru.nl

Abstract. The first generation of European e-passports will be issued
in 2006. We discuss how borders are crossed regarding the security and
privacy erosion of the proposed schemes, and show which borders need
to be crossed to improve the security and the privacy protection of the
next generation of e-passports. In particular we discuss attacks on Basic
Access Control due to the low entropy of the data from which the access
keys are derived, we sketch the European proposals for Extended Access
Control and the weaknesses in that scheme, and show how fundamentally
different design decisions can make e-passports more secure.

1   Introduction

After several years of preparation, many countries start issuing e-passports with
an embedded chip holding biometric data of the passport holder in 2006. This is
a major ICT-operation, involving many countries, most of them providing their
own implementation, using biometrics at an unprecedented scale. Passport security must conform to international (public) standards, issued by the International
Civil Aviation Organization (ICAO) [11, 10]. The standards cover confidentiality, integrity and authenticity of the passport data, including the facial image.
Additionally, the European Union (EU) has developed its own standards (called
"Extended Access Control").

The present paper reviews these developments (like in [14, 15]) especially from
a European perspective, with corresponding emphasis on fingerprint protection.
Also it tries to put these developments within a wider perspective of identity
management (IM) by governments, following [8]. This leads to a "revision" plan
for e-passports.

From an academic background we, the authors, closely follow the introduction of the e-passport in the Netherlands. We have advised the government on
several matters, and are involved in public debates on related issues. We have
received an early test version of the e-passport, and developed our own reader-
side software, based on the ICAO protocols. We have had access to confidential

---

* Id: passport.tex,v 1.44 2006/06/30 07:25:14 ronny Exp.

H. Yoshiura et al. (Eds.): IWSEC 2006, LNCS 4266, pp. 152–167, 2006.

material regarding the EU-protocols. However, the present paper is based solely on publicly available material, and is organised as follows.

We first discuss the main security requirements the new e-passport should satisfy. After a brief discussion of biometry in Sect. 3, we describe the standard security measures of the ICAO standard and the weaknesses associated with them in Sect. 4. Future European e-passports will be equipped with Extended Access Control, which we outline in Sect. 5, and whose shortcomings we also study. e-Passports enable new applications. Sect. 6 discusses the danger of such function creep but also investigates the new possibilities created by such applications. We study identity management issues of the e-passport in Sect. 7, and evaluate the realisation of the original goals in Sect. 8. We finish the paper with some proposals for more fundamental changes to the architecture of a second generation of e-passports that will increase both their security and their flexibility of use in new applications.

2   Aims and Security Goals

It is a fact that modern passports are hard to forge. Thus, many criminal organisations do not even try such fraud, but instead collect large numbers of genuine passports, and pick one that shows a reasonable resemblance to a member that needs a new identity. Similarly, passports are sometimes borrowed for illegal border crossing, and later returned to the rightful owner.

The original aim of the use of biometrics in travel documents is thus to combat "look-alike" fraud. Hence the emphasis is on biometric *verification* (instead of *identification*), involving a 1:1 check to make sure that a particular passport really belongs to a particular person.

The biometrics of the passport holder will be included in a chip that is embedded in the passport. Communication with the chip will be wireless, and not via contact points, because wireless communication allows higher data rates, does not involve wear, and does not require a change of the standard format of the passport to for instance credit-card size[1].

The wireless character does introduce new security risks (with respect to traditional passports), for the holder, the issuing state, and for the accepting state. At a high level of abstraction, the following three security goals seem reasonable. The first two focus on confidentiality for the passport holder. The last one mainly concerns the accepting (and also issuing) state.

1. A passport reader should identify itself first, so that only "trusted" parties get to read the information stored in the chip.
2. No identifying information should be released without consent of the passport holder.
3. The receiver of the information should be able to establish the integrity and authenticity of the data.

---

[1] A change of format for other official documents, like a drivers licence, is seen as less problematic, because such a document is not stamped.

The first goal relates to the situation where for instance a police officer wishes to check your identity. In most countries you have the right to ask the police officer in question to identify himself first, so that you can be sure that you are dealing with a genuine representative of the state. The second goal is relevant to prevent "RFID-bombs" [14] for instance, that are activated by the immediate presence of (the passport of) a particular person, or citizen of a particular country. Such information is also useful for a terrorist who is trying to decide whether to blow himself up in a particular bus. We shall evaluate the realisation of these goals later on, in Sect. 8

3   Biometry

This paper does not focus on the biometry involved, but a few words are in order. ICAO has opted for the use of facial images and fingerprints as primary biometrics because they are reasonably familiar, easy to use, and non-intrusive. A controversial issue—from a privacy perspective—is that the passport chip will not contain templates but pictures (actual JPEGs). The reason is that there is no well-established digital standard for such templates, and early commitment to a closed proprietary format is not desirable. This means that if a passport chip (or data base, or reader) is compromised, original biometric data leaks out, which may lead to reconstruction and additional (identity) fraud.

The effectiveness of biometry is highly overrated, especially by politicians and policy makers. Despite rapid growth in applications, the large-scale use of biometry is untested. The difficulty is that it is not only unproven in a huge single application (such as e-passports), but also not with many different applications in parallel (including "biometry for fun"). The interference caused by the diversity of applications—each with its own security policy, if any—may lead to unforeseen forms of fraud.

A basic issue that is often overlooked is fallback. What if my biometric identity has been compromised, and I am held responsible for something I really did not do, how can I still prove "it wasn't me"?

The Netherlands has recently conducted a field test for the enrolment procedures of the biometric passport, see [19], involving almost 15.000 participants. The precise interpretation of the outcome is unclear, but failure-to-acquire turns out to be a significant problem, especially for young and elderly people. Substantial numbers of people will thus not have appropriate biometric travel documents, so that fully automatic border crossing is not an option.

4   Standard Security Measures (ICAO)

The various ICAO standards for machine readable travel documents, notably [11] and [10], specify precise requirements for accessing and interpreting the contents of the embedded chip. Different security controls are described to ensure that different security goals are met. We discuss these in the order in which the mechanisms are used in a typical session between reader (or: inspection system,

Fig. 1. Example of a Dutch passport. The two bottom lines of text are the MRZ.

the computer that is attempting to read information from the document) and the European passport chip.

BAC: Basic Access Control. Before any information can be read from a passport, the reader needs to go through *basic access control* (BAC). This is a challenge-response protocol in which the reader proves to the passport that it has knowledge of the contents of the machine readable zone (MRZ). The MRZ consists of two lines of optically readable text containing among others the name of the holder, and the passport number. It is printed on the first page of the physical document (See Fig. 1).

The procedure is as follows. The reader optically reads the contents of the MRZ, and derives the *access key* seed $k_{IFD/ICC}$ from the data it reads. After that, the reader proves to the chip that it has optically read the MRZ by signing a random challenge from the chip using a key derived from the access key seed. Subsequently, passport and inspection system exchange some extra random data, which is then used to generate session keys and an initial counter for secure messaging. The session keys are fresh for each session.

BAC prevents so-called *skimming* of passports, i.e., reading the contents without the cardholder's knowledge. Note that BAC does not authenticate the reader: anyone who knows the MRZ can successfully complete BAC and continue reading other information on the chip.

SM: Secure Messaging. Confidentiality and integrity of all communication between reader and passport is provided by so-called *secure messaging*. Commands sent to the passport as well as responses sent back to the reader are encrypted and augmented with a message authentication code (MAC), using the keys established during BAC. A sequence counter is included to prevent replay of messages.

PA: Passive Authentication. The data stored on the passport is organised in a logical data structure (LDS), which consists of a number of files (called data groups). Typical examples of data groups are: a file containing the information in the MRZ, a file containing a JPEG image of the cardholder's face, and files containing other biometric features such as the cardholder's fingerprints.

Each data group in the LDS is hashed. All these hashes together form the (document) *security object* SO_{LDS}. The security object is signed by the issuing country and the result, SO_D, is stored on the passport as well. This means that the inspection system can check that the contents of the LDS have not been altered during communication, thus ensuring the integrity of the LDS. The standards refer to this integrity protection mechanism as *passive authentication*.

AA: Active Authentication. To prevent cloning of the chip, an integrity mechanism called *active authentication* is used, in which the passport proves possession of a private key k_{AA} using a challenge-response protocol. The corresponding public key, needed by the inspection system to check the response of the passport, is part of the LDS and can be read by the inspection system. A hash of this public key is signed through the SO_D, to ensure authenticity.

4.1   Guessing the Access Key

To access the passport without having its MRZ, one needs to guess the access key seed $k_{IFD/ICC}$, which is 128 bits long. The National Institute of Standards and Technology (NIST) [18] and the ECRYPT EU Network of Excellence on cryptology [3] recommend 80 bits for a minimal level of general purpose protection in 2005, and 112 bits ten years from now. In other words, the access key seed is long enough to provide adequate security.

But the fact that the access key seed is derived from information in the MRZ can be used to the attackers' advantage. The 'MRZ-information' consists of the concatenation of the passport number, date of birth and date of expiry, including their respective check digits, as described in [9]. Given a guess for the MRZ-information, the corresponding access key seed $k_{IFD/ICC}$ is easily calculated, and from that all other session keys can be derived as well. These keys can then be tried against a transcript of an eavesdropped communication session between this passport and the reader, to see if they deliver meaningful data.

To estimate the amount of work the attacker needs to perform for such an off-line attack, we estimate the amount of Shannon entropy of each of these fields. We should stress this is a very crude approach (unless we assume the underlying probability distributions are uniform). For lower bounds, we should in fact use the Guessing entropy [17] ($\sum_i i p_i$) or even the min-entropy ($\min_i - \log p_i$). The Shannon entropy only gives us an upper bound, but if that bound is small the security of the system is most certainly weak.

The entropy of the *date of birth* field is $\log(100 \times 365.25) = 15.16$ bits, as it can contain only the last two digits of the year of birth. If one can see the holder of the passport and guess his age correct within a margin of 5 years, the entropy of this field decreases to 10.83.

The *date of expiry* is determined by the date of issuing and the validity period of a passport. In the Netherlands, passports are valid for 5 years, and are issued only on working days (barring exceptional circumstances). For a *valid* passport, the entropy of this field becomes $\log(5 \times 365.25 \times 5/7) = 10.34$.

The MRZ field for the *passport number* can contain 9 characters. If the passport number is longer, the excess characters are stored in the MRZ optional data field (which is not used to derive the access key seed). The entropy of

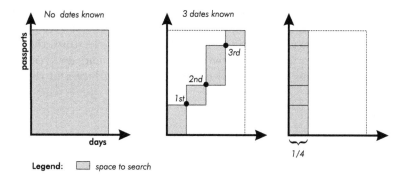

Fig. 2. Known dates of issuing reduce the search space

the passport number field, assuming digits and upper-case letters only, becomes $\log((26 + 10)^9) = 46.53$. Many countries have further restrictions on the format of their passport numbers. Passport numbers may contain check digits, or start with a common prefix to distinguish passport types (e.g., military passports).

At best, the total entropy of date of birth, date of expiry and passport number becomes $15.16+10.34+46.53 = 72.03$, which is less than 80 bits recommended by both NIST and ECRYPT [3, 18] to protect against eavesdropping and other off-line attacks. It *is* sufficient to protect against skimming attacks (where possible keys are tried on-line) because the passport is slow to respond to each individual key tried.

In certain countries the situation is even worse. Often, passport numbers are issued sequentially. This implies there is a correlation between the date of issue (and therefore date of expiry) and the passport number. Moreover, all currently valid passports numbers (ignoring stolen or otherwise invalidated ones) form a consecutive range, which is no longer than the total number of people of that nationality. For the Dutch passport for instance, bounding the population from above by 20 million, the passport number entropy drops to $\log(20 \times 10^6) = 24.25$.

With sequentially issued passports, the entropy drops even further with every known combination of a passport number and the expiry date. Suppose we know k such combinations. This gives rise to $k + 1$ intervals of possible passport numbers for a given date range Let us take the rather pessimistic approach that we do not assume anything about the distribution of passports over dates within those intervals (although it is very likely that passports are issued at a reasonably constant rate). On the optimistic side, let us assume the k known passports are issued evenly distributed over the validity period length. This reduces the search space by a factor $k + 1$ as illustrated in Fig. 2. Hence the entropy of expiry date plus passport number drops with $\log(k+1)$. For the Dutch passport, using $k = 15$ and the figures above, the entropy of the passport number becomes as small as 20.25, and the total entropy could be as small as $10.83 + 10.34 + 20.25 = 41.42$ (when we assume we can guess the age of the passport holder).

One obvious idea is to include the MRZ optional data field in the list of MRZ items that is used to derive the MRZ access key seed. This would increase the entropy of the MRZ access key seed, especially if this optional data field is filled with random data. Unfortunately some countries already use this field for other purposes. In the Netherlands, for instance, this field stores the social-fiscal number, which is uniquely linked to an individual and not very secret information. In fact, this idea was recently rejected for inclusion in the ICAO standards.

4.2   Traceability

To avoid collisions, contactless smart cards and RFID systems use unique low-level tag identifiers in the radio communication protocol. This is also true for the e-passports. If this identifier is fixed (which is usually the case in RFID tags and contactless smart cards), passports are clearly easily traceable. Note that because this identifier is used in the very first stages of setting up a connection between the passport and the reader, no form of access control or reader authentication can be performed.

Luckily, this anti-collision identifier does not have to be fixed. The number can also be randomly generated each time the passport comes within range of a reader. If the random generator is of sufficient quality (and this is certainly an issue in low-end RFID systems), the passport can no longer be traced through the anti-collision identifier.

However, the anti-collision identifier creates a possible subliminal channel. For instance, instead of simply generating a random number r, the passport could be instructed to generate an anti collision identifier like

$$id = E_{k_{NSA}}(r, passportnumber) \ .$$

The resulting string looks random, because of the randomness of r and the properties of the encryption function. But clearly it can be decrypted by the owner of k_{NSA} to reveal the passport number. Unless the passport chip is reverse engineered, the existence of such a subliminal channel cannot be detected.

Another subliminal channel exists when Active Authentication is used [5]. Recall that active authentication requires the passport to sign a challenge from a reader using its unique private key. Because the challenge is totally determined by the reader, the reader can embed information into this string, which is unknowingly signed by the passport. For instance, the challenge could contain the border crossing location, and the current date and time. A signature adds an extra layer of non-repudiability to the border crossing logs, and can be used to prove this fact to others. The challenge could also contain the passport number of the person verified ahead of you at border inspection, possibly linking you to the person you were travelling with.

Even if all the above issues are addressed, discriminating features of passports remain. Different countries may use different chip suppliers. Later batches of passports will use more advanced technology, or may contain different or additional information[2]. In the future, newer versions of chip operating systems

---

[2] Indeed, the first passports will be issued without fingerprints.

may be used. All these differences may be noticeable by looking carefully at the behaviour of the chip on the radio channel, at the chip's Answer To Reset (ATR), which is sent in reaction to a reset command by the reader, or at the responses the chip gives (or doesn't give) to specific card commands sent to it. We expect to see large differences in behaviour especially on unintended, unexpected or even unspecified input sent to the card. All these things are possible before BAC has been performed.

Other applications may be put on the passports (see Sect. 6) as well. These applications may even be accessible before BAC has been performed. The set of available applications may actually constitute a narrow profile that identifies a specific set of possible passport holders, and may reveal the place of work, or the banks the passport holder has accounts with.

We conclude that even without access to the MRZ, i.e., in the classic skimming scenario on streets, public transport, etc., passports still leak information that can be traced back to individuals, or groups of individuals.

5   Extended Access Control

Standardisation of the security features and biometrics to be used in European passports has been taken up independently (but of course in accordance with the ICAO standards) by the European Union [7]. In recognition of the fact that biometric information is quite sensitive, the European Union has mandated that such data should be protected by a so-called "Extended Access Control" mechanism. The technical specifications of the European e-passport are drafted by a special EU Committee, founded as a result of Article 6 of Regulation 1683/95 laying down a uniform format for visas [6].

Public information about the details of Extended Access Control has recently become available [5, 16]. This allows us to discuss certain shortcomings in the schemes under consideration, although we wish to stress that these schemes are a huge improvement over the extremely minimal security features imposed by the ICAO standards.

Extended Access Control consists of two phases, Chip Authentication followed by Terminal Authentication. Chip Authentication performs the same function as Active Authentication in the ICAO standards, i.e., proving the chip is genuine and thus protecting the passport against cloning. It avoids the problems associated with active authentication, like the challenge semantics discussed in the previous section. Chip authentication achieves its task by first exchanging a session key using a Diffie-Hellman key exchange. The chip uses a static key pair for this, the public part of which is part of the logical data structure (LDS) on the chip and thus signed through the security objects SO_D. The terminal uses a fresh key pair for each session. Authenticity of the chip is established once the chip proves that it knows the session key, which happens implicitly when the session key is used successfully to communicate with the chip.

Terminal Authentication aims to prove to the chip that the terminal is allowed to access the data on the chip. This access is granted through a chain of certifi-

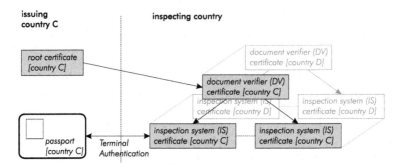

Fig. 3. Extended Access Control certificates

cates, the root of which is the issuer of the passport at hand (see Fig. 3). In other words, the issuer of the passport controls who can access the data on the passport. This root issues Document Verifier (DV) Certificates, one for each country that is granted access to the data on the passport. These DV certificates are used to generate Inspection System (IS) certificates, which can be distributed to inspection systems (e.g., readers/terminals) at border crossings. Each passport issued by a particular country can verify the authenticity of these DV certificates, and hence of the IS certificates issued through these DV certificates. A valid IS certificate grants access to certain data on the chip. All certificates have a limited validity period.

Terminal authentication, as proposed, does have a few weaknesses. First of all, the chip cannot keep time itself, and does not have access to a reliable source of time either. This makes it hard to check whether a certificate has expired or not. This, in turn, makes it practically impossible to revoke a certificate. The problem is the following. A terminal with a valid IS certificate and a valid DV certificate can access the sensitive data on many passports. When such a terminal is stolen, these access rights remain, even when the validity period of these certificates has expired: the chip does not know the correct time, and the terminal does not have to tell it the correct time. This is the case even if certificates have extremely short validity periods, like a single day. We see that one stolen terminal breaks the intended security goal of terminal authentication. Of course, stolen terminals do not make skimming attacks possible: a terminal still needs access to the MRZ in order to perform basic access control. To mitigate the problem somewhat, the standards propose that the chip keeps the most recent date seen on a valid certificate. In other words, the chip advances its idea of the current time each time it passes a border inspection system. This only saves the frequent travellers; people that barely use their passports stay vulnerable for a long time.

Secondly, the certificate hierarchy itself poses a problem. The hierarchy is quite shallow. It does not make it easy to allow access to the biometric data for other applications beyond border inspection, even though such applications are already being discussed today (see also Sect. 6 below). To acquire access, one has to apply for IS certificates at the country DV, or for a DV certificate at each issuing country. The latter would create a huge management overhead, as it would require each country to reliably verify the identity and trustworthiness of the requesting applicant and issue certificates in response. The first makes it impossible for countries to differentiate access rights among different applications, and would make the country DV responsible for the issuing of IS certificates for each and every terminal involved in the new application. This is clearly impractical, if we consider the use of passports for home banking or single sign-on systems that require terminals at each and every PC.

Making the certificate hierarchy larger and more flexible may not be an option. It means the chip has to verify even more certificates before it can grant access. This does put quite a burden on the processing capabilities of the chip, which should guarantee reasonably short transaction times. No one is willing to stand in the queue at border inspection for an even longer amount of time, simply because the new passports contain new, but slow, technology. A different, more flexible, approach is discussed in Sect. 9.

6   New Applications

The new e-passport requires an international infrastructure for biometric verification. This is a huge project, of which the effectiveness and risks are uncertain. The main driving force is political pressure: the logic of politics simply requires high profile action in the face of international terrorism. Once implemented, it inevitably leads to function creep: new possible applications emerge, either spontaneously or via new policy initiatives. We shall discuss two such applications, and speculate about the future.

Once we obtain a new passport with a high-end chip embedded with which we can communicate ourselves (via open standards), we can ask ourselves whether we can also use it for our own purposes. We briefly discuss two options: logon, and digital signatures.

The e-passport can be used to log on to your computer account. For instance, if you give your MRZ (or the associated keys) to your computer or local network, the logon procedure can set up a challenge-response session with your passport: activation of the chip happens via the MRZ, and checking of a signature written by the passport-chip on a challenge generated by your computer can proceed via the public key of the document signer. It allows your computer to check the integrity of the passports security object, which contains the public key corresponding to the private signature-key of your passport.

This authentication procedure only involves "something you have": anyone holding your passport can log in to your machine. You can strengthen the procedure by requiring a usual password, or even a biometric check based on a comparison of facial images (a freshly taken one, and the one on the chip).

You may also wish to use your e-passport to sign documents and emails using the embedded private key for Active Authentication. This is not such a good idea, for two reasons. First of all, the signature is obtained by exploiting the challenge-response mechanism for another purpose. Such interference should be avoided, because a challenge-response at a border inspection could then be misused to trick you into signing a certain document. Secondly, proving your identity after signing requires publication of your MRZ, together with the security object of your passport-chip (which is integrity-protected by a signature of the document signer): this object couples the public key (for your signature) to identifying information such as your name. But releasing the MRZ allows everyone to access your passport, through Basic Access Control.

The underlying problem is that the e-passport was not designed with an embedded useful certificate (such as X.509) for the holder.

Once there is an infrastructure for biometric verification, it becomes natural to ask: why not use it for identification as well? People may loose (willingly or unwillingly) their passport, or may apply for multiple copies, possibly under different names. Indeed, the government of the Netherlands is preparing legislation [1, 2] to set up a central database with biometric information, in order to "increase the effectiveness of national identification laws". Such a central database goes beyond what is required by European directives.

The possibility of biometric identification of the entire (passport-holding) population involves a change of power balance between states and their citizens. Consent or cooperation is then no longer needed for identification. Tracing and tracking of individuals becomes possible on a scale that we have not seen before.

Assuming the biometric passport leads to a reliable infrastructure for verification and identification of individuals, the societal pressure will certainly increase to use it in various other sectors than just border inspection. Such applications are not foreseen—or covered by—European regulations. Interested parties are police and intelligence forces, banks and credit card companies, social security organisations, car rental firms, casinos, etc. Where do we draw the line, if any?

We see that the introduction of the new e-passport is not only a large technical and organisational challenge, but also a societal one. Governments are implicitly asking for acceptance of this new technology. This acceptance question is not so explicit, but is certainly there. If some political action group makes a strong public case against the e-passport, and manages to convince a large part of the population to immediately destroy the embedded chip after issuance—for instance by putting the passport in a microwave—the whole enterprise will fail. The interesting point is that individuals do have decisive power over the use of the chip in their e-passport. Even stronger, such a political action group may decide to build disruptive equipment that can destroy the RFID-chips from some distance, so that passports are destroyed without the holder knowing (immediately). To counter such movements, governments may try to make it sufficiently unattractive or even impossible to cross borders for travellers without a functioning passport. This is only possible, however, if the numbers of broken chips is relatively low. And in any case, it will not improve popularity of the scheme to begin with.

7   Identity Management Issues

Identity management (IM) is about "rules-4-roles": regulation of identification, authentication and authorisation in and between organisations. The new e-passport is part of IM by states. It forms an identification and authentication mechanism that is forced upon citizens, primarily for international movement, but also for internal purposes.

Identification and authentication in everyday life is a negotiation process. When a stranger in the street asks for your biometric data, you will refuse. But you may engage in a conversation, discover mutual interests, and exchange business cards or phone numbers. Upon a next contact more identifying information may be released, possibly leading to a gradual buildup of trust.

The e-passport, in contrast, provides a rigid format. In certain situations it forms an overkill, for instance when you just need to prove that you are over eighteen. When IM goes digital and becomes formalised one would like to have more flexible mechanisms, with individual control via personal policies. In the future we may expect to be carrying identity tokens that flexibly react to the environment. Three basic rules for such systems are:

- The environment should authenticate itself first. For instance, when the environment can prove to be my home, my policy allows my token to release much personal information, for instance about my music preference or health.
- Authentication should be possible in small portions, for instance via certificates or credentials saying "this person is over eighteen", with a signature provided by a relevant authority.
- Automatic recognition of individuals, for instance via an implanted RFID chip that broadcasts your personal (social security) number, is excluded. Privacy is important for personal security—and not, as too often stated, only an impediment to public security.

8   Evaluation of Security Goals

In Sect. 2 we have formulated three security goals that we consider reasonable. In this section we evaluate whether the current system meets these goals.

Readers should identify themselves first. In the usual sense of "authenticated" or "trusted" readers, this goal is not reached. For instance, we managed to write our own terminal application that retrieves the public information like the facial image from the chip. And our reader is not considered trusted. The implemented BAC protocol only assures that the reader has knowledge of the MRZ on the passport. In the European implementation of EAC the reader must authenticate itself and hence this goal is more or less met for the information marked as sensitive, but weaknesses exist (see Sect. 5).

Consent by the passport holders. Theoretically this goal is reached. By use of BAC any terminal that tries to read information first needs to read the MRZ information printed on the inside of the passport. Hence the holder must give his consent for the transaction by opening his passport. However, as we have seen in Sect. 4.2 some subliminal channels exist that may leak information about the card even before BAC has been applied or in other words even before the holder has given his consent.

Proof of integrity and authenticity. The integrity part of this goal is reached by the secure messaging system, which is applied for all communication after BAC. As we have seen in Sect. 4 both commands and responses are encrypted and augmented with a message authentication code to provide integrity and confidentiality. Authenticity of the information is guaranteed through Passive Authentication (see Sect. 4)

9   e-Passport v2

Until now we have discussed several issues with the security and privacy protection of the current proposed standards for biometric passports, from both ICAO and, in particular, the EU. We have argued that protection mechanisms should be improved. However, improvements to such standards are at best incremental, and do not usually challenge the primary design decisions. In fact, such fundamental changes would certainly be backwards incompatible, and require a totally new standard. In our opinion, more fundamental changes are required to really provide strong security and proper privacy protection to the new generation of e-passports.

9.1   Avoiding Contactless Cards

The most fundamental change is to reconsider the choice for a wireless communication interface between the chip in the passport and the terminal at border inspection. Using a wireless interface makes skimming attacks possible. It is exactly the fear of this possibility that has sparked a huge controversy over the current e-passport proposals. Initially, the US passports would not even implement Basic Access Control. Now they are even considering to include metal shields in the cover pages of the passport to function as a Faraday cage, to physically disable the wireless communication link.

But all Basic Access Control really is, is a very elaborate way to achieve exactly the same as what is achieved when inserting a smart card with contacts into the slot of a reader: namely that the holder of the passport allows the owner of the terminal to read the data on the chip. Then, why not simply use smart cards with contacts for the new e-passport? The main arguments against this have been the form-factor of the passport, and the need for a sufficient bandwidth to quickly transmit the biometric data from the card to the terminal. However, identity cards and drivers licenses with dimensions similar to credit cards (ID-1) are already under consideration. And bandwidth concerns are no longer an issue either. Many smart card suppliers already sell smart cards with integrated USB 1.1 interfaces that allow for a much higher throughput, using the original [12] ISO contact module found on the card, and standardisation for this approach is underway [13]. Such a solution would take away all worries associated with using a wireless chip, and would keep the e-passport clear of all discussions surrounding the (perceived) privacy issues with RFID.

9.2 On-Line Terminal Authentication

Once a connection between passport and terminal is established, a decision has to be made regarding the access rights of the terminal and to determine which data on the passport it is allowed to read. Current EU proposals for extended access control are found wanting: stolen terminals cannot be revoked, and the shallow, rigid certificate hierarchy proposed to regulate access does not allow for flexible and/or dynamic access control policies (see Sect. 5). The EU approach was chosen to allow for off-line, mobile terminals, like those that are used by mobile border inspection units. But clearly such mobile terminals can be connected to the network over a wireless link, if only through GPRS, which is the standard on cell phones these days.

If we assume that terminals are always connected to the network, we can use on-line terminal authentication. The general idea is then the following.

Each terminal owns a private/public key pair. Each terminal is used for a particular application. This application is encoded in a certificate C_{AA} that contains the public key K_{TA} of the terminal, and which is signed by the application authority AA. Access rights are associated with application. Each country stores, for each application authority that it wishes to recognise, the access rights for that application. These access rights are stored in the back office. The back office also stores the public keys of all terminals that have been revoked.

On-line terminal authentication then proceeds as follows. First, the terminal sends the certificate C_{AA} (containing its public key K_{TA}) to the chip. The chip and the terminal perform a challenge-response protocol in which the terminal proves to the chip that it owns the private key corresponding to K_{TA}. This establishes the identity of the terminal. Next, the chip sets up an authenticated channel between itself and the back office of the issuing country. It can do so using a country certificate that is stored in the chip during personalisation. The channel should not be vulnerable to replay attacks. It sends C_{AA} (and K_{TA}) to the back-office. There, C_{AA} is verified against the known application authorities (this validates that K_{TA} was certified by such an authority) and K_{TA} is checked against the list of all revoked terminals. If these checks pass, the access rights for AA are sent back to the chip. If not, then the empty set (i.e., no access rights) is sent back to the chip. The chip interprets the access rights it receives and grants access to the terminal accordingly. Because the channel is authentic and does not allow replay attacks, the access rights received by the chip correspond to the certificate it sent to the back office.

With on-line terminal authentication, terminals can be revoked in real-time: as soon as they are marked as revoked in the back offices of the issuing country, no passport of that country will allow that terminal access to its data. Also, the access permissions can be changed dynamically, and can even be based on the exact time the request was made, or on the specific usage pattern of the passport. The general idea can be refined to also allow revocation of terminals by the countries that manage them, instead of requiring them to inform all other countries that a particular terminal should be revoked (because it was stolen, for instance). Also, more levels of certificates can be introduced, to make management of access rights easier.

9.3   Other Improvements

In Sect. 3 we have seen that real pictures are stored on the chip. With an immediate consequence that whoever is able to retrieve these images from the chip, has access to good biometric data, which he can use for identity theft. Using templates that work like a one-way function, it will be possible to check whether the template on the chip matches the template derived from the person who is claiming to be the holder of the passport. This leaking of real biometric data may not seem such a big deal in a time where many pictures are published on the Internet. The point here is that these pictures for the passports are taken under good conditions and hence provides highly accurate biometric information.

The entropy-related off-line attacks discussed in Sect. 4.1 are possible because a guess of MRZ-information directly leads to all keys used in a communication session. These keys can be checked against a transcript of that session to verify the guess. The situation is similar to many password-based authentication and session-setup protocols. Encrypted key exchange protocols, discovered by Bellovin and Merritt [4], do not suffer from this problem. There a low entropy password is used to exchange a high entropy secret that cannot efficiently be guessed using an off-line attack[3]. Using encrypted key exchange protocols for basic access control would strengthen the security of the passport considerably.

In Sect. 6 we have seen that it will be inevitable that other applications want to use the infrastructure available on the chip for other purposes than the original ones. In the current system it is already possible to sign things with a private key, but this causes some unwanted side effects as already described in Sect. 6. In order to prevent this the standards should be rewritten in such a way that at least these additional functions can be used and preferably in a disjoint setting from the border inspection functions. A possible implementation for this could be to have an X.509 certificate included with a public key that has nothing to do with the MRZ or other information needed for the border inspection tasks.

References

[1] Kamerstuk II 2004/2005, 25 764, nr. 26. (Official communication of the Dutch parliament).
[2] Kamerstuk II 2004/2005, 29 754, nr. 5. (Official communication of the Dutch parliament).

---

[3] Of course on-line attacks where all possible passwords are tried one by one can never be prevented.

[3] Yearly report on algorithms and keysizes (2005). Technical report, IST-2002-507932 ECRYPT, January 2006. D.SPA.10 Rev 2005-0.2.

[4] Steven M. Bellovin and Michael Merritt. Encrypted key exchange: Password-based protocols secure against dictionary attacks. In *IEEE Security & Privacy*, pages 72–84, Oakland, CA, USA, May 1992. IEEE.

[5] BSI. Advanced security mechanisms for machine readable travel documents – extended access control (eac). Technical Report TR-03110, BSI, Bonn, Germany, 2006.

[6] Proposal for a council regulation amending regulation (ec) no 1683/95 laying down a uniform format for visas. *OJ C*, 51:219–220, February 26 2002.

[7] Proposal for a council regulation on standards for security features and biometrics in eu citizens' passports. *OJ C*, 98:39, April 23 2004.

[8] Jaap-Henk Hoepman and Bart Jacobs. E-passports without the big picture. *eGov Monitor*, February 20 2006. http://www.egovmonitor.com/node/4716.

[9] ICAO. Machine Readable Travel Documents. Technical report, ICAO, 2003. 5th edition.

[10] ICAO. Development of a logical data structure - LDS for optional capacity expansion technologies, revision 1.7. Technical report, ICAO, May 2004.

[11] ICAO. PKI for machine readable travel documents offering ICC read-only access, version - 1.1. Technical report, Oct 2004.

[12] ISO 7816. ISO/IEC 7816 Identification cards – Integrated circuit(s) cards with contacts. Technical report, ISO JTC 1/SC 17.

[13] ISO 7816-12. ISO/IEC 7816 Identification cards – Integrated circuit(s) cards – Part 12: Cards with contacts – USB electrical interface and operating procedures. Technical report, ISO JTC 1/SC 17.

[14] A. Juels, D. Molnar, and D. Wagner. Security issues in e-passports. In *SecureComm 2005*, 2005.

[15] Gaurav S. Kc and Paul A. Karger. Security and privacy issues in machine readable travel documents (MRTDs). IBM Technical Report (RC 23575), IBM T. J. Watson Research Labs, April 2005.

[16] Dennis Kügler. Security mechanisms of the biometrically enhanced (eu) passport. Presentation at the Security in Pervasive Computing conference, Boppard, Germany, April 2005. www.spc-conf.org/2005/slides/SPC_Passport.pdf.

[17] J.L. Massey. Guessing and entropy. In *Proc. 1994 IEEE International Symposium on Information Theory*, page 204, 1994.

[18] National Institute of Standards and Technology. Recommendation for key management. Technical Report Special Publication 800-57 Draft, NIST, August 2005.

[19] Evaluation report biometrics trial 2B or not 2B, 2005. www.europeanbiometrics.info/images/resources/88_630_file.pdf.

A New Approach to Hide Policy for Automated Trust Negotiation*

Hai Jin, Zhensong Liao, Deqing Zou, and Weizhong Qiang

Cluster and Grid Computing Lab
Huazhong University of Science and Technology, Wuhan, 430074, China
hjin@hust.edu.cn

Abstract. Automated trust negotiation (ATN) is an important approach to establish trust between strangers through the exchange of credentials and access control policies. In practice, access control policy may contain sensitive information. The negotiation process becomes complicated when the access control policy is designed complex in order to avoid information leakage. Furthermore, if the access control policy has conflicts or cycles, normal negotiation strategies often fail. In this paper, a new approach to hide access control policy is proposed based on the study on the existing problems. In the approach, the policy consistency is checked so as to detect policy conflicts. 0-1 table is used to implement it as well as discover minimal credential-set. Meanwhile, a practical example shows that the approach is suitable and can effectively protect sensitive information in access control policy.

1 Introduction

As computer systems become more and more interconnected, many situations arise where different systems need to share data or resources [1][2][3]. For example, a provider who wants to supply online service over the web must decide how much a remote user with a certain set of credentials is to be trusted. Usually, in capability-based/identity-based/attribute-based access control systems, the access control decisions are decided by capabilities/identities/attributes of requesters.

Exchange of attribute credentials is a means to establish mutual trust relationship between strangers, who wish to share resources or conduct business transactions. ATN is invented as an effective method to regulate the exchange of sensitive information during such process [1][2][4][5][6][7]. In ATN, access control policy plays a key role in protecting resources from unauthorized access. Unlike in traditional trust management systems, the policy for a resource is usually unknown to the party, who requests access to the resource when trust negotiation starts. The approach of ATN differs from traditional identity-based access control systems mainly in the following aspects [2]:

---

* The paper is supported by National Natural Science Foundation of China under grant No.90412010 and No.60503040.

H. Yoshiura et al. (Eds.): IWSEC 2006, LNCS 4266, pp. 168–178, 2006.

- Trust between two strangers is established based on parties' properties, which are proven through disclosure of digital credentials. A digital credential is a verifiable, non-forgeable digitally signed assertion by a credential issuer about the properties of the parties;
- Each party can define access control policy to control outsiders' access to their sensitive resources;
- In the approaches to trust negotiation developed so far, two parties establish trust directly without involving trust third parties, other than credential issuers.

However, an access control policy itself may also contain sensitive information. Disclosing policies' contents unconditionally may leak valuable business information or jeopardize individual's privacy [4][6][7][8]. So the disclosure strategy of access control policy should take information protection into consideration. Meanwhile, the following situations pose a new challenge to ATN.

Problem 1. Conflicts in access control policy. In order to prevent sensitive information from leaking, the service/resource providers often place many constraints on the access such as requiring more credentials as possible, which sometimes lead to the policy conflicts. A simple case is that, $Policy=P_1 \wedge P_2$, where $P_1=p$ and $P_2=p'$, then $Policy=False$. It means that the policy itself is of no effect. However, the negotiation strategies cannot detect it and still occupy a lot of computational power (including network overhead and computing cost). As a result, the negotiation process fails.

Problem 2. Policy cycles in access control policy. The service's disclosure depends on user's credentials. The negotiator releases his credentials according to the access control policy. If the disclosure of credentials and policies relies on each other, then the deadlock generates. Surely, it results in the failed negotiation.

To take the above problems and privacy protection into consideration, a new approach to hide access control policy for ATN is proposed in this paper. In the approach, 0-1 table is adopted to check the policy consistency before the negotiation so as to detect whether access control policies are valid. During the checking process, it will produce basic minimal credential-set, which forms the credential disclosure sequence to meet the access requirements. Then, the negotiation process just matches the disclosed credentials with minimal credential-set to find whether any credential-set is in the credential disclosure sequence. Generally, the contributions of our work are as follows:

1) We present a new negotiation strategy to compute the credential disclosure sequence, which has the properties such as little overhead and loose-coupling computing. The example below shows that the approach can hide access control policy and effectively prevent sensitive information from omitting.
2) It is the first time for us to treat consistency of access control policy as an important issue. Previous work takes an assumption that the access control policy has no conflict and ignores the research on the policy consistency.
3) The approach offered can effectively deal with problems of policy cycle. Normal negotiation strategies fail if the policy cycle exists, because the existing strategies closely disclose the credentials and policies one by one, while the policy cycle makes it deadlocked.

The rest of this paper is organized as the following. Section 2 discusses the related work, which shows the recent and relevant research in this area. Section 3 is the main part of this paper. It gives a detailed description of the approach as well as how to implement it. Section 4 provides a practical example to illustrate how the approach works. Section 5 discusses the features of the approach. Section 6 concludes the paper.

2 Related Work

Our work is originally motivated from the existing automated trust negotiation research [1][2][4][5][6][7], whose goal is to enable trust establishment between strangers in a decentralized or open environment, such as Internet or grid. In ATN, each relying party publishes access control policies to regulate not only the granting of resources, but also the disclosure of credentials. We focus on privacy protection via hiding policies. Furthermore, we concentrate on handling the existing problems. So we mainly investigate two aspects in ATN: information protection and negotiation strategies.

Winsborough et al [1] presented ACK policy to control the disclosure of credentials and policies, and developed TTG protocol to construct policy tree so that it was easy to detect whether the credentials matched the policies or not. ACK policy is useful in protecting sensitive information, and TTG protocol enables two parties to do joint chain discovery in an interactive manner as well as the parties to use policies to protect sensitive credentials and the attribute information contained in the credentials. However, ACK policy and TTG are application-limited because of difficulty in constructing them in practical use.

Li et al [9] proposed OSBE protocol to prevent important information from leaking and being attacked. OSBE bases its idea on digital signature and examines the message's integrity so as to find whether the negotiator has the right signature. OSBE protects message from unauthorized access, but it is heavyweight to build and the signature computing has a great cost.

In [10], Bertino et al proposed a set of privacy preserving features to be included in any trust negotiation system, such as the support for the P3P standards, as well as different formats to encode credentials. Although they based their work on P3P standards, the methods could be adopted to handle similar questions and differed from our work.

Holt et al introduced hidden credentials in [11]. They gave a formal description for hidden credentials, including the concepts of credential and policy indistinguishability, and showed how to build them using IBE [12]. Their work also gave compelling examples of the utility of hidden credentials. In short, they provided a good model for trust negotiation to implement hidden credentials. Based on this, Robert et al [13] utilized hidden credentials to conceal complex policies, and Keith et al [14] made use of them to hide access control policies. Since hidden credential system cannot prevent from invalid inference, its implementation is restricted to some extend.

Li et al proposed the notions of OACerts and OCBE in [15]. OCBE protocol adopts the idea of zero-knowledge and ensures that if and only if the recipient is specified, he can get the resource, otherwise he gets nothing from the trust negotiation. However, the method did not discuss how to guarantee the security of messages during the transmission over the insecure Internet.

A negotiation strategy determines characteristics of a negotiation such as which credentials are requested and disclosed, and when the negotiation is halted. As far as the negotiation strategies were concerned, Winsborough et al [4] proposed two different categories of negotiation strategies: eager strategy and parsimonious strategy. The eager strategy allows flooding-style negotiation, where each party discloses a credential to the other party as soon as the policy of that credential is satisfied, therefore ensuring a successful negation can be found in the minimum possible number of rounds. Its disadvantage is that it usually results in disclosure of irrelevant credentials.

At the other extreme, parsimonious strategy does not allow credential disclosures until both parties know there exists a successful negotiation. When an incoming request for a credential is received and this credential has not been unlocked, an outgoing counter request is prepared according to the credential's access control policy and sent out in response.

Yu et al [16] proposed a brute-force backtracking strategy. The strategy backtracks whenever a circular dependency is detected. Given the sets of credentials and policies are finite at both parties, the search it conducts always terminates.

The existing negotiation strategies still base on the disclosure of credentials and policies, which will inevitably release some information and cannot handle policy cycles. In our approach, we hide the access control policy from revealing and match credentials with minimal credential-set, which can effectively protect the access control policy.

3   Hiding Policy

In this section, we depict our approach in detail. First, we review the concepts of ATN and describe the above problems. Then, we use 0-1 table to check policy consistency. This process examines conflicts in access control policy as well as generates minimal credential-set. Finally, we explain the importance and the meaning of minimal credential-set in hiding policy.

3.1   Basic Definitions

In ATN, the disclosure of service s is controlled by an access control policy p_s, which specifies the prerequisite conditions that must be satisfied in order for s to be disclosed. Generally, an ATN system includes the following elements:

- Client: the relying party who initiates the request to service s. Accordingly, server is the counterpart who possesses the service s. Note that the client and the server are not the traditional C/S model, on the contrary, they are peer-to-peer, they are just two different entities, and they are always treated as a negotiator and an opponent.

- C: credential set. Usually, C_c denotes client's credential set, while C_s stands for server's credential set. *Cred* contains all the credentials in negotiation process, i.e., $Cred=C_c\cup C_s$.
- P: policy set. P_c is used as the policy to protect client's credentials, and P_s denotes server's policy. Often, each policy P_s takes the form of $P_s :s\leftarrow f_s(c_1,...,c_k)$, $(c_1,...,c_k\in Cred)$, where $f_s(c_1,...,c_k)$ is a normal formula consisting of literals c_i, the Boolean operators $\wedge$ and $\vee$, and parentheses. f_s has the result in {*True, False*}. To better understand f_s, here gives an instance. Given a set of credentials $C\in Cred$ and a policy function $f_s(c_1,...,c_k)$. If $f_s=c_1\vee(c_2\wedge c_3)$, then $f_s(\{c_1,c_2\})=True$ while $f_s(\{c_2,c_4\})=False$. Policy P_s is satisfied by the credential set $C\in Cred$ if and only if $f_s(C)=True$. During the trust negotiation, the client discloses its credentials till $f_s(C')=True$ $(C'\subseteq C)$, then the negotiation succeeds; otherwise, the negotiation fails and the process terminates.

In ATN, a trust negotiation protocol is initiated by a client requesting a resource/service from the server. The server discloses some policies with the form of $s_i\leftarrow True$. Here are the basic definitions of ATN for policy conflict and policy cycle.

Definition 1 (Automated Trust Negotiation). Let C_c and C_s denote the credential sets of client and server. P_c and P_s are the policy sets of client and server. The negotiation is initiated by a request for $s\in C_s$ from the client. Before negotiation, the server discloses all the policies that have the form of $s_i\leftarrow True$. The goal of the trust negotiation is to find a credential disclosure sequence $(c_1, c_2, ..., c_n=s)$, where $c_i\in C_c\cup C_s$, and such that for each c_i $(1\leq i\leq n)$, the policy for c_i is satisfied by the credentials disclosed. In other words, $f_{ci}(\cup_{j<i}c_j)=True$. If the client and the server find a credential disclosure sequence, the negotiation succeeds, otherwise, it fails.

The sequence of the disclosed credentials depends on the decisions of each party. The decisions are decided by a negotiation strategy, which controls the credentials to be disclosed, when to disclose them, and when to terminate a negotiation.

Definition 2 (Policy Conflict). Let C_s and P_s denote the credential set and policy set of server. The negotiation is initiated by a request for $s\in C_s$ from the client. In order to protect important information of the access control policy, P_s has a complicated expression requiring client to disclose more credentials. P_s: $s\leftarrow f_s(c_1, c_2,..., c_n)$. If $f_s(c_1, c_2,..., c_n)\equiv False$ exists no matter $c_i=True$ or $c_i=False$, the policy is called conflicted, i.e., there exists a conflict in the access control policy.

Usually, $f_s(c_1, c_2,..., c_n)$ should be *True* or *False* when {c_i} sequence has different values. Surely, when $f_s(c_1, c_2,..., c_n) \equiv True$, the policy is still unacceptable, since it means the access control policy is always met no matter what credentials the client provides. In the next part, we classify the states of P_s into three types: incompatible, acceptable and non-recommended. Only the acceptable policy is valid, others are of no effect.

Definition 3 (Policy Cycle). Let C_c and C_s $(P_c$ and $P_s)$ denote the credential (policy) sets of client and server, respectively. The negotiation is initiated by a request for $s\in C_s$ from the client. If $P_{ci}:c_i\leftarrow g_{ci}(s_j)$ and $P_{sj}:s_j\leftarrow h_{sj}(c_i)$ appear in a trust negotiation, then the negotiation phase is deadlocked, in other words, there exists a policy cycle in the access control policy.

Policy cycle leads the trust negotiation deadlock and ends up with a result of failure. Normal negotiation strategies are unable to handle policy cycle, but still waste much network, computing and communication overhead. In the next part, we will illustrate how to minimize credential-set deals with policy cycle easily.

3.2 Checking Policy Consistency

Generally, the access control policy is consistent and can be satisfied by client's credentials. What will happen if the policy is self-contradictory or inconsistent? The result is obvious. In order to avoid undesirable unsuccessful negotiation, we adopt 0-1 table to detect policy conflict before negotiation. 0-1 table works as two steps:

- Decompose the original policies into many meta-policies. 0-1 table is used to list all possible results. In 0-1 table, 0 represents *False*, while 1 stands for *True*.
- Analyses the 0-1 results and classify them into three types: 1) Incompatible policy, i.e., the access control policy has conflicts, and the results are all *False*. For example, suppose a policy P can be expressed as $P=p_1 \wedge p_2$, where $p_1=p$, $p_2=p'$, then $P \equiv False$ and is incompatible. 2) Acceptable policy, i.e., the result includes some *True* and some *False*. Only the disclosure of right credentials can meet the requirements of acceptable policy. 3) Non-recommended policy, i.e., there exists no conflict in the policy, but all the results are *True*. Non-recommended policy means that the policy cannot control anything and deserves not being recommended.

0-1 table is an effective method to list all the possible results of a policy expression. To better understand 0-1 table, here gives an example to illustrate it.

Example 1. There exists a policy "The high performance computers of CGCL lab provide open cluster computing. Everyone who is a professor, a teacher or a PhD can use it directly. Otherwise, if a user is a graduate (Ms) and also a team-leader, he can use it too." This policy can be expressed as: $Policy=p_1 \vee p_2 \vee p_3 \vee (p_4 \wedge p_5)$, where $p_{si}:s_i \leftarrow c_i$ $(i=1,...,5)$ and $c_1:user.role=Professor$, $c_2:user.role=Teacher$, $c_3:user.role=PhD$, $c_4:user.role=Ms$, $c_5:user.role=Teamleader$. The corresponding 0-1 table can be expressed as Table 1, which shows that CGCL's policy is an acceptable one since the result contains 29 times of *True* and 3 times of *False*.

Table 1. 0-1 Table for Example 1 (0 represents False, 1 represents True, X represents 0 or 1)

p_1	p_2	p_3	p_4	p_5	*Policy*
1	X	X	X	X	1
X	1	X	X	X	1
X	X	1	X	X	1
X	X	X	1	1	1
0	0	0	0	X	0
0	0	0	X	0	0

3.3 Minimal Credential-Set

The goal of various negotiation strategies is to find credential disclosure sequence containing the requested service s. However, during the negotiation process, the credentials, including C_c and C_s, are required to be disclosed iteratively, which will inevitably bring information leakage problem. In this part, we use minimal credential-set to compute credential disclosure sequence.

Definition 4 (Minimal Credential-Set). Let P_s denote the policy set of server. $P_s = \cap P_{si} = P_{s1} \wedge ... \wedge P_{sn}$ and $P_{si}: s_i \leftarrow f_{si}(c_i)$. During the consistency detection process, 0-1 table lists all the possible results. Every credential sequence which makes P_s *True* is added into an effective credential set C_E. Minimal credential-set C_M is the simplification of C_E.

Definition 4 tells us that minimal credential-set C_M can be enough to meet the requirements of access control policy. In the above example, $P_1 = True$ can make P_s *True*, then $Seq_1 = \{c_1\} \subseteq C_E$. With the same, there exist $Seq_2 = \{c_1, c_2\} \subseteq C_E$, $Seq_3 = \{c_1, c_3\} \subseteq C_E$ etc. After a simplification towards C_E, the C_M will be $\{\{c_1\}, \{c_2\}, \{c_3\}, \{c_4, c_5\}\}$. The goal of simplification is to make C_E into the form of $C_E = Seq_1 \vee ... \vee Seq_n$. The principal the simplification must follow lies in that if $Seq_i \subseteq Seq_j$ ($i \neq j$), then remove Seq_j from C_E. The remainder items of C_E are the final minimal credential-set.

Minimal credential-set helps to find the credential disclosure sequence that the client should release. Now the trust negotiation process checks whether the client's credential set includes some items of minimal credential-set C_M. During the negotiation, the server does not need to disclose its access control policy any more; it only publishes the minimal credential-set.

3.4 Credential-Policy Matching

Minimal credential-set aims at checking whether the client has the satisfied credentials. It can also deal with policy cycle problem. The credential-policy matching process complies with **Theorem 1** described as the following.

Theorem 1. Let C_c and C_s denote the credential sets of client and server respectively. The negotiation is initiated by a request for $s \in C_s$ from the client. Let C_M be the minimal credential-set of P_s. if $\exists Seq \subseteq C_M$, and $Seq \subseteq C_c$, then the negotiation succeeds and the trust can be established, otherwise, the negotiation fails.

It is easy to prove Theorem 1. Note that $s \in C_s$, $P_s: s \leftarrow f_s(C)$. Since $\forall Seq \in C_M$, $f_s(Seq) = True$, then $f_s(C_M) = True$. $\exists Seq \subseteq C_M$ and $Seq \subseteq C_c \Rightarrow f_s(C_c) = True$, which equals to that negotiation succeeds. The algorithm is described as Fig.1. The function $MatchCreToPolicy(C_c, C_M)$ is to check whether credential set C_c belongs to minimal credential-set C_M. If $\exists Seq \subseteq C_M$ and $Seq \subseteq C_c$, then $MatchCreToPolicy(C_c, C_M)$ returns *True*. $isBelongTo(Seq, C_c)$ is a Boolean function to judge whether the sequence Seq of some credential set belongs to C_c.

Algorithm: MatchCreToPolicy(C_c, C_M)	Function: isBelongTo(Seq, C_c)
Input:	Input:
C_c: the credential set of the client	Seq: the disclosure sequence
C_M:the minimal credential-set	C_c: the credential set of the
Output:	client
True or *False*	Output:
Procedure:	*True* or *False*
For i=1, 2,…, *sizeof*(C_M)	Procedure:
$Seq_i \in C_M$;	For each $c \in Seq$
If (isBelongTo(Seq_i, C_c)==*True*)	If ($c \notin C_c$)
return *True*;	return *False*;
return *False*	return *True*

Fig. 1. Credential-Policy Matching Algorithm

Now, we give an example to illustrate how minimal credential-set handles policy cycle.

Example 2. Suppose the following access control policies exist between the client and server.

Client

p_{c1}: $c_1 \leftarrow s_2 \wedge s_3$
p_{c2}: $c_2 \leftarrow s_2$
p_{c3}: $c_3 \leftarrow s_6$
p_{c4}: $c_4 \leftarrow True$

Server

p_s: $s \leftarrow (c_1 \wedge c_4) \vee c_5$
p_{s1}: $s_1 \leftarrow c_6$
p_{s2}: $s_2 \leftarrow c_2$
p_{c3}: $c_3 \leftarrow c_4$

In the example, $C_c=\{c_1, c_2, c_3, c_4\}$ and $C_s=\{s, s_1, s_2, s_3\}$. Since c_2 and s_2 depend on each other so that the negotiation has policy cycle. Normal negotiation strategies cannot work well and will lead the negotiation failure. When minimal credential-set approach is taken, the process can go on. Since $s \leftarrow (c_1 \wedge c_4) \vee c_5$, then $\{c_1, c_4\} \subseteq C_E$, $\{c_5\} \subseteq C_E$. Meanwhile, $P_s=p_s=((p_{s2} \wedge p_{s3}) \wedge True) \vee False = p_{s2} \wedge p_{s3}$, then $\{c_2, c_4\} \subseteq C_E$, so the minimal credential-set $C_M=\{\{c_2, c_4\},\{c_1, c_4\},\{c_5\}\}$. Now $\{c_1, c_4\} \subseteq C_c$, the negotiation succeeds.

4   Use Case Study

In this section, we apply 0-1 table and minimal credential-set to handle a practical trust negotiation case.

4.1   Scenario Description

CGCL lab provides open high speed printing service. The printer is at the meeting room. During the meeting, no one except the meeting chair can use it. When there is no meeting at the working hours, teaching assistant can use it directly. Others can use it when the lab assistant is at present.

4.2 Policy Decomposition

Let *Policy* denote the access control policy. *Policy* can be described as *Policy*= $(p_1 \wedge p_2)$ $\vee(p'_1 \wedge p_3 \wedge p_4) \vee (p'_1 \wedge p_3 \wedge p_5)$. The corresponding credentials are: c_1:*Context.activity*= *meeting*, c_2:*user.role=meetingChair*, c'_1:*Context.Activity$\neq$meeting*, c_3:*Context. workinghours=True*, c_4:*user.role=teacherAssistant*, c_5: *labAssistant.atPresent=True*.

4.3 0-1 Table

The 0-1 table shows in Table 2 based on policy description.

Table 2. 0-1 Table for the Case

p_1	P'_1	p_2	p_3	p_4	p_5	*Policy*
1	0	1	X	X	X	1
1	0	0	X	X	X	0
0	1	X	1	1	X	1
0	1	X	1	X	1	1
0	1	X	0	X	X	0

As far as the results are concerned, the access control policy is acceptable since there are 14 times of *True* and 18 times of *False*.

4.4 Minimal Credential-Sets

From Table 2 we can see that $C_E=Seq_1 \vee Seq_2 \vee ... \vee Seq_{14}$, where $Seq_1=\{c_1, c_2\}$, $Seq_2=\{c_1, c_2, c_3\}$, $Seq_3=\{c_1, c_2, c_4\}$,..., $Seq_{14}=\{c_3, c_4, c_5\}$. After the simplification process, the final form is $C_E=\{c_1, c_2\} \vee \{c'_1, c_3, c_4\} \vee \{c'_1, c_3, c_5\}$. Then, the minimal credential-set $C_M=\{\{c_1, c_2\}, \{c'_1, c_3, c_4\}, \{c'_1, c_3, c_5\}\}$.

4.5 Negotiation Process

The negotiation process computes whether any credential sequence of C_M appears in C_c. The *MatchCreToPolicy(C_c, C_M)* algorithm is revoked to match the credentials to the access control policy. If *MatchCreToPolicy(C_c, C_M)=True* satisfies, the negotiation succeeds. Otherwise, the client's access will be denied.

5 Analysis

Based on the above description of 0-1 table and minimal credential-set, our approach has the following features:

1) Policy consistency detection. We adopt 0-1 table to check consistency of access control policy before the trust negotiation. We classify the access control policy into three types. Only the acceptable policy is meaningful while the others are not suitable.

2) Policy cycle disposal. Minimal credential-set can well handle the problem of policy cycle. Unlike other negotiation strategies, minimal credential-set treats client's credentials as a total integrity and compares them with credential sequence instead of disclosing the credentials and policies one by one.

3) Policy hiding as to protect sensitive information. After the policy consistency checking at the side of server, the access control policy is never disclosed to the client, which hides the policy from revealing and can greatly prevent sensitive information in policy from leaking.

4) Little cost. Since the approach does not need the gradual disclosure of credentials and policies, the overhead of network, communication and computing will reduce greatly. Meanwhile, if the access control policy has conflicts, our approach can prevent the negotiation from continuing, which can improve the rate of successful negotiation and enhance negotiation efficiency.

6 Conclusion

In this paper, we present a new approach to hide access control policy. In the approach, we adopt 0-1 table to check policy consistency and examine whether the access control policy is consistent or not. We classify the access control policy into three types according to its state. If the policy is an acceptable one, the trust negotiation can continue. Minimal credential-set is used to list all the possible credential disclosure sequences. If the client has the right credentials to include one of the items in minimal credential-set, the trust can be established and the access is allowed. In the paper, we describe the approach in detail and illustrate how it works through practical example.

References

[1] W. H. Winsborough and N. Li, "Towards practical automated trust negotiation", In *Proceedings of the 3rd International Workshop on Policies for Distributed Systems and Networks*, 2002, pp.92-103.

[2] T. Yu and M. Winslett, "A Unified Scheme for Resource Protection in Automated Trust Negotiation", In *Proceedings of IEEE Symposium on Security and Privacy*, 2003, pp.245-257.

[3] T. Yu, *Dynamic Trust Establishment in Open Systems*, PhD thesis, Department of Computer Science, University of Illinois. Sep, 2003.

[4] W. H. Winsborough, K. E. Seamons, and V. E. Jones, "Automated trust negotiation", In *Proceedings of DARPA Information Survivability Conference and Exposition*, 2000, pp.88-102.

[5] W. H. Winsborough and N. Li, "Protecting sensitive attributes in automated trust negotiation", In *Proceeding of ACM Workshop on Privacy in the Electronic Society*, 2002, pp.102-113.

[6] W. H. Winsborough and N. Li, "Safety in automated trust negotiation", In *Proceedings of the IEEE symposium on Security and Privacy*, 2004, pp.147-160.

[7] K. Seamons, M. Winslett and T. Yu, "Limiting the Disclosure of Access Control Policies during Automated Trust Negotiation", In *Proceedings of Network and Distributed System Security Symposium*, 2001, pp.45-56.

[8] P. Bonatti and P. Samarati, "Regulating Service Access and Information Release on the Web", In *Proceeding of 7th ACM Conference on Computer and Communications Security*, 2000, pp.78-87.

[9] N. Li, W.Du, and D. Boneh, "Oblivious signature-based envelope", In *Proceeding of the 22nd ACM Symposium on Principles of Distributed Computing*, 2003, pp. 182-189.

[10] E. Bertino, E. Ferrari, and A. C. Squicciarini, "Privacy-preserving trust negotiation", In *Lecture Notes in Computer Science*, Vol.3424, Springer-Verlag, 2005, pp.283-301.

[11] J. E. Holt, R. Bradshaw, K. E Seamons, and H. Orman, "Hidden credentials", In *Proceedings of 2nd ACM Workshop on Privacy in the Electronic Society*. 2003, pp.1-8.

[12] D. Boneh and M. Franklin, "Identity based encryption from the Weil pairing", In *Proceedings of Crypto2001, Advances in Cryptology*, Lecture Notes in Computer Science, Vol.2139, Springer-Verlag, 2001, pp.213-229.

[13] R. W. Bradshaw, J. E. Holt, and K. E. Seamons, "Concealing Complex Policies with Hidden Credentials", In *Proceedings of the 4th ACM Conference on Computer and Communications Security*, 2004, pp.245-253.

[14] K. Frikken, M. Atallah, and J. Li, „Hidden Access Control Policies with Hidden Credentials", In *Proceedings of the 3rd ACM Workshop on Privacy in the Electronic Society*, 2004, pp.130-131

[15] J. Li and N. Li, "OACerts: Oblivious Attribute Certificates", In *Proceeding of 3rd Conference on Applied Cryptography and Network Security*, 2003, pp.108-121.

[16] T. Yu, X. Ma, and M. Winslett, "PRUNES: An Efficient and Complete Strategy for Automated Trust Negotiation over the Internet", In *Proceeding of the 2000 ACM Conference on Computer and Communications Security*, 2000, pp.88-97.

Towards Remote Policy Enforcement for Runtime Protection of Mobile Code Using Trusted Computing

Xinwen Zhang, Francesco Parisi-Presicce, and Ravi Sandhu

George Mason University, Fairfax, Virginia, USA
{xzhang6, fparisip, sandhu}@gmu.edu

Abstract. We present an approach to protect mobile code and agents at runtime using Trusted Computing (TC) technologies. For this purpose, a "mobile policy" is defined by the mobile code originator, and is enforced by the runtime environment in a remote host to control which users can run the mobile code and what kind of results a user can observe, depending on the security properties of the user. The separation of policy specification and implementation mechanism in existing mobile computing platform such as Java Runtime Environment (JRE) enables the implementation of our approach by leveraging current security technologies. The main difference between our approach and existing runtime security models is that the policies enforced in our model are intended to protect the resources of the mobile applications instead of the local system resources. This requires the remote runtime environment to be trusted by the application originator to authenticate the remote user and enforce the policy. Emerging TC technologies such as specified by the Trusted Computing Group (TCG) provide assurance of the runtime environment of a remote host.

1 Introduction

Mobile code refers to programs and processes that migrate and execute at remote hosts, so that the execution environments are different for different instances. There is a wide range of mobile applications encompassing autonomous mobile agents which actively travel to remote hosts, Java applets, ActiveX, component software (e.g., COM/DCOM/ COM+ and Servlet/EJB), distributed ad hoc and sensor network applications,etcetera [16].

Runtime environments provide mechanisms to protect the user's and the system's sensitive information by enforcing security policies in a local host. The policies are based on the attributes of the code and of the user who is running it. Possible attributes include code sources, URLs, digital signatures, user groups, roles, and credentials. The two mainstream runtime environments currently adopted in industry are Common Language Runtime (CLR) in .Net and Java Runtime Environment (JRE) in Java. In Java, the security in JDK1.0 and JDK1.1 uses a sandbox model to restrict the access of Java Applets based on code source and digital signature, while in JDK1.2, a user-based access control model is introduced [10,15]. Similar to Java, .Net enforces a code access security model based on code source and location, as well as a role-based security model [16].

H. Yoshiura et al. (Eds.): IWSEC 2006, LNCS 4266, pp. 179–195, 2006.

The protection of mobile applications against malicious hosts and users is a more difficult problem. Current security models in runtime environments are used mainly to enforce the local host's security policy to protect the local system resources. However, there are cases in mobile applications where the originator may have some security requirements to protect the sensitive information brought or accessible by the mobile code. For example, a shopping application may carry a user's sensitive information while running in a remote site. The code originator may require that the code can only run in a specific protected domain, and the user who runs this code must have a specific role in an organization, or some other credentials. In this kind of situation, existing access control models for mobile code are not adequate.

In this paper we propose an approach to enforce the policy of the mobile application originator in remote host runtime environments to control accesses from users, by leveraging emerging client-platform-based Trusted Computing (TC) technologies. We call this kind of policy a "mobile policy" in our model, as compared with the remote host's local policy. A mobile policy is the security requirement provided by the originator to specify what kind of subject in a remote host can run this code, execute particular methods/components, or access some sensitive information included with the mobile application. We use the mechanisms in current runtime environments to enforce a mobile policy.

Since the subject of a mobile policy is a user or program that executes or accesses the mobile code in a remote site, the authentication of the subject is a key point to enforce the policy. Java authentication and authorization Service (JAAS) provides a general layer of user-based authentication and access control mechanism, beyond the sandbox model, which can be applied in our approach. One important advantage of our approach is that we try to reuse the runtime security technologies employed in current systems. A prerequisite for it is the basic assumption that all machines on which the code is intended to run guarantee a minimum of security regarding the correct behavior of the runtime environment. For an enterprise-wide environment, this is viable with on-site configuration of each host by the administrator. For multidomain distributed systems, a trusted runtime environment (TRE) is essential for our model. A TRE can be built on a Trusted Computing Base (TCB) and can be considered an extension of TCB. Emerging Trusted Computing (TC) technologies such as TCG's Trusted Platform Module (TPM) which provide hardware-based root of trust and extended trust to upper levels with verifiable platform characteristics, thus enabling remote policy enforcement in our architecture.

Our approach does not exclude ways other than mobile policies to distribute and enforce security requirements in different hosts within an organization. For example, a network administrator could install in each host, at the operating system level, the policy to be used to determine the specific users who can run a specific application. The use of mobile policies with mobile code has many advantages over this approach: (1) as the deployment and management of mobile code and agents is highly automated, the security management should also be automated and flexible, while administrator-involved configuration for individual platforms is burdensome for an organization; (2) extensibility and scalability of access control policy for a mobile application originator since a mobile policy can be updated/revoked easily with our approach; (3) specification of fine-grained access control for different users with different security properties in the same remote host, by allowing different users in the remote host to obtain different results from this application (beyond the simple "allowed/not allowed to execute); and (4) simplification of the specification and enforcement of global security policies in an organization.

The remainder of this paper is organized as follows: Section 2 shows some examples which can benefit from our approach but are difficult to implement with current runtime security technologies. Section 3 presents an overview of the security model in JRE. Section 4 proposes our trusted platform architecture to support remote policy enforcement in a distributed environment. Section 5 formulates our policy model specification and enforcement in JRE. Section 6 mentions some related work in the mobile code security area, and the differences between these and our approach. Section 7 summarizes this paper and presents our future work.

2   Motivating Examples

Example 1. In a mobile application intended to perform E-shopping services, the mobile code is transferred to a remote E-commerce server which collects related information, such as price, location, shipping fee, etc., and then returns it to the customer. The code carries the customer's information, such as credit card number, address, telephone number, etc., and some functions to perform specific work, such as data collecting and transporting, order transaction, etc. If the customer makes the decision to order, the mobile code places the order using the customer's information. In this example, the customer has access control requirements that his personal information can only be read by a clerk in a specific organization without modification, and the functions can only be executed in a particular domain. This objective cannot be achieved with current runtime security models based on code attributes and local host's policies to protect the host's resources. Also, the type safety and data encapsulation features of programming languages such as Java cannot solve this problem. With type safe language, a protected variable or class can be declared as a private element in object-oriented programming, but, with this mechanism, the resulting access control is "black or white" to all users, which is not suitable for fine-grained protection.

Example 2. Component-based software has been developed and applied in industry so widely that it has become the mainstream for enterprise computing during the last decade. A component is a software element that conforms to a component model and can be independently deployed and composed without modification according to a composition standard. Regarded as building blocks, components can be reused in many applications and deployed in different places. Consider a credit card company that has implemented a credit service component. The component, with the customer's information as input, will check the database in the credit card server and return some billing information. As a third party software, this component is deployed at an enterprise's application server and applied to build customized applications. As this component accesses the database, the owner of this component (e.g., the credit card company) has to make sure that only an authenticated and properly authorized application developer, deployer, or user can instantiate it and call it. With current technology, a component de-ployer or system administrator has some access control mechanisms to do this to some extent. For example, in Enterprise Java Bean (EJB), the deployment descriptor along with the component in the enterprise's application server controls what kind of roles can access the component and can activate its methods. But this XML-based descriptor is not generated by the component owner and cannot reflect his/her fine-grained access control policies, since the component owner normally is not aware of the security con-text of local roles in the enterprise. In this case, a mobile policy is a better solution, so that whenever the component is initialized and instantiated in the component container, the access control policy from the component owner can be enforced.

3   Java Runtime Security

This section presents an overview of the security mechanism in Java Virtual Machine (JVM) for Java mobile code, which is an example that we use to support runtime en-forcement of mobile policy in our framework.

3.1   Overview

JVM uses the sandbox model to enforce security policies at runtime. The sandbox model in JDK1.0 and JDK1.1 is based on code attributes such as the code's source, the URL, the signature, etc. While JDK1.0 simply prohibits any Java Applet from ac-cessing any of the local system's resources, JDK1.1 assigns to a Java Applet the same permissions as those of a local program if the host can trust the digital signature associ-ated with this applet (reverts to JDK1.0 otherwise). Starting with JDK1.2, the concept of protection domain based on code attributes is introduced with a complex sandbox model, and the Java Authentication and Authorization Service (JAAS) introduces user-based access control, and allows the local system's access control models and policies to be enforced in the runtime environment. Furthermore, a Java policy is augmented by the security policies of the local operating system, for example, to prevent mobile code executed by a user from accessing a file on the hard disk if the same user cannot read the file at the operating system level.

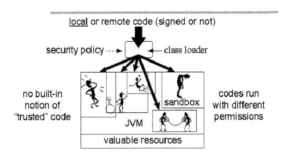

Fig. 1. JDK1.2 security model [10]

Figure 1 shows the semantic sandbox model in JDK1.2 [10]. In this model, the code is located in a protection domain which is defined by the code attributes and by the local access control policies. The protection domain represents the permissions that the code can hold during execution. The general process to run Java mobile code can be described schematically as follows: a Java binary code is loaded by a class loader and classes are defined with the *defineClass* method of the class loader. Each class is associated with a protection domain according to policy information. The code is ready to run or be called by other classes after being loaded; whenever it tries to access a local system's resource, it calls a Java API, which then calls the security manager (the access controller since JDK1.2) to check if this operation is allowable. If the security manager permits the operation, the Java API completes the call and returns to the original code, otherwise, the security manger throws an exception to the Java API, which in turn throws it to the user. Starting with JDK1.2, the operation permissions are determined by the access controller, which supplements the security manager.

The access controller in JRE can enforce fine-grained policies based on the attributes of the running code and of the user. Figure 2 illustrates an actual policy file in Java. The permission definition in Java includes two parts: the object and the access right. The objects are the local system's resources, such as the files and directories, sockets, registry keys and values, and so on. Access rights are defined based on object properties, such as "read" to file and directory ("*" means any operation). In Figure 2, the policy allows any code downloaded from "http://www.myuniversity.edu" to "read" files in "/tmp", and to accept connections on, to connect to, or to listen on any port between 1024 and 65535 on any host within "myuniversity.edu". The user has to be authenticated before being defined as "principal" in a policy file and the JAAS provides a mechanism to obtain the authentication context from the local platform. For example, the third item in Figure 2 specifies that "Alice", who is authenticated by Solaris, can access all files and directories within "/usr/home/Alice"; the last item states that an authenticated subject with Kerberos principal name "bob" with realm *foo.org* can call the *System.getProperty* method to access the user environment information. A customized permission class

```
grant codeBase "http://www.myuniversity.edu/"{
   permission java.io.FilePermission "/tmp", "read";
      };
grant signedBy "myuniversity" {
   permission java.net.socketPermission
   "*.myuniversity.edu:1024-",''accept,connect,listen";
   };
grant Principal com.sun.security.auth.SolarisPrincipal
      "Alice" {
      permission java.io.FilePermission
        "/usr/home/Alice", "*";
   }
grant Principal
      javax.security.auth.kerberos.KerberosPrincipal
      "bob@foo.org"  {
      permission java.util.PropertyPermission
        "user.home", "read";
      permission java.io.FilePermission "bar.txt", "read";
};
```

Fig. 2. Java policy example

can be defined for an application, thus greatly increasing the flexibility and expressive power of Java security policies.

Example 3. Consider the method shown below.

```
Public void sensitiveCall() {
  Permission permission = new
  java.net.SocketPermission("localhost:8080", "connect");
  AccessController.checkPermission(permission);
  // sensitive call
  Socket s = new Socket("localhost", 8080); }
```

In this example, a permission object (*permission*) is defined as a socket connection to local host port 8080. The single-instance class *AccessController* first checks the application's policy file. If this *permission* is granted in the policy or implied by any permission granted in the policy, the *AccessController*'s *checkPermission*[1] method keeps silent; otherwise, an access control exception is thrown to the caller method. Whether a permission is implied by another permission is defined in the *implies* method of the latter's *Permission* or *PermissionCollection* class. The details of defining a customized permission and implied permissions can be found in [9,21]. By default, the *Access-Controller*'s *checkPermission* method implements the *checkPermission* method implemented in *SecurityManager*.

3.2   JAAS

JAAS has been integrated into Java Standard Edition since J2SDK v 1.4. The two purposes of JAAS are to provide user-based authentication and authorization in Java. The original sandbox model in Java is code source-based, so that, a permission is determined by the location where the code comes from and a digital signature generated by the owner. In JAAS, security attributes of the user running the code are considered in access control.

Authentication. JAAS implements the Pluggable Authentication Module (PAM) standard with Java. Whenever a mobile application is loaded, the *Configuration* class stores all available *LoginModules* for this application, a *LoginContext* class is instantiated, and its *login* method invokes all *LoginModules* and attempts to authenticate the user. If successful, the user is authenticated as a *Subject* object with a set of *Principals* objects and credentials which represent the user's security attributes. *Principals* are names of identities with particular types, such as a SSN number, a group or domain name, a role, or a tickets. Credentials can be general security related attributes, such as password, public key certificates (X.509 or PGP), Kerberos tickets, etc. For example a successful authentication with *com.sun.security.auth.module.NTLoginModule* imports principals *userID*, *domainID*, and several *groupIDs* for a user.

Authorization. Starting with Java 2, the *SecurityManager* delegates security checks to *AccesssController*. After a user is authenticated, the method *Subject.doAs* dynamically associates this user with the *AccessControlContext*, which is retrieved by the *Access-Controller* to check if it has sufficient permissions for a sensitive operation based on the

---

[1] Actually this explicit permission check is redundant since any call to open a socket connection is checked by the *SecurityManager* by default.

principals and credentials associated with the subject. A *Subject* class interface has the form

```
Public final class Subject {
    ...
    public static Object doAs (Subject s,
    java.security.PrivilegedAction action) {}
}
```

4   Trusted Runtime Environment

As mentioned in Section 1, to correctly enforce a mobile policy, the application orig-inator needs to trust the runtime environment of the remote host. A trusted runtime environment (TRE) should not only detect any malicious modification of the policy, but also detect any change of the security components in the virtual machine, such as authentication and authorization modules. Specifically, a trusted runtime environment (TRE) should provide:

- *Integrity of mobile policy and code.*   Before being loaded, a mobile policy's in-tegrity should be attested and verified by the originator (the user who deploys the code) to ensure that the correct policy is used. This requires that the JVM correctly measures the integrity (e.g., with a hash function) and reports to the originator, upon a request to run the code. On the other side, a remote host may also need to verify the integrity and signature of the mobile policy, according to its local policies. For example, the digital signature of a mobile policy/code enables it to be launched in a JVM as a third party policy provider by means of code source-based authorization.
- *Trusted authentication of remote subjects.*   The authentication modules in the re-mote site must authenticate the user in the expected manner. While a uniform ap-proach to authentication may be viable in an organization-wide system, more gen-erally a trust mechanism is needed for multi-domain distributed systems.
- *Trusted authorization enforcement.*   After a mobile policy is loaded, the enforce-ment depends on the expected behavior of the remote JVM's authorization module, which is the policy enforcement point of the security system.

Therefore, a TRE is a prerequisite for our security model. It has been recognized for some time that software alone does not provide an adequate foundation for building a high-assurance trusted platform. The emergence of industry-standard Trusted Com-puting (TC) technologies promises a revolution in this respect by providing roots of trust upon which secure applications can be developed. These technologies offer a particularly attractive platform for security policy enforcement in general distributed systems. Many current efforts, especially the industry-led Trusted Computing Group (TCG), have focused on building trust rooted in hardware [5].

TCG has defined a set of specifications aimed at providing a hardware-based root of trust and a set of primitive functions that allow trust to propagate to application soft-ware, in addition to crossing over platforms. The root of trust in TCG is a hardware component on the platform called the Trusted Platform Module (TPM). Application-level trust requires strong integrity checks of binary code for running processes and a mechanism that allows other entities (applications or platforms) to verify that integrity as well. A TPM has the capabilities to measure and report runtime configurations of the platform, from BIOS to OS. TPM and TC-enhanced hardware technologies, such as Intel's LaGrande Technology (LT) [2] and AMD's Secure Execution Mode (SEM) [1], generally allocate isolated memory partitions to different application processes to prevent software-based attacks at runtime.

In our work, we abstract the underlying trusted computing technology, and focus on a high-level trusted runtime environment built beyond that. Since a runtime environment such as Java Virtual Machine is normally loaded after the OS is loaded, we consider the TRE as an application or service level trusted domain, which is built beyond the trusted hardware and OS of the remote host with the attestation mechanism of trusted computing technology, as shown in Figure 3. In this platform, the hardware layer (comprising a TCG compliant TPM and some other necessary hardware such as LT-enabled CPU and chipset) provides the root of trust for TC. The secure kernel (SK) provides the protected runtime environment for the JVM. This can be done through controlling DMA-enabled device drivers and memory management unit (MMU).

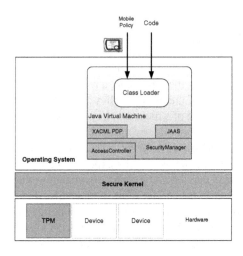

Fig. 3. Platform architecture to support trusted runtime environment for mobile code

4.1   The Trust Model

The integrity of SK is measured by the TPM when the system boots. Also, SK is protected in memory space by hardware so that its integrity is guaranteed at runtime. Before the JVM is started, SK measures the integrity of JVM and stores its hash value locally. In turn, when mobile code is loaded, the JVM measures the integrity of the program (Java bytecode) and the mobile policy, e.g., implemented by the class loader of JVM. Note that SK enhances the language-based security of the JVM by means of trusted hardware.

The measured integrity can be verified by the code originator with remote attestations, which is enabled by the TC hardware. A hash chain is constructed corresponding to an attestation challenge to establish the trust of JVM, the mobile code, and the mobile policy based on the root of trust provided by the hardware. Specifically, SK has a public-private key pair generated by the TPM when the platform is initialized, where the public key is certified by the attestation identity key (AIK) of TPM. SK also generates a public-private key pair for the JVM, where the public key is certified by the SK (by signing with its private key) and the private key is protected by JVM, e.g., with the sealed storage function of TPM. The key pair for JVM is generated for the first time when it is installed in the platform. When the platform receives an attestation challenge from a remote side to check a running code's environment state, TPM signs a set of platform configuration register (PCR) values with its AIK key[2], and SK signs the integrity value of JVM with its private key, while JVM signs the integrity value of the code. These three signatures are then sent to the attestation challenger. The challenger verifies all the signatures and the public key certificates of AIK, SK, and JVM, respectively. If all are valid and the integrity values match, the JVM is trusted, and the code and mobile policy's authenticity is verified. Thus, the code originator can trust the security enforcement of the remote JVM and the result generated by the code.

5 Mobile Policy Specification and Enforcement

The primary goal of our framework is to enforce the code originator's mobile policy in remote runtime environments. Policy management in our framework includes three phases: (1) policy specification by a mobile code originator, (2) policy distribution by the originator or a trusted third party (such as a central server), and (3) policy enforcement in the remote host. We mainly describe phases (1) and (3) in this paper. For phase (2), a mobile policy could be attached to the code and distributed along the network, in which the policy can be bound to the code itself, or the policy could be downloaded from a central repository only to sites where the code is actually run. In both cases the integrity of the mobile policy is critically important, as mentioned earlier.

5.1 Mobile Policy Specification

We have two levels of policy specification. The high-level phase is a logic specification with an authorization specification language (ASL) [14]. This provides a clear defini-tion and analysis, as well as confliction resolution, which is needed when the policies are derived or composed from different resources. For example, a policy can be de-rived from a policy in a group and another policy of an individual user, or a policy can be combined from several policies from different departments in an organization. The low-level phase is a concrete specification of the mobile policy with the extensible access control markup language (XACML) [3] format, enforced in a runtime environ-ment as an input. The separation of these two levels provides flexible deployment and decentralized policy specification and composition. Because of space limitations we only explain the XACML policy specification in this paper.

---

[2] We do not explicitly specify what PCR values are included in an attestation, since the re-quired properties of a platform (including hardware, BIOS, and OS configurations) are very application-specific.

XACML is an open-standard format to specify access control policies, and expected to be widely used thanks to the properties of interoperability and extensibility. A mobile policy can be described in XACML format as the following shows:

```
<Policy PolicyId="(policy-name)"
        PolicyCombinationAlg="rule-combining-algorithm:permit-overrides">
  <Target>
    <Subjects>(predicates over subject attributes)</Subjects>
    <Resources>(predicates over object attributes)</Resources>
    <Actions>(predicates over access rights such as read and write)</Actions>
  </Target>
  <Rule effect="permit"/> (Specification that this policy is positive)
  <Obligations>(Specification of attribute-update actions)</Obligations>
</Policy>
```

where the `<Subjects>` and `<Resources>` elements specify the attributes of the subjects and the objects, the rights are in `<Actions>` element, and the update actions are defined in `<Obligations>` element. Update of attributes result from granting the access thereby possibly changing the state of the subject or the object.

Subjects. A subject is a process running on behalf of a user or role that actually executes the code. In a mobile policy, subject attributes can be a username, or a role name, group name, certificate signed by a particular certificate authority, etc. Each subject or user attribute has to be authenticated by the runtime platform before running the code. JAAS, entrusted with enforcing the user-based access control, can be used within an enterprise or organization. For general distributed environment, a trusted third party subject attribute service may be needed for authentication.

Permissions. A pair (object, right) is regarded as a permission. The objects[3] in a mobile policy may be classes or methods of a mobile code, or information accessed or stored by a mobile code. Specifically, since a mobile policy is to protect a mobile application, possible objects include information on the state of the mobile code, results accumulated at other hosts by a mobile agent, sensitive information of the code originator, and functions to access other sensitive information, implemented as variables, classes, methods or components of a mobile application. Normally, the right associated with a function or component is to "execute", the right for any sensitive information, partial result, and individual variables may include "read" and "write", and the right to a class may be "instantiate" and "inherit". We assume that all the sensitive accesses of (object, right) are encapsulated in a method implemented in the classes, while the sensitive variables are private members of the classes. For example, to "read" a credit card number, a call to *getCredit* method is invoked, while "write" a credit number with *setCredit*. Thus, a permission must be granted to call a method to obtain sensitive information. So generally a permission is checked when a sensitive method is invoked and executed, or a protected object is instantiated or constructed.

5.2   Mobile Policy Enforcement

In a typical access control system, a policy decision point (PDP) evaluates access requests with subject and object attributes and sends results to a policy enforcement point

---

[3] Note that an object in a mobile policy is a different concept from the object (an instance of a class) in Java language.

(PEP). Using Sun's XACML library [4], the PDP module interprets XACML policies in the mobile policy file and makes access decisions, while the PEP can be just a simple interface of the enforcement mechanisms implemented in current JVM (refer to Figure 3). To re-use these functions, each mobile code needs to implement the permission classes for the protected access rights, which are application-specific.

Define Permission Classes. Although Java API provides some basic permission classes, most of them are used in local policy enforcement. Normally a mobile code originator has to define his/her own permissions according to the particular applications. For instance, in Example 1, a *creditPermission* class is needed with rights such as "read". Figure 4 is the skeleton to define a *CreditPermission* class for the E-Shopping example. In Java, an application-defined permission class inherits from the system class *Permission* and implements the *Serializable* interface. Each permission object has a type, name and action (access type). For *CreditPermission*, we only define "read" access type. Note that a permission instance does not imply that this permission is granted, but states that accessing this instance is checked by the access controller.

```
public final class CreditPermission extends Permission
 implements Serializable {
 public CreditPermission(string name, string actions){
 //Creates new CreditPermission object with the
 //specified actions. name is the method name that
 //represents the method to read credit card number,
 //such as "getCreditNo". actions is a list of the
 //desired actions granted to the object. In this example,
 //only "read" action to credit information.
    ...
    }
    public boolean implies(Permission permission){...}
    ...
}
```

Fig. 4. Sample permission class

The *implies* method specifies complex permission semantics, such as a prerequisite permission. For example, an "update" permission of an online account requires a "read" permission to that account object. Permission constraints such as separation of duty can also be specified in this method.

Import XACML Mobile Policy. From the XACML policy file, each subject in the mobile policy is mapped to principals defined in JAAS, such as role, group-name, etc, while the subject attributes and security related credentials such as password, ticket, public key certificate, etc., are associated with these principals after authentication. One of the advantages of using XACML for mobile policy is that XML provides flexible data specifications and semantics, and it is easy to extend it in future work if other information is needed to specify policies. Also, graph tools can be easily developed for policy composition and analysis.

Since the default policy implementation in Java is in a text file, we need to replace this with our alternative implementation. For this, an *XMLPolicy* class is defined which is a subclass of the abstract class *Policy* in Java, and is part of the PDP module to retrieve policy information from the XML file.

A mobile policy is defined by the code originator who is, in general, not the rightholder of the local host system. Therefore the JVM needs the permission from the local host system to load the mobile policy. In implementation, a mobile policy is loaded into a JVM dynamically as the code is loaded. Specifically, a third-party policy implementation can be inserted into a runtime environment by invoking the *setPolicy* method of the *Policy* class. A mobile policy file can be attached with a mobile code in a single Java Archive (JAR) file and captured by JVM, or it can be stored in a central server and a URL argument as the location is provided to load the application code in JVM. If a mobile policy is outside the remote side's domain, dynamically loading the policy requires *runtimePermission* checked by the *AccessController*. This requires that the remote host's default policy be configured to support a third-party policy provider. Code signature for authentication and integrity of the mobile policy is needed according to the host's local policy.

5.3   Policy Enforcement

After the permission and policy classes are loaded, and the user is authenticated with JAAS, a sensitive operation can be authorized to a particular subject at runtime. With JAAS, after a user is authenticated with a set of principals, the method *Subject.doAs* dynamically associates all the principals with the local *AccessController* (actually, it is *AccessControlContext* by calling *AccessController.getContext()*). Then, when a sensitive call is requested, the *AccessController* can make a decision based on the pre-defined policy. As shown in Section 3, a *Subject.doAs* method combines an authenticated subject and a *PriviledgedAction* object. Therefore to enforce a mobile policy, all sensitive operations should be encapsulated in *PriviledgedAction* classes. The following example shows a simple implementation.

Example 4. Consider an *eshop* mobile application where *creditPermission* is defined by the code originator and policy is specified as the following XACML format.

```
<Policy PolicyId="makeorder-policy"
        PolicyCombinationAlg="rule-combining-algorithm:permit-overrides">
  <Target>
    <Subjects>
      <Subject>
        <!-- The subject identity must include "OU=Org1". -->
        <SubjectMatch MatchId="function:x500Name-match">
          <AttributeValue DataType="string">OU=Org1</AttributeValue>
          <SubjectAttributeDesignator AttributeId="subject-id" DataType="x500Name"/>
        </SubjectMatch>
        <!-- The subject's rolename is PurchaseManager -->
        <SubjectMatch MatchId="function:regexp-string-match">
          <AttributeValue DataType="string">PurchaseManager</AttributeValue>
          <SubjectAttributeDesignator AttributeId="subject-rolename" DataType="string"/>
        </SubjectMatch>
      </Subject>
    </Subjects>
    <Resources>
      <Resource>
        <ResourceMatch MatchId="function:regexp-string-match">
          <AttributeValue DataType="string">creditPermission</AttributeValue>
          <ResourceAttributeDesignator AttributeId="permission-name" DataType="string"/>
        </ResourceMatch>
```

```
      <Resource>
    </Resources>
    <Actions>
      <!-- "GET" represents the read privilege. -->
      <Action>GET</Action>
    </Actions>
  </Target>
  <Rule effect="permit"/>
</Policy>
```

A *subject* is authenticated as a *Org1.PurchaseManager* role and trying to call the sensitive method *getCredit*. The following code shows the outline of the class.

```
public class EShop {
  public static void main(String[] args) {
    ...
    Subject.doAs(aPurchaseManager, new MakeOrder());
    // where aPurchaseManager is an authenticated Subject
    // with a principal of Org1.role named PurchaseManager.
    ...
  }
}
public class MakeOrder implements PrivilegedAction {
    public Object run() {
        ...
        //sensitive call
        String creditCardNo=CreditInfo.getCreditNo();
        ...
    }
}
```

In this example the sensitive code is encapsulated in the *MakeOrder* class, which implements *PriviledgedAction* class. The *CreditInfo* is a static class that stores a credit card information, which can be obtained by some methods. The *getCredit* method is a sensitive operation since as defined in the XML policy file. The *MakeOrder* will trigger an access control check when *getCredit* is called. According to the policy, the permission is granted. The general authorization in a mobile policy is similar to that in enforcing a local policy.

5.4   Access Control Algorithm

Java uses a stack-inspection mechanism to enforce the security policy in the runtime environment. In our model, the same stack-inspection mechanism is used, but the access controller checks the permissions based on the mobile policy file. Specifically, for each call in the stack frame, when there is a call to access protected objects in a mobile code, the call is forwarded to the access controller. The access controller determines if the operation is permitted according to the XML mobile policy: if the operation is not permitted, the access controller throws an exception back to the call, which in turn throws it back to the user running the code, otherwise the call completes the operation. Figure 5 shows the access control algorithm. For each call in the stack, the access control algorithm first checks its protection domain. If the target permission is not in the domain, an *AccessControlException* is thrown; otherwise, the algorithm in turn checks if this calling method is declared as a privileged action. If so, and an *AccessControlContext* is provided in the *doPrivileged* method, then the permission is checked with this

AccessControlContext, if not, this permission is granted. If a thread is created by a parent thread, the *AccessControlContext* of the parent is associated with the created thread. The permission is checked with the local thread's inherited context if it has not been granted or denied after the first two steps. More details on stack-inspection mechanism can be found in [9,27].

Access Control Algorithm:
checkPermission (permission) {
    //loop, from newest to oldest stack frame
    foreach (*stackFrame* in the stack of current thread) {
        if (*stackFrame* caller's protection domain does not
            have *permission* defined in the mobile policy)
        throw *AccessControlException*;
        else if (*stackFrame* calling method has been marked
                as privileged action with *permission*){
            if (an *AccessControllerContext context* is
                specified in the call to *doPrivildged*)
                context.checkPermission(permission);
        return; // allow access
        }
        else if(an *AccessControlContext inheritedContext*
                is inherited when this thread is created)
            inheritedContext.checkPermission(permission);
    return;
    }
}

Fig. 5. Access control with mobile policy

6   Related Work

Security is a basic problem in mobile computing. Generally, there are two distinct areas in mobile code security: (1) protection of the host from malicious mobile code and (2) protection of the mobile code from malicious hosts or users. Researchers have presented several models and mechanisms to deal with malicious code [20,29], such as Sandbox [19,10,15], code signing/code access [16], proof carrying code [17], etc. Protection of mobile code, however, is still an open problem. Vigna [26] proposes an execution tracing technology for mobile agents using cryptographic hash. Yee [28] presents mechanisms to detect tempering by malicious hosts with partial result authentication codes (PARCs) and forward-integrity security policy. Sander and Tschudin [22] formalize a theoretical result aimed at allowing an agent to preserve some secrecy from a malicious host by using encrypted forms of functions in mobile code. Algesheimer et al [6] introduce an approach for securely executing mobile code that relies on a minimally trusted third party. This third party cannot learn anything about the computing with guarantee of privacy and integrity to the code originator. The main difference between our approach and previous work is that we enforce the security policy in the runtime environment of the mobile code. Compatible with existing mechanism, fine-grained access control policies can be easily implemented in our approach, at the cost of a minimum of trust in the remote runtime environment.

Another line of work is reported in [12], where a Java Secure Execution Framework (*JSEF*) is proposed to support local user specific security policies and a global security policy defined by the administrator. The objective in *JSEF* is still to protect users from erroneous or malicious mobile code, and not to prevent malicious users from improperly accessing or using mobile code. An isolated program execution approach is presented in [18]. The isolation is achieved by delaying a sensitive operation such as file access to a "modification cache" that is invisible to others in the system. While this is practical in isolated applications to protect local system resources, it is not applicable in our approach since we aim at protecting resources brought in by mobile code, which can be not only an object in the virtual machine, but also a remote resource which can be accessed by the mobile code.

Venkatakrishnan et al [25] present a permission "empowering" mechanism to mobile code in the runtime environment instead of restricting the behavior. The scope of this work is still in the range of protecting resources in the local host from mobile code. Cubaleska et al [8] propose a method to build a trusted policy for a mobile agent owner. The policy indicates which host is malicious or not trusted anymore, so that the owner does not deploy mobile agents to these hosts. Since the trusted policy is a posteriori, the solution is useful only for some mobile applications which re-visit previous hosts. In our approach, the mobile policy is enforced in a trusted runtime environment, with no such limitation. Hohl [13] introduces a blackbox model to protect mobile agents from malicious hosts. In this idea, a parallel executable blackbox agent is generated from the original agent, which has a different structure. As declared by the author, this idea only partially solves the malicious host problem. However, our solution can be applied to any mobile code.

A trusted Java Virtual Macine (TrustedVM) is proposed in [11] to capture the behaviors of a remote computing entity. Similar to our approach, the virtual machine itself is attested by signed-hash mechanism. The main difference between this and our approach is that in TrustedVM, policies are used to confine the behavior of the Java program according pre-defined protocols in distributed environments, while the mobile policy in our framework is to protect the execution of mobile code at runtime, that is, the objects in mobile policy are the components of the code itself. Also, our architecture uses hardware-based TC technologies to enhance the security of the language-based JVM in a platform.

7   Conclusions

This paper presents a mobile policy framework to protect the information and resources imported by mobile code and agents in runtime environments with trusted computing technologies. This framework includes policy specification and definition, as well as a high-level implementation architecture in Java environment. For the implementation, the access control mechanism in the Java Runtime Environment is used with the existing stack-inspection mechanism. The benefit of this enforcement architecture is that we can define and implement the permission class in a mobile policy, maintaining the flexibility and compatibility with current runtime technologies. The extensibility of the Java authorization model, as well as the separation of policy specification and enforcement mechanism, makes our approach practical. A trusted computing architecture is proposed in our framework, to provide verifiable trusted behaviors of a remote host's runtime environment.

In future work we can consider development of a runtime policy analysis engine to dynamically answer permission checks. With this, permission derivation and inference, as well as policy analysis can be achieved in runtime. This benefits from scalability and development efficiency beyond the static policy specification and definition. For example, a policy for a code may be combined from several sources, and a real time check and analysis of these sources will improve the system performance by avoiding the redefinition of the static policy files and the restarting of the program.

References

1. AMD platform for trustworthy computing. Microsoft WinHEC, http://www.microsoft.com/whdc/winhec/pres03.mspx, 2003.
2. *LaGrande Technology Preliminary Architecture Specification, http://www.intel.com/technology/security/downloads/PRELIM-LT-SPEC_D52212.htm.*
3. OASIS XACML TC. *Core Specification: eXtensible Access Control Markup Language (XACML)*, 2005.
4. Sun's XACML implementation, http://sunxacml.sourceforge.net/.
5. *TCG Specification Architecture Overview*. https://www.trustedcomputinggroup.org.
6. J. Algesheimer, C. Cashin, J. Camenisch, and G. Karjoth, Cryptographic Security for Mobile Code, IEEE Symposium On Research in Security and Privacy, 2001.
7. D. Balfanz and L. Gong, Experience with Secure Multi-Processing in Java, International Conference on Distributed Computing Systems, 1998.
8. B. Cubaleska and M. Scheider, Applying Trust Policies for Protecting Mobile Agents Aganist DoS, 3rd Workship on Policies for Distributed Systems and Networks, 2002.
9. L. Gong, E. Gary, and D. Mary, Inside Java 2 Platform Security: Architecture, API Design, and Implementation, Addison-wesley, 2003.
10. L. Gong, M. Mueller, H. Prafullchandra, and R. Schemers, Going Beyond the Sandbox: An Overview of the New Security Arthitecture in the Java Development Kit 1.2, USENIX Symposium on Internet Technologies and Systems, 1997.
11. V. Haldar, D. Chandra, and M. Franz. Semantic remote attestation - a virtual machine directed approach to trusted computing. In *Proc. of the Third virtual Machine Research and Technology Symposium*. USENIX, 2004.
12. M. Hauswirth, C. Kerer and R. Kurmanowytsch, A Secure Execution Framework for Java, In Proc. of ACM Computer and Communication Security, 2000.
13. F. Hohl, Time Limited Blackbox Security: Protecting Mobile Agents From Malicious Hosts, Lecture Notes in Computer Science 1419, Springer-Verlag, Berlin, 1998.
14. S. Jajodia, P. Samarati, and V. Subrahmanian, and E. Bertino, A Unified Framework for Enforcing Multiple Access Control Policies, ACM SIGMOD, 1997.
15. C. Lai, L. Gong, L. Koved, A. Nadalin, and R. Schemers, User Authentication and Authorization in the Java Platform, Annual Computer Security Applications Conference, 1999.
16. B. LaMacchia, S. Lange, M. Lyons, R. Martin, and K. Price, .Net Framework Security, Addison-Wesley, 2002.
17. P. Lee and G. Necula, Research on Proof-carry Code for Mobile Code Security, DARPA workshop on Foundation for Secure Mobile Code, 1997.

18. Z. Liang, V. N. Venkatakrishan, and R. Sekar, Isolated Program Execution: An Application Transparent Approach for Executing Untrusted Programs, Annual Computer Security Applications Conference, 2003.
19. G. McGraw and E. Felten, Securing Java: Getting Down to Business with Mobile Code, Wiley, http://www.securingjava.com, 1999.
20. G. McGraw and G. Morrisett, Attacking Malicious Code: A Report to the Infosec Research Council, IEEE Software, Volume 17 Issue 5, Sep/Oct 2000.
21. S. Oaks, Java Security, O'Reilly, 2001.
22. T. Sander and C. F. Tschudin, Protecting Mobile Agent against Malicious Hosts, In G.Gigna, ed., Mobile Agents and Security, Lecture Notes in Computer Science 1419, 1998.
23. TCPA Design Philosphies and Concepts, http://www.trustedcomputing.org/home
24. Trusted Computing Group Home, https://www.trustedcomputinggroup.org/home
25. V. Venkatakrishnan, R. Peri, and R. Sekar, Empowering Mobile Code Using Expressive Security Policies, New Security Paradigms Workshop, 2002.
26. G. Vigna, Protecting Mobile Agents Through Tracing, In Proc. of the Workshop on Mobile Object systems, 1997.
27. D. S. Wallach and E. Felten, Understand Java Stack Inspection, IEEE Symposium On Research in Security and Privacy, 1998.
28. B. Yee, A Sanctuary for Mobile Agents, Secure Internet Programming: Security Issures for Mobile Code and Distributed Objects, J.Vitek and C.Jensen, eds., LNCS 1603, 1999.
29. J. Zachry, Protecting Mobile Code in the Wild, IEEE Internet Computing, March/April 2003.

IP Address Authorization for Secure Address Proxying Using Multi-key CGAs and Ring Signatures

James Kempf[1], Jonathan Wood[2], Zulfikar Ramzan[3], and Craig Gentry[4]

[1] DoCoMo Labs USA, 181 Metro Drive, Suite 300, San Jose, CA, 95110, USA
kempf@docomlabs-usa.com
[2] Nominum, Inc., 2385 Bay Road, Redwood City, CA, 94063, USA
jonwood@speakeasy.net
[3] Symantec, Inc., 1600 Seaport Blvd., Suite 200, Redwood City, CA, 94063, USA
zulfikar@alum.mit.edu
[4] Computer Science Dept., 353 Serra Mall, Stanford University, Stanford CA 94305, USA
cgentry@cs.stanford.edu

Abstract. *Address proxying* is a process by which one IP node acts as an endpoint intermediary for an IP address that actually belongs to another IP node. Address proxying serves many useful functions in IP networks. In IPv6, the Secure Neighbor Discovery Protocol (SEND) provides powerful tools for securing the mapping between the IP address and the link address which is the basis of local link address proxying; however, these tools don't work for address proxies. In this paper, we present an extension to SEND for secure proxying. As an example of how secure address proxying can be used, we propose a minor extension of the Mobile IPv6 protocol to allow secure proxying by the home agent. We then present measurements comparing SEND with and without the address proxying extensions.

Keywords: secure address proxy, ring signature, SEND, Mobile IPv6, multi-key cryptographically generated address.

1 Introduction

Address proxying is a process whereby one IP node acts as an endpoint intermediary for an IP address that is in some sense "owned" by another node. IP address proxies are used in a variety of ways. The original link layer protocol for converting IPv4 addresses to 48 bit Ethernet addresses, Address Resolution Protocol (ARP) [15], allowed network devices to proxy-resolve (Proxy ARP) addresses for hosts in order to support bridging and other functions. In IPv6, ARP was replaced by an IPv6 layer protocol called the Neighbor Discovery Protocol [9] which similarly allows routers and other network agents to perform proxy address resolution but at the IPv6 level.

As an example of the usefulness of address proxying, proxy IPv6 address resolution is used in the Mobile IPv6 protocol [6] to make it look like a mobile node is on its home link when it is not. The Mobile IPv6 home agent – a router in the home network of a mobile host – proxies the address of a mobile host on the home link –

H. Yoshiura et al. (Eds.): IWSEC 2006, LNCS 4266, pp. 196–211, 2006.

the home address – when the mobile host is not currently on the home link. This allows the home agent to intercept packets sent to the mobile host's home address and forward them to the mobile host's current address on the foreign link - the care-of address. Additionally, proxying prevents any other node on the home link from claiming the home address.

Despite its usefulness, address proxying is fraught with security problems. The underlying ARP protocol for translating between an IPv4 address and an Ethernet address never included any security measures. The sender of an ARP query therefore cannot tell whether a response comes from the legitimate owner of the IPv4 address, from a legitimate proxy (such as a router on the link), or from an attacker attempting to disrupt traffic to the legitimate owner. Such an attack is called "ARP spoofing"[1]. In IPv6, the Secure Neighbor Discovery Protocol (SEND) [1] allows a node to prove its authorization to claim ownership of an IPv6 address, but, as currently defined, the SEND protocol does not support address proxying either. Secure proxying, in effect, requires two nodes - the node claiming the address as its source address and the proxy - to be able to securely perform control signaling involving the address.

If a single IPv6 host is claiming ownership of the address, the requirements for IP address authorization in IPv6 are met fairly nicely with Cryptographically Generated Addresses (CGAs) [2] (sometimes called Statistically Unique and Cryptographically Verifiable (SUCV) addresses [8]). CGAs are used in the SEND protocol to secure the IPv6 to link address mapping on the local link [2]. CGAs are constructed by hashing the host's public key and some additional parameters into the bottom 64 bits of the IPv6 address, to form a cryptographically generated interface identifier. When a control protocol message is sent involving the address, the message is signed with the public key. The signature provides data origin authentication, while the cryptographically generated interface identifier in the address proves that the message was signed by the owner of the address.

While CGAs provide a fine solution for address ownership in IPv6 when one node can claim ownership of the address, they are less useful when multiple nodes might legitimately be viewed as owners since only the node generating the public key can claim the address. An example of multiple nodes being viewed as owners is address proxying. "Ownership" in this case means some kind of proof that the node in question is authorized to perform control signaling operations, such as routing updates, on the address. In order for the proxy node to be able to securely proxy the address, it must be able to present the same kind of cryptographic proof of ownership as the node that generated the address. CGAs only allow the node owning the public key and generating that address to present such proof.

1.1 Contribution

Our contribution in this paper is threefold:

1) We describe a technique that extends CGAs to addresses generated by keys from multiple hosts, called multi-key CGAs, in order to support address proxying and other functions where more than one node needs to claim

---

[1] The threat here is not hypothetical. One of the authors experienced an ARP spoofing attack at a prestigious international networking conference in 2003.

authorization for ownership. The technique uses a kind of group signature called a *ring signature* [5] [16] to secure the signaling.

2) We develop an extension of the SEND protocol using multi-key CGAs and a ring signature algorithm called Rivest-Shamir-Tauman (RST) [16] that allows a node autoconfiguring an IPv6 address to designate a router on the local subnet as a secure address proxy.

3) We compare the performance of IPv6 Neighbor Discovery without SEND, with SEND, and with SEND using multi-key CGAs and ring signatures instead of the standard RSA signature. We also present some performance figures comparing RST with RSA signatures, and characterize the scalability of the RST algorithm as the number of group members increases. To our knowledge, this is the first realistic application and first implementation of the RST ring signature algorithm.

2   Secure Neighbor Discovery and Proxy Address Resolution

In the basic Neighbor Discovery protocol, a node resolves an IPv6 address on the local link to a link layer address by multicasting a Neighbor Solicitation (NS) message. The node owning the IPv6 address replies with a Neighbor Advertisement (NA) containing the link layer address. This allows the soliciting node to forward packets using link layer routing on the last hop. Neighbor Discovery also allows a node to discover a router, by multicasting a Router Solicitation (RS). Routers on the link respond with Router Advertisements (RSs) containing their link layer addresses and other information about the link. This allows the soliciting node to find a router that can forward packets off the local link.

There are two basic attacks on Neighbor Discovery [13]. An attacker can respond to a NS message in lieu of the actual owner of the IPv6 address causing the sender to set up a mapping between the attacker's link address and the victim's IPv6 address, thereby allowing the attacker to siphon off the victim's traffic. An attacker can set up a fake router, advertise it on the link with a RA, and dupe victim nodes on the link to send traffic through the fake router, thereby allowing the attacker to control the victim's traffic. SEND [1][2] was designed to counter these threats to Neighbor Discovery.

Figure 1 illustrates the SEND protocol. In Step 1, a node coming on the link solicits a RA message by multicasting a RS message on the All Routers Multicast Address. A SEND router responds with an RA signed with the router's certified public key in Step 2, and containing IPv6 subnet prefixes for the link. If the node does not have the certificate for the router in its cache, in Step 3 the node sends out a Certificate Path Solicitation (CPS) to obtain the router's certificate path. The node includes in the CPS the names of trust anchors for certificate authorities for which the node has certificates in its cache. The router returns one Certificate Path Advertisement (CPA) per certificate for the entire chain, rooted in one of the trust anchors, and culminating with the CPA containing the router's own certificate. When the certificate path has been validated, the node can use the router's certified public key to validate the signature on the RA.

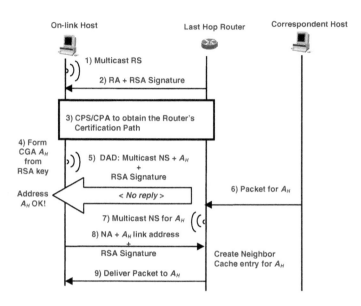

Fig. 1. Basic SEND prototcol

Once the RA has been certified, in Step 4 the node generates an RSA public key /private key pair for the CGA, and then generates the address using the public key and one of the subnet prefixes from the RA. In Step 5, the node uses Duplicate Address Detection (DAD) [17] to determine if the address is unique on the link. DAD requires the node to multicast a NS to the Solicited Node Multicast Address. Any node that also has the prospective address hears the NS and responds with a NA. The NS and NA must be signed with the respective RSA keys. The soliciting node then must use a different address. SEND allows three address conflicts to be reported before considering the node to be under attack. If DAD succeeds, the node is free to use the address.

In Step 6, a packet incoming from off link to the SEND router triggers the router in Step 7 to solicit for the link address so the packet can be delivered on the last hop. In Step 8, the node replies with a NA signed with the RSA key and using the CGA. The router checks these and establishes a Neighbor Cache entry for the CGA if the signature and CGA validate. In Step 9, the router finally delivers the packet to the node.

For proxy address resolution, the node replying with the NA to claim the IPv6 address in response to the DAD in Step 5 or the node replying with the NA for link address resolution in Step 8 is not the same the node that generated the address, it is the proxy. The proxy does not have access to the owning node's RSA private key and therefore the receiver cannot be sure that the proxy is authorized to claim the address. With no signature, an attacker could easily pose as an address proxy and steal the node's traffic. As a consequence, SEND cannot be used to secure proxy address resolution, and address proxying is therefore prohibited in the base SEND protocol. This is the basic address proxy security problem.

3 Previous Work

Two previous solutions have been proposed to solve the problem of proxy address resolution security. The simplest solution, proposed by Daley [4], is to allow a certified last hop router to sign the NA message on behalf of the owning node if the router is proxying. The router's public key certificate could be augmented with a property indicating permission from the certificate authority to proxy. Nikander and Arkko [12] propose having the owning node construct a signed attribute certificate delegating address proxying rights, and sending the attribute certificate to the proxy. The proxy then includes the attribute certificate in any signaling messages involving the proxied address, such as the NA, and signs the messages with its own private key.

Both these solutions have a problem with location privacy, which is important for applications such as the Mobile IPv6 example cited in Section 1. If the signature and security parameters on the message are not the same regardless of whether the proxy or the owning node are defending the address, the NA message has some indication that the message was signed by the proxy, and not by the owning node. A node receiving the NA can infer whether or not the owning node is on the local link. The location privacy of the owning node is thereby compromised. In contrast, by using the technique described in this paper, the receiving node cannot infer anything about the whether the owning node is on the local link or not, because the message looks the same regardless of whether the proxy or the owning node originated it. The ring signature itself does not reveal anything about which group member actually generated it, and the cryptographic parameters are the same in both cases.

The attribute certificate technique has an additional problem in that it requires a certain amount of preconfiguration between the proxy and the owning node before the address can be proxied. The owning node must send an attribute certificate to the proxy. With the technique described in this paper, the proxy must know the public key of the owning node, but it can learn that as part of the standard SEND protocol (for example, during DAD) if proxying is to be done without any additional signaling. The proxy group can be formed opportunistically because ring signatures allow the hosts in the ring to sign without any preconfiguration of cryptographic material or interaction with network infrastructure; although the hosts do need to agree on the membership of the group before the address is configured. Note, however, that the question of whether another node can actually be trusted to correctly proxy the address is not handled directly, and must be dealt with using certificates or another secure identity-determining technique.

4 Multi-key CGAs and Ring Signatures

In order to allow CGAs to be proxied securely, generation of the interface identifier portion of the address needs to be modified to include the public keys from more than one host. In addition, the signature algorithm must allow more than one signer. A group signature algorithm [3] is a good candidate, since group signatures typically allow multiple signers. For the address proxying application, we use a kind of group signature called a ring signature, because ring signature algorithms do not require a group manager or any preconfiguration on the members of the group (except that they must possess the public keys of all group members) and ring signatures are anonymous, protecting the location privacy of the node that originated the address.

4.1 Generating and Validating Multi-key CGAs

SEND [1] specifies an algorithm for constructing and verifying single key CGAs. The same algorithm can be used to generate and verify multi-key CGAs for unicast by simply replacing the single public key in the algorithm for SEND by the SHA-1 hash of the public keys in the group. A modification of the CGA algorithm in [2], appropriate for address proxying, is given below.

Generating a Multi-key CGA. The input parameters for constructing a multi-key CGA are the following:

- pk_1 through pk_n, the public keys of the n nodes in the group,
- The *Sec* parameter, which can have a value from 0 to 7. Increasing the value of the *Sec* parameter increases the cost of constructing a CGA, and therefore the cost of a dictionary attack [2].

In the following, | is the bit-wise concatenation function, and *SHA1()* is the SHA-1 cryptographic hash function [10]. A multi-key CGA is constructed as follows:

1) Compute the hash of the public keys for the nodes in the group:

$$ConcatVal = SHA1\ (\ pk1\ |\ pk2\ |\ ...\ |\ pkn\ )$$

2) Set the 128 bit value *modifier* to a random value.
3) Form the following difficulty test value:

$$Hash2 = SHA1_{112}\ (\ modifier\ |\ B9(0)\ |\ ConcatVal\ )$$

where $SHA1_n()$ indicates the left-most n bits of the SHA1 hash and $B9(0)$ indicates nine bytes set to zero.
4) Check the leftmost *Sec* times 16 bits of *Hash2*. If all bits are zero (or *Sec* itself is zero), go to the next step. Otherwise, increment *modifier* by one and redo Step 3.
5) Set *collision-count* to zero.
6) Using the final value of *modifier*, form the following CGA interface identifier:

$$Hash1 = SHA1_{64}\ (\ modifier\ |\ subnet\text{-}prefix\ |\ collision\text{-}count\ |\ ConcatVal\ )$$

where *subnet-prefix* is the 64 bit IPv6 subnet prefix for the address.
7) Replace the leftmost 3 bits of *Hash1* with *Sec* and set bits 6 and 7 (i.e. the "g" and "u" bits) in *Hash1* to zero.
8) Form the multi-key CGA as follows:

$$mCGA = subnet\text{-}prefix\ |\ Hash1$$

9) Perform DAD [17] on the address. If a collision is detected, increment *collision-count* and return to Step 6 if *collision-count* < 3. If *collision-count* ≥ 3, stop and report, since an attack or serious network misconfiguration is likely.

Validating a Multi-key CGA. The validation algorithm for multi-key CGAs is a modification of the SEND algorithm for single key CGAs, and follows from the generation algorithm above.

The input parameters for validating a multi-key CGA are the following:

- pk_1 through pk_n, the public keys of the n nodes in the group,
- The *modifier* random value and *collision-count* value used to generate the multi-key CGA,
- A multi-key CGA.

Note that nothing in an IPv6 address identifies it as a multi-key CGA, so this will have to be deduced from the context. In addition, the *modifier* and *collision-count* parameters need to be included in the control message in some fashion.

A multi-key CGA is validated as follows:

1) Check that *collision-count* ≤ 3. If not, the multi-key CGA verification fails. Exit.
2) Compute the hash of the public keys for the nodes in the group:

$$TestVal = SHA1 \ (\ pk_1 \mid pk_2 \mid ... \mid pk_n \ )$$

3) Form the following value:

$$Hash1 = SHA1_{64} \ (modifier \mid subnet\text{-}prefix \mid collision\text{-}count \mid TestVal \ )$$

4) Compare *Hash1* with the rightmost 64 bits of the address (the interface identifier bits), ignoring bits 6 and 7 and the leftmost 3 bits (i.e. the "g" and "u" bits and the *Sec* bits). If the comparison fails, the address does not match and the multi-key CGA verification fails. Exit.
5) Extract the security parameter from the three rightmost bits of the 64 bit interface identifier, treating the result as an unsigned integer *Sec*.
6) Form the following difficulty check value:

$$Hash2 = SHA1_{112} \ (\ modifier \mid B9(0) \mid TestVal \ )$$

7) Compare the leftmost *Sec* x 16 bits of *Hash2* to zero. If any are not zero, then the verification fails. Otherwise, the address is verified. Note that the verification never fails at this step if *Sec* is zero.

4.2   Ring Signature Background

Group signatures have been an object of investigation in the cryptographic community for some time [3]. Until recently, most group signature algorithms required one member of the group to be designated as the group manager, and additionally allowed the group manager to break anonymity on the signature. Rivest, Shamir, and Tauman [16] formalized the notion of a fully anonymous, ad-hoc group signature, called a ring signature. A ring signature does not require the intermediation of a group manager, allowing the group to form opportunistically. In fact, a group member can form a group and sign even without the active co-operation of other group members. The only requirement is that a signer possesses the individual public keys of the group members, and that the public keys are also available to the verifier. The signature is completely anonymous, so it is not possible to determine who the actual signer is. Verification of the signature requires the public keys of all members in the group. These properties make ring signatures an attractive approach for multi-host address authorization as applied to address proxying.

A theoretical disadvantage of the RST ring signature algorithm is that the size of the signature grows linearly as the number of members in the ring grows. Recently, work by Dodis, et. al. [5] describes a technique for generating constant sized ring signatures, based on the Strong RSA Assumption. The algorithm is not completely ad hoc because a group manager is needed and verification still requires possession of the public keys for all the group members, but the size of the signature itself is bounded. For address proxying, the requirement for a group manager makes the Dodis algorithm less practical than the RST algorithm, since it would require some amount of prior co-ordination between the proxy and the originating node. It is for this reason that the RST algorithm was selected for use in the secure address proxying extension to SEND.

4.3 Overview of How RST Signatures Work

This section gives a high-level overview of how RST ring signatures work [16], referencing the steps of the detailed procedure described below. Suppose that node i is wants to sign message m. Node i actually computes a standard RSA signature on a sequence of values $y_1, ..., y_n$ which will be related to m by means of a combining function (signing Step 4 below). The signature on each y_j will be valid with respect to the public key (N_j, e_j).

Since node i knows the i-th signing key corresponding to public key (N_i, e_i) it can easily compute the signature corresponding to y_i. The main question is how it can sign the remaining y_j values without knowing the private key corresponding to (N_j, e_j)? To accomplish this, the RST algorithm uses an interesting feature of RSA signatures: it is possible to come up with a valid message/signature pair by first generating the signature (e.g., at random) and then computing a message for which this signature is valid. This feature is relatively harmless in practice, since in practical applications of the RSA signature itself, one has to start with a meaningful message first and compute the resulting signature, not the other way around. In addition, hash functions like SHA-1 are applied to a message to create a digest which is signed, thereby making it harder for an attacker to generate a random forgery for which the pre-image of the digest is known. However, in the present case we can actually benefit from this feature.

Node i first generates random values x_j for all $j \neq i$ (signing Step3i). Node i essentially computes messages y_j for which x_j is a valid signature by exponentiating x_j

using the public exponent e_j (signing Step 3iii). Since we are dealing with different RSA moduli N_j, we have to exercise some care to make sure that the resulting values are in the right range (this issue is handled in Steps 3ii and 3iv of the signing algorithm). Next, node i calculates the value y_i for which $y_1, ..., y_n$ satisfies the combining function (Step 4). Finally, node i uses knowledge of the private key corresponding to (N_i, e_i) to compute a standard textbook RSA signature on y_i (step 6), again taking care of range issues associated with using different moduli (Steps 5 and 7).

At this point, the pairs $(x_1, y_1), ..., (x_n, y_n)$ are each valid RSA message/signature pairs under the respective RSA public keys $(e_1, N_1), ..., (e_n, N_n)$, so these pairs would constitute a legitimate ring signature on the message m. The verifier simply verifies each pair separately, taking care of range issues (verification, Step 2).

However, we can perform an optimization by noting that given $x_1, ..., x_n$, anyone can compute the corresponding $y_1, ..., y_n$ by exponentiating (respectively) by $e_1, ..., e_n$, modulo $N_1, ..., N_n$. So, the signer need not transmit $y_1, ..., y_n$. Instead, only the single value v in addition to the x_j values need to be transmitted, thereby allowing the verifier to construct $y_1, ..., y_n$, and to check that these values together with v satisfy the combining equation (verification, Step 3).

Note that the privacy property of ring signing is achieved because by looking at the signature, it is not possible to tell which value y_i the signer actually signed in Step 6 and which signatures were generated at random in Step 3.

4.4   Generating and Validating RST Signatures

The RST ring signature algorithm is based on the Rabin signature algorithm, which the authors describe as being preferable to a version based on RSA since signature verification for Rabin signatures is faster. However, we use a version of the RST algorithm based on RSA because RSA is more widely deployed.

This RSA-based ring signature algorithm is as secure as regular RSA-based signatures. Specifically, if an attacker is able to forge a ring signature which is valid for a group of signers that the forger does not belong to, with public keys pk_1 through pk_n, then such an attacker could break a regular RSA signature. The security proof of the ring signature algorithm is in the random oracle model and ideal cipher model. See [16] for the details.

In the following, let $E()$ be an encryption algorithm that uses d-bit keys and has b-bit input and output (we impose an additional condition on b below). Let t be a parameter – e.g., t may equal 80. Let $\oplus$ denote the XOR function.

Generating the Public Keys. The public keys in the RST ring signature algorithm are the same as public keys in RSA. Specifically $pk_i = (N_i , e_i)$, where N_i is a large (e.g., 1024-bit) composite integer that is the product of two large prime numbers p_i and q_i and where e_i is an integer that is relatively prime to $(p_i - 1)(q_i - 1)$. Let b be an integer such that $2^b > 2^t N_i$ for all i.

Generating a RST Signature. Let pk_i be the public key of the node constructing the signature. Form the ring signature as follows:

1) Set the symmetric encryption key k to be $SHA1(m)$, where m is the message to be signed.
2) Pick a random b-bit string v.
3) For j from 1 to n (except $j \neq i$) do:
  a) Pick random b-bit string x_j.
  b) Compute (q_j, r_j) such that $x_j = q_j N_j + r_j$ for $r_j \in [\,0, N_j\,]$.
  c) Compute $y_j' = x_j^{e_j}$ (mod N_j) for $y_j' \in [\,0,\ N_j\,]$.
  d) Set $y_j = q_j N_j + y_j'$.
  e) Go back to Step a if $y_j \geq 2^b$, otherwise exit loop.
4) Compute y_i such that:
$$E_k (y_n \oplus E_k (y_{n\text{-}1} \oplus E_k (... \oplus E_k (y_1 \oplus v)...))) = v.$$
5) Compute (q_i, r_i) such that $y_i = q_i N_i + r_i$ for $r_i \in [\,0,\ N_i\,]$.
6) Compute $x_i' = y_i^{1/e_i}$ (mod N_i) for $x_i' \in [\,0,\ N_i\,]$.
7) Set $x_i = q_i N_i + x_i'$.
8) Go to Step 3 if $x_i \geq 2^b$.
9) Output the ring signature (x_1, ..., x_n, v).

If t is large enough, there will be only a negligibly small probability that the signature generation algorithm will abort in Step 3e or Step 8 because y_j or x_i spills out of the permitted range $[\,0, 2^b\,)$. Regarding Step 4, notice that:

$$y_i = E_k^{-1} (y_{i+1} \oplus E_k^{-1} (... y_n \oplus E_k^{-1} (v))) \oplus E_k (y_{i\text{-}1} \oplus E_k (... \oplus E_k (y_1 \oplus v))).$$

Validating a RST Signature. Given the message m and public keys keys pk_1 through pk_n, the ring signature (x_1, ..., x_n, v) can be verified as follows:

1) Set the symmetric encryption key k to be $SHA1(m)$, where m is the contents of the signed message.
2) For j from 1 to n do:
  i) Compute (q_j, r_j) such that $x_j = q_j N_j + r_j$ for $r_j \in [\,0, N_j\,]$;
  ii) Compute $y_j' = x_j^{e_j}$ (mod N_j) for $y_j' \in [\,0,\ N_j\,]$.
  iii) Set $y_j = q_j N_j + y_j'$.
3) Calculate $v' = E_k(y_n \oplus E_k (y_{n\text{-}1} \oplus E_k (... \oplus E_k (y_1 \oplus v)...)))$.
4) If $v' = v$, the signature is verified.

5 Applying Multi-key CGAs and Ring Signatures to Secure Address Proxying

In this section, an extension of the SEND protocol to provide secure, location privacy-preserving address proxying on the last hop link [7] is described. An application of secure address proxying to mobility management, involving secure proxying of a mobile node home address by a Mobile IPv6 home agent is also presented.

5.1 Proxy SEND

Prior to forming a multi-key CGA, the host uses the SEND CPS/CPA exchange or some other means to obtain a certificate for its chosen default router, Step 3 in Figure 1 (for Mobile IPv6, the default router is the home agent). The host then uses the router's public key and its own RSA public key to generate the multi-key CGA, as described above, Step 4 in Figure 1. Use of the router certificate ensures that the node selected for proxying can, in fact, be trusted. In Steps 5 and 8 of Figure 1 - where SEND requires the host to use an RSA signature in the NA or NS message - proxy SEND uses an RST signature. No new protocol messages are required. The use of a RST requires a new Ring Signature Option to hold the new signature instead of the standard RSA Signature Option in SEND. In addition, the host sends the public key for the router along with its own public key in the CGA Parameters Option, since both keys are needed to validate the signature. The router uses the CGA when proxying; otherwise, a receiving node can detect if the owning node is on link or not. For backward compatibility, the host needs some indication that the router supports secure proxying, so that it knows whether to use SEND or proxy SEND. An extension to the router's certificate can provide this information.

The security of this extension is the same as SEND. Validation of the RST signature indicates that a node owning one of the public keys in the CGA signed the message with its private key, and the multi-key CGA indicates that the message was sent from a source address that can claim authorization to send control signaling affecting the source address (i.e. that the address is not being spoofed). An attacker can't construct an RST signature for the same CGA because the attacker doesn't possess the private key for the owning node or the proxy. The attacker could forge a CGA, but failure to validate the signature would tip off the receiver.

5.2 Mobile IPv6 Secure Proxying

As mentioned, Mobile IPv6 [6] requires the home agent to act as a proxy for all home addresses when their owners are off link. The home agent discovers that a mobile host is off link when it receives a Binding Update (BU) message containing an off-link care-of address. The BU requests that the home agent establish a binding between the home address and care-of address, and that any traffic arriving on the link for the home address should be forwarded through a tunnel to the care-of address. The mobile host also sends traffic back to its correspondents by reverse tunneling through the home agent. The BU is secured by an IPsec security association to prevent an unauthorized node from changing the binding.

Again, no change is required in the basic Mobile IPv6 binding update protocol for secure proxying. Figure 2 illustrates the protocol. If the home agent is capable of doing proxy SEND, in Step 1 of the figure, the mobile host sends its public key ("MN Key") and the home agent's public key ("HA Key") along with the BU in a new Binding Update Option, the Secure Proxy Mobility Option, through an IPsec ESP tunnel to the home agent. The two public keys are used to calculate the multi-key CGA. The home agent uses this information to check that it is the owner of the public key and therefore capable of proxying.

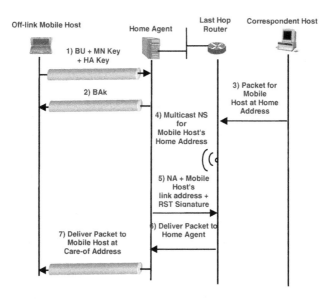

Fig. 2. IPv6 Binding Update with secure proxying

In Step 2 of the figure, the home agent replies with a Binding Acknowledgement (BAk), again through an IPsec ESP tunnel, indicating that the routing to the care-of address has been established. At this point, the home agent is prepared to securely proxy the mobile node's home address. A packet from a correspondent host directed to the home address of the mobile host arrives at a last hop router on the link, in Step 3. The last hop router solicits the mobile host's link address in Step 4 using the NS. In Step 5, the home agent securely proxies the home address by replying with a signed NA including the link address, the multi-key CGA, the two public keys, and the RST signature. Note that the NA contains exactly the same information and is formatted exactly the same as if it had been sent by the mobile node itself, so the router can't tell from the NA contents whether the mobile node is off the link or not. The router then delivers the packet to the home agent in Step 6, and in Step 7 the home agent tunnels the packet to the mobile host at its care-of address, using either an IP-IP tunnel or an IPsec ESP tunnel.

6   Implementation Results

We implemented the proxy SEND algorithm described above and ran performance tests comparing it with insecure Neighbor Discovery and with SEND which uses a standard RSA signature. The RST implementation was done on OpenSSL version 0.9.8 running on Linux version 2.6.14.3. In order to make the comparison fair, we used our own custom implementation of RSA that was very basic rather than the version of RSA provided with OpenSSL, because the OpenSSL implementation contains many features to increase the security and performance of RSA. Such features could ultimately be included in a release version of RST too. Tests were run on 2 GHz Pentium M laptops with 1 GB of RAM and a 1 Gbit Ethernet connection. For the tests, 1024 bit keys were used and the block cipher was AES128 [11]. The reported measurements are the average of twenty runs.

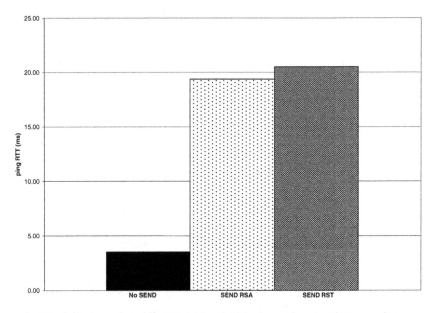

Fig. 3. Performance of IPv6 Neighbor Solicitation with and without security

Figure 3 compares the performance of the three cases. Note that in this figure and Table 1, SEND with RST signatures uses two keys, the mobile node key and the router key. The performance test was done by running ping to discover the link address of the neighbor node when the IPv6 to link address map was not in the Neighbor Cache. Note that the performance of SEND with RST is not substantially worse than SEND with RSA. The big difference in performance occurs when security is enabled for Neighbor Discover. Since Neighbor Discovery is only performed if the IPv6 address to link address map is not in the Neighbor Cache, however, the hit taken by adding security is not critical. After the Neighbor Cache entry is available, the address is resolved from the cache entry until it either times out or is invalidated by the owning node, and therefore no network traffic is required.

Table 1. Comparison of SEND RSA and SEND RST Cryptographic Operations Performance

	SEND RSA	**SEND RST**
Signature Calculation	7.973 ms	8.331 ms
Verification Calculation	0.174 ms	0.350 ms

Table 1 contains a more detailed comparison between SEND with standard RSA and with the RST ring signature algorithm. As can be seen from the table, signing and verification performance are all slightly slower than RSA performance.

Figures 4 and 5 illustrate the time required to generate and verify (respectively) an RST signature for between 1 and 10 hosts (1 host corresponds to a standard RSA signature). As expected, signature generation and verification times increase linearly as the number of group members increases However, the rate of increase is not particularly large, and for the purposes of address proxy security – where the group size is most likely to be exactly 2 – the signing and verification performance appear to be acceptable.

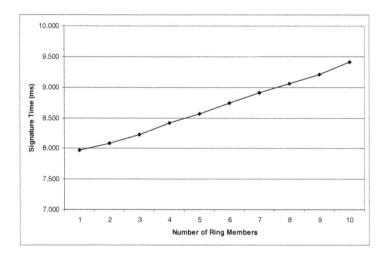

Fig. 4. RST signature generation time as a function of ring size

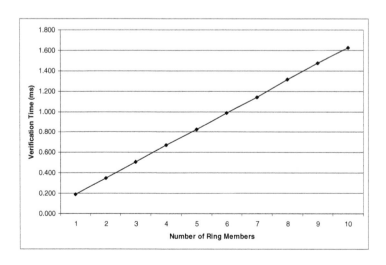

Fig. 5. RST signature verification time as a function of ring size

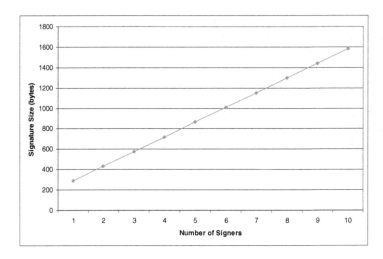

Fig. 6. RST signature size as a function of the number of signers

Figure 6 illustrates the size of the RST signature for between 1 and 10 hosts. As expected, the signature size also increases linearly with the number of signers. As mentioned above, the Dodis [5] ring signature algorithm maintains a constant signature size as the number of members increases and could be used in an application where group sizes are considerably larger. The disadvantage of the Dodis algorithm is that it requires a group manager and therefore preconfiguration on the nodes in the group, resulting in more protocol support to set up.

7 Conclusions

In this paper, we have described a scheme by which cryptographically generated addresses (CGAs) can be extended to support multiple hosts. We utilize the resulting multi-key CGAs and ring signatures to extend the SEND protocol to support secure address proxying. The SEND extension allows a router on the link to proxy a CGA when the host owning the address is off link. We also described how proxy SEND can be used to provide address proxy security on the home link for home addresses in Mobile IPv6. Both applications require no additional protocol messages. Finally, we presented some measurements from a Linux/OpenSSL implementation of multi-key CGA SEND and the RST ring signature algorithm. The measurements suggest that the RST algorithm could be a practical solution for proxy SEND security, since the group size is usually 2. The results of this work promise to firmly ground the security of address proxying; a function that today is basically insecure, and may be applicable to other IPv6 protocols where multiple hosts can claim a single address.

References

1. Arkko, J. (ed.), Kempf, J., Zill, B., and Nikander, P., "SEcure Neighbor Discovery (SEND)", RFC 2971, March, 2005.
2. Aura, T., "Cryptographically Generated Addresses (CGA)", RFC 3972, March, 2005.

3. Chaum, S., and van Heyst, E., "Group Signatures", Eurocrypt, 1991.
4. Daley, G., "Securing Proxy Neighbour Discovery Problem Statement", Internet Draft, work in progress, 2004.
5. Dodis, Y., Kiayias, A., Nicolosi, A., and Shoup, V., "Anonymous Identification in Ad-Hoc Groups", Eurocrypt 2004, LNCS 3027, pp. 609-626, Springer, 2004.
6. Johnson, D., Perkins, C., and Arkko, J., "Mobility Support in IPv6", RFC 3775, June, 2004.
7. Kempf, J., and Gentry, C., "Secure IPv6 Address Proxying using Multi-Key Cryptographically Generated Addresses (MCGAs" Internet Draft, work in progress.
8. Montenegro, G., and Castellucia, C., "Crypto-Based Identifiers (CBIDs): Concepts and Applications", ACM Transactions on Information and System Security, 7(1), pp. 97-127, Feburary, 2004.
9. Narten, T., Nordmark, E., and Simpson, W., "Neighbor Discovery for IP version 6 (IPv6)", RFC 2461, December, 1998.
10. National Institute of Standards and Technology, "Secure Hash Standard", Federal FIPS 180-1, April,1993.
11. National Institute of Standards and Technology, "Specification for the Advanced Encryption Standard (AES)", FIPS 197, November, 2001.
12. Nikander, P., and Arkko, J., "Delegation of Signalling Rights", in B. Christianson, et al. (editors), *Security Protocols*, Springer Lecture Notes in Computer Science 2845, pp. 203-214, 2004.
13. Nikander, P., Kempf, J., and Nordmark, E., "IPv6 Neighbor Discovery (ND) Trust Models and Threats", RFC 3756, May, 2004.
14. O'Shea, G., and Roe, M., "Child-proof Authentication for MIP6 (CAM)", ACM SIGCOMM Computer Communication Review, 31(2), pp. 4-8, April, 2001.
15. Plummer, D. C., "Ethernet Address Resolution Protocol", RFC 826, November, 1982.
16. Rivest, R., Shamir, A., and Tauman, Y., "How to Leak A Secret", ASIACRYPT 2001, pp. 552--565. Lecture Notes in Computer Science 2248, Colin Boyd, ed., Springer, 2001.
17. Thompson, S., and Narten, T., "IPv6 Stateless Address Autoconfiguration", RFC 2462, December, 1998.

A Study of Detection Method of Printed Image Alteration Using Digital Watermark

Junji Onishi and Tsukasa Ono

National Universities Corporation Tsukuba University of Technology, Tsukuba,
Ibaraki 305-8521, Japan
`ohnishi@cs.k.tsukuba-tech.ac.jp`, `ono@cs.k.tsukuba-tech.ac.jp`

Abstract. The digital watermark is used for detection of digital image alteration. However, most of digital images are printed on the paper document for submitting. Once digital images are printed on the paper, it is hard to detect alteration of it. In this paper, the detection method of printed image alteration by using digital watermark is proposed.

1   Introduction

Today's digital imaging systems provide sophisticated processing capabilities, flexibility, and reliability at lower costs and competitive quality when compared with the analog systems of yester-year. As a result, digital image acquisition, processing, storage and reproduction systems have been steadily replacing their analog counterparts. Nevertheless, the lack of built-in integrity and quality verification mechanisms often raises doubts about the use of digital imaging systems.

Traditionally, due to the limited processing abilities in analog media, malicious manipulation of images has been a tedious task with only inferior results being realized without prohibitively expensive professional equipment. However, digital images, unlike their analog counterparts can be easily manipulated using a variety of sophisticated signal processing tools that are readily available as commercial packages. Photo-realistic manipulations can be created by virtually everyone using low cost hardware and software components. (Fig. 1 shows a example of such manipulations, which is created by the author using a personal computer system.) The ease and extent of such manipulations raise serious questions about the integrity and authenticity of digital images. Potential security loopholes of shared information networks, e.g. Internet, on which digital images are commonly posted and distributed further exacerbates the problem. As a result, there is a need for secure image authentication techniques in applications where verification of integrity and authenticity of the image content is essential.

Digital watermarking[1] offers a promising alternative to digital signatures in image authentication applications. The use of watermarks instead of digital signatures typically affords additional functionality by exploiting inherent properties of image content. One such advantage is the direct embedding of authentication information into the image data. As a result, the authentication information survives even when the host image goes under format conversions.

H. Yoshiura et al. (Eds.): IWSEC 2006, LNCS 4266, pp. 212–226, 2006.

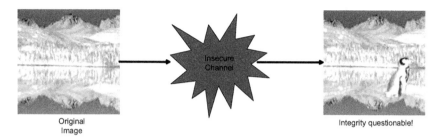

Original
Image

Insecure
Channel

Integrity questionable!

Fig. 1. Integrity and authenticity of digital image are questionable without additional security mechanisms

In contrast, a digital signature appended in the header of an image file maybe easily stripped off, when the file is opened and saved in a different format. This functionality is known as the tamper localization property.

In the development of integrity verification for digital image, two approaches have been proposed. One solution is to use digital signatures which is a data string which associates a message with some originating entity. Image authentication in this manner, however, requires an auxiliary channel for the storage and transmission of a digital signature for each image. This increases the bandwidth requirements and imposes restrictions on implementation. In practical implementations, the signatures and other helper information are kept either as a separate file/bit-stream or as a part of the image header[2]. A second solution is to use digital watermarks which are designed to be easily destroyed if the watermarked image is manipulated in the slightest manner. Many fragile watermarks are also capable of localization, where the areas of the watermarked image that have been tampered with can be determined and distinguished from areas where the watermarked image has not been modified. Early fragile watermarking[3] systems embedded checksums[4] or pseudo-random sequences[5] in the least significant bit (LSB) plane of an image while more recent systems apply more sophisticated embedding mechanisms including the use of cryptographic hash functions[6] to detect changes to a watermarked image.

On the other hand, digital images can be used for printing to a photo paper. Digital photographs look like traditional photographs when printed, displayed on a monitor or projected on a television. Most of people react with the same trust to digital photographs as they do to traditional photographs. In most of case, it is impossible to detect alteration of printed image without comparison to the original digital image, if a source digital image has been altered before printing. Unfortunately, most of recent works for detecting the alteration image is target to the digital image data. They will not be available for printed image such as analog data. Oki Electric Industry Co., Ltd. has developed the integrity verification system for paper documents under printing[7]. However, their system is not available for photo printing, because their system can distort the image under printing process.

Our goal is to detect printed image alteration. In this paper, we propose the detection method for printed image alteration by using digital watermark which is based on extending a simple spread-spectrum watermarking technique[8] with a modified detector in the spatial domain. The detection process is performed on each block of the image so regions of alterations can be identified.

2   Definition of Image Alteration

Generally, digital images can be manipulated using a variety of sophisticated signal processing tools by owner. These manipulation can be considered as alteration. Thus, let us define the our target of image alteration clearly. In this paper, our target of image is described the below.

- Original image is a color image taken by the digital camera without manipulating.
- Original image has been embedded the signal for detecting image alteration by using our proposed method.

The definition of image alteration is described the below.

- Replacement of some objects in the source image by using another photo data.
- Overwriting a part of image in order to remove or add some objects on the original source image from another image which is taken the same scene.

Our method do not consider as image alteration in cases described the below.

- Cropping the apart of image from original.
- Image manipulate processing without image alteration described the above.

3   Overview of Technique Relationship with Watermark

In this paper, digital watermark is applied for detecting of printed image alteration. The watermark embedded into the original image is required the robustness under printing process. Therefore, a digital watermark based on a spread-spectrum technique is used in order to embed the signal for detecting the image alteration. The signal for detecting the image alteration is attached into the middle frequency domain of the source digital image which is divided by several blocks. To extract the signal, the signal is extracted from each blocks of the source image. The image alteration can be detected to verify the signal on each blocks of the source image. Then, the block of image alteration can be detected. On the other hand, to use the property of Fourier Transform, the embedded signal can have the property of translation invariant, which is useful for detecting the detail domain of image alteration. On the other hand, it is higher possible to have error detection under extracting the signal from printed image, even if the target image is not altered. Our goal is to detect printed image alteration correctly. Thus, in order to avoid the error detection, our method creates the gray scale mask image which shows the domain of image alteration under extracting

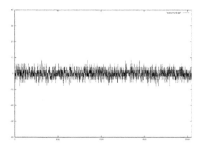

Fig. 2. An example of a spread spectrum signal used as an alteration detection signal

the signal. To observe the mask image, we can understand which domain on the target image has lots of error detection under extracting process. Therefore, the mask image will help us to find out the domain of image alteration more correctly.

3.1 Spread Spectrum of the Alteration Detection Signal

A method for encoding the signal for detecting image alteration which can later be recovered given knowledge of the key used is described here. A sequence of N randomly generated real numbers $X = x_1, x_2, \ldots, x_n$ is a random number defined as

$$x_n \longleftarrow a \cdot m_n \quad (0 \leq n < N) \tag{1}$$

where m_n is a pseudo random noise and $a (> 0)$ is a real number. The alteration detection signal is written in the form of a sequence of symbols $S_1, S_2, \ldots, S_K$, most generally by a change in a number base with L. The next stage is to encode each symbol S_k in the form of a zero mean pseudo random vector of length N. The alteration detection signal is defined as

$$x_n \longleftarrow x_n + m_{L \cdot k + S_k + n + 1} \quad (0 \leq n < N) \tag{2}$$

Fig. 2 shows a spread spectrum signal of the alteration detection signal as given by equation 2. Let us decode the alteration detect signal from y_n which extracted mark. A sequence of N randomly generated real numbers m_n as same as encoding steps with the same key is a random number. q_n is the sequence of detection symbol defined as

$$q_n \longleftarrow m_{L \cdot k + l + n + 1} \quad (0 \leq n < N) \tag{3}$$

where, $l = 0, \ldots, L - 1$ is a range value of symbol. The next stage is to calculate each q_n in the form of a zero mean pseudo random vector of length N. We measure the similarity of y_n and q_n by

$$Z_l \longleftarrow \left(\sum_{n=0}^{N-1} q_n \cdot y_n \right) / \left(\sqrt{\sum_{n=0}^{N-1} y_n^2} \right) \tag{4}$$

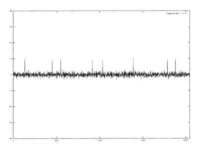

Fig. 3. An example of detection alteration detect signal

The symbol of alternation detect signal is l where Z_l is the maximum value among each Z_l calculated by the equation 4. Fig. 3 shows the detection of alteration detect signal as given by equation 4.

3.2 FFT: Translation

Let the image be a real valued continuous function $f(x, y)$ defined on an integer-valued. $F(u, v)$ is the Discrete Fourier Transform coefficient value of $f(x, y)$. Shifts in the spatial domain cause a linear shift in the phase component.

$$F(u, v)exp[-j(au + bv)] \longleftrightarrow f(x + a, y + b) \tag{5}$$

Note that both $F(u, v)$ and its dual $f(x, y)$ are periodic functions so it is implicitly assumed that translations cause the image to be "wrapped around". We shall refer to this as a circular translation or a cyclic shift. From property 5 of the Fourier transform it is clear that spatial shifts affect only the phase representation of an image. This leads to the well known result that the magnitude of the Fourier transform is a circular translation invariant. This property allow to extend for the detection of alteration domain of printed image by using watermark. Fig. 4 illustrates the property of translation invariant of Fourier Transform.

4   Algorithm

4.1   Embed the Signal for Detecting Image Alteration

Let the image be a function $f(x, y)$. A function $b(n_1, n_2)$ is a block image divided by $M \times M$ from the image $f(x, y)$. A function $F(u, v)$ is the Discrete Fourier Transform of $b(n_1, n_2)$ given by

$$F(u, v) = \sum_{n_1=0}^{M-1}\sum_{n_2=0}^{M-1} b(n_1, n_2)e^{-j2\pi n_1 u/M - j2\pi n_2 v/M} \tag{6}$$

The DFT of a real image is generally complex valued. This leads to magnitude and phase representaton for the image:

$$Amp(u, v) = [F(u, v)] \tag{7}$$

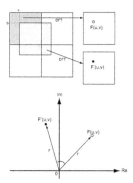

Fig. 4. The property of translation invariant of Fourier Transform

$$\Phi(u, v) = \angle F(u, v) \tag{8}$$

The next stage, the integer number group $(u_n, v_n)(0 \leq n < N)$ is defined by the pseudo-random sequence with the key value $key2$, where a point (u_n, v_n) is contained in the middle frequency domain of DFT. The spread signal for alteration detect x_n is embedded into $Amp(u, v)$ by

$$Amp(u_n, v_n) \longleftarrow Amp(u_n, v_n) + p \cdot x_n \tag{9}$$

$$Amp(M - u_n, M - v_n) \longleftarrow Amp(M - u_n, M - v_n) + p \cdot x_n \tag{10}$$

where, p is real number. The reconstruction of the image $b'(n_1, n_2)$ is given by Inverse Discrete Fourier Transform. To apply the above process for all block images on the original image, The image which is embedded the alteration detect signal $f'(x, y)$ is created. Fig. 5 illustrates this processing of embedding of alteration detect signal.

4.2 Extraction of the Signal for Detecting Image Alteration

Let the image which is target for detecting image alteration be a function $f'(x, y)$. $b'(n_1, n_2)$ is a block image divided by $M \times M$ from the image $f'(x, y)$. Let the function $F'(x, y)$ denote the Discrete Fourier Transform of $b'(n_1, n_2)$. The integer sequence group (u_n, v_n) is generated by the key value $key2$ which is the same key as embedding process. The magnitude elements $Amp'(x, y)$ is computed from the target image $f'(x, y)$ by DFT. The sequence of y_n which includes the signal of alteration detect is given by

$$y_n \longleftarrow Amp(u_n, v_n) \quad (0 \leq n < N) \tag{11}$$

The sequence of q_n for detecting symbol code is generated by

$$q_n \longleftarrow m_{L \cdot k + l + n + 1} \quad (0 \leq n < N) \tag{12}$$

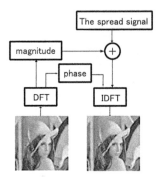

Fig. 5. Outline of embedding process of alteration detect signal

The sequence of q_n is adjusted to be zero-meaning. To extract the embedded symbol data, the symbol response function Z_l is computed with following the equation 4, where $l = 0, 1, \ldots, L-1$. The symbol data is l, when Z_l becomes the maximum value among each Z_l values. The embedded signal S_k is determined the value which transformed l by base L. Fig. 6 illustrates the outline of extracting the signal.

4.3   Detect the Domain of Image Alteration

Let the mask image which shows the domain of alteration be a function $D(x, y)$ which is determined by

$$D(x, y) \longleftarrow 0 \tag{13}$$

The symbol of alteration detect signal S_k is extracted by the process described in the previous section at the offset position (o_x, o_y) on the image $f'(x, y)$. If S_k cannot be extracted correctly, the process defined the below is carried out.

$$D(o_x + t, o_y + t) \longleftarrow D(o_x + t, o_y + t) + \delta \tag{14}$$

where δ is real number and t consists of the integer number which range is $(0 \leq t < M)$. To carry out these process described the above with shifting

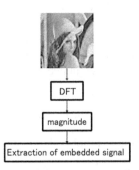

Fig. 6. Outline of extracting the signal

the offset position by α, where α is the integer number, the function $D(x,y)$ shows the measurement of the domain which the alteration detect signal is not extracted. If $D(x,y)$ is satisfied with the inequality:

$$D(x,y) \geq \delta \tag{15}$$

then, it stands for possibility of image alteration domain at position (x,y) of the image. As the result, to investigate $D(x,y)$, the domain of image alteration can be detected. Then, the accuracy of the detection depends on the value of α.

5   Experimental Results

To evaluate the proposed technique, let two nature images be used shown in Fig. 7 which image size is 512×512 pixels. The parameters for this evaluation are $M = 128, N = 512, a = 0.12, L = 256$, $p = 1000.0C\delta = 5.0C\alpha = 8$, and (u_n, v_n) which is given by $32 \leq \sqrt{u_n^2 + v_n^2} \leq 64$. Some of these parameters except of the parameters which stands for image size and block size for DFT are defined manually by the performance of image quality and its robustness based on our pre-evaluation. Note that the automatic definition of parameters system has not been proposed in our method. The number of bits of the signal for detecting image alteration is 8 bits. The images embedded the signal by our method following these parameters are shown in Fig. 8. In this evaluate, the devices for printing and capturing which used in this evaluate are described the below

- Canon BJ-F850 for photo printing.
- EPSON LP-7000C for color or gray scale printing.
- EPSON GT-X800 for capturing the image from printed image.

(a) Test image No.1   (b) Test image No.2

Fig. 7. Original image. (512×512 pixels).

(a) Test image No.1   (b) Test image No.2

Fig. 8. The images embedded the signal for detectiong image alteration

5.1 Evaluation of the Influences of Adjusting Gamma Factor

The purpose of the evaluation in this section is to know robustness of watermark which we use under manipulating the digital image for printing. One of favorite manipulation is to adjust gamma factors for fine printing. This manipulation does not mean image alteration under our definition of image alteration. However, it is possible to fail to extract the embedded signal correctly. The signal for detecting image alteration has to be robustness against the adjust of gamma factors and so on which do not stand for image alteration. Thus, let us evaluate the robustness of the signal for detecting image alteration. In most of case, gamma adjustment is used for perceptually fine veiw. Then, gamma factor takes from

(a) Test image No.1   (b) Test image No.2

Fig. 9. The image of adjustment of gammer factor

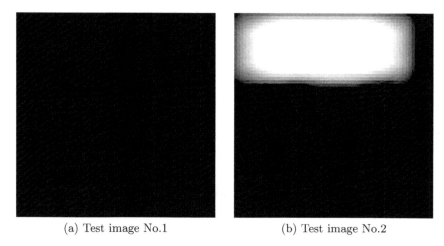

(a) Test image No.1   (b) Test image No.2

Fig. 10. Extraction of the area of image alteration

0.8 to 1.2 which depends on the target image. In this evaluation, we choose 1.2 for adjusting gamma factor. Fig. 9 are the images that adjusted gamma factor which value is 1.2 from the images shown in Fig. 8 by using Adobe Photoshop. These images are not altered. Fig. 10 shows the result of the detection of image alteration which stands for the function $D(x, y)$. The domain of black color stands for the domain which is not altered. To observe Fig. 10(a), we consider that Fig. 9(a) is not altered. On the other hand, Fig. 10(b) shows the domain which is detected as alteration on the image shown in Fig. 9(b). That domain corresponds to the region of cloudy on the original image. This domain is almost composed by white color only, and which includes low frequency component on DFT. Therefore, it is possible that the signal has been lost under the embedding processing because this signal is embedded into the elements of middle frequency components on the original image. Therefore, we understand that most of detection errors may occure on the simple color pattern domain of the image. We are under studying in order to solve this issue. In this paper, we suppose that the region of cloudy of test image No.2. will not be altered in this evaluation.

5.2   The Alteration Detect of Photo Printed Images

Let the image alteration be created from Fig. 8 by using Adobe Photoshop which are shown in Fig. 11. These images are printed to photo papers by printer device. Fig. 12 shows the images captured by the scanner device from printed photo papers. To detect the alteration, the function $D(x, y)$ are computed, and which result is shown in Fig. 13. Fig. 14 shows the object or region which is altered on the images by using both Fig. 11 and Fig. 13. As this result, our proposed method is available for detecting image alteration.

(a) Test image No.1   (b) Test image No.2

Fig. 11. Altered image

5.3   The Alteration Detect for Printed Images

Let us to evaluate the performance of our method against printed image on the non-photo paper. Printed images is created from the images shown in Fig. 11 by the printer device. Fig. 15 is the result of alteration detect. This evaluation shows our method works against the target of paper printed image.

5.4   The Alteration Detect for Paper Printed Gray Scale Images

Let us consider the case of gray scale printed image. In order to evaluate the capability of our method, gray scale image shown in Fig. 11 is printed by the same

(a) Test image No.1   (b) Test image No.2

Fig. 12. Printed image captured by scanner

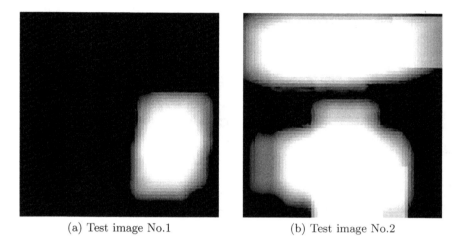

(a) Test image No.1   (b) Test image No.2

Fig. 13. Result of detection image alteration

printer device as section 5.3. To carry out our method, the detector performance is shown in Fig. 16. This result is almost the same as section 5.3, because the alteration detect signal is embedded into the intensity of the original image. Therefore, detector performance shows the same as the case of color printed image.

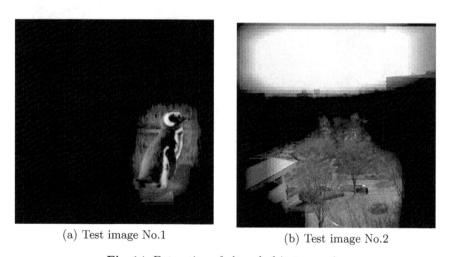

(a) Test image No.1   (b) Test image No.2

Fig. 14. Extraction of altered object or region

5.5   Compensating for Rotation Capturing

In this section, we described the steps required to locate the template given the following scenario: When the target printed image is captured, it is then rotated shown in Fig. 17. In this case, we evaluate to detect image alteration. Fig. 18 shows the result of detection. To observe it, our method even works good.

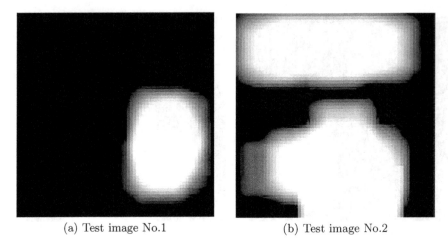

(a) Test image No.1   (b) Test image No.2

Fig. 15. Result of detection of the area of alteration

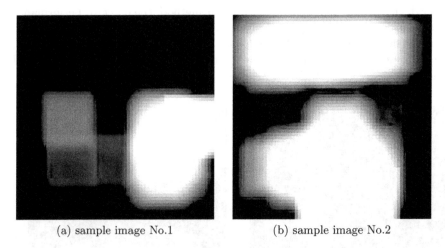

(a) sample image No.1   (b) sample image No.2

Fig. 16. Result of detection of the area of alteration

6   Conclusions

Unlike robust watermarks, fragile watermarks are designed to be easily destroyed if the watermarked image is manipulated in the slightest manner. This property is ideal for image authentication applications, where the objective is to determine if watermarked image has been tampered with or modified. In this paper, the alteration detect algorithm for printed natural images based on the watermark techniques are proposed. As the experimental result, our proposed method can detect the object or domain on the printed image alteration. To apply our method to the digital camera devices, the source of digital image can be included the

(a) sample image No.1   (b) sample image No.2

Fig. 17. Rotated image captured by scanner

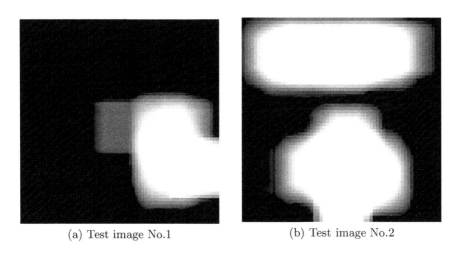

(a) Test image No.1   (b) Test image No.2

Fig. 18. Result of detection of alteration domain

signal for detecting image alteration automatically. It also supports to detect the fake image created by an owner. Our method helps to reduce the fake images on the public official documents.

On the other hand, as the experimental result shows, our method has some issues that cannot support white or black color flat pattern domain. The image alteration detected by our method stands for integrity questionable. To make a reliable detection system for printed image alteration, the key certificate system and so on based on cryptograph theory are needed for watermark encoder and detector of our method. Future work will focus on the construction of trust detector system against printed image alteration.

References

[1] I. Cox, M. Miller, and J. Bloom: Digital Watermarking. Morgan Kaufmann Publishers (2002)

[2] ISO/IEC 15444-8: Information technology JPEG 2000 image coding system part 8: JPSEC (2004).

[3] Fragile and Robust Watermarking by Histogram Specification. D. Coltuc, P. Bolon and J. Chassery: Proceeding of the SPIE Security and Watermarking of Multimedia Contents IV, Edward J. Delp III, Ping W. Wong, Editors, vol.4675 (2002), 701-710

[4] S. Walton: Information authentication for a slippery new age. Dr. Dobbs Journal vol.20 no.4 (1995) 18–26

[5] R. B. Wolfgang and E. J. Delp: Fragile Watermarking Using the VW2D Watermark. Proceedings of the SPIE/IS&T International Conference on Security and Watermarking of Multimedia Contents. vol.3657 (1999) 204–213

[6] P. Wong: A watermark for image integrity and ownership verification. Final Program and Proceedings of the IS&T PICS99 (1999) 374–379

[7] Oki Electric Industry Co., Ltd.: TrustPaper http://www.oki.com/en/otr/198/downloads/otr-198-R15.pdf (2005)

[8] Bijan G. Mobasseri: Exploring CDMA for watermaking of digital video. Proc. SPIE, vol.3657 (1999) 96–102

Real-Time Watermark Embedding for High Resolution Video Watermarking

In-Koo Kang[1], Dong-Hyuck Im[1], Young-Ho Suh[2], and Heung-Kyu Lee[1]

[1] Department of EECS, Korea Advanced Institute of Science and Technology,
Guseong-dong, Yuseong-Gu, Deajeon, Republic of Korea
{ikkang, iammoni, hklee}@mmc.kaist.ac.kr
[2] Digital Content Research Division, Electronics and Telecommunications Research
Institute, Gajeong-dong, Yuseong-gu, Daejeon, Republic of Korea
syh@etri.re.kr

Abstract. This paper addresses implementation issues for real-time watermark embedding scheme of High Definition(HD) resolution videos on personal computers. In most watermark applications, an embedding procedure should be built at low costs and at the same time the embedded watermarks should have robustness against signal and image processing as well as malicious attacks. This paper provides some performance optimization guidelines and a simplified Human Visual System (HVS) method for fast and robust watermark embedding. This work demonstrates a real-time watermark embedding process including HD MPEG-2 video decoding, watermark embedding and displaying on Intel architecture personal computers. Experimental results show optimized embedding performances and robustness against several malicious attacks commonly happened to videos.

1 Introduction

In proportion to developments of digital infrastructures and industries, digital watermarking technologies are also advanced to protect the copyright of those contents from illegal distributions and reproductions. In these days, people can easily access digital contents from various sources, furthermore, their requests for high quality contents are rising rapidly. In watermark applications, watermarking schemes should be implemented at low cost, especially real-time embedding systems are required for authentication, fingerprinting, copy protection systems. Real-time watermarking systems for high quality contents are not an exception any more.

In this work, we implemented a real-time watermark embedding system for 1920×1080 high resolution MPEG-2 video contents on an Intel Pentium® system. We will present some general tips for system optimization in section 2. In the next section, we will define our watermark embedding scope and specify implementation details and optimization issues for a real-time embedding scheme. In section 4, experimental results are presented to verify our embedding scheme is suitable for real-time processing and robust against video attacks.

H. Yoshiura et al. (Eds.): IWSEC 2006, LNCS 4266, pp. 227–238, 2006.

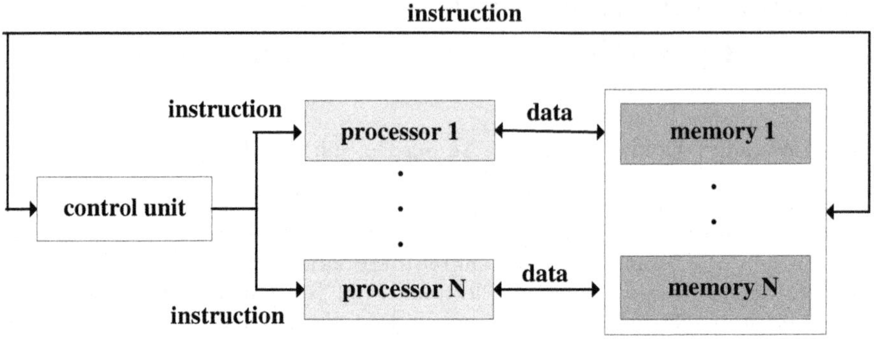

Fig. 1. SIMD structure : A SIMD structure includes several processors and those processors are controlled by one control unit. Even if all processors are assigned one instruction from one control unit, they use different data from different memories.(In some cases, processors share memories.)

2   General Optimization Guidelines

Many multimedia applications in these days are implemented for a real-time processing according to their purposes. However, due to intensive computing volumes for multimedia data, applications are used to be implemented with application specific integrated circuits(ASICs) or digital signal processors. Things are changed owing to the introduction of Single-Instruction-Multiple-Data(SIMD) extensions to general-purpose processors. With this, the following optimizations are possible [5]:

1. Use a current generation compiler that will produce an optimized application. This will help you generate good codes from the start.
2. Maximize memory access performance:
   - Minimize memory references,
   - Maximize register usages,
   - Prefetch data,
   - Arrange code to minimize instruction cache misses and optimize prefetch,
   - Align frequently executed branch targets on 16-byte boundaries,
   - Make sure all data are aligned
3. Minimize branching penalties:
   - Minimize branch instructions, for instance, unroll small loops,
   - Arrange code to minimize the misprediction in the branch prediction algorithm, for example, forward conditional branches are usually not taken and backward conditional branches are usually taken.
4. Use software pipelining to schedule latencies and functional units. Unroll small loops to schedule more instructions.

With multimedia instruction set extensions such as Intel's MMX(Multi-Media eXtension) technology, we can speed up the computing time up to eight times faster[1][4]. The SIMD technique is the reason to make it possible. Earlier version of CPUs which do not use the SIMD technique process one data using one instruction, where as in SIMD one instruction can handle several data concurrently. That is to say, MMX technology offers much greater capabilities of speed up to multimedia data owing to eight data, each of eight-bits, concurrency processing power using 64-bits data buffers. Nevertheless, advantages of MMX technique, this technique cannot be adopted to all of implementation areas because the MMX technique is best-suitable to simple and steady data structures or iterative data processing like multimedia data. This method, for that reason, is regarded as a second majority technique to improve system performances, not main methodology for data process enhancements. Under this circumstances, it is an important work to recognize possible areas of MMX optimization for performance improvements. The followings are three basic steps [5]:

1. Understand where the application spends most of its execution time: The benefit of optimizing computationally-intensive parts is larger than that of optimizing non-intensive parts. We should start optimizations from the most computationally-intensive components.In our watermarking system, we found the most time-spending part that bothers the real-time embedding processing and modified it.
2. Understand which algorithm is the best for MMX technology in this application: Matching the algorithms to MMX instruction capabilities is the key to extracting the best performance. Once the computationally-intensive sections of code are identified, an evaluation should be done to determine whether the current algorithm or a modified one will give the best performance. There could be many algorithms for a same application. In some cases, it is possible to improve performance by changing the types of operations in the algorithm.
3. Understand where data values in the application can be converted to integer (fixed-point) while maintaining the required range and precision if the data values are not originally of an integer type: The MMX instructions offer the best support for 8-bit and 16-bit integer data types. While some DSP can be done in the integer domain, some must be done in the floating-point domain. MMX can provide significant speedup in certain DSP and multimedia application, even over hand-optimized floating-point assembly code. MMX seems well-suited for image processing applications because of the large amount of contiguous, 8-bit data to process and precision requirements that rarely extend beyond 8 bits.

3   Optimization Issues for Real-Time Embedding

In this section, first we will define real-time scope of our watermarking system and describe optimization issues and our solutions for those problems. For an optimum system, we analyzed time complexities of a watermarking system implemented using pure C code. Then, we decided which parts of the system should be rebuilt to reduce the execution time suitable for real-time processing and modified those modules.

3.1   Real-Time Performance Scope

First in this session, we would like to define the term "real-time" in our work. The term "real-time" is cited in many applications in slightly different meanings. The word in our work defines that a watermark embedding process should not be recognizable during video playing time. That means watermark embedding time should be shorter than a frame processing time. In case of 30 fps(frames per second) framerates videos, a frame is decoded and displayed on a screen in around 0.03 second. It is obvious that watermark embedding time should be more shorter than 0.03 second. Furthermore, we manipulate 1920×1080 size HD contents to embed watermarks.

Our real-time watermarking system consists of three major parts as shown in figure 2: a decoding unit of HD MPEG-2 video bitstreams into raw frames, a watermark embedding unit and a video display unit on a screen. More specifically, our watermarking unit includes subunits such as a HVS masking function, watermark multiplication to HVS masked frames and addition of the watermarks to raw frames on a spatial domain, etc. In our real-time scheme, these three units are scope of real-time processing.

We included a video display unit to our scope for two reasons. One is that our real-time solution could be used in other applications. For example, in digital fingerprinting systems, the unique fingerprint code assigned to each different customer is embedded to contents at the end-users' computers, not on suppliers' servers. In this case, the fingerprint codes should be embedded while videos are being displayed on a screen. The other is our solution could be adopted to real-time watermark detection systems. In most of watermarking systems, watermark detection complexities are lower than embedding complexities. That means if a embedding scheme can be executed in real-time, a detection routine can be also executed in real-time.

Encodings of watermarked raw frames to MPEG-2 video streams are beyond of our scope. A real-time encoding to HD MPEG-2 bitstreams on personal computers is too heavy work and it cannot be implemented by software approaches, without any MPEG-2 encoding specific hardware. It, however, should be noted that our embedding scheme including decodings of HD MPEG-2 stream, HVS masking function and watermark addition to decoded frames have merits in watermark applications. Because all these steps should be performed within theoretically 0.03 second in case of 30 fps videos and software approaches of watermarking systems are more efficient over hardware approaches when modifications or updates are needed.

3.2   Use of the MMX Technique to Reduce Computing Time

The MMX instructions offer the best support for 8-bit and 16-bit integer data types. MMX can provide significant speedup in certain DSP and multimedia

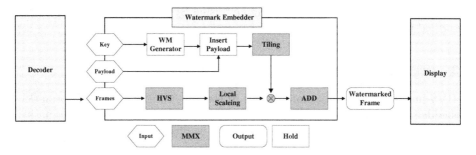

Fig. 2. High-level view of real-time watermarking system. Our real-time scope consist of a HD MPEG-2 decoding, a watermark embedding and displaying of video. In the watermark embedder, routines that need fast processing are implemented with MMX instructions.

applications. MMX seems well-suited for image processing applications because of the large amount of contiguous, 8-bit data to process and precision requirements that rarely extend beyond 8 bits. With the MMX technique, the following optimization guideline will be applicable for real-time programming [4][5][6][7]:

1. Do not intermix MMX instructions and floating-point instructions. MMX instructions do not mix well with floating-point instructions. MMX registers and states are aliased onto the floating-point registers and state, so no new registers or states are introduced by MMX.
2. MMX code sections should end with "emms" instructions if floating-point operations are to be used later in the program.
3. MMX shift/pack/unpack instructions do not mix well with each other. In general, two MMX instructions can be executed at the same clock. However, only one MMX shift/pack/unpack instruction can be executed at one clock because there is only one shifter unit.
4. MMX multiplication instructions "pmull/pmulb/pmadd" do not mix well with each other. Currently, there is only one multiplication unit.
5. MMX instructions, which reference memory or integer registers, do not mix well with integer instructions referencing same memory or registers.
6. It is important to arrange data in the best way for MMX processing, e.g., structure of array, array of structure, row-wise, or column-wise arrangements. Column-wise processing in general is better than sequential row-wise processing.

We applied the MMX technology to several embedding modules that spend much time and need to be rebuilt for speedup as shown in figure 2. This includes watermark tiling, a HVS masking, watermark addition to source frames and other miscellaneous operations such as multiplications or additions as depicted in grayed rectangles. These modules have some common features which are suitable to be manipulated by the MMX instructions: they are frequently and regularly used, conduct simple and repeatable operations and need fast processing time. The MMX implementation of such heavy modules produced great performance improvements especially at HVS (Human Visual System) masking function as described in Table 1.

3.3   Use of Simplified HVS Function

A HVS function plays an important role in watermarking systems. Watermarks embedded in flat areas can be notified easily, so we have to embed watermarks into those areas weakly. On the other hand, watermarks in edge or textured areas are not noticeable compared to flat areas, so we can embed watermarks more strongly into those areas. That says a HVS function adjusts watermark strength according to local features of source images. While the HVS function is the most important part for robust and invisible watermarking methods, it is the heaviest processing step over the rest of other embedding steps.

In many literatures, a NVF (Noise Visibility Function) is a commonly used HVS function [2]. The NVF function measures flat areas and edge(textured) areas of source images by calculating local variance and mean values. Despite of its popularity for the purpose of a HVS mask, this function takes bunch of processing time than that of other embedding modules due to heavy calculations for local mean, local variance values and division operations as shown in equation 1, where σ_x^2 is a local variance of source images, $\sigma_x^2{}_{max}$ is the maximum local variance for a given image and $D \in [50, 100]$ is an experimentally determined parameter. Even if sophisticated computations of local measures in NVF provide more exact estimation of source images, a number of computations prevent watermark embedding from real-time processing. We confirm this effect in a table 1. In the pure C code implementation of watermarking system, the HVS function took the most longest time in the embedding processes and its processing time(0.05sec.) is already over the 0.03 second, upper bound frame processing time in our application.

$$NVF(i, j) = \frac{1}{1 + \theta \sigma_x^2(i, j)}, \quad where \ \theta = \frac{D}{\sigma_x^2{}_{max}}. \tag{1}$$

For a real-time embedding, the HVS function should be lightened. To reduce the time complexity, we would rather use an edge detector than NVF function in our system for following reasons:

- As described above, the NVF function is too heavy in real-time video processing.
- The NVF function results in floating point values between 0 and 1, i.e. $0 \leq NVF \leq 1$. That means the NVF function cannot be implemented by the MMX instructions, because the MMX code can process floating point value data. Furthermore, floating point data operations decrease the processing time.
- Edge detectors can be also used as a HVS function, because edge detectors also extract highly textured area of source images and watermarks can be strongly embedded in those area.

$$1)\begin{bmatrix} 1 & 1 & 1 \\ 1 & -2 & 1 \\ -1 & -1 & -1 \end{bmatrix} \quad 2)\begin{bmatrix} 1 & 1 & 1 \\ 0 & 0 & 0 \\ -1 & -1 & -1 \end{bmatrix} \quad 3)\begin{bmatrix} 5 & 5 & 5 \\ -3 & 0 & -3 \\ -3 & -3 & -3 \end{bmatrix} \quad 4)\begin{bmatrix} 1 & 2 & 1 \\ 0 & 0 & 0 \\ -1 & -2 & -1 \end{bmatrix}$$

(a)

$$\begin{matrix} 1 & 1 & 1 \\ 0 & 0 & 0 \\ -1 & -1 & -1 \end{matrix} \qquad \begin{matrix} 1 & 1 & 0 \\ 1 & 0 & -1 \\ 0 & -1 & -1 \end{matrix} \qquad \begin{matrix} 1 & 0 & -1 \\ 1 & 0 & -1 \\ 1 & 0 & -1 \end{matrix} \qquad \begin{matrix} 0 & -1 & -1 \\ 1 & 0 & -1 \\ 1 & 1 & 0 \end{matrix}$$

(N)   (NW)   (W)   (SW)

$$\begin{matrix} -1 & -1 & -1 \\ 0 & 0 & 0 \\ 1 & 1 & 1 \end{matrix} \qquad \begin{matrix} -1 & -1 & 0 \\ -1 & 0 & 1 \\ 0 & 1 & 1 \end{matrix} \qquad \begin{matrix} -1 & 0 & 1 \\ -1 & 0 & 1 \\ -1 & 0 & 1 \end{matrix} \qquad \begin{matrix} 0 & 1 & 1 \\ -1 & 0 & 1 \\ -1 & -1 & 0 \end{matrix}$$

(S)   (SE)   (E)   (NE)

(b)

Fig. 3. Edge Detectors of our HVS module(compass operators): With a "separable" feature and MMX instructions, we implemented the HVS function at a low complexity. (a) shows four different edge detectors and (b) depicts eight compassed kernels of the second kernel of (a).

- Furthermore, we also consider flat regions of source images as well as edge or highly textured area using equation 2 like that used in a NVF function.
- Some edge detectors have a "separable" property which makes its computation more faster and are also more suitable for a MMX instructions.

In our system, we adopted a compass operator as an edge detector. Compass operators measure gradients in as selected number of directions. Figure 3 (a) shows four different compass gradients for north-going edges. An anti-clockwise circular shift of the eight boundary elements of these masks gives a 45 degree rotation of the gradient direction. For example, the eight compass gradients corresponding to the second operator of figure 3 (a) are shown in figure 3 (b).

This compass operator can be transformed to be separable. A 2D filter is "separable" if the kernel $[h_{2D}]$ can be decomposed into two 1D kernels which are applied successively. The filtering is performed in one dimension (rows), followed by filtering in another dimension (columns) : $[h_{2D}] = [h_{1D}^{(V)}] \otimes [h_{1D}^{(H)}]$, where $\otimes$ stands for a convolution operator. The rows and the columns in the original image are thus separately filtered. Whatever the first 1D filtering performed, the output image $I_S(m, n)$ is still the same. To be separable, a 2D filter must have proportional elements on the rows and the columns: mathematically that is seldom true, however, several usual 2D filters are separable. In figure 4, properties of separable filters and some examples are presented.

The complexity is low for 2D separable filters because the number of operations (multiplications and additions) is reduced, thus the computation time is faster. Typically if the kernel size is $M \times N$, we need only $(M + N)$ multiplications and $(M + N - 2)$ additions instead of $(M \times N)$ multiplications and

$$[h_{2D}] = [h_{1D}^{(V)}] \otimes [h_{1D}^{(H)}]$$

$I_S(m, n) = h(m, n) \otimes I_e(m, n)$: 2D linear filter

$I_S(m, n) = h_V(m, n) \otimes [h_H(n) \otimes h_e(m, n)]$: convolution of two 1D filters

Constraint : columns and rows of h_{2D} must have proportional elements.

$$[a\ b\ c] \otimes \begin{bmatrix} \alpha \\ \beta \\ \gamma \end{bmatrix} = \begin{bmatrix} a\alpha & b\alpha & c\alpha \\ a\beta & b\beta & c\beta \\ a\gamma & b\gamma & c\gamma \end{bmatrix} \qquad [a\ b\ a] \otimes \begin{bmatrix} a \\ b \\ a \end{bmatrix} = \begin{bmatrix} a^2 & ab & a^2 \\ ab & b^2 & ab \\ a^2 & ab & a^2 \end{bmatrix}$$

Examples :

Averaging :

$$\frac{1}{3}[1\ 1\ 1] \otimes \frac{1}{3}\begin{bmatrix} 1 \\ 1 \\ 1 \end{bmatrix} = \frac{1}{9}\begin{bmatrix} 1 & 1 & 1 \\ 1 & 1 & 1 \\ 1 & 1 & 1 \end{bmatrix}$$

Binomial :

$$\frac{1}{4}[1\ 2\ 1] \otimes \frac{1}{4}\begin{bmatrix} 1 \\ 2 \\ 1 \end{bmatrix} = \frac{1}{16}\begin{bmatrix} 1 & 2 & 1 \\ 2 & 4 & 2 \\ 1 & 2 & 1 \end{bmatrix}$$

Fig. 4. Separable filter properties and examples. $I_e(M, N)$ is a original image, $h_H(n)$ and $h_V(m)$ are 1D horizontal and vertical filters, respectively. $I_S(m, n)$ is a 2D filtered image of $I_e(M, N)$.

$(M + N - 1)$ additions for a non-separable 2D filter. Often the term "MAP" is preferred (multiplications and accumulations per pixel): there are $(M + N)$ MAP for a separable filter instead of $(M \times N)$ MAP for a non-separable filter.

When applying edge detectors to get a HVS masked image, the result shows only edged areas or highly textured areas are strongly highlighted. On the other hand, pixel values of flat areas approach zero. That means watermarks embedded in only textured areas are emphasized and easily visible, but the watermark information is nearly lost in flat areas. We should concern both textured areas and flat areas for robust and invisible watermarks. As a consequence of this consideration, we adopted the contents-adaptive embedding rule in the NVF method and slightly modified it suitable for our HVS [2]:

$$\Lambda = (C - HVS) \cdot \alpha + HVS \cdot \beta, \tag{2}$$

where C is a constant value that limits the upper bound of HVS energies, α is a strength parameter for edged areas(textured areas) and β is a strength parameter for flat regions. As a result of this embedding rule, watermarks have a strength range between α and β. So watermarks could be embedded with a at least β strength in the very flat areas and the watermark strength could be controlled by adjusting the parameters α and β according to a tradeoff of a watermark visibility and robustness.

4   Experiments

We experimented our embedding scheme on an Intel Pentium IV processor 3.6GHz and with a 1 GB RAM. The decoding time of HD bitstreams and the display time after watermark embedding is constant as shown in table 1 and these values are beyond of our analysis scope because they are already optimized for the best performance. We embedded watermarks into 1920×1080 size HD MPEG-2 videos using the same watermarks and embedding ways as the method described in [3]. We adjusted the Λ value in equation 2 between 1 to 7, that says watermarks were embedded in strength 7 on textured areas and strength 1 on flat areas. An average PSNR after watermark embedding was around 45dB, so image visual degradations due to watermark embedding were not perceptual. We tested five MPEG-2 HD videos in the fields of movies, entertainment shows, documentaries, etc. which contain more than 20 different scenes and features as shown in figure 5.

Fig. 5. Snapshot examples of test videos: All test videos have 1920×1080 resolutions(HD). This test set contains a number of scenes and different features.

First, we measured time complexities of subfunctions for a embedding process. As mentioned earlier, the decoding process and the display process took a constant time during all experiments and time complexities for embedding steps such as a HVS masking function, multiplication and addition operations are varied according to the implementation methods and programming languages as shown below:

All the three experiment systems consist of three subfunctions: decoding of bitstreams to raw frames, watermark embedding and a display of watermarked frame to a screen. The watermark embedding unit includes taking a HVS masking function to decoded raw frames, multiplication and addition operations for watermark manipulations and other miscellaneous operations which do not take serious time for an analysis. The first experiment was designed to measure processing time taken for units, each of which is implemented using pure C programming language. In this test, the NVF masking function was used as a HVS method. As we mentioned earlier, the NVF masking method with C code implementation is inappropriate for a HD real-time video watermarking

Table 1. Time complexity comparisons between experiment systems that implemented with pure C code and MMX code. Execution time taken for each subfunction is shown in the table. The total time is the time complexity taken for watermark processing per frame.

[sec.]

	Decoding time	Watermark Embedding Time			Display Time	Total Time
		HVS function	MUL, ADD function	miscellaneous		
System 1.		0.050 (NVF)	0.006	0.003		0.0770
System 2.	0.0132	0	0.002	0.001	0.0048	0.0210
System 3.		0.006 (our HVS)	0.002	0.002		0.0280

application: the NVF process time is 0.050 second and the total processing time is 0.077 second, beyond of the time limit per frame.

A MMX code implementation considerably drops processing time compared with C code implementation. In the second experiment, all units were implemented with MMX code but a HVS function. We observe that the MMX coding considerably reduced the time complexity of a whole embedding process and the real-time watermark embedding is feasible. However, watermarks that were simply added to source frames without any HVS processing were not robust to various well-known watermark attacks.

Our proposed HVS method conducted its job fast under MMX implementation. In the third experiment, we applied an edge detector as a HVS mask, the second one in figure 3 (a) and its compassed ones like (b) with a "separable" feature. Our masking function took only 0.006 second to get masked images and the total processing time is 0.028 second, still under the processing limit time per frame. That means our implementation can decode HD-resolution bitstreams, embed robust watermarks with HVS masking and display the watermarked frames on a screen within 0.03 second. From the results, the total processing time of system 1, 0.077 sec., was decreased to 0.028 sec. of system 3, thus we achieved about 63% performance enhancement.

We tested robustness of our watermarks against several common attacks to videos. Various video processing attacks in the table 2 are expected to occur to HD videos owing to its high resolution and excellent visual qualities. People may scale down HD contents to VGA files for efficient playing on personal computers, convert the MPEG-2 format to various MPEG-4 formats to reduce file sizes for easy manipulations or network transference. Watermarks embedded in our method survived against various kinds of attacks as shown in below table.

It should be noted that we selected attack items by focusing on video manipulations which could be happened frequently to HD videos, so we did not consider common image(signal) processing attacks or geometric attacks of

Table 2. Summarization of performance of our watermark robustness in the real-time system. After various attacks, watermarks were survived with the following normalized correlation values.

[Normalized Correlation]

	Average	Minimum	Maximum
Original (1920x1080)	0.63	0.37	0.73
Resize to VGA with padding (640x360)	0.28	0.15	0.45
Resize to VGA (640x480)	0.35	0.14	0.45
Cropping	0.56	0.20	0.69
Framerate Conversion (30 to 24 fps)	0.62	0.25	0.74
Color Conversion (RGB to Gray)	0.58	0.25	0.70
White-noise Addition	0.18	0.10	0.31
MPEG-1 Conversion	0.48	0.10	0.72
MPEG-4 Conversion	0.60	0.50	0.70
Slow Motion	0.60	0.30	0.73

image watermarking. However, we applied robust watermarking methods such as spread-spectrum method in [3] or human visual masking method in [2], thus we expect our watermarks would be robust against those kind of attacks.

5   Conclusion

As digital content markets and infrastructures are emerging, high quality contents are becoming the center of market shares. Digital watermarking techniques should come up with the market currencies. In this paper, we proposed real-time video watermarking implementation guidelines for HD videos. We suggested a system implementation using the MMX technique to decrease processing time and increase multimedia manipulation efficiency, a simplified HVS method for robust watermark embedding. The MMX implementation offers significant speedup in multimedia data processing and certain DSP instructions because MMX instructions are well-suited for manipulating large amount of contiguous 8-bit data that are common forms of multimedia data.

Our HVS method provides low time complexities and high performance capabilities. By using an edge detector for the purpose of HVS mask, we achieved the real-time embedding requirement as well as robustness. The "separable" feature of edge detectors reduces multiplication and addition complexities and its structure is well-suited for the MMX implementation.

We measured the processing time of our embedding units and experimented the robustness of our watermarks against various video dedicated attacks. The watermarking system that was implemented with MMX instructions and applied with the simplified HVS function presented the best performances in both real-time processing and robustness. With our implementation, watermarks are embedded into HD-resolution high quality videos in real-time, 0.03 second per frame, and robust against video manipulation attacks. All these techniques could be applied to other video watermarking schemes and other video signal processing applications.

Acknowledgment. This work is financially supported by the Ministry of Education and Human Resources Development(MOE),the Ministry of Commerce, Industry and Energy(MOCIE) and the Ministry of Labor(MOLAB) through the fostering project of the Lab of Excellency.

References

[1] A. Peleg and U. Weiser : The MMX Technology Extension to the Intel Architecture, IEEE Micro, Vol. 16, no. 4, pp. 42-50, Aug. 1996.

[2] S. Voloshynovskiy, A. Herrigel, N. Baumgartner and T. Pun : A stochastic approach to content adaptive digital image watermarking, In International Workshop on Information Hiding, Vol. LNCS 1768, pp. 212-236, Springer Verlag, Dresden, Germany, 1999.

[3] Ingemar J. Cox, Joe Kilan, F. Thomson Leighton and Talal Shamoon : Secure spread spectrum watermarking for multimedia, in IEEE Trans. on Image Processing, Vol. 6, No. 12, Dec., 1997.

[4] The complete guide to MMX technology, McGraw-Hill, 1997.

[5] Yen-Kuang Chen, Matthew Holliman, William Macy and Minerva Yeung : Real-time Detection of Video Watermark o nIntel Architecture, Proceeding of SPIE, Vol. 3971, pp. 198-208, May 2000.

[6] R. Ceolho and M. Hawash : DirexX®, RDX, RSX and MMX Technology : a Jumpstart Guide to High Performance APls, MA, Addison-Wesely, April 1998.

[7] Intel Architecture MMX Technology Developer's Manual, IL, Intel Corporation, Order Number 243006, 1996.

Inhibiting Card Sharing Attacks

Michael Tunstall, Konstantinos Markantonakis, and Keith Mayes

Smart Card Centre, Information Security Group,
Royal Holloway, University of London,
Egham, Surrey TW20 0EX, UK
{m.j.tunstall, k.markantonakis, keith.mayes}@rhul.ac.uk

Abstract. The satellite TV industry relies heavily on the use of smart card technology at the very heart of broadcasted services that are protected by legacy conditional access systems. The process of Satellite TV signal protection is distributed amongst a number of system components, e.g. smart cards, receivers, Conditional Access Modules (CAM) and the content provider. However, the introduction of "Open" Satellite Receivers, providing a highly configurable environment with software emulation of conditional access systems, enabled the implementation of whole range of new attacks. A widely deployed attack is often referred to as the "card sharing" attack, by which one legitimate user colludes to provide protected content to a larger group of unauthorised users. This paper proposes a countermeasure that increases the bandwidth requirements of this attack to the point where it is no longer practical with a standard internet connection, with a minimal impact on existing protocols and architectures.

1 Introduction

During the early development of the satellite TV industry it became evident that in order to protect its investment and revenue streams it was necessary to encrypt digital content. Protection of the digital content traditionally relied on a number of system components including Set-Top-Boxes (STB), smart cards and content encryption boxes at the service provider level. Encryption, in the context of the satellite TV industry, is often defined as "the process of protecting the secret keys that have to be transmitted with the scrambled signal in order for the descrambler to work". The above procedure requires the existence of a conditional access system [19,13] that combines a signal encryption algorithm and key protection algorithm in order to prevent unauthorised signal reception. Many providers follow the DVB-S standard [9] and tailor the necessary configuration parameters [11] to their own particular needs.

The recent technological advances of the computer industry, along with the continued requirements for more advanced and powerful set of services means that satellite TV providers are all trying to differentiate their offerings, each with their own STB software and hardware. Conversely, consumers are constantly looking for ways that will allow them to use more flexible and powerful equipment that will simplify or even enhance their viewing experience.

H. Yoshiura et al. (Eds.): IWSEC 2006, LNCS 4266, pp. 239–251, 2006.

The natural market response was the introduction of open satellite receivers [30] that allowed consumers to purchase the STB that met their viewing and personal requirements. These STBs are highly configurable environments based on open operating systems such as Linux. Basically, they can be considered as traditional computer workstations enhanced with satellite TV signal processing capabilities. However, the fact that they are powerful and open devices has introduced a number of new threats. At the very least, it has enabled a more efficient realisation of a number of already identified and well-documented attacks [20,22,16]. The market trend towards open receivers along with current hardware restrictions (e.g. at the card level) has forced the satellite TV content providers to mitigate their protection mechanisms away from the underlying STB hardware and bring it closer to the smart card and Conditional Access Module (CAM). The latter two are often seen as a single component.

The purpose of this paper is to briefly introduce how these recent technological advances are affecting the satellite TV industry and then to propose a relevant countermeasure for a specific type of attack i.e. the card sharing attack [22].

The aforementioned open satellite receivers can be used to share one subscriber's rights with numerous people. A subscriber can start a server on a STB that will accept connections from other open STBs. These client STBs belong to people that are not subscribers and therefore have no rights to view a given broadcast. Every time the client STB receives an encrypted key from the broadcaster, it is sent to the server STB that deciphers it and returns the key necessary to decipher the broadcast. As the maximum frequency that this key can be changed is once every two seconds, the amount of bandwidth required for this is negligible (a maximum of 5 bytes of information per second in each direction). With the bandwidth requirement being so small synchronisation issues can be minimised.

Furthermore, it implies that one receiver can act as a server and provide numerous clients with the sequence of keys necessary to watch a given broadcast. As an open receiver can simulate a CAM it is difficult to base a solution at this level as any behaviour can be simulated. The CAM should therefore be regarded as an untrustworthy entity within the protocol. This paper will propose a smart card based solution to this sharing attack that will mean that all users watching a given broadcast will need to have a smart card issued by the broadcaster.

The remainder of the paper is structured as follows: Section 2 provides all the necessary background information that will enable the reader to understand how content encryption works in the satellite TV industry along with the recent smart card attacks in the light of the introduction of open STBs. In Section 3 we provide an overview of the proposed countermeasures and how different communication protocols change the countermeasure. Section 4 discusses how the proposed countermeasure affects users with various different types of countermeasure. This is followed by the conclusion in Section 5.

2 Issues Around Content Provision for the Satellite TV Industry

In the following sections we provide an overview of how the situation is changing in the light of the recent technological advances in the smart card, STB and satellite TV industries. Subsequently, the main characteristics of two widely used satellite TV attacks are highlighted in order to provide a reference point for the proposed countermeasure.

2.1 A Changing World – New Requirements for Open Receivers

An Open Receiver (OR) or Open Set-top-Box (OSTB) is a highly reconfigurable computer system that offers the capability to receive and decrypt the scrambled TV signals. These receivers often come with a number of pre-installed Conditional Access Module (CAMs) along with a Linux operating system. Furthermore, they also come pre-installed with a number of "images" containing all the necessary software to watch subscribed TV channels, along with various other tools for recording and organising channels using a variety of graphical interfaces.

However, the hacking communities are taking advantage of these open receivers by developing their own "images" containing all the necessary hacking tools that will enable them to circumvent the security around a protected TV signal. These images reside in the EEPROM or flash memory of the OSTB and can be easily upgraded, deleted and modified by connecting the receiver to another computer through a network or serial cable. A variety of the plug-in images enable the receivers to access USB tokens, hard disks, connected cameras or keyboards and to use the network or modem cards. All this functionality along with the plethora of freeware hacking tools makes the open receiver a very powerful tool in the hands of illegitimate users.

2.2 Recent Satellite TV Attacks

Over the last decade a number of satellite TV attacks have emerged. Some of them are based on cards being cloned, communication being logged and on-card elements being emulated by software residing in the STB. In the following paragraphs we provide a very brief overview of the main type of attack that has particular significance in the light of the proposed countermeasure.

The Card Sharing attack [20], see Figure 1, belongs in a set of simple, powerful and effective satellite TV attacks. This attack requires an OSTB with a legitimate card (i.e. the Server CAM), sharing its secrets with a number of illegitimate receivers (i.e. Client CAM) in order to provide them with access to unauthorised content. The user with the legitimate card runs a Card Server image on their OSTB.

The server image enables the OSTB server to accept connections from a number of OSTB clients (Client CAM) across a number of communication mechanisms including the Internet. As soon as an Electronic Management Message

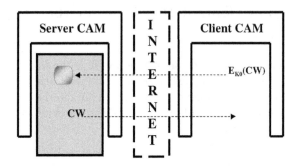

Fig. 1. Overview of the card sharing attack

(EMM) or an Electronic Code word Message (ECM) is received by an OSTB client it is forwarded to the corresponding OSTB server and in turn to the corresponding smart card in order to be processed. The server subsequently carries out the message decryption and forwards back to each client the decrypted CW or other relevant messages. This type of attack is often referred to as the jugular attack [22].

2.3   The Concept of Secure Content Provision for the Satellite TV Industry

Satellite communication is considered a very expedient vehicle for broadcasting a large amount of valuable information over wide geographical areas. The satellite TV industry needs to rigorously safeguard its revenue streams, i.e. the content or "Services". Various sources [18,7] estimate that in Australia, for example, approximately 4-5% of all satellite TV subscriptions were illegal resulting in a direct loss in the realm of 50 million Australian dollars. Broadcasters wanting to protect their revenue streams will therefore have to employ some effective and robust means to control access to the transmitted services.

The process of satellite TV signal transmission is often divided into two distinct phases: The first begins with the service provider encrypting or "scrambling" the signal and the second when the subscriber uses the necessary equipment, i.e. STB, in order to decrypt the signal. There are several systems that can provide access control for satellite TV; the most widely used ones are presented in [15,21].

Digital Video Broadcast (DVB) is a broadcasting standard developed by the major European satellite TV producers. The DVB standard is based on the MPEG-2 standard [1] that organises broadcasts into packets separating multiplexed information from program streams. The most commonly deployed satellite TV broadcasting methods involves a STB, a satellite dish responsible for receiving the encrypted signal, a Conditional Access System (CAS) [6] which often includes a CAM and a smart card that is responsible for the service decryption.

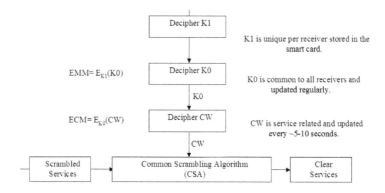

Fig. 2. Summarised process of DVB signal de-scrambling and cryptographic key hierarchy

The process is simplified in Figure 2 and summarised as follows. The service signal is encrypted/scrambled (by using the DVB Common Scrambling Algorithm) using a cryptographic key, called a Code Word (CW), that is generated by a Control Word Generator.

In turn, the CW is encrypted and encapsulated within an ECM, in order to protect the CW during transmission to all legitimate recipients. The encryption of the CW is often defined as "the process of protecting the keys that will be transmitted with the scrambled signal in order for the descrambler to work". A CAS offers all the necessary flexibility to satellite TV operators to operate proprietary conditional access systems that better fit their security and operational requirements. Some of the most commonly used CAS systems include VIAaccess [29], Irdeto [17], Cryptoworks [8], and Seca [26]. In principle, the CAS prohibits brute force attacks from taking place as the signal encryption key is changing every 2–10 seconds [5], i.e. the crypto period. The details of the CAS remain confidential but the basic idea that a chain of encryptions is taking place on the CW to guarantee protection of keys and avoid brute force attacks.

The role of the STB is to receive the satellite TV signal through the satellite dish and return the descrambled stream. This actually involves the utilisation of both the smart card and the CAM. The multiplexed/scrambled services and ECM are forwarded to the CAM residing within the STB. The actual ECM is forwarded from the CAM to the smart card. A Service Key (K0) is stored in the smart card and it is used in order to decrypt the CW. An Electronic Management Message (EMM) updates these keys, and their validity period is usually one month but varies from one broadcaster to another. The newly obtained CW is also used within the CAM in order to decrypt the signal and return it back to the STB. The ECM and EMM can be used in order to send commands and new keys to the smart cards. In the above architecture the STB can host multiple CAMs in order to match the individual broadcaster requirements.

In terms of the DVB data broadcast the following process is incorporated: the DVB transmission is an encrypted signal that has a bandwidth of 1 to 4 Mbits per second in packets of 188 bytes. The encrypted signal is accompanied by series of control words (CW) that can be deciphered by receivers to provide a key (CK) that can be used to decipher the broadcast. The CW can be updated during a broadcast so that more than one key is needed to decipher the broadcast. The maximum frequency this can occur is once every two seconds [5]. The keys for transforming CW to CK from a set of 292 keys that are distributed and updated by the broadcaster. This key is then used to decipher the payload of the DVB packets being delivered to each STB.

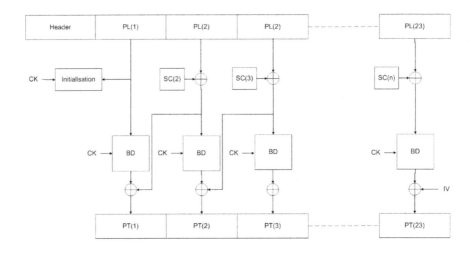

Fig. 3. Deciphering the contents of DVB packets using key CK

Figure 3 shows the deciphering process that comprises of two layers. The payload (PL(i) for $i \in [0, 23]$) of the packet is first deciphered by a stream cipher (SC) and then by a block cipher (BD) using the CBC chaining method. This produces the plaintext of the signal (PT(i) for $i \in [0, 23]$). The value for i can take values in the interval $[0, 23]$ as the stream cipher and block cipher treat the data in blocks of eight bytes. Further information on this process is available at [2], although the authors admit that in an actual implementation the details may vary.

In most cases this process takes place in a controlled environment where the STB and CAM are provided by the broadcaster. If an OSTB is used the whole process can be simulated and each incoming CW is sent to a server OSTB that will return CK, that can then be used to decipher a given broadcast. Every time CW is changed the client OSTB is required to send and receive a message of 10 bytes. If CW is changed every 2 seconds (the maximum frequency) this gives a bandwidth of 40 bits per second in each direction.

3   Increasing the Bandwidth Requirements

A way of raising the difficulty of this attack would be to use the fact that a smart card contains all the keys necessary for deciphering the arriving CWs. It is assumed that these keys can be delivered securely and are not at risk once stored within the smart card.

The smart card could be used to create a stream of values for CK rather than one value that is valid for 2–10 seconds. As the deciphering key changes much more frequently a server OSTB would have to provide much more information to enable a client OSTB to decipher a broadcast. This would have two effects, the amount of bandwidth necessary to share viewing rights becomes prohibitively large, and as the smart card is constantly communicating (i.e. it's bandwidth is saturated) it can no longer be asked to decipher arbitrary CWs as it can only create one stream at a time.

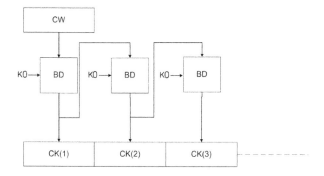

Fig. 4. Generating a series of values for CK

For a given CW a smart card can deliver a series of CKs, as shown in Figure 4, that are used to decipher the signal until the delivery of another CW. The arriving CW is deciphered with a block cipher (BD) using the key (K0) to produce a CK, this is again deciphered to produced the next CK etc. The value for K is chosen from the 292 available by the header delivered with CW. This means that an attacker would be obliged to share each CK as it is generated to enable someone else to decipher the same signal. New values can be generated by continuing to decipher the delivered CW to produce other values of CK. When a new CW is delivered the process restarts with the new CK.

Two different possibilities for implementing this idea are discussed below: using a standard smart card and using a card with a fast protocol to provide the sequence of CK values.

3.1   Using a Standard Smart Card

In order to ask a smart card for a new value for CK the CAM will need to send an APDU and then receive the procedure byte, the data, and status word [23].

This gives an overhead of 8 bytes for each request to the card for a new value for CK. In order to minimise the effect of this, numerous values of CK can be delivered by the same APDU to minimise the amount of protocol bytes sent. These keys will be stored on the CAM and used as necessary. Table 1 gives the set of keys that can be generated per second for every amount of keys that can be delivered in 1 APDU. The bandwidth requirement is shown as a function of the number of CKs provided per APDU.

Each CK value is assumed to be 8 bytes long as this is the key length required by the block ciphers if DES or the proprietary CSA algorithm is used. The maximum number of CK values that can be delivered by one APDU is

Table 1. The bandwidth requirements for different length commands

CKs per APDU	Clock cycles per command	CKs per second	Bandwidth required (Kbits/s)
1	3072	1627.6	104.2
2	4608	2170.1	138.9
3	6144	2441.4	156.2
4	7680	2604.1	166.7
5	9216	2712.6	173.6
6	10752	2790.1	178.6
7	12288	2848.3	182.3
8	13824	2893.5	185.2
9	15360	2929.6	187.5
10	16896	2959.2	189.4
11	18432	2983.9	191.0
12	19968	3004.8	192.3
13	21504	3022.6	193.5
14	23040	3038.1	194.4
15	24576	3051.7	195.3
16	26112	3063.7	196.1
17	27648	3074.3	196.8
18	29184	3083.8	197.4
19	30720	3092.4	197.9
20	32256	3100.1	198.4
21	33792	3107.2	198.9
22	35328	3113.6	199.3
23	36864	3119.5	199.7
24	38400	3125	200
25	39936	3130.0	200.3
26	41472	3134.6	200.6
27	43008	3138.9	200.9
28	44544	3142.9	201.1
29	46080	3146.7	201.4
30	47616	3150.2	201.6
31	49152	3153.4	201.8

$\lfloor 255/8 \rfloor = 31$ (i.e. the maximum data size possible in one APDU divided by 8). If this algorithm is replaced with an AES the same table can be used. In this case the number of CKs per APDU will be divided by 2, so only the rows corresponding to an even number of CKs per APDU need be considered. This is because an AES key will require twice the number of bytes as a DES key.

These calculations are based on a smart card with an external clock of 5 MHz and an ETU[1] of 16 clock cycles, which is the fastest speed provided for in the ISO standards [23]. A faster clock speed can sometimes be used but the behaviour of a smart card cannot be predicted (some smart cards will refuse to function), this case is therefore not taken into account.

The values given in Table 1 also assume that data is constantly being sent or received across the I/O between the CAM and the smart card i.e. processing time is not taken into account. This requires that the I/O is being conducted by an UART[2] in the smart card and the block cipher is being done with a crypto-coprocessor i.e. the I/O and algorithm calculation are not dependent on the CPU. The CPU is therefore just required to send data from the UART to the crypto-coprocessor and *vice versa*, as the UART and crypto-coprocessor will be separate blocks on the chip. In the case of proprietary algorithms a hardware implementation is unlikely to be available, which will significantly lower the amount of keys that can be delivered per second, as CPU cycles will need to be used to calculate the block cipher. It will still be possible to calculate values of CK while the UART is communicating but the performance will be significantly slower than a hardware implementation. As the performance of the proprietary CSA algorithm on a smart card is not known it is not possible to predict the effect this will have on the proposed countermeasure.

To use a smart card in this manner will require a special mode, where the smart card will only respond to commands asking for more keys or to exit this mode. Otherwise the command dispatcher will take too much time and the performance will drop.

As can be seen the bandwidth required to share the CKs is greatly increased from 40 bits per second. It may still be feasible for an attacker to share the series of CKs with one other person if they have a fast enough internet connection, but will be unable to act as a server for numerous people. The client OSTB will also be obliged to decipher the same broadcast as the server OSTB. Even if an attacker is sharing this data with one other person there are likely to be synchronisation difficulties streaming this data from one receiver to another, which will lower the quality of the signal that can be produced by the client receiver.

---

[1] An ETU is an Elementary Time Unit in the $T = 0$ protocol [23] and is the amount of clock cycles required to send one byte. 12 ETU's are required to send 1 byte.

[2] A Universal Asynchronous Receiver-Transmitter (UART) is an autonomous block on the chip that will receive and and send signals on the I/O pin based on instructions from the CPU. This greatly simplifies I/O routines as the CPU does not need to concern itself with the state of the I/O pin at any given time.

3.2   Using Fast Protocols

The countermeasure proposed above is based on a standard smart card using the $T = 0$ protocol. The smart card industry is currently working on several solutions to the bandwidth problems posed by this protocol. With a fast protocol it should be possible to have a card that deciphers the broadcast on-the-fly. These are summarised below, with a brief description on how this would change or replace the proposed countermeasure:

Proprietary Protocols: A method of using a standard smart card with a proprietary protocol, and therefore a proprietary reader, was presented by Gemplus at Cartes 2003 [12]. This protocol allowed music from a CD player to be deciphered on-the-fly. Using this technology to implement the above countermeasure a smart card would be able to produce 11000 keys per second [12], given the bandwidth required to decipher a CD on-the-fly, which gives a required bandwidth to share the series of CKs of 680.8 Kbits per second. This is potentially too fast as the CK will change 3 times for each DVB packet treated by the CAM, assuming that the broadcast is arriving at its maximum bandwidth of 4 Mbits/s. It may not be possible to re-key the CAM this often. The major draw back is the use of a proprietary protocol means that substantial changes will be required in the CAM to be able to communicate with this card.

USB Smart Cards: Some chip manufacturers propose smart cards with a USB interface that will allow for a larger bandwidth between a smart card and reader [28]. These chips include a USB interface conforming to USB 1.1 that will provide a bandwidth of 10 Mbits/s. This is more than enough to handle a DVB broadcast, although problems may arise with deciphering the signal. The specification of an example smart card chip can be found at [27] based on ST Microelectronic's ST19 chip family. The internal clock frequency can be raised to 10 MHz, which will not be enough to decipher a broadcast at 4 Mbits/s on-the-fly. If we assume that a hardware DES takes 16 clock cycles (i.e. 1 clock cycle per round) the deciphering will take about a tenth of the CPU time, leaving enough time for data transfer etc. In the case of proprietary protocols this chip is unlikely to be able to provide deciphering on-the-fly due to the amount of CPU time that will be required. In practice industry has found these cards inadequate to increase the bandwidth between a smart card and reader due to the complexity of the host interface [25], although this view may no longer be valid.

Secure MultiMediaCards: A more recent initiative is the Secure MultiMediaCards (Secure-MMC) [10] that aims to blend smart card technology with MultiMediaCards [3]. These chips aim to provide secure storage in devices, such as mobile phones, principally for digital rights management. The advantage of this technology in the context of this paper is that MultiMediaCards generally have a bus rather than a serial interface. The MMC standard allows for a bandwidth of up to 416 Mbits/s depending on the clock frequency and the size of the bus used. It is assumed that a Secure-MMC will be able to decipher several megabytes per second on-the-fly [24]. The Secure-MMC is a relatively new technology so no specifications are currently available. It is assumed that such cards will be able to decipher broadcasts on-the-fly as the new generation of MultiMediaCards are designed to accept clock speeds up to 52 MHz [4].

The use of any of these fast protocols is going to be a difficult choice for a broadcaster. The use of feature rich chips increases the price of each smart card, as each extra block will require more silicon and development time. This extra cost will have to be included in the subscription fees, which may drive customers away. However, it is anticipated that revenue would increase over time if such a solution was chosen as only subscribers would be able to view broadcasts. The proposed countermeasure will provide the most cost effective solution until USB cards or Secure-MMCs become more affordable.

4 Connection Speeds

There are several different connection speeds offered by internet providers. A summary of these connections is shown in Table 2, where the majority of the information is taken from [14].

Table 2. The bandwidth available with different connection types

Type of Internet Connection	Download Bandwidth Kbits/s	Upload Bandwidth Kbits/s
ADSL 256	256	128
ADSL 512	512	128
ADSL 1024	1024	256
T1	1500	1500
T3	45000	45000

The proposed countermeasure should be effective in stopping the card sharing attack for ADSL users. A smart card with over 2 keys per APDU will easily be a able to saturate the upload bandwidth of a "slow" speed ADSL connection. An ADSL connection with an upload bandwidth of 256 Kbits/s is more problematic. In theory this would make it possible to share one channel with one other person. However, in practice it is unlikely to to be practical as ADSL internet connections will not consistently attain their theoretical maximums. The headers and footers of all the protocol layers will also add to the bandwidth requirements.

This countermeasure will not stop a the card sharing attack where an attacker has access to a T1/T3 connection. These connections provide enough bandwidth that the stream of keys could be shared with another user. It is assumed that each extra client will add the same bandwidth requirements as the same data needs to be sent to each client. A T3 connection would therefore be able to supply key information to a small group of clients. The proposed countermeasure will not prevent the card sharing attack in this case.

This does not mean that the countermeasure is worthless, as T1/T3 connections are generally only used by businesses. There is also no way of preventing a user with a T3 connection from sharing the broadcast they are watching with at least one other user. Broadcasts are delivered to a user with a bandwidth of between 1 and 4 Mbits/s. An attacker could potentially decipher the broadcast and deliver it in clear to a third party.

5   Conclusion

A method of inhibiting the card sharing attack is described that functions by increasing the bandwidth required to the point where it is less practical to share the information required to conduct the attack. The communication with the card is saturated so the only information that an attacker is able to share is the broadcast being watched rather than an arbitrary channel. It has been shown that sharing the information required to continue conducting the attack is prohibitive unless the attacker uses a T1/T3 connection, which are normally only used by businesses and are not affordable by everybody.

The proposed countermeasure provides a way of inhibiting the card sharing attack until USB and Secure-MMC devices become readily available and affordable. For this reason the countermeasure has been designed to minimise the impact on the existing protocol as major changes to the protocol will be expensive, and may be unnecessary if more powerful secure devices are going to be used in the near future.

The principle problem of using this countermeasure is that one smart card is required per screen. It will not be possible to view one broadcast and video another, or have two televisions viewing different broadcasts, etc. In order to record a second broadcast a viewer would be required to store the data and CWs and have this deciphered on-the-fly at viewing time. This is a possible advantage for broadcasters as they are sure that only legitimate users can view their emissions, as a smart card needs to be present.

References

1. ETR 154:. Digital video broadcasting (DVB): Implementation guidelines for the use of MPEG-2 systems; video and audio in satellite, cable and terrestrial broadcasting applications.
2. Anonymous. CSA – known facts and speculations. http://CSA.irde.to.
3. MultiMediaCard Association. http://www.mmca.org.
4. MultiMediaCard Association. Application note, an0501-1.00, April 2005. http://www.mmca.org/compliance/buy_spec/AN_MMCA050419.pdf.
5. EBU Project Group B/CA. Functional model of a conditional access system. EBU technical Review, Winter 1995.
6. CENELEC. Common interface specification for conditional access and other digital video broadcasting decoder applications. Technical Report CENELEC Standard 50221, European Committee for Electrotechnical Standardization (CENELEC), Brussels, Belgium, February 1997.

7. V. Chachiere. Man ordered to pay $180m restitution for TV signal piracy. Naples Daily News. http://www.naplesnews.com.
8. Cryptoworks. http://www.digitalnetworks.philips.com.
9. D. J. Cutts. DVB conditional access. *IEE Electronics and Communications Engineering Journal*, 9(1):21–27, February 1997.
10. Giesecke & Devrient. Secure and mobile storage media – the memory card with smart card technology. http://www.gi-de.com/, 2005.
11. ETSI. Digital video broadcasting (DVB); support for use of scrambling and conditional access (CA) within digital broadcasting systems. Technical Report ETSI Technical Report ETR 289, European Telecommunications Standards Institute (ETSI), Sophia Antipolis, France, October 1996.
12. Gemplus. Cryptomotion. presented at Cartes 2003, 2003. review available at http://www.prnewswire.co.uk/cgi/news/release?id=112260.
13. L. C. Guillou. Smart cards and conditional access. In T. Beth, N. Cot, and I. Ingemarsson, editors, *Advances in Cryptology - EUROCRYPT '84*, volume 209 of *Lecture Notes in Computer Science*, pages 480–485. Springer-Verlag, 1984.
14. helpwithpcs.com. Internet connections explained, a guide to dial-up, adsl and cable connections. http://www.helpwithpcs.com/internet/internet-connections.htm#adsl-connections.
15. R. Hewitt. North american MPEG-2 information, July 2003. http://www.coolstf.com/mpeg.
16. D. Holankar and M. Stamp. Secure streaming media and digital rights management. In *Proceedings of the 2004 Hawaii International Conference on Computer Science*, pages 85–96. ACM Press, 2004.
17. Irdeto. http://www.irdetoaccess.com.
18. P. Kalina. No-pay TV costs industry $50m. The Age Journal. http://www.theage.com.um.
19. D. W. Kravitz and D. M. Goldschlag. Conditional access concepts and principles. In M. K. Franklin, editor, *Financial Cryptography – FC '99*, volume 1648 of *Lecture Notes in Computer Science*, pages 158–172. Springer-Verlag, 1999.
20. M. Kuhn. Attack on pay-tv access control systems. Security Seminar talk. University of Cambridge, London, UK., 1997.
21. G. C. Langelaar. Overview of protection methods in existing TV and storage devices. Technical University of Delft, July 1996.
22. J. McCormac. European scrambling system. Waterford University Press, 1996.
23. International Standards Organisation. ISO7816–3 smart card standard: Part 3: Electronic signals and transmission protocols.
24. D. Praca. Next generation smart card: New features, new architecture and system integration. 6th e-Smart Conference, Sophia Antipolis, France, September 2005.
25. D. Praca and C. Barral. From smart cards to smart objects: The road to new smart card technologies. *Computer networks*, 36(4):381–389, July 2001.
26. Seca. http://www.securityit.com.
27. STmicroelectronics. Smartcard solutions ST19 multi-application smartcard ICs. http://www.st.com.
28. STmicroelectronics. STmicroelectronics delivers world's first USB-certified smart card chips. http://www.st.com, 2002.
29. VIAccess. http://www.viaccess.com.
30. Dream Multimedia Worldwide. Dreambox DM7000s user manual. http://www.dream-multimedia-tv.de/manual/manual_eng.zip.

A Flooding-Based DoS/DDoS Detecting Algorithm Based on Traffic Measurement and Prediction*

Shi Yi, Yang Xinyu, and Zhu Huijun

Dept. Computer Science & Technology, Xi'an Jiaotong University,
Xianning West Road 28#, Xi'an, P.R.C.
yxyphd@mail.xjtu.edu.cn

Abstract. This paper analyzed the features of the flooding-based DoS/DDoS attack traffic, and proposed a novel real-time algorithm for detecting such DoS/DDoS attacks. In order to shorten the delay of detection, short-term traffic prediction was introduced, and prediction values were used in the detecting process. Though we use real-time traffic data to calculate the mean and variance, few periods of data need to be stored because the algorithm is a recurring process, therefore the occupied storage space is less. Moreover, the complex and cost of the recurring process is less than calculating the whole sequence, so the load of the server would not increase much. Although we focus our research on detecting flooding-based DoS/DDoS attacks, the simulation shows that the approach also can deal with DDoS attacks that zombies start without simultaneousness.

1 Introduction

Flooding-based DoS/DDoS attacks, such as SYN-flooding, ICMP-flooding, UDP flooding, DNS flooding, and so on, have already become a major threat to the stability of the Internet [1]. In these attacks, attackers send a large stream of packets to a victim to consume its key resources, and then the victim fails to provide services to legitimate clients [2].

It is found by our experiments that the flooding-based DoS/DDoS attacks behaves such features --- traffic burst and remaining of comparative smooth for some time, and this can be described by calculating the global average value and the variance of the traffic. In this paper, we simplify the variance calculating by just calculating the variance of difference sequence of the traffic, and propose a novel method to detect the flooding-based DoS/DDoS attacks. Furthermore, to accelerate the attack detecting, we also give an adjusted detecting algorithm with short-term traffic prediction.

The rest of this paper is organized as follows. Section 2 describes the traffic features during flooding-based DoS/DDoS attacks. Section 3 proposes the basic

---

* This work is supported by the NSFC (National Natural Science Foundation of China -- under Grant 60403028), NSFS (Natural Science Foundation of Shaanxi -- under Grant 2004F43), and Natural Science Foundation of Electronic and Information Engineering School, Xi'an Jiaotong University.

H. Yoshiura et al. (Eds.): IWSEC 2006, LNCS 4266, pp. 252–267, 2006.

DoS/DDoS detection algorithm based on the traffic features presented in Section 2. Section 4 introduces the short-term traffic prediction into the basic detecting algorithm and gives an adjusted method. Experiment results are shown in section 5 to testify the feasibility of the algorithm and to analyze the sensitivity of the algorithm by different parameter values. Section 6 expresses related works. Finally, conclusions are drawn in Section 7.

2   Traffic Features During Flooding-Based Dos/DDos Attacks

Under flooding-based DoS/DDoS attacks, the traffic arrived at a victim behaves differently from normal traffic. The normal traffic fluctuates violently, and the average value of it is far from the bandwidth capacity. Whereas the flooding-based DoS/DDoS attack traffic behaves two distinct features: the burst of traffic and the trends to be smooth, i.e., it behaves flat-burst. Described by statistical values, it means the traffic volume measured at the traffic burst is much greater than its global average value before the burst; and the variance presents a decreasing trend in a small range after the traffic burst. These features can be clarified by a set of data as follows.

Fig. 1 shows the measured network traffic data of an FTP server opened to the public in our lab. The data set is a time series with the unit *packets/s*. The length of the sequence is 4000 seconds. During some periods, DoS attacks were launched by using a program launching syn-flooding attacks to the server. The start moment and attacking duration of each attack are listed in Table 1.

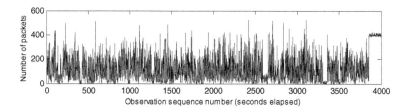

Fig. 1. Original observed traffic

Table 1. The start moment and attacking duration of each attack

Attack	Start Moment (s)	Attacking Duration (s)
Attack A	341	3
Attack B	1428	3
Attack C	2009	5
Attack D	2508	5
Attack E	3855	145

Local features around the periods under attacks are demonstrated from Fig. 2 to Fig. 4:

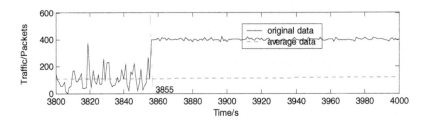

Fig. 2. The real traffic and mean traffic around Attack E(3855s~4000s)

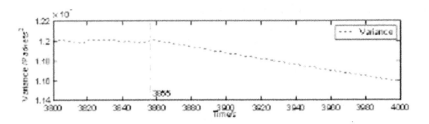

Fig. 3. The difference variance traffic around Attack E(3855s~4000s)

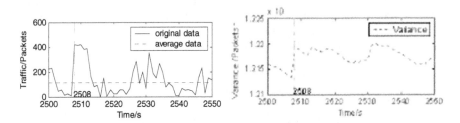

Fig. 4. (left) The real traffic and mean traffic around Attack D(2508s~2512s) (right) The difference variance traffic around Attack D(2508s~2512s)

In Fig. 2 and the left of Fig. 4, the blue solid lines and red dotted lines represent original data and average data respectively, and during attacks original data are much higher than average data compared with normal situations. In Fig. 3 and the right of Fig. 4, the red dotted lines represent the difference variance (defined in Equation 3) of the data set, and they decrease during the attacks.

In Probability Theory, the formula to calculate the variance of a sequence X with the length t is

$$\text{var}(t) = \frac{1}{t}\sum_{i=1}^{t}(X(i) - \overline{X})^2 \tag{1}$$

In Equation 1, $X(i)$ means the observed value at the moment i, and $\overline{X}$ means the expectation of the sequence X. In practical calculations, the expectation of the traffic is substituted by the mean of X, which is computed after acquiring every traffic datum, thus it is not stable. However, what is worth concerned about is the relative and local fluctuation of the data, rather than concrete values. On the other hand, the mean of the difference of a large sequence can be considered as 0, the proof is as follows.

Let d_X be the difference sequence of X, namely for every $i>1$, $d\_X(i)=X(i)-X(i-1)$. Let d_mean be the mean of d_X, then

$$
\begin{aligned}
d\_mean &= \frac{1}{t}\sum_{i=2}^{t} d\_X(i) \\
&= \frac{1}{t}\sum_{i=2}^{t}(X(i)-X(i-1)) \\
&= \frac{1}{t}(X(2)-X(1)+X(3)-X(2)+\cdots \\
&\quad + X(t-1)-X(t-2)+X(t)-X(t-1)) \\
&= \frac{1}{t}(X(t)-X(1))
\end{aligned}
\tag{2}
$$

At least, d_mean is much closer to 0 than $\overline{X}$ is, and when $t\to\infty$, $d\_mean\to0$. So we regard it as 0 to simplify the calculation.

Therefore, the variance of difference sequence of the traffic (called "difference variance" in this paper, and represented by d_var) can reflect the fluctuation as well. And the function to calculate d_var is

$$
\begin{aligned}
d\_var(t) &= \frac{1}{t-1}\sum_{i=2}^{t}(d\_X(i)-d\_mean)^2 \\
&= \frac{1}{t-1}\sum_{i=2}^{t}d\_X(i)^2 \\
&= \frac{1}{t-1}\sum_{i=2}^{t}(X(i)-X(i-1))^2
\end{aligned}
\tag{3}
$$

Calculating the variance of the difference sequence in Equation 3 is simpler than calculating the variance of the original traffic sequence in Equation 1.

3 The Basic Attack Detecting Algorithm

According to the features of flooding-based DoS/DDoS attack traffic given above, a recursive algorithm to detect such attacks is proposed in the following subsections.

3.1 The Calculation of Statistical Values

In order to satisfy the real-time demands of the algorithm, statistical values are calculated by a recursive way.

Suppose at the moment t, the original traffic is $C(t)$, the global average value (the mean of all $C(i), i<=t$) is $c\_mean(t)$, the difference of the traffic is $z(t)$, and the difference variance (the variance of all $z(i), i<=t$) is $d\_var(t)$. The mean of $z(t)$ is $d\_mean(t)$, which can be considered as 0 according to Equation 2. The calculations of these statistical values are:

1) $c\_mean(t)=1/t*((t-1)*c\text{-}mean(t-1)+C(t))$, considering the traffic under attacks may cause the global traffic mean to be greater, the calculation should be stopped when an attack is detected, and be resumed after it ends. Such measures can mitigate t gdhe impacts of attacking traffic to the global mean, so make it much closer to the natural scenario of the network.

2) $z(t)=C(t)\text{-}C(t-1),\ (t>1)$

3)
$$d\_var(t)=\frac{1}{t-1}\sum_{i=2}^{t}(z(i)-d\_mean(t))^2$$
$$=\frac{1}{t-1}\sum_{i=2}^{t}z(i)^2$$
$$=\frac{1}{t-1}\left(\sum_{i=2}^{t}z(i)^2+z(t)^2\right)$$
$$=\frac{1}{t-1}\left((t-2)\cdot d\_var(t-1)+z(t)^2\right)$$

4)   In order to weigh the volume of the traffic at the moment t, a function $\mu_G(t)$ is defined as:

$$\mu_G(t)=\begin{cases}0 & ,C(t)<lt\cdot c\_mean(t)\\[2mm]\dfrac{C(t)}{(ht-lt)\cdot c\_mean(t)}-\dfrac{lt}{ht-lt} & ,C(t)\in[lt\cdot c\_mean(t),\ ht\cdot c\_mean(t)]\\[2mm]1 & ,C(t)>ht\cdot c\_mean(t)\end{cases}$$

This definition borrows the concept of "membership function" in Fuzzy Arithmetic, but much simpler. In the definition, $lt*c\_mean(t)$ means the lower limit of "great" traffic; if the traffic volume is less than $lt*c\_mean(t)$, it can be considered to be "not great", namely the weight of "great" is 0. If $C(t)\in[lt*c\_mean(t),\ ht*c\_mean(t)]$, its weight of "great" is defined by the function $\mu_G(t)=C(t)/((ht-lt)*c\_mean(t))-lt/(ht-lt)$. And $ht*c\_mean(t)$ means the upper limit of "great" traffic; if the traffic volume exceeds the global mean by ht times, it can be considered to be "very great", namely its weight of "great" is 1. In real applications, the parameters lt and ht should be assigned according to the performance of networks. For example, according to long-term measured data of the network, and the definition of lt may have more significant.

3.2 Judging Process

According to the definition of $\mu_G(t)$, if $\mu_G(t)=0$, it is regarded that no attacks occur; if at the moment t, $\mu_G(t)>0$, it is a hint of the beginning of an attack, and the judging process is triggered immediately to verify its occurrence.

The following is the description of judging process. There are two predefined two variables: one is *interval*, representing the detecting period; another is *accumulate_volume*, representing a volume threshold for a host to tolerate, for example, the size of buffer[1]. For each time slot t during detection, $A(t)$ represents the attack intensity at that slot. And let *accumulate_steps* be the largest integer less than *(accumulate_volume*interval)/C(t)*. The variables *attack_count* cooperates with *accumulate_steps* to decide when to alarm. Once the judging process starts up, if the attack intensity enhances $(A(t)>=A(t-1))$, *attack_count* increases by 1, otherwise it decreases by 1. If *attack_count* accumulates to or surpasses *accumulate_steps*, the process alarms. The calculation of attack intensity at the moment t is shown in the following pseudo code. The influences on detecting results by the value of *accumulate_volume* discussed in Section 5.

```
for each t-th time slot of detection do
    accumulate_steps = floor((interval*accumulate_volume)
                       /C(t)) ;   /*(1)*
    if(accumulate_steps == 0)
        alarm( );  /*(2)*/
    else{
        if(μG(t) > 0){
            attack_count++;   /*(3)*/
            if(d_var(t) >= d_var(t-1))
                A(t) = μG(t);   /*(4)*/
            else A(t) = max(μG(t-1), μG(t));   /*(5)*/
        }else attack_count = 0;   /*(6)*/
        if (attack_count > =accumulate_steps){
            if (A(t) >= A(t-1))   /*(7)*/
                alarm();
            else attack_count=accumulate_steps-1;   /*(8)*/
        }
    }
}
```

Explanations to the algorithm:

(1) This sentence calculates the largest integer that is less than or equal to *(accumulate_volume*interval)/C(t)* and assign to *accumulate_steps*;

(2) If large pulsing attacks or flash-crowd-type attacks happen, $C(t)$ would be extremely huge (larger than *accumulate_volume*interval*), causing *accumulate_steps* to equal to 0, and the process alarms immediately;

(3) If the traffic is "great", it means an occurrence of a traffic burst, probably a beginning of an attack, increase *attack_count* by 1;

(4) If the difference variance increases or remains at the moment t compared with that at $t-1$, it means that the fluctuation of the traffic is not weakened. There are two possibilities causing the fluctuation: a) the traffic increases, so $\mu_G(t) > \mu_G(t-1)$, and the probability of attacks enhances as well, then $A(t)$ should be assigned the larger μ_G,

---

[1] The unit of buffer size should be the same as the unit to measure the traffic in the algorithm. For example, if the measuring unit is the number of packets per time slot, buffer size can be the number of packets with average size to replete the buffer; if the measuring unit is monitored bytes per time slot, buffer size can be the whole byte number of the buffer. In this paper, we use the number of packets in both trace experiments and simulation.

namely $\mu_d(t)$; b) the traffic decreases, so $\mu_d(t) < \mu_d(t-1)$, and the probability of attacks reduces, then $A(t)$ is assigned the smaller μ_c, which is also $\mu_d(t)$;

(5) If the difference variance decreases at the moment t compared with that at $t-1$, it means that the traffic changes little, therefore the probability of attack enhances, thus the larger μ_c is assigned to $A(t)$;

(6) If the traffic is "not great", reassign 0 to *attack_count*, and the process enters the next time slot of detection;

(7) The coincidence of *attack_count>=accumulate_steps* and $A(t)>=A(t-1)$ indicates that the attack possibility has already increased or at least remained for no less than *accumulate_steps* time slots, and the possibility continues to enhance, so the process alarms;

(8) While *attack_count>=accumulate_steps*, but $A(t)<A(t-1)$, it indicates that although the attack possibility has increased or remained for a while, it reduces at the moment t, the process continues to observe and waits for verification.

According to the recurring of statistical values and the judging process, the only data needed at a time slot t are $C(t-1)$, *c_mean(t-1)*, *d_var(t-1)*, $\mu_d(t-1)$, and $A(t-1)$. The data $C(t)$, *c_mean(t)*, *d_var(t)*, $\mu_d(t)$, and $A(t)$ are stored for the next time slot.

4 The Ajusted Detecting Algorithm with Short-Term Traffic Prediction

4.1 The Feasibility of Introducing Short-Term Traffic Prediction into Flooding-Based DoS/DDoS Attacks Detection

Treating the traffic as a time series, we can establish an adaptive AR model on it and predict its values based on the model. The predicting approach is Error-adjusted LMS (EaLMS), which has shorter predicting delay and less prediction error for the short-term real-time prediction to smoother traffic than to violent fluctuating traffic [3]. The main intent of introducing short-term traffic prediction into DoS/DDoS detection is to obtain some data in advance, thus to accelerate detecting. Under flooding-based DoS/DDoS, the arriving traffic of a victim is smoother than normal. Therefore, if

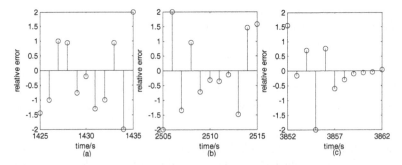

Fig. 5. Relative prediction errors (a) around Attack B(1428s~1430s) (b) around Attack D(2508s~2512s) (c) around Attack E(3855s~4000s)

EaLMS is applied to predict traffic values, the prediction under attacks is more accurate than that under normal situations, namely the prediction error is less. Demonstrated in Fig. 5, the relative prediction error during an attack is smaller than normal cases (to show clearly, the values more than 2 or less than -2 are cut to 2 or -2).

For each $C(t)$, suppose its prediction value is $C\_p(t)$, then $r\_p\_err(t)$ (the relative prediction error at moment t) is defined as $r\_p\_err(t)=(C\-p(t)\-C(t))/C(t)$. From the Table 2 showing the average $|r\_p\_err(t)|$, it is clear that prediction errors during attacks are much smaller than global prediction errors.

Table 2. The comparison of relative prediction error among global traffic and attacking cases

	Average $|r\_p\_err(t)|$
Global	2.49
Attack A	0.23
Attack B	0.64
Attack C	0.32
Attack D	0.51

4.2 Adjustments to the Algorithm

After obtained the difference of current traffic (presented by $z(t)$), the single step prediction $z\_predict(t+1)$ for $z(t+1)$ is calculated. Then let $C\_p(t+1)$ be the prediction value for the traffic at $t+1$. The $z\_predict(t+1)$ is regarded as $z(t+1)$ and be used for calculating $d\_var(t+1)$ and $\mu_d(t+1)$.

1)
$$d \_ var(t + 1) = \frac{1}{t}\sum_{i=2}^{t+1} (z(i) - d \_ \text{mean} (t))^2$$

$$= \frac{1}{t}\sum_{i=2}^{t+1} z(i)^2$$

$$= \frac{1}{t}(\sum_{i=2}^{t} z(i)^2 + z(t+1)^2)$$

$$= \frac{1}{t}((t-1)\cdot d \_ var(t) + z\_predict(\ t+1)^2)$$

2) $C \_ p(t+1) = C(t) + z \_ predict(t+1)$

3)
$$\mu_G(t) = \begin{cases} 0 & , C \_ p(t+1) < lt \cdot c \_ \text{mean}(t) \\ \dfrac{C \_ p(t+1)}{(ht-lt)\cdot c\_\text{mean}(t)} - \dfrac{lt}{ht-lt} & , C\_p(t+1) \in [lt \cdot c\_\text{mean}(t),\ ht \cdot c\_\text{mean}(t)] \\ 1 & , C \_ p(t+1) > ht \cdot c \_ \text{mean}(t) \end{cases}$$

For the algorithm in Section 3.2, replace $d\_var(t)$ and $\mu_d(t)$ by $d\_var(t+1)$ and $\mu_d(t+1)$ respectively. Without short-term prediction, if at the moment $t+1$ an attack is detected, it could be detected at the moment t with short-term prediction, because the relevant data at $t+1$ is obtained by prediction at t, consequently the attack is detected in advance. If multi-step prediction is applied, the time of detecting the attack will be ahead more. However, such advance could not be unlimited. For one thing, the more steps to predict, the more errors to occur. For another thing, only if attacks do occur, the prediction value are worthy in detection algorithm. Thus multi-step prediction should be carefully deployed in practice. It is important to point that $d\_var(t)$ and $\mu(t)$ are calculated at the moment $t-1$ according to the data at that time, so they should be recomputed based on the real datum at the moment t.

5   Experiment Results and Discussion

5.1   The Basic Algorithm Without Short-Term Prediction

Without the loss of generality, set the parameters $accumulate\_volume=1200$, $lt=2.5$ and $ht=3.5$, and the algorithm shows perfect detection performances on the data set of Fig. 1. The effects are demonstrated in Fig. 6 and Table 3, in which the rate of successful detection (the times of correct detections/the total times of attack) is 100%, and the rate of false detection (rate of considering normal traffic as attack) is 0.

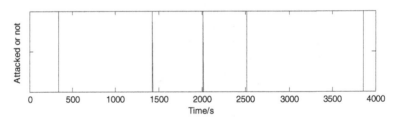

Fig. 6. The detection effects when $accumulate\_volume=1200$, $lt=2.5$ and $ht=3.5$

Table 3. The detection effects when $accumulate\_volume=1200$, $lt=2.5$ and $ht=3.5$

Attack	Start Moment (s)	Detected Moment (s)	Detected Delay(s)
Attack A	341	344	3
Attack B	1428	1431	3
Attack C	2009	2012	3
Attack D	2508	2510	2
Attack E	3855	3859	4

1)   The detection results of different values of $accumulate\_volume$

According to the definition in Section 3.2, $accumulate\_volume$ is a parameter to evaluate the protected host's tolerable capacity. In real application, it can be set the buffer size of the host, or any value that the administrator considered as a threshold for the host to tolerate.

a) $accumulate\_volume=1100$, $lt=2.5$ and $ht=3.5$, see Table 4.

Table 4. The detection effects when *accumulate_volume=1100, lt=2.5* and *ht=3.5*

Attack	Start Moment (s)	Detected Moment (s)	Detection Delay (s)
Attack A	341	343	2
Attack B	1428	1431	3
Attack C	2009	2011	2
Attack D	2508	2510	2
Attack E	3855	3858	3
-	-	2074	-
-	-	3588	-

The rate of successful detection is 100%, and the delays of detection are shorter in Attack A, C and E than those in Table 3, but there are two false detections. Because reducing *accumulate_volume* means a smaller tolerable threshold for traffic of a host, although there are no attacks at 2073s and 3587s, the large volumes at those moments make the algorithm generate alarms. So if the value of *accumulate_volume* is assigned smaller, it is possible to detect an attack faster, but enhance the probabilities of false alarms.

  b)   *accumulate_volume=1500, lt=2.5* and *ht=3.5*, see Table 5.

Table 5. The detection effects when *accumulate_volume=1500, lt=2.5* and *ht=3.5*

Attack	Start Moment (s)	Detected Moment (s)	Detection Delay (s)
Attack A	341	344	3
Attack B	1428	Undetected	-
Attack C	2009	2014	5
Attack D	2508	2511	3
Attack E	3855	3859	4

Augmenting *accumulate_volume* has two impacts to the results. Firstly, Attack B is undetected in this experiment, because it is the weakest attack (with the least average intensity) among the five, and the algorithm believes that such intensity fails to reach the tolerable threshold. Secondly, the delay of Attack C is prolonged. So, larger *accumulate_volume* would reduce the sensitivity of the algorithm.

The analysis in a) and b) indicates that the value of *accumulate_volume* can influence the response speed of alarms and the probability of false alarms. Small *accumulate_volume* value helps to shorten the delays of alarms, but enhances the chances of false alarm. Large *accumulate_volume* value increases the delays of alarms to some extent, and may omit attacks. However, because *accumulate_volume* is assigned due to the process capacity, the ignorant attacks would not impact the host's performance seriously. So it is important to assign a proper value to *accumulate_volume* to protect the host efficiently by this algorithm.

  2)   The detection results of different values of *lt*

  a)   *lt=2, accumulate_volume=1200*, and *ht=3.5*, see Table 6

Table 6. The detection effects when *lt=2, accumulate_volume=1200,* and *ht=3.5*

Attack	Start Moment (s)	Detected Moment (s)	Detection Delay (s)
Attack A	341	343	2
Attack B	1428	1431	3
Attack C	2009	2012	3
Attack D	2508	2510	2
Attack E	3855	3859	4
-	-	900	-
-	-	2074	-
-	-	2419	-
-	-	2654	-
-	--	2757	-
-		2900	-

   b)   *lt=3, accumulate_volume=1200,* and *ht=3.5,* see Table 7.

Table 7. The detection effects when *lt=3, accumulate_volume=1200,* and *ht=3.5*

Attack	Start Moment (s)	Detected Moment (s)	Detection Delay (s)
Attack A	341	344	3
Attack B	1428	Undetected	-
Attack C	2009	2012	3
Attack D	2508	2510	2
Attack E	3855	3859	4

According to the results of a) and b), the assignment of *lt* also determines the sensibility of the detection. Small value of *lt* means lower tolerance to traffic bursts of the network, thus attacks can be detected correctly, but less intensity bursts would be considered as attacks by the process. Contrarily, large value of *lt* means higher scale of traffic bursts to bear, thus false alarms would be avoided to some extent, whereas some attacks would be omitted.

3)   The detection results of different values of *ht*
   a)   *ht=3, lt=2.5* and *accumulate_volume=1200*
   The results are the same to Fig. 7 and Table 3.
   b)   *ht=4, lt=2.5* and *accumulate_volume=1200*
   The results are the same to Fig. 7 and Table 3.

According to the experiments in a) and b), the value of *ht* has few influences on the results while *lt* and *accumulate_volume* remain.

4)   Sum up

The algorithm refers to three parameters: *accumulate_volume, lt* and *ht.* Among them *accumulate_volume* and *lt* have important influences on the experiment results, determines the sensitivity of the algorithm. And the value of *ht* only need to satisfy the condition to make $\mu_4(t)$ resoluble when $C(t)>=lt*c\_mean(t)$.

5.2 The Algorithm with Short-Term Traffic Prediction

5.2.1 The Experiment Results of the Data in Fig. 1

The results of applying the adjusted algorithm with short-term prediction on the data in Fig. 1 are shown in Fig. 7 and Table 8. The parameters here are still *accumulate_volume=1200*, *lt=2.5* and *ht=3.5*.

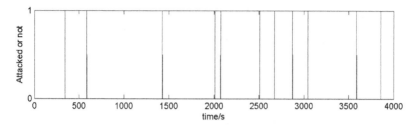

Fig. 7. The detection effects of Fig. 1 with single-step prediction when *accumulate_volume=1200, lt=2.5* and *ht=3.5*

Table 8. The detection effects of Fig. 1 with single-step prediction when *accumulate_volume= 1200, lt=2.5* and *ht=3.5*

Attack	Start Moment (s)	Detected Moment (s)	Detection Delay (s)
Attack A	341	343	2
Attack B	1428	1430	2
Attack C	2009	2011	2
Attack D	2508	2510	2
Attack E	3855	3858	3
-	-	588	-
-	-	2074	-
-	-	2673	-
-	-	2876	-
-	-	3046	-
-	-	3588	-

Compared with the algorithm without prediction, the adjusted algorithm can detect attacks in advance in most situations if the detections are correct, and the detection delays are shortened(see Attacks A,B,C and E). But on account of inevitable prediction errors, false detections occurred sometimes.

The two algorithms have advantages respectively. The one that completely relies on current and former data without any prediction has a higher accuracy, while the one with predictions has a faster response if the attacks are detected correctly. Accuracy and high velocity in detection are conflicting, but we believe that the speed of detecting is more important in DoS/DDoS attacks detecting. In order to obtain a high response speed and avoid additional cost for false alarm as more as possible, we apply both algorithms in every detecting period. An alarm should be generated when either algorithm detects an attack at first, then corresponding processes (such as source orientation [4]) start immediately. If an alarm is from the algorithm without prediction, it is regarded correct, and running corresponding processes continue without any interruption in the following time. On contrast, there are two possibilities if the algorithm with prediction alarms at first. For one thing, the algorithm without prediction alarms in the next period, it is testified that the alarm in the previous period is correct, so corresponding processes continues. For another thing, if there is not any alarm from the algorithm without prediction in the following period, it is testified that the alarm of the previous period is wrong, and corresponding processes should stop.

The detection effects with the combination of the two algorithms are demonstrated in Table 9. It is shown that the delay situations are the same as those in Table 8, but the false alarms are amended.

Table 9. The detection effects of Fig. 1 using the basic algorithm and the combined algorithms when *accumulate_volume=1200*, *lt=2.5* and *ht=3.5*

Attack	Start Moment (s)	Basic Algorithm		Combined Approach	
		Detected Moment (s)	Detection Delay (s)	Detected Moment (s)	Detection Delay (s)
A	341	344	3	343	2
B	1428	1431	3	1430	2
C	2009	2012	2	2011	2
D	2508	2510	2	2510	2
E	3855	3859	4	3858	3

5.2.2   The Analysis on the Traffic Sequence of LLS_DDOS_1.0

LLS_DDOS_1.0 is a data set provided by Lincoln Laboratory, MIT to evaluate DDoS detection [5]. In the final phase of the scenario, the attacker manually launches the "mstream DDOS" to 131.84.1.31 from three servers simultaneously. The "mstream DDOS" consists of many, many connection requests to a variety of ports on the victim. All packets have a spoofed, random source IP address. The traffic is shown in Fig. 8.

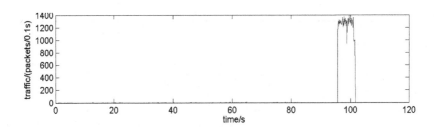

Fig. 8. The traffic data of LLS_DDOS_1.0 phase 5

In this data set, the normal traffic is much less than attack traffic. Table 10 shows the detection results with 0.1s as its detection period.

Table 10. The detection results of Fig. 8 when *accumulate_volume=15000*, *lt=2.5* and *ht=3.5*

Start Moment	95.8s
Detected Moment	95.9s
Detection Delay	0.10s

5.3 Simulating Experiments in NS-2

5.3.1 Simulation Framework

The experiments in this section are simulations in NS-2 [6]. With the architecture concerning syn-flooding attack detecting, source orientating and defense proposed in [4]. The algorithm proposed in this paper works as detecting component in this system. Its topology is shown in Fig. 9:

The nodes in Fig. 9 are classified into two groups, end-host nodes and router nodes. Nodes 5, 15, 16, 17, 18, 19, 21, 22, 23 and 24 are end-host nodes, among which nodes 15 and 17 are attacking nodes, with node 16 as their fake source address during attacking, and nodes 18 and 23 are normal nodes. Node 5 is a protected node (a victim). For other purposes in this simulation, node 5 forwards all the packets it receives to node 20 which is deployed the detection algorithm, so node 20 is the same node as node 5 logically.

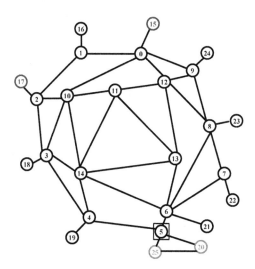

Fig. 9. The topology of NS-2 simulating experiments

5.3.2 Simulation Results

The steps of the experiments are:

- At the 0th second, nodes 15, 17, 18 and 23 start to request normal TCP connections, and the detecting algorithm starts.
- At the 4th second, nodes 15 and 17 launch syn-flooding attacks to node 20 (node 5) by requesting TCP connections with node 16 as their fake source thus to destruct normal TCP connections.
- At the 30th second, the simulation stops.

Table 11 shows detection results with different attack intensity. The average rate of normal connection is 20 packets/s each node and the average rate of attacking is changing. Detection parameters are *accumulate_volume=400*, *lt=2.5* and *ht=3.5*.

Table 11. The two attacking nodes start at 4.0s simultaneously

Average Attacking Rate per Node	Detected Moment	Detection Delay
200 packets/s	4.1s	0.1s
160 packets/s	4.2s	0.2s
100 packets/s	4.2s	0.2s
60 packets/s	4.3s	0.3s

Table 11 shows the sensitivity of the detecting algorithm to different attack intensities, the larger the attacking rate is, the faster the detecting algorithm responses. In Table 12, the two attacking nodes start at different moments, causing the traffic to reach a high level in several time slots rather than at once, and the algorithm can also detect the attacks. So the algorithm shows a valuable performance in DoS/DDoS attack detecting.

Table 12. The two attacking nodes start at different time with the rate 100 packets/s each

Node 15 Start Moment	Node 17 Start Moment	Detected Moment	Detection Delay
4.0s	4.1s	4.3s	0.3s
4.0s	4.2s	4.3s	0.3s
4.0s	4.3s	4.3s	0.3s

6   Conclusion

Through analyzing the time series of the traffic arriving at a host, it is clarified in this paper that the flooding-based DoS/DDoS attacks behaves such features --- traffic burst and remaining of comparative smooth for some time. According to these features, a novel real-time approach to detect such attacks is proposed. The approach contains a membership function to express the degree of how great a current traffic value is. It calculates the global average value and the difference variance based on data obtained in real time, and then judges the occurrence of attacks according to the following ideas: when the traffic is "great", the judging process is triggered; then if the difference variance decreases, or the volume remains "great", an attack alert is generated. In order to shorten the delay of detection, short-term traffic prediction was introduced, and prediction values were used in the detecting process. The feasibility of the algorithms and their sensitivity to parameter values are analyzed experimentally. Although we focus our research on detecting flooding-based DoS/DDoS attacks, the simulation shows that the approach also can deal with DDoS attacks that zombies start without simultaneousness. We will research this in depth in future.

References

[1] Comp. Emergency Response Team, "Results of the Distributed-Systems Intruder Tools Workshop," http://www.cert.org/reports/dsit_workshop-final.html.

[2] Jelena Mirkovic, Janice Martin and Peter Reiher, "A Taxonomy of DDoS Attacks and DDoS Defense Mechanisms", *ACM SIGCOMM Computer Communication Review Volume 34, Issue 2* (April 2004)

[3] YANG Xinyu, ZENG Ming, ZHAO Rui, SHI Yi, "A Novel LMS Method for Real-time Network Traffic Prediction", *Lecture Notes in Computer Science, Springer-Verlag Heidelberg, ISSN: 0302-9743, Volume 3046 / 2004* (April 2004) 127 – 136, *Computational Science and Its Applications - ICCSA 2004: International Conference*(Assisi, Italy, May 14-17, 2004) Proceedings, Part IV

[4] YANG Wen-jing, YANG Xin-yu, SHI Yi, ZENG Ming, ZHENG Shou-qi, "A Novel Algorithm of SYN Flooding Attack Source Orientation & Defense based on Network Traffic and its Description using Petri Network", *Microelectronics & Computer, Vol.22, No.1, 2005*,20-24

[5] http://www.ll.mit.edu/IST/ideval/data/2000/LLS_DDOS_1.0.html

[6] The Network Simulator - ns-2. http://www.isi.edu/ns

Hardware Stack Design: Towards an Effective Defence Against Frame Pointer Overwrite Attacks

Yongsu Park[1], Younho Lee[2], Heeyoul Kim[2], Gil-Joo Lee[1], and Il-Hee Kim[1]

[1] The College of Information and Communications, Hanyang University,
17 Haengdang-dong, Seongdong-gu, Seoul 133-791, Korea
{yongsu, kjlee, ihkim}@hanyang.ac.kr
[2] Division of Computer Science, Department of Electrical Engineering and Computer
Science, Korea Advanced Institute of Science and Technology (KAIST), 373-1
Guseong-Dong, Yuseong-Gu, Daejeon, Korea
{yhlee, hykim}@camars.kaist.ac.kr

Abstract. Currently, a buffer overflow attack is one of the most serious and widely utilized assaults in computer systems. Defense methods against this attack can be classified as three: compiler modification, system software modification, and hardware modification. Among them, most of the cases, hardware modification methods aim at detecting or tolerating alternation of return addresses in the memory stack. However, to the best of our knowledge, the previous methods cannot defend against frame pointer overwrite attacks, where an adversary can control the execution at his/her will by modifying the saved frame pointers in the stack. In this paper, we present a new reliable hardware stack to detect alternation of saved frame pointers as well as return addresses. We show that the proposed method can defend against both frame pointer overwrite attacks and stack smashing attacks.

Keywords: computer security, buffer overflow attack, computer architecture.

1 Introduction

Buffer overflow occurs when a process tries to store more data in a buffer than its maximum capacity, by which an adversary can execute a malicious code or make the process operate in an unintended way [4]. In spite of countless methods designed to cope with buffer overflow vulnerabilities, new attacks are continuously appeared such as format string attacks [8], heap overflow attacks, or multiple free errors. Up till now, buffer overflows are still major cause of exploited vulnerability.

To cope with this problem, numerous researches have been conducted, which can be classified as three ways: compiler modification, system software modification, and hardware modification.

Among them, we focus on modifying the hardware to enhance security and to defend against some types of buffer overflow attacks. Up till now, hardware

H. Yoshiura et al. (Eds.): IWSEC 2006, LNCS 4266, pp. 268–277, 2006.

modification schemes have focused on protecting mainly memory stack contents. Currently, commercial CPUs such as Pentium-4 or Athlon 64 have the NX (No-eXecute) bit [3] (Intel calls it the Execute Disable Bit), by which we can prohibit execution of instructions in the stack. While this helps to defend against some of buffer overflow attacks where the attack code is injected and executed in the stack, it cannot defend against various indirect attacks where most of the cases execution is redirected to system() library function with argment "/bin/sh".

In addition to the NX-bit, recently several hardware modification methods have been devised and developed. They use a specially designed RAS (Return Address Stack) in the CPU to detect modification of the return address in the memory stack [12,7] or they rely on an additional hardware stack in the CPU to detect/evade the modification [10,12].

To the best of our knowledge, all the hardware modification methods (except for the NX bit) focus on protecting only the return address in the stack from alternation. Hence, they are vulnerable to the frame pointer overwrite attack, where an adversary modifies only the saved frame pointer to control the execution (including running a shell).

In this paper, we present a new reliable hardware stack that is located in the CPU to defend against the frame pointer overwrite attack as well as the stack smashing attack. In our scheme the hardware stack stores 3-tuples: (saved frame pointer, return address, stack pointer), by which we can detect the frame pointer overwrite attack and deal with several exceptional cases such as the context switch, setjmp/longjmp problem [10], etc.

To examine feasibility of our method, first a stack smashing attack is given and we show that the proposed scheme can detect it. Then, by slight modification, we change it into the frame pointer overwrite attack. After that, we show that the proposed method can also detect the modified attack.

Our scheme can be viewed as an approach to increase trustworthiness as well as to enhance security of the systems to be protected. The rest of this paper is organized as follows. In Section 2 we describe the stack smashing attack and the frame pointer overwrite attack. In Section 3 we describe the proposed method and in Sections 4 we examine feasibility of our scheme. Finally, we offer some conclusions in Section 5.

2   Stack Smashing Attack and Frame Pointer Overwrite Attack

In this section we briefly explain the stack smashing attack and the frame pointer overwrite attack. Furthermore, we show the relation between them, i.e., with slight modification the stack smashing attack can be easily changed into the frame pointer overwrite attack.

2.1   Brief Description of Stack Smashing Attacks [9]

First, we explain the stack smashing attack [9]. Let us consider the vulnerable code below, which is written in the ANSI C language.

```
#include <stdio.h>
func(char *sm) {
    char buffer[256];
    int i;
    strcpy(buffer, sm);
}

main (int argc, char *argv[]) {
    func(argv[1]);
}
```

Code 1. An example of vulnerable code

Fig. 1 shows the activation record (a. k. a. stack frame) when the function func() is called in the above code. Note that in Fig. 1 the activation record of func() is below that of main() and that the stack grows downward (by successive function calls). On the contrary, the buffer is filled upward (from buffer[0] to buffer[255] by memory copy operations such as strcpy() or memcpy()).

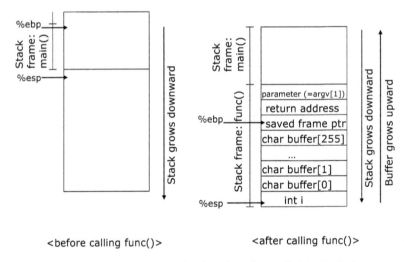

<before calling func()>   <after calling func()>

Fig. 1. Activation records when func() is called in Code 1

We briefly explain how the stack frame of func() is constructed as follows. Initially, the stack pointer register %esp points out the top of the stack and the frame pointer register %ebp indicates the base of the main() stack frame.

First, when the func() is called in the main() function, the parameter (=argv[1]) is pushed in the stack and then the return address is pushed on the stack. After that, at the beginning of func() execution, the frame pointer register %ebp is pushed into the stack (we call this value the *saved frame pointer* hereafter) and the %ebp is changed to point out the address of the saved frame pointer. After the all the local variables (buffer[256] and i) are allocated in the stack, finally, the body code of the func() is executed.

When the execution of func() is finished, immediately before the exit of func(), the %ebp is copied to the %esp and then the saved frame pointer is popped into the %ebp (i.e., %ebp is restored to point out the base of the main() stack frame). Finally, the instruction pointer register %eip has the return address value to resume the execution of the main().

Now assume that the local buffer buffer[] is overflowed during executing str-cpy() in the func() and the return address is modified as the value x. Then at the exit of function func(), the instruction pointer register %eip is changed into x, which means that the code in the address x is executed. By this way, the adversary can control the execution, e.g., he can execute the shell code by inserting it into buffer[] and redirecting into it [6]. Up till now, there have been devised countless variants of stack smashing attacks and all of them have the one common objective, overwriting the return address at their will.

To cope with these attacks several defense methods have been devised [5,4,11,2,1,12,7,10] and most of them focus on protecting the return address or detecting alternation of the return address. For example, they use specially designed RAS (Return Address Stack) in the CPU to detect modification of the return address in the memory stack [12,7] or they rely on an additional hardware stack in the CPU to detect/evade the modification [10,12].

2.2   Frame Pointer Overwrite Attack [6]

In the previous subsection, we showed how the stack smashing attack can be done. With slight modification of that attack scenario, an adversary can evade the defense against the stack smashing attack (such as checking the modification of the return addresses in the stack [12,7,10]). The modification attack overwrites the frame pointer while leaving the return address untouched, from which we call this a frame pointer overwrite attack [6].

Let us consider the vulnerable code, Code 1 in Section 2.1. Recall that Fig. 1 shows the activation record when the function func() is called in Code 1. Recall that in Fig. 1 the activation record of func() is below that of main(). At this time, we explain how this structure is constructed by using the following disassembled code of the above program. In the main() function, command 'pushl %edx' puts the parameter (=argv[1]) in the stack and 'call 0x8048134 <func>' pushes the return address. At the beginning of func(), 'pushl %ebp' saves the frame pointer into the stack. Immediately before the exit of func(), commands 'popl %ebp' restores the frame pointer and command 'ret' returns the execution to the main function. Then, in main(), the commands 'addl $0x04, %esp; movel %ebp, %esp; popl %ebp; ret' are sequentially executed.

Assume that the local buffer buffer[] is overflowed during executing strcpy() in the func() and the saved frame pointer is modified as the value x. Then at the exit of function func(), the frame pointer register %ebp has the value x. After the return to the main function, the commands 'addl $0x04, %esp; movel %ebp, %esp; popl %ebp' increase the value of %esp by 4, move the value of %ebp to %esp, change the value of %ebp. Finally, the command 'ret' changes the instruction pointer %eip into the value that is pointed by the stack pointer %esp ($= x + 4$).

```
0x8048180 <main>: pushl %ebp        <- beginning of the function main()
0x8048181 <main+1>: movel %esp, %ebp
...
0x80481a8 <main+40>: pushl %edx
0x80481a9 <main+41>: call 0x8048134 <func>
0x80481ae <main+46>: addl $0x4, %esp
0x80481b1 <main+49>: movl %ebp, %esp
0x80481b3 <main+51>: popl %ebp
0x80481b4 <main+52>: ret            <- end of the function main()
...
0x8048134 <func>: pushl %ebp        <- beginning of the function func()
0x8048135 <func+1>: movel %esp, %ebp
0x8048137 <func+3>: subl %0x104, %esp
...
0x804817c <func+72>: movl %ebp, %esp
0x804817e <func+74>: popl %ebp
0x804817f <func+75>: ret            <- end of the function func()
```

Code 2. Disassembled instructions of Code 1

If an attacker wants to execute the code having the address y, then he carefully overflows the local buffer buffer[] such that the frame pointer register %ebp has the value $x = y - 4$. Then, at the exit of the function 'main()', the instruction having address y is executed. By using this abnormal behaviour, the attacker can execute the shell code by inserting and redirecting into it [6] or can perform the return-into-libc() attack or the GOT (Global Offset Table) attack, etc.

3   Proposed Method

As mentioned in the abstract, defense methods against buffer overflow attacks can be classified as three: compiler modification, system software modification, and hardware modification. Among them, we believe that hardware modification is more effective than the others because we need not recompile the user program and only slight modification of system softwares is required, i.e., if we use the enhanced CPU that contains the proposed scheme and then slightly patch the system softwares, security of the entire system can be strengthened. (This approach is identical to that of the NX-bit (No-eXecute) bit [3] in Pentium-4 or Athlon 64, which is the most practically and widely used defense method against buffer overflow attacks.)

Unlike hardware modification methods, compiler modification techniques such as StackGuard [5] or PointGuard [4] need recompilation of each application. System software modification methods such as ASLR (Address Space Layout Randomization) provided by the PAX project [11] or Bhatker et al.'s scheme [2] require complex modification of system softwares (operating system kernel, application loader, etc).

Note that our method is the way to extend the facility in the existing CPU architecture while preserving compatibility, not to modify the ISA (Instruction Set Architecture) to break compatibility.

Moreover, we suggest that this hardware enhancement technique can be used to only the privileged processes to minimize the security risk and to reduce the performance degradation. (e.g., for the NX bit major operating systems such as Windows Server 2003 can selectively use it to the privileged/important processes).

In this section we describe the proposed hardware stack. This stack resides in the CPU, has the fixed size, and supports overflow/underflow detection facilities. The stored value is 3-tuple: <saved frame pointer, stack pointer, return address>. Fig. 2 shows the structure of the hardware stack.

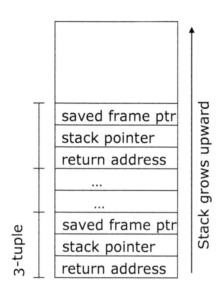

Fig. 2. Hardware stack in the proposed scheme

When the call instruction is executed, a 3-tuple is pushed into the hardware stack and when the ret instruction is executed, the 3-tuple is popped. Detailed description is as follows.

1. **Call Instruction Execution:** First, the return address and the value of stack pointer %esp are stored into the hardware stack. Then, the original call operation is performed: the return address is stored in the memory stack and the instruction pointer %eip is set to the starting address of the callee function. After the call instruction is executed, the CPU observes the fetched instructions until 'pushl %ebp' appears. If so, after this instruction is executed, the hardware stack stores the value of %ebp (= the saved frame pointer) and completes the 3-tuple.

2. **Ret Instruction Execution:** When the CPU fetches 'popl %ebp', it triggers a certain internal status bit, called *check_ebp*. This status bit is turned off when the value of the register %ebp is changed (by instructions addl/movl/incl, etc). In the case of the execution of 'ret', if the check_ebp bit is on, the CPU compares the value of %ebp and the saved frame pointer in the hardware stack. If two values are identical, then the CPU performs the following 2 comparisons: the saved stack pointer in the hardware stack and the value of the register %esp, the return address in the hardware stack and the return address in the memory stack. If they are identical to each other, the CPU executes the ret instruction. Otherwise, it terminates the execution and raises an exception.

3.1   Handling Overflow/Underflow in the Hardware Stack

Since the size of the hardware stack is finite, it can be overflowed if deeply-nested functions are called. If an exception is raised due to overflow, the CPU raises an exception and the operating system should swap the entire content of the hardware stack into the main memory.

Because the swapped memory should be protected under alternation by adversaries, we suggest that it is saved in the PCB (Process Control Block), which cannot be directly accessed by the user process. The swapping procedure can be done by the special CPU instruction or regular load/store instructions by using the memory mapped I/O, just as in [10].

If underflow occurs, the operating system catches the exception and restores the swapped context in the PCB into the hardware stack.

3.2   Handling the Context Switch

When a context switch occurs in the operating system, all status including register values should be saved and restored. In addition to this, the operating system should save the content of the hardware stack for the saved process/thread and restore the saved content for the resumed process/thread. The saving or restoring procedure is already mentioned in Subsection 3.1.

3.3   Setjmp()/Longjmp() Problem

When a C-language source code contains setjmp() or longjmp(), multiple activation records should be popped together, which causes inconsistency between the hardware stack and the memory stack (for further explanation, refer to [10]). We choose [10]'s solution, where longjmp() should be modified to use indirect jump (i.e., we should modify the shared library, libc.so) and in the case of execution of call instruction, the value of the stack pointer is stored in the hardware stack. We omit the detailed the procedure to handle the setjmp()/longjmp(). Refer to [10].

4   Security Analysis

In this section, we show that the proposed scheme can defend against both the stack smashing attack and the frame pointer overwrite attack. Fig. 3 shows the structure of the execution parameter by which an adversary can invoke the stack smashing attack in the code described in Section 2.

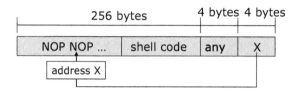

Fig. 3. Parameter for the stack smashing attack

If the execution is done by using the above parameter, during the strcpy() execution in func(), the return address in Fig. 1 is changed to the value X. Hence, at the return of func(), shell code is executed.

However, in the proposed scheme, at the func() call, both the return address and the value of the stack pointer (=%esp) are stored in the hardware stack. After that, the return address in the memory stack is overwritten to X. Finally, at the return of func(), an exception is raised due to inconsistency between the return address in the hardware stack and that in the memory stack.

From now on, consider the frame pointer overwrite attack that was described in Section 2. Fig. 4 shows the structure of the execution parameter by which an adversary can invoke the frame pointer overwrite attack in the code described in Section 2.

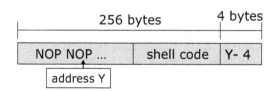

Fig. 4. Parameter for the frame pointer overwrite attack

As explained in Section 2, by using the above parameter, an adversary can overwrite the saved frame pointer as $Y - 4$ and eventually the shell code is executed.

If the above attack is done in the proposed scheme, at the function call of func(), the return address and the value of stack pointer %esp are stored in the hardware stack. Then, call operation is performed (the return address is stored in the memory stack and the instruction pointer is set to the starting address of func()). After the call instruction is executed, the CPU fetches 'pushl %ebp' instruction and the hardware stack stores the value of %ebp. Then, during execution of strcpy(), the saved frame pointer in the memory stack is overwritten to $Y - 4$. At the return of func(), the CPU fetches 'popl %ebp' and sets the check_ebp bit on. Then, CPU fetches 'ret' and the CPU compares the value of %ebp and the saved frame pointer in the hardware stack. Since the two values are different, execution is terminated and an exception is raised.

5   Conclusion

In this paper we have designed a new hardware stack to defend against both the stack smashing attack and the frame pointer overwrite attack by storing 3-tuples: (return address, stack pointer, frame pointer). Moreover, we have dealt with how to handle the problems due to the context switch, stack underflow/overflow, and setjmp()/longjmp(). To examine the feasibility of our method, first a stack smashing attack is given and we show that the proposed scheme can detect it. Then, by slight modification, we change it into the frame pointer overwrite attack and show that the proposed method can also detect the modified attack. Our scheme can be viewed as an approach to increase trustworthiness as well as to enhance security of the systems to be protected.

Acknowledgement

This work was partially supported by Korea Information Security Agency and National Security Research Institute. The content of this work does not necessarily reflect the position or policy of the government.

References

1. Gabiela Barrantes, David H. Ackley, Stephanie Forrest, Trek S. Palmer, Darko Stefanovic, and Dino Dai Zovi. Randomized Instruction Set Emulation to Disrupt Binary Code Injection Attacks. In *10th ACM Conference on Computer and Communication Security*, pages 281–289, October 2003.
2. Sandeep Bhatkar, Daniel C. DuVarney, and R. Sekar. Address Obfuscation: an Efficient Approach to Combat a Broad Range of Memory Error Exploits. In *12th USENIX Security Symposium*, pages 105–120, August 2003.
3. NX bit. from wikipidia, free enclopedia. avaliable at http://en.wikipedia.org/wiki/NX_bit.
4. Crispin Cowan, Steve Beattie, John Johansen, and Perry Wagle. PointGuard: Protecting Pointers From Buffer Overflow Vulnerabilities. In *12th USENIX Security Symposium*, pages 91–104, August 2003.
5. Crispin Cowan, Calton Pu, Dave Maier, Jonathan Walpole, Peat Bakke, and Steve Beattie. StackGuard: Automatic Adaptive Detection and Prevention of Buffer-overflow Attacks. In *7th USENIX Security Symposium*, pages 63–78, January 1998.
6. klog. The Frame Pointer Overwrite, Phrack Magazine, Vol. 9, Issue 5, 1999.

7. R. B. Lee, D. K. Kang, J. P. McGregor, and Z. Shi. Enlisting Hardware Architecture to Thwart Malicious Code Injection. In *International Conference on Security in Pervasive Computing*, 2003.

8. T. Newsharm. Format String Attacks, GUARDENT Technical Report, 2000.

9. Aleph One. Smasing The Stack For Fun And Profit. Phrack 49, File 14 of 16, 1996.

10. H. Ozdoganoglu, T. N. Vijaykumar, and C. A. Jalote et al. SmashGuard: A Hardware Solution to Prevent Security Attacks on the Function Return Address. Technical report, TR-ECE-03-13, Purdue University, School of ECE, 2003.

11. PaX team. The PaX Project. avaliable at http://pageexec.virtualave.net, 2001.

12. J. Xu, Z. Kalbarczyk, S. Partel, and R. K. Iyar. An Architecture Support for Defending Against Buffer Overflow Attacks. In *Workshop on Evaluating and Architecting System Dependability*, 2002.

Modeling of Network Intrusions Based on the Multiple Transition Probability*

Sang-Kyun Noh[1], DongKook Kim[2], Yong-Min Kim[3], and Bong-Nam Noh[2],**

[1] Interdisciplinary Program of Information Security,
Chonnam National University, Korea
guru@lsrc.chonnam.ac.kr
[2] Div. of Electronics Computer Engineering,
Chonnam National University, Korea
{dkim, bbong}@chonnam.ac.kr
[3] Dept. of Electronic Commerce,
Chonnam National University, Korea
ymkim@chonnam.ac.kr

Abstract. In the TCP network environment, all unit transmissions are constructed using sessions. In the session, packets are transmitted sequentially. In this case, the previous and next packets contain causality mutually. Thus, we propose a method that models network transmission information based on transitions of packet states. In addition to the transition model, a probability matrix for the multiple state-transition models of all sessions is represented. The matching of the models is achieved using the maximum log-likelihood ratio. Evaluation of the proposed method for intrusion modeling is conducted by using 1999 DARPA data sets. The method is also compared with Snort-2 which is misuse-based intrusion detection system. In addition, the techniques for advancing proposed method are discussed.

Keywords: Network-based intrusion detection, multiple transition probability, Ergodic model, probability-based modeling, likelihood measure.

1 Introduction

The set of TCP network packets transmitted depending on one activity is called a session, which is the sequential transmission group of a series of packets from connection opening to closing. In the session, all packets include sequential characters. This means that there is causality between a previous packet and the next packet, and this causality is represented as state-transition information. The states of TCP packets are composed of field values of several pieces of header information. In a session, statistical transition information of all packet states can be shown as a frequency matrix.

---

* This research was supported by the MIC(Ministry of Information and Communication), Korea, under the ITRC(Information Technology Research Center) support program supervised by the IITA(Institute of Information Technology Assessment).
** Correspondent author.

H. Yoshiura et al. (Eds.): IWSEC 2006, LNCS 4266, pp. 278–291, 2006.

To combine such frequency matrices for multiple sessions, we propose a probability matrix for multiple state-transition information. In this case, we use the ergodic model [1] are applied using Markov chains of Markov models for multiple (independent) observation sequences. Each state can reach any other state of the model in a single step. We also detect on the model matching method using the maximum log-likelihood ratio [2].

In this paper, experiment of the proposed model is achieved using 1999 DARPA Intrusion Detection Evaluation Data Sets (DARPA99) [7]. We show the possibility of our modeling technique through analysis of detection results. And the effectiveness of our intrusion detection system is compared with Snort-2, which is a packet-based misuse detection system. Moreover, ideas for advancing the effectiveness of the proposed model are introduced.

This paper is structured as follows: In Sect. 2, characteristics of intrusion detection using Markov models are represented. In Sect. 3, the frequency model of state-transition of each packet in a TCP session is proposed. In Sect. 3.1, selected features are introduced. In Sect. 3.2, state information of packets is shown. In Sect. 3.3, state-transition information using a frequency matrix is presented. In Sect. 4, the modeling method of multiple state-transition information is represented. In Sect. 4.1, a model for multiple transition probability is proposed. In Sect. 4.2, the method of model matching is represented. In Sect. 5, the effectiveness of the proposed method is analyzed using several experimental results. Finally, this paper is concluded and future ideas for improvements are discussed in Sect. 6.

2   Related Works

The two main Markov models are the left-to-right model and the ergodic model. In the left-to-right model, the probability of going back to the previous state is set to zero, and therefore the model will always start from a certain state and end in an exiting state. In the ergodic model of every state can be reached from any other state in a finite number of time steps [1].

In [4], Otsuka and Ohya used left-to-right models with three states to model each type of facial expression. The advantage of using this model lies in the fact that it appears natural to model a sequential event with a model that also starts from a fixed starting state and always reaches an end state. It also involves fewer parameters, and therefore is easier to train. However, it reduces the degrees of freedom the model in an attempt to account for the observation sequence. There has been no study to indicate that the facial expression sequence is indeed modeled well by the left-to-right model. On the other hand, using the ergodic model allows more freedom for the model to account for the observation sequences, and in fact, for an infinite amount of training data it can be shown that the ergodic model will reduce to the left-to-right model, if that is indeed the true model. In this work both types of models were tested with various numbers of states in an attempt to study the best structure for modeling facial expressions.

[5] has proposed an anomaly-based IDS using the privilege transition flows data and combining multiple hidden Markov models. This method can open a new way of utilizing the computation-intensive anomaly detection technique in the real world, based on behavioral constraints imposed by security policies and on models of typical behavior of users. However, this method is not suitable for network data.

Estevez-Tapiador, et al. [8] proposed anomaly detection methodology applied to TCP and disposed in two steps. First, a quantization of the TCP header space is accomplished, so that a unique symbol is associated with each TCP segment, and then represented by a sequence of symbols. The second step is the modeling of these sequences by means of a Markov chain. The model is built using the normal usage of the protocol, so that deviations from the behavior provided by the model are detected. However, this approach simply models using the flags of TCP header without information about transmission directions of the packets and so on. It is difficult to clearly define the characteristics of a mutual communication. Moreover, the model is not complete because the probabilities of all transitions are not computed.

3   State-Transition Information of Packets in a TCP Session

A session in the TCP network environment is formed by packets of the same socket pair[1], and these packets which are included in the session, have correlated sequences such as the stream of network traffic. It is assumed that previous packet and next packet (in other words, current packet or observed packet), are closely connected in a session.

3.1   Feature Selection

To indicate the property of each TCP packet, we extract important features from the packet header fields. [6] described the causality of protocol measures for network-based intrusion detection, using DARPA99. The causality analysis system has some fault to extract specific measures depending on a change of a network environment; nevertheless, we could have gained hints about general characteristic measures in a TCP/IP network.

IP-flag offers the fragmentation information of packets. *TCP-flag* also can reveal the role information of packets. In this case, *Direction* of the transmission is important.

3.2   State of a Packet

We select the state of each packet from the protocol header fields. The state information is presented in Table 1.

---

[1] The socket pair is a way to uniquely specify a connection in a TCP/IP network, i.e., source IP address, source port, destination IP address, and destination port.

Table 1. Bits-based state information for each network packet. The state has a value of 9-bits composed of *IP-flag*, *TCP-flag*, and *Direction*. Thus, it can represent 512 (2^9) kinds of states.

		State Information by 9-bits							
Composition	Direc-tion	TCP-flag						IP-flag	
sub-States	DIR	URG	ACK	PSH	RST	SYN	FIN	DF	MF
sub-Values	256	128	64	32	16	8	4	2	1

IP-flag (*flag* field of IP protocol header) consists of a total of 3-bits, i.e., *R* (Reserved), *DF* (Don't Fragment), and *MF* (More Fragments). Only a space of 2-bits is allocated to *IP-flag* sub-state information, because the *R* bit is not used. *TCP-flag* (*flag* field of TCP protocol header) consists of a total of 6-bits, i.e., *URG* (Urgent Pointer field significant), *ACK* (Acknowledgment field significant), *PSH* (Push Function), *RST* (Reset the connection), *SYN* (Synchronize sequence numbers), and *FIN* (No more data from sender). If it is the packet transmitted from client to server, the *Direction* bit is set, otherwise the bit is zero.

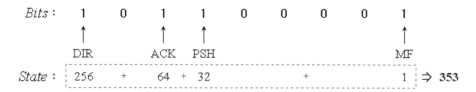

Fig. 1. Operation example for the state of a network packet. A packet transmitted from client to server has *TCP-flag* of *ACK|PSH* and *IP-flag* of *MF*. And the state value is 353.

The state of a packet transmitted from client to server, has *TCP-flag* of *ACK|PSH* and *IP-flag* of *MF* is gained as shown in Fig. 1. The bits-based state of the packet is $101100001_{(2)}$, and thus the state value becomes $353_{(10)}$. These states can be represented as 512 (2^9) kinds of states in $0 \leq state \leq 511$.

3.3 State-Transition Information

A state-transition matrix is generated based on state information. We save the transition information of an observed state that is changed from a previous state in a session. The matrix is composed of previous-states row and observed-states column. The matrix has information of the statistical frequencies of each state-transition. Fig. 2 represents a frequency matrix for the state-transition information of the following:

$$(264 \rightarrow 72 \rightarrow 322 \rightarrow 354 \rightarrow 66 \rightarrow 354 \rightarrow 66 \rightarrow 324 \rightarrow 66 \rightarrow 68 \rightarrow 322)$$

which is transition information of states the packets have in a session. In this way, a session has a frequency matrix for its state-transition information. We can attempt statistical learning based on state-transition information of all the training sessions.

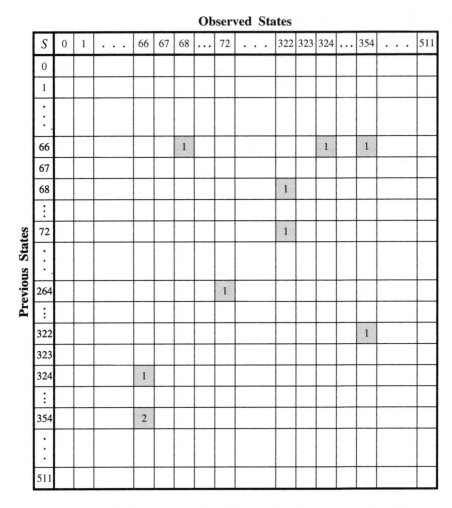

Fig. 2. Frequency matrix for state-transition. The matrix represents the statistical frequency numbers of state-transition information of all packets in a session.

4   Modeling for the Multiple State-Transition Information

The method of using a frequency matrix has the defect that it must maintain the matrix for all sessions. We thus describe a technique that generates only a single state-transition matrix for all training sessions, and is based on Markov models theory.

Markov models contain each state and the associated transition probability. We propose a specific model for state-transition on the basis of the ergodic model shown in Fig. 3. The model contains statistical causalities between states of sequential packets in a session.

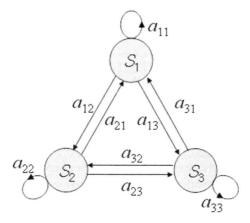

Fig. 3. Ergodic model of Markov chains

4.1 Multiple State-Transition Probability Model

The transition probability from previous state p to observed state o is defined as the following equation:

$$a_{po} = \Pr(S_i = o \mid S_{i-1} = p), \quad \forall p,o : a_{po} \geq 0 \text{ and } \forall p : \sum_{o=1}^{N} a_{po} = 1 \qquad (1)$$

where N is total number of possible states. And the probability of the initial state π is defined as the following:

$$\pi_p = \Pr(S_1 = p), \quad \sum_{p=1}^{N} \pi_p = 1 \qquad (2)$$

On the other hand, the transition probability is calculated by frequency, as the following:

$$a_{S_{i-1}S_i} = \Pr(S_i \mid S_{i-1}) = \frac{\mathrm{Fr}(S_i \mid S_{i-1})}{\sum_{j=1}^{N} \mathrm{Fr}(S_j \mid S_{i-1})}, \quad \forall i : i \geq 2 \qquad (3)$$

where $\sum_{j=1}^{N}\mathrm{Fr}(S_j|S_{i-1})$ is total frequency of all observed states about the previous state. This is proposed in order to indicate the relationship with the previous states. If it is divided by total frequency of all previous states, it will have a relationship with the observed state, of all previous states. However, the operation leads to results of $\Pr(S_{i-1}|S_i)$ against transition probability of equation (1).

The probability of sequence $S = \{S_1, S_2, ..., S_T\}$ can be defined by Markov properties as the follows:

$$Pr(S) = Pr(S_1, S_2,..., S_T) = Pr(S_1) Pr(S_2 \mid S_1)...Pr(S_T \mid S_{T-1}) \tag{4}$$

In other words, we have:

$$Pr(S) = \prod_{i=1}^{T} Pr(S_i) = Pr(S_1) \prod_{i=2}^{T} Pr(S_i \mid S_{i-1}) = \pi_{S_1} \prod_{i=2}^{T} a_{S_{i-1}S_i} \tag{5}$$

The probability defined in equation (5) is the likelihood it can be used as the criterion for recognizing models. Here, the probability of initial state π is ignored, because the start of TCP connections is almost a transmission of SYN packet that is the first step for 3-way handshake. The first step is not important. However, we must take precautions because thereafter repeated transmissions of the SYN packet might be a *DoS* attack, such as SYN flooding.

Therefore, the likelihood (L) can be defined by the following equation:

$$L = \prod_{i=2}^{T} a_{S_{i-1}S_i} \tag{6}$$

However, the likelihood may result in an underflow by multiplications of the probabilities. Thus, ultimately, log-likelihood (LL) is specified as:

$$LL = \log(L) = \sum_{i=2}^{T} \log(a_{S_{i-1}S_i}) \tag{7}$$

The log-likelihood is the sum of the transition log-probabilities of states. This is our method for model matching, and the model is built for multiple state-transition information as the probability matrix. Fig. 4 presents an example for building the probability matrix. In the example, the three training sessions have four sub-states, i.e., 0, 1, 2, and 3. The trained sessions are as follows:

- Session #1 = {2,2,2,3,3,1}   : $2 \rightarrow 2 \rightarrow 2 \rightarrow 3 \rightarrow 3 \rightarrow 1$
- Session #2 = {2,2,2,3,3,0,1} : $2 \rightarrow 2 \rightarrow 2 \rightarrow 3 \rightarrow 3 \rightarrow 0 \rightarrow 1$
- Session #3 = {3,3,2,0,1}   : $3 \rightarrow 3 \rightarrow 2 \rightarrow 0 \rightarrow 1$

If a frequency is zero, we give a minimum value for including all cases of the state-transition among the proposed model. The minimum frequency (Fr_{min}) value must be a low number such as 0.001.

As an additional example, the log-likelihood between an arbitrary session {2,2,3,0,1} with the probability matrix of Fig. 4, is calculated by the following:

$$LL = \log(a_{22}) + \log(a_{23}) + \log(a_{30}) + \log(a_{01})$$

$$= \log \frac{4}{7.001} + \log \frac{2}{7.001} + \log \frac{1}{6} + \log \frac{2}{2.003}$$

$$= -1.566$$

This demonstrates that the greater the log-likelihood, the greater the similarity.

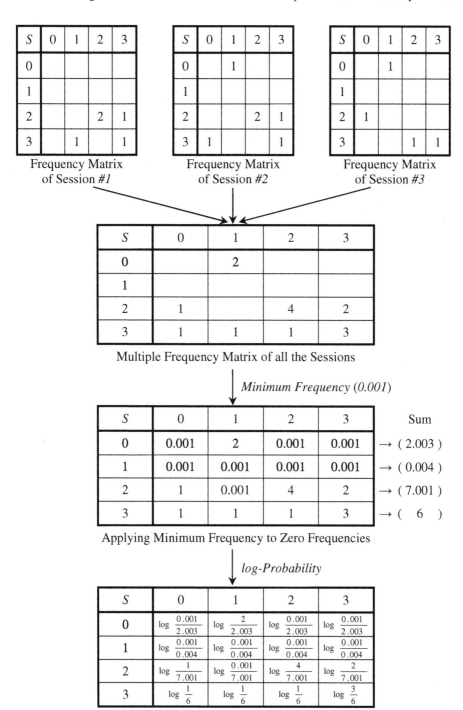

Fig. 4. Example of probability matrix for multiple state-transition of sessions *#1*, *#2*, and *#3*

4.2 Matching for the Detection

We represent a method for detecting intrusions using model matching. We ultimately calculate a ratio with normal model, for determining the attacks. The log-likelihood ratio (*LLR*) is defined as:

$$LLR = \log(\frac{L(M)}{L(N)}) = LL(M) - LL(N), \quad M \in \{A_1, A_2, ..., A_K, A, N\} \tag{8}$$

where will also be referred to as "normalized scaled log-likelihood". The usual normalized likelihood is typically used to obtain posterior estimates from likelihoods (as often used, e.g., to estimate confidence measures) [3]. The log-likelihood ratio is defined as the ratio of log-likelihood with the trained models M, $LL(M)$, and log-likelihood with normal model N, $LL(N)$. A is an integrated model of all trained attacks $\{A_1, A_2, ..., A_K\}$.

In this paper, we propose the intrusion detection system (Fig. 5) based on the method of the maximum log-likelihood ratio (*MLLR*). The multiple state-transition probability models (i.e., matrices) of the three kind of learning sets are built, these are: each attack, all attacks, and normal sessions. And then we detect trough the model matching. The input data are matched by the model with the greatest likelihood. In this case, data matched by model of all attacks can be classified as unknown attacks, because these are not included in each of the trained attacks or normal data.

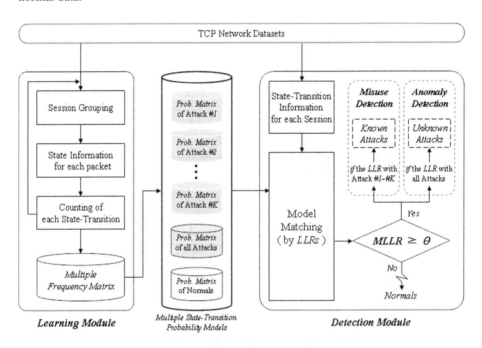

Fig. 5. The overview of the proposed intrusion detection system

The decision process of the detection module is shown above. It is detected when MLLR is bigger than zero. This is achieved as follows.

$$MLLR = \max(LLR), \quad MLLR \geq 0 \tag{9}$$

If *MLLR* is zero, the matched target is a normal session, because *LLR* computed by matching with the trained normal model is zero always. The model matching process is described in Fig. 6.

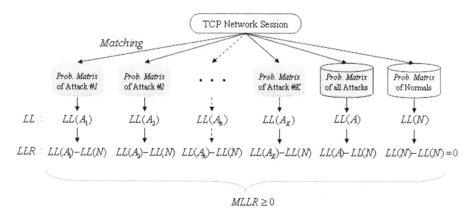

Fig. 6. The process of model matching. Normalized scaled *MLLR* has range bigger than or equal to zero.

In other words, the input data are determined as normal if *MLLR* = 0, otherwise, these can be detected in the case of *MLLR* > 0. In order to apply the threshold concept, it is detected when *MLLR* is bigger than or equal to θ ($\theta > 0$).

5   Experimental Results

We have used the DARPA99 data sets for evaluation of the proposed model. This includes old data sets, but the trust of this data for intrusion detection can still be beneficial. It is sufficient to guess the possibility of the proposed modeling technique.

Attacks from week2 data sets (Table 2) and normal data sets of week1 were used for training in the preprocessing stage of the learning module. Attacks of week4 data sets (Table 3) were also used for testing in the detection module. The data consists of three attack classes, which are Denial-of-Service (*DoS*), *Probes*, and Remote-to-Local (*R2L*). And sessions of TCP protocol were extracted from traffic of the data sets. In the training data sets, attack sessions are not sufficient except for *mailbomb* and *neptune* attacks. To gain more correct models of attacks, more training data is required.

The testing data sets include unknown attacks. Generally, the propensities of attacks of the *DoS* class are similar with one other, and *Probes* is also the same. We can see the possibility of worm detection from their unknown detection ability,

Table 2. Training data sets of week2 attacks

Attack Class	Attack Name	Number of Sessions
DoS	back	80
	crashiis	4
	land	2
	mailbomb	1000
	neptune	20480
Probes	NTinfoscan	14
	portsweep	33
	satan	55
R2L	ftpwrite	6
	httptunnel	4
	phf	2

Table 3. Testing data sets of week4 attacks. These sets also include unknown attacks.

Attack Class	Attack Name	Number of Sessions
DoS	crashiis	2
	dosnuke	1
	land	1
	mailbomb	1366
	sshprocesstable	501
Probes	NTinfoscan	15
	portsweep	26
	satan	16
R2L	ftpwrite	3
	guest	18
	httptunnel	10
	imap	1
	named	6
	ncftp	27
	phf	2
	xlock	4
	xsnoop	2

because the behaviors of worm attacks are similar to them. In addition, the DSI (deep stream inspection) method will be useful in detecting such spread attacks.

We have compared the detection rates and the false-positive error rates for verifying the trained models in the Receiver Operating Characteristic (ROC) curve as shown in Fig. 7. The results of the several attacks (mainly, *mailbomb* and *satan*) were not available. They are attacks of the *DoS* and the *Probes* class. We can assume that the reason for this is due to training data sets not containing sufficient data.

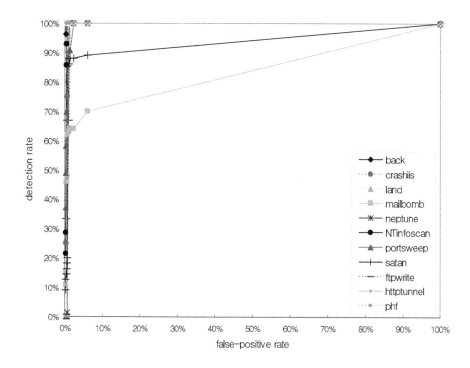

Fig. 7. ROC for each of all training data sets

For the probability matrix, in all experiments, the minimum frequency of (Fr_{min} = 0.001), is used.

Three modeling modes for all the trained attacks were used in the experiment. First, we have built models for each attack. Second, we have built three attack models for each class (*DoS*, *Probes*, *R2L*). Third, we have built one integrated model for all attacks.

Such as Table 4, the first modeling method reveals the best results, and the detector is more efficient than Snort-2. The false-positive rate was given equally. It is possible to make improvements by analyzing differences in the attacks and the normal models. Details of the detection results are described in Table 5. The proposed detection system shows better effectiveness in *DoS* and *Probes* attacks. These attacks are difficult to be detected in Snort-2, the typical packet-based IDS.

Table 4. The result of detections in the testing data sets. These include both known and unknown attacks.

	Snort-2	Multiple Transition Probability Model		
		for each Attack	for each Class	for all Attacks
Detection rate	65 %	84 %	61 %	30 %
False-Positive rate	0.5 %	0.5 %	0.5 %	0.5 %

Table 5. Details of the detection results

Attack		Snort-2	Multiple Transition Probability Model		
			for each Attack	for each Class	for all Attacks
DoS	crashiis	100 %	100 %	100 %	0 %
	dosnuke	0 %	100 %	100 %	100 %
	land	100 %	100 %	100 %	0 %
	mailbomb	0 %	62 %	48 %	48 %
	sshprocesstable	0 %	100 %	100 %	0 %
Probes	NTinfoscan	100 %	100 %	100 %	26 %
	portsweep	33 %	100 %	100 %	100 %
	satan	100 %	81 %	31 %	31 %
R2L	ftpwrite	100 %	100 %	33 %	0 %
	guest	0 %	100 %	100 %	77 %
	httptunnel	0 %	80 %	80 %	0 %
	imap	100 %	100 %	0 %	0 %
	named	67 %	50 %	17 %	17 %
	ncftp	100 %	33 %	25 %	11 %
	phf	100 %	100 %	0 %	0 %
	xlock	100 %	20 %	0 %	0 %
	xsnoop	100 %	100 %	100 %	100 %
experimental Threshold			2.0	4.5	2.5

6   Conclusions and Future Works

In this paper, we proposed a modeling technique of network intrusions based on the probability matrix for multiple state-transition information. The states of TCP packets are composed of field values of protocol header information, and in a session, statistical transition information of all packet states can be shown as a frequency matrix. To combine such frequency matrices for multiple sessions, the ergodic model was used for Markov chains. We also detected to be based on the model matching method using the maximum log-likelihood ratio.

We demonstrated the possibility of our modeling technique through analysis of detection results of DARPA99 data sets. The model had better effectiveness in the detection of *DoS* and *Probes* attacks. It is assumed that the proposed technique is also useful in detection of worm spread. On the other hand, the detection rate still remained as a task that must be improved.

In order to gain better effectiveness, it is necessary to extract features containing a lot of differences in attack and normal models. In this case, the distance between distributed features is computed. Moreover, in order to advance the performance of model matching, methods that detect data before the complete session is constructed are required. It can be implemented by detecting the beginning of sequential transition.

References

1. Sheldon M. Ross, *Introduction to Probability Models*, Academic Press, 8th Edition, 2002.
2. Carl W. Helstrom, *Statistical Theory of Signal Detection*, London: Pergamon Press, 2nd Edition, 1968.
3. A. F. Shchervinin, "Conditional normalized likelihood estimators of parameters of the normal distribution," Measurement Techniques, Springer New York, 1992.
4. T. Otsuka and J. Ohya. "Recognizing multiple persons' facial expressions using HMM based on automatic extraction of significant frames from image sequences," In Proc. Int. Conf. on Image Processing (ICIP'97), pages 546–549, Santa Barbara, CA, USA, October 1997.
5. S-B Cho and S-J Han, "Two Sophisticated Techniques to Improve HMM-Based Intrusion Detection Systems," Recent Advances in Intrusion Detection (RAID'03), Lecture Notes in Computer Science, Pittsburgh, USA, September 2003.
6. I-A Cheong, Y-M Kim, M-S Kim, and B-N Noh, "The Causality Analysis of Protocol Measures for Detection of Attacks based on Network," The Intl. Conf. on Information Networking, Proc. Vol. III, February 2004.
7. Lincoln Laboratory, MIT, DARPA Intrusion Detection Evaluation Data Sets, http://www.ll.mit.edu/IST/ideval/data/data_index.html.
8. Juan M. Estevez-Tapiador, Pedro Garcia-Teodoro, and Jesus E. Diaz-Verdejo, "Stochastic Protocol Modeling for Anomaly Based Network Intrusion Detection," The First IEEE International Workshop on Information Assurance (IWIA'03), Darmstadt, Germany, March 2003.

Chosen Ciphertext Security from Identity-Based Encryption Without *Strong* Condition

Chik How Tan

NISlab, Department of Computer Science and Media Technology
Gjøvik University College, Norway
chik.tan@hig.no

Abstract. Recently, Canetti et al [11] gave a generic construction (called CHK construction) of public key encryption (PKE) from a selective identity-based encryption scheme combined with a strong one-time signature scheme. Later, few schemes were proposed to improve the efficiency of CHK construction [11], for example, Boneh-Katz scheme [8] replaced a strong one-time signature with a message authentication code and Boyen-Mei-Waters scheme [9] was constructed directly from Waters' IBE scheme. But, both constructions have either trade-off the publicly verifiable property or security against adaptive chosen-ciphertext attack. We ask a question whether it is possible to construct an efficient and publicly verifiable PKE scheme from a selective IBE scheme with a weak one-time signature scheme. In this paper, we provide an affirmative answer and construct a public key encryption scheme which preserves the publicly verifiable property and is secure against adaptive chosen-ciphertext attack. The construction of the proposed scheme is based on Boneh-Boyen identity-based encryption (IBE) scheme [5] and a weak one-time signature scheme (using Waters' signature scheme [24]) built within Boneh-Boyen IBE scheme. In this construction, one-time signature scheme is not required to be strongly existential unforgeable as Waters' signature scheme is not a strongly existential unforgeability. We also show that the proposed scheme is "almost" as efficient as the original Boneh-Boyen IBE scheme.

Keywords: Cryptography, public key encryption, bilinear map.

1 Introduction

After Rackoff and Simon [22] introduced the security notion for encryption scheme against adaptive chosen ciphertext attack (CCA2) in 1991, this security notion was widely accepted to provide the right level of security for public key encryption (PKE) scheme, which is also referred to IND-CCA2 secure scheme. The first provably secure public key encryption schemes against adaptive chosen ciphertext attack under the standard assumptions in the standard model was proposed by Rackoff and Simon [22]. But the scheme was impractical. The first practical and provably secure PKE scheme against CCA2 under the standard assumption in the standard model was proposed by Cramer and Shoup [12] in

H. Yoshiura et al. (Eds.): IWSEC 2006, LNCS 4266, pp. 292–307, 2006.

1998. Their scheme is based on the hardness of decisional Diffie-Hellman problem. Cramer and Shoup [13] further generalized and extended [12] to obtain a new and practical encryption schemes that are secure against CCA2 under two different standard assumptions, that is, Paillier's decision composite residuosity assumption and the classical quadratic residuosity assumption. These schemes [13] are provably secure against CCA2 in the standard model. Since then, many attempts were made to construct new public key encryption scheme based on different assumptions in the standard model.

Related Works and Our Contributions

Recently, Canetti, Halevi and Katz [11] gave a generic construction of an IND-CCA2 secure public key encryption scheme (PKE) from a secure selective identity based encryption scheme (IND-sID-CPA IBE) against chosen-plaintext attack. In their construction, they used a strong one-time signature scheme to convert a CPA secure scheme into a IND-CCA2 secure scheme. As mentioned in [21], Canetti-Halevi-Katz construction is relatively efficient as Cramer-Shoup scheme [14] if the underlining one-time signature scheme is efficient and Boneh-Boyen identity-based encryption scheme (BB-IBE) [5][1] is used in the construction. The main advantage of Canetti-Halevi-Katz PKE construction over Cramer-Shoup scheme [12] is that the validity of a ciphertext can be verified publicly; while Cramer-Shoup scheme could only be verified with a private key. Since then, few attempts were made to construct an efficient PKE scheme based on a selective IBE scheme. In 2005, Boneh and Katz [8] improved the Canetti-Halevi-Katz construction by replacing a one-time signature with a message authentication code; however Boneh-Katz construction is no longer publicly verifiable. Later, Boyen, Mei and Waters [9] constructed a secure PKE which is only secure against direct chosen ciphertext in the standard model and not adaptive chosen ciphertext attack. Their construction is based on Waters' IBE scheme [24]. Hence, both constructions have either trade-off the publicly verifiable property or security against adaptive chosen-ciphertext attack. We ask a question whether it is possible to construct an efficient and publicly verifiable PKE scheme from a selective IBE scheme with a weak one-time signature scheme. In this paper, we provide an affirmative answer and construct a public key encryption scheme which preserves the publicly verifiable property and is secure against adaptive chosen-ciphertext attack. The construction of the proposed scheme is based on Boneh-Boyen identity-based encryption (IBE) scheme [5] and a weak one-time signature scheme (using Waters' signature scheme [24]) built within Boneh-Boyen IBE scheme. In this construction, one-time signature scheme is not required to be strongly existential unforgeable as Waters' signature scheme is not a strongly existential unforgeability. We also showed that the proposed scheme is secure against adaptive chosen ciphertext attack and it is "almost" as efficient as original Boneh-Boyen IBE scheme.

---

[1] The identity-based encryption scheme defined in [5] is a simplified version of [2] without admissible hash function and is different from [3] which is based on decision q-BDHI assumption.

Organization of Paper

The paper is organised as follows: In Section 2, we briefly describe bilinear maps and its properties; and bilinear Diffie-Hellman assumptions. A definition of a strong/weak one-time signature scheme and a secure PKE against adaptive chosen ciphertext attacks are also given in Section 2. In Section 3, we construct a public key encryption scheme with a weak one-time signature scheme; the construction is based on the Boneh-Boyen identity-based encryption (IBE) scheme and Waters' signature scheme. Section 4 gives a detailed proof of the proposed scheme which is secure against CCA2 under the hardness of decisional bilinear Diffie-Hellman assumption (DBDH) in the standard model. In Section 5, the computational complexity of the proposed scheme is compared with other schemes which are based on Canetti-Halevi-Katz construction. We showed that the proposed scheme is "almost" as efficient as Boneh-Boyen IBE scheme.

2   Preliminaries

2.1   Bilinear Maps and Assumptions

Let G_1 and G_2 be cyclic groups of prime order p and g be a generator of G_1. Let e be an admissible bilinear map from $G_1 \times G_1$ to G_2 satisfying the following:

a. Bilinear: for all $u, v \in G_1$ and integers a, b, then $e(u^a, v^b) = e(u, v)^{ab}$.

b. Non-degenerate: $e(g, g) \neq 1$.

c. Computability: $\forall u, v \in G_1$, $e(u, v)$ is efficiently computable.

Definition 1. (Bilinear Diffie-Hellman Problem (BDH)). *Given a quadruple* $(g, g^a, g^b, g^c) \in G_1^4$ *where* $a, b, c \in Z_p$, *output* $e(g, g)^{abc}$.

Definition 2. (Decisional Bilinear Diffie-Hellman Problem (DBDH)). *Given a 5-tuple* $(g, g^a, g^b, g^c, T) \in G_1^4 \times G_2$ *where* $a, b, c \in Z_p$, *decide* $T = e(g, g)^{abc}$. *We say that an algorithm has an advantage* ϵ *in solving DBDH if*

$$\left| \Pr[\mathcal{A}(g, g^a, g^b, g^c, e(g, g)^{abc}) = 1] - \Pr[\mathcal{A}(g, g^a, g^b, g^c, Z) = 1] \right| \geq \epsilon,$$

where the probability is over the random choice of $a, b, c \in Z_p$, *the random choice of* $Z \in G_2$.

Definition 3. (DBDH Assumption). *We say that* (t, ϵ)-*DBDH assumption holds if no* t-*polynomial time algorithm has an advantage of at least* ϵ *in solving the DBDH problem.*

Now, we give a definition of a collision resistant hash function and a target collision resistant hash function as follows.

Definition 4. (Collision Resistance). *Let $\bar{w}$ and $\bar{n}$ be two positive integers. We say that a family of hash function $\mathcal{H} = \{H_k : \{0,1\}^{\bar{w}} \to \{0,1\}^{\bar{n}}\}_{k \in K}$ is (t, ϵ_H)-collision resistance hash function if the probability of any t-polynomial time algorithm $\mathcal{A}$ is*

$$\Pr[\, H_k(x) = H_k(y) \text{ and } y \neq x \;:\; k \leftarrow K;\; x,\, y \leftarrow \mathcal{A}(H_k)\,] < \epsilon_H.$$

Definition 5. (Target Collision Resistance). *Let $\bar{w}$ and $\bar{n}$ be two positive integers. We say that a family of hash function $\mathcal{H} = \{H_k : \{0,1\}^{\bar{w}} \to \{0,1\}^{\bar{n}}\}_{k \in K}$ is (t, ϵ_H)-target collision resistance hash function if the probability of any t-polynomial time algorithm $\mathcal{A}$ is*

$$\Pr[\, H_k(x) = H_k(y) \text{ and } y \neq x \;:\; \text{given } x \in \{0,1\}^{\bar{w}},\, k \leftarrow K;\, y \leftarrow \mathcal{A}(k)\,] < \epsilon_H.$$

2.2   Signatures

A digital signature scheme $(\mathcal{K}, \mathcal{S}, \mathcal{V})$ involves three algorithms, that is, key generation $\mathcal{K}$, signature generation $\mathcal{S}$ and signature verification $\mathcal{V}$. A digital signature scheme is said to be secure if it is existentially unforgeable under a chosen message attack, and was first defined in [16]. This definition normally refers to a weak existential unforgeable. In some applications, such as, encrypt-then-sign scheme [1] and CHK construction [11], a strong notion of signature scheme is required, which is called strong existential unforgeability. Strong existential unforgeability means that an adversary is unable to produce a new signature of an old message which was signed before. The formal definition of a weak and a strong existential unforgeability are given below:

Definition 6. *A digital signature scheme $(\mathcal{K}, \mathcal{S}, \mathcal{V})$ is (t, q_s, ϵ)-weak existentially unforgeable secure against adaptive chosen-message attacks if no forger $\mathcal{F}$ outputs a valid forgery with probability of at least ϵ after at most q_s signatures queries and t processing time, where a forger $\mathcal{F}$'s probability is defined as*

$$\Pr \left[\begin{array}{l} (pk, sk) \leftarrow \mathcal{K}(1^l); \\ \text{for } i = 1, \cdots, q_s; \\ m_i \leftarrow \mathcal{F}(pk, m_1, \sigma_1, \cdots, m_{i-1}, \sigma_{i-1}),\ \sigma_i \leftarrow \mathcal{S}(sk, m_i); \\ (m, \sigma) \leftarrow \mathcal{F}(pk, m_1, \sigma_1, \cdots, m_{q_s}, \sigma_{q_s}), \\ m \neq m_i \text{ for all } i \in \{1, \cdots, q_s\} \text{ and } \mathcal{V}(pk, m, \sigma) = \text{accept.} \end{array} \right].$$

Definition 7. *A digital signature scheme $(\mathcal{K}, \mathcal{S}, \mathcal{V})$ is (t, q_s, ϵ)-strong existentially unforgeable secure against adaptive chosen-message attacks if no forger $\mathcal{F}$ outputs a valid forgery with probability of at least ϵ after at most q_s signatures queries and t processing time, where a forger $\mathcal{F}$'s probability is defined as*

$$\Pr \left[\begin{array}{l} (pk, sk) \leftarrow \mathcal{K}(1^l); \\ \text{for } i = 1, \cdots, q_s; \\ m_i \leftarrow \mathcal{F}(pk, m_1, \sigma_1, \cdots, m_{i-1}, \sigma_{i-1}),\ \sigma_i \leftarrow \mathcal{S}(sk, m_i); \\ (m, \sigma) \leftarrow \mathcal{F}(pk, m_1, \sigma_1, \cdots, m_{q_s}, \sigma_{q_s}), \\ (m, \sigma) \neq (m_i, \sigma_i) \text{ for all } i \in \{1, \cdots, q_s\} \text{ and } \mathcal{V}(pk, m, \sigma) = \text{accept.} \end{array} \right].$$

It is noted that $(m, \sigma) \neq (m_i, \sigma_i)$ means that it can be $m = m_j$ and $\sigma \neq \sigma_j$ for some j.

One-time signature is referred to the signing key which is only used once. This means that a signature produced each time uses a different signing key. We say that a one-time signature scheme is weak/strong existential unforgeability secure is same as above definitions except that it is only allow to query once in the above definitions.

2.3   Secure Encryption

A public key encryption scheme PE= $(\mathcal{K}, \mathcal{E}, \mathcal{D})$ consists of three algorithms. The key generation algorithm $\mathcal{K}$ generates a pair $(pk, sk) \leftarrow \mathcal{K}$, where pk is a public key and sk is a private key. The encryption algorithm $\mathcal{E}$ takes a public key pk and a plaintext m, then returns a ciphertext $c \leftarrow \mathcal{E}(pk, m)$. The decryption algorithm $\mathcal{D}$ takes a private key sk and a ciphertext c, then returns $m = \mathcal{D}(sk, c)$ or reject.

Definition 8. (Adaptive Chosen Ciphertext Attack (CCA2)) *Let* PE $=$ $(\mathcal{K}, \mathcal{E}, \mathcal{D})$ *be a public key encryption. Let $\mathcal{A}$ be an attacker modeled as a probabilistic Turning machine. Consider the following game played by a challenger $\mathcal{C}$ and an adversary $\mathcal{A}$.*

Set Up. *$\mathcal{C}$ takes a security parameter and runs the key generation algorithm to obtain a public key pk and private key sk. It gives pk to $\mathcal{A}$ and keeps sk secret.*

Phase 1. *In this phase, $\mathcal{A}$ adaptively makes a decryption queries on a ciphertext C. The challenger $\mathcal{C}$ responds with $\mathcal{D}(sk, C)$ or reject.*

Challenge. *$\mathcal{A}$ outputs two equal length plaintexts (m_0, m_1). The challenger $\mathcal{C}$ picks a random $b \in \{0, 1\}$, computes a target ciphertext $C^* = \mathcal{E}(pk, m_b)$ and gives it to $\mathcal{A}$.*

Phase 2. *The adversary $\mathcal{A}$ continues to make decryption queries on a ciphertext C as in* **Phase 1** *except $C \neq C^*$. The challenger $\mathcal{C}$ responds with $\mathcal{D}(sk, C)$ or reject.*

Guess. *$\mathcal{A}$ outputs a bit $b' \in \{0, 1\}$. It wins if $b' = b$.*

The advantage of an adversary $\mathcal{A}$ of the above game is defined as

$$\mathbf{Adv}_{\mathrm{PE}}^{\mathrm{IND-CCA2}}(\mathcal{A}) = |\Pr[b' = b] - 1/2|.$$

An encryption scheme is said to be secure against adaptive chosen ciphertext attack, if no polynomial time bounded adversary has non-negligible advantage in the game described above.

Definition 9. *A public key encryption scheme* PE $= (\mathcal{K}, \mathcal{E}, \mathcal{D})$ *is said to be (t, q_d, ϵ)-IND-CCA2 secure if the advantage of any t-polynomial time adversary $\mathcal{A}$ is*

$$\mathrm{Adv}_{\mathrm{PE}}^{\mathrm{IND-CCA2}}(t, q_d) = \max_{\mathcal{A}}\{\mathrm{Adv}_{\mathrm{PE}}^{\mathrm{IND-CCA2}}(\mathcal{A})\} < \epsilon,$$

where the maximum is over all $\mathcal{A}$ which runs in time t and makes at most q_d queries to the decryption oracle.

3   Propose Encryption Scheme

In this section, we construct a public key encryption scheme which is called EO. The proposed scheme is constructed from Boneh-Boyen IBE scheme [5] with a one-time signature scheme (using Waters' signature scheme [24]) built within the Boneh-Boyen IBE scheme. In this construction, the one-time signature scheme is not required to be strongly existential unforgeable. We also show that the proposed scheme is almost as efficient as Boneh-Boyen IBE scheme with only an increase of two exponentiations and one multi-exponentiation in encryption and decryption respectively.

Let G_1 and G_2 be groups of prime order p, let g be a generator of G_1 and e be an admissible bilinear map from $G_1 \times G_1$ into G_2. Let a family of hash function $\mathcal{H}_1 = \{H_{\bar{k}_1} : \{0,1\}^{\bar{w}_1} \to \{0,1\}^{\bar{n}_1}\}_{\bar{k}_1 \in K_1}$ be a target collision resistant hash function and a family of hash function $\mathcal{H}_2 = \{H_{\bar{k}_2} : \{0,1\}^{\bar{w}_2} \to \{0,1\}^{\bar{n}_2}\}_{\bar{k}_2 \in K_2}$ be a collision resistant hash function, where $\bar{w}_1$, $\bar{w}_2$, $\bar{n}_1$ and $\bar{n}_2$ are integers such that $\bar{n}_1 < \log_2 p$ and K_1 and K_2 are key spaces.

Keygen: Choose random integers x, y, $z \in Z_p$ and compute $g_1 = g^x$, $g_2 = g^y$, $h_1 = g^z$ and $Z = e(g_1, g_2)$. Choose a random $u' \in G_1$ and a random n-dimensional vector $U = (u_1, \cdots, u_n)$ where element u_i is randomly chosen from G_1 for $i \in \{1, \cdots, n\}$. Select $H_{\bar{k}_1} \in \mathcal{H}_1$ and $H_{\bar{k}_2} \in \mathcal{H}_2$ for fixed $\bar{k}_1 \in K_1$ and $\bar{k}_2 \in K_2$ respectively such that $\bar{n}_2 = n$. For simplicity, denote $H_{\bar{k}_1}$ and $H_{\bar{k}_2}$ as H_1 and H_2 respectively. Then the public key is $PK = (g_1, g_2, h_1, Z, u', U, H_1, H_2)$ and the private key is $SK = (x, y, z)$.

Encryption: To encrypt a message m, first choose random integers s, $\alpha \in Z_p$ such that $g^\alpha \neq g_1$. Then, compute the following:

$$c_0 = g^\alpha, \quad c_1 = Z^s m, \quad c_2 = g^s, \quad c_3 = (g_1^v h_1)^s, \quad c_4 = g_2^\alpha (u' \prod_{i=1}^n u_i^{w_i})^s,$$

where $v = H_1(c_0, c_2)$, $w = H_2(c_1, c_3)$ and $w = (w_1, \cdots, w_n) \in \{0, 1\}^n$. Then, the ciphertext is $C = (c_0, c_1, c_2, c_3, c_4)$.

Decryption: Upon receipt of ciphertext $C = (c_0, c_1, c_2, c_3, c_4)$, the receiver first computes $v = H_1(c_0, c_2)$, $w = H_2(c_1, c_3)$. Let the binary representation of w be $(w_1, \cdots, w_n)$. The receiver first checks $e(c_4, g) = e(u' \prod_{i=1}^n u_i^{w_i}, c_2) \cdot e(g_2, c_0)$ and $e(c_3, g) = e(g_1^v h_1, c_2)$ (or $c_3 = c_2^{xv+z}$). If one of them is not equal, output reject symbol $\perp$, otherwise decrypt the ciphertext as either

A.   Choose a random $r \in Z_p$ and compute a decryption key $DK = (d_1, d_2)$ as $d_1 = g_2^x \cdot (g_1^v h_1)^r$ and $d_2 = g^r$ and compute the plaintext as $m = c_1 \cdot \frac{e(c_3, d_2)}{e(c_2, d_1)}$.

B.   Compute the plaintext as $m = \frac{c_1}{e(c_2, g^{xy})}$.

It is noted that (c_1, c_2, c_3) is a ciphertext of Boneh-Boyen identity-based encryption scheme if v is an identity. (c_2, c_4) is a signature of Waters' signature scheme with the public key (c_0, g_2). It is worth to mention that c_2 is commonly shared by both Boneh-Boyen IBE encryption scheme and Waters' signature scheme.

From the above two decryptions, method B is more efficient than method A, which requires two exponentiations and four pairing. Method A is basically followed from Boneh-Boyen identity-based encryption scheme [5]. In fact, the computational complexity of decryption can be further optimized if one chooses $\aleph = (\mu', \mu_1, \cdots, \mu_n) \in Z_p$ such that $u' = g^{\mu'}$ and $u_i = g^{\mu_i}$ for $i \in \{1, \cdots, n\}$ and store $\aleph$ as a part of private key. Then, Waters' signature scheme can be verified by $c_4 = c_0^y c_2^{\mu' + \sum_{i=1}^n w_i \mu_i}$ instead of using three pairings. Therefore, the decryption of the proposed scheme requires only one pairing, two exponentiations and one multi-exponentiation. Hence, the proposed scheme only increases two exponentiations (one of these is multi-exponentiation) and one multi-exponentiation in encryption and decryption respectively as compared to Boneh-Boyen IBE encryption scheme.

4   Security Proof

Before we state the main theorem, we first list the following useful lemma which was called "Difference Lemma" and was defined by Cramer and Shoup in [23].

Lemma 1. ([23], Difference Lemma) *Let S_1, S_2 and F be events defined on some probability space. Suppose that the event $S_1 \wedge \neg F$ occurs if and only if $S_2 \wedge \neg F$ occurs. Then*

$$\big|\Pr[S_1] - \Pr[S_2]\big| \leq \Pr[F].$$

Theorem 1. *The proposed encryption scheme EO is (t, q_d, ϵ)-IND-CCA2 secure, assuming that the (t', ϵ')-DBDH assumption, the (t'', ϵ'')-weak existentially unforgeable one-time Waters' signature scheme, and the (t_1, ϵ_1)-target collision resistant hash function H_1 and the (t_2, ϵ_2)-collision resistant hash function H_2 holds, such that*

$$\epsilon \leq \epsilon' + 2\epsilon'' + \epsilon_1 + \epsilon_2 + \frac{2q_d}{p},$$

where t', t'', t_1 and t_2 are essentially the same as t and $q_d < p$.

Proof. The proof of the theorem is by reductionist proof. Suppose there exists a t-polynomial time adversary $\mathcal{A}$ who breaks the proposed encryption scheme EO in the sense of IND-CCA2, then we build an algorithm $\mathcal{B}$ that solves the decisional bilinear Diffie-Hellman (DBDH) assumption in a random instance with advantage ϵ'. First, algorithm $\mathcal{B}$ is given an input of 7-tuple $(G_1, G_2, g, g^x, g^y, g^{s^*}, T)$, where T is either $e(g, g)^{xys^*}$ or a random element from G_2. The algorithm $\mathcal{B}$'s goal is to output 1 if $T = e(g, g)^{xys^*}$ and 0 otherwise. The algorithm $\mathcal{B}$ interacts with $\mathcal{A}$ in the IND-CCA2 game as follows:

Set Up: First, $\mathcal{B}$ sets $g_1 = g^x$, $g_2 = g^y$, $g_3 = g^{s^*}$ and $Z = e(g_1, g_2)$. Then, $\mathcal{B}$ chooses random integers α^*, γ, μ', μ_1, $\cdots$, $\mu_n \in Z_p$ such that $g^{\alpha^*} \neq g_1{}^2$ and computes $v^* = H_1(g^{\alpha^*}, g_3)$, $u' = g^{\mu'}$ and $u_i = g^{\mu_i}$ for $i \in \{1, \cdots, n\}$. Let H_1 be a target collision hash function chosen from $\mathcal{H}_1$ and H_2 be a collision hash function chosen from $\mathcal{H}_2$. The algorithm $\mathcal{B}$ gives $\mathcal{A}$ the public key $PK = (g_1, g_2, h_1, Z, u', U, H_1, H_2)$ where $U = (u_1, \cdots, u_n)$. The private key of $\mathcal{B}$ is $(x, y, \gamma - xv^*)$ which are unknown to $\mathcal{B}$. The algorithm $\mathcal{B}$ also keeps the secret elements $(\mu', \mu_1, \cdots, \mu_n)$ for decryption in this simulation.

Phase 1: The adversary $\mathcal{A}$ makes a number of decryption queries on $C = (c_0, c_1, c_2, c_3, c_4)$. If $c_2 = g_3$ (g_3 will be defined as c_2^* in the challenge ciphertext later), then the simulation aborts, otherwise $\mathcal{B}$ computes $v = H_1(c_0, c_2)$ and $w = H_2(c_1, c_3)$ and checks $e(c_2, g_1^v h_1) = e(g, c_3)$ and $e(c_4, g) = e(u' \prod_{i=1}^n u_i^{w_i}, c_2) \cdot e(c_0, g_2)$ where $w = (w_1, \cdots, w_n) \in \{0, 1\}^n$. If one of them is not equal, return reject symbol $\perp$, otherwise chooses a random $r \in Z_p$ and generates a decryption key $DK = (d_1, d_2)$ for decryption as follows:

$$
\begin{aligned}
d_1 &= g_2^{-\frac{\gamma}{v-v^*}} \cdot (g_1^{v-v^*} \cdot g^\gamma)^r = g_2^x \cdot g_1^{-y} \cdot g_2^{-\frac{\gamma}{v-v^*}} \cdot (g_1^{v-v^*} \cdot g^\gamma)^r \\
&= g_2^x \cdot (g_1^{v-v^*} \cdot g^\gamma)^{r - \frac{y}{v-v^*}} = g_2^x \cdot (g_1^v \cdot h_1)^{\bar{r}} \\
d_2 &= g_2^{-\frac{1}{v-v^*}} \cdot g^r = g^{\bar{r}},
\end{aligned}
$$

where $\bar{r} = r - \frac{y}{v-v^*}$. Then, $\mathcal{B}$ returns the plaintext m as follows:

$$
m = c_1 \cdot \frac{e(c_3, d_2)}{e(c_2, d_1)}.
$$

Challenge: After the number of queries in phase 1, $\mathcal{A}$ outputs two equal length messages m_0 and m_1 on which it wishes to be challenged. $\mathcal{B}$ flips a fair coin $b \in \{0, 1\}$, and responds with the challenge ciphertext $C^* = (c_0^*, c_1^*, c_2^*, c_3^*, c_4^*)$ as follows:

$$
c_0^* = g^{\alpha^*}, \quad c_1^* = T \cdot m_b, \quad c_2^* = g_3, \quad c_3^* = g_3^\gamma, \quad c_4^* = g_2^{\alpha^*} \cdot g_3^{\mu' + \sum_{i=1}^n w_i^* \mu_i},
$$

where $w^* = H_2(c_1^*, c_3^*)$ and $w^* = (w_1^*, \cdots, w_n^*) \in \{0, 1\}^n$. It is noted that $c_3^* = g_1^{v^* s^*} \cdot h_1^{s^*}$ and $c_4^* = g_2^{\alpha^*} \cdot (u' \prod_{i=1}^n u_i^{w_i^*})^{s^*}$.

Phase 2: The adversary $\mathcal{A}$ continues to make its decryption queries on ciphertext C except $C \neq C^*$.

Guess: After the number of decryption queries, the adversary $\mathcal{A}$ returns a bit $b' \in \{0, 1\}$. If $b = b'$, the simulator return $\beta' = 1$, else it returns $\beta' = 0$. This completes the description of the simulator. Note that the simulator behaves exactly as in the original public key encryption except the abort in Phase 1, we will discuss this in detail below.

---

[2] If $g^{\alpha^*} = g_1$, then $x = \alpha^*$ and it is easy to check whether $T = e(g^y, g^{s^*})^x$. In this case, $\mathcal{B}$ will output the correct result and stop.

In order to analyse the success probability of $\mathcal{B}$, we consider a sequence of the "indistinguishable" modified games, from game G_0 to game G_6, where G_0 is the original game and the last game G_6 clearly gives no advantage to the adversary $\mathcal{A}$. Let $b' \in \{0,1\}$ be the output of $\mathcal{A}$ and T_i be the event that $b' = b$ in the game G_i for $0 \le i \le 6$. Then, we have

$$\text{Adv}_{\text{EO}}^{\text{IND}-\text{CCA2}}(\mathcal{A}) = \left| \Pr[T_0] - 1/2 \right|$$

and the sequence of games are described as follows:

Game G_1: First, game G_0 is modified to a new game G_1 such that the decryption oracle in **Phase 1** is modified with the rejection rule $\mathcal{R}_1$ as follows : If the adversary submits a ciphertext $C = (c_0, c_1, c_2, c_3, c_4)$ with $c_0 = c_0^*$ or $c_2 = c_2^*$, the decryption oracle immediately outputs reject and halt. In **Phase 1**, since the adversary has no information (in a statistical sense) about c_0^* or c_2^* from the challenge ciphertext C^*, and if the adversary makes at most q_d decryption queries in **Phase 1**, then the probability of having $c_0 = c_0^*$ or $c_2 = c_2^*$ is $\frac{2q_d}{p}$. Therefore, by Lemma 1, we have

$$\left| \Pr[T_1] - \Pr[T_0] \right| \le \frac{2q_d}{p}.$$

Game G_2: To turn game G_1 to a new game G_2, the decryption oracle in **Phase 2** is modified such that the rejection rule $\mathcal{R}_2$ is applied as follows: If the adversary $\mathcal{A}$ submits a ciphertext $C = (c_0, c_1, c_2, c_3, c_4)$ with $(c_0, c_2) \ne (c_0^*, c_2^*)$ and $v = v^*$ where $v = H_1(c_0, c_2)$, then the decryption oracle immediately outputs reject and halt. Let R_2 be the event that the decryption oracle in game G_2 rejects a ciphertext using the rule $\mathcal{R}_2$. As games G_2 and G_1 proceed identically until the event R_2 occurs, therefore the event $T_2 \wedge \neg R_2$ and $T_1 \wedge \neg R_2$ are identical. Hence, by Lemma 1, we have $\left| \Pr[T_2] - \Pr[T_1] \right| \le \Pr[R_2]$.

Lemma 2. $\Pr[R_2] \le \epsilon_1$.

Game G_3: In this game, the decryption oracle in **Phase 2** is further modified such that the ciphertext is not rejected by the rule $\mathcal{R}_2$ before and the rejection rule $\mathcal{R}_3$ of this game is applied as follows : If the adversary submits a ciphertext $C = (c_0, c_1, c_2, c_3, c_4)$ with either $c_1 \ne c_1^*$ or $c_3 \ne c_3^*$; and $w = w^*$ where $w = H_2(c_1, c_3)$, the decryption oracle immediately outputs reject and halt. Let R_3 be the event that the decryption oracle in game G_3 rejects a ciphertext using the rule $\mathcal{R}_3$. So, by Lemma 1, we have $\left| \Pr[T_3] - \Pr[T_2] \right| \le \Pr[R_3]$.

Lemma 3. $\Pr[R_3] \le \epsilon_2$.

Game G_4: The decryption oracle in **Phase 2** is further modified from game G_3 to obtain a new game G_4 with the rejection rule $\mathcal{R}_4$. It rejects those ciphertexts that are not be rejected by rules $\mathcal{R}_2$ and $\mathcal{R}_3$ before and is as follows : If the adversary submits a ciphertext $C = (c_0^*, c_1, c_2, c_3, c_4)$ with $C \ne C^*$ and $v \ne v^*$, the decryption oracle immediately outputs reject and halt. Let R_4 be the event that the decryption oracle in game G_4 rejects a ciphertext using the rule $\mathcal{R}_4$. So, by Lemma 1, we have $\left| \Pr[T_4] - \Pr[T_3] \right| \le \Pr[R_4]$.

Lemma 4. $\Pr[R_4] \leq \epsilon''$.

Game G_5: In game G_5, the decryption oracle is further modified so that it rejects all the invalid ciphertext $C = (c_0, c_1, c_2, c_3, c_4)$ in **Phase** 2 with $v \neq v^*$, where $v = H_1(c_0, c_2)$. This rejection rule rejects those ciphertext which are not rejected under game G_2, G_3 and G_4 before. Let R_5 be the event that the decryption oracle in game G_5 rejects a ciphertext using the rule $\mathcal{R}_5$. So, by Lemma 1, we have $\left|\Pr[T_5] - \Pr[T_4]\right| \leq \Pr[R_5]$.

Lemma 5. $\Pr[T_5] \leq \epsilon''$.

Game G_6: In this game, the encryption oracle is modified so that c_1^* is replaced by random c_1' in G_2. Due to this change, c_1' is independent of the challenge bit b, and does not provide any information in the adversary's view. Therefore, we have $\Pr[T_6] = 1/2$. As game G_6 does not depend on T, therefore, we have

$$\left|\Pr[T_6] - \Pr[T_5]\right| \leq \epsilon'.$$

Combine the results from the above games, we immediately obtain the following:

$$\epsilon \leq \epsilon' + 2\epsilon'' + \epsilon_1 + \epsilon_2 + \frac{2q_d}{p}.$$

5 Performance Comparisons

In this section, we compare the performance of the proposed PKE scheme to those PKE schemes using Canetti-Halevi-Katz's construction [11] with a strong one-time signature scheme. As Canetti-Halevi-Katz's construction is generic on any selective-identity IBE scheme, in order to have better understanding of the comparison, we give a brief description of Canetti-Halevi-Katz's construction on Boneh-Boyen IBE encryption scheme [5] as follows:

CANETTI-HALEVI-KATZ'S CONSTRUCTION ON BONEH-BOYEN IBE SCHEME

Keygen: The key generation is similar to Section 3 except $PK_2 = (u', U, H_2)$, which is only particular to Waters' signature scheme. Therefore, the public key is $PK_1 = (g_1, g_2, h_1, Z, H_1)$ and the private key is $SK = (x, y, z)$.

Encryption: To encrypt a message m, one chooses a random integer $s \in Z_p$ and random one-time private key sk_o and compute its public key pk_o. Then, one computes the following:

$$c_0 = pk_o, \quad c_1 = Z^s m, \quad c_2 = g^s, \quad c_3 = (g_1^v \, h_1)^s, \quad c_4 = Sg_o(sk_o, c_1, c_2, c_3),$$

where $v = H_1(c_0)$ and c_4 is a signature of (c_1, c_2, c_3) with the signing key sk_o. Then, the ciphertext is $C = (c_0, c_1, c_2, c_3, c_4)$.

Decryption: Upon receipt of ciphertext $C = (c_0, c_1, c_2, c_3, c_4)$, the receiver first computes $v = H_1(c_0)$ and checks the validity of the signature c_4 with the public key c_0 and $e(c_3, g) = e(g_1^v h_1, c_2)$ (or $c_3 = c_2^{xv+z}$). If the signature is not valid or the equality does not hold, then output reject symbol $\perp$, otherwise the plaintext is computed as $m = \frac{c_1}{e(c_2, g^{xy})}$.

As a one-time signature scheme requires to be strong existential unforgeable, we consider two such signature schemes for comparisons, that is, the strong Waters' signature scheme (BSW) [10] (By Boneh-Shen-Waters' transformation from a weak existential unforgeability to a strong existential unforgeability) and Boneh-Boyen signature scheme (BB) [4]. Up to now (up to my knowledge), these two signature schemes based on bilinear maps are provable to be strongly existential unforgeable in the standard model. We first briefly described the strong Waters' signature scheme [10] as follows:

STRONG WATERS' SIGNATURE SCHEME

Keygen: The basic parameter setting is same as that in Section 3, that means g, G_1, G_2 are same as that of Section 3. Choose random $\alpha \in Z_p$ and $\bar{g}_2, h \in G_1$. Set $\bar{g}_1 = g^\alpha$ and choose random $u' \in G_1$ and random n-dimensional vector $U = (u_1, \cdots, u_n)$ where element u_i is randomly chosen from G_1 for $i \in \{1, \cdots, n\}$. Let $H_{\bar{k}} \in \mathcal{H}$ be a collision hash function for fixed $\bar{k} \in K$ and denote $H_{\bar{k}}$ as H. Then, the public key is $pk_o = (\bar{g}_1, \bar{g}_2, h, u', U, H)$ and the private key is $sk_o = (\bar{g}_2^\alpha)$.

Sign: To sign a message M, choose random integers $r, d \in Z_p$ and compute the following sequentially

$$\sigma_2 = g^r, \quad t = H(M, \sigma_2), \quad m = H(g^t h^d), \quad \sigma_1 = \bar{g}_2^\alpha (u' \prod_{i=1}^n u_i^{m_i})^r,$$

where m is written as $(m_1, \cdots, m_n) \in \{0, 1\}^n$. Then, the signature is (σ_1, σ_2, d).

Verify: Upon receipt of signature (σ_1, σ_2, d) on message M, the receiver first computes $\bar{t} = H(M, \sigma_2)$ and $\bar{m} = H(g^{\bar{t}} h^d)$. Write $\bar{m}$ as $(\bar{m}_1, \cdots, \bar{m}_n)$. The receiver checks $e(\sigma_1, g) = e(u' \prod_{i=1}^n u_i^{\bar{m}_i}, \sigma_2) \cdot e(\bar{g}_1, \bar{g}_2)$. If they are equal, accept the signature, otherwise reject.

As all the compared encryption schemes are based on Boneh-Boyen IBE encryption scheme, we only need to compare the additional computation cost incurred by the one time signatures, that is, c_0 and c_4 in all the schemes under comparison. As PK_2 is only for Waters' signature scheme and is not generated during the encryption phase, therefore it can be included as part of the public key of PKE scheme. Hence, the public key of PKE scheme based on Waters' signature scheme and the proposed scheme will be longer than the CHK construction with one-time BB signature scheme [4].

Let l_1 be the length of the representation of an element in G_1 and $l_p = \log_2 p$. The efficiency comparisons are listed below:

Table 1. Efficiency Comparisons

	pk_o length c_0	sk_o length	Signature length c_4	Signature Generation[1]	Signature Verification
Strong Waters[3] [10]	$2l_1$	l_1	$2l_1 + l_p$	3 exp[2], 2 m-exp	2 pairings, 1 exp, 1 m-exp
BB[4] [4]	$2l_1$	$2l_p$	$l_1 + l_p$	3 exp	1 pairings, 1 m-exp
Prop Scheme	l_1	l_p	l_1	1 exp, 1 m-exp	1 m-exp

Note :

1. The signature generation also includes public/private key generation.

2. exp is the usual exponentiation and m-exp denotes the multi-exponentiation.

3. In a strong Waters' scheme [10], (u', U) is part of public key of the encryption scheme. Therefore, the signature verification is $e(\sigma_1 \sigma_2^{-(\mu' + \sum_{i=1}^n w_i \mu_i)}, g) = e(\bar{g}_1, \bar{g}_2)$ which reduces the original 3 pairings to 2 pairings.

4. In BB scheme, $e(g, g)$ is part of the public key, therefore, the number of pairings in signature verification is reduced to one instead of two.

From Table 1 above, the proposed scheme required an addition of two exponentiations and one multi-exponentiation in encryption and decryption respectively; and there is no additional pairing. While two pairings and one pairings are required in strong Waters' signature scheme and BB signature scheme respectively. Therefore, the proposed scheme is more efficient than CHK construction with Waters' signature scheme and BB signature scheme respectively. Below we list the timings of the respective schemes which run on MIRACL software [18] on 3.0GHz Pentium IV computer. The elliptic curve and size of finite fields are same as that of [7].

Table 2. Timing of PKE Schemes

	CHK with Waters Scheme [10]	CHK with BB Scheme [5]	Proposed Scheme	CS Scheme [12]
Encryption	$32.66ms$	$17.17ms$	$21.07ms$	$3.12ms$
Decryption	$84.42ms$	$57.86ms$	$35.04ms$	$2.73ms$

From Table 2, the encryption of CHK construction with BB signature scheme is slightly faster than the proposed scheme. This is because that computing $c_4 = g_2^\alpha (u' \prod_{i=1}^n u_i^{w_i})^s$ takes more time and we did not optimize this. But the decryption of the proposed scheme is faster than the CHK construction with BB signature scheme. From Table 2, Cramer-Shoup scheme [12] is still faster than other schemes as there is no pairing in decryption and the length of prime number is 1024-bit, while the finite field in the proposed scheme is 512-bit.

6 Conclusion

In this paper, we constructed an efficient public key encryption with a weak one-time signature scheme and publicly verifiable. The security depends on the hardness of decisional bilinear Diffie-Hellman problem, secure one-time Waters' signature scheme, the collision resistance hash function and the target collision resistance hash function. Furthermore, the computational complexity is almost as efficient as Boneh-Boyen IBE encryption scheme with only an increase of two exponentiations and one multi-exponentiation in encryption and decryption respectively.

Acknowledgments

The author wishes to thank Jens-Are Amundsen for providing the timings of Table 2 using MIRACL software run on 3.0GHz Pentium IV computer. The author also wishes to thank the anonymous reviewers for invaluable suggestions to improve this revised paper.

References

[1] J.-H. An, Y. Dodis and T. Rabin, "On the security of joint signature and encryption," Advances in Cryptology - Eurocrypt'02, Lecture Notes in Computer Science, vol.2332, pp.83-107, Springer-Verlag, 2002.

[2] D. Boneh and X. Boyen, "Secure identity based encryption without random oracles," Advances in Cryptology - Crypto'04, Lecture Notes in Computer Science vol.3152, pp.443-459, Springer-Verlag, 2004.

[3] D. Boneh and X. Boyen, "Efficient selective-id secure identity based encryption without random oracles," Advances in Cryptology - Eurocrypt'04, Lecture Notes in Computer Science vol.3027, pp. 223-238, Springer-Verlag, 2004.

[4] D. Boneh and X. Boyen, "Short signatures without random oracles," Advances in Cryptology - Eurocrypt'04, Lecture Notes in Computer Science, vol.3027, pp. 56-73, Springer-Verlag, 2004.

[5] D. Boneh, R. Canetti, Shai Halevi, and J. Katz, "Chosen-Ciphertext Security From Identity-Based Encryption," Accepted to SIAM Journal on Computing. Available from http://www.cs.umd.edu/~jkatz/papers/id-cca-journal/pdf.

[6] D. Boneh and M. Franklin, "Identity-based encryption from Weil pairing," Advances in Cryptology - Crypto'01, Lecture Notes in Computer Science vol.2139, pp.213-229, Springer-Verlag, 2001.

[7] D. Boneh and M. Franklin, "Identity-based encryption from Weil pairing," SIAM J. Comput., vol.32(3), pp.586-615, Springer-Verlag, 2003.

[8] D. Boneh and J. Katz, "Improved efficiency for CCA-secure cryptosystems built using identity based encryption," Topics in Cryptology – CT-RSA 2005, Lecture Notes in Computer Science vol.3376, pp. 87-103, Springer-Verlag, 2005.

[9] X. Boyen, Q. Mei, and B. Waters, "Direct chosen ciphertext security from identity-based techniques,"   In ACM Conference on Computer and Communications Security   CCS 2005, pp. 320-329, ACM Press, 2005. Full version available at http://eprint.iacr.org/2005/288.

[10] D. Boneh, E. Shen, and B. Waters, "Strongly unforgeable signatures based on computational Diffie-Hellman,"   Public Key Cryptography - PKC'06, Lecture Notes in Computer Science vol.3958, pp.229-240, Springer-Verlag, 2006.

[11] R. Canetti, S. Halevi and J. Katz, "Chosen-ciphertext security from identity-based encryption,"   Advances in Cryptology - Eurocrypt'04, Lecture Notes in Computer Science vol.3027, pp. 207-222, Springer-Verlag, 2004.

[12] R. Cramer and V. Shoup, "A practical public key cryptosystem provably secure against adaptive chosen ciphertext attack," Advances in Cryptology - Crypto'98, Lecture Notes in Computer Science vol.1462, pp. 13-25, Springer-Verlag, 1998.

[13] R. Cramer and V. Shoup, "Universal hash proofs and paradigm for adaptive chosen ciphertext secure public-key encryption," Advances in Cryptology - Eurocrypt'02, Lecture Notes in Computer Science vol.2332, pp.46-64, Springer-Verlag, 2002.

[14] R. Cramer and V. Shoup, "Design and analysis of prractical public-key encryption schemes secure adaptive chosen ciphertext attack," SIAM J. Comput., vol.33, no.1, pp.167-226, 2003.

[15] D. Dolev, C. Dwork, and M. Naor, "Non-malleable cryptography," The $23rd$ Annual ACM Symposium on Theory of Computing – STOC'91, pp.542-552, ACM press, 1991.

[16] S. Goldwasser, S. Micali and R. L. Rivest, "A digital signature scheme secure against adaptive chosen-message attacks,"   SIAM J. Computing, vol.17, no.2, April, pp.281-308, 1988.

[17] E. Kiltz, "On the limitation of the spread of an IBE-to-PKE transformation," Public key Cryptography - PKC'06, Lecture Notes in Computer Science vol.3958, pp. 274-289, Springer-Verlag, 2006.

[18] MIRACL, Multiprecision integer and rational arithmetic C/C++ library, Shamus Software Ltd. Available from http://indigo.ie/~mscott/.

[19] D. Naccache, "Secure and practical identity-based encryption," Available from http://eprint.iacr.org/2005/369.

[20] N. Noar and M. Young, "Universal one-way hash functions and their cryptographic applications," The 21st ACM Symposium on Theory of Computing – STOC'89, pp.33-43, ACM Press, 1989.

[21] T. Okamoto, "Cryptography based on bilinear maps," The 16th International Symposium on Applied Algebra, Algebraic Algorithms and Error-Correcting Codes - AAECC-16, Lecture Notes in Computer Science Vol.3857, pp.35-50, Springer-Verlag, 2006.

[22] C. Rackoff and D. Simon, "Non-interactive zero-knowledge proof of knowledge and chosen ciphertext attack," Advances in Cryptology - Crypto'91, Lecture Notes in Computer Science Vol.576, pp.46-64, Springer-Verlag, 1991.

[23] V. Shoup, "Sequences of games: a tool for taming complexity in security proofs," manuscript, 2004. Available from http://eprint.iacr.org/2004/332.

[24] B. Waters, "Efficient identity-based encryption without random oracles,"   Advances in Cryptology - Eurocrypt'05, Lecture Notes in Computer Science vol.3494, pp.114-127, Springer-Verlag, 2005.

Appendix A

Proof of Lemma 2

We construct an algorithm $\mathcal{A}'$ which acts as a simulator and interacts with $\mathcal{A}$ as follows. First, algorithm $\mathcal{A}'$ takes $(G_1, G_2, g, g^x, g^y, g^{s^*}, T)$ as input, it constructs a public and private key-pair for the encryption scheme which is similar to the key generation algorithm as before. The construction of encryption and decryption is same as before. Assume that the challenge ciphertext is $C^* = (c_0^*, c_1^*, c_2^*, c_3^*, c_4^*)$, if $\mathcal{A}$ submits a decryption query on $C = (c_0, c_1, c_2, c_3, c_4)$ with $v = v^*$ where $v = H_1(c_0, c_2)$, then $\mathcal{A}'$ applies the rejection rule $\mathcal{R}_2$ in the game G_2. $\mathcal{A}'$ will reject C and halt. In this case, $\mathcal{A}'$ has obtained a collision of H_1. Therefore, the lemma is proved.

Proof of Lemma 3

The proof of this lemma is similar to Lemma 2 and we omit the proof here.

Proof of Lemma 4

Let $w = H_2(c_1, c_3)$, we consider the following two cases.

Case i: $w \neq w^*$. In this case, we show that there is a forgery of Waters' signature scheme. We construct an algorithm $\mathcal{A}''$ which provides an environment for $\mathcal{A}$ and interacts with $\mathcal{A}$ as follows. Algorithm $\mathcal{A}''$ takes $(G_1, G_2, g, g^x, g^y, g^{s^*}, T)$ as input, it first constructs a public and private key-pair for the encryption scheme which is similar to the key generation algorithm as before. The construction of encryption and decryption is same as before. Assume that the challenge ciphertext is $C^* = (c_0^*, c_1^*, c_2^*, c_3^*, c_4^*)$, if $\mathcal{A}$ submits a decryption query on $C = (c_0^*, c_1, c_2, c_3, c_4)$ with $C \neq C^*$ and $e(c_4, g) = e(u' \prod_{i=1}^n u_i^{w_i}, c_2) \cdot e(c_0, g_2)$, then $\mathcal{A}''$ applies the rejection rule $\mathcal{R}_4$ in the game G_4. $\mathcal{A}''$ will reject C and halt. In this case, $\mathcal{A}''$ has obtained a valid signature (c_2, c_4) of the message $M = (c_1, c_3)$. Therefore, we have $\Pr[R_4] \leq \epsilon''$ in this case.

Case ii: $w = w^*$. As this case is not the same as game G_3, therefore, $c_1 = c_1^*$ and $c_3 = c_3^*$. Now, we consider the following two sub-cases:
Subcase a: $c_2 = g^s$ such that the adversary $\mathcal{A}$ controls s. If the adversary $\mathcal{A}$ is able to produce a valid signature, then the adversary could obtain the secret key $g_2^{\alpha^*} = c_4 \cdot (u' \prod_{i=1}^n u_i^{w_i})^{-s}$. This means that the adversary could compute the secret key $g_2^{\alpha^*}$ or Diffie-Hellman problem for given (c_0, g_2). This contradicts to the hardness of Diffie-Hellman problem, so, the adversary is not able to submit a correct c_4. Hence, we have $\Pr[T_4] = \Pr[T_3]$ in this sub-case.
Subcase b: $c_2 = g^s$ such that the adversary $\mathcal{A}$ does not fully know s (s depends on s^*). Assume that the adversary $\mathcal{A}$ knows $k = s - s^*$ where $c_2 = g^s$, otherwise, the adversary $\mathcal{A}$ is still not able to gain any information about T as the decryption oracle returns a message as $c_1 \cdot e(g_1, g_2)^{-s}$. Since $c_3 = c_3^*$ and $c_3 = (g_1^v h_1)^s$, we

have $(g_1^{v^*}h_1)^{s^*} = (g_1^v h_1)^s$. Let $a = v(v^*)^{-1} \bmod p$, then, we have $g_1^{v^*s^*-vs} = h_1^k$ and

$$g_1^{(1-a)v^*s^*} = (h_1 g_1^{av^*})^k,$$
$$g_1^{s^*} = (h_1 g_1^{av^*})^{\frac{k}{v^*(1-a)}}.$$

This shows that given g_1 and c_2^*, the adversary $\mathcal{A}$ can compute $g_1^{s^*}$ which is a Diffie-Hellman problem. Consequently, the adversary can easily compute $e(g_1, g_2)^{s^*}$ which is a Bilinear Diffie-Hellman problem. Hence, we conclude that the adversary is not able to produce a valid c_2 and $c_3 = (g_1^v h_1)^s$ such that $c_3 = c_3^*$. Therefore, we have $\Pr[T_4] = \Pr[T_3]$ in this sub-case.

From the above two cases, we have $\Pr[T_4] \le \epsilon''$.

Proof of Lemma 5

In this proof, we consider the following two cases:

Case i: The adversary $\mathcal{A}$ has full control of c_0. Here, we consider two sub-cases.
Subcase a: $c_2 = g^s$ such that the adversary $\mathcal{A}$ controls s. As the adversary also controls c_0, the adversary $\mathcal{A}$ is able to produce a valid signature (c_2, c_4). Then the actual decryption oracle will returns a message as $c_1 \cdot e(g_1, g_2)^{-s}$. If c_1 is related to T, the adversary $\mathcal{A}$ will not gain any useful information about T from this query as he/she can only get back to c_1. Therefore, we have $\Pr[T_5] = \Pr[T_4]$ in this sub-case.
Subcase b: $c_2 = g^s$ such that the adversary $\mathcal{A}$ does not fully know s (s depends on s^*). If the adversary $\mathcal{A}$ is able to produce $c_3 = (g_1^v h_1)^s$ for $v \ne v^*$ with either $s = k+s^*$ or $s = ks^*$, where $\mathcal{A}$ knows k. If $\mathcal{A}$ does not know k, $\mathcal{A}$ will not gain any information about T even if c_1 is related to T as the decryption oracle returns a message as $c_1 \cdot e(g_1, g_2)^{-s}$. Now, consider $s = k + s^*$, let $a = v(v^*)^{-1} \bmod p$ and we have $c_3^* c_3^{-1} = g_1^{v^*s^*-vs}h_1^{-k}$ and

$$c_3^* c_3^{-1} h_1^k = g_1^{(1-a)v^*s^*} g_1^{-av^*k},$$
$$g_1^{s^*} = (c_3^* c_3^{-1} h_1^k g_1^{av^*k})^{\frac{1}{v^*(1-a)}}.$$

If $s = ks^*$, we obtain $g_1^{s^*} = (c_3^* c_3^{-1})^{1/(v^*-v)}$. This shows that given g_1 and c_2^*, the adversary $\mathcal{A}$ can compute $g_1^{s^*}$ which is a Diffie-Hellman problem. Hence, we conclude that the adversary is not able to produce a valid c_2 and $c_3 = (g_1^v h_1)^s$. Therefore, we have $\Pr[T_5] = \Pr[T_4]$ in this sub-case.

Case ii: The adversary $\mathcal{A}$ has no full control of c_0. That means that $\mathcal{A}$ does not know the exponent of c_0 and so does not know the private key of the one-time signature. Then, we consider two sub-cases: $w = w^*$ and $w \ne w^*$. The proof of these two cases is similar to the two cases in Lemma 4, we omit the proof here. Therefore, we have $\Pr[T_5] \le \epsilon''$ in this case.

Combine the above two cases, we have $\Pr[T_5] \le \epsilon''$.

Ciphertext-Auditable Public Key Encryption

Satoshi Hada[1] and Kouichi Sakurai[2]

[1] Tokyo Research Laboratory, IBM Research, 1623-14, Shimotsuruma, Yamato,
Kanagawa 242-8502, Japan
[2] Dept. of Computer Science and Communication Engineering, Kyushu University,
Hakozaki, Fukuoka 812-81, Japan

Abstract. Loss of backup tapes containing personal information (PI) is
a potential breach of privacy and encryption is the typical way to prevent
the breach. This paper considers an attack scenario where an adversary
who encrypts the PI for backup purpose tries to hide the plain PI in a
valid-looking ciphertext without being detected. We show that the standard security notion IND-CCA2 does not capture such a scenario. For example, the Cramer-Shoup scheme is vulnerable to such an attack. To capture such a scenario, we define a new notion of "ciphertext-auditability"
as a new property of public key encryption schemes (PKESs). It requires
that, given a public key and a ciphertext, anyone should be able to verify whether the ciphertext was actually generated using the public key.
Also, it requires that, given a public key and a plaintext, no adversary
should be able to generate a valid-looking ciphertext so that the verification passes, but nevertheless the plaintext can be recovered from the
ciphertext without the corresponding secret key. We propose a general
construction of such PKESs based on standard cryptographic primitives
in the random oracle model.

1 Introduction

1.1 Motivating Scenario

Recently, the number of enterprises that collect personal information (PI) from
their customers and that use it for various purposes, including advertising and
marketing, has been increasing. At the same time, the number of cases where
the collected PI is leaked by malicious employees is also increasing. To prevent
such leakages by insiders, *network security* such as firewalls is widely used. For
example, it prohibits employees from sending the PI out by email. In addition
to network security, *physical security* also needs to be addressed to prohibit
employees from taking storage devices such as CDs, DVDs, and backup tapes
out of the building.

One of the typical data leakage scenarios is as follows: An enterprise copies
the PI to a backup tape and asks a transport service (TS) to transport it to a
secure warehouse. There are a lot of cases where backup tapes get lost in transit[1]

---

[1] For example, a major American bank announced that backup tapes containing federal workers' customer and account information were somehow lost during shipment
to a backup data center (February 25, 2005).

H. Yoshiura et al. (Eds.): IWSEC 2006, LNCS 4266, pp. 308–321, 2006.

and are potentially leaked to outsiders. In order to prevent this kind of potential leakages, the PI needs to be encrypted. Does encryption really help here? We consider an attack scenario, where traditional encryption does not help. In our scenario, the backup operation is performed by the following three entities in an enterprise:

1. Backup manager BM who provides the enterprise-wide backup management service. According to a corporate backup policy, BM periodically (e.g., every three months) sends to every department a request that it must backup its PI database and transport it to a secure warehouse. Also, BM is responsible for managing encryption keys.
2. An operator O who maintains the PI database in a department. O is responsible for encrypting the PI using a right encryption key before copying it to a backup tape.
3. An auditor A in the same department. A is responsible for auditing the backup tape to ensure that it is encrypted under a right encryption key. Note that, when BM and O are in different locations, BM has no physical access to the backup tape and cannot play the role of A.

Our basic assumption is that the PI database is protected by both network and physical security so that it is difficult for O to take the PI and related information out of the building. An exception is the case where O needs to backup the PI and transport it to a warehouse. In our scenario, a public key encryption scheme (PKES) is used to encrypt it in the following steps:

Step 1: BM sends a backup request with a public key to both O and A in an authenticated way (e.g., over SSL).

Step 2: O uses the public key to encrypt the PI and copies the encrypted PI to a backup tape.

Step 3: A audits the backup tape to check whether O used the right public key to encrypt the PI (and of course to check that it contains only the encrypted PI). The purpose of this audit is to ensure that the PI cannot be recovered from the backup tape without the corresponding secret key (even if O is malicious).

Step 4: If it passes the audit, then O is authorized to ask the TS to transport the backup tape to a warehouse.

We assume that BM is always trusted and that O could be malicious and collude with the TS for the PI theft. In this scenario, we need to satisfy the following two requirements:

1. Since no one checks whether A audits the backup tape appropriately, A should have no chance to leak the PI to outsiders. That is, A should have no access to the PI database and corresponding secret key. Therefore, the first requirement is that A should be able to check whether O used the right public key to encrypt the PI without having access to the secret key and PI database. In other words, given the public key and backup tape, anyone should be able to play the role of A.

2. Consider the following attack by malicious O. It tries to *forge* a valid-looking encryption of the PI (a valid-looking ciphertext) such that it passes the audit by A, but nevertheless it is easy for the malicious TS to recover the PI from the forged ciphertext without the corresponding secret key. Intuitively, O tries to hide the PI in a ciphertext without being detected by A (as in steganography [15]). Therefore, the second requirement is that O should not be able to succeed in this attack.

In general, traditional public key encryption schemes do not satisfy these two requirements. Actually, as we will see in Section 3.2, the IND-CCA2 scheme suggested by Bellare and Rogaway [4] and the Cramer-Shoup scheme [7] are vulnerable to a forgery attack by malicious O.

Remark 1. We can consider a similar scenario using symmetric encryption instead of public key encryption. In this case, BM generates a secret key and sends it to both O and A in a secure manner. Since our basic assumption does not allow malicious O to leak the secret key to TS, such a scenario would make sense. However, it is still true that malicious O has a chance to leak it. This is why we focus on the public key encryption scenario, where O does not have such a chance at all unless O breaks the encryption scheme. We believe that the notion of ciphertext-auditability would be useful in the symmetric encryption setting, too.

1.2 Our Contribution

In order to address the two requirements, this paper proposes a new notion of *ciphertext-auditable* public key encryption. In ciphertext-auditable PKESs, encryption algorithms output not only a ciphertext but also an associated proof string for the validity of the ciphertext. Ciphertext-auditability is defined as the following two properties corresponding to the two requirements:

Verifiability: Given a public key and a ciphertext, anyone having the associated proof string should be able to verify whether the ciphertext was actually generated using the public key.

Unforgeability: No adversary should be able to *forge* a valid-looking pair of a ciphertext and a proof string such that the verification passes, but nevertheless the plaintext can be recovered from the ciphertext without the corresponding secret key.

Ciphertext-auditability ensures that as long as a ciphertext is verified to be a valid one the plaintext cannot be recovered from the ciphertext without the corresponding secret key. We give a formal definition of such a PKES in Section 3. Also, as mentioned above, we will show that IND-CCA2 security does not imply ciphertext-auditability.

In Section 4, we propose a general construction in the random oracle model [4], where we use as building blocks a non-interactive zero-knowledge (NIZK) proof of knowledge for NP and a trapdoor one-way permutation. We give a brief overview of our construction. Consider an encryption algorithm $\mathcal{E}(pk, M; r)$ and a forgery strategy called the semi-honest strategy where, given a plaintext M, an adversary somehow selects a *dummy* pair of a plaintext M' and a set of random coins r' and outputs the ciphertext $\mathcal{E}(pk, M'; r')$ as a valid-looking ciphertext. We will construct an encryption scheme such that, no matter how an adversary selects such a dummy pair (M', r'), the original plaintext M cannot be recovered from the ciphertext without the secret key (as long as the adversary follows the semi-honest strategy). Given any trapdoor permutation, we will construct such an encryption scheme in the random oracle model. The encryption algorithm behaves close to a random oracle on a pair of a plaintext and a set of random coins. That is, no matter how an adversary selects such a dummy pair (M', r'), the resulting ciphertext becomes close to a random string. As a result, the original plaintext M cannot be recovered from the ciphertext without the secret key. Intuitively, this implements unforgeability. Given such an encryption scheme, what remains is to force adversaries to follow the semi-honest strategy. For this purpose, we can use an NIZK proof of knowledge to append to each ciphertext a proof of its "well-formedness" as in [18,19,10,17]. Such a proof string is used to implement verifiability.

Remark 2. Under our basic assumption, the backup tape (encrypted PI) is the only thing that O is allowed to take out of the building. Otherwise, malicious O can take the plain PI out and there is nothing to solve. Our formal definition of ciphertext-auditability captures this basic assumption (See Remark 6).

1.3   Related Work

Refer to [1] for the standard security notions of public key encryption such as IND-CPA, IND-CCA1, IND-CCA2. There is a sequence of works that provide plausibility results for IND-CCA1 and IND-CCA2 schemes based on NIZK proofs [18,19,10,17]. Since our focus is not on such notions, we don't review the definitions in this paper.

Bellare et al. investigated the notion of key-privacy, which requires that ciphertexts should reveal no information on the public key used [2,13]. Ciphertext-auditability is a property contradicting key-privacy.

Bellare et al. defined a similar notion called ciphertext-verifiability in a different context [3]. Ciphertext-verifiability contradicts IND-CPA security (See Remark 4), but ciphertext-auditability does not contradict any standard security notions. Indeed, as shown in Section 4, ciphertext-auditability and IND-CCA2 can be satisfied simultaneously.

A notion of unforgeability of encryption is implicit in the design of IND-CCA2 schemes [18,19,10,17], where the purpose is to make the decryption oracle *useless*. Also, Katz and Yung explicitly defined such a notion in the context of symmetric key encryption [14]. Their purpose is different from ours. Our unforgeability implies some ability to prevent steganography (although it is impossible to prevent it perfectly [15]).

Desmedt investigated how to prevent steganography in many cryptographic protocols including encryption, but the proposed solution requires that the auditor must be involved in the encryption process and so the auditor must be trusted [8]. On the other hand, the auditor in our proposed scheme needs not be trusted. Also, there are recent works on how to prevent it perfectly in the context of zero-knowledge and mix networks [16,6].

2   Preliminaries

We say that a function $\nu(\cdot) : \mathbb{N} \to \mathbb{R}$ is negligible in n if for every polynomial $p(\cdot)$ and all sufficiently large n's, it holds that $\nu(n) < 1/p(n)$.

We let the string ATK be instantiated by any of CPA, CCA1, and CCA2. PPTM stands for "probabilistic polynomial time machine" and PSCF stands for "polynomial-size circuit family".

Given a probability distribution S, we denote by $x \leftarrow S$ the operation of selecting an element according to S. If A is a probabilistic machine then $A(x_1, x_2, \ldots, x_k)$ denotes the output distribution of A on inputs $(x_1, x_2, \ldots, x_k)$. Let $\Pr[x \leftarrow S_1; x_2 \leftarrow S_2; \ldots; x_k \leftarrow S_k : E]$ denote the probability of the event E after the processes $x_1 \leftarrow S_1, x_2 \leftarrow S_2, \ldots, x_k \leftarrow S_k$ are performed in order. Similarly, let $\mathrm{E}[x \leftarrow S_1; x_2 \leftarrow S_2; \ldots; x_k \leftarrow S_k : f(x_1, x_2, \cdots, x_k)]$ denote the expectation of $f(x_1, x_2, \cdots, x_k)$ when the processes $x_1 \leftarrow S_1, x_2 \leftarrow S_2, \ldots, x_k \leftarrow S_k$ are performed in order. We say that a probability distribution ensemble $\{D_n\}$ is *well-spread* if the largest probability of an element, i.e., $\max_v \Pr[x \leftarrow D_n : x = v]$, is negligible in n [5].

We review the definition of trapdoor one-way permutations. A permutation generator is a PPTM $\mathcal{G}$ such that $\mathcal{G}(1^n)$ outputs (the descriptions of) a pair of deterministic polynomial-time algorithms (f, f^{-1}) specifying a permutation and its inverse on $\{0,1\}^n$.

Definition 1. *We say that a permutation generator $\mathcal{G}$ is a trapdoor one-way permutation generator if, for every non-uniform PSCF M, $\Pr[(f, f^{-1}) \leftarrow \mathcal{G}(1^n); x \leftarrow \{0,1\}^n : M(f(x)) = x]$ is negligible in n.*

Finally, we recall the definition of efficient adaptive NIZK proofs of knowledge [19,11,10].

Definition 2. *We say that $\pi = (f, \mathcal{P}, \mathcal{V}, \mathcal{S} = (\mathcal{S}_1, \mathcal{S}_2), \mathcal{EXT} = (\mathcal{EXT}_1, \mathcal{EXT}_2))$ is an efficient adaptive NIZK proof of knowledge for a language $L \in NP$ with witness relation R if f is a polynomial and $(\mathcal{P}, \mathcal{V}, \mathcal{S}, \mathcal{EXT})$ are PPTMs such that:*

Efficient Completeness: *For all $x \in L$ and all w such that $R(x, w)$ is true, for all strings σ of length $f(|x|)$, we have that $\mathcal{V}(x, \mathcal{P}(x, w, \sigma), \sigma) = \mathsf{Acc}$.*

Witness Extractability: $\{\mathcal{EXT}_1(1^n)\}$ *and the uniform distribution on $\{0,1\}^{f(n)}$ are statistically indistinguishable. For all adversaries A, we have that*

$$\Pr\left[\begin{array}{l} \sigma \leftarrow \{0,1\}^{f(n)}; \\ (x, p) \leftarrow A(\sigma) : \\ \mathcal{V}(x, p, \sigma) = \mathsf{Acc} \end{array}\right] - \Pr\left[\begin{array}{l} (\sigma, aux) \leftarrow \mathcal{EXT}_1(1^n); \\ p \leftarrow A(x, \sigma); \\ w \leftarrow \mathcal{EXT}_2(\sigma, aux, x, p) : \\ (x, w) \in R \end{array}\right]$$

is negligible in n, where x is any string in L of length n.

Adaptive ZK: *For all non-uniform PSCFs* $A = (A_1, A_2)$, *we have that*

$$\left| \Pr \begin{bmatrix} \sigma \leftarrow \{0,1\}^{f(n)}; \\ (x, w, \tau) = A_1(\sigma); \\ p \leftarrow \mathcal{P}(x, w, \sigma) : \\ A_2(p, \tau) = \text{true} \end{bmatrix} - \Pr \begin{bmatrix} (\sigma, aux) \leftarrow \mathcal{S}_1(1^n); \\ (x, w, \tau) = A_1(\sigma); \\ p \leftarrow \mathcal{S}_2(x, aux) : \\ A_2(p, \tau) = \text{true} \end{bmatrix} \right|$$

is negligible in n, *where* x *is any string in* L *of length* n.

3 Ciphertext-Auditability

In this section, we present a formal definition of ciphertext-auditable PKESs and show that some IND-CCA2 schemes do not satisfy ciphertext-auditability.

3.1 A Formal Definition

Let $\mathcal{AE} = (\mathcal{K}, \mathcal{E}, \mathcal{D})$ be a PKES, which consists of three algorithms $(\mathcal{K}, \mathcal{E}, \mathcal{D})$. The key generation algorithm $\mathcal{K}$ is a randomized algorithm that takes as input the security parameter 1^n and returns a pair of public and secret keys (pk, sk). The encryption algorithm $\mathcal{E}$ is a randomized algorithm that takes a public key pk and a plaintext $M \in \{0,1\}^*$ to return a ciphertext C, and the encryption process is denoted by $C \leftarrow \mathcal{E}(pk, M)$. When we need to make explicit the random coins r used by $\mathcal{E}$, we write $C = \mathcal{E}(pk, M; r)$. The decryption algorithm $\mathcal{D}$ is a deterministic algorithm that takes a secret key sk and a ciphertext C to return the plaintext M, and the decryption process is denoted by $M = \mathcal{D}(sk, C)$. It is required that, for every key pair (pk, sk) generated by $\mathcal{K}$ and every plaintext $M \in \{0,1\}^*$, it holds that $\mathcal{D}(sk, \mathcal{E}(pk, M)) = M$ with probability 1.

We syntactically extend the encryption algorithm so that it outputs not only the ciphertext but also a proof string for its validity, that is, we write $(C, p) \leftarrow \mathcal{E}(pk, M)$, where p denotes the proof string. The idea is that knowledge of p enables anyone to verify whether C was actually generated using pk. We assume that p is not required for decryption and so we make no syntactic change to the decryption algorithm. Since we can view p as part of the generated ciphertext, we can apply the standard security notions such as IND-CPA to this syntactically extended formulation. Basically, this requires that the pair of C and p should not reveal any information about M. We say that a PKES is "standard" when the encryption algorithm does not output any proof string, i.e., when the proof string is empty.

Let $\mathcal{X}(1^n)$ denote a well-spread distribution over $\{0,1\}^{m(n)}$, where $m(n)$ is a polynomial. We use it as a source of plaintexts. We consider an adversary who consists of two algorithms, which we call an encryption adversary A^e and a decryption adversary A^d. Given a pair of a public key pk and a plaintext M generated by $\mathcal{X}(1^n)$, A^e tries to *forge* a valid-looking pair of a ciphertext C and a proof string p such that the verification passes, but nevertheless A^d can recover M from C without the corresponding secret key. Ciphertext-auditable public-key encryption is formally defined as follows:

Definition 3. *We say that a PKES* $\mathcal{AE}$ *is* ciphertext-auditable *if it has the following two properties:*

Verifiability: *There exists a PPTM* $\mathcal{CV}$ *(verification algorithm) such that, for every* $M \in \{0,1\}^*$, $\Pr[(pk, sk) \leftarrow \mathcal{K}(1^n); (C, p) \leftarrow \mathcal{E}(pk, M) : \mathcal{CV}(pk, C, p) = \mathsf{Acc}] = 1$.

Unforgeability: *For every pair of non-uniform PSCFs* $A^e = \{A_n^e\}$ *and* $A^d = \{A_n^d\}$ *and every well-spread distribution* $\mathcal{X}(1^n)$, $\Pr[(pk, sk) \leftarrow \mathcal{K}(1^n); M \leftarrow \mathcal{X}(1^n); (C, p) = A_n^e(pk, M) : \mathcal{CV}(pk, C, p) = \mathsf{Acc}$ *and* $A_n^d(pk, C) = M]$ *is negligible in* n.

Note that adversaries A^e and A^d correspond to the malicious operator and transport service in our motivating scenario, respectively. Also, the auditor can be implemented using the verification algorithm.

Several remarks are as follows:

Remark 3. Like key-privacy [2], verifiability is a property orthogonal to the standard security notions such as the semantic security and indistinguishability of encryptions. On the other hand, unforgeability seems to imply some kind of one-wayness of encryption. It is an open issue to investigate relations between unforgeability and known security notions.

Remark 4. The verification algorithm is not allowed to take as input the plaintext M. If we allow it then the definition contradicts IND-CPA security. Such a property is defined in a different context in [3], where it is called "ciphertext-verifiability".

Remark 5. The decryption adversary A^d is not allowed to take as input the proof string p for the reason that we will describe in Remark 10. This is the reason why we made explicit the existence of p in our formulation. This means that, in our motivating scenario, p is not copied to the backup tape by the operator, but the auditor must be able to access it. Also, see Remark 10.

Remark 6. There is no information flow allowed from A^e to A^d except for the public key pk and ciphertext C. If arbitrary information flow is allowed, the definition makes no sense at all. This is because A^e can pass the plaintext M to A^d and A^d can output it as it is. This restriction corresponds to our basic assumption (See Remark 2). Also, due to this restriction, A^d has no access to any data generated internally in the encryption process, e.g., a hash value of the plaintext. Remark 11 will discuss this issue from the perspective of our proposed general construction.

Remark 7. We need to assume that $\mathcal{X}(1^n)$ is well-spread in the definition of unforgeability. Otherwise, the definition makes no sense. For example, if a sequence of messages $\{M_n\}$ is generated by $\mathcal{X}(1^n)$ with probability at least $\frac{1}{2}$ (for infinitely many n's), then A^d that always outputs such a message breaks the unforgeability.

Remark 8. The current definition captures a minimalistic requirement. It is a future research issue to investigate how we can strengthen the definition. For example, the definition is very weak in the sense that it only requires that decryption adversaries should not be able to recover the whole plaintext. Ideally, we want to require that no decryption adversary should be able to recover even a single bit of the plaintext. However, such a stronger definition could make no sense. For example, it could be easy for A^e to hide the last bit of plaintexts in a *valid* ciphertext. That is, A^e can repeat the (randomized) encryption using the right public key until the ciphertext becomes an odd value if and only if the last bit is 1, and A^d outputs 1 if and only if the ciphertext is odd. From the perspective of steganography [15], it is impossible to prevent such an attack perfectly since encryption must be randomized.

Remark 9. Unlike the standard security notions such as the semantic security and indistinguishability of encryptions [12, Section 5.2.4], ciphertext auditability is not *robust* in the sense that it cannot be extended to the setting where multiple messages are encrypted. For example, consider a situation where an adversary has an opportunity to encrypt multiple messages $(M_1, M_2, \cdots, M_n)$, each of length n. The adversary could hide M_1 in the ciphertexts by hiding the i-th bit of M_1 in M_i in the way described in the previous remark.

3.2   IND-CCA2 Does Not Imply Ciphertext-Auditability

We show that some IND-CCA2 schemes do not satisfy ciphertext-auditability. Take for example, the IND-CCA2 scheme suggested by Bellare and Rogaway [4], where pk is a trapdoor permutation f and $C = (C_1, C_2, C_3) = \mathcal{E}(pk, M; r) = (f(r), \mathcal{H}_1(r) \oplus M, \mathcal{H}_2(M, r))$, where $\mathcal{H}_1$ and $\mathcal{H}_2$ are random oracles. If an encryption adversary uses a fixed string R as the random coins r to forge a valid-looking ciphertext, i.e., $C = (f(R), \mathcal{H}_1(R) \oplus M, \mathcal{H}_2(M, R))$, then a decryption adversary having the fixed R can always recover M from C, i.e., $M = C_2 \oplus \mathcal{H}_1(R)$ (Note that Definition 3 allows A^e and A^d to share a priori information). In this case, the forged ciphertext would be considered as *valid* no matter how we implement a verification algorithm. It is easy to see that the same attack can be applied to some encryption schemes in the standard model, too. Examples include the ElGamal and Cramer-Shoup schemes [9,7].

4   A General Construction

In this section, we propose a general construction of ciphertext-auditable PKESs in the random oracle model [4]. We will do so in two steps. Intuitively, verifiability and unforgeability are implemented in the first and second steps, respectively. The first step works in the standard model while the second step works in the random oracle model. Before describing it, we would like to point out that, given an arbitrary secure PKES, verifiability is easy to implement, i.e., we can just append the used public key to each ciphertext as the proof string. So the non-trivial task is to satisfy unforgeability at the same time.

4.1   Step 1: Implementation of Verifiability

Let $\mathcal{AE} = (\mathcal{K}, \mathcal{E}, \mathcal{D})$ be a *standard* PKES. We consider a specific strategy for encryption adversaries to forge valid-looking ciphertexts, which we call the *semi-honest strategy*. It is a generalization of the attack described in Section 3.2. In this strategy, given a pair of a public key pk and a plaintext M, an encryption adversary A^e somehow selects a plaintext M' and a set of random coins r' and then outputs $C = \mathcal{E}(pk, M'; r')$, where M' may not be equal to M. In the case of the attack described in Section 3.2, $M' = M$ and r' is a fixed string R.

We consider a standard PKES for which the semi-honest strategy does not work, that is, no matter how an encryption adversary selects (M', r'), it is difficult for any decryption adversary to recover M. We define it formally as follows:

Definition 4. *We say that a standard PKES* $\mathcal{AE} = (\mathcal{K}, \mathcal{E}, \mathcal{D})$ *is secure against the semi-honest strategy if, for every pair of non-uniform PSCFs* $F = \{F_n\}$ *and* $DA = \{DA_n\}$ *and every well-spread distribution* $\mathcal{X}(1^n)$, $\Pr[(pk, sk) \leftarrow \mathcal{K}(1^n); M \leftarrow \mathcal{X}(1^n); (M', r') = F_n(pk, M); C = \mathcal{E}(pk, M'; r') : DA_n(pk, C) = M]$ *is negligible in* n.

Basically, F and DA play the roles of A^e and A^d in Definition 3, respectively. A general construction of such a scheme is presented at Step 2 (in the random oracle model) and Theorem 1 says that we can use such a scheme as a building block to construct a ciphertext-auditable PKES. Specifically, we can convert a standard PKES that is secure against the semi-honest strategy into a ciphertext-auditable PKES by appending to each ciphertext an NIZK proof of its "well-formedness" as in [18,19,10,17] in order to force F to follow the semi-honest strategy.

Theorem 1. *Let* $\mathcal{AE}$ *be a standard PKES that is secure against the semi-honest strategy. If there exist efficient adaptive NIZK proofs of knowledge for NP, then we can transform* $\mathcal{AE}$ *into a ciphertext-auditable PKES* $\mathcal{AE}'$ *while preserving the IND-ATK security.*

Proof: Let $\mathcal{AE} = (\mathcal{K}, \mathcal{E}, \mathcal{D})$ be a standard PKES that is secure against the semi-honest strategy. Given a public key pk for $\mathcal{AE}$, define an NP language $L = \{(pk, C) : \exists(M, r) \text{ such that } C = \mathcal{E}(pk, M; r)\}$. L is the set of "well-formed" ciphertexts in the sense that they are an encryption of a plaintext under a public key. Let $\pi = (f, \mathcal{P}, \mathcal{V}, \mathcal{S} = (\mathcal{S}_1, \mathcal{S}_2), \mathcal{EXT} = (\mathcal{EXT}_1, \mathcal{EXT}_2))$ be an efficient adaptive NIZK proof of knowledge for L.

We apply a well-known technique to $\mathcal{AE}$, that is, we use π to append to each ciphertext an NIZK proof of its "well-formedness" as in [18,19,10,17]. This will force encryption adversaries to follow the semi-honest strategy. Formally, $\mathcal{AE}$ is converted into $\mathcal{AE}' = (\mathcal{K}', \mathcal{E}', \mathcal{D}')$ as follows:

- $\mathcal{K}'(1^n)$ generates $((pk, \sigma), sk)$, where $(pk, sk) \leftarrow \mathcal{K}'(1^n)$ and $\sigma \leftarrow \{0, 1\}^{f(n)}$ (σ is the common reference string for π and is part of the public key).
- $\mathcal{E}'(pk, M)$ generates (C, p), where $C \leftarrow \mathcal{E}(pk, M)$ $(C = \mathcal{E}(pk, M; r))$ and $p \leftarrow \mathcal{P}((pk, C), (M, r), \sigma)$.
- $\mathcal{D}'(sk, C) = \mathcal{D}(sk, C)$.

Note that $\mathcal{K}$ and $\mathcal{E}$ are modified for appending the proof, but $\mathcal{D}$ is not.

It is easy to see that $\mathcal{AE}'$ preserves the IND-ATK security (Recall that the conversion is based on the standard technique for security enhancement [18,19,10,17]). Also, it is easy to see that $\mathcal{AE}'$ satisfies verifiability, that is, we can use $\mathcal{CV}((pk, \sigma), C, p) = \mathcal{V}((pk, C), p, \sigma)$ as the verification algorithm.

It remains to show that $\mathcal{AE}'$ satisfies unforgeability. For contradiction, assume that there exists a pair of non-uniform PSCFs $A^e = \{A_n^e\}$ and $A^d = \{A_n^d\}$ and a well-spread distribution $\mathcal{X}(1^n)$ such that $\Pr[((pk, \sigma), sk) \leftarrow \mathcal{K}'(1^n); M \leftarrow \mathcal{X}(1^n); (C, p) = A_n^e((pk, \sigma), M) : A_n^d((pk, \sigma), C) = M$ and $\mathcal{V}((pk, C), p, \sigma) =$ Acc] is not negligible in n. We construct from (A^e, A^d) a pair of non-uniform PSCFs $F = \{F_n\}$ and $DA = \{DA_n\}$, which contradicts the assumption that $\mathcal{AE}$ is secure against the semi-honest strategy. For simplicity, we describe F as a *probabilistic* non-uniform PSCF. The idea is that F uses the knowledge extractor of π to extract the pair of plaintext and random coins that A^e used and DA just simulates A^d.

Circuit: F_n
Input: pk, M
Step1: Generate $(\sigma, aux) \leftarrow \mathcal{EXT}_1(1^n)$.
Step2: Generate $(C, p) = A_n^e((pk, \sigma), M)$.
Step3: Generate $(M', r') \leftarrow \mathcal{EXT}_2(\sigma, aux, (pk, C), p)$.
Step4: Output (M', r').

Circuit: DA_n
Input: pk, C
Advice: σ_n (this is the σ generated by F_n)
Step1: Output $A_n^d((pk, \sigma_n), C)$

Note that we can derandomize F so that all random coins including (σ, aux) are fixed. It is easy to see that $\Pr[(pk, sk) \leftarrow \mathcal{K}(1^n); M \leftarrow \mathcal{X}(1^n); (M', r') = F_n(pk, M); C = \mathcal{E}(pk, M'; r') : DA_n(pk, C) = M]$ is not negligible in n. This contradicts the assumption that $\mathcal{AE}$ is secure against the semi-honest strategy.
□

Remark 10. The proof of Theorem 1 depends on the fact that A^d is not allowed to have access to the proof string p. Note that our construction rules out the possibility that an adversary can hide the plaintext in the ciphertext, but does not necessarily rule out the possibility that an adversary can somehow hide the plaintext in the proof string p. It is an interesting open problem whether we can construct a ciphertext-auditable scheme such that A^d is allowed to have access to p, in other words, p is always empty. See Remark 5.

4.2   Step 2: Implementation of Unforgeability

We show how to construct a standard PKES that is secure against the semi-honest strategy. Unfortunately, we don't know if we can construct such a scheme in the standard model. Alternatively, we will construct it in the random oracle model, where we allow encryption/decryption algorithms and the two PSCFs (F, DA) in Definition 4 to have oracle access to random oracles.

Our proposed scheme $\mathcal{AE} = (\mathcal{K}, \mathcal{E}, \mathcal{D})$ is a modification of the IND-CCA2 scheme suggested by Bellare and Rogaway [4]. Let $\mathcal{H}_1 : \{0,1\}^* \to \{0,1\}^n$, $\mathcal{H}_2 : \{0,1\}^n \to \{0,1\}^\infty$, and $\mathcal{H}_3 : \{0,1\}^* \to \{0,1\}^n$ be random oracles. Let $\mathcal{G}$ be the generator for a trapdoor one-way permutation, denoted by $(f, f^{-1}) \leftarrow \mathcal{G}(1^n)$. $\mathcal{AE}$ is defined as follows:

- $\mathcal{K}(1^n)$ is the same as $\mathcal{G}(1^n)$, where $pk = f$ and $sk = f^{-1}$.
- $\mathcal{E}(pk, M; r) = (C_1, C_2, C_3) = (f(\mathcal{H}_1(M, r)), \mathcal{H}_2(\mathcal{H}_1(M, r)) \oplus M, \mathcal{H}_3((\mathcal{H}_1(M, r), M)))$, where r is chosen uniformly at random from $\{0,1\}^n$.
- $\mathcal{D}(sk, (C_1, C_2, C_3)) = C_2 \oplus \mathcal{H}_2(f^{-1}(C_1))$ if $C_3 = \mathcal{H}_3((f^{-1}(C_1), C_2 \oplus \mathcal{H}_2(f^{-1}(C_1))))$, decryption fails otherwise.

If we omit the hashing by $\mathcal{H}_1$, i.e., if we replace $\mathcal{H}_1(M, r)$ by r, then $\mathcal{AE}$ is the same as the IND-CCA2 scheme suggested by Bellare and Rogaway. Therefore, it is easy to see that the IND-ATK security of $\mathcal{AE}$ is reducible to the security of their IND-CCA2 scheme. Also, it is important to note that $\mathcal{E}(pk, \cdot; \cdot) : \{0,1\}^{m(n)+n} \to \{0,1\}^{m(n)+2n}$ behaves close to a random oracle unless F can find an $\mathcal{H}_1$-collision, where $m(n)$ is the length of plaintexts. Therefore, no matter how F selects (M', r'), the probability that the ciphertext $C = \mathcal{E}(pk, M'; r')$ is contained in the set of ciphertexts from which DA can recover M is negligible in n. This means that $\mathcal{AE}$ is secure against the semi-honest strategy.

Theorem 2. *Assume that $\mathcal{G}$ is a trapdoor one-way permutation generator. Then $\mathcal{AE}$ is a standard IND-CCA2 PKES that is secure against the semi-honest strategy in the random oracle model.*

Proof: If we omit the hashing by $\mathcal{H}_1$, i.e., if we replace $\mathcal{H}_1(M, r)$ by r, then $\mathcal{AE}$ is the same as the IND-CCA2 scheme suggested by Bellare and Rogaway. Given a plaintext M, the distributions of its ciphertexts generated by the two schemes are statistically close as long as r is chosen uniformly at random. This implies that the IND-ATK security of $\mathcal{AE}$ is reducible to the security of Bellare and Rogaway's scheme. Therefore, $\mathcal{AE}$ is IND-CCA2.

It remains to show that $\mathcal{AE}$ is secure against the semi-honest strategy. Given a PSCF $DA = \{DA_n\}$, a public key pk, a plaintext M, and three random oracles $(\mathcal{H}_1, \mathcal{H}_2, \mathcal{H}_3)$, let $S_{DA_n^{\mathcal{H}_1, \mathcal{H}_2, \mathcal{H}_3}}(pk, M)$ be the set of the ciphertexts from which DA_n can recover M, i.e., $S_{DA_n^{\mathcal{H}_1, \mathcal{H}_2, \mathcal{H}_3}}(pk, M) = \{C \mid M = DA_n^{\mathcal{H}_1, \mathcal{H}_2, \mathcal{H}_3}(pk, C)\}$. When $\mathcal{X}(1^n)$ is well-spread, its expected size is negligibly small. That is, for every non-uniform PSCF DA, every well-spread distribution $\mathcal{X}(1^n)$, every public key pk, and every three oracles $(\mathcal{H}_1, \mathcal{H}_2, \mathcal{H}_3)$,

$$Size_{DA_n^{\mathcal{H}_1, \mathcal{H}_2, \mathcal{H}_3}}(\mathcal{X}, pk) = E\left[M \leftarrow \mathcal{X}(1^n) : \frac{|S_{DA_n^{\mathcal{H}_1, \mathcal{H}_2, \mathcal{H}_3}}(pk, M)|}{2^{m(n)+2n}}\right]$$

is negligible in n, where $m(n)$ is a polynomial that represents the output length of $\mathcal{X}(1^n)$.

Note that, given a public key pk and a plaintext M, F_n tries to find a pair (M', r') such that $\mathcal{E}(pk, M'; r')$ is contained in the $S_{DA_n}{}^{\mathcal{H}_1, \mathcal{H}_2, \mathcal{H}_3}(pk, M)$. We need to prove that it succeeds only with negligible probability. That is, we will show that, for every pair of non-uniform PSCFs (F, DA) and every well-spread distribution $\mathcal{X}(1^n)$, the probability

$$Success_{F_n, DA_n}(\mathcal{X}) = \Pr \begin{bmatrix} (\mathcal{H}_1, \mathcal{H}_2, \mathcal{H}_3) \leftarrow 2^\infty; \\ (pk, sk) \leftarrow \mathcal{K}(1^n); \\ M \leftarrow \mathcal{X}(1^n); \\ (M', r') = F_n^{\mathcal{H}_1, \mathcal{H}_2, \mathcal{H}_3}(pk, M): \\ \mathcal{E}(pk, M'; r') \in S_{DA_n}{}^{\mathcal{H}_1, \mathcal{H}_2, \mathcal{H}_3}(pk, M) \end{bmatrix}$$

is negligible in n, where 2^∞ denotes the set of all random oracles from which $(\mathcal{H}_1, \mathcal{H}_2, \mathcal{H}_3)$ is chosen.

Without loss of generality, we can assume that

- F_n outputs one of the queries that it made to $\mathcal{H}_1$ and the number of queries is at most $q_1(n)$. The $q_1(n)$ queries may be adaptively chosen.
- The number of queries to $\mathcal{H}_2$ and $\mathcal{H}_3$ is at most $q_2(n)$ and $q_3(n)$, respectively. Again, the queries may be adaptively chosen.
- When F_n makes the i'th query (M_i, r_i), if at least one of the following conditions holds, then F_n runs a *special program*.

  1. A pair of (M_i, r_i) and $(M_j, r_j)(j < i)$ is a collision under $\mathcal{H}_1$, i.e., $\mathcal{H}_1(M_i, r_i) = \mathcal{H}_1(M_j, r_j)$.
  2. F_n has already made the query $\mathcal{H}_1(M_i, r_i)$ to $\mathcal{H}_2$.
  3. F_n has already made the query $(\mathcal{H}_1(M_i, r_i), M_i)$ to $\mathcal{H}_3$.

Let $SP_{F_n}{}^{\mathcal{H}_1, \mathcal{H}_2, \mathcal{H}_3}(pk, M)$ denote the event that F_n, given a pair of a public key pk and a plaintext M, runs the special program. It is easy to see that, for every pair of pk and M, the probability of the event occurring, i.e., $\Pr[(\mathcal{H}_1, \mathcal{H}_2, \mathcal{H}_3) \leftarrow 2^\infty : SP_{F_n}{}^{\mathcal{H}_1, \mathcal{H}_2, \mathcal{H}_3}(pk, M)]$, is negligible in n. We denote by $\nu(n)$ the negligible probability, which does not depend on any pair of pk and M.

When F_n makes the i'th query (M_i, r_i) to $\mathcal{H}_1$, the conditional probability that the corresponding ciphertext is contained in $S_{DA_n}{}^{\mathcal{H}_1, \mathcal{H}_2, \mathcal{H}_3}(pk, M)$ assuming that $SP_{F_n}(pk, M)$ has not occurred is at most

$$P_{DA_n}(pk, M) = E \begin{bmatrix} (\mathcal{H}_1, \mathcal{H}_2, \mathcal{H}_3) \leftarrow 2^\infty : \\ \frac{|S_{DA_n}{}^{\mathcal{H}_1, \mathcal{H}_2, \mathcal{H}_3}(pk, M)|}{(2^n - q_1(n) - q_2(n) - q_3(n))2^{m(n)+n}} \end{bmatrix}.$$

Therefore, for every pair of non-uniform PSCFs (F, DA) and every well-spread distribution $\mathcal{X}(1^n)$, $Success_{F_n, DA_n}(\mathcal{X})$ is bounded from above as follows:

$$Success_{F_n, DA_n}(\mathcal{X}) \leq E \begin{bmatrix} (pk, sk) \leftarrow \mathcal{K}(1^n); \\ M \leftarrow \mathcal{X}(1^n) : \\ 1 - (1 - P_{DA_n}(pk, M))^{q_1(n)} \end{bmatrix} (1 - \nu(n)) + \nu(n).$$

$$\leq \mathrm{E}\left[\begin{array}{l}(pk, sk) \leftarrow \mathcal{K}(1^n); \\ M \leftarrow \mathcal{X}(1^n): \\ q_1(n) P_{DA_n}(pk, M)\end{array}\right] + \nu(n).$$

$$= q_1(n)\mathrm{E}\left[\begin{array}{l}(pk, sk) \leftarrow \mathcal{K}(1^n); \\ M \leftarrow \mathcal{X}(1^n); \\ (\mathcal{H}_1, \mathcal{H}_2, \mathcal{H}_3) \leftarrow 2^\infty: \\ \dfrac{|S_{DA_n^{\mathcal{H}_1, \mathcal{H}_2, \mathcal{H}_3}}(pk, M)|}{(2^n - q_1(n) - q_2(n) - q_3(n))2^{m(n)+n}}\end{array}\right] + \nu(n).$$

$$= \frac{q_1(n)2^n}{2^n - q_1(n) - q_2(n) - q_3(n)}\mathrm{E}\left[\begin{array}{l}(pk, sk) \leftarrow \mathcal{K}(1^n); \\ (\mathcal{H}_1, \mathcal{H}_2, \mathcal{H}_3) \leftarrow 2^\infty: \\ Size_{DA_n^{\mathcal{H}_1, \mathcal{H}_2, \mathcal{H}_3}}(\mathcal{X}, pk)\end{array}\right] + \nu(n).$$

Since $q_1(n)$, $q_2(n)$, and $q_3(n)$ are polynomials, the value is negligible in n. □

Remark 11. What if an encryption adversary uses a fixed string R as in the attack described in Section 3.2? If the encryption adversary is allowed to pass the value of $\mathcal{H}_1(M, R)$ to the decryption adversary, M can be easily recovered from C. However, Definition 3 does not allow it (See Remark 6). From the perspective of our motivating scenario, passing the value of $\mathcal{H}_1(M, R)$ is as difficult as passing the plaintext M itself under our basic assumption.

5   Concluding Remarks

Motivated by a privacy breach scenario, we have proposed a new notion of ciphertext-auditable PKESs, which is not captured by the standard security notion IND-CCA2. We have shown a plausibility result for the new notion, that is, it can be realized using as building blocks an NIZK proof of knowledge for NP and a trapdoor one-way permutation in the random oracle model. We have the following research issues: (1) construct *practical* schemes based on number-theoretic assumptions such as discrete logarithm and factoring problems, and (2) investigate general construction in the standard model rather than in the random oracle model. Also, we have already mentioned some open issues in Remarks 1, 3, 5, 8, and 10.

Also, as we have already mentioned, it would be interesting to investigate:

- ciphertext-auditability in the symmetric encryption setting (See Remark 1).
- relations between ciphertext-auditability and standard security notions such as IND-CPA (See Remark 3).
- whether it is possible to construct a ciphertext-auditable PKES with empty proof string (See Remarks 5 and 10).
- how to strengthen the definition of ciphertext-auditable PKESs (See Remark 8).

References

1. M. Bellare, A. Desai, D. Pointcheval, and P. Rogaway, "Relations among Notions of Security for Public-key Encryption Schemes," Proceedings of Crypto'98, 1998.
2. M. Bellare, A. Boldyreva, A. Desai, and D. Pointcheval, "Key-Privacy in Public-Key Encryption," Proceedings of ASIACRYPT'01, 2001.
3. M. Bellare, A. Boldyreva and A. Palacio, "An Uninstantiable Random-Oracle-Model Scheme for a Hybrid-Encryption Problem," Proceedings of Eurocrypt'04, 2004.
4. M. Bellare and P. Rogaway, "Random Oracles are Practical: a paradigm for designing efficient protocols," Proceedings of the 1st ACM Conference on Computer and Communications Security, pp. 62-73, 1993.
5. R. Canetti, "Towards Realizing Random Oracles: Hash Functions that Hide All Partial Information," Proceedings of CRYPTO'97, pp.455-469, 1997.
6. J. Y. Choi, P. Golle, and M. Jakobsson, "Auditable Privacy: On Tamper-evident Mix Networks," Proceedings of Financial Crypto'06, 2006.
7. R. Cramer and V. Shoup, "A practical public key cryptosystem provably secure against adaptive chosen ciphertext attack," Proceedings of CRYPTO'98, pp.13-25, 1998.
8. Y. Desmedt, "Abuses in Cryptography and How to Fight Them," Proceedings of CRYPTO'88, pp.375-389, 1988.
9. T. ElGamal, "A public key cryptosystem and signature scheme based on discrete logarithms," IEEE Trans. Inform. Theory, Vol. 31, pp.469-472, 1985.
10. A. De Santis, G. Di Crescenzo, R. Ostrovsky, G. Persiano and A. Sahai, "Robust Noninteractive Zero-Knowledge," Proceedings of CRYPTO 2001, 2001.
11. A. De Santis and G. Persiano, "Zero-Knowledge Proofs of Knowledge without Interaction," Proceedings of the 33rd FOCS, 1992.
12. O. Goldreich, "Foundations of Cryptography: Volume II Basic Applications," Cambridge University Press, 2004.
13. S. Halevi, "A sufficient condition for key-privacy," Cryptology ePrint Archive, Report 2005/005, 2005.
14. J. Katz and M. Yung, "Unforgeable Encryption and Chosen Ciphertext Seucre Modes of Operation, " Proceedings of FSE 2000, 2001.
15. J. Langford, N. Hopper, and L. Ahn, "Provably Secure Steganography," Proceedings of CRYPTO'02, 2002.
16. M. Lepinski, S. Micali, A. Shelat, "Fair-Zero Knowledge," Proceedings of TCC'05, 2005.
17. Y. Lindell, "A Simpler Construction of CCA2-Secure Public-Key Encryption Under General Assumptions," Proceedings of Eurocrypt'03, 2003.
18. M. Naor and M. Yung, "Public-key Cryptosystems Provably Secure Against Chosen Ciphertext Attacks," Proceedings of the 22nd STOC, 1990.
19. A. Sahai, "Non-Malleable Non-Interactive Zero Knowledge and Adaptive Chosen-Ciphertext Security," Proceedings of the 40th FOCS, 1999.

Provably-Secure Two-Round Password-Authenticated Group Key Exchange in the Standard Model*

Jeong Ok Kwon[1], Ik Rae Jeong[2], and Dong Hoon Lee[1]

[1] Graduate School of Information Security CIST, Korea University,
Anam-dong Seongbuk-Gu, Seoul, 136-701 Korea
{pitapat, donghlee}@korea.ac.kr
[2] ETRI (Electronics and Telecommunications Research Institute),
161 Gajeong-dong, Yuseoung-Gu, Daejeon, 305-700 Korea
jir@etri.re.kr

Abstract. Password-authenticated group key exchange (PAGKE) allows group users to share a session key using a human-memorable password *only*. The fundamental security goal of PAGKE is security against dictionary attacks. Several solutions have been proposed to solve this problem while most ones require rounds linearly increasing in the number of group users, so they are neither scalable nor practical. Recently a provably-secure constant-round PAGKE protocol overcoming this shortcoming is proposed at PKC '06. However current PAGKE protocols have been proven secure in the *ideal* model. The ideal model assumes that some functions are "ideal" functions (or random functions). In the ideal cipher model, we assume a block cipher is an ideal cipher and in the ideal hash model (also the so-called the random oracle model), we assume a hash function is an ideal hash function. However it is well-known that a provably-secure scheme in the ideal model may be insecure if the ideal functions are implemented by the real functions. In this paper we propose the first provably-secure PAGKE protocol in the *standard* model. Our protocol is a two-round protocol and the security of the protocol is reduced to the Decisional Diffie-Hellman (DDH) problem.

1 Introduction

To communicate securely over an insecure public network it is essential that secret keys are exchanged securely. The shared secret key may be subsequently used to achieve some cryptographic goals such as confidentiality or data integrity. Password-authenticated key exchange (PAKE) protocols are used to share a secret key between two or more specified users using *only* a human-memorable password. PAKE has many merits in views of convenience, mobility, and less

---

* This work was supported by the MIC (Ministry of Information and Communication), Korea, under the ITRC (Information Technology Research Center) support program supervised by the IITA (Institute of Information Technology Assessment) and was done while the first author was visiting Kyushu University in Japan.

H. Yoshiura et al. (Eds.): IWSEC 2006, LNCS 4266, pp. 322–336, 2006.

hardware requirement. Because in PAKE protocols, each party remembers only an easily memorable password and the parties do not need any additional devices like smart cards or hardware tokens, and any additional trusted third party.

Protocols for password-authenticated group key exchange (PAGKE) can be used in several environments, especially in mobile networks. In mobile networks session key exchange for the secure group communication services, such as electronic conferences [4,39], personal networking [13,27], military operations, and emergency rescue [38,39,40], has to be done efficiently using relatively small resources. Since protocols for PAGKE provide a way to authenticate users of a group and derive cryptographically secure keys for users from low-entropy passwords in environments where a security infrastructure like the PKI (Public-Key Infrastructure) is not deployed, PAGKE protocols can be more easily implemented and efficiently used for the applications. The main efficiency issues in real applications over mobile networks is how to reduce the number of rounds, the computing time, and the size of the transmitted message since wireless clusters have memory and processing constraints, and the networks have limited bandwidth. Especially the number of rounds is very important factor in case that the size of group users is large or group keys have to be exchanged frequently.

Compared to other security models, the most distinguishable characteristic of the PAKE security model is that the model must incorporate dictionary attacks. The dictionary attacks are possible due to the low entropy of the password space. In practice, a password consists of 4 or 8 characters such as natural language phrase to be easily memorized. The set of these probable passwords is small, so there exists a relatively small dictionary. Usually dictionary attacks are classified into two classes: *on-line* and *off-line* dictionary attacks. In on-line dictionary attacks, an adversary attempts to use a guessed password by participating in a key exchange protocol. If the protocol run is failed, the adversary initiates a new protocol run using another guessed password. These on-line attacks require the participation of an adversary. In off-line dictionary attacks, an adversary selects a password from a dictionary and verifies his guess in the off-line manner, i.e., the adversary uses only recorded transcripts from a successful run of the protocol. So such off-line attacks are undetectable. The on-line dictionary attacks are always possible, but these attacks can not become a serious threat because the on-line attacks can be easily detected and thwarted by counting access failures. However, off-line dictionary attacks are more difficult to prevent. Even if there exist tiny amounts of redundancy information in flows of the scheme, then adversaries may mount an off-line dictionary attack by using the redundancy as a verifier for checking whether a guessed password is correct or not. The main security goal of schemes for PAKE is to restrict the adversary to on-line dictionary attacks only. If a PAKE scheme is secure, an adversary can not obtain any advantage in guessing the passwords and the session keys of users through the off-line dictionary attacks.

One of the most basic security requirements of PAKE protocols is key secrecy, which guarantees that no computationally bounded adversary should learn anything about the session keys shared between honest users by eavesdropping or sending messages of its choice to parties in the protocol. Other desirable security goals are as follows (formal definitions are given in Section 4). The importance of the following attributes depends on the real applications. *Forward Secrecy* means that even with the password of the users any adversary does not learn any information about session keys which are successfully established between honest parties without any interruption. A PAKE protocol is secure against *known-key attacks* if compromise of multiple session keys for sessions other than the one does not affect its key secrecy. This notion of security means that session keys are computationally independent from each other. A bit more formally, this security protects against "Denning-Sacco" attacks [23] involving compromise of multiple session keys (for sessions other than the one whose secrecy must be guaranteed). Security against known-key attacks also implies that an adversary cannot gain the ability to perform the off-line dictionary attacks on the passwords from the compromised session keys which are successfully established between honest parties.

2 Our Work in Relation to Prior Work

Related Work. There are several works about how to make the PAGKE protocol [4,16,34,24,2]. In [4], Asokan *et al.* have proposed a PAGKE protocol based on the group key exchange protocol of Becker and Wille [11] without a formal proof. A forward-secure key exchange guarantees that the expose of a password does not compromise the previous session keys. Bresson *et al.* have suggested the first provably forward-secure PAGKE protocol in both the ideal hash/cipher model under the TG-CDH and M-DDH assumptions [16]. The protocols in [4] and [16] requires $O(n)$ rounds and $O(n)$ exponentiations per each user, where n is the number of group users, and the protocols are *asymmetric*. Asymmetric group key exchange protocol places an unfair computational burden to any specific user of the key exchange. [24] proposed a password-based variant of the Kim-Lee-Lee group key exchange protocol [31]. The PAGKE protocol requires constant-round and uses an ideal cipher. However, in [2] Abdalla *et al.* show that the protocol is vulnerable to an off-line dictionary attack since the encryption key used by each user is unique. Very recently, Abdalla *et al.* [2] have provided a symmetric PAGKE protocol with consant-round and a security proof without forward secrecy in both the ideal hash/cipher model under the DDH assumption. The protocol is built on the protocol of Burmester and Desmedt.

Motivation. All previous PAGKE protocols have been constructed in the *ideal model*. The ideal model is a security model, where we assume that a certain function is an "ideal" function. In the ideal cipher model, a block cipher ideally behaviors through encryption/decryption oracles as follows: Let $\mathcal{G}$ and $\mathcal{C}$ to be finite sets of strings where $|\mathcal{G}| = |\mathcal{C}|$ and fix $\mathcal{K} \in \{0,1\}^*$. The encryption oracle $\mathcal{E}$ produces a truly random value $c \in \mathcal{C}$ for each new query ($m \in \mathcal{G}, k \in \mathcal{K}$) and identical answers if the same query is asked twice. The decryption oracle $\mathcal{D}$ produces a truly random value $m \in \mathcal{G}$ for each new query ($c \in \{0,1\}^*, k \in \mathcal{K}$) and identical answers if the same query is asked twice. In the ideal hash model (also called the random oracle model [6]) a hash function is a true random function. The hash function produces a truly random value for each new query and identical answer if the same query is asked twice.

The security proof of a protocol in the ideal model gives an insight in analyzing the protocol, but does not guarantee that the protocol is secure in the real world. In fact, many results [20,37,26,21,10] on the ideal hash methodology show that a scheme secure using ideal hash oracles may be not secure if the oracles are replaced by real functions; Canetti, Goldreich and Halevi [20] point out that although the ideal hash methodology formulated by Bellare and Rogaway [6] seems to be useful in practice, it is unclear how to put the methodology on the real world. They showed that there exist a signature scheme and an encryption scheme, which are secure in the ideal hash model but result in insecure schemes for any implementation of the ideal hash in the real world. A secure PAGKE scheme in the ideal cipher model only guarantees that the PAGKE protocol is secure against general attacks that do not exploit a particular implementation of the block cipher. Added to that, in practice current block ciphers are far from being random permutations. Thus a protocol seems to be more reliable, if we do not use ideal functions such as an ideal hash and an ideal cipher. Thus, a protocol is more reliable, if we do not use ideal functions such as an ideal hash and an ideal cipher. This is the motivation of our work.

Table 1. Comparisons of complexity and security with the related PAGKE protocols

Scheme	Asokan et al. [4]	Bresson et al. [16]	Abdalla et al. [2]	Our Protocol
Round	$n+1$	n	3	2
Exponentiation	$O(n)$	$O(n)$	4	4
Communication	$O(n \cdot |p|)$	$O(n \cdot |p|)$	$2 \cdot |p| + |N|$	$2 \cdot |p|$
Security	−	KK and FS	KK	KK and FS
Assumption	−	IH and IC	IH and IC	Standard

We use a group $\mathbb{Z}_p^*$ where p is a prime. n is the number of users in a group and $|N|$ is the length of a random number. An FS protocol is a forward-secure key exchange protocol and a KK protocol is a secure key exchange protocol against known-key attacks. IH denotes the ideal hash model and IC denotes the ideal cipher model.

Our Result. Our main contribution is the first provably-secure constant-round PAGKE protocol in the standard model under the DDH assumption. The protocol also provides forward secrecy and is symmetric. The suggested protocol is based on the protocol of Burmester and Desmedt [19]. The Burmester and Desmedt protocol is not a password-authenticated key exchange protocol, and the security of the protocol in the passive adversarial model was proved by Katz and Yung [30]. In [30], Katz and Yung also proposed a forward-secure constant-round group key exchange protocol against active adversaries in the standard model, which is based on the group key exchange protocol of Burmester and Desmedt. They use signatures to authenticate the messages of the protocol of [19]. To use a signature scheme, all group users have an associated public-/private-key pair known to all other users in the network. Due to the critical assumption for possessing of public-/private-key pair, the approach in [30] can not be applied to PAGKE.

We note that converting a group key exchange protocol secure against passive adversaries into a PAGKE protocol secure against dictionary attacks is not easy at all. Because PAGKE must provide authentication using only a password, redundancy information in the flows of the PAGKE protocols can provide a clue to mount an off-line dictionary attack. To solve this problem, instead of using signatures to authenticate the protocol messages of [19], we use a multiplicative function as in [32,3,1], where the multiplicative function multiplies the protocol messages of [19] by a value which is made with a password and a pseudo random function to generate a session key.

We compare the efficiency and the security of our protocol with the protocols of Asokan *et al.* in [4], Bresson *et al.* in [16], and Abdalla *et al.* in [2]. Table 1 summarizes the comparisons in which communication cost is the total number of bits that each user sends during a protocol run. In the comparisons, we consider the protocol [2] by omitting the mutual authentication part (However, the omission does not affect the main mechanism of the protocol because the protocol is analyzed in the ideal cipher and the ideal hash models).

3   Primitives

Decisional Diffie-Hellman Assumption. Let $\mathbb{G} = \langle g \rangle$ be any finite cyclic group of prime order q. The DDH problem is defined as follows: given a triple (U, V, W), determine that the triple is a Diffie-Hellman triple (g^a, g^b, g^{ab}) or a random triple (g^a, g^b, g^r). The advantage of an algorithm $\mathcal{A}$, $\mathsf{Adv}_{\mathbb{G},\mathcal{A}}^{\mathsf{ddh}}(t)$, running in time t is ϵ, if

$$|\Pr[a, b \leftarrow \mathbb{Z}_q : \mathcal{A}(g, g^a, g^b, g^{ab}) = 1] - \Pr[a, b, r \leftarrow \mathbb{Z}_q : \mathcal{A}(g, g^a, g^b, g^r) = 1]| \geq \epsilon.$$

We say the DDH assumption holds in $\mathbb{G}$ if no probabilistic polynomial time algorithm $\mathcal{A}$ can solve the DDH problem with non-negligible advantage. We let $\mathsf{Adv}_{\mathbb{G}}^{\mathsf{ddh}}(t)$ denote the maximum advantage which is over all adversaries $\mathcal{A}$s running in time at most t.

Pseudorandom Functions. Let $F : Keys(F) \times D \to R$ be a family of functions, and $g : D \to R$ a random function. $\mathcal{A}$ is an algorithm that takes an oracle access to a function and returns a bit. We consider two experiments:

$$
\begin{array}{|c|c|}
\mathbf{Exp}_{F,\mathcal{A}}^{\mathsf{prf}\text{-}1} & \mathbf{Exp}_{F,\mathcal{A}}^{\mathsf{prf}\text{-}0} \\
K \stackrel{R}{\leftarrow} Keys(F) & g \stackrel{R}{\leftarrow} Rand^{D \to R} \\
d \leftarrow \mathcal{A}^{F_K(\cdot)} & d \leftarrow \mathcal{A}^{g(\cdot)} \\
\text{return } d & \text{return } d
\end{array}
$$

The advantage of an adversary $\mathcal{A}$ is defined as follows:

$$\mathsf{Adv}_{F,\mathcal{A}}^{\mathsf{prf}} = \Pr[\mathbf{Exp}_{F,\mathcal{A}}^{\mathsf{prf}\text{-}1} = 1] - \Pr[\mathbf{Exp}_{F,\mathcal{A}}^{\mathsf{prf}\text{-}0} = 1].$$

The advantage function is defined as follows:

$$\text{Adv}_F^{\text{prf}}(\kappa, T, q, \mu) = \max_{\mathcal{A}}\{\text{Adv}_{A_{F,\mathcal{A}}}^{\text{prf}}\},$$

where $\mathcal{A}$ is any adversary with time complexity T making at most q oracle queries and the sum of the length of these queries being at most μ bits. The scheme F is a secure pseudo random function family if the advantage of any adversary $\mathcal{A}$ with time complexity polynomial in κ is negligible.

The protocol of Burmester and Desmedt [19]. Our protocol is based on the Burmester and Desmedt's conference key exchange protocol in broadcast networks. Let $U_1, \ldots, U_n$ be a group of n users wishing to generate a session key. The indices are cyclic, i.e., U_{n+i} is U_i.

$\mathcal{BD}$

Round 1. Each user U_i chooses a random $r_i \in \mathbb{Z}_q^*$ and broadcasts $z_i = g^{r_i} \bmod p$.

Round 2. Each useer U_i broadcasts $X_i = (z_{i+1}/z_{i-1})^{r_i} \bmod p$.

Key computation. Each user U_i computes the session key as follows:

$$K_i = (z_{i-1})^{nr_i} \cdot X_i^{n-1} \cdot X_{i+1}^{n-2} \cdots X_{i-2} \bmod p.$$

It may be easily verified that all honest users compute the same key,

$$K = g^{r_1 r_2 + r_2 r_3 + \ldots + r_n r_1} \bmod p.$$

The following characterizes the security of $\mathcal{BD}$. The proof of below theorem appears in the proof of Theorem 3 of [30].

Theorem 1. Let $\mathbb{G}$ be a group in which the DDH assumption holds. Then $\mathcal{BD}$ is a secure group key exchange (GKE) protocol achieving forward secrecy in an authenticated channel model (i.e., secure against only passive adversaries). Concretely,

$$\text{Adv}_{\mathcal{BD}}^{\text{gke-fs}}(k, t, 1) \leq 2n \cdot \text{Adv}_{\mathbb{G}}^{\text{ddh}}(t),$$

where t is the maximum total game time including an adversary's running time, and an adversary makes only a single execute query. n is the upper bound of the number of the parties in the game.

4   Model

The model described in this section is based on Bresson *et al.*'s model in [15,16] and Katz *et al.*'s model in [30] which follow closely the model established by Bellare and Rogaway [7,8]. In the paper, we assume that the network is a broadcast network, where the users can simultaneously broadcast messages to each other. But we do not assume that the broadcast network guarantees that all users receive identical messages, i.e., we allow that a malicious adversary may intercept the broadcast messages and substitute his own messages for some of them. In our model, we assume that the group users do not deviate from the protocol and the adversary is not a group user.

Initialization. We fix a nonempty set $\mathcal{U} = \{U_1, \ldots, U_n\}$ of potential users, where n is the number of users. A user $U_i \in \mathcal{U}$ may have many instances of the protocol. An instance of U_i is represented by an oracle Π_i^s, for any $s \in \mathbb{N}$. A set of users shares a password pw obtained at the start of the protocol using a password generation algorithm $\mathcal{PG}(1^\kappa)$ which on input a security parameter 1^κ outputs a password pw uniformly distributed in a password space of size $\mathcal{PW}$.

Partnering. We define *partnering* for broadcast networks. We do not assume a synchronous network, and a round number is appended to a broadcast message. We assume that a sender's identity is also appended to the message to indicate the sender of the message. Let sid_i^s be the concatenation of all (broadcast) messages that oracle Π_i^s has sent and received. For the concatenation we assume that the messages are lexically ordered according to the sender's identity. Let a partner identifier pid_i^s for instance Π_i^s be a set of the identities of the users with whom Π_i^s intends to establish a session key. pid_i^s includes U_i itself. The oracles Π_i^s and Π_j^t are *partnered* if:

- $\mathsf{pid}_i^s = \mathsf{pid}_j^t$ and $\mathsf{sid}_i^s = \mathsf{sid}_j^t$.

Queries. An adversary $\mathcal{A}$ is a probabilistic polynomial-time machine that controls all the communications and makes queries to any oracle. The queries that $\mathcal{A}$ can use are as follows:

- Execute($\mathcal{U}$): This query models passive attacks, where the adversary gets the instances of honest executions of a protocol by $\mathcal{U}$.
- Send(Π_i^s, m): This query is used to send a message m to Π_i^s and get the response from Π_i^s. The adversary can initiate a new instance Π_i^s with a set of communicating users $U_1, \ldots, U_n$ by calling $\mathsf{Send}_0(U_i, (U_1, \ldots, U_n))$.
- Reveal(Π_i^s): This query models the adversary's ability to obtain session keys (*known-key attacks*). If a session key $sk_{\Pi_i^s}$ has previously been constructed by Π_i^s, it is returned to the adversary.
- Corrupt(U_i): This query models the adversary's ability to obtain long-term keys of parties (*forward secrecy*). The adversary is assumed to be able to obtain long-term keys of parties, but cannot control the behavior of these players directly (of course, once the adversary has asked a query Corrupt(U_i), the adversary may impersonate U_i in subsequent Send queries.) We restrict that on Corrupt(U_i) the adversary only can get the password pw, but cannot obtain any internal data of U_i.
- Test(Π_i^s): This query is used to define the advantage of the adversary. This query is allowed only once by the adversary $\mathcal{A}$, and only to *fresh* oracles, which is defined later. On this query a simulator flips a coin b. If b is 1, then the session $sk_{\Pi_i^s}$ is returned. Otherwise a string randomly drawn from a session key distribution is returned.

A *passive adversary* can use the Execute, Reveal, Corrupt and Test queries while an *active adversary* additionally can use the Send query. Even though the Execute query may seem to be useless since it can be simulated by repeatedly using the Send queries. Yet the Execute query is essential to distinguish on-line dictionary attacks from off-line dictionary attacks. The Send queries are directly asked by the adversary and the number of those dose not take into account the number of Execute queries. Thus, the number of on-line dictionary attacks can be bounded by the number of Send queries.

PAGKE Security. Consider a game between an adversary $\mathcal{A}$ and a set of oracles. $\mathcal{A}$ asks the above queries to the oracles in order to defeat the security of a protocol P, and receives the responses. At some point during the game a Test query is asked to a fresh oracle, and the adversary may continue to make other queries. Finally the adversary outputs its guess b' for the bit b used by the Test oracle, and terminates. We define CG to be an event that $\mathcal{A}$ correctly guesses the bit b. The advantage of adversary $\mathcal{A}$ must be measured in terms of the security parameter k and is defined as follows:

$$\mathsf{Adv}_{P,\mathcal{A}}(k) = 2 \cdot \Pr[\mathsf{CG}] - 1.$$

The advantage function is defined as follows:

$$\mathsf{Adv}_P(k, t) = \max_{\mathcal{A}} \{\mathsf{Adv}_{P,\mathcal{A}}(k)\},$$

where $\mathcal{A}$ is any adversary with time complexity t which is polynomial in k.

Freshness. We define a notion of *freshness* considering forward secrecy which means that an adversary does not learn any information about *previously* established session keys when making a Corrupt-query. We say an oracle Π_i^s is *fresh* if the following conditions hold:

- Π_i^s has computed a session key $sk \neq$ NULL and neither Π_i^s nor Π_j^t have been asked for a Reveal query, where Π_i^s and Π_j^t are partnered.
- No Corrupt query has been made by the adversary since the beginning of the game.

Definition 1. We say a protocol P is a *secure password-authenticated group key exchange protocol* if the following two properties are satisfied:

- Validity: if all oracles in a session are partnered, the session keys of all oracles are same.
- Key secrecy: $\mathsf{Adv}_P(k, t)$ is bounded by $q_{se}/\mathcal{PW} + \epsilon(k)$, where $\epsilon(k)$ is negligible, q_{se} is the number of Send queries, and $\mathcal{PW}$ is the size of the password space.

(1) We say a protocol P is a secure PAGKE protocol if validity and key secrecy are satisfied when no Reveal and Corrupt queries are allowed.
(2) We say a protocol P is a secure PAGKE-KK protocol if validity and key secrecy are satisfied when no Corrupt query is allowed.

(3) We say a protocol P is a secure PAGKE-FS protocol if validity and key secrecy are satisfied when no Reveal query is allowed.

(4) We say a protocol P is a secure PAGKE-KK&FS protocol if validity and key secrecy are satisfied.

5   A Two-Round Protocol for PAGKE

In this section, we present protocol $\mathcal{PAGKE}$ which requires only two rounds, achieves forward secrecy, and is secure against known-key attacks. $\mathcal{PAGKE}$ is designed without using the random oracle model and its security is proved under the DDH assumption. In order to convert the unauthenticated Burmester and Desmedt's group key exchange protocol to a PAGKE protocol, we use a multiplicative function; the user U_i's ephemeral Diffie-Hellman value $g_1^{r_i}$ is multiplied by $g_2^{H(pw\|U_i)}$ in the first round.

$\mathcal{PAGKE}$

Public information: Let $U_1, \ldots, U_n$ be the identities in lexical order of n users. A finite cyclic group $\mathbb{G}$ of order q in $\mathbb{Z}_p^*$. Two primes p, q such that $p = 2q + 1$, where p is a safe prime such that the DDH problem is hard to solve in $\mathbb{G}$. g_1 and g_2 are generators of $\mathbb{G}$ both having order q, where g_1 and g_2 must be generated so that their discrete logarithmic relation is unknown. A hash function H from $\{0,1\}^*$ to $\mathbb{Z}_q^*$. F is a pseudo random function family.

Round 1: Each user U_i chooses a random number $r_i \in \mathbb{Z}_q^*$, computes $x_i = g_1^{r_i} \bmod p$ and $X_i = x_i \cdot g_2^{H(pw\|U_i)} \bmod p$. U_i broadcasts $U_i\|1\|X_i$, where 1 represents the broadcast message in the first round.

Round 2: Each user U_i computes x_{i-1} and x_{i+1} using pw and the senders' identities U_{i-1} and U_{i+1}, respectively. U_i computes $Y_i = (x_{i+1}/x_{i-1})^{r_i} \bmod p$ and broadcasts $U_i\|2\|Y_i$.

Key computation: Each user U_i computes the secret key for F as $k_i = (x_{i-1})^{nr_i} \cdot Y_i^{n-1} \cdot Y_{i+1}^{n-2} \cdots Y_{i-2} \bmod p$ and the session key $sk_i = F_{k_i}(\mathcal{U}\|\mathsf{sid})$, where $\mathcal{U} = (U_1, \ldots, U_n)$, $\mathsf{sid} = 1\|\mathsf{X}\|2\|\mathsf{Y}$, $\mathsf{X} = (X_1, \ldots, X_n)$, and $\mathsf{Y} = (Y_1, \ldots, Y_n)$.

If everything works correctly in $\mathcal{PAGKE}$, the session key computed by U_i is $sk_i = F_{k_i}(\mathcal{U}\|\mathsf{sid})$, where $k_i = g_1^{r_1 r_2 + r_2 r_3 + \ldots + r_n r_1} \bmod p$.

6   Security Analysis

We now present that under the intractability assumption of the decisional Diffie-Hellman (DDH) problem and if F is a secure pseudo random function, the proposed group key exchange protocol is secure against dictionary attacks and known-key attacks and provides forward secrecy.

Theorem 2. Let $\mathbb{G}$ be a group in which the DDH assumption holds and F is a secure pseudo random function family. Then $\mathcal{PAGKE}$ is a secure PAGKE-KK&FS protocol. Concretely,

$$\mathsf{Adv}_{\mathcal{PAGKE}}^{\text{pagke-kk\&fs}}(k, t, q_{ex}, q_{se}) \leq 2(n + 2n \cdot N_s + q_{se}) \cdot \mathsf{Adv}_{\mathbb{G}}^{\text{ddh}}(t) + \mathsf{Adv}_{\mathcal{F}}^{\text{prf}}(\kappa, T, q, h)$$

$$+ \frac{2q_{se}}{\mathcal{PW}} + \frac{|\mathcal{U}|(q_{ex} + q_{se})^2}{2q},$$

where t is the maximum total game time including an adversary's running time, and an adversary makes q_{ex} Execute queries and q_{se} Send queries. n is the upper bound of the number of the parties in the game, N_s is the upper bound of the number of sessions that an adversary makes, and $\mathcal{PW}$ is the size of the password space.

Proof of Theorem 2. Consider an adversary $\mathcal{A}$ attacking $\mathcal{PAGKE}$ in the sense of forward secrecy and security against known-key attacks. In this proof, we prove that the best strategy $\mathcal{A}$ can take is to eliminate one password from the password dictionary per initiated session. Assume that $\mathcal{A}$ breaks $\mathcal{PAGKE}$ with a non-negligible probability. An adversary may get information about a particular session key if a collision appears on the transcripts (for the same set of users) during the experiment; i.e., there exists a user $U_i \in \mathcal{U}$ and t, s ($t \neq s$) such that the transcript used by instance Π_i^s is equal to the transcript used by instance Π_i^t. The other cases allow us to solve the DDH problem and break a pseudo randomness of a pseudo random function family with probability related to the adversary's success probability. We now proceed with a more formal proof. Let Col be the event that a transcript is used twice by a particular user.

The advantage with the event Col is bounded by the birthday paradox:

$$\mathsf{Adv}_{\mathcal{PAGKE}}^{\text{pagke-kk\&fs-Col}}(k, t, q_{ex}, q_{se}) = 2\Pr[\mathsf{CG} \wedge \mathsf{Col}] - 1 \leq 2\Pr[\mathsf{Col}] \leq \frac{|\mathcal{U}|(q_{ex} + q_{se})^2}{q},$$

$$(1)$$

where q is the size of the group $\mathbb{G}$.

The advantage without the event Col is from the following two cases:

(Case 1) For the Test oracle Π_i^s, all parties in pid_i^s have a partner oracle.
(Case 2) For the Test oracle Π_i^s, there exists at least one party U_j ($j \neq i \wedge U_j \in \mathsf{pid}_i^s$) such that U_j does not have a partner oracle.

For $i \in \{1, 2\}$, let $\mathsf{Adv}_{\mathcal{PAGKE}}^{\text{pagke-kk\&fs-Case } i}(k, t, q_{ex}, q_{se})$ be the advantage of an adversary from Case i. Then we have

$$\mathsf{Adv}_{\mathcal{PAGKE}}^{\text{pagke-kk\&fs}}(k, t, q_{ex}, q_{se}) = \mathsf{Adv}_{\mathcal{PAGKE}}^{\text{pagke-kk\&fs-Col}}(k, t, q_{ex}, q_{se}) +$$
$$\mathsf{Adv}_{\mathcal{PAGKE}}^{\text{pagke-kk\&fs-}\overline{\text{Col}}}(k, t, q_{ex}, q_{se})$$
$$= \mathsf{Adv}_{\mathcal{PAGKE}}^{\text{pagke-kk\&fs-Col}}(k, t, q_{ex}, q_{se}) +$$
$$\mathsf{Adv}_{\mathcal{PAGKE}}^{\text{pagke-kk\&fs-Case 1}}(k, t, q_{ex}, q_{se}) +$$
$$\mathsf{Adv}_{\mathcal{PAGKE}}^{\text{pagke-kk\&fs-Case 2}}(k, t, q_{ex}, q_{se}).$$

If the advantage of an adversary is from Case 1, the password of the parties may be revealed by Corrupt queries. Although Corrupt queries are allowed by the definition of freshness, for the Test oracle Π_i^s, all instances in pid_i^s are executed by Execute queries. This case can be seen that there is no the password in the protocol, and thus we may ignore Corrupt queries. Therefore, computing the upper bound of the advantage from Case 1 is similar to that of Theorem 3 of [30] (Theorem 1 in this paper) and hence we omit the details.

$$\mathsf{Adv}_{\mathcal{PAGKE}}^{\text{pagke-kk\&fs-Case 1}}(k, t, q_{ex}, q_{se}) \leq N_s \cdot \mathsf{Adv}_{\mathcal{BD}}^{\text{gke-fs}}(k, t, q_{ex}) \leq 2n \cdot N_s \cdot \mathsf{Adv}_{\mathbb{G}}^{\text{ddh}}(t). \quad (2)$$

To compute the upper bound of the advantage from Case 2, we assume an adversary $\mathcal{A}$ gets the advantage from Case 2. In this case, the password of the parties is not revealed by freshness conditions. Informally, there are only two ways an adversary can get information about a particular session key; either the adversary successfully breaks the authentication part, which means that the adversary correctly guesses the password, or correctly guesses the bit b involved in the Test query. The advantage from Case 2 is bounded as follows:

$$\mathsf{Adv}_{\mathcal{PAGKE}}^{\text{pagke-kk\&fs-Case 2}}(k, t, q_{ex}, q_{se}) \leq 2(n + n \cdot N_s + q_{se}) \cdot \mathsf{Adv}_{\mathbb{G}}^{\text{ddh}}(t) + \mathsf{Adv}_{\mathcal{F}}^{\text{prf}}(\kappa, T, q, h)$$
$$+ \frac{2q_{se}}{\mathcal{PW}}. \quad (3)$$

From Equations (1),(2) and (3) lead to

$$\mathsf{Adv}_{\mathcal{PAGKE}}^{\text{pagke-kk\&fs}}(k, t, q_{ex}, q_{se}) = \mathsf{Adv}_{\mathcal{PAGKE}}^{\text{pagke-kk\&fs-Case1}}(k, t, q_{ex}, q_{se}) +$$
$$\mathsf{Adv}_{\mathcal{PAGKE}}^{\text{pagke-kk\&fs-Case 2}}(k, t, q_{ex}, q_{se}) + 2\Pr[\mathsf{Col}]$$
$$\leq 2(n + 2n \cdot N_s + q_{se}) \cdot \mathsf{Adv}_{\mathbb{G}}^{\text{ddh}}(t) + \mathsf{Adv}_{\mathcal{F}}^{\text{prf}}(\kappa, T, q, h) +$$
$$\frac{2q_{se}}{\mathcal{PW}} + \frac{|\mathcal{U}|(q_{ex} + q_{se})^2}{2q}.$$

The detailed proof of the theorem appears in the full version of the paper [33].

7   Explicit Authentication

$\mathcal{PAGKE}$ is a PAGKE protocol with *implicit authentication*; A key exchange protocol is said to provide implicit key authentication if users are assured that no other users aside from partners can possibly learn the value of a particular secret key. Note that the property of implicit key authentication does not necessarily mean that the partners actually have computed the key. Another notion is *explicit authentication*, which guarantees to each user that it actually shares the same session key with all the others. To convert $\mathcal{PAGKE}$ with implicit authentication into the protocol $\mathcal{PAGKE}'$ that provides explicit authentication, we use the well-known approach which generates an "authenticator" for the other users by using a message authentication code (MAC) keyed by the shared session key [22]. We now present the modification $\mathcal{PAGKE}'$ providing implicit authentication which is the same as $\mathcal{PAGKE}$ except the following points.

$\mathcal{PAGKE}'$

Public information: A message authentication code (MAC), Mac = (Mac.gen, Mac.ver). Given a random key k, Mac.gen computes a tag τ for a message M; we write this as $\tau = \text{Mac.gen}_k(M)$. Mac.ver verifies the message-tag pair using the (shared) key, and returns 1 if the tag is valid or 0 otherwise.

Key computation: Each user U_i computes the secret key for F as follows:

$$k_i = (x_{i-1})^{nr_i} \cdot Y_i^{n-1} \cdot Y_{i+1}^{n-2} \cdots Y_{i-2} \bmod p.$$

Each user U_i broadcasts his authenticator $\tau_i = \text{Mac.gen}_{k_i}(\mathcal{U}||1||\mathsf{X}||2||\mathsf{Y})$, where $\mathcal{U} = (U_1, \ldots, U_n)$, $\mathsf{X} = (X_1, \ldots, X_n)$, and $\mathsf{Y} = (Y_1, \ldots, Y_n)$.

Key confirmation: Upon receiving τ_j ($j \neq i$), each user U_i checks the validity of τ_j ($1 \leq j \leq n$). If all are valid, each user U_i computes the session key as $sk_i = F_{k_i}(\mathcal{U}||\mathsf{sid})$, where $\mathsf{sid} = (1||\mathsf{X}||2||\mathsf{Y}||3||\tau)$ and $\tau = (\tau_1, \ldots, \tau_n)$.

---

8 Concluding Remarks

A previous constant-round PAGKE protocol has been proven secure in both the ideal hash model and the ideal cipher model [2]. However, a provably-secure protocol using ideal functions may be insecure if the ideal functions are implemented by the real-world functions. Thus a protocol without using ideal functions in proving its security is more desirable. In the paper, we have proposed the first provably-secure two-round PAGKE protocol without using any ideal function. This result is the best solution since the security of the protocol is based on weaker and more reasonable assumptions and the protocol achieves constant-round complexity, yet much work remains to be done to improve the computational efficiency.

References

1. M. Abdalla, E. Bresson, O. Chevassut, A. Essiari, B. M öller, and D. Pointcheval, *Provably Secure Password-Based Authentication in TLS*, In Proc. of ASIACCS'06, ACM Press, pages 35-45, ACM Press, 2006.

2. M. Abdalla, E. Bresson, O. Chevassut, and D. Pointcheval. *Password-based Group Key Exchange in a Constant Number of Rounds*, In Proc. of PKC '06, LNCS ??, pages ??-??, 2006.

3. M. Abdalla and D. Pointcheval. *Simple password-based encrypted key exchange protocols*, In Proc. of CT-RSA 2005, LNCS 3376, pages 191-208. Springer-Verlag, 2005.

4. N. Asokan and P. Ginzboorg. *Key Agreement in Ad-hoc Networks*, Journal of Computer Communications 23(17), pages 1627-1637, 2000.

5. S. Bellovin and M.merritt. *Encrypted Key Exchange: Password-Based Protocols Secure against Dictionary Attacks*, In Proc. of the Symposium on Security and Privacy, pages 72-84. IEEE Computer Society, 1992.

6. M. Bellare and P. Rogaway. *Random oracles are practical: a paradigm for designing efficient protocols*, In Proc. of 1st Conference on Computer and Communications Security, pages 62-73, ACM, 1993.

7. M. Bellare and P. Rogaway. *Entity authentication and key distribution*, In Proc. of CRYPTO '93, LNCS 773, pages 232-249, Springer-Verlag, 1993.

8. M. Bellare and P. Rogaway. *Provably secure session key distribution-the three party case*, In Proc. of the 27th ACM Symposium on the Theory of Computing, 1995.

9. M. Bellare, D. Pointcheval, and P. Rogaway. *Authenticated key agreement secure against dictionary attacks*, In Proc. of EUROCRYPT '00, LNCS 1807, pages 139-155. Springer-Verlag, 2000.

10. M. Bellare, A. Boldyreva and A. Palacio. *An Uninstantiable Random-Oracle-Model Scheme for a Hybrid-Encryption Problem*, In Proc. of EUROCRYPT '04, LNCS 3027, pages 171-188, 2004.

11. K. Becker and U. Wille. *Communication Complexity of Group Key Distribution*, In Proc. of the 5th ACM confernce on Computer and Communications Security, pages 1-6, 1998.

12. J. Black and P.Rogaway. *Ciphers with Arbitrary Finite Domains*, In Proc. of the RSA Data Security Conference, Cryptographer's Track (RSA CT '02), LNCS 2271, pages 114-130, Springer-Verlag, 2002.

13. Bluetooth. *Specification of the Bluetooth System*, December 1999, Available at http://www.bluetooth.com/developer/specification/specification.asp.

14. V. Boyko, P. MacKenzie, and S. Patel. *Provably Secure Password-Authenticated Key Exchange Using Diffie-Hellman*, In Proc. of EUROCRYPT '01, LNCS 1807, pages 156-171, Springer-Verlag, 2001.

15. E. Bresson, O. Chevassut, D. Pointcheval, and J.-J. Quisquater. *Provably Authenticated Group Diffie-Hellman Key Exchange*, In Proc. of the 8th ACM conference on Computer and Communications Security, pages 255-264, 2001.

16. E. Bresson, O. Chevassut, and D. Pointcheval. *Group Diffie-Hellman Key Exchange Secure Against Dictionary Attacks*, In Proc. of ASIACRYPT 2002, LNCS 2501, pages 497-514, Springer-Verlag, 2002.

17. E. Bresson, O. Chevassut, and D. Pointcheval. *Security Proofs for an Efficient Password-Based Key Exchange*, In Proc. of the 10th ACM Conference on Computer and Communications Security, ACM, pages 241-250, 2003.

18. E. Bresson, O. Chevassut, and D. Pointcheval. *New Security Results on Encrypted Key Exchange*, In Proc. of PKC 04, LNCS 2947, pages 145-158, Springer-Verlag, 2004.

19. M. Burmester and Y. Desmedt. *A Secure and Efficient Conference Key Distribution System*, In Proc. of EUROCRYPT '94, LNCS 950, pages 275-286, Springer-Verlag, 1995.

20. R. Canetti, O. Goldreich, and S. Halevi. *The random oracle methodology, revisited*, In Pro. of the 32nd Annual ACM Symposium on Theory of Computing, pages 209-218, 1998.

21. R. Canetti, O. Goldreich and S. Halevi. *On the Random-Oracle Methodology as Applied to Length-Restricted Signature Schemes*, In Pro. of 1st Theory of Cryptography Conference (TCC), LNCS 2951 , pages 40-57, 2004.

22. R. Canetti and H. Krawczyk. Universally Composable Notions of Key Exchange and Secure Channels. In *Eurocrypt '02*. Full version available at http://eprint.iacr.org/2002/059.

23. D. Denning and G. M. Sacco. *Timestamps in Key Distribution Protocols*, Communications of the ACM, 24(8), pages 533-536, 1981.

24. R. Dutta and R. Barua. *Password-based encrypted group key agreement*, International Journal of Network Security, 3(1):30-41, July 2006. http://isrc.nchu.edu.tw/ijns.

25. O. Goldreich and Y. Lindell. *Session-Key Generation using Human Passwords Only*, In Proc. of CRYPTO '01, LNCS 2139, pages 408-432. Springer-Verlag, 2001.

26. S. Goldwasser and Y. Taumen. *On the (in)security of the Fiat-Shamir Paradigm*, In Proc. of STOC '03, pages 102-115, IEEE Computer Society, 2003.

27. M. Jakobsson and S. Wetzel. *Security Weaknesses in Bluetooth*, In Proc. of the RSA Data Security Conference, Cryptographer's Track (RSA CT '01), LNCS 2020, pages 176-191, Springer-Verlag, 2001.

28. J. Katz, R. Ostrovsky, and M. Yung. *Efficient Password-Authenticated Key Exchange using Human-Memorable Passwords*, In Proc. of EUROCRYPT '01, LNCS 2045, pages 475-494, Springer-Verlag, 2001.

29. J. Katz, R. Ostrovsky, and M. Yung. *Forward secrecy in Password-only Key Exchange Protocols*, In Proc. of SCN '02, LNCS 2576, pages 29-44,Springer-Verlag, 2002.

30. J. Katz and M. Yung. *Scalable Protocol for Authenticated Group Key Exchange*, In Proc. of CRYPTO '03, LNCS 2729, pages 110-125, Springer-Verlag, 2003.

31. H. J. Kim, S. M. Lee, and D. H. Lee. *Constant-round authenticated group key exchange for dynamic groups*, In Proc. of ASIACRYPT 2004, LNCS 3329, pages 245-259, 2004.

32. K. Kobara and H. Imai. *Pretty-simple password-authenticated key-exchange under standard assumptions*, IEICE Transactions, E85-A(10): 2229-2237, Oct. 2002. Also available at http://eprint.iacr.org/2003/038/.

33. J. O. Kwon, I. R. Jeong and D. H. Lee. *Full version of this paper*, Available at http://cist.korea.ac.kr/new/Publication.

34. S. M. Lee, J. Y. Hwang and D. H. Lee. *Efficient Password-Based Group Key Exchange*, In Proc. of TrustBus '04, LNCS 3184, pages 191-199, Springer-Verlag, 2004.

35. P. MacKenzie. *More Efficient Password Authenticated Key Exchange*, In Proc. of the RSA Data Security Conference, Cryptographer's Track (RSA CT '01), LNCS 2020, pages 361-377, Springer-Verlag, 2001.

36. M. Naor and O. Reingold. *Number-Theoretic Constructions of Efficient Pseudo-Random Functions*, In Proc. of the 38th IEEE Symposium on Foundations of Computer Science, pages 458-467, IEEE Computer Society, 2004.

37. J. B. Nielsen. *Separating Random Oracle Proofs from Complexity Theoretic Proofs: The Non-Committing Encryption Case*, In Proc. of CRYPTO '02, LNCS 2442, pages 111-126, 2002.

38. K. Obraczka, G. Tsudik, and K. Viswanath. *Publishing Limits of Multicast in Ad Hoc Networks*, In Proc. of International Conference on Distributed Computing Systems, 2001.

39. C. E. Perkins. *Ad Hoc Networking*, Addison Weseley, 2001.

40. L. Zhou and Z. J. Haas. *Securing Ad Hoc Networks*, IEEE Networks Magazine 13(6), pages 24-30, 1999.

On the Effectiveness of TMTO and Exhaustive Search Attacks

Sourav Mukhopadhyay[1] and Palash Sarkar[2]

[1] Projet CODES, INRIA Rocquencourt
B.P. 105 78153 Le Chesnay Cedex, France
Sourav.Mukhopadhyay@inria.fr
[2] Applied Statistics Unit
Indian Statistical Institute
203 B.T. Road, Kolkata-700 108, India
palash@isical.ac.in

Abstract. In this paper, we consider time/memory trade-off (TMTO) and exhaustive search attacks and analyze their effectiveness on various key sizes. The first part of the paper is an overview of TMTO methodology and summarizes earlier work on hardware implementation of TMTO and exhaustive search attacks. The second part of the paper develops a cost model for analysing the effectiveness of generic attacks. Analysis of the cost model shows that 128-bit keys seem safe for the present. However, key sizes less than 96 bits do not provide comfortable security assurances. This is particularly relevant for the 80-bit stream ciphers in the Ecrypt call for stream ciphers as well as for the A5/3 encryption algorithm used in GSM mobile phones.

Keywords: one-way function, cryptanalysis.

1 Introduction

Cryptographic algorithms such as block and stream ciphers require the use of a secret key to ensure confidentiality of transmitted messages. The basic goal of a cryptanalytic attack is to recover the secret key from publicly available information. Very often a successful attack exploits weakness in the design of the specific algorithm being considered.

On the other hand, a generic approach to cryptanalysis is to try every possible key until the correct one is found. This is called an exhaustive search attack. The importance of such an approach arises from the fact that if a cryptographic algorithm is not secure against exhaustive search, then it cannot be considered secure at all. The resistance against exhaustive search depends on the size of the key space. However there are other factors to consider: Implementation in software or special purpose hardware; the number of parallel processors available; the speed at which each key can be processed; the cost of each processor and the overall cost of implementing the attack. (There are other issues like power consumption and mean time between failures to consider.) Implementation of exhaustive search is most feasible in special purpose hardware. In 1998,

H. Yoshiura et al. (Eds.): IWSEC 2006, LNCS 4266, pp. 337–352, 2006.

a remarkable achievement was made when the Electronics Frontier Foundation built a machine for cracking DES at a cost of US \$200,000 and which cracked a DES problem in 3 and 1/2 days.

One disadvantage of using exhaustive search is that it has to be repeated separately for each target. Hellman [12] introduced an approach to avoid this problem. In his approach, one performs an exhaustive search once in an offline pre-computation phase. The actual attack, i.e., finding the key corresponding to a target is done in an online phase and is significantly faster then exhaustive search. Also, one can repeat the attack on different targets without going through the pre-computation each time. This approach has been called a time-memory trade-off (TMTO) attack. A TMTO attack is a generic attack which can be carried out against any one-way function f. The online target consists of an image y and the goal of the attack is to find a k, such that $f(k) = y$.

This paper has two parts. The first part is a summary of state of the art on implementation of TMTO and exhaustive search attacks. We present an overview of TMTO algorithms and summarize the work done so far on software and hardware implementation of such algorithms. In this part we also describe the work done on special purpose hardware for exhaustive search with special emphasis on DES. In the second part of the paper, we develop a cost-time-data trade-off model and analyze the effectiveness of exhaustive search and TMTO pre-computation for s-bit keys with $s \leq 128$. This analysis shows that $s \leq 96$ does not afford comfortable security while $s = 128$ appears to be secure in the foreseeable future. We apply our trade-off model to stream ciphers and find that the 80-bit stream ciphers does not provide adequate protection against TMTO attacks. Further, we show that the A5/3 encryption algorithm used in GSM mobile phone also does not provide adequate security.

2   TMTO Methodology

In 1980, Hellman [12] presented a cryptanalytic time/memory trade-off attack which can viewed as a generic one-way function $(f : \{0,1\}^s \rightarrow \{0,1\}^s)$ inverter. Hellman's attack consists of two steps: precomputing the tables and searching (table lookups) in the tables. In a precomputed table, we generate a chain of length t from a start point k_0 as,

$$k_0 \xrightarrow{f} k_1 \xrightarrow{f} k_2 \rightarrow \ldots \rightarrow k_{t-2} \xrightarrow{f} k_{t-1}.$$

For an $m \times t$ table, m chains of length t are generated. We store start and end points in the table, sorted in the increasing order of end points. Using matrix stopping rule, we choose m and t such that $mt^2 = N$, where $N = 2^s$. So one table can cover only a fraction $\frac{mt}{N} = \frac{1}{t}$ of N. Hence, we need t different (unrelated) tables to cover all N keys. For the ith table, we choose a function $f_i(k) = \phi_i(f(k))$, which is a simple output modification of $f(k)$. The functions f_i, $i = 1, 2, \ldots, t$ are unrelated. In the ith table, we randomly select m distinct keys from the key space, generate m chains taking each key as a start point with the same function f_i.

Given a target $y = f(k)$, we need to find its pre-image k. Suppose k is in one of the constructed tables. For all $i = 1, 2, \ldots, t$, we repeatedly apply f_i to $y' = \phi_i(y)$ at most t times, each time we check whether it reaches an end point of ith table. The number of table lookups for this is at most t. If it reaches an end point, we have the position of k. Then we come to the corresponding start point and repeatedly apply the function until it reaches y. The previous value it visited is k. Hence, the total number of f invocations $= t^2 + t \approx t^2$. The total number of table lookups required is t^2. The Hellman method can recovers a key in time T (total number of f invocations) using M memory such that $TM^2 = N^2$, this is called the trade-off curve.

Rivest introduced the distinguished point (DP) property in time/memory trade-off attack. We can define a DP property on the key space K as follows: a key k satisfies the DP property if its first p bits are zero. In the DP method, we stop a chain after reaching a DP. So the chains are of variable lengths. Given a cipher text, in the search phase we generate a chain, until we reach a DP. After reaching a DP, we perform a table lookup, and so the number of table lookups reduces from t^2 (for t Hellman tables) to t.

In 2003, Oechslin [16] proposed the rainbow method to reduce the runtime cost to one-half of Hellman method. This method can obtain the key using the same trade-off curve as Hellman method, i.e., $TM^2 = N^2$ for $1 \leq T \leq N$. The rainbow method replaces t Hellman tables of size $m \times t$ into a single rainbow table with size $mt \times t$. Each row of a rainbow table is a rainbow chain,

$$k_0 \xrightarrow{f_1} k_1 \xrightarrow{f_2} k_2 \to \ldots \to k_{t-2} \xrightarrow{f_{t-1}} k_{t-1}.$$

Given a target y, to find the pre-image, rainbow method does the following: Apply f_{t-1} to y' and lookup the value in the endpoints of the table. If found, then we get the position of the key in the last column. Otherwise, we apply f_{t-2}, f_{t-1} to check whether the key is in the second last column of the table. This way we apply f_{t-3}, f_{t-2}, f_{t-1} and so forth. After getting the position of the key (assuming that it is in the table) we come to the corresponding start point and apply the functions $f_1, f_2, \ldots$ until it reaches y'. Then the previous value it visited is k. So, the total number of f invocations required is $\frac{t(t-1)+2t}{2} \approx \frac{t(t-1)}{2}$.

TMTO was applied to stream ciphers by Babbage [4] and Golić [10]. This attack is jointly known as the BG attack. Later, Biryukov and Shamir [7] combined the Hellman and the BG attack to obtain TMTO with multiple data. They obtained the curve $TM^2D^2 = N^2$. In [9], a rigorous time/memory trade-off construction is given that works for any function f. Unfortunately, the trade-offs obtained in [9] are worse than the Hellman trade-offs. Hence, [9] is primarily of theoretical interest.

3   Implementation of TMTO Attack

3.1   Software Implementation

In 2003, Oechslin [16] described the implementation of *rainbowcrack* which is a general purpose implementation of rainbow method. Rainbowcrack can attack

MS-Windows password hashes and crack 99.9% of all aphanumerical password hashes (out of 2^{37}) in 13.6 seconds using 1.4 GB data.

There is an elegant application of TMTO in [6], which uses a special type of sampling technique called the BSW sampling. This technique uses only part of the available online data and also reduces the search space. Use of this technique allowed particularly efficient attacks on A5/1 which is a 64-bit stream cipher. After a 2^{48} parallelizable data preparation stage (which has to be carried out only once), the actual attacks can be carried out in real time on a single PC.

3.2 Hardware Implementation

In 1988, Amirazizi and Hellman [3] proposed time/memory/processor trade-off where more than one processors execute in parallel, sharing a large memory through a switching/sorting network. This requires $n \log n$ switching elements, n being both the number of processor and blocks of memory. The emphasis of the work is to minimize the runtime of the cryptanalytic attacks in time/memory trade-off cryptanalysis by running the processors in parallel. The cost of the wires (number of wires required) is one of the dominating cost in the switching/sorting network. Amirazizi and Hellman [3] assumed that the cost of the wires is less than $n \log n$ and left this as an open problem for further study. Recently, Wiener [21] investigated the problem and proved that the wiring cost can not be less than $\Theta(n^{\frac{3}{2}})$ for any switching/sorting network to connect n processors with n memory blocks.

Quisquater and Standaert [19] provide a sketch of a generic architecture based on their two previous works [17, 20]. They suggest a pipelined architecture for implementing a multi-round function f. This builds on Wiener's design [22] of implementing DES in his exhaustive search attack on DES.

Nele Mentens et al [14] propose a hardware architecture for key search based on rainbow method. They have *estimated* that an FPGA implementation of the machine can run at 17.5 Unix password tests/second on a Virtex-4. Their design targets Unix passwords of length 48 bits (out of 56 bits). In 11 days, using 56 Gigabyte with 16 FPGAs, the precomputation for one salt and recovering an individual password takes a few minutes. A problem with this approach is the inherent difficulty of implementing a single large table.

4   Exhaustive Search on DES

In 1977, Diffie and Hellman [8] proposed an exhaustive search machine for DES which consists of 10^6 DES chips. The cost of the machine was estimated to be around 20M USD and it was expected to find the key in 12 hours. An improvement of this exhaustive search technique was proposed by Quisquater and Delescaille [17] in 1989, followed by a suggestion for distributed computation by Quisquater and Desmedt [18] in 1991.

A gate-level design of DES chip was proposed by Wiener [22] in 1993. In this design, every chip has 16 pipeline stages with a clock frequency of 50 Mhz. A machine consists of 57600 DES chips and was expected to recover the key in 3.5 hours and the total expected cost was 1M USD.

In 1997, a prize for cracking DES was announced at the annual RSA Cryptographic Trade Show. As a result, in 1998 DES was broken in 39 days using exhaustive search on a network of PCs.

In 1998, EFF (Electronics Frontier Foundation) built a machine for cracking DES [2] in 3 days with a total cost of 200,000 USD (80,000 USD for man power + 120,000 USD for production) by exhaustive search. The DES cracker is a ciphertext only attack where a PC drives many *search units*. Each search unit is a DES chip and searches 2.5 million keys per second. A total of 24 search units fit inside a custom chip and searches 60 million keys per second. A large circuit board contains 64 chips which searches 3.8 billion keys per second and 12 boards are mounted into a chassis which searches 46 billion keys per second. They use two chassis to search 92 billion keys per second, i.e., covering half of the key space in about 4.5 days. Recently, Quisquater and Standaert [19] gave a rough estimate that a 12000 USD machine could break DES in 3 and 1/2 days by exhaustive search.

Very recently, Bernstein [5] describes the pre-computation phase of two known TMTO attacks (rainbow; Hellman+DP) as parallel brute force search algorithms. Exhaustive search normally does not require sorting. However, since Bernstein adapts TMTO to brute force, he requires parallel sorting. Bernstein does not provide architectural details.

5   Cost Analysis

Let f be the one-way function that we want to invert and N is the size of its domain. We would like to perform a cost-time analysis of TMTO and exhaustive search attacks. To do this, we need to identify the dominant components of both the attack time and the costs. This is relatively easy to do for exhaustive search. The function f has to be applied on every possible input in the domain. Hence, the dominant component of the time is the time required to apply f a total of N times; for parallel implementation, this time is scaled down by the number of processors used. The dominant cost component is the cost of implementing the parallel f-invocation units (or processors). The cost should also include the manpower cost, but this is harder to estimate.

A TMTO algorithm is more complex than exhaustive search and deriving an appropriate cost model is more difficult. The precomputation phase of the TMTO algorithm has several time components – time required to obtain the (start-point, end-point) pairs; memory access time required to store these pairs into the table; and the time required to sort the tables. The online time has two major components – time to obtain the end-points; and the time for table look-up. Similarly, the cost has several components – the cost of the parallel f-invocation units; and the cost of storage media. In the online stage, the wiring cost of connecting processors to memory can also be substantially high [21].

To a large extent, the appropriate choice of the cost model depends on the underlying architecture used for the implementation. Following Wiener's work,

it is currently believed that the dominant cost of the hardware will be the interconnection cost of connecting a set of processors to a set of memory locations.
However, this assumes a particular architecture, i.e., all the processors will actually be connected to all the memory locations. This is not the only possible
architecture. Below we provide a sketch of a pipelined architecture for which
the interconnection cost will be minimal. Similarly, for the time component, the
current belief is that the dominant factor is the time required for memory access. This is true for a sequential implementation on a PC connected to a single
disk. On the other hand, with special purpose hardware, there are several ways
to efficiently pipeline the operations such that the cost of memory access can
actually be ignored. We discuss this in more details below with respect to the
Hellman with distinguished point (Hellman+DP) method.

Pre-Computation Phase: Let us consider the tasks performed in the pre-computation phase. At a top level this consists of the following two separate tasks for
each table.

1. Compute the chains and write the (start-point, end-point) pairs to the table.
2. Sort the table.
3. Write the table into a DVD

Let us call the first task, chain-computation, the second task sorting, and third
task DVDwrite. We take the following issues in consideration.

- Chain computation and sorting hardware should be designed so that they
  complete simultaneously. In any case, sorting should not take more time than
  chain computation.
- Both chain computation and sorting phase will require memory writes. For
  the chain computation stage, batching can be used to reduce number of memory accesses. Also chain computation and memory access can be pipelined
  to some extent.
- We use few blocks of high speed memory while keeping the actual tables
  into DVDs. The completed table in a high speed memory will be written
  to a DVD and then the high speed memory will be cycled back into fresh
  memory.
- If the DVD writing time is more than the time required for chain computation for a table, then we use more than one DVD writers (running in parallel)
  to synchronize the chain computation and DVD write.

In the Hellman+DP method, a total of r tables are to be prepared. Let us denote
the tables by $T_1, \ldots, T_r$. Consider the following algorithm.

1. Perform chain-computation for T_1;
2. do in parallel
       perform chain-computation for T_2;
       perform sorting for T_1;
3. for $i = 3$ to r do in parallel
       perform chain-computation for T_i;

        perform sorting for T_{i-1};
        initiate DVDwrite for T_{i-2} ;
4. end do;
5. do in parallel
        perform sorting for T_r;
        perform DVDwrite for T_{r-1};
6. perform DVDwrite for T_r.

This algorithm pipelines the chain computation for T_i with the sorting of T_{i-1} and DVD writing for T_{i-2}. Under the reasonable assumption that the sorting time is at most the chain computation time, the major time component is at most the time required for chain-computation of r tables plus the time required to sort a table and write to DVD. The chain-computation itself has two tasks – parallel f-invocations and writing to high speed memory. These two tasks can also be pipelined as we discuss below.

Suppose n many f-invocation units are available. Each table has a total of m many (s-p, e-p) pairs. These are divided into m/n blocks $B_1, \ldots, B_{m/n}$, where each block contains n pairs. The n many f-invocation units will be operating in parallel to produce one block.

1. Generate block B_1;
2. for $i = 2$ to m/n do in parallel
        Generate block B_i;
        Write block B_{i-1} to the table;
3. end do;
4. Write block $B_{m/n}$ to the table;

Producing each block B_i requires $n \times t$ many f-invocations. We may assume that the time for nt many f-invocations is more than the time to write a block of n pairs to the table. Hence, the dominant time is the time required to compute all the chains in a table, which is time required for $m \times t$ many f invocations.

Let us consider the time required to prepare all the tables. Using the above two algorithms, the total time will essentially be mrt many f-invocations done in parallel by n many f-invocation units. The cost has several components–cost of the f-invocation units; cost of input/output (I/O) units to write the blocks B_i's to the table; cost of storing r tables; and cost of the sorting unit. The dominant cost components are the cost of the f-invocation units and the cost of storage (memory).

On-Line Phase: We would like to avoid the lower bound on the wiring cost obtained by Wiener [21]. An architecture which avoids this cost can be described as follows. There is a set of n many f-invocation units, which produce DPs and write them to a buffer. There is another set of q many I/O processors, which read from this buffer and perform look-up into the tables.

At a time, the q I/O processors are connected to q tables. Once look-up on q tables are completed, the tables are moved out and a new set of q many tables are moved into place. Thus, the system operates as follows: Look-up on $T_1, \ldots T_q$

are completed, then look-up on $T_{q+1}, \ldots, T_{2q}$ are completed, and so on. Once a table is replaced, it is never loaded again for this data set. Thus, if we have D targets, then the look-up into table T_i for all these targets are completed before T_i is replaced.

In the above scenario, the following two tasks are performed in parallel.

- Apply f-invocations to the D targets and write the final DPs to the buffer.
- Read from the buffer; perform look-up in the q tables; and then replace the tables.

With a suitable design and choice of the parameters q and n, we can make the assumption that the above two tasks require approximately the same time. Under this assumption, the total time required in the online phase can be taken to be the total time for all the f-invocations. Further, in this architecture, the wiring cost is minimal and the dominant cost is the cost of implementing the f-invocation units. The task of an I/O processor is relatively simple and also we will have q to be much less than n. Hence, the cost of implementing q I/O processors can be ignored with respect to the cost of implementing the n many f-invocation units. *See [15] for more details.*

We summarize the above discussion with respect to the cost and time measures.

Pre-computation phase:
- Time: time required for rmt many f-invocations;
- Cost: cost of implementing n many parallel f-invocation units and cost of storing r many tables.

Online phase:
- Time: time required for rtD many f-invocations;
- Cost: cost of implementing n many parallel f-invocation units.

5.1   Approximate Cost Analysis

In CHES 2005, Good and Benaissa [11] proposed a new FPGA design for AES using Xilink Spartan-III (XC3S2000). The cost of a Xilink Spartan-III FPGA device whose cost is around 12 USD (see [19]). The speed of encryption of the design in [11] is 25Gbps=0.2×2^{32} AES-128 encryption/sec. Under the assumption that the cost and time scale linearly as we move from one processor to n processors, the total processor cost for n processor units is $H_p = 12n$ USD and the speed is $n \times 0.2 \times 2^{32}$ AES-128 encryptions/sec. Let T_{sec} be the pre-computation time in seconds. In T_{sec} time, the number of encryptions will be, $T_{sec} \times n \times 0.2 \times 2^{32}$.

For a general s-bit ($s \leq 128$) cipher, attacking $D = 2^d$ online data points, the number of encryptions required at the pre-computation stage is 2^{s-d}. *We assume that for an s-bit cipher with $s \leq 128$, the throughput and chip area will remain same as for the best AES-128 implementation.* Hence, in T_{sec} time, the number of encryptions will be, $T_{sec} \times n \times 0.2 \times 2^{32}$ and we get,

$$T_{sec} \times n \times 0.2 \times 2^{32} = 2^{s-d}. \tag{1}$$

Using $H_p = 12n$, we get $T_{sec}H_p = 60 \times 2^{s-d-32}$, or

$$2^{32}T_{sec}H_pD = 60N. \tag{2}$$

This gives a new type of trade-off involving pre-computation time T_{sec}, processor cost H_p and data D whereas usual trade-off curve involves online time (number of f invocations), data and memory.

Memory Cost: We assume that one table will fit into one memory block. This simplifies the table management and in particular the design of the sorting algorithm. The latest cheap high density storage is DVD with storage capacity between 4 and 20 Gbyte. In the near future, SONY will launch the paper disk with capacity of 100 Gbytes. At present, we consider 4Gbyte ($= 4 \times 2^{32}$ bytes) DVD with cost around 1 USD. Since, for a table we need $\frac{2sm}{8}$ bytes storage, so $\frac{2sm}{8} \leq 4 \times 2^{32}$, or,

$$sm \leq 2^{36}. \tag{3}$$

DVD write time: At present, we consider the writing time for a 4GB DVD is 1min[1] ($\approx 2^6$sec). The total number of f-invocations required for a single table is mt and the time required for this is $t_1 = \frac{mt}{n \times 0.2 \times 2^{32}}$. Let $W_1, \ldots W_k$ be the DVD writers which are running in parallel. At each of time $T = it_1$ for $i = 2, \ldots r+1$, one table will be ready for DVD write. At time $T = (i+1)t_1$, the table T_i will be assigned to W_i for $i = 1, 2, \ldots, k$. The next table T_{k+1} will be ready for DVD write at time $T = (k+2)t_1$. If we choose $kt_1 \geq 2^6$, then at time $T = (k+2)t_1$, W_1 will be free (since the time difference between the present time and the time when W_1 was assigned the table is $(k+2)t_1 - 2t_1 = kt_1 \geq 2^6 =$ DVD write time). So the table T_{k+1} will be assigned to W_1 for DVD write. In this way the next table will be assigned to W_2 and so on. So in this case all the processors and DVD writers will remain busy at all the time. Hence from the above discuss we have $kt_1 \geq 2^6$, or,

$$k \times \frac{mt}{n \times 0.2 \times 2^{32}} \geq 2^6. \tag{4}$$

or,

$$k \geq \frac{n2^{36}}{mt}. \tag{5}$$

Note the there are r table to be written into r DVDs and each DVD write takes 2^6 seconds. The total time required for DVD write is $\frac{r2^6}{k}$ while k many DVD writers are running in parallel. This time must be less than or equal to the pre-computation time, i.e., $\frac{r2^6}{k} \leq T_{sec}$, or,

$$k \geq \frac{r2^6}{T_{sec}}. \tag{6}$$

We take $k = max\left(\frac{n2^{36}}{mt}, \frac{r2^6}{T_{sec}}, 1\right)$. Then k satisfies both the inequalities 5 and 6. At present, we consider the DVD writer cost is 100 USD each. The total DVD writer cost is $H_w = 100k$ USD. For r tables, memory cost is $H_m = r$ USD and

---

[1] For example writing speed of Samsung SH-W162 is 21.6MB/sec (16X).

Table 1. Trade-off for different values of s with $D = 1$

s	r	m	t	T_{sec}	n	H_p	H_m	k	H_w	τ_{sec}
56	2^{19}	2^{19}	2^{19}	$2^{16.5}$	2^{10}	$2^{13.6}$	2^{19}	$2^{8.5}$	2^{15}	0.31
64	2^{21}	2^{21}	2^{21}	$2^{16.5}$	2^{18}	$2^{21.6}$	2^{21}	2^{12}	$2^{18.5}$	0.03
80	2^{27}	2^{27}	2^{27}	2^{25}	2^{25}	$2^{28.6}$	2^{27}	2^{8}	$2^{14.5}$	0.62
86	2^{29}	2^{29}	2^{29}	2^{25}	2^{31}	$2^{34.6}$	2^{29}	2^{10}	$2^{16.5}$	0.61
96	2^{32}	2^{32}	2^{32}	$2^{38.3}$	2^{28}	2^{32}	2^{32}	1	$2^{6.5}$	80
128	2^{32}	2^{64}	2^{32}	$2^{70.3}$	2^{28}	2^{32}	2^{32}	1	$2^{6.5}$	80

total hardware cost $C = H_p + H_m + H_w = (12n + r + 100k)$ USD. Let us consider the following cases.

Case 1: $D = 1$ $(d = 0)$. We choose the Hellman table parameters as: $r = m = t = N^{1/3} = 2^{s/3}$. The total number of f invocations required at the online stage $= r \times t$ and the time required for this is $\tau_{sec} = \frac{r \times t}{n \times 0.2 \times 2^{32}}$, running n processors in parallel with the speed of 0.2×2^{32} encryptions/sec. Suppose we want to finish the pre-computation within a day, then $T_{sec} = 2^{16.5}$ (the number of seconds in one day). From Equation 1, we get, $n = 5 \times 2^{s-48.5}$. For 1 year pre-computation time, i.e., $T_{sec} = 2^{25}$ (the number of seconds in one year) we need the number of processors, $n = 5 \times 2^{s-57}$. In Table 1, we summarize some of the trade-offs with different values of s.

Case 2: $D > 1$. The memory cost increases with the number of tables. We consider the following table parameters as in [7]: $r = \frac{N^{1/3}}{D} = 2^{\frac{s}{3}-d}$ and $m = t = N^{1/3} = 2^{s/3}$. The total number of f invocations required for online search $= rtD$ and the time required for this is $\tau_{sec} = \frac{r \times t \times D}{n \times 0.2 \times 2^{32}}$, running n processors in parallel with speed of 0.2×2^{32} encryption/sec. From Equation 1 we get, $n = \frac{5 \times 2^{s-d-32}}{T_{sec}}$. Table 2 summarizes some of the trade-offs with different values of s and $d = \frac{s}{4}$. The rows of the tables were calculated by fixing some of the parameters as mentioned below.

- Table 1 $(d = 0)$
  - *rows 1 and 2*: Fix T_{sec} to be one day.
  - *rows 3 and 4*: Fix T_{sec} to be one year.
  - *rows 5 and 6*: Fix $H_p = H_m = 2^{32}$.

Table 2. Trade-off for different values of s and $d = \frac{s}{4}$

s	r	$m = t$	T_{sec}	n	H_p	H_m	k	H_w	τ_{sec}
80	$2^{6.7}$	$2^{26.7}$	$2^{16.5}$	2^{14}	$2^{17.6}$	$2^{6.7}$	1	$2^{6.5}$	845
86	$2^{6.7}$	$2^{28.6}$	$2^{16.5}$	2^{18}	$2^{21.6}$	$2^{6.7}$	1	$2^{6.5}$	776
96	2^{8}	2^{32}	$2^{16.5}$	2^{26}	$2^{29.6}$	2^{8}	1	$2^{6.5}$	320
96	2^{8}	2^{32}	2^{25}	2^{17}	$2^{20.6}$	2^{8}	1	$2^{6.5}$	$2^{17.3}$
128	2^{11}	2^{43}	2^{25}	2^{41}	$2^{44.6}$	2^{11}	1	$2^{6.5}$	$2^{15.3}$
128	2^{32}	2^{32}	2^{25}	2^{41}	$2^{44.6}$	2^{32}	2^{13}	$2^{19.5}$	$2^{25.3}$
128	2^{32}	2^{32}	2^{38}	2^{28}	2^{32}	2^{32}	1	$2^{6.5}$	$2^{38.3}$

- Table 2 ($d = s/4$)
  - *rows 1, 2 and 3*: Fix T_{sec} to be one day.
  - *rows 4 and 5*: Fix T_{sec} to be one year.
  - *row 6*: Fix T_{sec} to be one year and $H_m = 2^{32}$.
  - *row 7*: Fix $H_p = H_m = 2^{32}$.

Discussion: From Tables 1 and 2, we conclude the following.

- 56-bit and 64-bit f's are completely insecure.
- For $d = 0$, with one year pre-computation time and around 500M USD investment it is possible to crack 80-bit f in online time less than one second. For multiple targets (data) with $d = s/4$, attacking 80-bit becomes easier.
- For $s = 96$, and with a single data point, pre-computation time is more than 4000 years. This is at a cost of around 1 billion USD. It is possible to bring down the pre-computation time to a few years by increasing the cost to around 1 trillion dollar. Another problem is that the size of single table becomes large and barely fits in a single storage unit (see the bound 3). In the presence of multiple data of the order of 2^{24} ($d = s/4$), the attack becomes reasonable. Hence, 96-bit f also does not provide comfortable security.
- For $s = 128$, and with a single data point ($d = 0$), at least one of the parameters among (T_{sec}, H_p, H_m) become infeasible. Also even with $d = s/4 = 32$, one of the above parameters continue to remain infeasible. Increasing d beyond 32 is not practical. Hence, 128-bit can be considered to provide adequate security margin, at least until a new technological revolution invalidates the analysis performed here.

General Case: For the general case, let us assume that C_1 and C_2 are the costs of one search unit and one storage unit respectively and ρ, δ are the rate of encryption and size of one storage unit in Gbyte respectively. Then Equation 1 becomes,

$$T_{sec} \times n \times \rho = 2^{s-d} \qquad (7)$$

and, $H_p = C_1 n$ and $H_m = C_2 r$. Using $H_p = C_1 n$ in Equation 7, we get $T_{sec} \times H_p \times \rho = 2^{s-d} C_1$, or $\rho T_{sec} H_p D = C_1 N$. Since for a table we need $\frac{2sm}{8}$ bytes storage, so $\frac{2sm}{8} \leq \delta \times 2^{32}$, or,

$$sm \leq \delta 2^{34}. \qquad (8)$$

This constraint is required because we are fitting one table into one storage unit. Let ϵ be the DVD (storage) writing time. Then equation 4 becomes, $k \times \frac{mt}{n \times \rho} \geq \epsilon$, or, $k \geq \frac{n \times \rho \times \epsilon}{m \times t}$ and equation 6 becomes, $k \geq \frac{r\epsilon}{T_{sec}}$. Thus we take $k = max\left(\frac{n \times \rho \times \epsilon}{m \times t}, \frac{r\epsilon}{T_{sec}}, 1\right)$. Let C_3 be the cost of one DVD writer, then $H_w = kC_3$USD.

5.2   Cost of Exhaustive Search

Cost analysis of exhaustive search is same as the cost analysis for TMTO pre-computation except the memory cost and DVD writer cost. Note that the processor cost H_p is required for both exhaustive search and TMTO pre-computation. The factor H_m is additionally required for TMTO. Hence, the trade-off for exhaustive search is same as Equation 2, i.e.,

$$2^{32}THD = 60N \tag{9}$$

where T denotes the time in seconds required for exhaustive search, H is the total processor cost and D is the number of data points. The general equation is the following.

$$\rho THD = C_1 N \tag{10}$$

5.3   Rainbow Method

The rainbow method replaces t Hellman table of size $m \times t$ into a single rainbow table with size $m' \times t$, where $m' = mt$. Let us consider the case when $s = 56$ (DES). Then $N = 2^{56}$, taking $m = t = N^{1/3}$, we get $m' = 2^{36}$, i.e. $sm' = 56 \times 2^{36} > 2^{36}$. This violates the constraint 3 ($sm' \leq 2^{36}$). Hence a single large rainbow table has to be stored into the more than one memory block (the number of memory block will increase with the value of s). Then the sorting algorithm becomes much more complicated since it has now to sort the table which is split into different memory blocks. On the other hand, if we break the large single rainbow table into several number of small mutually disjoint rainbow tables the online time increases by a factor of r, where r is the number of rainbow tables. In view of this, rainbow method is not a good choice for hardware implementation.

6   Application to Stream Ciphers with IV

Application of TMTO to stream ciphers with IV was analysed in [13]. For a k-bit stream cipher using an l-bit IV, consider the following $(k+l)$-bit one-way function f:

$$(k\text{-bit key}, l\text{-bit IV}) \mapsto (k+l)\text{-bit keystream prefix.} \tag{11}$$

As pointed out in [13], inverting this one-way function f will provide the secret key. Since many IVs are used with the same key, and since IVs are public, one can apply multiple data TMTO to f, using D many publicly available IVs. It has been shown in [13], that if IV length is less than key length, then this the online time of TMTO is less than exhaustive key search. (This has resulted in the recent Ecrypt call for stream ciphers, to mandate IV length to be at least equal to the key length.) However, the pre-computation time becomes 2^{k+l} which is more than exhaustive key search. On the other hand, the importance of IV in a TMTO attack matters more than its length. The effective length of IV is also crucial and has been pointed out in [13]. Let us consider this point in more details.

The usual requirement on IV is that it should be a nonce, i.e., no value should be repeated. Thus, for example, one can fix a key and use the numbers $1, 2, \ldots$, as IVs for different messages. Suppose at most 2^λ messages are encrypted before a key change. The above appears to be a valid protocol for using stream cipher. The problem is that in this approach, only the last λ bits of the IV ever change. If we put the (arbitrary) restriction that at most 1000 messages are encrypted before a key change, then $\lambda \approx 10$.

Suppose, for a particular key we have access to the keystream segment for about $32 = 2^5$ messages. This gives $D = 2^5$. Since we know all the IVs, we can apply TMTO to a search space of size $N = 2^{k+10}$ with $D = 2^5$. The precomputation time is $N/D = 2^{k+10}/2^5 = 2^{k+5}$ and the online time then comes to around $2^{2(k+5)/3}$. If $k = 80$, then the precomputation can be completed in one year at a cost of 2^{32} USD and the online time is around a minute. While the cost is quite high, it is not out of reach of powerful organizations.

We interpret this situation as indicating that to resist TMTO, it is *not* sufficient to have IV length to be equal to key length. The protocol must ensure that the entire IV length is actually used. One simple way of doing this can be to choose a random nonce as IV for the first msg encrypted using a particular key and then use nonce + 1, nonce + 2, ... as IVs for subsequent msg.

6.1   GSM

For the GSM mobile phones [1], A5/3 stream cipher is used which is based on the iterated block cipher KASUMI. The cipher A5/3 uses 64-bit key and 22-bit effective IV size (others bits of IV are fixed). The following one-way function f from 86-bit to 86-bit has been considered in [13]:

$$(64\text{-bit key}, 22\text{-bit effective IV}) \mapsto 86\text{-bit keystream prefix}. \qquad (12)$$

The size of the search space for exhaustive search attack is 2^{64}. From Table 1 (see row 2), we have the time for exhaustive search attack which is same as the pre-computation time for TMTO to be $2^{16.5}$ sec with a 2^{21} USD investment.

This is certainly doable and hence GSM mobile phone communications cannot be considered secure for more than a day. However, can we consider such communications to be secure for a shorter duration such as an hour. For example, a stock order is placed over a phone and the order is executed within an hour. Once the order is executed, there is no need for secrecy. Thus, it is enough to ensure secrecy from the point of the order being placed and it being executed, which is at most an hour. If we consider only exhaustive search attacks, then such communication over GSM phones appears to be secure. However, if we apply TMTO to the search space of the function f defined in (12), then this might not be true.

The size of the search space f is $N = 2^{86}$. From Equation 1 we get, $n = \frac{5 \times 2^{86-d-32}}{T_{sec}}$ where 2^d is the number of data points availible to the attacker. Table 3 summarizes some of the trade-offs with different values of D where the table parameters are taken as: $r = \frac{N^{1/3}}{D} = 2^{\frac{s}{3}-d}$ and $m = t = N^{1/3} = 2^{s/3}$. From Table 3, we conclude that the A5/3 algorithm of GSM provides inadequate security.

Table 3. Trade-off of GSM for different values of D

D	r	$m = t$	T_{sec}	n	H_p	H_m	k	H_w	τ_{sec}
1	2^{29}	2^{29}	2^{25}	2^{31}	$2^{34.6}$	2^{29}	2^{10}	$2^{16.5}$	0.61
2^8	2^{21}	2^{29}	2^{25}	2^{23}	$2^{26.6}$	2^{21}	2^2	$2^{8.5}$	32
2^{16}	2^{13}	2^{29}	$2^{16.5}$	2^{24}	$2^{27.6}$	2^{13}	2^3	$2^{9.5}$	16
2^{22}	2^7	2^{29}	$2^{16.5}$	2^{18}	$2^{21.6}$	2^7	1	$2^{6.5}$	2^{10}

7   TMTO Versus Exhaustive Search

In this section, we provide a comparison between TMTO and exhaustive search. Note that the size of the search space is same irrespective of whether we use TMTO or exhaustive search. The availability of multiple data (targets) bring down both the precomputation and online time of TMTO. The same is true for exhaustive search which of course does not have separate online and offline phases.

1. TMTO is a chosen plaintext attack which can be converted to weak known plaintext or ciphertext only attack (see [12]). On the other hand, exhaustive search can be a ciphertext only attack [2].
2. TMTO pre-computation phase is also an exhaustive search. However it additionally requires the following,
   – Memory is required to store the table(s).
   – Memory access is needed to write the (start point, end point) pairs into the table. Unless suitably pipelined, the memory access time can be substantial overhead.
   – Sorting is performed on the table(s) to sort (start point, end point) pairs in the increasing order of the end points. Again unless suitably pipelined, this is a substantial overhead.

Possible advantages of TMTO over exhaustive search. Pre-computation of TMTO is a one-time activity. Once completed, the online stage is much faster than exhaustive search for target available at different times. In the case of exhaustive search, the entire attack has to be repeated every time.

Rechannelising the memory cost of TMTO into processor cost for exhaustive search does not significantly reduce the exhaustive search time. To justify this, we consider a TMTO which can find the key in time τ_{sec} with T_{sec} precomputation time, H_p processor cost and H_m memory cost. We also consider an exhaustive search attack which can find the key in time T with the processor cost $H = H_p + H_m$. Then we will have the following three cases:

Case 1: If $H_p > H_m$, then $H \approx H_p$. Eq. (2) and (9) yield $T = T_{sec} > \tau_{sec}$.

Case 2: If $H_p \approx H_m$, then $H \approx 2H_p$. Eq. (2) and (9) yield $T = \frac{1}{2}T_{sec} > \tau_{sec}$.

Case 3: If $H_p < H_m$, then $H \approx H_m$. This case occurs only when the key size is small. For instant consider $s = 56$. Then from Table 1, we see that $H_p = 2^{13.6}$ and $H_m = 2^{19}$. So $H \approx 2^{19}$ and from Equation (9), we get $T = 480$ sec $> 0.31 = \tau_{sec}$

The above three cases show that the exhaustive search time will be more than the online search time for TMTO. Hence, transferring the cost of memory to the processor and performing only exhaustive search does not bring down search time to make it comparable to online phase of TMTO.

8   Conclusion

In this paper, we have considered the effectiveness of time/memory trade-off and exhaustive search attacks. For TMTO, we have outlined a possible pipelined architecture, in which the dominant cost is the total number of f-invocations. The hardware cost of TMTO is the cost of implementing parallel f-invocation units and the cost of memory. On the other hand, the hardware cost of exhaustive search is just the cost of the f-invocation units.

To study the effectiveness of these attacks, we have developed a cost-time-data trade-off model based on the currently best known AES-128 implementation. We conclude that while 128-bit keys appear to be secure, key sizes less than 96 bits do not offer comfortable security. A possible future work is to reconsider our cost estimates and develop designs targeted for special purpose hardware at a lower cost and/or at higher speed. Additionally, for TMTO approach, one has to consider the possibility of lower cost bulk storage technology.

References

[1] 3GPP TS 55.215 V6.2.0 (2003-09), A5/3 and GEA3 Specifications. Available from http://www.gsmworld.com

[2] Electronics Frontier Foundation, Cracking DES, O'Reilly and Associates, 1998.

[3] H. R. Amirazizi and M. E. Hellman. "Time-memory-processor trade-offs", in *IEEE Transactions on Information Theory*, vol. 34, no. 3, pp. 505-512, 1988.

[4] S. H. Babbage. "Improved exhaustive search attacks on stream ciphers", in European Convention on Security and Detection, IEE Conference publication, no. 408, pp. 161-166, IEE, 1995.

[5] D. J. Bernstein. "Understanding brute force", http://cr.yp.to/papers. html#bruteforce, 2005.

[6] A. Biryukov and A. Shamir and D. Wagner. "Real Time Cryptanalsis of A5/1 on a PC", in the proceedings of FSE 2000, LNCS 1978, pp. 1-18, 2000.

[7] A. Biryukov and A. Shamir. "Cyptanalytic Time/Memory/Data Tradeoffs for Stream Ciphers", in the proceedings of Asiacrypt 2000, LNCS 1976, pp. 1-13, 2000.

[8] W. Diffie and M. Hellman. "Exhaustive Cryptanalysis of the NBS Data Encryption Standard", in *Computer*, vol. 10, no. 6, pp. 74-84, June 1977.

[9] A. Fiat and M. Naor. "Rigorous time/space tradeoffs for inverting functions", in STOC 1991, pp. 534-541, 1991.

[10] J. Dj. Golić. "Cryptanalysis of alleged A5 stream cipher", in the proceedings of Eurocrypt 1997, LNCS 1233, pp. 239–255, 1997.

[11] T. Good and M. Benaissa. "AES on FPGA from the Fastest to the Smallest", in the proceedings of CHES 2005, LNCS 3659, pp 427-440, 2005.

[12] M. Hellman. A cryptanalytic Time-Memory Trade-off, IEEE Transactions on Information Theory, vol 26, pp 401-406, 1980.

[13] J. Hong and P. Sarkar. "New Applications of Time Memory Data Tradeoffs", in the proceedings of Asiacrypt 2005, LNCS 3788, pp. 353-372, 2005.

[14] N. Mentens, L. Batina, B. Preneel, and I. Verbauwhede. "Cracking Unix passwords using FPGA platforms", in the proceedings of SHARCS'05, 2005.

[15] S. Mukhopadhyay and P. Sarkar. "Hardware Architecture and Trade-offs for Generic Inversion of One-way Functions", in 2006 IEEE International Symposium on Circuits and Systems (ISCAS 2006), 2006. Full version available as (Indian Statistical Institute Techinical Report No. ASD/2006/2).

[16] P. Oechslin. "Making a faster Cryptanalytic Time-Memory Trade-Off", in the proceedings of Crypto 2003, LNCS 2729, pp. 617-630, 2003.

[17] J.J. Quisquater and J.P. Delescaille. "How easy is collision search? Application to DES", in the proceedings of Eurocrypt 1989, LNCS 434, pp 429-434, 1990.

[18] J.J. Quisquater and Y.G. Desmedt, "Chinese Lotto as an Exhaustive Code-Breaking Machine", in *Computer*, vol. 24, issue 11 (November 1991), pp. 14-22, 1991.

[19] J.J. Quisquater and F.X. Standaert. "Exhaustive Key Search of the DES: Updates and Refinements", presented at SHARCS'05, 2005.

[20] J.J. Quisquater, F.X. Standaert, G. Rouvroy, J.P. David and J.D. Legat. A Cryptanalytic Time-Memory Tradeoff: First FPGA Implementation, in the proceeding of FPL 2002, LNCS 2438, pp 780-789, 2002.

[21] M. J. Wiener. "The Full Cost of Cryptanalytic Attacks", in *Journal of Cryptology*, vol. 17, no. 2, pp. 105-124, 2004.

[22] M. J. Wiener. "Efficient DES Key Search", Crypto 1993 (rump session presentation), Santa Barbara, California, USA, August 1993. Reprint in Practical Cryptography for Data Internetworks, William Stallings editor,IEEE Computer Society Press, pp. 31-79, 1996.

Low Power AES Hardware Architecture for Radio Frequency Identification

Mooseop Kim[1], Jaecheol Ryou[2], Yongje Choi[1], and Sungik Jun[1]

[1] Electronics and Telecommunications Research Institute (ETRI)
161 Gajeong-dong, Yuseong-gu, Daejeon, 305-700, South Korea
{gomskim, choiyj, sijun}@etri.re.kr
[2] Division of Electrical and Computer Engineering, Chungnam National University
220 Gung-dong, Yuseong-gu, Daejeon, 305-764, South Korea
jcryou@home.cnu.ac.kr

Abstract. We present a new architecture of Advanced Encryption Standard (AES) cryptographic hardware which can be used as cryptographic primitives supporting privacy and authentication for Radio Frequency Identification (RFID). RFID is a technology to identify goods or person containing the tags. While it is a convenient way to track items, it also provides chances to track people and their activities through their belongings. For these reasons, privacy and authentication are a major concern with RFID system and many solutions have been proposed. M. Feldhofer , S. Dominikus, and J. Wolkerstorfer introduced the Interleaved Protocol which serves as a means of authenticating RFID tag to reader devices in [14]. They designed very small and low power AES hardware as a cryptographic primitive. In this contribution, we introduce a novel method to increase the operating speed of previous method for low power AES cryptographic circuits. Our low power AES cryptographic hardware can encrypt 128-bit data block within 870 clock cycles using less than 4000 gates and has a power consumption about or less than 20 μW on a 0.25 μm CMOS process.

1 Introduction

Radio Frequency Identification (RFID) is a technology for automated identification of objects and people with electromagnetic fields. Conceptually, RFID is similar to a bar-code system, but its wireless communication allows significant qualitative advances. The reader need not have line-of-sight to the tag and interrogates multiple tags at the same time. The tag can store many more bits of information. There are various applications for low-cost and low power tags such as logistics, point-of-sales, animal identification, item management, and so on. Thanks to advances in the capabilities of tags, drastic decreases in the cost of RFID system, and many efforts to adapt it in the real world, RFID system seems to replace optical bar-code and proliferate in the near future.

However, the radio communications between RFID tag and readers raise a number of security issues. Basically, RFID tags send their identifier without further security verification when they are powered by electromagnetic waves from

H. Yoshiura et al. (Eds.): IWSEC 2006, LNCS 4266, pp. 353–363, 2006.

a reader. For these reasons, the security and privacy aspects of RFID systems have become a major issue. Current RFID systems do not protect the unique identifier so that unauthorized readers in the proximity can gather identity data. The collected identifying data could be accumulated and linked with location information in order to generate a customer profile. The threat to privacy grows when a tag serial number is combined with personal information.

Over the past few years, several efforts have been made to protect privacy problems of RFID systems. The first step to protect user privacy in RFID systems was physical approaches such as Kill Tag, Faraday cage, Blocker tag techniques [2], [3], [4]. But these methods have weak points such as reusability and operating range restriction.

Another approaches are to design an authentication protocol using cryptographic solutions. The Hash-Lock and Randomized Hash Lock scheme [2], [3], [4] was introduced to prevent an exposure of tag identity by using cryptographic hash functions. However, these schemes do not fully protect location privacy.

Other approaches are more secure than above presented methods because these methods use symmetric cryptography to protect tag data. In [14], M. Feldhofer, S. Dominikus, and J. Wolkerstorfer introduced the Interleaved Protocol which serves as a means of authenticating RFID tag to reader devices. They used AES cryptographic algorithm for their authentication protocol. Considering the constraints of tag, data encryption requires high computation cost especially in power consumptions. They designed very small AES hardware circuit as a cryptographic primitive. The proposed circuit requires about 1,000 clock cycles and consumes below 9 μA to encrypt a 128-bit block of data.

In general, small and inexpensive RFID tags are passive. Passive tags derive their transmission power from the signal of an interrogating reader because they have no on-board power source. For these architectural features, RFID systems have very stringent limitations with respect to available power, physical circuit area, and costs. Therefore special architecture and design methods for low power AES circuit are required.

In this paper, we introduce a novel method to increase the operating speed of previous method [14] for low power AES cryptographic hardware. As a result, a compact and low power AES implementation capable of supporting the Interleaved Protocol for RFID authentication was developed and evaluated.

This paper is constructed as follows. Section 2 describes some related works for low power design of AES circuit. Section 3 describes AES algorithm reviews and architecture of our low power AES circuits. Section 4 describes synthesis and implementation results. Finally, in Section 5, we conclude this work.

2   Related Works

The National Institute of Standard and Technology (NIST) selected the Rijndael algorithm as the Advanced Encryption Standard (AES) [8] in 2001. Numerous FPGA and ASIC implementations [10], [11], [12], [13] of the AES were previously proposed and evaluated. Most of these implementations feature high speeds and high costs suitable for high-performance usages. The need for secure data exchange will become more important in the low-end devices such as RFID, sensor network systems and many other embedded systems. Most of these low-end embedded systems do not require high speed encryption functions and have very strict environment in power consumption and in circuit area. For these reasons, compact and low power AES hardware design became a new trend in the cryptographic hardware design.

The first effort to compact design of AES was proposed by V. Rijmen [9]. AES S-box is based on the mapping $x \rightarrow x^{-1}$, where x^{-1} is the multiplicative inverse in the field. He suggested an efficient method to calculate the multiplicative inverse using composite fields which can reduce an 8-bit computing to several 4-bit ones. J. Wolkerstoefer [15] introduced an ASIC implementation of the S-box based on finite field arithmetic rather than using lookup-tables. In contrast to Rijmen's idea, they used the polynomial representation of finite filed elements for more flexible hardware architecture. M. Feldhofer [14] proposed a symmetric challenge-response authentication protocol which can be integrated into the existing ISO/IEC 18000 standard. They introduced an efficient architecture for a low power and low die-size implementation of the AES algorithm. For compact and low power design, they adapted previous methods of S-box using combinational logic and suggested using a submodule in the crucial step of computing MixColumn operation. A. Satoh [16] further extended the idea of Rijnmen [9]. They introduced a new composite field to optimize the S-box structure suited for compact ASIC design. In this scheme, they reduced the 4-bit calculation to 2-bit ones. D. Canright [18] improved the compact implementation of [16] using normal basis representation. To achieve a more compact S-box, he examined many choices of basis for each subfield, not only polynomial bases but also normal bases. This approach leads to a whole family of 432 implementation cases. He also find out that replacing some XORs and NANDs with NORs gives further saving of logic area. The best implementation case of S-box is 20% smaller than previous work of [16], which resulted in the smallest AES S-box architecture to date.

3   Low Power AES Hardware Architecture

The AES algorithm is a symmetric block cipher with a variable block length and a variable key length. The block length and the key length can be independently specified to 128, 192, 256 bits. The corresponding number of rounds for each key size is 10 rounds, 12 rounds, and 14 rounds, respectively. Our implementation uses a fixed size of 128 bits data block and key length because 128-bit length of key gives sufficient security level for RFID systems.

We began the design of the low power AES architecture by analyzing the basic architecture of AES algorithm [7], [8]. Each data block of AES is modified by several predefined rounds of processing, where each round involves four functional steps. As figure 1 indicates, the four steps in each round of data encryption are called SubBytes, ShiftRows, MixColumn, and AddRoundKey. Before the first round operation, the input data block is processed by AddRoundKey. Also, the last round skips the MixColumn operation. Otherwise, all rounds are process the same functions, except each round uses a different round key.

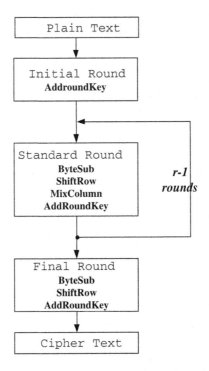

Fig. 1. Operating steps of AES algorithm

M. Feldhofer [14] designed a data path to reduce these four steps to three ones. The first step of each round operation is SubByte function. During the execution of SubByte, the controller addresses the data memory to operate ShiftRow function at the same time. Then MixColumn and AddRoundKey functions are executed.

Our innovative method to optimize our AES circuit is the reordering and modifying of the AES round operation steps. The primitive functions SubByte and ShiftRow are based on byte-oriented arithmetic, and AddRoundKey is a simple 128-bitwise XOR operation. Their operating order is not important because SubByte operates on one single byte, and ShiftRow reorders byte data without changing them. We use these arithmetic features of AES algorithm to reduce AES round operation to two functional steps by reordering and merging AddRondKey, SubByte, and ShiftRow into a single step. The modified AES processing steps are shown in figure 2. By reducing functional steps, we can save clock cycles which are consumed to operate a separate AddRoundKey function.

The efficiency of a low-cost AES cryptographic hardware in terms of circuit area, power consumption, and throughput is mainly determined by the data

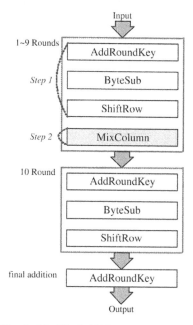

Fig. 2. Modified AES processing steps

path structure of AES circuit and by the implementation of MixColumn and Sboxes. We use 8-bit architecture for our low power AES circuit. This approach for a low power AES cryptographic circuit implementation is motivated by two reasons. First, RFID system offers very strict circuit design environment such as circuit area and limited power. Second, an 8-bit architecture enables to decrease the number of S-box to save silicon area. To compute AES encryption, 128-bit data block is divided into sixteen 8-bit data state, and is processed through 8-bit data buses.

In order to optimize our low power AES cryptographic circuit, resource sharing in the data path is fully employed. We also used some low power circuit design technologies. At the gate level, gated clock is used to reduce switching activity of latches and flip-flops. Data gating is used to decrease unwanted switching in combinational logic blocks. At the architectural level, we try to optimize the data path by reordering and integrating the functional steps of AES algorithm. The main goal of these low power circuit design methods are to reduce dynamic power consumption by reducing unwanted switching activities.

For our low power AES circuit, the first step was to find a minimal architecture. This part was done by hand. A set of key components thus obtained. Components of AES circuit then designed and applied aforementioned low power techniques to each component. The architecture of our 8-bit based low power AES cryptographic circuit is represented in figure 3. It unrolls only one round operation, and iteratively loops data through this round operation until the entire encryption is completed. There are several key components for our low power AES cryptographic circuit: a controller, data and key memory, S-box, and data path.

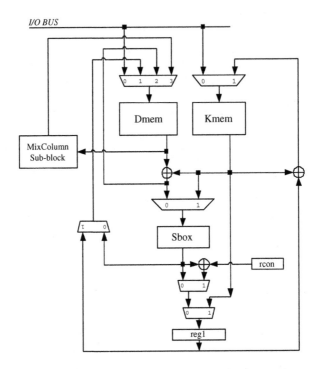

Fig. 3. Architecture of low power AES circuit

Although it is not illustrated in figure 3, the controller is one of the most important components. Controller communicates other modules to receive data and control signals through interface modules. It also sequences the ten rounds of AES operation. Therefore, it addresses data memory and key memory accordingly and generates control signals for proper data path selection and round key generation.

We separate a data memory (Dmem) and a key memory (Kmem) for efficient control. They store intermediate sate data and round keys of each round operation. By separate data and key memory, parallel processing for data encryption and round key calculation is possible. These memories are register based and single port 128-bit memory using standard logic cells. Gated clock is applied every memory cell registers to reduce unwanted switching activity. Each memory uses multiplexer to select data between initial input data and intermediate round operation data.

The data path of low power AES contains combinational logic to calculate the AES SubByte functions. We use a novel method and a data path to execute SubByte, ShiftRow, and AddRoundKey at the same time. An additional 8-bit register is used to store modified state and calculated round key before they overwrite previous values in memories. By choosing the read and write address of memory properly, and controlling the data path effectively to write data of register to current address of memory, we combined efficiently SubByte, ShiftRow, and AddRoundKey functions. The combined function of AddRoundKey, Sub-Byte, and ShiftRow takes 42 clock cycles to calculate one round operation.

Another important part of AES data path is S-box which is used for the SubByte. During the MixColumn operation, it also used to generate round key which used for next round operation. There are several methods to implement an AES S-box. The most naive method is using 256 × 8-bit ROM to implement lookup table. But, using a lookup table requires very large silicon area. Fortunately, J. Wolkerstofer [15] presented an alternative method. It used combinational logics to implement AES S-box. We adapted this combinational S-box for our low power AES cryptographic circuit. However, combinational logic always consumes current whenever data signal is inputed. To solve this problem, we use additional 8-bit register as a data gating circuit to prevent unwanted dynamic power consumption.

The MixColumn multiplies the input polynomial by a constant polynomial $c(x)$, given by

$$c(x) = \{03\}x^3 + \{01\}x^2 + \{01\}x + \{02\}. \tag{1}$$

As shown in equation 2, the MixColumn operation for one column is written as

$$
\begin{aligned}
q(x) &= c(x) \otimes a(x) \\
q_0 &= (\{02\} \cdot a_0) \oplus (\{03\} \cdot a_1) \oplus (\{01\} \cdot a_2) \oplus (\{01\} \cdot a_3) \\
q_1 &= (\{02\} \cdot a_1) \oplus (\{03\} \cdot a_2) \oplus (\{01\} \cdot a_3) \oplus (\{01\} \cdot a_0) \\
q_2 &= (\{02\} \cdot a_2) \oplus (\{03\} \cdot a_3) \oplus (\{01\} \cdot a_0) \oplus (\{01\} \cdot a_1) \\
q_3 &= (\{02\} \cdot a_3) \oplus (\{03\} \cdot a_0) \oplus (\{01\} \cdot a_1) \oplus (\{01\} \cdot a_2)
\end{aligned}
\tag{2}
$$

The equation shows that all output byte data of MixColumn are calculated using the same function except the order of the input column bytes. For our low power AES architecture, we designed a sub-block which calculates one forth of the full MixColumn operations. Figure 4 depicts a detailed structure of the sub-block.

By accessing the sub-block four times, one column of data is calculated. A 32-bit shift register and several combinational XOR logics are used for an efficient implementation of MixColumn operation. In contrast to M. Feldhofer [14], we use a 32-bit shift register for its convenient control. Additional reason of using a shift register is clock gating and data gating which reduce unwanted switching activity of register and reduce unwanted switching of sub-block's combinational logics. The sub-block needs eight clock cycles to process one column of MixColumn operation. Among these clock cycles, four clock cycles are used to load a column data stored in the data memory(Dmem) to the shift register and the other clock cycles are used to shift the register's data and overwrite the output data of sub-block to Dmem. Therefore, a complete MixColumn function takes 32 clock cycles.

Remaining modules of the data path are used to generate round keys. Round keys are derived from previous one by using Sbox, rcon, two XOR gates, and several data multiplexors of the data path. Rcon is a simple circuit to generate predefined round constant used for round key computation. The round keys are

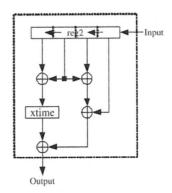

Fig. 4. Sub-block of MixColumn operation

computed in between the rounds of the cipher, so called on-the-fly method, and therefore the key generation operation is repeated for every round operation execution. More accurately, round keys are calculated during the MixColumn operation. It takes 36 clock cycles to calculate a round key. Because round key calculation is processed with the MixColumn function in parallel, our architecture requires only four clock cycles to generate a round key.

4   Synthesis and Implementation Results

The implementation of our low power AES cryptographic circuit, which combines SubByte, ShiftRow, and AddRoundKey from AES algorithm, is a standard-cell circuit on a 0.25 μm CMOS process from Hynix Corp. and Samsung Electronics. For synthesis of our low power AES circuit, we used the Synopsys Design Compiler. It needs 870 clock cycles to encrypt a 128-bit data block. The required hardware complex is estimated to be 3,900 gates from Hynix process and 3,868 gates from Samsung process.

Table 1 shows the synthesis results of our AES circuit using Samsung 0.25 μm CMOS process. All presented results come from simulations and synthesis on transistor level.

The clock cycles of each functional step for a single round operation are required as follows:

– AddRoundKey/ByteSub/SiftRow: 42 clock cycles
– MixColumn: 32 clock cycles
– KeySchedule: 4 clock cycles

There are several additional clock cycles for entire AES encryption operation.

– data and key IO: 70 clock cycles
– final round key addition: 16 clock cycles
– interrupt signal for end of operation: 1 clock cycle
– command check: 3 clock cycles

Considering overall ten rounds of AES operation, the total operating clock cycles for 128-bit data block encryption are calculated as follows:

Table 1. Logic blocks and their complexity from Samsung 0.25 μm CMOS process

Logic Block	Gate count	Clock cycle
Interface	144	70
S-box	413	
Memory	1,940	
AddRoundKey/ByteSub/ShiftRow	192	440
MixColumn	441	320
KeySchedule	157	40
Controller	581	
Total	3,868	870

Total clock cycles
$$= (\text{AddRoundKey/ByteSub/SiftRow}) + \text{MixColumn}$$
$$+ \text{KeySchedule} + \text{Interface}$$
$$= (42 \times 10 + 17 + 3) + (32 \times 10) + (4 \times 10) + 70$$
$$= 870 \text{ clocks}$$

Table 2. Logic blocks and their power consumptions

Logic Block	Samsung[†]		Hynix[†]	
	power	percentage	power	percentage
Interface	0.008	≈ 0	0.033	0.7
S-box	14.61	68.3	4.36	89.9
Memory	2.87	13.4	0.307	6.3
AddRoundKey/ByteSub/ShiftRow	0.52	2.43	0.054	1.1
MixColumn	0.45	2.11	0.036	0.74
KeySchedule	0.23	1.06	0.018	0.36
Controller	2.71	12.7	0.042	0.9
Total	$21.4\mu W$	100%	$4.85\mu W$	100%

[†] All process use 0.25 μm CMOS technology.

After synthesis, Synopsys PowerCompiler was used for assessing the performance of our low power AES circuit. Table 2 shows the results of power estimations. The standard cell library was 0.25 μm technology from Hynix Corp. and Samsung Electronics. The applied voltage was 2.5V and the operating frequency was 100 KHz.

The table 2 shows that the combinational S-box is the major power consumer because it is shared in both data path computing for integrated function of AddRoundKey, ByteSub, and ShiftRow and for round key generation.

Table 3 presents a comparison of our design with some previous results. For fair comparison, our results of power consumption converted to current representation. Our result shows 14% reduction of clock cycles with a similar or less power consumption, but shows about 7.5% increase in the circuit area against the results of M. Feldhofer [14]. The increase of circuit area is mainly due to the using of gated clock and data gating used for memory cells and other registers.

Table 3. Comparison with previous works based on power consumption, gate count, and clock cycles

128-bit encryption	μA at 100 KHz	Gate counts	Clock cycles
This work[†]	1.94	3,900	870
M. Feldhofer [14]	8.15	3,628	1,016
S. Mangard [10]	47.24	10,799	64
I. Verbauwhede [11]	307	173K	10

[†] Test results using 0.25 μm CMOS process from Hynix Corp.

5   Conclusions

In this work, we proposed a compact yet high-speed architecture for a low power AES cryptographic circuit and evaluated through simulation and synthesis for ASIC implementation. In order to minimize the hardware size and to optimize the throughput, the order of SubByte, ShiftRow, and AddRoundKey arithmetic functions were changed and integrated into a single step.

Our architecture provides a compact and high performance AES cryptographic hardware for low power RFID system authentication. Our AES hardware has a chip size of 3,868 gates from Samsung and 3,900 gates from Hynix 0.25 μm CMOS process. It has a power consumption of 21.4 μW on Samsung and 4.85 μW on Hynix process respectively at the operating frequency of 100 KHz. Low power techniques used are mainly based on clock and data gating. The encryption of 128 bits data requires 870 clock cycles.

The results of power consumption, throughput, and functionality make our low power AES cryptographic hardware practical and suitable in RFID applications and other low-end embedded systems.

Acknowledgements

The second author of this research was supported by the MIC (Ministry of Information and Communication), Korea, under the ITRC (Information Technology Research Center) support program supervised by the IITA (Institute of Information Technology Assessment) (IITA-2005-(C1090-0502-0020)).

References

1. K. Finkenzeller. *RFID-Handbook*. 2nd edition, Carl Hanser Verlag Munchen 2003.
2. S.A. Weis. Security and Privacy in Radio-Frequency Identification Devices. Master's thesis, Massachusetts Institute of Technology, Cambridge, MA 02139, May 2003.
3. S.E. Sarma, S.A. Weis, and D.W. Engels. RFID Systems and security and privacy implications. In *CHES2002*, volume 2523 of *Lecture Notes in Computer Science*, pages 454-469. Springer, 2002.

4. K.P. Fishkin, S. Roy, and B. Jiang. Some Methods for Privacy in RFID Communication. In *ESAS2004*, volume 3313 of *Lecture Notes in Computer Science*, pages 42-53. Springer, 2004.
5. L. Sumi, H. Youngju, L. Donghoon, and L. Jongin. Efficient Authentication for Low-Cost RFID Systems. In *ICCSA2005*, volume 3480 of *Lecture Notes in Computer Science*, pages 619-627. Springer, 2005.
6. J. Daemen and V. Rijmen. *The Design of Rijndael: AES - The Advanced Encryption Standard*. Springer-Verlag, ISBN 30540-42580-2, 2002.
7. J. Daemen and V. Rijmen. *AES Proposal: Rijndale*. available at: http://csrc.nist.gov/encryption/aes/rijndael/Rijndael.pdf
8. NIST. Specification for the ADVANCED ENCRYPTION STANDARD (AES). Technical Report FIPS PUB 197, 2001.
9. V. Rijmen. Efficient Implementation of the Rijndael SBox. available at: http://www.esat.ku-leuven.ac.be/ rijmen/rijndael/sbox.pdf, 2001.
10. S. Mangard, M. Aigner, and S. Dominikus. A Highly Regular and Scalable AES Hardware Architecture. *IEEE Transactions on Computers*, 52(4) pages 483-491, April 2003.
11. I. Verbauwhede, P. Schaumont, and H. Kuo. Design and Performance Testing of a 2.29 Gb/s Rijndael Processor. *IEEE Journal of Solid-State Circuits*, pages 569-572, March 2003.
12. S. Morioka and A. Satoh. A 10 Gbps full-AES crypto design with a twisted-BDD S-box architecture. *IEEE International Conference on Computer Design*. IEEE, 2002.
13. N. Weavwe and J. Wawrzynek. High Performance, compact AES implementations in Xilinx FPGAs. available at: http://www.cs.Berkeley.edu/~nweaver/papers/AES_inFPGAs.pdf, September 2002.
14. M. Feldhofer, S. Dominikus, and J. Wolkerstorfer. Strong Authentication for RFID Systems Using the AES Algorithm. In *CHES2004*, volume 3156 of *Lecture Notes in Computer Science*, pages 357-370. Springer, 2004.
15. J. Wolkerstorfer, E. Oswald, and M. Lamberger, An ASIC Implementation of the AES Sboxes, In *CT-RSA 2002*, volume 2271 of *Lecture Notes in Computer Science*, pages 67-78. Springer, 2002.
16. A. Satoh, S. Morioka, K. Takano, and S. Munetoh. A Compact Rijndael Hardware Architecture with S-Box Optimization. In *ASIACRYPT2001*, volume 2248 of *Lecture Notes in Computer Science*, pages 239-254. Springer, 2001.
17. P. Chodowiec and K. Gaj. Very Compact FPGA Implementation of the AES Algorithm. In *CHES2003*, volume 2779 of *Lecture Notes in Computer Science*, pages 319-333. Springer, 2003.
18. D. Canright. A Very Compact S-Box for AES. In *CHES2005*, volume 3659 of *Lecture Notes in Computer Science*, pages 441-455. Springer, 2005.
19. K. Wonjong, K. Seungchul, B. Younghwan, J. Sungik, P. Youngsoo, and C. Hanjin. A Platform-Based SoC Design of a 32-bit Smart Card. *ETRI Journal*, vol.25, no.6, pages 510-516, December 2003.
20. W. Stallings. *Cryptography and Network Security: Principles and Practice*. 3rd edition, Pearson Education Inc., 2003.
21. K.C. Chang. *Digital Systems Design with VHDL and Synthesis: An Integrated Approach*. IEEE Computer Society Press, 1999.

The High-Speed Packet Cipher System Suitable for Small Sized Data

Sang-Hyun Park[1], Hoon Choi[2], Sang-Han Lee[1], and Taejoo Chang[1]

[1] National Security Research Institute
161 Gajeong-dong, Yuseong-gu, Daejeon, 305-350, Korea
{sanghyun, freewill71, tchang}@etri.re.kr
[2] Department of Computer Engineering, Chungnam National University
220 Gung-dong, Yuseong-gu, Daejeon 305-764, Korea
hc@cnu.ac.kr

Abstract. Since all data input and output to a cryptographic module must occur through its interface, performance degradation coming from interface constraints is inevitable for small data packets even the best-performing cipher chip. This paper proposes the High-Speed Packet Cipher System that encrypts even small packet data at high speed by improving the packet data processing method used in existing cryptographic modules. Looking at the test result, we see that speed of 68Mbps better than 0.5Mbps of 4-step Procedure is achieved for 32-byte packets.

Keywords: Packet Cipher, SoC(System on Chip), Cryptographic module, Security API.

1 Introduction

The openness of the ubiquitous computing environment - wherein users can access a network anytime, anywhere - facilitates information sharing. Still, its downside includes the exposure to misuse, wiretapping, forgery, and alteration by malicious users. Protecting user data from such risks requires encryption. The high-performance cryptographic module performing the hardware-based cipher algorithm using the cipher chip has recently been enjoying growing popularity.

Under the ubiquitous computing environment, the cryptographic module features the SoC(System on Chip) type to satisfy requirements such as low cost, small size, and low power consumption. PCI is currently used as the external interface of SoC for high-performance servers or network devices. For portable devices in particular, the USB interface is widely used for its flexibility, scalability, and usability. It is also expected to be very popular under the ubiquitous computing environment.

USB1.1 and USB2.0 standards govern the USB interface. In particular, USB2.0 can theoretically transmit data at a maximum of 480Mbps[1]. PCI standards include PCI 2.1, PCI-X, and PCI Express whose transmission support ranges from the Gbps level to tens of Gbps level[2][3]. Still, the maximum performances of these standards are realized only when massive volumes of data are transmitted

H. Yoshiura et al. (Eds.): IWSEC 2006, LNCS 4266, pp. 364–377, 2006.

simultaneously by the host. When only a small amount of data is transmitted, however, actual performance is quite different. Since all data inputs and outputs of the cryptographic module occur through the interface, even the best-performing cipher chip cannot display maximum performance given small data size owing to interface constraint.

This paper proposes the High-Speed Packet Cipher System that encrypts even small packet data at high speed by improving the packet data processing method used in existing cryptographic modules.

The rest of this paper is organized as follows: Chapter 2 reviews related works; Chapter 3 analyzes the USB interface as the most popular interface for portable cryptographic modules as well as the packet processing performance of cryptographic modules with the USB interface; Chapter 4 presents the design of the High-Speed Packet Cipher System; Chapter 5 analyzes the performance of the portable cryptographic module applying the proposed system to prove the appropriateness of the high-speed packet processing system proposed in this paper for both large and small amounts of data; finally, Chapter 6 presents the conclusion.

2   Review of Related Works

According to the report of the Tolly Group, a world-renowned network performance test agency, the packet transmission performance of NETSAQ F2000 is 1.684Gbps for 1,518 bytes but only 177Mbps for 128 bytes, or a tenfold difference[4]. Similar tenfold difference in performance is noted when the AES128 block cipher algorithm is used for SECUi.com's VPN device called NXG 2000: 1.9Gbps for 1,400 bytes but 221Mbps for 64-byte ciphering[5]. A large difference in packet size is also noted for Future System's FSC2003 [6].

Figure 1 shows the result of the test conducted by the Tolly Group for SECUi.com's NXG 2000. NXG 2000 uses a PCI-X v1.0 interface with maximum transfer speed of 8Gbps. For the block cipher algorithm, 3DES and AES128 are used as the 2Gbps class cipher chip. As shown in the figure, performance of 1.9Gbps for 1,400 bytes and 221Mbps for 64 bytes data is observed, a tenfold difference in data size. Such difference is attributed to the effect of the communication overhead, i.e., the time required by the cryptographic module in order to transmit the packet is almost the same regardless of the data size. Therefore, the relative effect of the overhead increases as data size decreases; hence deteriorating overall system performance.

3   Analysis of Packet Data Performance

3.1   USB2.0 Standard Analysis

In the USB2.0 standard, the basic unit of time for communication is called a micro frame; one micro frame is $125\mu s$ long. In other words, data communication occurs in units of micro frame under the USB2.0 standard, with even the smallest data consuming $125\mu s$ for data input/output activity.

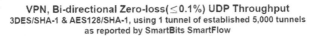

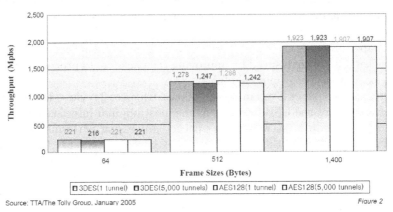

Figure 2

Fig. 1. Performance per packet size(NXG 2000)

Since it takes at least $125\mu s$ even for the smallest data size under the USB2.0 standard, transfer performance deteriorates when small sized data is transferred. For example, since the maximum data size for transmitting 1,500-byte data in each transaction is 512 bytes, only 3 transactions occur within 1 micro frame; the remaining 10 transactions merely consume time without actual data transfer. Therefore, the theoretical transfer speed of a 1,500-byte data becomes $(1500 \times 8)/125\mu s = 96$Mbps, which is $1/5$ of the maximum speed of 480Mbps. Figure 2 depicts such phenomenon.

Fig. 2. Conceptual diagram of 1,500-byte data transmission in 1 micro frame

Table 1 shows the theoretical maximum data transfer speed based on data size under the USB2.0 standard[1]. Given a payload size of 512 bytes, up to 13 data transactions are realized in 1 micro frame. Therefore, the data transfer speed is $(512 \times 8(bit)) \times 13/125\mu s = 426.0$Mbps, approximating the theoretical maximum (480Mbps). For data payload of 4 bytes, up to 127 transfers are enabled, however; thus the transmission speed decreases to $(4 \times 8(bit)) \times 127/125\mu s = 32$Mbps.

Figure 3 shows the transfer speed with respect to varying data sizes under the USB2.0 standard. Transfer performance deteriorates with small sized data, with the maximum transfer speed of 480Mbps approximated when data size is a multiple of 6,656 bytes. Since all data transactions of the cryptographic module with the USB 2.0 interface occur through USB2.0's matching functions, the data cipher/decipher cannot exceed the data transfer speed under the USB2.0 standard.

Table 1. USB2.0 High-speed Bulk Transaction Limits

Protocol Overhead		(3 X 4) SYNC bytes 3PID bytes 2EPADDR+CRC bytes 2 CRC16 and 3 X (1+11)bytes interpacket delay		
Data Payload	Max Bandwidth (Mbps)	Microframe Bandwidth per Transfer(%)	Max Number of Transfer	Byte/Microframe Useful Data
1	8.512	1	133	133
4	32.512	1	127	508
16	107.52	1	86	2,752
128	327.68	2	40	5,120
512	426.00	8	13	6,656

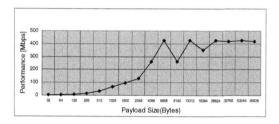

Fig. 3. Data transfer speed given varying payload data sizes under the USB2.0 standard

3.2 Encryption Speed Based on Data Size

Although it differs by cryptographic module and command type, the cryptographic module generally communicates with the host device through the USB interface based on the procedure in Table 2 for implementing the ciphering process:

All inputs and outputs of the command and data occur through USB communication; even reading small command consumes one micro frame of $125\mu s$.

Since ciphering occurs between ③ the data read for ciphering and ④ the cipher result output steps, ① the command read and ② response output steps are additional steps causing the deterioration of overall cipher performance. Specifically, such steps may cause the performance to deteriorate considerably when encrypting small sized data.

Table 2. Procedure for Ciphering

Process	Content
① Command Reading	Read the command of cipher processing transmitted by the host.
② Response Output	transmit the result of the command interpretation to the host.
③ Data Read for Ciphering	Read the data for ciphering from the host and start the ciphering process of the input data.
④ Cipher Result Output	Transmit the cipher result to the host.

Figure 4 depicts byte data ciphering under USB2.0 communication. As shown in the figure, command read and response output require 1 micro frame each for a total of 2 micro frames. Since 6,656 bytes can be transferred per micro frame, ($\lceil N/6656 \rceil$) micro frames are required for each data read and response output. Therefore, the total number of frames transferred is $\{2+(2 \times \lceil N/6656 \rceil)\}$. Performance can be expressed as:

$$Performance(Mbps) = \frac{N \times 8}{\{2 + (2 \times \lceil N/6656 \rceil)\} \times 125} \tag{1}$$

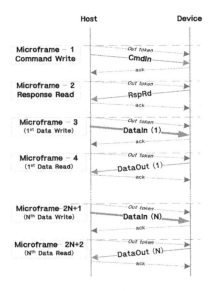

Fig. 4. N bytes ciphering process

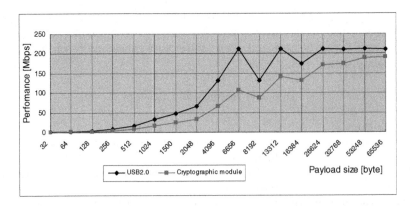

Fig. 5. Ciphering performance vs USB 2.0 standard data transfer performance

Given a sufficiently large N, the time required by two micro frames for command read and for response output will be negligible; otherwise, it may be longer than the time required for actual cipher processing.

Figure 5 compares the data transfer performance of the USB2.0 standard and ciphering performance of the cryptographic module per data size based on Equation 1. Here, the transfer performance of USB 2.0 and ciphering performance of the cryptographic module drastically deteriorate with small sized packet data to be encrypted. The transfer performance of USB 2.0 is highest when data size is a 6,656 bytes or multiples of 6,656bytes.

4   High-Speed Packet Cipher System Design

4.1   System Design Overview

To design the High-Speed Packet Cipher System, the cause of performance deterioration of the existing cryptographic module was analyzed, and improvement has been made accordingly. Key features of the High-Speed Packet Cipher System of the new cryptographic module include:

- Minimization of the USB communication
  - The 4-step procedure of "Command Read⇒Response Output⇒Data Read for ciphering⇒Cipher Result Output" is simplified into a 2-step procedure of "Command and Data Read⇒Response and Cipher Result Output"
  - A packet is structured with the command and cipher/decipher data.
  - Command and data read is performed through the data input channel, and response and data output is through the data output channel.
- Addition of a separate hardware in order to handle command interpretation, processing, and response which used to be handled by CPU
  - Command Interpretation: Command and data are separated from the packet that transmitted by the host.
  - Command Processing: The cipher process is executed to interpret the command and to appropriately control the block cipher processing engine based on such interpretation.
  - Response Output: Response data is created according to the command interpretation and result and sent to the host.
- Grouping of the multiple packet data into 6,656 bytes for batch processing
  - Multiple packets are grouped to form data size of a multiple of 6,656 bytes and sent to the cryptographic module in 1 USB communication.

In this paper, we define three packet processing system as follows.

- 4-step Procedure
  - Command interpretation, processing, and response handled by CPU
  - The 4-step procedure of "Command Read⇒Response Output⇒Data Read for ciphering⇒Cipher Result Output"

- Proposed Method 1
    - Addition of a separate hardware for command interpretation, processing, and response
    - The 2-step procedure for ciphering
- Proposed Method 2(High-Speed Packet Cipher System)
    - Grouping of the multiple packet data for batch processing in addition to the Proposed Method 1

4.2   Hardware Circuit Design

The High-Speed Packet Cipher System hardware consists of the USB controller, CPU, and FPGA containing the block cipher processing engine (Figure 6).

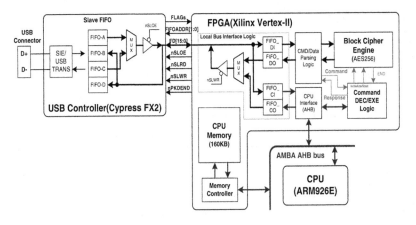

Fig. 6. Hardware design of the High-Speed Packet Cipher System

Widely used for SoC development, ARM926EJ CPU from ARM is used to perform cipher engine initialization, generation and management of the cipher/decipher key, and general control of the hardware.

For the USB controller, Cypress's CY7C68013 is used to match USB2.0 with the external host device. This chip features the local slave FIFO bus; the system uses a total of 4 FIFOs.

FPGA uses the XC2V8000 chip from Xilinx. As shown in Figure 6, the main blocks of the FPGA circuit include the local bus interface logic, block cipher engine, cmd/data parsing logic, and command DEC/EXE logic plus CPU memory of 160 KB using the distributed SelectRAM of FPGA, memory controller, and CPU interface logic with the AHB interface function.

The local bus interface logic handles the interface to the external USB controller and contains 4 internal FIFO (FIFO_CI, FIFO_CO, FIFO_DI, FIFO_DO) as in the USB controller.

CPU receives the block cipher engine initialization command sent by the host device through FIFO_CI, executes the initialization process, and sends the result back to the host through FIFO_CO.

On the other hand, the host device sends the high-speed packet processing command delivered to the command/data parsing logic through FIFO_DI. The command/data parsing engine then separates the command for delivery to the command DEC/EXE Logic, confirms the packet completion flag of the command, and sends the completion signal to the local bus interface block to initiate the generation of the packet completion signal (nPKDEND). The USB controller confirms the packet completion signal and initiates USB communication to output the cipher processing result data efficiently at the time requested by the host.

The command DEC/EXE logic interprets the delivered command, delivers the generated key to the block cipher engine, controls the initiation and completion of the processing action, and delivers the command execution result to the cmd/data parsing block. The cmd/data parsing logic then transmits the command response along with cipher result data delivered from the command DEC/EXE logic and block cipher engine to the host device through FIFO_DO.

4.3   Software Design

This section describes the design of software for the High-Speed Packet Cipher System. The security API(Application Programming Interface) for high-speed packet processing is first designed, and the specification of each command, defined.

Security API is a library enabling the use of the cipher function that protects against security risks even without extensive knowledge of security mechanism. In other words, a security library is a security toolkit that enables the easy addition of the cipher service such as encryption and authentication to the software even without expertise in the cipher algorithm.

Widely known cipher APIs include GSS-API by IETF, CGS-API by X/OPEN, CryptoAPI by Microsoft, Cryptoki by RSA, and CDSA by Intel. Recently, however, CryptoAPI by Microsoft and Cyptoki by RSA become popular. CryptoAPI runs on MS Windows. This paper uses Cryptoki[7] in designing the security API to make it portable to other operating systems.

Security API's general model is illustrated in Figure 7. The model begins with one or more applications that need to perform certain cryptographic operation, and ends with one or more cryptographic modules, on which some or all of the operations are actually carried out. Security API provides an interface to one or more cryptographic modules that are active in the system through a number of "slots". Each slot may contain a token. A token is typically "present in the slot" when a cryptographic module is present in the reader. It is possible that multiple slots may share the same physical reader. The point is that a system has some number of slots, and applications can connect to tokens in any or all of those slots. A cryptographic module can perform some cryptographic operations, following a certain command set; these commands are typically passed through standard device drivers.

Security API makes each cryptographic module look logically like every other device, regardless of the implementation technology. Thus the application need

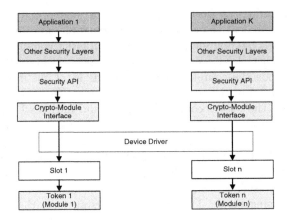

Fig. 7. Security API usage

not interface directly to the device drivers; Security API hides these details. Indeed, the underlying "module" may be implemented entirely in software -no special hardware is necessary.

Application can receive security services including encryption, decryption and digital signature from one or multiple cryptographic module using security API.

We define CI(Crypto-module Interface) as the logical specification that transforms the API command by application program into something that can be understood by the cryptographic module. The CI sends it to the cryptographic module and transmits the response of the command to API. Table 3 describes the CI command/Response block structure and elements for the High-Speed Packet Cipher System.

CMD, PE, hSession, data length, and ACK are collectively called command header. These fields commonly appear in all packets. As shown in Table 3, the header takes up 8 bytes. Therefore, cipher performance deteriorates with shrinking cipher data size. For example, the header occupies 20% of packet when ci-

Table 3. Command/Response block

Category	Byte Size	Description
CMD	8	Command Code
PE(Packet End)	1	Flag bit indicating whether the currently transmitted command is the last packet data
reserved	7	Reserved for future expansion
hSession	16	Session identifier
Data length	16	Data length in bytes 0xFFFF for a command block
ACK/RV	16	Cipher result as the return value defined in PKCS #11 specification for the response block
Data	Variable	Data for cipher

phering 32 data bytes since the total packet size will be 40 bytes. With increasing data size, however, the effect of the header becomes negligible.

The PE flag in the command and response blocks indicates whether the currently transmitted command is the last one. In other words, when the host device groups the multiple packets, the last packet has a PE flag of "1" to let the cryptographic module know that the current command is the last packet cipher command. Cipher result data of less than the maximum payload size under the USB 2.0 standard are stored by the cryptographic module in the buffer until the PE flag becomes "1". At this time, the collected cipher result data are sent to the host simultaneously; thus minimizing unnecessary USB communication considerably.

Figure 8 shows how multiple packets are processed. API stores the packets transmitted from the application program in the buffer and sends them to the cryptographic module after setting the PE value of the last data header to "1" once the stored data reaches the largest size or Chunk time expires. Chunk Time is time to accumulate the packet transmitted and MAX_SIZE is the maximum size of packets transmitted. The cryptographic module then encodes the received data of less than the maximum payload and stores them in the output buffer until the PE value is "1". Data accumulated in the output buffer are then transmitted to the host simultaneously.

In the High-Speed Packet Cipher System, it is very important to set the Chunk time and MAX_SIZE appropriately. The MAX_SIZE value should be set to match the interface used. For example, as was calculated in Section 3, MAX_SIZE should be set to 6,656 for the USB 2.0 interface.

Appropriate value for Chunk time will depend on the environment the cryptographic module is used in. For the server environment, where there is a con-

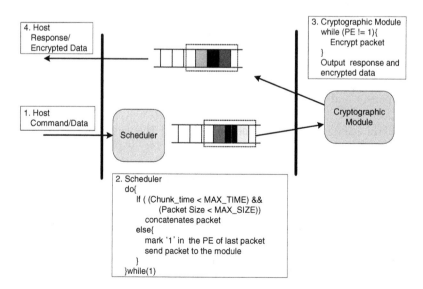

Fig. 8. Software design of the High-Speed Packet Cipher System

tinuous stream of packets to encrypt, it should be set to the time it takes to encrypt MAX_SIZE bytes. In the opposite case, where packet occurrence is less frequently, Chunk time should be set as small as possible. It is advisable to set it to 0 in the personal environment, so that the scheduler relays the packet to the cryptographic module as soon as it receives without holding it in the buffer.

5   Performance Analysis

Figure 9 shows the test environment. The USB host and the analyzer PC are a general-purpose PC with Windows XP and Pentium 4 3.0GHz CPU. The USB protocol analyzer uses LE-620HS from LINEEYE, with the cryptographic module employing ARM926EJ CPU with 33MHz clock. The AES algorithm is applied to Xilinx XC2V8000 FPGA.

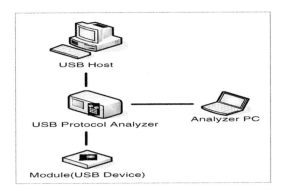

Fig. 9. Test environment

The USB host generates the packet for sending to the cryptographic module, which then sends the cipher result to the host. The USB protocol analyzer monitors the packet and reports it to the analyzer PC to display the analysis result on the screen.

We set the value of Chunk time to 1ms and the value of MAX_SIZE to 6,656 bytes. Figure 10 shows the packet monitoring display generated by the USB protocol analyzer (LE-620HS). Here, 6,656-byte long data are encrypted through the 4-step Procedure. The cipher speed shows a performance of $(6656 \times 8)bit/(1264.375 - 1263.500)ms = 60.85Mbps$. Since the theoretical maximum performance as presented in Figure 5 in section 3.2(Encryption speed based on data size) for ciphering 6,656 bytes is 106Mbps, this means that only 60% of the theoretical maximum performance is achieved.

On the other hand, Figure 11 shows the test result for ciphering 6,656 bytes by Proposed Method 1. The test result reveals that it takes 0.5ms to cipher 6,656 bytes, which is equivalent to the cipher speed of $(6656 \times 8)bit/(1236.625 - 1236.125)ms = 106Mbps$. About 70% improvement is achieved by reducing the

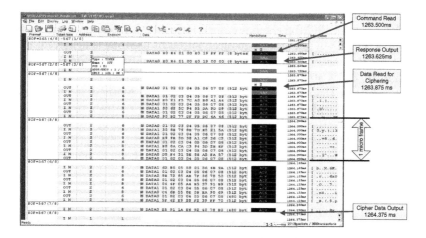

Fig. 10. Ciphering by 4-step Procedure

number of communications and by addition of a separate hardware for command interpretation, processing, and response.

The reason not to achieve the theoretical performance 480Mbps (maximum performance under USB2.0 standard) as calculated in Section 3.2 (Encryption speed based on data size) in Figure 10 and Figure 11 is due to the number of transactions per frame. Only 9 transactions are transferred per frame instead of 13. This is because of the immature performance of the cipher chip which is only a prototype in FPGA logic. Therefore, 13 transactions transfer per frame is expected show the improved cipher chip performance.

Figure 12 depicts the performance measurements from the 4-step Procedure, Proposed Method 1, and Proposed Method 2. It shows a 200% performance increase of Proposed Method 1 over 4-step Procedure for small packet data.

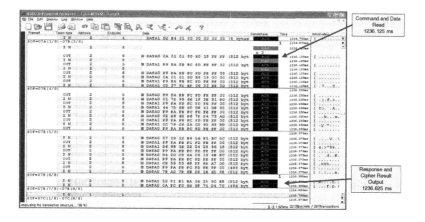

Fig. 11. Ciphering by Proposed Method 1

Looking at the data for Proposed Method 2, we see that the maximum cipher chip performance of 100Mbps is maintained for packet sizes larger than or equal to 128 bytes. For 32-byte packets, reduced speed of 68Mbps is achieved, due to the 8-byte packet header taking up 20% of data, but this performance is still better than that of 4-step Procedure and Proposed Method 1.

We can also see that the performance of Proposed Method 1 and Proposed Method 2 are identical for packets of 4,096-byte and 6,656-byte sizes. This is because a concatenation of two 4,096 bytes would result in something larger than 6,656 bytes and hence Proposed Method 2 sends a 4,096 byte packet to the cryptographic module without concatenating it with the next packet.

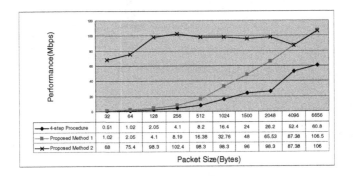

Fig. 12. Cipher performance per packet size

6   Conclusion

Since all data input and output to a cryptographic module must occur through its interface, performance degradation coming from interface constraints is inevitable for small data packets. This paper proposes the High-Speed Packet Cipher System that encrypts even small packet data at high speed by improving the packet processing method used in existing cryptographic modules.

Base on the observation that the transfer rate of a USB 2.0 interface is at its highest when data is sent in packets of 6,656-bytes size, we have designed the High-Speed Packet Cipher System to concatenate data before sending them to the USB interface in a single USB communication step. Test shows that it maintains the maximum cipher chip performance of 100Mbps regardless of the packet size. The High-Speed Packet Cipher System may be used in encryption of small packet data at high speed in PCI interface.

Performance of the High-Speed Packet Cipher System proposed in this paper depends on the frequency of pack occurrence. In the server environment with frequent packets, its performance is good. In the opposite environment, if Chunk time is set to be too large, performance deteriorates due to the buffering. Therefore, Chunk time must be set to a small value in this environment. A possible future study would be on the optimal Chunk time value.

References

1. Universal Serial Bus Specification Revision 2.0, Compaq, Hewlett-Packard, Intel, Lucent, Microsoft, NEC, Philips, Apr.27, 2000
2. PCI DMA Chaining Reference Design, QuickLogic, Application Note 63
3. DMA Chaining Performance when using the QL5064, QuickLogic, Application Note 56
4. NETASQ F2000 IPS-Firewall Multiservice Security Appliance Performance Evaluation. http://www.tollygroup.com/TS/2005/NETASQ/F2000/TollyTS205120NETA SQF2000IPS-FirewallJune2005.pdf
5. SECUi.COM NXG 2000 Evaluation of Gigabit Ethernet Firewall & VPN Performance. http://www.tolly.com/ts/2005/Secui/NXG2000/TollyTS205102-TTA-SECUI-NXG2000-Feb2005.pdf
6. Future Systems, Inc. FSC2003 SoC(System on a Chip) in Future Systems RenoGate, Fire-wall and VPN Performance Evaluation. http://www.tolly.com/TS/2005/ FutureSystems/FSC2003/TollyTS205147FutureSystemsFSC2003December2005.pdf
7. PKCS#11 v2.10 : Cryptographic Token Interface Standard, RSA Lab., Dec. 1999

A Tool for Managing Security Policies in Organisations

Anna V. Álvarez[1], Karen A. García[1], Raúl Monroy[1],
Luis A. Trejo[1], and Jesús Vázquez[2]

[1] Tecnológico de Monterrey, Campus Estado de México,
Km 3.5 Carretera al Lago de Guadalupe,
Col. Margarita Maza de Juárez, Atizapán de Zaragoza,
Estado de México, Mexico, 52926
{A00472185, kazurim, raulm, ltrejo}@itesm.mx
[2] Banco de México
Avenida 5 de Mayo, Col. Centro, Del. Cuauhtémoc
México D.F., Mexico, 06059
jjesusvg@banxico.org.mx

Abstract. Security policies are rules aimed at protecting the resources of an organisation from the risks associated with computer usage. Designing, implementing and maintaining security policies are all error prone and time consuming. We report on a tool that helps managing the security policies of an organisation. Security policies are formalised using first-order logic with equality and the unique names assumption, closely following the security policy language suggested in [1]. The tool includes a link to an automated theorem prover, Otter [2], and to a model finder, Mace [2], used to formally verify a set of formal security policies. It also includes a GUI and a number of links to read information and security policies from organisation databases and access control lists.

1 Introduction

Security policies are rules that prescribe how to manage IT resources in order to protect them from risks associated with computer usage. If properly defined, they help ensuring the goals of computer security, namely: integrity, confidentiality, and availability of IT resources.

Crafting proper security policies is a very difficult task, for two reasons. First, security policies may be ambiguous or clash one another, therefore they ought to be formalised. This formalisation, however, is tedious and error-prone. Second, policies quickly become obsolete, thus maintaining security policies is never-ending and also time-consuming. This situation prompts the construction of a tool that could help a user to readily design and develop proper security policies.

This paper reports on a security policy manager, called *e-policy manager*, portraying the following features:

1. It captures security policies using a language similar to the security policy language $\mathcal{L}_7$, defined by Halpern and Weissman [1]. Our language has a clear and precise semantics, namely: first-order logic with equality, together with the unique names assumption.

H. Yoshiura et al. (Eds.): IWSEC 2006, LNCS 4266, pp. 378–388, 2006.

2. It reasons about security policies simultaneously running Otter [2], a first-order theorem prover, and Mace [3], a first-order model finder.
3. It eases the capture of security policies, reading information from different sources, including database systems, access control lists, etc. E-policy manager also comes with a GUI for human interaction.

Currently, e-policy manager deals only with security policies of type *access control*. E-policy manager is *not* a security model[1] for a security policy, but a means of capturing, managing and ensuring logical consistency of a set of security policies.

Paper overview

The rest of this paper is organised as follows: In Section 2, we describe how to express security policies using first-order logic with equality and the unique names assumption. We also introduce the verification tasks we are interested in. In Section 3, we recapitulate Halpern and Weissman's results, namely: a first-order logic language for the specification of security policies and a characterisation of the computational complexity of verification tasks. In Section 4, we show how to apply the pair Otter and Mace to conduct the verification process. In Section 5, we describe how to use e-policy manager. We also present a graphical user interface for easily capturing security policies. In Section 6, we report on the results we have obtained from a psychological validity test carried on the e-policy manager. In Section 7, we compare related work and in Section 8, we present the conclusions drawn from our research.

2 Expressing Security Policies Using First-Order Logic

Hereafter, we assume the reader is familiar with the syntax of first-order logic, including terms, atoms, literals and well-formed formulae, the semantics of first-order logic, including models and valuations, and with validity and satisfiability of first-order formulae.

In this paper, security policies are mainly of either of two types: *permitting* or *denying*. A permitting (respectively denying) security policy conveys the *conditions* under which someone, the *subject*, is allowed (respectively forbidden) to perform an *action* on some *object*. Accordingly, the vocabulary of our language is assumed to contain at least four collection of predicate relations, one denoting subjects (agents, processes, officers, etc.), one denoting objects (files, directories, databases, applications, etc.), one denoting actions (read, write, execute, etc.), and another denoting constraints (roles, etc.) The vocabulary also contains a reserved binary predicate, called *permitted*. The literal *permitted(S, A)* means S, a term of type subject, is allowed to carry out A, a (compound) term representing an action over some term of type object.

A security policy is a sentence of the form:[2]

$$\forall X_1{:}T_1, \ldots, X_n{:}T_n. \ (C \rightarrow [\neg]permitted(S, A)) \tag{1}$$

---

[1] A *computer security model* consists of a set of underlying protection mechanisms, security issues of a computing environment, and formal models that provide a framework for a security policy.

[2] We sometimes find it convenient to abbreviate $\forall X. \ (T(X) \rightarrow P(X))$ and $\exists X. \ (T(X) \wedge P(X))$ by $\forall X{:}T. \ P(X)$ and $\exists X{:}T. \ P(X)$, respectively.

where C is a conjunction of literals, S and A are terms, and where $[\neg]$*permitted*(S, A) indicates that *permitted* may or may not be negated. A policy of the form (1) is called a *standard policy* [1]. Standard policies are generally enough to express most security policies. For example, the policies "only security officers may edit the password file", "anyone who is allowed to edit a file may read it", "anyone who is forbidden to read a file may not edit it" and "employees may read all the information associated with their department of affiliation" can be expressed as follows:

$$\forall X{:}staff,\ Y{:}posts.\ (post(X,\ officer,\ sec) \rightarrow permitted(X,\ write(passwords)))$$

$$\forall X{:}staff,\ Y{:}posts.\ (\neg post(X,\ officer,\ sec) \rightarrow \neg permitted(X,\ write(passwords)))$$

$$\forall X{:}staff,\ F{:}info.\ (permitted(X,\ write(F)) \rightarrow permitted(X,\ read(F)))$$

$$\forall X{:}staff,\ F{:}info.\ (\neg permitted(X,\ read(F)) \rightarrow \neg permitted(X,\ write(F)))$$

$$\forall X{:}staff, Y{:}posts, Z{:}dpt, F{:}info.(post(X,Y,Z) \wedge blng2(F,Z) \rightarrow permitted(X,read(Z))).$$

The *environment* is a non-empty set of relevant facts describing the organisation [1]. "John is a manager", "managers are employees", "file F is of security clearance l", etc. are all example facts of a typical environment. Formally, an environment is a set of sentences, each of which does not contain the *permitted* predicate. The environment is said to be *standard*, if it can be partitioned into two sets, E_0 and E_1, where E_0, called a *basic environment*, contains only ground literals, while E_1 contains only universally quantified formulae.

The verification tasks we are interested in are formalised as follows: Let E and $P_1,...,P_n$ respectively denote an environment and some policies and let S and A be closed terms, then we want to address the following queries:

1. Is individual S allowed (respectively forbidden) to carry out action A? This query amounts to ask whether $E \wedge P_1 \wedge ... \wedge P_n \rightarrow permitted(S, A)$ (respectively $\neg permitted(S, A)$) is valid.
2. What is the individual profile of individual S? This query amounts to ask whether, and how many times, $E \wedge P_1 \wedge ... \wedge P_n \rightarrow permitted(S, X) \vee ans(X)$ is valid, where X is an answer literal for the associated fill-in the blank question.
3. Are the policies consistent amounts to ask if $E \wedge P_1 \wedge ... \wedge P_n$ is satisfiable.
4. Are the policies Bell-LaPadulla compliant? This query amounts to ask if $E \wedge P_1 \wedge ... \wedge P_n$ satisfies the simple security condition, $clearance(S) \leq clearance(O) \rightarrow permitted(S, read(O))$, and the *-property, $permitted(S, write(O)) \rightarrow clearance(S) \leq clearance(O)$, of the Bell-LaPadulla model.

3 Tractability Results

Halpern and Weissman have shown that the problem in which we are interested is in general undecidable [1]. For the decidable part, it cannot be answered efficiently unless we impose severe restrictions. Halpern and Weissman have, in particular, shown that the language $\mathcal{L}_7$ is the most amenable to computation:

Theorem 4.3. [1]: Let ϕ be a vocabulary that contains *permitted* (and possibly other predicate, constant, and function symbols). Let $\mathcal{L}_7$ consists of all closed formulas F in $\mathcal{L}^{FO}(\phi)$ of the form $E_0 \wedge E_1 \wedge P_1 \wedge \ldots \wedge P_n \rightarrow permitted(S, A)$, where E_0 is a Basic environment, E_1 is a conjunction of universal formulas, $P_1 \wedge \ldots \wedge P_n$ is a conjunction of standard policies, and both S and A are closed terms of the appropriate sort, such that:

1. E_0 has m constants,
2. no conjunct in $E_1 \wedge P_1 \wedge \ldots \wedge P_n$ has an inequality in its antecedent, and
3. each conjunct in $E_1 \wedge P_1 \wedge \ldots \wedge P_n$ has at most one literal that is bipolar in $E_1 \wedge P_1 \wedge \ldots \wedge P_n$ relative to the equality statements in E_0.[3]

Halpern and Weissman determined that the validity of a query of type 1 can be answered in:

$$O(|E_1 \wedge (P_1 \wedge \ldots \wedge P_n)|\log|E_1 \wedge (P_1 \wedge \ldots \wedge P_n)| + b|C_l| + T)$$

where b is the number of bipolar pairs in F relative to the equality statements in E_0, C_l is the longest conjunct in F, and T depends on the number of variables that appear as an argument to an instance of *permitted* (see [1] for further details).

Unfortunately, our security policies are not part of $\mathcal{L}_7$, because they might not satisfy condition 2. We have been forced to include inequalities in the antecedent of a policy for the sake of completeness. We illustrate this by means of a simple example. Consider again the set of security policies defined in the previous section. To decide whether these policies permit (respectively forbid) *anna* to edit the password file, we must know if the statement *post(anna, officer, sec)* is true (respectively false). But if *anna* is a head of department, neither of these queries can be decided unless we explicitly assert ¬*post(anna, officer, sec)*.

To get around this incompleteness issue, we adopt a conservative meta-rule: *any action is forbidden, unless it is explicitly allowed*. This meta-rule is implemented by (automatically) including the closure of every permitting security policy. The *closure* of a permitting policy P, denoted $R(P)$, is the smallest set of denying policies that are logically consistent with P. Consider, for example, the policy "all head of departments are permitted to read information that is classified as confidential (*clearance(F)* = 4)", in symbols:

$$\forall X{:}staff,\ Z{:}dpt.\ (post(X,mgr,Z)\ )\wedge clearance(F)=4 \rightarrow permitted(X,read(F)))$$

The closure of this policy is given by:

$$\forall X{:}staff,\ Y{:}posts,\ Z{:}dpt.\ (post(X, Y, Z) \wedge Y \neq mgr\ \wedge clearance(F) = 4$$
$$\rightarrow \neg permitted(X,read(F)))$$

which is then complemented with another policy stating that "anyone who is forbidden to read a file may not edit it or share it or print it (see Section 3).

---

[3] A literal ℓ is said to be *bipolar in a formula F*, written in conjunctive normal form, if ℓ is in F, and if there is another literal ℓ' in F such that ℓ and $\neg\ell'$ unify; that is, $\exists\sigma.\ (\ell'\dot{=}\neg\ell')\sigma$. If $(\ell'\dot{=}\neg\ell')\sigma$ follows from a set E of equality statements, then ℓ is said to be *bipolar in a formula F relative to E*.

The unique names assumption is used to establish the inequality of two objects with distinct names. Unfortunately, $R(P)$ cannot be characterised logically, only procedurally.

Even though our security policies cannot be accommodated in $\mathcal{L}_7$, our experiments show that our 4 verification tasks can be carried out quickly, as discussed below.

4 Reasoning About Security Policies

Once captured, both the policies and the environment are given to an automated first-order theorem prover. We have chosen to use Otter [2], since it is well-established. Otter's main inference rules are resolution and paramodulation. Resolution is well-known to be refutation complete: if a formula is unsatisfiable then resolution will eventually deduce the proposition false, the empty clause.

First-order logic is semi-decidable: if a formula is satisfiable, then the resolution procedure may not terminate. To partly approach this problem, we simultaneously apply Mace, *models and counter-examples*, a searcher for finite models of first-order and equational statements [3]. Mace serves as a complementary companion to Otter: given an input first-order conjecture, Otter will search for a proof and Mace will search for a counter-example. Mace's engine is a Davis-Putnam-Loveland-Logemann propositional decision procedure.

Our 4 verifications tasks are then tackled as follows. Let E_0 be a conjunction of ground formulae, E_1 be a conjunction of universal formulas, $P_1 \wedge \ldots \wedge P_n$ be a conjunction of standard policies, and let S and A be closed terms representing a subject and an action over some object, respectively. Then:

1. Is individual S allowed to carry out action A amounts to giving both Otter and Mace $E_0 \wedge E_1 \wedge P_1 \wedge \ldots \wedge P_n \wedge \neg permitted(S, A)$. If the conjecture is a theorem, Otter will hopefully deduce the empty clause; otherwise, Mace will hopefully find a counter-example. We proceed similarly to verify whether S is forbidden to carry out action A.

2. To determine the individual profile of an individual S, we give Otter the conjecture $E_0 \wedge E_1 \wedge P_1 \wedge \ldots \wedge P_n \wedge (\neg permitted(S, X) \vee ans(X))$ and ask it to find as many proofs as possible.

3. Are the policies consistent amounts to give both Otter and Mace the conjecture $E_0 \wedge E_1 \wedge P_1 \wedge \ldots \wedge P_n$. If Otter deduces the empty clause, we use the proof to automatically hint the user which security policies are thought to be in conflict. Otherwise, Mace will hopefully find a counter-example.

4. Whether the security policies are Bell-LaPadulla compliant amounts to giving Otter and Mace two formulae: i) for the simple security condition $E_0 \wedge E_1 \wedge P_1 \wedge \ldots \wedge P_n \wedge clearance(S) \leq clearance(O) \wedge \neg permitted(S, A)$, and ii) for the *-property, $E_0 \wedge E_1 \wedge P_1 \wedge \ldots \wedge P_n \wedge \neg permitted(S, A) \wedge \neg(clearance(S) \leq clearance(O))$.

In our experiments, Otter was able to quickly find inconsistencies in the input security policies, (deriving the empty clause), if there was any, but usually spent a while, otherwise. Notice that, if the input security policies are not inconsistent, then Otter may run forever.

When asked a specific query about what a specific user can do, Otter also replied quickly. Our experiments confirm the theoretical results of [1]. Otter has been made to run in automatic mode, applying binary resolution, unary resolution or UR-Resolution, hyper-resolution, and binary paramodulation. Otter works searching for the empty clause, which, in the case of a verification task of type 3, is an evidence of contradiction amongst the security policies.

5 Using E-Policy Manager

The basic environment, E_0, which is a conjunction of ground formulae, is usually built using a simple, three-view approach. In the first view, the organisation is character-ised as a collection of employees. Each employee is described in terms of the standard attributes, e.g. name, surname, etc. In the second view, the organisation is character-ised in terms of a structure, which usually consists of several departments and their relations. Relations, e.g. *staff(X)*, *post(Y)*, *dpt(Z)*, *post(X, Y, Z)*, etc., are used to named departments, employees, etc. At this point, each employee is affiliated with some department and given a role. In the third view, the organisation is described in terms of its resources, information in our case. Files, directories and all kinds of information resources are then incorporated into the environment.

Using the unique names assumption, we may express and prove simple properties of the basic environment. Proven properties include "every employee is affiliated to one and only one department", "every employee has one and only one password", etc.

5.1 Linking E-Policy Manager with a Database Management System

Mostly, the basic environment is captured through a database management system. E-policy manager can be linked, so far, to read information from Access or SQL server. To fulfil the intended interpretation, the basic environment is assumed to come from the following tables:

- Subject<identifier, name, department of affiliation, position>
- Object<identifier, name, department this object belongs to, class>
- Action<identifier, action description, object this action is applied to>
- Security_mechanism<identifier, access mechanism>

The second part of the environment, which is a conjunct of universally quantified formulae, together with the security policies, is captured via a GUI, which we de-scribed below. Notice, though, that security policies can be also captured by means of a collection of control access lists. An *access control list* (ACL) is a concept in com-puter security used to enforce privilege separation. It is a means of determining the appropriate access rights to a given object depending on certain aspects of the process that is making the request, principally the process's user identifier.[4]

5.2 A Graphical User Interface

Writing, developing and maintaining security policies are all responsibilities of a secu-rity officer, who can not be assumed to be acquainted with formal methods. Formal

---

[4] http://en.wikipedia.org/wiki/Access_control_list

methods require both significant skill and time (and therefore financial resources) to use. To get around this problem, e-policy manager comes with a graphical user interface (GUI) that makes it easy to capture security policies by means of wizards and other graphical techniques. Also the GUI makes it easy both to correctly interpret the input security policies and to formalise them in FOL.

Through the GUI, a security officer can capture a set of security policies at a high, abstract level, by means of schemata. Although schemata restrict the expressiveness of our policy language, the output security policies contain the necessary ingredients for guaranteeing a simple but correct translation into our first-order language. Moreover, the GUI hides formal methods and knowledge representation out of the user, who no longer needs to be acquainted with these techniques.

To provide flexibility to the user, we maintain a database of action names synonymous. So a user may write (or select) "change", "manipulate", "alter", etc. rather than the default "access". To avoid slowing down the deduction process, we normalise all the synonymous of an action to a designated, default action name. This way, we do not perform additional, unnecessary applications of paramodulation or rewriting.

Using the capturing schema, each security policy is translated into both a first order formula and a semi-natural language expression. The formula is regarded as the formal model of the associated security policy. The expression is used for documentation purposes. It is part of the security policies manual of the associated organisation.

Given that a policy specifies the conditions under which a subject is allowed (respectively forbidden) to perform an action on some object, the GUI portrays a schemata, based on wizards, through which the user conveys several pieces of information. This involves the subject, e.g. users, processes, etc., the action, e.g. reading, writing, creating, etc., the object, an information file, the restrictions under which the action is permitted, e.g. a user role, a user affiliation, etc., and whether the action should be denied or permitted. The subject of a security policy can be a specific individual or a group of individuals that are related by some condition.

The GUI also allows the introduction of a modifier, we call the *purpose modifier*. If the purpose modifier is on, the interpretation of the security policy at hand is changed so that it now reads "*only* subject is allowed (respectively forbidden) to perform the associated action on the object under the given conditions".

Using the GUI, a user is thus able to capture a security policy through a suitable schema. Schematically, the wizard enables the user to convey six pieces of information: i) the subject of the policy, ii) number of purposes (use only to denote exclusiveness, otherwise this field is left apart), iii) the type of policy (permitting or denying), iv) the action to be carried out, v) the object the action should be performed on, and vi) the constraints.

As an example policy capturing, consider that, after interacting with the wizard, the user has input the following information: subject = *staff*, condition on the subject = *officer*, department = *sec*, purpose modifier = *on*, policy type = *permitting*, action = *read*, object = *passwords* (the password file), and object constraints = none, then the policy manager records the following formulae within the policy database:

$$\forall X{:}staff.\ (post(X, officer,\ sec) \rightarrow permitted(X,\ read(passwords)))$$

$$\forall X{:}staff.\ (\neg post(X, officer,\ sec) \rightarrow \neg permitted(X,\ read(passwords)))$$

As another example of security policy capturing, consider that, after interacting with the wizard, a security officer has input the following information: `subject` = *staff*, `subject constraints` = *affiliated2(subject, it)*, `purpose modifier` = off, `policy type` = *permitting*, `object` = *information*, `object constraint` = *belongs2(object, it)*, `action` = *read*. Then, e-policy manager outputs:

$$\forall X{:}staff, Y{:}dpt, F{:}info. \ (post(X, Y, it) \wedge blngs2(Y, it) \rightarrow permitted(X, read(Y)))$$

Each policy can be added or removed from the database by means of a wizard, which pops up a table containing all existing policies. A user only has to select an unwanted policy, by clicking on it, and then indicate policy removal or edition.

The design of both the interface and the security policy schemata of e-policy manager was largely inspired by LaSCO [4]. LaSCO is an object oriented programming language which expresses a security policy by means of a constraint imposed on an object. Other policy languages were also considered, e.g. [5], but none of them provides as much a solid theoretical foundation as that of [1]. We have more to say about related work in Section 5.

6   Testing Psychological Validity

E-policy manager was used to capture a number of security policies found in books or gathered from practitioners. Although they impose severe constraints on the policy language, schemata were found to be enough to capture all these security policies. Our experiments show that the verification process may take a few milliseconds.

E-policy manager was also evaluated for psychological validity. We run a test on six security officers, who answered a survey and interacted with the tool prototype. Our results from this experiment are encouraging. The answers provided by these security officers point that e-policy manager has achieved its two primary design goals, namely: i) to make it easy to capture a security policy while guaranteeing it is correct in the sense of interpretation, and ii) to provide a means for formally verifying the security policies are consistent. Rather than an adverse opinion, we were urged to include an account for policies about other resources.

E-policy manager is available upon request by sending e-mail to the first author. In the next section, we will review existing languages for the specification of security policies.

7   Related Work

A policy specification language aims at formalising the intent of a policy designer into a form that can be read and interpreted by both people and machines [5]. It is especially designed to specify the relations amongst system entities in terms of actions and the conditions upon which these actions are denied or performed. There exist several policy specification languages. In what follows, we review the main features of four policy specification tools and associated languages: i) Keynote, ii) SPSL [5], iii) LaSCO [3], and iv) the General Computer Security Policy Model [6].

Keynote and SPSL [5] are used to specify security policies about network applications. Neither Keynote nor SPL provide a visual tool for policy capturing. However, they are both equipped with a policy compiler, which produces a user profile that the intended application can use for denying or permitting the execution of an action. Keynote cannot be used to specify facts about the environment. Keynote does not scale properly, as it is difficult to foresee the state that results when enforcing a number of security policies. E-policy manager can be used to capture facts about the environment but was never thought as a mechanism for enforcing security policies.

LaSCO [3] is based on a model where a system consists of objects and events and works by conveying restrictions on objects. This language represents the policies by means of directed graphs which describe a specific state of the system (domain) and specific access constraints (requirements) and in mathematic logic. The nodes represent system objects and the edges represent system events. LaSCO [3] can be used to express a wide variety of standard and customised security policies, including access control and other history-based and context-dependent policies. Our work has been inspired in this language. For example, for the graphical user interface, we have adopted the use of graphs facilitating the security policies representation, as well as denoting information access control. LaSCO expressions can be translated into a low-level language for security policy enforcement. However, the tool does not involve the use of a mechanism to guarantee that the policies are consistent or that they meet certain properties.

Krsul, Spafford and Tuglualar [6] have presented a functional approach to the specification of security policies that allows policy stepwise refinement. The model makes the explicit assumption that policies and the value of the system objects are related. This model expresses policies as algorithmic and mathematical expressions. The specification policy explicitly lists the objects and attributes that are needed to enforce the policy. The model helps identifying the components that are relevant to the policy and hence provides a better policy understanding.

These languages are all adequate for the specification of security policies. However, they are not this effective, since, except for [6], they do not have a formal semantics, with which to reason about the security policies. Also security policy capturing using no visual aid has proven to be error prone, making it necessary to verify the written policies. Languages have been developed for the integration of local and distributed security policies oriented towards the interoperability of several computer sites [9,10]. They do not help ensuring that policies do not contradict one another.

Halpern and Weissman have shown that (a subset of) first order logic is enough to express and efficiently reason about security policies [1]. They represent a security policy as a relation between three sorts, *Actions* (e.g. accessing a file), *Subjects* (the agents that perform actions) and *Times*. This contrasts with our work, where we denote a policy as a relation amongst *Subjects*, *Objects* and *Actions*. Halpern and Weissman are much more interested in using a user profile in order to enforce security policies; they argue that their security policy schema (which we have borrowed for our work) makes it easier for a user to write proper policies. They have not paid attention to checking policy consistency. As we can see, our work is also based on Halpern and Weissman's. Indeed, in [1] it is mentioned these two researchers are working on developing a user-friendly interface for security policy capturing, but no report has been published yet.

E-policy manager ensures that the set of security policies are unambiguous and do not contradict each other; that is, it guarantees that the security policies are, what we call, *consistent*. This contrasts with related work where methods are proposed to ensure that the security policies are consistent *across* a distributed environment [11,12].

More related to ours is the work of Zanin *et al.* [13], where a formal model, called SELinux Access Control (SELAC), is proposed for analyzing an arbitrary security policy configuration for the SELinux system.[5] SELAC defines a semantics for the constructs of the SELinux configuration language and models the relationships occurring among sets of configuration rules. Zanin *et al.* have developed an algorithm based upon SELAC, which, given an arbitrary security policy configuration, can verify whether or not a given subject can access a specific object in a particular mode. They are planning on extending the model and the tool functionalities to support the analysis of data confidentiality and integrity.

E-policy manager is a second-generation of that presented in [14]. In particular, the newer e-policy manager has much better reasoning capabilities, a better interface and more linking capabilities to interact with other systems.

8 Conclusions and Future Work

To secure the most significant resources of an organisation, it is necessary to have a set of appropriate policies. Managing security policies is not an easy task and currently it does not have computer support. The goal of our work is to provide a tool that supports this task and gives a basis for future research. The tool, called e-policy manager, includes a graphical user interface that makes it easy to capture security policies and a module that formalises these policies to be verified by a first-order theorem prover, Otter, and a first-order model finder, Mace.

Further work includes using a natural language processor so as to allow a user to input security policies as he would in an informal document. This interface would significantly increment the acceptance of E-policy manager from potential users. Further work also considers expressing and reasoning about policies regarding resources other than information.

References

[1] Joseph Y. Halpern and Vicky Weissman. Using first-order logic to reason about policies. In *Proceedings of the 16th IEEE Computer Security Foundations Workshop CSFW 2003*, pages:187-201. IEEE Computer Society, 2003.
[2] William McCune. Otter 2.0 In Mark E. Stickel, editor, *Proceedings of the 10th Conference on Automated Deduction*, volume 449 of *Lecture Notes in Computer Science*, pages 663-664. Springer, 1990.
[3] William McCune. Mace4 Reference Manual and Guide. *The Computing Research Repository (CoRR)* CS.SC/0310055, 2004.
[4] James A. Hoagland. Specifying and enforcing policies using LaSCO, the language for security constraints on objects. *The Computing Research Repository*, CS.CR/0003066, 2000.

---

[5] SELinux (Security Enhanced Linux) consists of a collection of security enhancements in the Linux kernel.

[5] Renato Iannella. ODRL: The open digital rights language initiative. Technical report.

[6] Minna Kangasluoma. Policy Specification Languages. Department of Computer Science, Helsinki University of Technology, 1999.

[7] Ivan Krsul, Eugene Spafford, and Tugkan Tuglular. A New Approach to the Specification of General Computer Security Policies. COAST *Techical Report 97-13.*, 1998, West Lafayette, IN 47907–1398.

[8] E. Davies, *Representation of Commonsense Knowledge*, Courant Institute for Mathematical Sciences, 1990.

[9] T. Ryutov, C. Neuman. Representation and evaluation of security policies for distributed system services. In *Proceedings of DARPA Information Survivability Conference and Exposition 2000 (DISCEX '00)*, pages:172-183, vol. 2, 2000.

[10] R. Bhatti, A. Ghafoor, E. Bertino, J. Joshi. X-GTRBAC: an XML-based policy specification framework and architecture for enterprise-wide access control. *ACM Transactions on Information and System Security (TISSEC)* 8(2):187-227, 2005.

[11] S. Ngamsuriyaroj, T.F. Keefe, A.R. Hurson. Maintaining consistency of the security policy using timestamp ordering. In *Proceedings of the 2002 International Conference on Information Technology: Coding and Computing*, pages:164–170. IEEE Computer Society, 2002.

[12] S. Ngamsuriyaroj, T.F. Keefe, A.R. Hurson. Maintaining consistency of the security policy in distributed environment. In *Proceedings of the 21st IEEE International Performance, Computing, and Communications Conference*, pages:179-186. IEEE Computer Society, 2002.

[13] G. Zanin, L. Vincenzo Mancini. Security analysis: Towards a formal model for security policies specification and validation in the selinux system. In *Proceedings of the ninth ACM symposium on Access control models and technologies*, pages:126-135. ACM Press, 2004.

[14] K. García, R. Monroy and J. Vázquez. An Artificial Manager for Security Policies in Organizations. *Journal of Research in Computing Science* 17:97-106, 2005.

Information Flow Query and Verification for Security Policy of Security-Enhanced Linux

Yi-Ming Chen and Yung-Wei Kao

Department of Information Management, National Central University
300, Jungda Rd., Joungli, 32054, Taiwan, ROC
{cym, 93423010}@cc.ncu.edu.tw

Abstract. This paper presents a Colored Petri Nets (CPN) approach to analyze the information flow in the policy file of Security-Enhanced Linux (SELinux). The SELinux access control decisions are based on a security policy file that contains several thousands of security rules. It becomes a challenge for policy administrator to determine whether the modification of the security policy file conforms to the pre-specified security goals. To address this issue, this paper proposes a formal information flow model for SELinux security policy file, and presents a simple query language to help administrators to express the expected/unexpected information flow. We developed a method to transform the SELinux policy and security goal into Policy CPN Diagram and Query CPN Diagram. A tool named SEAnalyzer that can automatically verify the SELinux policy has been developed and two application examples of this tool will be presented in the context.

Keywords: Colored Petri Nets, information flow, SELinux, security policy.

1   Introduction

OS security is considered to be the basis of the computer security [1]. In 1983, the Department of Defense published the TCSEC (Trusted Computer System Evaluation Criteria). In TCSEC, there are seven levels for security computer system, from D to A1. In 2001, NSA (National Security Agency) proposed the SELinux (Security-Enhanced Linux) [2] system, which has reached the B1 level of TCSEC [3]. It is considered to be secure, because that most of the popular OS, like Windows or Linux, do not even satisfy the requirement of B1 level.

Although the SELinux is secure, the policy of SELinux is complex to make. For example, in the SELinux example policy file which associated with the distribution of SELinux, there are more than 30,000 policy statements. In different situation, different applications running in the system, or different resources allocation, the security policy should be modified to adapt the current environment and ensure the security of the whole system. So this is a problem for policy administrator, who has the responsibility to handle thousands of policy statements and make sure that these policy statements

H. Yoshiura et al. (Eds.): IWSEC 2006, LNCS 4266, pp. 389–404, 2006.

will exactly behave as what he expects. Several researches have tried to solve this problem [4][5][6][7][8][9][10][11], and we will compare our approach to theirs in the last two sections.

The aim of this paper is to provide a more intuitive for users to analyze the information flow of SELinux security policy. We first propose a formal information flow model for SELinux security policy file, then presents a simple query language to help administrators to express the security flow that he/she concerns. We have developed a method that transform the information flow related rules and security query to Colored Petri Net (CPN) diagram. We have implemented a tool named SEAnalyzer and will illustrate its uses by several examples in the context.

The paper is organized in 9 sections. Section 2 introduces the SELinux security model. Section 3 presents the system definition. Section 4 explains the security goal and security query. Section 5 presents the verification tool and process. Section 6 describes our CPN diagram transformation methodology. Section 7 gives analysis examples to the application of our approach and Section 8 compares our work with related work. Finally we make conclusions and give future research directions in Section 9.

2 SELinux Security Model

2.1 SELinux MAC Operation

The key factor to make SELinux a more secure system than many other popular operating systems is that SELinux adopt the MAC (Mandatory Access Control) mechanism, not the DAC (Discretionary Access Control). DAC only depends on the user ID and ownership of this user to decide whether the subject (e.g. process) can access the object (ex. file) or not. On the other hand, MAC depends on labels to make the decision. The label contains a variety of security-relevant information [13]. Subject and object are the most basic terms in the literature on access control. Subject refers to the active component in a system, usually the process, while object refers to any system resource accessed by subject, such as file, directory, network socket, or even another process. If any subject intents to access any object, only the behavior of access that is clearly defined to be allowed in the MAC policy can be conducted.

MAC is an important feature that makes the main difference between level C and level B in TCSEC. However, traditional MAC architecture has some limitations. For example, the MAC mechanism is typically tightly coupled to a MLS (multi-level security) policy. That makes the system very inflexible. To overcome this problem, NSA and SCC (Secure Computing Corporation) worked with University of Utah's Flux research group to develop Flask architecture [13], which provides the support of dynamic security policies.

Figure 1 shows the Flask architecture. The Flask architecture separates the definition of the policy logic from the enforcement mechanism. Two components, Security Server and Object Manager, respond in those tasks respectively.

In the SELinux implementation, all the kernel subsystems (e.g. process management, filesystem, socket IPC, System V IPC), except the Security Server, are Object Managers. If any subject intends to access some objects, Object Manager will query the Security Server first. After the Security Server send the decision of this access back, Object Manager then conduct the enforcement to accept or deny the access depends on the Security Server decision. Security Server stores the security policy. Security Server receives the query sent by the Object Manager, checks the rules defined in the security policy, and makes the decision for this query.

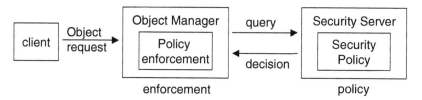

Fig. 1. Flask architecture

2.2 Security Context

Security context is one of the policy-independent data type for security labels in Flask architecture [13]. The security context is a variable-length string, and the security identifier is an integer that is mapped to a security context. SELinux associates a security context with every subject and object in the system. Here a security context is a 3-tuple *(user, role, type)*. The notion of *user* is the person who makes the process running if it is in the subject security context, and is the owner of object in the object security context. The notion of *role*, derived from the literature on role-based access control, is used to represent a set of permissions that the user can be granted. The notion of *type* is also known as domains, which divides subjects or objects into groups [14]. The information stored in security context is used as the representation of environment by SELinux for making authorization decisions.

3 System Definition

3.1 CPN Definition

CPN is proposed by Kurt Jensen in 1980s [12]. The difference between Petri Nets and CPN is that CPN involve the concept of *color set* that just is similar to the concept of data type in general purpose programming languages. CPN is a graphic-oriented language, which use oval to represent the place, rectangle to the transition, and arrow to the arc. Arc expression represents the condition for the transition occurs. There may be zero, one, or many tokens in each place. If the value of the token matches to the condition on the arc expression, the transition will be initiated.

CPN can be formally defined by a tuple $N = (\Sigma, P, T, A, N, C, G, E, I)$ which satisfies the following requirements:

1. *Σ is a finite set of non-empty data types, called color sets.*
2. *P is a finite set of places.*
3. *T is a finite set of transitions.*
4. *A is a finite set of arcs.*
5. *$N : A \rightarrow P \times T \cup T \times P$ is a node function that associates arcs with two nodes.*
6. *$C : P \rightarrow \Sigma$ is a color function that associates places with data types.*
7. *$G : T \rightarrow EXP$ is a guard function that associates transitions with expressions such that: $\forall t \in T$, $(type(G(t)) = bool) \wedge (type(var(G(t))) \subseteq \Sigma)$*, where type(e) denotes the data type of an expression e, type({e1,e2, . . .}) denotes the set of data types of expressions e1,e2, . . ., var(e) denotes the set of free variables of an expression e, and EXP denotes the set of all expression.
8. *$E : A \rightarrow EXP$ is an arc expression function that associates arcs with expressions such that: $\forall a \in A$, $(type(E(a)) = C(p(a))_{MS}) \wedge (type(var(E(a))) \subseteq \Sigma)$,*
   where p(a) is the place of N(a), and 't_{MS}' denotes type 'multi-set of type t'.
9. *$I : P \rightarrow EXP$ is an initialization function that associates places with expressions such that: $\forall p \in P$, $type(I(p)) = C(p)_{MS}$.*

3.2 Security Policy Definition

In order to define what the security policy is, we have to define several basic sets first. Here are several sets defined for the SELinux policy:

Pu : the set of users in SELinux policy
Pr : the set of roles in SELinux policy
Pt : the set of types in SELinux policy
Pc : the set of classes in SELinux policy
Pp : the set of permissions in SELinux policy

After these sets were defined, several relations of these sets can be defined to represent some declarations and rules which are used in the SELinux policy. Here are several relation definitions:

1. *User declaration relation υ:*

   $\upsilon(u, r_1, r_2,..., r_n)$, *where $u \in Pu$, for each $1 \leq i \leq n$, $i \in N$, $r_i \in Pr$*
   Relation υ represents that user u play the role $r_1, r_2,...,$ or r_n. For example: *user root roles { user_r sysadm_r };*

2. *Role declaration relation ρ:*

   $\rho(r, t_1, t_2,..., t_n)$, *where $r \in Pr$, for each $1 \leq i \leq n$, $i \in N$, $t_i \in Pt$*
   Relation ρ represents that role r is declared, and r can access type $t_1, t_2,...,$ or t_n. For example: *role user_r types user_t;*

3. *Class declaration relation χ:*

   $\chi(c_1, c_2, p_1, p_2,..., p_n)$, *where $c \in Pr$, for each $1 \leq i \leq n$, $i \in N$, $p_i \in Pp$.*

Relation χ represents that class c_1 is defined that it inherits from c_2 and contains the permission set $\{p_1, p_2, \ldots, p_n\} \cup$ permission set of c_2. For example: *class dir inherits file { add_name }*

4. *Allow rule relation α:*

$\alpha(t_1, t_2, c, p_1, p_2, \ldots, p_n)$, *where* $t_1 \in Pt$, $t_2 \in Pt$, $c \in Pc$, *for each* $1 \leq i \leq n$, $i \in N$, $p_i \in Pp$. Relation α represents that type t_1 can access type t_2 with operation of class c and permission $p_1, p_2, \ldots,$ or p_n. For example: *allow crond_t locale_t:dir { read getattr lock search ioctl };*

3.3 Security Context Definition

SELinux uses security context to summarize the security-relevant information of resources. Here is the definition of the legal security context set S:

$S = \{ (u,r,t) \mid u \in Pu,\ r \in Pr,\ t \in Pt,\ \upsilon(u,r),\ \rho(r,t) \}$

3.4 Information Flow Definition

The most important control in SELinux is the access control from subject to object. After the basic sets and relations have been defined, we can define the direct information flow that flows from some security context to another, but doesn't pass trough any security context in the middle. The direct information flow δ is defined as:

$\delta(u_1, r_1, t_1, u_2, r_2, t_2, c, p)$, *where,*
  $(u_1, r_1, t_1) \in S$, $(u_2, r_2, t_2) \in S$, $\chi(c, p), \alpha(t_1, t_2, c, p)$ *if write_like(p), or*
  $(u_1, r_1, t_1) \in S$, $(u_2, r_2, t_2) \in S$, $\chi(c, p), \alpha(t_2, t_1, c, p)$ *if read_like(p)*

Function *write_like* returns *true* if p is a write-like permission and *false* if read-like. Also, function *read_like* returns *true* if p is read-like permission and *false* if write-like. However, usually the information flow doesn't come alone. For example, the httpd_t is allowed to access log_t to log something in the log file, so there exits one information flow form httpd_t to log_t. After that, maybe the sysadm_t is allowed to check the log file, so there will be one information flow from log_t to sysadm_t. In this example, the information flow can flow from httpd_t, through log_t, and into sysadm_t. Such successive information flow is called *Sequenced Information Flow*. The sequenced information flow σ can be defined as:

$\sigma(u_1, r_1, t_1, u_n, r_n, t_n)$, *where,* $\exists \{(u_1, r_1, t_1) \ldots (u_n, r_n, t_n)\} \subseteq S$, $\{ c_1, c_2, \ldots, c_{n-1} \} \subseteq Pc$, $\{ p_1, p_2, \ldots, p_{n-1} \} \subseteq Pp$, $1 \leq i \leq n$, $i \in N$, *so that* $\delta(u_1, r_1, t_1, u_2, r_2, t_2, c_1, p_1), \delta(u_2, r_2, t_2, u_3, r_3, t_3, c_2, p_2), \ldots, \delta(u_{n-1}, r_{n-1}, t_{n-1}, u_n, r_n, t_n, c_{n-1}, p_{n-1})$.

Moreover, if the information flow flows to any security context that is passed through before, we name this kind of information flow as *Recursive Information Flow*. For example, if there is a user writes something into a file, and reads the file later, then the information flow will flow form the user's security context to the file's, and back to the user's, as the event of reading. The Recursive Information Flow ρ is defined as:

$\rho(u_1, r_1, t_1, u_n, r_n, t_n)$, where $\sigma(u_1, r_1, t_1, u_n, r_n, t_n)$, $1 \leq n$, $n \in N$,
and $(u_1, r_1, t_1)=(u_n, r_n, t_n)$.

4 Security Goal and Security Query

4.1 Security Goal

One of the challenges to address the SELinux policy analysis problem is how to express the security goal. Here the security goal indicates the security condition that the administrator wants to know whether it exists in the policy configuration file. With security goal, we can validate the policy, and examine that is there exist any wrong-made policy which conflicts the goal we expect. For this reason, we need a kind of expression to represent the security goal, or so-called security policy specification. For example, after the administrator installs a SAMBA service in a SELinux server, he/she wants to know whether the samba program would access the password file that it is permitted to access. In this case, we may describe the security goal as:

"Only the information flow which starts from samba_t and directly flows into passwd_t is the legal information flow"

However, there will several situations that are considered to be illegal information flows under this description:

1. *The information flow which starts from samba_t, and flows to another type, but enters into passwd_t.*
2. *The information flow which starts from samba_t, but doesn't flow through passwd_t.*
3. *The information flow doesn't flows through samba_t, but enters into passwd_t.*
4. *The information flow which flows through neither samba_t nor passwd_t.*

It is obvious that, many of these situations could be unreasonable. For example, in the fourth case, most of the information flows in the policy should be illegal. Hence, the representation of this security goal is very improper. The reason of this improper representation is that it is a *positive representation*. Positive representation means that it describes the legal information flow of the security goal. On the other hand, if the *negative representation* is used, that will be more specific. The negative representation describes the illegal information flow of the security goal. For example, the negative representation of security goal in the samba_t-passwd_t case maybe as:

"Only the information flow that starts from samba_t, and flows to another type, but enters into passwd_t is the illegal information flow"

However, not all of the security goals are suitable to be described in negative representation. For example, consider the following security goal:

"There must be information flow flowing from samba_t to passwd_t"

This is a positive representation of security goal. If we use negative representation instead, we will find that it is difficult and complex. In such situation, positive representation is the better choice. In conclusion, the selection of positive or negative representation to describe security goal depends on the property of this security goal.

SLAT [8][9] supports a security goal description language, called Diagram. The Diagram in SLAT must be made in positive representation, and SLAT will convert this Diagram into negative representation automatically. This is a dangerous step because that there maybe one positive representation of the security but many negative representations that conflict the positive one. SLAT only chose one of them to verify the security policy. So it is likely that the result of SLAT verification (the information flow that matches the converted security goal) is talking about the wrong story about the illegal information flows.

4.2 Security Query

Query is a neuter way because that it can be used in both positive and negative representation. In the positive case, query can be used to find legal information flow. If any result was found in positive query, then the security goal is satisfied. In the negative case, query can be used to find illegal information flow. If any result was found in negative query, then the security goal is violated.

In Order to allow the administrator easily expresses the security goal, we develop a simple query language which expresses the information flow that administrator wants to query, no matter it is a positive or negative query. The BNF form [15] of the query language is expressed as follows:

```
Goal ::= IF IFP type";"
IF ::= IF IFP type
    | type
IFP ::= ":(" Perm "," Operator ", !(" Not_List ")):"
    | ":(" Perm "," Operator ", !()):"
Perm ::= "WL" | "RL" | "ALL"
Operator ::= "+" | "-"
Not_List ::= Not_List "," type
        | type
type ::= ([a-z,A-Z] | "_")+
```

"IF" represents the information flow, and *"IFP"* represents the information flow path. The direction of information flow is from the left type of the information flow path to the right type of the same information flow path.

"Perm" represents all the permissions in this information flow. If "Perm" is *"WL"*, that means all the permissions in information flow path are write-like permissions, and *"RL"* means read-like permissions. At last, if "Perm" is *"ALL"*, then permission type is not checked.

"Operator" represents the direct information flow in *"-"*, and sequenced information flow in *"+"*. *"Not_List"* represents the SELinux types that are not

included in the information flow path. Finally, *"type"* represents the SElinux type name. For example, if the query is formulated as:

a_t:(WL,+,!()):b_t:(RL,-,!()):c_t:(ALL,+,!(d_t)):e_t;

Then this query is made to find the information flow that:

1. a_t can access b_t with write-like permissions in sequenced information flows
2. c_t can access b_t with read-like permission in direct information flow
3. c_t can access e_t with the information flow that doesn't pass through type d_t

It is noticeable that c_t access b_t by read-like permission, not b_t access c_t. The reason is that the direction of information flow is from left to right, in other words, from b_t to c_t. So only when c_t accesses b_t with read-like permission, the information flow direction is matched.

5   Verification Tool and Verification Process

In order to verify the user maintained SELinux security policy with user specified security goal, we need a verification tool which can automatically parse the policy, parse the query, construct the model to simplify the policy, and deduce the model automatically to conclude that whether the security policy satisfies the security goal or not. We propose the tool, named *SEAnalyzer*, to responds for theses tasks. In SEAnalyzer, CPN is used to model the security policy and query separately, into the *Policy CPN Diagram* and *Query CPN Diagram*. Allow relation is the majority part of SELinux policy, and it is the most important relation in the information flow. Hence, the SEAnalyzer only focus on allow relations and model information flow with allow relations in Policy CPN Diagram.

6   CPN Diagram Transformation

Before the usage of CPN, the colors and variables should be defined first. We define the following colors and variables that would be used in information flow analysis using *CPN ML notation* [16].

```
color Match = BOOL;
color SELinux_type = string;
color Perm_type = string;
color Pre_Query_Type = string;
color Type_List = list SELinux_type;
color Perm_List = list Perm_type;
color INFO= product
Match*Pre_Query_Type*Type_List*Perm_List;
var selinux_type : SELinux_type;
var pre_query_type : Pre_Query_Type;
var type_list : Type_List;
```

```
var info : INFO;
var pre_query_type : Pre_Query_Type;
var match : Match;
```

6.1 Policy CPN Diagram Transformation

First of all, the allow relation will be extracted from SELinux policy and transformed into Policy CPN Diagram. For each allow relation, the source type and destination type will be transformed into CPN place with the name as the SELinux type name. Each of the permission in the allow relation will be transformed into place named *"RL"* if this is a read-like permission and *"WL"* if write-like permission. For example, the following two allow relations (1) and (2) will be transformed into Table 1 individually for each of the permission.

$$allow\ p1,\ p2:c\ \{\ read,\ write\ \};\tag{1}$$

$$allow\ p1,\ p2:c\ \{\ read\ ,write\ \};\tag{2}$$

After these Diagrams were transformed individually, then combine these Diagrams into one Policy CPN Diagram as Figure 2.

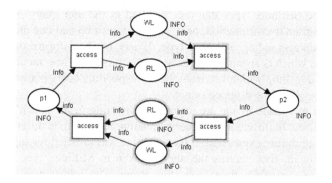

Fig. 2. Combined Policy CPN Diagram for (1) and (2)

Finally, for each of the arc which direct to any SELinux type, the arc expression should be altered to put some information into the token and check the recursive information flow. For example, the allow relation in (3) will be modeled as Figure 3.

$$allow\ user\_t\ fsadm\_t : file\ \{\ write\ \};\tag{3}$$

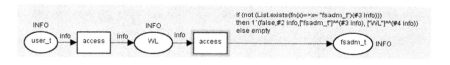

Fig. 3. Security Policy Diagram for (3)

Table 1. CPN Diagram transformed from (1) and (2) for each of the permission

Types and permission	CPN Diagram
p1 read p2	
p1 write p2	
p2 read p1	
p2 write p1	

6.2 Query CPN Diagram Transformation

The verification methodology is designed to check all of the information flows which flow through the SELinux types that are specified in the user query. Hence, in the Query CPN Diagram transformation, one *"match"* transition and one place should be added for the corresponding SELinux type. If any of the information flow flows through the type which is specified in query, this information flow should be checked by the "match" transition with token from the corresponding query place to decide this information flow should be dropped or not.

The decision was made by the arc expression directing from "match' transition to SELinux type place. In different user query situation, there will be different condition in *"if"* decision of the arc expression. If the condition was satisfied for any information flow passes through, then returns the altered token to SELinux type place. If the condition was not satisfied, then drops this token. The information flow will be terminated after the token was dropped, and this information flow will be excluded from the result information flow set for the user query. Table 2 lists different conditions

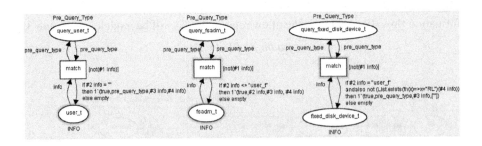

Fig. 4. Security Query Diagram for (4)

that should be added in the "if" decision of the arc for different user query. For example, if the query is defined as (4):

$$user\_t :(WL, +,!(fsadm\_t)):fixed\_disk\_device\_t; \qquad (4)$$

Then the Security Query Diagram for (4) will be modeled as Figure 4.

Table 2. Different conditions that should be added in "if" decision for different query

User Query	Condition to be added
First type of query type	#2 info = ""
Not first type and not Not_List type	#2 info = *previous not Not_List_Type*
Not_List type	#2 info <> *previous not Not_List_Type*
Not Not_List type, and exist "RL" Perm in previous IFP	andalso not (List.exists(fn(x)=>x="WL")(#4 info))
Not Not_List type, and exist "WL" Perm in previous IFP	andalso not (List.exists(fn(x)=>x="RL")(#4 info))
Not Not_List type, and exist "ALL" Perm in previous IFP	*Do nothing*
Not Not_List type, and exist "+" Operator in previous IFP	andalso List.exists(fn(x)=>x= *previous not Not_List_Type*)(#3 info)
Not Not_List type, and exist "-" Operator in previous IFP	andalso List.nth(#3 info,0) = *previous not Not_List_Type*

6.3 Diagram Combination

After the Policy CPN Diagram and Query CPN Diagram were transformed successfully, the Combined CPN Diagram should be established. First, the SELinux

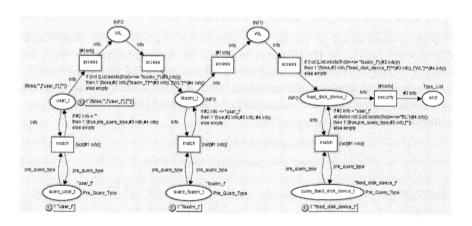

Fig. 5. Combined CPN Diagram for policy (5), (6) and query (4)

type in Query CPN Diagram should be replaced by the type with the same name in Security Policy Diagram. Second, add the *"security"* transition and *"end"* place at the end of the SELinux type in query. Finally, put initial tokens on all query types and the SELinux type that corresponding to the first query type. For example, if (5) and (6) are only two policy statements in SELinux policy, and the security goal is defined as (4), then the Combined CPN Diagram will be modeled as Figure 5.

$$\text{allow } user\_t\ fsadm\_t{:}process\ \{\ write\ \};\qquad\qquad (5)$$

$$\text{allow } fsadm\_t\ fixed\_disk\_device\_t{:}\ file\ \{\ write\ \};\qquad\qquad (6)$$

7 Analysis Examples

The analysis of SELinux security policy is performed when the administrator modifies the security policy file after changing the system configuration. The administrator has to guarantee that the modified policy file would not conflict with some specific security goal. In this section, we give an application example.

First of all, suppose one of the security goals for the SELinux is that:

$$\textit{"For all the sequenced information flows which start from user\_t and flow to}\atop\textit{fixed\_disk\_device\_t must flow through the trusted type fsadm\_t "}\qquad (7)$$

By the analysis method mentioned in Section 5, we transform this security goal to a security query, as shown below:

$$user\_t :(ALL, +,!(fsadm\_t)){:}\ fixed\_disk\_device\_t;\qquad\qquad (8)$$

Assume the original policy statements in the security policy file contains only the following statements:

allow user_t httpd_t:file { write };
allow httpd_t fsadm_t:file { write };
allow fsadm_t fixed_disk_device_t : file { write};

The above statements indicate that the system permits the user to write something to HTTP server, permits the HTTP server to access the trusted program *fsadm_t*, and permits the *fsadm_t* to write the low security level disk type *fixed_disk_device_t*.

Now suppose the administrator installs an audit program to audit the web logs and allows this audit program to access hard disks, he/she may add the following two policy statements to reflect the system changes:

$$\text{allow } httpd\_t\ log\_t : file\ \{\ write\ \};\qquad\qquad (9)$$

$$\text{allow } log\_t\ fixed\_disk\_device\_t : file\ \{\ write\};\qquad\qquad (10)$$

Above statements implies that the system permits the HTTP server to write something to *log_t* for auditing, and the *log_t* to write *fixed_disk_device_t*. After the addition of above statements, the administrator would like to check whether this addition conforms to the security goal of (7). Using the SEAnalyzer, he/she can make the query of (8) and obtained the results as shown in Figure 7.

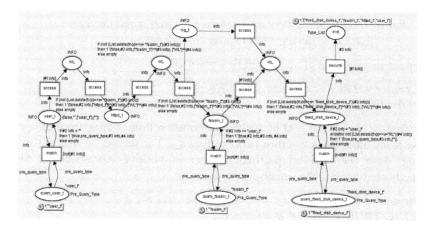

Fig. 7. A query result with a token flown in the end place

Note that in Figure 7, there is one token flowing into the *end* place. From the contents of that token's list: *["fixed_disk_device_t", "log_t", "httpd_t", "user_t"]*, the administrator could easily be mentioned that the security conflict comes from the flow between *httpd_t* and *log_t*, and the flow between *log_t* and *fixed_device_t*. He/she can then locate the problematical policy statements (9) and (10), and readjust the configuration of audit program to delete these two statements from the policy file. After above conflict resolution steps, he/she can repeat the same security query of (8) by the SEAnalyzer again. The new result shown in Figure 8 indicates that there is no token flown into the *end* place, i.e. no security violation exists, so the security goal of (7) is verified.

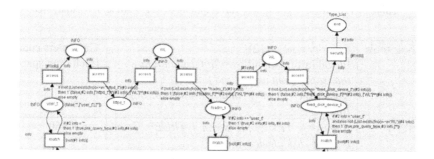

Fig. 8. A query result with no token flown in the end place

8   Related Work

SLAT [8][9] and PAL [10], like ours, are tools that come with a security goal/query language. A SLAT goal is like a kind of regular expression that specifies the expected form of information-flow paths between two specified security contexts. For example, if there is a security goal

> *"For each information-flow which starts from user_t and flows to*   (11)
> *fixed_disk_device_t has to pass through fsadm_t"*

Then the security goal of SLAT will be written as:

[t=user_t, TRUE+; t=fsadm_t, TRUE+;]
t=fixed_disk_device_t;

The first "+" inside the goal means that information flow starting from *user_t* can traverse many other types and then flows to *fsadm_t*. The second "+" has the similar meaning. After the goal is specified by user in positive representation, SLAT improperly converts it to the negative representation as:

!(t=user_t & E[t !=fsadm_t ∪ t= fixed_disk_device_t &
EF (k=TRUE & t= fixed_disk_device_t)])

This negative representation means that the information flow which starts from user_t, flows through fsadm_t, and flows to fixed_disk_device_t is the illegal information flow. However, if the administrator consider that the information flow which starts from user_t, pass trough fsadm_t, and flows to fixed_disk_device_t is the illegal one, then SLAT is unable to come out the right verification. PAL, unlike SLAT, has to transform the security goal to a security query program. For example, for the same security goal (12), the query of PAL is:

init(fdisk_automaton, [user_t, R, U]).
trans(fdisk_automaton,[T0,R0,U0],(Class,Perm),[T1,R1,U1],[neq(T1,fsadm_t)]).
trans(fdisk_automaton,[T0,R0,U0],(Class,Perm),[fixed_disk_device_t,R1,U1], []).
final(fdisk_automaton, [fixed_disk_device_t,_R,_U], []).

Table 3. The different goal/query forms among SLAT, PAL and SEAnalyzser

Analysis tools	Security goal = (12) Illegal information flow="*information flow that starts from user_t and flows to fixed_disk_device_t but doesn't pass through fsadm_t*"	Characters count (including space)
SLAT	*[t=user_t, TRUE+; t=fsadm_t, TRUE+;]* *t=fixed_disk_device_t;*	60
PAL	*init(fdisk_automaton, [user_t, R, U]).* *trans(fdisk_automaton,[T0,R0,U0],(Class,Per m),[T1,R1,U1],[neq(T1,fsadm_t)]).* *trans(fdisk_automaton,[T0,R0,U0],(Class,Per m),[fixed_disk_device_t,R1,U1], []).* *final(fdisk_automaton,* *[fixed_disk_device_t,_R,_U], []).*	249
SEAnalyzser	*user_t:(ALL,+!(fsadm_t)):fixed_disk_device_t*	45

Note that there is a *neq* operator in the second line of above query. The above program means that administrator wants to *"find all information-flow which starts from user_t and flow to fixed_disk_device_t without passing through fsadm_t"*. The disadvantage of PAL is that its query is much more complicated than SLAT's and ours. It looks more like a small program than a simple query.. In addition, the analysis engine behind PAL and ours are very different. PAL use the logic program to deduce the results, while ours uses the CPN to perform the analysis. The graphic property of CPN graph and the data type design in the token flown from place to place can give users more useful information in the course of query formulation and security analysis. Table 3 compares the different goal/query forms among SLAT, PAL and SEAnalyzser.

9 Conclusion

This paper presents a CPN approach to analyze the information flow in the policy file of SELinux. All of the power of SELinux depends on a set of well defined access control policies. Unfortunately, the large number of policy statements within the SELinux example security policy file and the complex relationships among these statements make the verification of security policy correctness for SELinux difficult, thus constrains the wide-spread use of SELinux. In this paper, we propose a CPN approach to analyze the security policy of SELinux. The use of a well established CPN model enables the administrators to formally model a security query. In addition, the graphic property of CPN model allows the administrators to easily use and comprehend the analysis results. Therefore, in comparison with alternative approaches, such as SLAT and PAL, our approach has the advantages of intuitive use and powerful analysis and verification capabilities. Our contribution in this paper includes: (1) propose a model to transform the allow-rule police statement to Policy CPN Diagram, (2) propose a intuitive and powerful query language to express the information flow that the administrators may concern, and (3) propose a method to combine the Policy CPN Diagram of security policy file and Query CPN Diagram of user query in respective as an Combined CPN Diagram to let our CPN engine to perform analysis automatically.

Currently, we only analyze allow rules. We assume that the SELinux types don't change in the operation. However, the types do change in the real world with type transition rules .The address of other rules will be the direction of our future research. Moreover, we only consider about one query a time. The research of multi-query analysis and multi-query conflict resolution is also the interesting future research.

References

1. Peter A. Loscocco, Stephen D. Smalley, Patrick A. Muckelbauer, Ruth C. Taylor, S. Jeff Turner, John F. Farrell., The Inevitability of Failure: The Flawed Assumption of Security in Modern Computing Environments. *Proceedings of the 21st National Information Systems Security Conference* (1998) 303-314.
2. NSA SELinux, http://www.nsa.gov/selinux/

3. TCSEC, http://www.radium.ncsc.mil/tpep/library/rainbow/5200.28-STD.html
4. P.A. Loscocco, and S.D. Smalley, Meeting critical security objectives with Security-Enhanced Linux. *In proceedings of the 2001 Ottawa Linux Symposium* (2001)
5. M. Archer, E. Leonard and M Pradella, Towards a Methodology and tool for the Analysis of Security-Enhanced Linux Security Policies. *NRL Memorandum Report NRL/MR/5540-02-8629* (2002)
6. T. Jaeger, R. Sailer, and X. Zhang, Analyzing integrity protection in the SELinux example policy. *In Proc. USENIX Security Symposium* (2003) 59-74
7. T. Jaeger, R. Sailer, and X. Zhang, Resolving Constraint Conflicts. *Proceedings of the 2004 ACM Symposium on Access Control Models and Technologies.* (2004)
8. J.D. Guttman, A.L. Herzog, and J.D. Ramsdell, Information Flow in Operating Systems: Eager Formal Methods. *Workshop on Issues in the Theory of Security* (WITS'03) (2003)
9. J.D. Guttman, A.L. Herzog, and J.D. Ramsdell, SLAT: Information Flow Analysis in Security Enhanced Linux. Included in the SLAT distribution, available from http://www.nsa.gov/SELinux (2005)
10. B. Sarna-Starosta and S.D. Stoller, Policy Analysis for security-Enhanced Linux. *Workshop on Issues in the Theory of Security* (WITS) (2004)
11. G. Zanin and L.V. Mancini, Towards a Formal Model for Security Policies Specification and Validation in the SELinux System. *In the Proceeding of SACMAT'04, Yorktown Heights, New York, USA 136-145*
12. Kurt Jensen: Coloured Petri Nets. Basic Concepts, Analysis Methods and Practical Use". Vol. 1 : Basic Concepts. *In EATCS Monographs on Theoretical Computer Science, Spring-Verlag* (1992) 1-234
13. P.A. Loscocco, and S.D. Smalley, Integrating Flexible Support for Security Policies into the Linux Operating System. *USENIX Annual Technical Conference* (2001)
14. Bill Mccarty, *SELinux NSA's Open Source Security Enhanced Linux.* ISBN: 0-596-00716-7, 256 pages, published by O'Reilly
15. Tony Stubblebine, *Regular Expression Pocket Reference.* ISBN: 0-596-00415-X, 112 pages, published by O'Reilly (2003)
16. Gutnik, G. and Kaminka, G.A., Representing Conversations for Scalable Overhearing. *JAIR Volume 25* (2006) 349-387

The Complexity of Discretionary Access Control

Stephen Dranger, Robert H. Sloan*, and Jon A. Solworth

Dept. of Computer Science
University of Illinois at Chicago
stdrange@alumni.uchicago.edu, {sloan, solworth}@uic.edu

Abstract. A recent paper presented an access control scheme for discretionary access controls with a decidable safety problem. This paper deals with the complexity analysis of that access control, and finds it to be, in its worst cases, PSPACE-complete, but polynomial time for practical cases. The PSPACE-hardness reduction uses the theory of succinct problems in a more general manner than circuit representation.

1 Introduction

In a computer system, *access controls* restrict subjects (users and/or processes) to performing only those operations on objects (e.g., files) for which they are authorized. For each such operation, the access controls either allow or disallow that operation to be performed. In *Discretionary Access Controls (DACs)*, each *object* has an owner who exercises primary control over the object. DACs are oldest and most widely used class of access controls, the access controls for both Windows and UNIX are DAC. The Unix DAC, for example, has the well known three primitive permissions read, write, and execute.

In the late 1970s, Harrison, Ruzzo, and Ullman (HRU) introduced a seemingly very simple general-purpose language for Discretionary Access Control (DAC). In spite of the simplicity of the HRU language, a *safety* property with parameters a specific permission p, subject s, and object o:

$$\text{``Always } s \text{ does not have permission } p \text{ for } o\text{''} \tag{1}$$

is undecidable [3].

Recently Solworth and Sloan gave a group-based mechanism for designing DACs for which the safety problem (Equation 1) *is* decidable [10], and showed that that mechanism is expressive enough to construct any particular DAC from a taxonomy of DACs given by Osborne et al. (OSM) [8].

That group-based access control scheme was the first general access control model proved both to have a decidable safety property and to be capable of implementing the full range of DAC models. From HRU's work in the 1970s though the early 2000s, general access control models were published that have both decidable (but relatively weak) and undecidable (but more expressive) variants. This includes HRU, Sandhu's 1992 Typed Access Model (TAM) [9], and

---

* Partially supported by NSF grant No. CCF-0431059.

H. Yoshiura et al. (Eds.): IWSEC 2006, LNCS 4266, pp. 405–420, 2006.

Koch et al.'s 2002 graph-based model [5,4]. In each of these cases, decidability is obtained by requiring a type of monotonicity: an operation can add or remove privileges but not both. Thus, for example, changing a user's group membership is not permitted in the decidable version of those access control schemes, since changing groups typically both adds and removes privileges.

In this paper we consider the precise complexity of the safety problem in the Solworth and Sloan access control scheme. We show that for the implementation of any DAC in Osborne et al.'s taxonomy, the safety problem can be decided in polynomial time, and that for the mechanism in its full generality, the safety problem is PSPACE complete. The proof of PSPACE hardness may have some interest in its own right. As we mention very briefly in Section 6, it generalizes the theory of succinct graph problems [2].

In the next section we quickly sketch the group-based access control model of [10] (full details are given in that paper). Section 3 describes the sliding marker net, a new marked graph model, which is the appropriate abstraction of the key part of the group-based access control system. Section 4 gives the polynomial-time result, and Section 5 gives the PSPACE-completeness result. We conclude in Section 6.

2   Review of the Access Control Scheme

Solworth and Sloan's group-based access control model is a general purpose scheme that allows one to describe a wide variety of particular access control systems. It corresponds to what they called "Layer 1" [10], and to what Li and Tripunitara [6] call an *access control scheme*. An access control scheme has a set of states and family of transition functions, and possible permissions. A particular access control system specifies a particular transition function, and the specific permissions, and typically narrows the set of states as well.

In all particular access control systems in the Solworth-Sloan scheme, processes derive authority to perform operations from the *user* on whose behalf they execute. Every *object*—or entity that can be accessed by a process—has a *label* that (indirectly) defines the *privilege* (also called *permission* or *right*) that various users have to perform operations on the object. (A file is the typical example of an object.) Objects are disjoint from users.

In defining a particular system, a fixed constant number of privileges is chosen (e.g., read, write, and execute). Privileges map labels to *groups* of users; the mapping is fixed when the label is created, although the membership of the group is *not* fixed. Protection is at the granularity of labels.

The group mechanism is the novel part of the scheme. A *group set* is a collection of one or more *groups*; a group is a set of users.[1] Every group set has a set of users, a set of group tags, and a set of pairs, $\langle u, t \rangle$ where u is a user ID and t is a group tag, which determine group membership.

---

[1] What we describe in this section are "*native* groups and group sets" in [10]; to implement a particular DAC policy one typically uses more than one of these native groups to implement one group in the specified policy.

2.1   Formal Description of Solworth-Sloan Scheme

In this subsection, for completeness, we give a fairly detailed description of the relevant parts of the Solworth-Sloan access control scheme. However, the reader can probably follow the main points of this paper without reading these details.

Formally, in the Solworth-Sloan scheme, every state (in any possible system) is a tuple with the following (many) components:

- The set U of current users
- The set O of current objects
- The set L of current labels of objects
- A map $\ell : O \to L$ giving the label of every object
- The set GS of current group sets
- The set G of current groups
- The set of privileges, and for each privilege, a map $p : L \to G$ telling which group of users has that privilege
- A map $\text{gs} : G \to GS$ that determines the group set of each group
- The set T^G of current group tags, and a map $f : T^G \to GS$ that gives the group set of each group tag.
- The set $GL \subset U \times T^G$ of all user–group tag pairs. Each ordered pair $\langle u, t \rangle$ can be thought of as a "group label" on a notional group object.
  Each user has at most one group tag for each group set at any time; that is, if both $\langle u, t \rangle, \langle u, t' \rangle \in GL$ then $f(t) \neq f(t')$. The current set of users of a given group set is exactly the set of users that have a an group tag associated with the group set; that is, the users of groups set gs are exactly $\{u : \exists t : f(t) = gs \text{ and } \langle u, t \rangle \in GL\}$.
- A relation $r \subset T^G \times G$ relating group tags to groups. User u is a member of group g iff there is a $t \in T^G$ such that $\langle u, t \rangle \in GL$ and $r(t, g)$.
  We require that group tags give membership only in groups in the tags group set; that is, that if $r(t, g)$, we have $f(t) = \text{gs}(g)$.
- A set of triples $rules \subset T^G \times T^G \times G$. Each triple $\langle t, t', g \rangle$ gives a group label relabel rule of the form $Relabel(t, t') = g$, which means that any member of group g can, for any u change group label $\langle u, t \rangle$ to $\langle u, t' \rangle$.
  A relabel rule must be inside of a single group set; that is, if $\langle t, t', g \rangle \in rules$, then $f(t) = f(t')$. However, we do *not* require that the group administering the relabel be in the group set; that is, we do not require $\text{gs}(g) = f(t)$.
- The current set $N \subset T^G$ of *new user group tags*. When a new user u_n is added to the system, for each $t \in N$ a new group label $\langle u_n, t \rangle$ is created.

2.2   Key Points About Groups and Group Sets

In this paper, we are not concerned with any state transitions that add new groups or group sets to a system. We are concerned exclusively with those transitions that change the membership of existing groups. There are two types of transitions that change group membership: the addition of new users, and the application of group tag relabel rules to change the user–group tag pairs. These transition rules are the same in any system using the Solworth-Sloan access control scheme—what varies from system to system are the groups and group sets that can be created. In obtaining the hardness results in this paper, we assume that arbitrary groups and groups sets can be created.

Roughly speaking (see the previous subsection for more details), every system is comprised of a set of users U, a set of objects O, a set of labels L, a mapping $\ell : O \to L$, and group sets, groups, and permissions. We describe group sets in detail shortly, but each group set has some (unique) groups, and the set of all groups in all groups sets is denoted G. Now for each primitive privilege (e.g., read, write) we have a map $p : L \to G$ specifying the group of users that have that permission for objects with a particular label.

Each group set includes the following components:

1. Its set of groups. Every group belongs to exactly one group set.
2. Its set of group tags. Every group tag is associated with exactly one group set.
3. The current group tag–user pairs.
4. An optional new user tag.
5. Its set of users.[2]
6. The relation of the group set's group tags to its groups.
7. Group tag relabel rules.

All components are finite, and all components except the group tag–user pairing are specified and fixed for the life of the group set when the group set is created. An initial group tag–user pairing is specified when the group set is created, but it evolves over time.

Each user in the group set has exactly one group tag at any time. The group-tag–user pairs are referred to as *group labels*, and are thought of as labels on notional objects. Thus, if group tag G is associated with groups g_1 and g_3, and user u has group tag G in group set $\mathcal{G}$, then (at that time) u is a member of groups g_1 and g_3, and not a member of any other group of $\mathcal{G}$ (From this information alone, we cannot tell which groups of *other* group sets u is in.)

The definition of the group set tells which users are initially in the group set, and the group tag for each user. If $\mathcal{G}$ has new user tag G_n, then all users added to the system are added to group set $\mathcal{G}$ with tag G_n.

For any two group tags G_1, G_2 in group set gs, a group relabel permission $Relabel(G_1, G_2) = g$ may be defined at gs's creation that enables any member of group g to change the group tag of any user u in $\mathcal{G}$ from G_1 to G_2. Group g may be either in gs or an existing group in another group set.

2.3   Safety Problem in This Setting

In this setting, the safety problem of Equation 1 becomes, "Can user s become a member of group $g = p(\ell(o))$?", where $l = \ell(o)$ is the label of object o and $p(l)$ is the group having permission p for label l. This in turn becomes the question, "for each group tag G associated with group g in group set gs, could user u be paired with tag G?"

---

[2] Formally, the set of users is induced by the set of group tag–user pairs.

3   Abstract Model of Problem

To model the safety problem for this access control system, we introduce the *sliding marker net* model. Group tags form the vertices of a digraph, with the edges corresponding to the existence of a relabel rule. Markers on the vertices represent users. Thus k markers in a vertex representing group tag G correspond to k users having a user–group-tag pair with G. Each edge is *governed* by a set of vertices—corresponding to the tags for the group that has the relabel permission for that edge. A marker can be moved across an edge only if at least one vertex in the set of vertices governing that edge contains a marker. A set of new marker vertices that can have markers added to them models the new user tag mechanism for adding new users. More formally:

Definition 1. *A **sliding marker net** is a 5-tuple, (V, E, A, M_0, N), where V and E are the vertices and edges of a directed graph, A is a function $A : E \to 2^V$, mapping each edge to a vertex set, $M_0 : V \to \mathbb{N}$ is the* initial marking, *and $N \subseteq V$. (N represents the group of new users.) We say vertex set $A(e)$ governs edge e (if $|A(e)| = 1$ we may say a vertex governs an edge). The underlying digraph is called the* sliding marker graph.

The marking of a sliding marker net is its state. For marking M we say that vertex v is *nonempty* if $M(v) > 0$ and *empty* if $M(v) = 0$.

Given a marking M of a sliding marker net, we can obtain a new marking M', or make a *move*, in two ways. One is by "sliding a marker" over edge $(u, v) \in E$. This move requires that $M(u) > 0$ and that there is a $w \in A(u, v)$ s.t. $M(w) > 0$ (i.e., $A(u, v)$ has at least one nonempty vertex in marking M), and decreases $M(u)$ by 1 and increases $M(v)$ by 1. The other kind of move is to add 1 to $M(v)$ for every $v \in N$, which models adding new users.

The VERTEX SET NONEMPTINESS problem for sliding marker nets is as follows: Given a sliding marker net (V, E, A, M_0, N) and a vertex set S, is there a sequence of moves that yields a new marking in which at least one $v \in S$ is nonempty? This has the same complexity as VERTEX NONEMPTINESS (ignoring a multiplicative factor of at most $|V|$), whether a particular $v \in V$ can be made nonempty, and we work with this slightly simpler problem. To the best of our knowledge, sliding marker net VERTEX NONEMPTINESS is a novel graph problem.

We are in fact analyzing the complexity of a slightly different problem than the analog of the stated safety problem (1). The sliding marker net analog of the safety problem in this context is, "Can a *specific, named marker* reach vertex v?" However, this problem and VERTEX NONEMPTINESS are both PSPACE-complete. A slightly messier version of Theorem 1's construction would show this problem is in PSPACE as well. In the other direction, there is a simple reduction of VERTEX NONEMPTINESS to the specific-marker version: Given a sliding marker net and vertex v^*, add two new vertices v_1 and v_2 with an edge (v_1, v_2), and add the specific named marker to v_1 in the initial marking. Finally set $A((v_1, v_2)) = \{v^*\}$. The VERTEX NONEMPTINESS instance has a solution iff the named marker can reach v^*.

4   The OSM DACs Can Be Decided in Polynomial Time

The group mechanism of Sloan and Solworth can be used to implement some intricate access control policies that go beyond what are conventionally considered DAC systems. To obtain the PSPACE hardness result we show in Section 5, we construct an artificial access control system that certainly goes beyond a normal reasonable DAC system. In this section we briefly argue that the safety question for conventional DAC systems can be answered in polynomial time.

The result needed for sliding marker nets is that VERTEX NONEMPTINESS can be decided quickly for an sliding marker net with a simple structure. We say vertices $U \subset V$ of sliding marker net (V, E, A, M_0, N) form an *isolated component* iff both (1) there is no directed edge between U and $\bar{U}$ in the underlying graph and (2) every edge e within U has $A(e) \subseteq U$.

Theorem 1. *If the underlying digraph of sliding marker net (V, E, A, M_0, N) consists of isolated components where each component has only a constant number of vertices, then* VERTEX NONEMPTINESS *can be solved in linear time.*

Proof. We need consider only the component with the vertex in question; let its size be c. To decide its nonemptiness, first, add c markers to every vertex in the set N. If any vertex in the component has more than c markers, reduce its number of markers to c. Then exhaustively construct the portion of the state space obtained only by sliding markers in the component. The required bookkeeping can be done in time linear in the size of the sliding marker net.

Now OSM gave a taxonomy intended to include all reasonable DAC systems. In all of them, the owner of an object can grant or revoke ordinary permissions (e.g., read, write, and execute) to the object. The various OSM DACs allow the following variations: (1) Whether or not a owner of an object can give it away (change ownership). (2) Whether the owner of an object can delegate the right to grant ordinary permissions to other users. The case where the owner can delegate is called liberal DAC, and it has a number of variations: (a) who can revoke ordinary permissions, and (b) whether the delegation propagates. OSM propose no propagation ("one-level grant"), that an owner can make either a grant that cannot be propagated, or a grant that can be propagated once ("two-level grant"), and arbitrary propagation (multi-level grant).

Solworth and Sloan [10] sketched the implementation of any of these DAC mechanisms on top of their group mechanism. Objects are protected at the granularity of *labels*. For each label l and each ordinary permission, two group sets are used, one for the ordinary permission and one for the administration. The ordinary permission group set has two group tags, and the administrative group set has only two tags in all cases except for liberal DAC with 2-level grant, when it has three tags. In all cases, all group tag relabel permissions within those two group sets are held by members of the administrative group set. The group tags correspond to vertices. Relabeling of a users group tag occurs only among group tags inside one group set. The sets $A((u, v))$ correspond to the users allowed to relabel an arbitrary user's group tag from u to v. Thus the construction gives isolated components of 4 vertices for each OSM DAC except for 5 vertices for liberal DAC with two-level grant.

Thus we have sketched the argument for:

Corollary 1. *The safety problem can be decided in polynomial time for all the OSM DACs.*

Remark: The extension to OSM to allow n-level grants for any constant n is also decidable.

5   General Problem is PSPACE Complete

In this section we will show that sliding marker net VERTEX NONEMPTINESS is PSPACE complete.

5.1   Vertex Nonemptiness Is in PSPACE

Theorem 2. *Sliding marker net* VERTEX NONEMPTINESS $\in PSPACE$.

Proof. We argue VERTEX NONEMPTINESS is in PSPACE = NPSPACE. Consider net (V, E, A, M_0, N). Vertices having more than one, as opposed to exactly one, marker affect the emptiness/nonemptiness of vertices in reachable markings only because some of those "extra" markers could later move, creating additional nonempty vertices. Thus we can treat markings with more than $|V|$ markers in a vertex as if they had only $|V|$ in that vertex. Hence we may modify M_0 to a marking M_0' by first adding $|V|$ markers to every vertex in N ("new users"), and then reducing the marking of any vertex u with more than $|V|$ markers to $|V|$.

Thus we have at most $|V|^2$ markers. So the total number of distinct markings is less than the number of ways we can fit $|V|^2$ indistinguishable markers into $|V|+1$ containers, or $\binom{|V|^2+|V|}{|V|^2} < (|V|^2 + |V|)^{|V|}$. (We add another container to represent the markers that are not on the sliding marker net yet.) To solve the problem nondeterministically, we simply choose a legal move, increment a counter, and repeat. This requires $O\left(|V|\log|V| + \log\left((|V|^2 + |V|)^{|V|}\right)\right) = O(|V|\log|V|)$ space: $O(|V|\log|V|)$ to keep track of where the markers are (i.e., we need to store $|V| + 1$ integers in the range of 0 to $|V|^2$) and $O\left(\log\left((|V|^2+|V|)^{|V|}\right)\right)$ to keep to keep track of the binary counter.

5.2   Vertex Nonemptiness Is PSPACE Hard

Our reduction for PSPACE hardness is loosely inspired by succinct representations of graphs [2,7]. In that theory, a graph is represented by a (sometimes) exponentially smaller circuit describing the graph. Here, the state space of the sliding marker net is exponentially bigger than the sliding marker net itself.

Theorem 3. *Sliding marker net* VERTEX NONEMPTINESS *is PSPACE-hard.*

We will reduce QUANTIFIED BOOLEAN FORMULA (QBF) to VERTEX NON-EMPTINESS. The reduction is rather involved; we give it here, and then sketch the argument for its correctness.

Reduction

Throughout let n be the number of variables in the given QBF

$$\psi = Q_1 x_1 Q_2 x_2 \cdots Q_n x_n \phi(x_1, \ldots, x_n) \tag{2}$$

where each Q_i is either $\exists$ or $\forall$, and ϕ is some 3CNF formula.

We implicitly use but do not construct a "QBF graph" of ψ that has a path from a designated source to a designated sink iff ψ is satisfiable. This graph is adopted from [7]; here we construct a digraph. We construct a sliding marker net such that it has designated vertex that can become nonempty iff the QBF graph has a source to sink path. We will rely on:

Proposition 1 ([7]). *A QBF is satisfiable if and only if its QBF graph has a path from s to t.*

QBF graph. The QBF graph is a digraph with source s and sink t; every vertex is either "s-side" or "t-side." Each vertex corresponds to a partial assignment to the n Boolean variables. A vertex's *level* m, for $0 \leq m \leq n$, tells how many variables are set. The only level 0 vertices are s and t. For $1 \leq m \leq n$, in a level m vertex, the first m variables are set. We give each vertex a $2n + 1$ bit label: First, n bits for the level m in (padded) unary; then 1 bit for s or t; then m bits for the setting of the first m variables; and lastly $(n - m)$ 0s if on the s side, or 1s if on the t side.

The edges are (roughly) as follows. For $m < n$, each s-side level $(m - 1)$ vertex has one or two level m successors on the s-side: two successors setting x_m to each of 0 and 1 if Q_m is $\exists$, and one successor setting $x_m = 0$ if Q_m is $\forall$. For each (complete) variable assignment a that satisfies ϕ, there is an edge from the level n s-side to the level n t-side vertex with assignment a. For $0 < m \leq n$, the edges out of each t-side vertex with level m are as follows. If $Q_m = \exists$ or the assignment to $x_m = 1$, then the vertex has a level $m - 1$ t-side successor with the same assignment to the first $m - 1$ variables and with $x_m = 1$ (though the level $m - 1$ means that this is not considered part of the partial assignment). If $Q_m = \forall$ and $x_m = 0$, then the vertex has a level m s-side successor with the same assignment except $x_m = 1$.

We now make one modification, so that there are no edges where both the level and the truth setting changes. For existential variables on the s side, for the successor that corresponds to setting the variable to 1, we use two vertices— the immediate successor has a label with the level *not* increased and the truth setting changed to 1, and that vertex has one successor with the level increased. Similarly, for the t side we decrease the level, then change the truth setting to 0 when we unset an existential variable. See Figure 1.

Sliding marker net construction. We do not construct the QBF graph. We do construct a sliding marker net of size polynomial in n that has certain special markings corresponding to vertices of ψ's QBF graph. Our construction will allow it to move from one special marking to another if and only if there is a

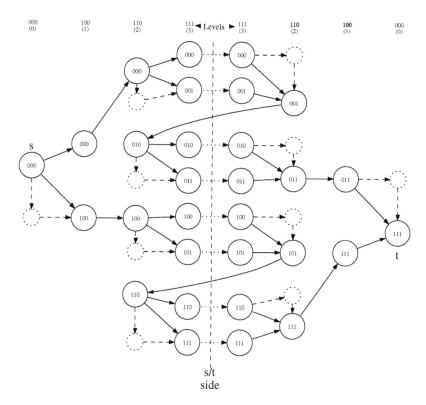

Fig. 1. QBF graph for $\exists x_1 \forall x_2 \exists x_3 \phi$. The vertex labels shown are the values of x_i, written $x_1 x_2 x_3$. (Full vertex label doesn't fit in this diagram.) Vertex levels are shown above in both unary and decimal. The line through the center of the graph divides the s and t sides. The dotted horizontal lines through that line represent edges that exist exactly when ϕ is true for that particular value of $x_1 x_2 x_3$. Dashed vertices and dashed edges show the minor modification in our construction. Notice that unset variables are always 0 on the s side and 1 on the t side.

corresponding edge in the QBF graph. From there, we will show this construction therefore allows a designated vertex v^* to be marked if and only if there is an s-to-t path in the QBF graph.

The sliding marker net has two isolated vertices, *empty* (with no marker) and *full* (with one marker). We lay out the remaining vertices in rows within $3n + 2$ numbered columns: first n *level columns*, then one *s/t column*, then n *truth (assignment) columns*, then n *ON/OFF columns*, and lastly one *final column*. We denote the ith column by C_i. All columns except the s/t column have $3n + 2$ vertices. (The number of vertices in the s/t column depends on the number of clauses in the formula.) The initial marking puts one marker in each column, in the top-most vertex. Each column has both directed edges between every pair of (vertically) adjacent vertices, except the final column which has only the down directed edge. There are no other edges. We refer to edges from vertex m to

$m + 1$ in a column as *down (side)* edges, and edges from vertex $m + 1$ to m as *up (side)* edges. See Figure 2 for the layout of the sliding marker graph.

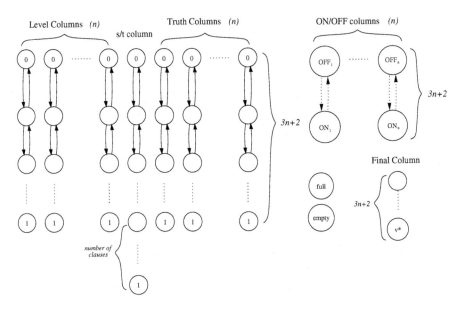

Fig. 2. Overall layout of constructed sliding marker graph for n-variable formula

The top-most and bottom-most rows play a special role. We refer to the top row of the ON/OFF columns as the OFF row and the bottom row as the ON row. For the other columns we refer to the top row as the 0 row and the bottom row as the 1 row; we also speak of ON, OFF, 0, and 1 vertices. (It may help to remember that QBF graph we are modeling starts at 0 and ends at 1.) The notation 0_m (respectively 1_m) stands for the top (respectively bottom) vertex of column C_m; $0/1_m$ denotes the vertex set $\{0_m, 1_m\}$. Somewhat inconsistently, OFF_i (respectively ON_i) stands for the OFF (respectively ON) vertex of the ith ON/OFF column, which is column C_{2n+1+i}. When clear from context we also use the term for a vertex for the singleton set containing that vertex.

A marking of this sliding marker net is a **QBF marking** if every marker is in the top or a bottom row of its column. A QBF marking corresponds to a QBF vertex whose label is obtained from the bits of the level, s/t, and truth columns of the sliding marker net. See Figure 3 for an example of a QBF marking.

We give some more notation; then describe the governing sets for the edges. For simplicity's sake, we call an edge (in either direction) between rows r and $r+1$ the "rth edge." (Row 1 is the top row.) Besides vertex sets mentioned already, we need $n - 1$ additional OFF vertex sets: $\{OFF_1, OFF_2\}, \ldots, \{OFF_1, \ldots, OFF_n\}$. We refer to these vertex sets as $OFF_{1\ldots2}, \ldots, OFF_{1\ldots n}$.

There is a correspondence between the rth edge of an arbitrary column (excluding the final column) and the rth column for $1 \leq r \leq 3n + 1$. First, for any

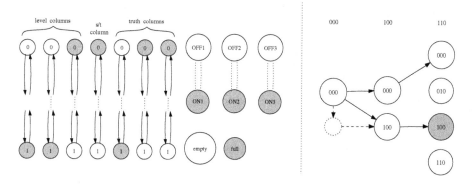

Fig. 3. Example of a marking of the sliding marker net that corresponds to a vertex in the QBF graph. In this figure, the shaded circles in the sliding marker net represent vertices with markers on them and the shaded circle in the QBF graph represents the vertex that the sliding marker net marking corresponds to.

column C_m, we can speak of the first n *edges* of column C_m as being the "level edges" of C_m. Similarly, edge $n+1$ is the "s/t edge", and then we have n "truth" edges followed by n ON/OFF edges. Second, if the rth edge of column C_m is not governed by *empty, full,* or some OFF group, then it must be governed by a vertex set contained in the corresponding column C_r.

That is, for any column C_m, if the rth edge of C_m for $1 \le r \le 3n + 1$ is not governed by one of *empty, full,* or some OFF group, then the *rth edge of column C_m* (between rows r and $r + 1$) *must be governed by one of the vertex sets* 0_r, 1_r, $0/1_r$ *of column* r. Thus we often use the shorthand of saying that edge e has $A(e) = 0$ (or 1 or 0/1 or ON) without specifying the column for the set $A(e)$, because $A(e)$'s column is determined by e's row.

We now specify the governing vertex set of each edge. First, every ON/OFF edge is governed by ON unless otherwise stated.

The level columns. Our goal is that a marking with a marker in 1_i for $i \le m$ and in 0_i in the remaining $n - m$ level columns should correspond to a QBF graph vertex with level m.

Level column C_m, down edges: The first $m - 1$ level edges are governed by 1; the mth by *full*, and the remaining $n - m$ level edges by 0. That is, the rth down edge in *column C_m* is governed by the 1 vertex of *column C_r* for $r < m$, and by the 0 vertex of *column C_r* for $r > m$. This forces the level columns to move their markers from the 0 to the 1 row in order—C_m can move its marker down the first n rows from its 0 vertex only if $C_1, \ldots, C_{m-1}$ all have markers in their 1 vertices, and $C_{m+1}, \ldots, C_n$ all have markers in their 0 vertices.

The s/t down edge is governed by 0 (s), insuring that we can move down this edge only there is a marker in the s/t column corresponding to the s side of the QBF graph.

The n truth edges depend on Q_m. If $Q_m = \forall$, the xth truth edge is governed by the 0/1 vertex set $1 \le x \le m-1$, and by the 0 vertex set for $m \le x \le n$. This corresponds to allowing either setting of the first $m - 1$ Boolean variables and requiring the remaining variables to be 0 in the universal case. The case $Q_m = \exists$ is the same *except* that the mth truth edge is governed by the 0/1 rather than the 0 vertex set, because for existential quantifiers, m Boolean variables would have been set already.

Level column C_m, up edges: These are the same as the down edges with two exceptions. First, the s/t edge is governed by 1 (t), corresponding to being on the t side of the QBF graph for decreasing of level. Second, those truth edges that must be governed by the 0 vertex for the down edges must instead be governed by the 1 the vertex. This is because instead of making sure variables have been set, we must make sure variables have been unset.

The s/t column. The s/t column is special in this construction: it has a different number of vertices (and edges). This column is used to control the edges between the s and t sides. There is a path from s to t if the Boolean formula ϕ is true for the particular variables; edges from t back to s are needed to handle universally quantified variables.

The s/t column, C_{n+1}, starts with $3n + 2$ vertices with $3n + 1$ edges just like the level columns. The s/t column's down level edges are governed by 1, since we must be at level n to evaluate the Boolean formula. The s/t down edge is governed by *full*. The truth edges are governed by the 0/1 vertex set. The governing vertex sets for the up edges of this s/t column are the same as for the down direction except that edges governed by ON on the down side are governed by $OFF_{1...n}$ on the up side.

Going downwards from vertex $3n + 2$, this column should "compute" whether ϕ is true on the truth setting encoded in the truth columns in the current marking (i.e., Boolean x_i is 1 (respectively 0) if the 1 (respectively 0) vertex of the ith truth column is marked). We add one additional vertex to the column for each clause of ϕ. To govern the down edge for each of these these additional vertices, we use a vertex set of three vertices (from the truth columns) for the clause. If the clause contains x_i (respectively $\bar{x}_i$), then the vertex set contains truth column i's 1 (respectively 0) vertex.

The corresponding up edges are all governed by the *full*.

The truth columns Column C_{n+1+m} is the mth of the n truth columns.

Truth column m, down edges: The first $m - 1$ level edges are governed by 1. Edge m is governed by 0_m if $Q_m = \exists$ and 1_m if $Q_m = \forall$. (If x_m is existential, our QBF graph sets $x_m = 1$ immediately *before* incrementing the level to m.) The remaining $n - m$ level edges are governed by 0. The s/t edge is governed by 0/1 if $Q_m = \exists$ and 1 if $Q_m = \forall$.

The first $m - 1$ truth edges are governed by 0/1, and the mth by *full*. The last $n - m$ truth edges are governed by the 0/1 vertex set if $Q_m = \exists$, and the 1 vertex if $Q_m = \forall$.

If $Q_m = \forall$, the mth ON/OFF edge is governed by OFF_m.

Truth column m, up edges: The first $m - 1$ level edges are governed by 0/1; the remaining level edges by 0. This is to allow x_m to revert to false if a universal

x_i for $i < m$ needs to *reset* itself. The s/t edge is governed by 1 (t) to make sure we are on the t side of the graph.

The truth edges are governed by 0/1 except that the mth truth edge is governed by *full*. The first $m - 1$ ON/OFF edges are all governed by $OFF_{1...m-1}$. (All the truth edges of the first truth *column* are governed by *empty*.)

ON/OFF columns. The n ON/OFF columns are designed to be ON/OFF switches. Intuitively they are used to *turn off* the sliding marker net—put it into a QBF marking not corresponding to an QBF graph vertex. This is used when we have two QBF vertices u and v that differ in more than one area of information, which happens when we need to test the second value of a universally quantified variable. The governing vertex sets are assigned so that we can move ON/OFF switch m from ON to OFF only at level m.

ON/OFF column m up edges: We first give the rules for the up edges. The first m level edges are governed by 1 and the remaining level edges by 0. This ensures that we can move a marker down over these edges only at level m. The mth level is the point in the graph where we must retest the x_m with the other Boolean value if $Q_m = \forall$.

The s/t edge is governed by 1 (t), because we must be on the t side of the graph. The first $m - 1$ truth edges are governed by 0/1; the mth truth edge by 0; the remaining $n - m$ truth edges by 1. The mth ON/OFF edge is governed by *full*.

ON/OFF column m down edges: If $Q_m = \exists$, then *empty* is the governing group for every edge of the mth ON/OFF column. Thus x_m can never be turned on after being turned off.

Otherwise $(Q_m = \forall)$, the level edges are the same as for the down edges of this column, and the s/t edge is governed by 0 (s), because to turn back on, we must be on the s side of the QBF graph. The first $m - 1$ truth edges are governed by 0/1, the mth truth edge by 1, and the remaining $n - m$ truth edges by 0. The mth ON/OFF edge is governed by *full*.

The final column. The final column has $3n + 2$ vertices; its bottom vertex the special designated vertex v^*.

The final column's first n edges are level edges governed by the 1 vertex, its next n edges behave as a second set of level edges, governed by 0, its next n edges behave as truth edges, governed by 1, and its last edge as an s/t edge governed by t.

This ensures that the rest of the net first enters a marking with level n, and then later enters a marking with level 0. Then we make sure that we have the right Boolean values for the end and we are on the correct side.

Sketch of why reduction is correct

Let $G(\psi)$ be the QBF graph of ψ of the form of Equation (2), and let SM be the constructed sliding marker net. Then SM is of size $O(n^2 + |\phi|)$, and can be constructed in polynomial time.

By Proposition 1, ψ is satisfiable if and only if $G(\psi)$ has an s to t path. Thus we need to argue that a marker can reach the bottom vertex of the final row of SM if and only $G(\psi)$ has an s to t path.

A QBF marking is a ***QBF ON marking*** if all the markers in the ON/OFF columns are in ON. The point of our construction is that each QBF ON marking of the sliding marker net corresponds to a vertex of the QBF graph whose level, s/t, and truth labels match the marking of the level, s/t, and truth-setting columns of the sliding marker net. In this correspondence, the initial marking of SM is a QBF ON marking that corresponds to the vertex s of $G(\psi)$.

To show that an s to t path in $G(\psi)$ implies that a marker can reach the bottom vertex of the final column of SM, it suffices to show that if there is a directed edge from vertex u to vertex v in $G(\psi)$, then from a QBF ON marking corresponding to the label of u, there is a series of legal moves to a QBF ON marking corresponding to the label of v. In fact, this can be done without moving any of the markers in the ON/OFF columns in all cases except when u is on the t side and v is on the s side. In that case, then exactly one ON/OFF column has to have its marker move from the ON to the OFF column and then back again, as well as markers moving in at least one truth column, as SM passes through one or more QBF markings.

Secondly, we have to show that for any QBF ON marking of SM that corresponds to the label of a vertex v that is in $G(\psi)$, then for every QBF ON marking reachable directly (without any intervening QBF ON marking) in SM, there is a corresponding successor of v in $G(\psi)$.

The following technical lemma says that we can always restrict our attention in SM to moves that move one marker from one end of a column all the way to the other end, without any moves in other columns in between, and would be used in a formal proof of both directions.

Lemma 1. *If the constructed sliding marker net can go from QBF marking M_1 to QBF marking M_2, then it can do so with moves such that a marker always moves from one top/bottom vertex to the opposite top/bottom vertex before any other marker moves at all.*

Proof. Given any QBF marking M and any two columns C_c and C_d, if the marker in C_c moves, and stops at row x in between column C_c's top and bottom vertices, then the marker in column C_d cannot move from one to the other top/bottom vertex because (exactly) one edge of column C_d is governed either by a vertex set consisting of one or two top/bottom vertex vertices of column C_c or by *empty*. Therefore, if the marker in column C_c moves, then C_d's marker cannot move until the marker in column C_c reaches a top/bottom vertex (and thus sliding marker net reaches a QBF marking again).

If the marker in c begins to move, then the most any other column d can do until c reaches a top/bottom vertex is to move only part of the way from top/bottom vertex of its column to the other. Therefore, when c's marker finally reaches one top/bottom vertex of the column, the graph is not in a QBF marking; however, the marker in column d could have reached the same vertex had it waited until c "finished" its move.

6   Concluding Remarks

In this paper, we have determined the complexity of the safety problem for the group-based access control system of [10]. For Osborne et al.'s exhaustive catalog of DAC systems [8], it is polynomial time. In general, it is PSPACE-complete.

This in fact creates an important open problem for practical access control systems, because there are numerous access control policies that have aspects of discretionary access control, but are not purely discretionary. The group-based mechanism appears to be powerful enough to implement any of the access control policies discussed in the literature, discretionary, mandatory, or otherwise. In considering any particular such policy, say, Chinese Wall [1], we have been able to make some sort of particular argument similar to Section 4 that that policy's implementation gives a safety problem that can be decided in polynomial time. However, we would like to find a characterization of some group structure that could implement any of these more exotic access control policies in addition to DAC policies, while still having a polynomial-time safety problem.

In the area of complexity theory, we think the time may be ripe to revisit the area of succinct graph representations, taking a much broader view of representations, and, simultaneously, a view that is more tied to application areas. In the original theory [2], a graph is represented by an exponentially smaller circuit that recognizes the graph. Here "recognize" meant that the circuit returns 1 for those binary numbers that encode an edge of the graph. In this paper we showed an application from computer access controls where a group membership system could represent, through its state space, an exponentially larger graph. Perhaps similar results can be obtained for various structures used in contemporary artificial intelligence, such as Bayes nets (belief nets).

References

1. D. F. C. Brewer and M. J. Nash. The Chinese Wall security policy. In *Proc. IEEE Symp. Security and Privacy*, pages 206–214, 1989.
2. Hana Galperin and Avi Wigderson. Succinct representations of graphs. *Information and Control*, 56:183–198, 1983.
3. Michael A. Harrison, Walter L. Ruzzo, and Jeffrey D. Ullman. Protection in operating systems. *Communications of the ACM (CACM)*, 19(8):461–471, 1976.
4. Manuel Koch, Luigi V. Mancini, and Francesco Parisi-Presicce. Decidability of safety in graph-based models for access control. In *Proc. European Symp. Research in Computer Security (ESORICS)*, pages 229–243. LNCS, Springer-Verlag, 2002.
5. Manuel Koch, Luigi V. Mancini, and Francesco Parisi-Presicce. A graph-based formalism for RBAC. *ACM Transactions on Information and System Security (TISSEC)*, 5(3):332–365, 2002.
6. Ninghui Li and Mahesh V. Tripunitara. Security analysis in role-based access control. In *Proc. of ACM Symposium on Access Control Models and Technologies (SACMAT)*, 2004.
7. Antonio Lozano and José L. Balcazár. The complexity of graph problems for succinctly represented graphs. In *Proc. of Graph-Theoretic Concepts in Computer Science*, volume 441 of *Lecture Notes in Computer Science*, pages 277–285, 1990.

8. Sylvia Osborn, Ravi Sandhu, and Qamar Munawer. Configuring role-based access control to enforce mandatory and discretionary access control policies. *ACM Transactions on Information and System Security (TISSEC)*, 3(2):85–106, 2000.
9. Ravi S. Sandhu. The typed access matrix model. In *Proc. IEEE Symp. Security and Privacy*, pages 122–136, 1992.
10. Jon A. Solworth and Robert H. Sloan. A layered design of discretionary access controls with decidable properties. In *Proc. IEEE Symp. Security and Privacy*, pages 56–67, 2004.

Traceroute Based IP Channel
for Sending Hidden Short Messages

Zouheir Trabelsi[1], Hesham El-Sayed[1], Lilia Frikha[2], and Tamer Rabie[1]

[1] United Arab Emirates University
College of Information Technology
PO Box 17555
Al Ain, United Arab Emirates
[2] College of Telecommunications (SupCom)
The University of Tunisia
Cité Technologique des Communications
Route de Raoued Km 3, 5 – 2083 El Ghazala, Ariana, Tunisia
trabelsi@uaeu.ac.ae

Abstract. The paper proposes a novel IP channel for sending hidden short messages, based mainly on the use of the "traceroute" command and the IP header Record route options. Instead of encrypting a hidden message or embedding it into a multimedia object, as in traditional multimedia steganography, we process the entire message and generate several IP packets with different types to carry the secret message. Thereby we foil an eavesdropper who is primarily applying statistical tests to detect encrypted communication channels. We show that our approach provides more protection against Steganalysis and sniffing attacks. A friendly graphical tool has been implemented to demonstrate the proposed secret IP channel.

Keywords: Covert channel, Hidden information, IP header Record route option, Steganalysis, Traceroute.

1 Introduction

Steganography is the technique of hidden communication. It relies on hiding covert message in unsuspected multimedia data. It is generally used in secret communication between acknowledge parties. It is a method of encryption that hides data among the bits of a covert file, such as a graphic or an audio file. The technique replaces unused or insignificant bits with the secret data. A covert channel is a mechanism that can be used to communicate data across network or between processes within the system in a manner that goes unnoticed [23]. An effective covert channel is the one that is undetectable by the adversary and can provide high degree of privacy. The goal of the covert channel is to communicate data from one host to another host in a way that receiving host can detect the data but the eavesdropper won't even get the hint that some secret data was being communicated. Some features of the TCP/IP protocol suite can be used to send covert messages as discussed in [6]. Encrypted or non-encrypted information can be

H. Yoshiura et al. (Eds.): IWSEC 2006, LNCS 4266, pp. 421 – 436, 2006.

encapsulated within otherwise normal TCP/IP packets. The TCP/IP header information can also be modified to encode secret messages. There are some fields in the packet headers that are not used by the current communication networks. These fields can be used as message carries.

These covert channels are an immense cause of security concern because they can be used to pass malicious messages. These messages could be in the form of computer virus, spy programs, terrorist messages, etc. Therefore, detecting these covert channels is an important issue that needs to be addressed [10]. However, covert channels can also be used to exchange hidden information, such as e-commerce transaction data or governmental confidential information, so that a hacker or any one spying the communication channel will not be able to detect that the captured packets carry hidden information. The sheer volume of Internet traffic provides a higher bandwidth vehicle for covert communications which leads to a plethora of applications.

This paper proposes a novel IP channel for sending hidden short messages, based mainly on the use of the "traceroute" command and the IP header Record route options. It will be demonstrated that the hidden message or information exchanged over the secret IP channel is protected against Steganalysis and sniffing. That is, a hacker or any one spying the communication will not notice the existing of hidden information in the packets exchanged.

The rest of the paper is organized as follows. Section 2 discusses the related works in the literature. Section 3 provides the necessary background information to understand the principle of the proposed IP channel which is described in Section 4. Section 5 presents a mechanism to protect the proposed covert channel against Steganalysis and sniffing. Section 6 discuses an example of how a hidden message is inserted in the covert memory. Section 7 shows a comparison between the covert memories available in several existing covert channels. Section 8 presents a friendly tool, implemented to demonstrate the proposed covert channel. The tool provides the user with a friendly interface to send and receive hidden messages. Finally, Section 9 provides the conclusion and future work.

2 Related Work

The concept of a covert channel was first introduced by Lampson [4] as a channel that is used for information transmission, but that is not designed nor intended for communication. Then, Girling [5] analyzes covert channels in a network environment. His work focuses on local area networks (LANs) in which three *obvious* covert channels (two storage channels and one timing channel) are identified. The first uses the bits reserved for addresses, the second uses the bits reserved for the length and the third uses the time difference between the packets. In [14], Wolf presents results applied to LAN protocols. He highlights the relationship between covert storage channels and protocol format, and the link between covert timing channels and protocol procedure elements taking into account the frame layouts of the LAN protocols. Covert storage channels utilize the *reserved fields, padding fields* and *undefined fields* of the frames. In [22], Handel and Sanford take a broader perspective and focus on covert channels within the general design of network communication protocols. They employ the OSI (Open System Interconnection) network model as a basis for their development in which they characterize system elements having potential to be used for data hiding.

Covert channels are discussed more generally in a variety of papers. A generalized survey of information-hiding techniques is described in "Information Hiding- A Survey", [15]. Theoretical issues in information hiding are considered in [7] and [17]. In [12], John McHugh provides a wealth of information on analyzing a system for covert channels.

Many covert channels have been identified in the IP and TCP protocols [26], using fields like: the IP identification field, the TCP initial sequence number field, the TCP acknowledge sequence number field, windowing bits, and protocol identification field ([2, 3, 6]). These papers focused on finding places where covert data could potentially be sent but did not work out the details of how to send it.

Kamran [2, 3] discussed also a covert channel based on the flags bits (URG, ACK, PSH, RST, SYN, FIN) in the TCP header. This covert channel offers only few bits as a covert memory per TCP packet. Techniques for detecting covert channels, as well as possible places to hide data in the TCP stream, are discussed (the sequence numbers, duplicate packets, TCP window size and the urgent pointer) in [24]. In [8], the idea of using IP checksums for covert communication is discussed. Katzenbeisser and Petitcolas [21] have also observed the potential for data hiding in the TCP/IP protocol suite. Katzenbeisser and Petitcolas use the term *Internet Steganography* for this potential scenario and indicate that the ongoing research work includes the embedding, recovering and detecting information in TCP/IP packet headers.

In [13], the idea of hiding data in TCP timestamps is discussed. By imposing slight delays on the processing of selected TCP packets, the low order bits of their timestamps can be modified. The low bit of the TCP timestamp, when modified in this way, provides a covert channel.

Also, some research works propose to use ICMP packet [11] to carry hidden information in the ICMP header [1, 2]. These covert channels involve putting hidden data and messages in the data fields of the ICMP packets, mainly in Ping ICMP packets. Obviously, the existence of hidden data and messages in such data fields can be easily identified. However, such covert channels exploit the fact that network devices usually do not apply filters on the data fields of the ICMP headers.

Unfortunately most of the existing covert channels in literature are not efficient and/or practical. They either provide very limited covert memory such as TCP-based covert channels, or not robust enough against Steganalysis such as ICMP-based covert channels. The covert channel proposed in this paper addresses the above drawbacks and provides a more practical and robust covert channel for hiding information.

3 Background

In order to introduce the terms used in this paper and lay the groundwork for what follows, we will introduce briefly the option field in the IP protocol header.

3.1 The Fields of the IP Header Option

The IP option field in the IP header is not required in every IP datagram. Options are included primarily for network testing or debugging. Options processing is an integral part of the IP protocol, and all standard implementations must include it.

Figure 1 shows the structure of the IP header option.

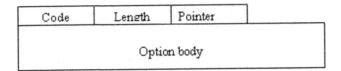

Fig. 1. The IP header Option structure

The field *Code* indicates the type of the option in the IP header. The field *Length* indicates the size of the field *Option*. The *Pointer* field plays a particular function, depending on the type of the option. There are eight possible types of options in an IP datagram. The four most used options are:

- *Loose source routing*: used to route a datagram along a specific path.
- *Record route*: used to trace a route.
- *Strict source routing*: used to route a datagram along a specified path.
- *Internet timestamp*: used to record timestamps along a route.

For the proposed covert channel in this paper, we are only interested in the *Record route* option.

3.2 The Record Route Option in an IP Header

The *Record route* option in an IP datagram allows the source host to create an empty list of IP addresses and arrange for each router that handles the datagram to add its IP address to the list. Figure 2 shows the format of the *Record route* option.

The *Code* field is set to the value 7. The *Length* field specifies the total length of the *Record route* option in an IP datagram, including the first three bytes. The *Pointer* field specifies the offset within the *Record route* option of the next available slot. That is, it specifies the position in the *Record route* option where the next gateway can insert its IP address.

Whenever a router handles an IP datagram that has the *Record route* option set, the router adds *its* IP address to the record route list. It is clear that enough space must be allocated in the *Record route* option by the original source host to hold all the IP addresses of the routers. To add its IP address to the list, a router first compares the

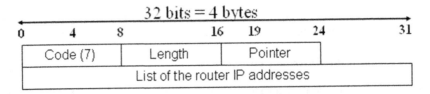

Fig. 2. The format of the *Record route* option in an IP datagram

values in the *Pointer* and *Length* fields. If the value in the *Pointer* field is greater than the value in the *Length* field, this means that the list is full, then the router forwards the IP datagram without inserting its IP address. If the list is not full, the router inserts its 4-bytes IP address at the position specified by the *Pointer* field, then increments the *Pointer* by four. When the IP datagram reaches its destination, the destination host extract and process the record route list of IP addresses.

3.3 Classes of IP Addresses

In order to provide the flexibility required to support different size networks, the Internet designers decided that the IP address space should be divided into three different address classes - Class A, Class B, and Class C [18, 19]. This is often referred to as "*classful*" addressing because the address space is split into three predefined classes, groupings, or categories. Each class fixes the boundary between the network-prefix and the host-number at a different point within the 32-bit address.

In addition to the three most popular classes, there are two additional classes. Class D addresses have their leading four-bits set to 1-1-1-0 and are used to support IP Multicasting. Class E addresses have their leading four-bits set to 1-1-1-1 and are reserved for experimental use.

4 A Covert Channel Based on the Record Route Option

The idea behind the proposed covert channel is to allow a source host to use the available bytes in the Record route option to insert hidden information, and at the same time prevent any router (along the path to the destination host) from inserting its IP address to keep the hidden information intact.

When the IP header option designates a record route, the Code and Pointer fields should be set to the standard values 7 and 4, respectively. Also, the maximum value in the Length field should be 39.

In its way to its destination, any packet with such an IP header option would ask each router to write its IP address in the 4-bytes field pointed by the *Pointer* field (Fig. 3). Then, the value of the *Pointer* field in the IP header option is increased by 4. So that, the next router would write its IP address in the next 4-bytes field in the IP header option. However, if the value of the *Pointer* field becomes greater than the value of the *Length* field, then no more routers can write their IP addresses.

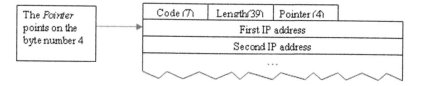

Fig. 3. A normal *Record route* option header

Therefore, we may establish a covert channel for sending hidden messages if the initial value of the *Pointer* field is greater than the value of the *Length* field (Fig. 4.a), or just greater than the length of the hidden message (Fig. 4.b).

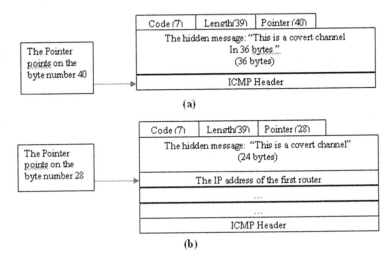

Fig. 4. The different values of the *Pointer* field used for the covert channel

If we set the initial value of the *Pointer* field greater than the value of the *Length* field, then no router can write its IP address. In this case, we can use all the 36 bytes of the IP header option to put hidden data or messages. However, if we set the initial value of the *Pointer* field just greater than the length of the hidden message, then a number of routers can write their IP addresses in the remaining bytes of the IP header option.

This covert channel has the following features:

- *Considerable covert memory*: In the proposed covert channel, we have nearly 40 bytes of covert memory per packet. This provides more flexibility compared to the existing TCP-based covert channels such as in [6], which offer a maximum of 4 bytes of covert memory per packet.
- *Flexibility*: The proposed covert channel may use ICMP, TCP and/or UDP packets to exchange hidden information. This removes any restrictions imposed by the only use of TCP packets (such as synchronisation, flow and congestion control) as in the case of TCP-based covert channels [6].
- *Undetectability*: Inserting the hidden information in the Record route options will in general not alert users who are analyzing the traffic about the presence of the hidden information in those packets. Most of these users would assume that this hidden information represents a valid list of IP addresses of the routers along the connection path. However, an advanced Steganalysis process may be able to notice that these IP addresses are not valid and generate a suspicious situation. In Section 5, we propose a

mechanism to further protect the covert channel form such Steganalysis. But, the available covert memory will be reduced in order to offer protected covert channel against Steganalysis.

5 Protection Against Steganalysis and Sniffing

The information in the covert channel is packaged in the form of IP addresses of routers. However, it is possible for one to verify the validity of these IP addresses in the connection path which immediately offers a means for Steganalysis. For example, if we want to send the hidden message *"RDV at 9pm"* in an IP packet, then the contents of the Record route option would appear as shown in Figure 5. However, a Steganalysis process may identify that the IP addresses in the Record route option (82.68.86.32, 97.116.32.57, 112.109.0.0) are not valid IP addresses.

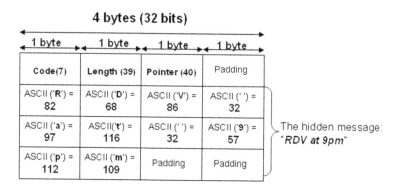

Fig. 5. The contents of the Record route option

To protect the scheme from such potential Steganalysis process, it is clear that the IP addresses used in the Record route option should look-like valid router IP addresses. Hence, a mechanism is proposed to generate packets carrying hidden information and satisfying the above condition.

The proposed mechanism is based on two steps. The purpose of the first step is to collect the IP addresses of the routers that will most likely be in the connection path. The purpose of the second step is compute the number of IP packets needed to carry the hidden information and generate the contents of the Record route options in these packets.

Step 1: Collection of the IP addresses

Before generating any packet carrying hidden information, we collect the list of IP addresses of the routers that will most likely be in the connection path. Unix command 'traceroute', Windows command 'tracert' [20], or any program that provides the same functionality can be used to collect such a list as shown in Figure 6. In theory, this path may not be identical for all packets sent to the same destination. However, in practice all packets that belong to the same flow always follow very similar paths, if not the same path. So, this should not raise any concern.

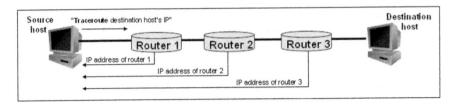

Fig. 6. Unix command *"traceroute"*

Step 2: Generation of the contents of the Record route options

To generate packets carrying hidden information and protect them from any Stega-nalysis process, the following two requirements should be satisfied:

➤   First, the IP addresses inserted in the Record route options should look-like valid router IP addresses. That is, they should be very similar to the router IP addresses collected by commands such as *"traceroute"* or *"tracert"*.

➤   Second, the hidden information should be included in the IP addresses inserted in the Record route options.

Hence, we developed an algorithm for generating IP packets carrying the hidden information and satisfying the above two requirements. The algorithm takes two pa-rameters as input:

a)   a hidden message of k characters; $HM = \{c1,...,ck\}$, and
b)   the collected list of IP addresses of the routers that most likely will be in the connection path. This list can have a mixture of Class A, B and C IP ad-dresses: $List\_IP = (\{IP1,...,IP_{nB}\},\{ IP1,...,IP_{nC}\})$, where nB = number of Class A and B IP addresses, and nC = number of Class C IP addresses. It is important to note that a maximum of nine IP addresses can be inserted in a Record route option, since the maximum available space in the Record route option is 39 bytes, and each IP address needs four bytes.

As output, the algorithm produces:

➤   The number of IP packets that are needed to carry the hidden text,
➤   The contents of the Record route option in each packet to be sent.

The algorithm is defined as follows:

Algorithm generatePackets (HM, List_IP)

Step 1: calculate the number of IP packets needed to hide *HM* using the following formula:

$$P(k,nB,nC) = \text{int}\left(\frac{k}{2nB+nC}\right) + round\left(\frac{k\%(2nB+nC)}{2nB+nC} + 0.4\right)$$

*where int(.) denotes integer division where the fraction part is discarded, round(.) denotes rounding to the nearest whole number [e.g. round(0.5)=1], and % denotes the modulus operator [in general: a%b = a - int(a/b) * b].*

Step 2: Repeat for each packet to be sent
   Step 3: Construct an IP packet with a random type.
     // This is important to further confuse and mislead someone who is sniffing the
     // communication channel
   Step 4: Insert the list of IP addresses (*List_IP*) in the Record route option
   Step 5: Repeat for each IP address in the Record route option
     ➤ If there is no more characters in *HM*, exit.
     ➤ *If* the IP address belongs to Class C
       Replace the least significant byte by the next character from *HM*
     ➤ *Else // Class B or Class A*
       Replace the least significant two bytes by the next two characters from *HM*
   End // repeat step 5
  End // repeat step 2
End // Algorithm generatePackets

Using this algorithm, the secret information will be hidden inside valid IP addresses to protect the covert channel against Steganalysis. However, this would require more packets to be generated since the algorithm uses only one or two bytes in each IP address in the Record route options. If further secrecy is deem important, the confidentiality of the hidden information can be enhanced further using any crypto technique.

6 Example

Assume that we want to send the hidden message (*HM*) "*RDV at 9pm*", which has 10 characters from a source host (190.100.20.10) to a destination host 195.95.40.10 as shown in Figure 7. The command '*traceroute*' retrieves the following two IP addresses of Class B and two IP addresses of Class C from the connection path:

  1. Class B addresses:
   ➤ 190.100.20.1
   ➤ 190.100.30.1
  2. Class C addresses:
   ➤ 195.95.37.1
   ➤ 195.95.40.1

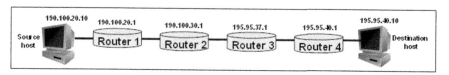

Fig. 7. An example of a connection path

By applying the algorithm, the number of packets that should be sent to carry the *HM* is computed as follow:

$$P(10,2,2) = int(10/6) + round(0.67 + 0.4) = 1 + 1 = 2 \text{ packets.}$$

The contents of the Record route options of the two packets that are generated by the algorithm are shown in Figure 8.

Packet 1

1 byte	1 byte	1 byte	1 byte
Code(7)	Length (39)	Pointer (40)	Padding
190	100	ASCII ('R') = 82	ASCII ('D ') = 68
190	100	ASCII ('V') = 86	ASCII (' ') = 32
195	95	37	ASCII ('a ') = 97
195	95	40	ASCII ('t ') = 116

Packet 2

1 byte	1 byte	1 byte	1 byte
Code(7)	Length (39)	Pointer (40)	Padding
190	100	ASCII (' ') = 32	ASCII ('9') = 57
190	100	ASCII ('p ') = 112	ASCII ('m') = 109
195	95	37	1
195	95	40	1

Fig. 8. The contents of the Record route options of the two packets

As shown in Figure 8, the hidden message HM will be sent to the destination host in two separate packets. Packet 1 will carry the string "*RDV at*" and Packet 2 will carry the remaining string " *9pm*". For Class C IP addresses, we modified only the least significant byte, and the least significant two bytes for Class B IP addresses. It is clear from Figure 8 that even if the traffic is sniffed and analyzed, it will be very difficult to notice that the IP addresses in the Record route options are not valid addresses that carry hidden message.

Compared with the contents of the Record route option of Figure 5 (which was generated without using the *generatePackets* Algorithm), Figure 8 shows clearly the strength of the algorithm in protecting the covert channel against Steganalysis. Figure 5 includes non-valid addresses such as 112.109.0.0, which is quite suspicious to be included in any Record route option. On the contrary, all IP addresses appear in Figure 8 look -like valid router IP addresses.

7   Covert Memory Per Packet

The proposed covert channel offers more covert memory per packet than the existing available covert channels. The number of bytes in the covert memory depends on the classes of the IP addresses of the routers between the source host and the destination host. The following formula computes the number of bytes (n) available in the covert memory per packet:

$$n = (2 * m1) + m2$$

Where:
- *m1* is the number of Class A and Class B's IP addresses of the routers between the source host and the destination host.
- *m2* is the number of Class C's IP addresses of the routers between the source host and the destination host.

Table 1 gives examples of the number of bytes (n) available in the covert memory per packet.

Table 1. The number of bytes (n) in the covert memory per packet

Number of routers between the source host and the destination host	Number of Class A and B's IP addresses of the routers ($m1$)	Number of Class C's IP addresses of the routers ($m2$)	Number of bytes in the covert memory per packet (n)
1	1	0	2 bytes
1	0	1	1 bytes
2	1	1	3 bytes
3	2	1	5 bytes
4	2	2	6 bytes
5	1	4	5 bytes
5	3	2	7 bytes

Table 2 shows the covert memory per packet in a number of existing covert channels. The proposed covert channel in this paper offers the highest covert memory, when there are more than three routers between the source host and the destination host (Table 1). In addition, it is not limited to any particular protocol type. For example, the packets carrying the hidden information can be a combination of ICMP, TCP and UDP packets.

Table 2. Available covert memory per packet in some existing covert channels

Protocols of the covert channels	The fields carrying the hidden information	Covert memory / Packet
IP protocol	The *Identification* field in the IP header	2 bytes / packet
TCP protocol	The *Initial Sequence Number (ISN)* field in the TCP header	4 bytes / packet
TCP protocol	The *Acknowledge Sequence Number* field in the TCP header	4 bytes / packet
TCP protocol	The *TCP Options* field in the TCP header (TCP timestamp)	4 bytes / packet
TCP protocol	*TCP flags Bits* (URG, ACK, PSH, RST, SYN, FIN)	Few bits / packet
ICMP protocol	**The Data field in the ICMP Header**	4 bytes / packet

8 Implementation

A friendly graphical tool has been developed based on the proposed covert channel, using Visual C++ and Winsock library. At the source host, the tool allows a user to write his hidden message and then generates the necessary packets that will carry the hidden message. At the destination host, the tool extracts the hidden messages from the received packets and displays their contents to the user.

The following steps describe the process of sending an example hidden message to a destination host using the tool. Figure 9 shows the network's architecture used in this example. The network has two Cisco routers (2600 series) connected via a serial interface. The first router is connected to the source host via subnetwork 2.2.2.x, and the second router is connected to the destination host via subnetwork 1.1.1.x.

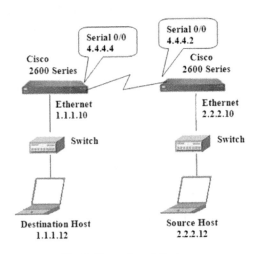

Fig. 9. Network architecture

Step 1: At the source host, as soon as the user invokes the tool, he will get the main screen shown in Figure 10. The source IP address of the source host will be

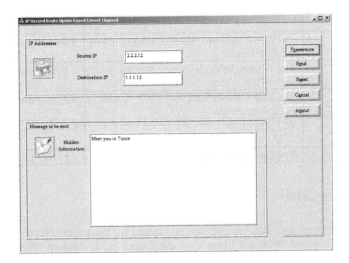

Fig. 10. Main screen of the Covert channel tool

displayed automatically by the tool. The user needs only to write the IP address of the destination host (1.1.1.12), and his hidden message ("*Meet you in Tunis*") as shown in Figure 10.

Step 2: The user clicks on the "*Traceroute*" button to get the list of the IP addresses of the routers between the source host (2.2.2.12) and the destination host (1.1.1.12). In response, the tool will automatically execute the "traceroute" command and retrieve the list of IP addresses along the path to destination. Then it computes the minimum number of packets required to send the hidden message, and displays this information as shown in Figure 11.

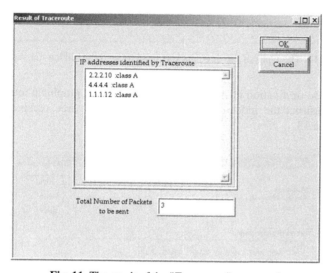

Fig. 11. The result of the "*Traceroute*" command

To compute the minimum number of packets needed to carry the hidden message, it is important to note that, although the number of characters in the hidden message is 17, the tool will use 18 bytes to send the message. The first byte will include the number of character in the hidden message and the remaining 17 bytes will include the ASCII codes of the 17 characters of the hidden message. Since there are three class-A IP addresses identified along the path to the destination, and the tool uses the two least significant bytes of each class-A IP address to carry two characters of the message (see the algorithm *generatePacket in, Section 5*), then each packet will carry 6 characters of the hidden message. Consequently, three packets are required to send the hidden message.

Step 3: Once the user agrees with the identified list of IP addresses and the number of packets to be used (Figure 12), the tool will automatically generate the three packets with random types, which could be ICMP and/or UDP. The types of the ICMP packets are also chosen randomly, in order to avoid one type of packets carrying the hidden message. This would contribute considerably to further protect the covert channel from Steganalysis. Figure 17 shows that two ICMP packets (Type = 15 and Type = 13) and one UDP packet will be generated to carry the hidden message "*Meet you in Tunis*".

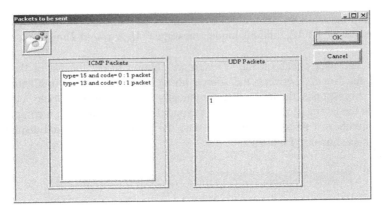

Fig. 12. The types of the three packets used to send the hidden message

Step 4: At the destination host (1.1.1.12), the tool uses a graphical interface to extract and reconstruct the hidden message inserted in the three received packet as shown in Figure 13.

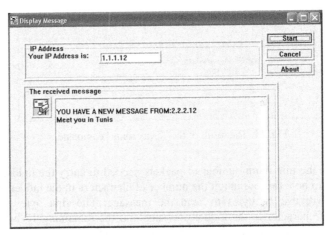

Fig. 13. The hidden message displayed to destination user

9 Conclusion

This paper discusses a novel IP channel for sending hidden short messages, based mainly on the use of the "traceroute" command and the IP header Record route options The IP channel is protected against Steganalysis and sniffing by hiding the secret message inside valid IP addresses in the Record route options. An algorithm has been developed to generate the necessary packets to carry the secret information. In order to avoid one type of packets carrying the hidden message, the types of the packets are chosen randomly, and could be ICMP and/or UDP. This would contribute considerably to further protect the covert channel from Steganalysis. Compared to the existing covert channel proposed in literature, our covert IP channel offers more covert memory than any of the existing covert channels, especially when there are more than three routers between the source host and the destination host. It also exploits the simplicity of the ICMP and UDP tunnelling to avoid the restriction and rules (synchronisation, flow and congestion control) imposed by TCP-based covert channels.

A friendly graphical tool has been developed to demonstrate the proposed covert IP channel. The tool allows a user to write his hidden message and then generates the necessary packets that will carry the message. At the destination host, the tool extracts the hidden messages from the received packets and displays their contents to the user.

Currently, we are developing new mechanisms to further protect the scheme from other advanced Steganalysis, especially in networking environments that are highly protected by Firewalls (using filtering rules) and intrusion detections systems.

References

1. Abhishek Singh ,Ola Nordström, Chenghai Lu, Andre L M dos Santos, "Malicious ICMP Tunnelling : Defence against the Vulnerability", in Proceedings of the 8th Australasian Conference: Information Security and Privacy (ACISP 2003), Wollongong, Australia, pp. 226 – 236, July 9-11, 2003.
2. Ahsan Kamran, "Covert Channel Analysis and Data Hiding in TCP/IP", Master Thesis, University of Toronto, 2002.
3. Kamran Ahsan and Deepa Kundur, "Practical data hiding in TCP/IP", In Proceedings of the Workshop on Multimedia Security at ACM Multimedia, December 2002.
4. B. W. Lampson, "A note on the confinement problem," in Proceedings of the Communications of the ACM, number 16:10, pp. 613–615, October 1973.
5. C. Girling, "Covert channels in LAN's," Vol. SE-13 of 2, IEEE Transactions on Software Engineering, February 1987.
6. C. H. Rowland, "Covert channels in the TCP/IP protocol suite," Tech. Rep. 5, First Monday, Peer Reviewed Journal on the Internet, July 1997.
7. Christin Cachin, "An information-theoretic model for steganography", In David Aucsmith, editor, Information Hiding, 2nd International Workshop, volume 1525 of Lecture Notes in Computer Science, pages 306-318, Springer, 1998.
8. Christopher Abad, "IP checksum covert channels and selected hash collision", Technical report, 2001.
9. D. Wu and F. Wong., "Remote Sniffer Detection". Computer Science Division, University of California, Berkeley. December 14, 1998.
10. Gina Fisk , Mike Fisk , Christos Papadopoulos, Joshua Neil, "Eliminating Steganography in Internet Traffic with Active Wardens", In the Proceedings of the 5th International Workshop on Information Hiding, p.18-35, October 07-09, 2002.
11. J. Postel, "Internet Control Message Protocol", Protocol Specifications, DARPA Internet Program, September 1984.
12. John McHugh, "Covert Channel Analysis", Portland State University, December, 1995.
13. John Giffin, Rachel Greenstadt, Peter Litwack, and Richard Tibbetts. Covert messaging through TCP timestamps. In Workshop on Privacy Enhancing Technologies, San Francisco, volume 2482, pages 194--208, April 2002.
14. M. Wolf, "Covert channels in LAN protocols," in Proceedings of the Workshop on Local Area NetworK Security (LANSEC'89), pp. 91 – 102, 1989.

15. Markus G. Kuhn Fabian A.P. Petitcolas, Ross J. Anderson, "Information hiding – a survey." In Proceedings of the IEEE, special issue on protection of multimedia content, 87(7):1062–1078, July 1999.

16. Richard Stevens – "TCP/IP Illustrated: Volume 1", 2001.

17. Ross Anderson and Fabien A.P. Petitcolas. "On the limits of steganography", IEEE Journal on Selected Areas in Communications, 16:474-481, May 1998.

18. RFC 950 - Internet Standard Subnetting Procedure.

19. RFC 1466 - Guidelines for Management of IP Address Space.

20. RFC 1393 - Traceroute message.

21. S. Katzenbeisser and F. Petitcolas, "Information Hiding Techniques for Steganography and Digital Watermarking", Computer Security Series, 685 Canton Street, Norwood, MA 02062: Artech House, Inc., 2000.

22. T. Handel and M. Sandford., "Hiding data in the OSI network model,", Cambridge, U.K., First International Workshop on Information Hiding, May-June 1996.

23. U.S.D.O.D., "Trusted computer system evaluation criteria", 1985.

24. Uc davis denial of service (dos) project, meeting notes. <http://seclab.cs.ucdavis.edu/projects/denial-service/meetings/01-27-99m.html>, January 27, 1999.

25. Regunathan Radhakrishnan, Kulesh Shanmugasundaram, Nasir D. Memon, "Data masking: a secure-covert channel paradigm". IEEE Workshop on Multimedia Signal Processings, 339-342, 2002

26. Steven J. Murdoch, Stephen Lewis, "Embedding Covert Channels into TCP/IP", the 7th Information Hiding Workshop, Barcelona, Catalonia (Spain) 6 – 8 June 2005.

Author Index

Lecture Notes in Computer Science

For information about Vols. 1–4182

please contact your bookseller or Springer

Vol. 4224: E. Corchado, H. Yin, V. Botti, C. Fyfe (Eds.), Intelligent Data Engineering and Automated Learning – IDEAL 2006. XXVII, 1447 pages. 2006.

Vol. 4223: L. Wang, L. Jiao, G. Shi, X. Li, J. Liu (Eds.), Fuzzy Systems and Knowledge Discovery. XXVIII, 1335 pages. 2006. (Sublibrary LNAI).

Vol. 4222: L. Jiao, L. Wang, X. Gao, J. Liu, F. Wu (Eds.), Advances in Natural Computation, Part II. XLII, 998 pages. 2006.

Vol. 4221: L. Jiao, L. Wang, X. Gao, J. Liu, F. Wu (Eds.), Advances in Natural Computation, Part I. XLI, 992 pages. 2006.

Vol. 4219: D. Zamboni, C. Kruegel (Eds.), Recent Advances in Intrusion Detection. XII, 331 pages. 2006.

Vol. 4218: S. Graf, W. Zhang (Eds.), Automated Technology for Verification and Analysis. XIV, 540 pages. 2006.

Vol. 4217: P. Cuenca, L. Orozco-Barbosa (Eds.), Personal Wireless Communications. XV, 532 pages. 2006.

Vol. 4216: M.R. Berthold, R. Glen, I. Fischer (Eds.), Computational Life Sciences II. XIII, 269 pages. 2006. (Sublibrary LNBI).

Vol. 4215: D.W. Embley, A. Olivé, S. Ram (Eds.), Conceptual Modeling - ER 2006. XVI, 590 pages. 2006.

Vol. 4213: J. Fürnkranz, T. Scheffer, M. Spiliopoulou (Eds.), Knowledge Discovery in Databases: PKDD 2006. XXII, 660 pages. 2006. (Sublibrary LNAI).

Vol. 4212: J. Fürnkranz, T. Scheffer, M. Spiliopoulou (Eds.), Machine Learning: ECML 2006. XXIII, 851 pages. 2006. (Sublibrary LNAI).

Vol. 4211: P. Vogt, Y. Sugita, E. Tuci, C. Nehaniv (Eds.), Symbol Grounding and Beyond. VIII, 237 pages. 2006. (Sublibrary LNAI).

Vol. 4210: C. Priami (Ed.), Computational Methods in Systems Biology. X, 323 pages. 2006. (Sublibrary LNBI).

Vol. 4209: F. Crestani, P. Ferragina, M. Sanderson (Eds.), String Processing and Information Retrieval. XIV, 367 pages. 2006.

Vol. 4208: M. Gerndt, D. Kranzlmüller (Eds.), High Performance Computing and Communications. XXII, 938 pages. 2006.

Vol. 4207: Z. Ésik (Ed.), Computer Science Logic. XII, 627 pages. 2006.

Vol. 4206: P. Dourish, A. Friday (Eds.), UbiComp 2006: Ubiquitous Computing. XIX, 526 pages. 2006.

Vol. 4205: G. Bourque, N. El-Mabrouk (Eds.), Comparative Genomics. X, 231 pages. 2006. (Sublibrary LNBI).

Vol. 4204: F. Benhamou (Ed.), Principles and Practice of Constraint Programming - CP 2006. XVIII, 774 pages. 2006.

Vol. 4203: F. Esposito, Z.W. Raś, D. Malerba, G. Semeraro (Eds.), Foundations of Intelligent Systems. XVIII, 767 pages. 2006. (Sublibrary LNAI).

Vol. 4202: E. Asarin, P. Bouyer (Eds.), Formal Modeling and Analysis of Timed Systems. XI, 369 pages. 2006.

Vol. 4201: Y. Sakakibara, S. Kobayashi, K. Sato, T. Nishino, E. Tomita (Eds.), Grammatical Inference: Algorithms and Applications. XII, 359 pages. 2006. (Sublibrary LNAI).

Vol. 4200: I.F.C. Smith (Ed.), Intelligent Computing in Engineering and Architecture. XIII, 692 pages. 2006. (Sublibrary LNAI).

Vol. 4199: O. Nierstrasz, J. Whittle, D. Harel, G. Reggio (Eds.), Model Driven Engineering Languages and Systems. XVI, 798 pages. 2006.

Vol. 4198: O. Nasraoui, O. Zaiane, M. Spiliopoulou, B. Mobasher, B. Masand, P. Yu (Eds.), Advances in Web Minding and Web Usage Analysis. IX, 177 pages. 2006. (Sublibrary LNAI).

Vol. 4197: M. Raubal, H.J. Miller, A.U. Frank, M.F. Goodchild (Eds.), Geographic, Information Science. XIII, 419 pages. 2006.

Vol. 4196: K. Fischer, I.J. Timm, E. André, N. Zhong (Eds.), Multiagent System Technologies. X, 185 pages. 2006. (Sublibrary LNAI).

Vol. 4195: D. Gaiti, G. Pujolle, E. Al-Shaer, K. Calvert, S. Dobson, G. Leduc, O. Martikainen (Eds.), Autonomic Networking. IX, 316 pages. 2006.

Vol. 4194: V.G. Ganzha, E.W. Mayr, E.V. Vorozhtsov (Eds.), Computer Algebra in Scientific Computing. XI, 313 pages. 2006.

Vol. 4193: T.P. Runarsson, H.-G. Beyer, E. Burke, J.J. Merelo-Guervós, L.D. Whitley, X. Yao (Eds.), Parallel Problem Solving from Nature - PPSN IX. XIX, 1061 pages. 2006.

Vol. 4192: B. Mohr, J.L. Träff, J. Worringen, J. Dongarra (Eds.), Recent Advances in Parallel Virtual Machine and Message Passing Interface. XVI, 414 pages. 2006.

Vol. 4191: R. Larsen, M. Nielsen, J. Sporring (Eds.), Medical Image Computing and Computer-Assisted Intervention – MICCAI 2006, Part II. XXXVIII, 981 pages. 2006.

Vol. 4190: R. Larsen, M. Nielsen, J. Sporring (Eds.), Medical Image Computing and Computer-Assisted Intervention – MICCAI 2006, Part I. XXXVVIII, 949 pages. 2006.

Vol. 4189: D. Gollmann, J. Meier, A. Sabelfeld (Eds.), Computer Security – ESORICS 2006. XI, 548 pages. 2006.

Vol. 4188: P. Sojka, I. Kopeček, K. Pala (Eds.), Text, Speech and Dialogue. XV, 721 pages. 2006. (Sublibrary LNAI).

Vol. 4187: J.J. Alferes, J. Bailey, W. May, U. Schwertel (Eds.), Principles and Practice of Semantic Web Reasoning. XI, 277 pages. 2006.

Vol. 4186: C. Jesshope, C. Egan (Eds.), Advances in Computer Systems Architecture. XIV, 605 pages. 2006.

Vol. 4185: R. Mizoguchi, Z. Shi, F. Giunchiglia (Eds.), The Semantic Web – ASWC 2006. XX, 778 pages. 2006.

Vol. 4184: M. Bravetti, M. Núñez, G. Zavattaro (Eds.), Web Services and Formal Methods. X, 289 pages. 2006.

Vol. 4183: J. Euzenat, J. Domingue (Eds.), Artificial Intelligence: Methodology, Systems, and Applications. XIII, 291 pages. 2006. (Sublibrary LNAI).